ART of the DEFEAT

ART of the DEFEAT

FRANCE 1940–1944

LAURENCE BERTRAND DORLÉAC

TRANSLATED BY JANE MARIE TODD

PUBLISHED BY THE GETTY RESEARCH INSTITUTE

THE GETTY RESEARCH INSTITUTE PUBLICATIONS PROGRAM
Thomas W. Gaehtgens, *Director, Getty Research Institute*
Gail Feigenbaum, *Associate Director, Programs*
Julia Bloomfield, *Head, Publications Program*

Thomas Crow, Jeffrey M. Hurwit, Jacqueline Lichtenstein, Alex Potts, and Mimi Hall Yiengpruksawan, *Publications Committee*

ART OF THE DEFEAT, FRANCE 1940–1944
Serge Guilbaut, *Editorial Consultant*
Michelle Bonnice, *Manuscript Editor*

Originally published in France as *L'art de la défaite, 1940–1944*

PUBLISHED BY THE GETTY RESEARCH INSTITUTE, LOS ANGELES
Getty Publications
Gregory H. Britton, *Publisher*
1200 Getty Center Drive, Suite 500
Los Angeles, California 90049-1682
www.getty.edu

12 11 10 09 08 5 4 3 2 1

COVER
French artists leaving on the trip to Germany organized by Arno Breker and Otto Abetz, Gare de l'Est, Paris, October 1941. See p. xiv. Photo: © LAPI/Roger-Viollet

LIBRARY OF CONGRESS CATALOGING-IN-PUBLICATION DATA
Bertrand Dorléac, Laurence, 1957–
[Art de la défaite, 1940–1944. English]
Art of the defeat, France 1940–1944 / Laurence Bertrand Dorléac ; translated by Jane Marie Todd.
p. cm.
Originally published: L'art de la défaite, 1940–1944. Paris : Editions du Seuil, c1993.
Includes bibliographical references and index.
ISBN 978-0-89236-891-4 (hardcover)
1. Art, French—20th century. 2. Art—Political aspects—France. 3. France—History—German occupation, 1940–1945. 4. Artists—France—Public opinion. 5. Public opinion—France. I. Title.
N6848.B39513 2008
709.44'09044—dc22
2008012025

CONTENTS

ACKNOWLEDGMENTS

This study could not have been accomplished without the generous aid of the administrators and staff of various archives, museums, and libraries: Chantal de Tourtier-Bonazzi, chief librarian of the contemporary section at the Archives nationales; Janine Irigoin, Isabelle Vernus-Moutin, and Brigitte Blanc, managers of the archives of the fine arts administration; Sylvie Le Clech; Jean Astruc, conservator of the library at the Institut d'histoire du temps présent; Yveline Cantarel-Besson, manager, and Danièle Kriser, historian, at the archives of the Musées nationaux; Jean Coural, general administrator of Mobilier national and of the Manufactures nationales des Gobelins et de Beauvais; Cécile Coutin, librarian at the Bibliothèque nationale de France; Jean-Pierre Defrance, librarian of the archives of the Ministère de l'intérieur; François Gasnault, librarian of the Service des archives économiques et financières du Ministère de l'économie et des finances; Nathalie Genet-Rouffiac, librarian of the archives of the Ministère de la culture; Laurent Gervereau, librarian of the Bibliothèque de documentation internationale contemporaine; Sarah Halperyn and Vidar Jacobsen, curators of the Centre de documentation juive contemporaine; Marie Hamon, manager of the archives and library of the Ministère des affaires étrangères; Anne-Marie Laffitte-Larnaudie, chief librarian of the archives of the Institut de France; Jean-Marc Léri, chief librarian of the Bibliothèque centrale du Louvre; Mme Malherbe, at the archives of the Ministère de la culture; France-Odile des Mazery and Monsieur Guérin, researchers at the Archives de la Ville de Paris; and Didier Schulmann, curator at the Musée national d'art moderne.

I am equally indebted to those who have conserved priceless personal archives, especially Véronique Chabrol, Colette Dreyfus, André Fougeron, Henriette and Maurice Guy-Loë, Michel Kellermann, Françoise Landowski, and Christine Manessier, as well as to the managers of the Galerie Louis Carré, Galerie Brame et Lorenceau, Galerie Jeanne-Bucher, and Galerie de France, and, finally, to Mme Robert Lallemant.

I would like to thank as well all those who, through their research or their experience, have helped me to tease out various threads and solve various problems over the years: Maurice Agulhon, Claire Andrieu, Daniel Arsand, Serge Barcellini, Rémi Baudouï, Françoise Bertaux, Chantal Bizot, Gabrielle Blot, Gilles Blot, Franck Blot, Dominique Buffier, Françoise Buisson, David Butcher, Anne Cazalis, Daniel Cordier, David Curtis, Mme Decourdemanche, Véronique Denis, Christian Derouet, Jean Dewasne, Roland Donneger, Élisabeth Dussaud, Dominique Egret, Serge Fauchereau, Anna Fedorovskaia, Sophie Fouriaud, Marie-Bernadette Gassien, Thierry Gassien, Ursula Gauthier, Laurent Gervereau, Jean-Pierre Greff, Jean-François Jaeger, Stéphane Kerjean, Jean Lacambre, Annick Lantenois, Hervé Le Boterf, Elizabeth Lebovici, Nathalie Leleu, Germaine Lelièvre, Jacqueline Lichtenstein, Éric Martin, Martine Martin, Michelle Michel, Jean-Pierre Monsu, Ruth Néray, Mme Ogilvie, Pascal Ory, Brigitte Pain-Kozine, Anne Simonin, Danièle Voldman, François Wehrlin, and Olivier Wieviorka.

I thank in addition all those who were quick to point me toward new information, a fresh track, or a witness to be met: Nerses Aslanian, Patrick Bongers, Daniel Catan, Jean-Marc Felzenszwalbe, Serge Garnier, Sirarpi Kurkjian, Fernand Madar, Yves Mairot, Jean-Yves Mock, Frédérique Mompelier, Gilbert Mompelier, Henri Noguères, Emmanuel Pernoud, Paul Pittman, Françoise Py, Alain Rubens, and Rurik.

At Editions du Seuil, Catherine Rambaud, Odile Serre, Claude Hénard, Janine Lescarmontier, and Karine Benzaquin worked on the original edition of this book with assiduous good will. At the Getty Research Institute, the publication of this translation was facilitated by Gail Feigenbaum, Julia Bloomfield, Michelle Bonnice, Michele Ciaccio, Rachelle Okawa, Jannon Stein, and Sylvie Young.

This work could not have been completed without the watchful eye of my thesis director, Pierre Milza, and the encouragement of my teachers, professors Jean-Pierre Azéma, Serge Berstein, Robert Bonnaud, Marc Le Bot, Jean Laude, Jean-Pierre Rioux, and Fanette Roche-Pézard. I have benefited from the support of Thomas W. Gaehtgens, now director of the Getty Research Institute; the Institut Universitaire de France; and the Centre d'histoire de Sciences Po, especially its director, Jean-François Sirinelli.

I am indebted to Michel Winock, Jean-Loup Champion, Serge Guilbaut, and Brigitte Pain-Kozine for having been thoughtful advisers regarding my work. Finally, I am most grateful to my family, to my friends, to Stéphane, to Jean, to Jean-François.

FOREWORD

Serge Guilbaut

Maurice Papon, who died at the age of ninety-six, was buried in Paris on 21 February 2007. Like many French people, he was buried with insignias of honor and accomplishment, in his case with his beloved badge of a commander of the Légion d'honneur, given to him by Charles de Gaulle in 1962. What was rather interesting is that this ordinary ritual became the object of violent diatribe in the French media at the time. That this man was going to wear his medal around his neck forever turned into a political confrontation. Papon was, of course, not a neutral figure. He had a shadowy and controversial history over the course of his long career as a civil servant and politician, during which he worked for several ministers and presidents of the French republic. He had served as chief of the Paris police under de Gaulle and as budget minister under Raymond Barre and Valéry Giscard d'Estaing.[1] But it was his most problematic activities that put him in the public spotlight in 2007: he had been convicted of complicity in crimes against humanity in 1998, after the disclosure in 1981 of heretofore hidden information about his role during the German occupation. To make matters worse, the revelation was initially aired by the satirical weekly newspaper *Le canard enchaîné*,[2] widely read for its investigative reporting of scandals in the French political and business sectors. According to the rediscovered archival documents, while working diligently for the Vichy regime in Bordeaux in the early 1940s, Papon sent approximately sixteen hundred Jewish people to the internment center at Drancy and, hence, to their death in Auschwitz and other Nazi concentration camps. Though formally dismissed from the Légion d'honneur in November 1999, Papon seemingly still wore the boutonniere of a commander of the order on his lapel during an interview with the press in February 2004, to the displeasure of a large part of French society.[3] Thus, when it became known that Papon was to be buried with his Légion d'honneur badge, there was a general outcry and some attempt was made to stop this from occurring. What is fascinating about this strange and morbid story is the fetishistic interest surrounding a medal inscribed with the words "Honneur et Patrie"—for honor was what was profoundly at stake at this time. The political maneuvering around Papon's coffin in many ways not only represented the last chance for the war generation to settle scores but also kept the entire unsavory subject of wartime collaboration very much alive in French memory.

As Papon's trial had vividly demonstrated, it was a very complex history indeed. The issue of collaboration, especially by Vichy officials, had long been left very fuzzy. Papon, like so many others, thanks to a very complicated strategy of shadowy alliances and back-door dealings during the occupation, had contact with all the players, both Vichy and Resistance as well as German. In fact, at the war's end, he was vouched for by several heroes of the Resistance. In a complex and deadly situation such as the occupation, everybody able to survive the regime became, it was understood, part of the structural process of surveillance and pacification. Some would play several roles, collaborator on the surface and resister at heart if not in action. The truth of what one did, what one thought, what one said while, as it was common to say then, "the walls had ears" became difficult to sort out. Nobody knew anything for sure; people talked in code to one another, public spaces were eloquent with anonymous graffiti and propaganda posters. Indeed, the society constructed by the Pétain regime was one of secrecy, veiled discourses, manipulative statements, suspicion, and double-talk. Even images by Pablo Picasso, such as his nine still lifes of a potted tomato plant on an urban balcony, all painted in August 1944, could send mute but intelligible messages about suffering, resistance, and survival, as he also proposed in his *Aubade* (1942). The embarrassed and heavy silence about the occupation experience was rarely broken in public in France due to the fact that so many were directly or indirectly implicated. Papon's saga shows that the memory of this period is still very fresh and active, and for that reason alone, it is necessary to come to grips with those who should be held responsible. Resentment is still profound even if not verbalized, and with it comes the desire for revenge—in this case, against the collaborators before it is too late, before all are freed by death. But due to the muddied political situation during the occupation, and due also to the smart ideological apparatus put in place by Vichy that in many ways continued, though with key differences, the cultural policies devised by the Front populaire, it has always been difficult to adopt a clear-cut position, to cleanly distinguish between the guilty and the less guilty, the less guilty and the absolved. That is why honor became so central in Papon's story. France lost everything during the war except, some said, its honor, thanks to a few independent minds. Hence it was imperative that the public recognition of honor should not be bestowed lightly or indiscriminately in the postwar era. Given the autocratic situation enforced by the Vichy regime and the comprehensive and fragile status quo, in which the majority of people had to conform to the new situation in order to survive, it was crucial to be extremely careful in rewarding only those who, by their implacable opposition to the occupation, deserved the trust and gratitude of the entire nation.

Some forty years after the occupation, with French memory still fresh and revenge still an active emotion, Laurence Bertrand Dorléac had the daring idea to look into that past through the lens of the production and reception of art in France during the dark years. What she discovered in archives and by interviewing participants is laid bare here in her book, ironically called *L'art de la défaite*, or *Art of the Defeat*. The double entendre of the title is precisely the pivot on which this important and sophisticated historical statement turns: it recognizes that artists in France were, after all, very good at art and thus able to paint France's defeat in many colors, but it also concedes that the French were used to dealing with defeat, with compromise, with survival.[4]

The fact is that for so long the occupation period has been in France like a bandaged wound that throbs every time it is touched, however lightly. Bertrand Dorléac's book manages to calmly air that sore, naming names, unearthing a relentless series of telling original sources, analyzing sharply for the first time the fascinating imbroglio of the art scene. It was a scene replete with confiscations of art collections from Jewish families, with destruction by fire of so-called degenerate works by artists such as André Masson, Joán Miró, Francis Picabia, and Paul Klee, but also with carefully crafted critical statements by young modern painters. The book is an intelligent and necessary if somewhat painful exposure of a mixture of petty actions and subdued yet heroic statements.

At a time when it seems ever more difficult to avoid superficial, market-oriented exhibitions and coffee-table art books with a minimum of historical understanding and writing, it is refreshing to have a book such as this one, whose author does not refuse to tackle embarrassing issues and difficult political and moral situations. *Art of the Defeat* is exemplary in the sense that for the first time an art historian seriously examines, without bias, this important era in the history of art in France. Bertrand Dorléac represents a new type of French art history, developed out of interest in sociology, knowledge of the "new history," and a flair for original research. What gives the book its formidable appeal is not only the extraordinary archival work, which is in itself a feat when one knows the proverbial bureaucratic slalom one has to negotiate in France to gain access to material, but also the cautious and discerning use of these archives. What Bertrand Dorléac helps us understand through her research is that the situation in the art world was profoundly complicated, as complicated as a chess game, in which the players have to constantly keep in mind the implications of each move if they are to advance or simply stay put without being wiped out, to survive when, in this case, the endgame was almost anyone's guess.

Art of the Defeat is, then, not only a description of what happened but a precise analysis of the moves made by the sophisticated Nazi and Vichy regimes, by individual artists and bureaucrats, as the players sought to create a viable, somewhat acceptable environment for themselves. And that is where the shoe pinches, where the sore spot originated—because to go on living, many had to further racist and reactionary activities or look the other way when all the structures of power that had been left intact, including museums and the press, were filled with often xenophobic, chauvinist, and fascist voices. Bertrand Dorléac takes us by the brain, archives to hand, and leads us through the maze of the occupied country and its government, describing the field of possibilities, the ideological traps and blind alleys, and some of the paths taken by the different players. She offers an impressive analysis of how the Nazi regime was able to create a false sense of continuity with the French past for the French people thanks to the Germans' flexibility and their shrewd relations with the established powers in France. They worked, in part, by encouraging the Vichy regime to exploit values already put in place and defended by the Front populaire before the war. What is protected and even developed, with a twist, is the love for a distinctively French patrimony, for gymnastics, for an art for the people that Vichy, through the production of personalized and kitsch imagery, transformed into a populist cult of Pétain. And looming behind all of this was the rhetoric of the all-encompassing love for the land, for the pure nation, for the sacred, for the heroic old leader. What we have at first sight is a form of return to established French artistic values and genres, such as the landscape and the nude. Yet we can also discern a perverted acceptance, by the occupiers, of a form of light modernism, which worked to prove that France was a culturally degenerate entity after all. For great art was done in Germany, by German artists following the taste of the Führer, in the form of pastiche of great art of the past with bigger but emptier ambition. One can see how under the weight and framing power of the Nazis, in this airless environment, artists and intellectuals who stayed in France had a very thin margin in which to work.[5] In this situation, even the most traditional studies such as those concerning the Middle Ages became controversial. In 1943, Pierre Francastel's *L'humanisme roman* was banned by Vichy, when it was understood that his analysis of

Romanesque art was a different and dangerous call for the recognition of a foundational and modern early French identity in opposition to the archaic and passive vision of Romanesque culture devised by Pétain's regime. Francastel's vision of Romanesque art was in fact a sort of power-sapping machine targeting Vichy's description of French identity as based on passive peasant communities. His medieval French identity was rather surprisingly based on a more aggressive individualism akin to the modern notion of the avant-garde, something which could not fit well with the Révolution nationale but which could spark, as it did, a series of counterrepresentations of France through modern art, albeit of a mild and subtly indicated sort.

Bertrand Dorléac also analyzes in depth and detail the trip to Germany made in 1941 by a group of well-known French artists corralled to support and advertise Vichy's friendly relationship with the Third Reich (Belmondo, Bouchard, Derain, Despiau, Dunoyer de Segonzac, Friesz, Landowski, Legueult, Lejeune, Oudot, van Dongen, Vlaminck). So symbolically important and mediatized was this trip that the artists who participated would forever be marked by infamy in French memory. Using this notorious example, Bertrand Dorléac deconstructs the indirect and often recurring mechanisms of subjugation put in play during the occupation which were so difficult to avoid. Without evading the matter of different levels of participation, she renders thorough account of this far-reaching social and political web, which in 1941 also encompassed the appearance and development of a loosely knit and mildly oppositional group of artists, the so-called Jeunes peintres de tradition française, whose name was designed to conceal the avant-garde and resistant nature of their art. Through the use of blue, white, and red, their bright, semiabstract works were able to express a form of individual symbolic resistance for a select few to relish in private.

This era was, of course, of extreme importance for American art, as many artists and intellectuals from France were in exile in New York City during this time, helping to produce there—and not in Europe—one of the most powerful schools of art that developed after the war. But Bertrand Dorléac, by analyzing both the circumscribed purge of the art world immediately following the liberation of France and the liberation Salon d'Automne's heroic presentation of Picasso, the modernist artist and recently avowed Communist, not only shows that revenge was sweet and very selective but also suggests why the new French art scene being forged would not be heard internationally. France could not disentangle itself from the divisions and ambiguities resulting from a long occupation, and Paris could not re-create the clear international image it had before the war.

An examination of a very painful time in French art history, this book discusses particularly well the myriad mechanisms of subjugation in occupied France by bringing into the light so many shadowy figures in order to understand how its people could rest between Scylla and Charybdis for so long. The fact that many who survived the occupation (or at least their representatives) refused to allow war-era photographs and works of art to be published in the French edition of *Art of the Defeat* shows how Bertrand Dorléac has succeeded in disturbing—in a healthy way—a peace that was in fact never there.

NOTES

1. Among many other problematic things, let us remember that Papon was chief of the Paris police in February 1962 when nine CGT trade unionists were killed at the Charonne metro station by police during an anti-OAS demonstration organized by the French Communist Party. The Organisation de l'armée secrète (OAS) was a militant far-right underground group that advocated armed struggle to prevent Algeria's independence from France; the leftist and then Communist-oriented Confédération générale du travail (CGT) was one of the five major French confederations of trade unions.
2. See the issues of *Le canard enchaîné* for 6, 13, and 20 May 1981.
3. Maurice Papon, "Le dernier plaidoyer de Papon," *Le point*, 19 February 2004; and, for example, "Les lecteurs écrivent," *Le point*, 4 March 2004; and Sandra Calme, "France in Uproar about Nazi Collaborator's Legion of Honour," European Jewish Press (EJP), 17 September 2007, http://www.ejpress.org/article/14356.
4. Bertrand Dorléac's book is the first study of the French art scene during the occupation in a field that has only lately been under investigation in France, after the pioneering, and to some controversial, work by Robert O. Paxton titled *Vichy France: Old Guard and New Order, 1940–1944* (New York: Knopf, 1972; reprint, Columbia Univ. Press, 1982; reprint, with a new introduction, Columbia Univ. Press, 2001).
5. Among those who stayed were many like the hunted surrealists, some of whom left for the south of France and from there went to New York.

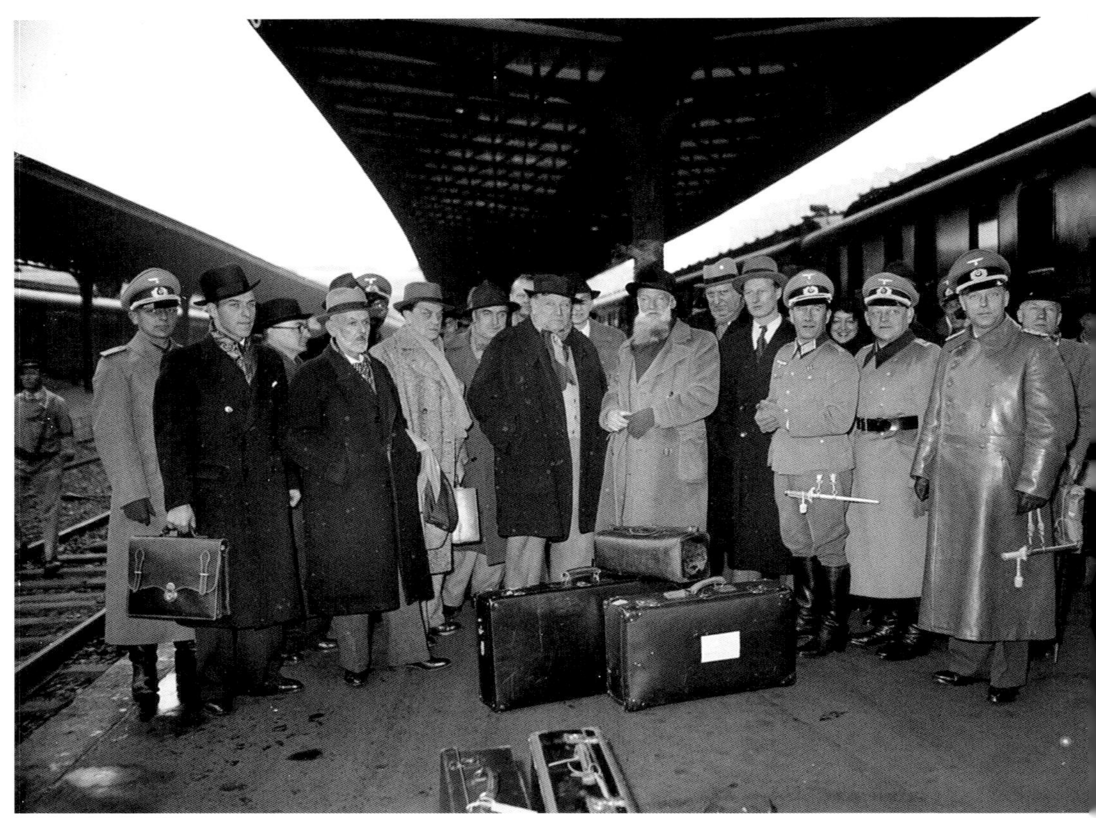

French artists leaving on the trip to Germany organized by Arno Breker and Otto Abetz, Gare de l'Est, Paris, October 1941: *left to right (excluding the unidentified six German officers, four other men, and one woman)*, Roland Oudot (behind, wearing glasses), Charles Despiau (in front, bearded), Othon Friesz (in front, long scarf), André Dunoyer de Segonzac (behind, dark hat), Henri Flammarion (behind, hatless), Maurice de Vlaminck (in front, short scarf), Kees van Dongen (in front, long beard), André Derain (behind, light hat), Raymond Leguelt (in front, white shirt)

INTRODUCTION

False Continuities

Any return to France's dark years, the period of the Nazi occupation, entails not only putting the nation's memory to the test but also exposing the limits of a grand republic downtrodden by the enemy and in crisis. For my generation, it necessarily means raising the question of responsibility for the sinister process that began with Philippe Pétain and Adolf Hitler's handshake at Montoire-sur-le-Loir, establishing the collaborationist regime in Vichy, and culminated in a nightmare. It also means revisiting the nature of totalitarianism as well as the historiographical and political debate that has raged in Germany but has spared France for a long time.

In art history as elsewhere, it is still primarily the monolith of the Nazi model that deflects our vision of the French scene between 1940 and 1944. The French experience is usually judged, with emphasis given to Vichy's limits, in relation to that most fully realized of the totalitarian experiments, despite the inroads made by functionalism toward relativizing the coherence of Nazism and its genocidal projects. And, indeed, when compared to swaggering Germany and its triumphant dogma, France easily passes for a body fractured by defeat, an entity that made endless alarming declarations and legislated at every possible opportunity without ever fully implementing the authoritarian program it proclaimed. When looked at more closely, however, that incompletion cannot obscure the larger aberrations that made of Vichy a regime whose emergency powers were sustained by false continuities. If we confine ourselves just to artistic matters, we need only think of the new status for artists and works of art that the regime contrived despite the fact that it did not always have to yield to the occupier's demands.

The grand discourse whose aim was to condemn freedom in art; the exclusion of Jews and Freemasons; the overhaul of education; the Ordre des artistes; the Service artistique du Maréchal; the mass distribution of Pétain's image; the transformation of artistic signs and symbols into political propaganda; the selling off of art collections, by Pierre Laval in particular; the transfer of Georges Hilaire, Laval's trusted man, from the police to the fine arts administration: these Vichy specialties remind us that the regime, despite lacking a "program" like Hitler's or a definitive plan announced by its leaders, still hoped to put an end to disorder. It had a relatively short life, but its actions proved all the more effective because it deployed continuities like so many assets to carry out its policy. It celebrated traditional figures and major themes (landscapes, human figures, still lifes), retained a good part of the fine arts administration, reopened the museums, and glorified French artistic greatness. These many conventional reference points could be held up as proof of the permanence of the past and of *the tradition*—a tradition to which everyone, whether in favor of the regime or against it, whether a collaborator or not, whether modern or antimodern, stubbornly clung. One of the peculiarities of the dark years is that they blurred distinctions while revealing old rifts. Hence, at a time when France's tradition of republican universalism was being flouted, references to past glories and a call to arms for a strong and pure French identity were soured by the humiliation of defeat and by the fear that the nation would be definitively crushed by the occupying forces.

As a totalitarian state, France was far from the equal of Nazi Germany, with its exhibitions of "degenerate art" and its autos-da-fé of paintings, its masterly processes for negating the *strangeness of the world* and its binding of the masses to the supreme will. All the same, in France too, nothing and no one escaped the chaos, the exacerbation of tensions, the illusions of the time. Neither the decision makers (French or German) nor the intermediaries (critics or administrators) nor the artists, abruptly recalled to the bedside of the body politic, nor the public was spared. Everyone was confident that art ought to be able to ward off the crisis by edifying the multitudes and healing their souls. Of course, that agenda was not new, and the crisis had already struck France head-on before the war. The end of color, the love of *fine craftsmanship* and the favoring of design, the call for a new humanism and the return to the portrait, the taste for the sacred and the reconciliation of art and the *common people*, the recourse to an unadulterated identity: all these had sprung into being earlier, in the wake of World War I. And yet, all these were now being dangerously perverted. Under Vichy even the reforms implemented by the Front populaire were accommodated, but the observer of the regime's four years soon detects, beyond the putative continuities, a tremendous change of scale and the materializing of a tragic situation whereby, in theory at least, art could no longer exist in accordance with its imperatives: a taste for adventure and permanent movement, debate, critique, the extolling of conflict. The French situation was undoubtedly unique, in that the ruling powers, French and German, proceeded carefully and empirically, counting on the passage of time and on grassroots initiatives that seemed to "anticipate" official decisions. It was the rank and file that, very early on, called for a program to restore the old order long ago engraved on a collective imagination prepared to accept catastrophe and to both blame and instrumentalize art and artists.

That the collective imagination ultimately resisted, that many artists provided proof that deep down France was not ready to renounce its legacy of freedom, that the majority of the ruling class balked at taking things to the extreme: these too are conclusions that we will reach, without calling into question the exceptional character of the regime. In this dreary waiting game, reality was far from cut-and-dried; it was inexorably dependent on small acts of courage and cowardice by each player. In following an established chronology, we must not neglect either the hidden movements of minor figures or the unprecedented impact of traditions illuminated by a new situation quickly perceived as "abnormal." At every level of daily and cultural life, France played for high stakes, but the call for change had to contend with its heritage. In art, the short and lugubrious history of the triumph of norms and barbarism was also the history of a nation's eyes collectively riveted on the images of a bucolic past filled with hope. To the majority of those eyes, there was nothing appealing about the brutality of *fascist* figures. In France's darkest hours, it was Aristide Maillol's fleshy and nurturing Graces who made them dream.

CHAPTER ONE

The Vanquisher's Eye

THE SCENE AT RETHONDES

The occupation of France began in the vanquisher's eye, when Adolf Hitler came to his new territories to take possession of what interested him most: not the people, who for him never played more than a minor role, but the space, the monuments, the commemorative symbols, the works of art, everything that assuaged his thwarted ambition as a painter and the shame of a soldier defeated in 1918.[1] In June 1940, his orchestration of the armistice negotiations at Rethondes and his journey to Paris in the guise of an aesthete provided a foretaste of the fate he reserved for the French, who were particularly humiliated by what had been a crushing defeat.

In reality, no one had imagined that France would be beaten so quickly. In 1938, General der Artillerie Ludwig Beck, chief of the German army's general staff, had asked Hitler to reconsider his decision to annex part of Czechoslovakia, since Beck judged that French forces were still first-rate. In fact, the armies were equally matched, save for a few things. The French had just as many armored vehicles as their adversaries, and their soldiers were braver than has been reported. But they also had outmoded ways of doing things and a command that panicked at the first setbacks. They could not withstand the modernity or the swiftness of German tanks and airplanes. Surging forward at great speed,[2] enemy troops secured victory within six weeks, and the French government left Paris for Bordeaux on 10 June, just before the arrival of the army commanded by General der Artillerie Georg von Küchler. On 14 June, he hoisted the flag of Nazi Germany atop the Eiffel Tower.

At the end of the rout, French leaders had to make a choice. Instead of surrender, which would have left them free to continue the fight from North Africa but with no certainty about what Germany would make their country endure—instead of leaving things to chance, that is—they preferred the meager assurances of a truce that seemed to guarantee limits on the vanquisher's rights even as it hamstrung the French government.[3] On 16 June, the French interior minister, Georges Mandel, announced that the Conseil d'Etat was divided, that there were those who wanted to fight and those who did not. Citing the need to face realities, those against fighting prevailed for the most part, withdrawing from the Anglo-French accord of 31 March 1939, which guaranteed armed support for Poland, and passing off Britain's attempts at rapprochement as a desire to turn France into a dominion. On the evening of 16 June, Albert Lebrun, president of the French republic, designated Philippe Pétain as the new head of state, and his government was formed the next day. That did not prevent the French cabinet from deciding on 19 June that some ministers and both legislative houses would leave for Morocco, since there was a risk that Bordeaux would be invaded before any negotiations could begin. In the end, only about twenty deputies and one senator (plus a few high officials, including Georges Huisman, director general of the fine arts administration) boarded the *Massilia* for North Africa on 21 June, thereby joining the ranks of the "émigrés."[4]

This meant that Hitler no longer had to worry about deploying his military forces to North Africa or occupying all of continental France. He could dedicate himself to staging his revenge: a peace negotiated in the circular clearing at Rethondes, in the forest of Compiègne, where, on 11 November 1918, Germany had surrendered to France and its allies. In his desire to ritually mark the reversal of fortunes, Hitler made history repeat itself, with nothing left to chance, meticulously studying the ceremonial of the armistice that led to the Treaty of Versailles.[5] In June, armed with pneumatic drills, German engineers demolished the wall of the structure where the railway carriage used by the maréchal de France Ferdinand Foch was enshrined and pushed that relic to the middle of the clearing, to the precise spot where he had signed the armistice in 1918.

On 21 June, Hitler arrived at Rethondes, accompanied by Hermann Göring, Walther von Brauchitsch, Wilhelm Keitel, Rudolf Hess, Erich Raeder, Paul Schmidt, and Joachim von Ribbentrop. Mindful that, from that moment on, each of his gestures had the eloquence of myth, Hitler glanced in passing at the monument to the liberators of Alsace-Lorraine, now covered with German war banners to conceal the Hohenzollern imperial eagle transfixed by the victor's sword. Once he had reached the clearing and hoisted his personal pennant, his gaze rested on the monument commemorating the Allied victory. He approached the thick block of blue granite to read the inscription engraved on it (he would have it effaced three days later):

> HERE SUCCUMBED, ON 11 NOVEMBER 1918,
> THE CRIMINAL ARROGANCE OF THE GERMAN EMPIRE,
> VANQUISHED BY THE FREE PEOPLES
> IT ASPIRED TO SUBJUGATE.

Witnesses report his contemptuous expression as he boarded the railway car where the previous armistice was signed (he would soon have the car "returned" to Germany).[6] What followed is well known: the astonishment of the French delegation, headed by général d'armée Charles Huntziger, at the vanquisher's grotesque staging; its vain protests upon hearing the merciless conditions of the armistice; the intransigence of Keitel and his deputy Generalmajor Alfred Jodl, who deviated not one iota from Hitler's directives; the final signature, at 6:50 P.M. on 22 June, after much delay, on a treaty that gave the advantage to Hitler but which he would not respect in any case.

The treaty accomplished the political, economic, and military imperatives of the Third Reich. It stipulated German occupation of three-fifths of France, determined by a line of demarcation that privileged overland communication routes with Germany and Spain; German control of the Atlantic coast and the coast along the English Channel, which was indispensable for pursuing the war against England; de facto collaboration between the French authorities and the occupier; French payment of "occupation costs"; the return of German prisoners and exiles; and so on.

"France has been handed over, plundered, enslaved," thundered Charles de Gaulle against Pétain on 26 June, just after the armistice agreement had taken effect. That was his reaction to the tragedy grounded in a forced accord, whose consequences were bluntly drawn by the Third Reich's propaganda ministry on 6 July 1940:

> Germany is not concluding a "chivalrous" peace with France. Germany does not consider France an ally but a state with which old accounts will be settled in the peace treaty. In the future, France will play for Europe the role of an "enlarged Switzerland" and will become a tourist destination potentially being allowed to produce fashionable products. . . . Any form of government that seems suited to restore France's might will be prevented by the [Third] Reich. In Europe, Germany has the only say.[7]

Was France a country of landowners or of artists? The Nazi imagination did not settle the question and took France en bloc once it was reduced to an inferior position. The roles were assigned and the division of labor strictly set out: in the perverse couple born of defeat, France would play the female part, the passive and nurturing matron who could be distracted from her troubles by fashion. Was art included among the ephemera to be produced? Yes, without a doubt, if we are to believe subsequent events and the strange fascination that art exerted on lovers of French culture and on Hitler himself, who was excited by the exoticism of a model he had first discovered in books. Paris especially fascinated him, all the more so after the defeat, when it took on the mortified look of a beautiful "European cultural document."[8] His taste for ruins and monuments devoid of all humanity was seconded by the political imperatives of the moment. While awaiting final victory, he spared the French the humiliation of a lavish parade up the Champs-Elysées—which he postponed—preferring a quick trip made incognito, just after the armistice, in the early morning hours, between six and nine, of 23 June 1940.[9]

HITLER PINXIT

In coming to Paris, Hitler claimed to be realizing "a lifelong dream," in reality, a longtime dream that predated World War I and that he had had to postpone after his first failures. In 1907, at age eighteen, he had failed the entrance exam to the Akademie der Bildenden Künste in Vienna. Accompanying his rating was the notation, "Adolf Hitler, Braunau am Inn. 20 April 1889. Catholic. Father customs foreman. Four years of Realschule. Not very bright. Drawing insufficient...." "It struck me as a bolt from the blue," Hitler protested to the rector at the time.[10] He redirected his energies to architecture, which he seems by far to have preferred to portraits. But, once again, he was turned down, this time penalized for his academic deficiencies: he could not be admitted without the equivalent of a high school diploma.[11] When he applied the next year, his drawings were judged so poor that he was not even allowed to take the entrance exam.

His life as a failed artist began then,[12] during the period to which most historians date the birth of his political interests and his anti-Semitism. It was also a time when he preferred to dodge military service under the flags of Austria-Hungary, which he saw as a "Babylon of races": he dreamed of serving exclusively a greater Germany. Working as an interior decorator and as a day laborer on construction sites, living in Vienna at a sordid shelter in the Meidling district, then at a hostel for young singles on Meldemannstrasse, Hitler the artist persevered.[13] He made drawings and watercolors in minuscule formats with cold, meticulous gestures,[14] recopying postcards or old prints exactly, mimicking every detail and not allowing himself any original interpretation. Only genre scenes, landscapes, and especially cities and monuments inspired his assembly-line art. Its monotony would undoubtedly have deterred his petit bourgeois clientele had Hitler not thought to individualize his little pictures. He had only to shift the shadows cast by the buildings—or the hands of his folkish clocks. All human representations banished or reduced to puny marionettes, his art worked its charm on tipsy provincials and minor collectors infatuated with and proud of the Ringstrasse, the renovated center of Vienna, or of Munich, with its Asamkirche, Theatinerkirche, and Hofbräuhaus am Platzl,[15] which ten years later served as the meeting place for the Nazi Party. Did Hitler the artist see these pastiches as just the beginning? He managed, in any case, to be satisfied with them until 1914, just as he agreed, for lack of anything better, to draw billboards advertising the antiperspirant powder Teddy and to reproduce ad infinitum the annex to Munich's city hall, where weddings were held, after which Hitler the art dealer would sell the newlyweds a "souvenir" of the place.[16]

On the eve of World War I, though he had not abandoned his artistic pretensions, he no longer wanted to be a painter and was content to mechanically execute the reproductions that were his livelihood. He now called himself an architect and had immersed himself in a large-scale project: to build the largest assembly hall in the world, seventeen times the size of Saint Peter's in Rome and large enough to accommodate a crowd of 180,000 people. He moved abruptly from the infinitely small to the gigantic, gave up the cozy world of his petit bourgeois enthusiasts, imagined an art for the use of the masses, and went into politics—at last.

Even though his blueprints displayed an affected academicism reminiscent of his first experiments as a painter, Hitler's vision was colossal. While still living with his mother in Linz, he had begun to fill his notebook with sketches inspired, in all likelihood, by the work of the architect of the day: at the end of the nineteenth century, Camillo Sitte had advocated a mix of neoclassical and neogothic monumentalism, very much in vogue in official Viennese circles, of which the Ringstrasse was a faithful illustration. According to the architect, every urban construction should comply with a unified artistic model, patterned on the Wagnerian project of the total synthesis of the arts (*Gesamtkunstwerk*).[17] Hitler had become infatuated with its application in architecture, but he could not find the master builder and the patron who would give him the opportunity. He had to wait until he rose to power to assign to a mimetic double his grandiose projects, supposed to finally embody the unhappy consciousness of the Germans. This role was played by Paul Ludwig Troost, and, after his death, by Albert Speer, who was at Hitler's side in Paris on 23 June 1940.

A DEAD PARIS

Hitler, who had planned to see the French capital only "as an artist among artists," with the sculptor Arno Breker and the architects Speer and Hermann Giesler, let himself be convinced by Keitel to invite "politicians" as well: Luftwaffe Generalleutnant Karl Bodenschatz, the physician and SS Obersturmbannführer der Waffen-SS Karl Brandt, Adjutant des Heeres Gerhard Engel, and NSDAP Reichsleiter Martin Bormann.[18] In fact, he was more obsessed by the "great lessons" to be drawn from his historic visit than by the political show. It was for him a matter of seizing on a model whose moderation fascinated him, though he wanted "his artists" to double its size to embody his worldwide hegemony. The style of the Third Reich had to be an oversized version of the academic neoclassicism that was then in vogue throughout the West and whose advantage was to be reassuring by virtue of its robust air and its references to the golden age of classical civilization. For a regime that wanted to do away with history and live in the *pure present*, art was to take over the sacred rites of the past without regard for the purity of genres but in accordance with the apparent meaning of forms. Then everything, from Wilhelmine banalities to the architecture of the French Revolution, whether that of Étienne-Louis Boullée or Claude-Nicolas Ledoux, could contribute to the project of Speer and his ilk: these earlier architects, too, had attempted to build a new, willful man, not just a "sensitive" one. Any model could be rehabilitated so long as its forms proved eloquent—but gigantism, sharp angles, orthogonality, and shoddy historicity captured the Nazi ideal better than any other forms. One has only to compare them with the roundness of American streamlining,[19] which embodied the reverse: a collective ideal that was individualistic and oriented toward comfort. Excluding anything that would have too explicitly recalled "collective relaxation," Nazism assimilated at least three different registers, which were to be linked to the variants, more or less sharp, more or less technocratic, of a heterogeneous ideological system: neoclassicism (for the masses), regionalism (for everyday use), and functionalism (reserved for industrial life).[20]

In fact, far from being new and monolithic, Nazi style was an appropriation, a copy, a pastiche whose incoherence was amply revealed in Hitler's imaginary museum and in his own petit bourgeois interiors. His tour of Paris reflected his eclecticism. He wanted to begin his visit with the baroque architecture of the Opéra, his favorite building, where "he was enthused…his eyes glittering, lost in ecstasy," which "troubled" even Speer. After admiring the site down to the smallest recesses that he had seen in books, he had someone ask the old French guard to show him the chief of state's "reception room" and theater box. Since the one was nonexistent and the other hard to reach, he commented on democracy's contempt for its leaders as he continued his visit, prior to whispering in his aide-de-camp's ear that they were going to take their leave, having offered the French "guide" a tip that he flatly refused.[21] It made them wonder, Breker especially, whether they were witnessing a harbinger of a disastrous "collaboration."

The next phase was devoted to visiting the highlights of Paris: the Champs-Elysées, which they went up slowly, thinking of the spectacular echo, in Berlin, of the north-south axis, two and a half times the size, then under construction; the Arc de Triomphe, which must have reminded them of the enormous arch, double the size of the French one, that Speer was supposed to build, following Hitler's drawings, and for which Breker was finishing the decorations; the Eiffel Tower, which the Führer considered a fine example of a piece of modern architecture able to elicit strong sensations. The visitors then posed on the esplanade of the Trocadéro, before their mood turned dark as they passed the dome of the Invalides, near the commemorative monument to Charles Mangin, the general whose troops had occupied the Ruhr in 1921.[22]

In effect, all Paris was covered in the itinerary followed by Hitler, who, according to Speer, spent too little time at the place des Vosges, Musée du Louvre, Palais de Justice, and Sainte-Chapelle, preferring to waste time at Sacré-Coeur de Montmartre and to press on to Montparnasse, the famous bohemian district that Breker had praised to him.

GERMAN FRANCE

The import of Hitler's visit became clear that evening, when he summoned Speer and dictated a decree in which he ordered all construction in Berlin to resume. Having often wondered if Paris would not have to be destroyed,[23] he was delighted to have finally seen it "in good condition." Berlin was supposed to vie with it, to the point of making people forget the French miniature, whose only import was to inspire the major public works projects to which Hitler would devote all the time not set aside for the war and politics. Speer helped him realize plans that would become intelligible to Hitler's architect only after the fall of the Nazi regime. In their French "frivolousness," the buildings of the latter, designed in 1939, belonged to a neo-Empire genre, "comparable to the style that prevailed a hundred and twenty-five years before, shortly before Napoleon's fall. They were marked by excessive ornamentation, a mania for gilding, a passion for pomp, and total decadence,"[24] all of which made Hitler's drawings more comprehensible to Speer but also presaged the Führer's fall. Until then, Speer adhered to his leader's decisions, even though Hitler had tipped his hand to the architect, a few months before the outbreak of World War II, by asking him to substitute a terrestrial globe for the swastika the imperial eagle clasped in its claws on the model for the Volkshalle in Berlin.

After his visit in June 1940, Hitler never returned to Paris. He delegated to his administration in France the task of bringing the culture of the defeated nation into line. If he was told that French culture did not correspond to the norms imposed in Germany, he took the news in stride, never giving any weight to what seemed to go counter to Nazi hegemony. He reckoned that the passage of time would impose his new cultural order. As for the dross of European decadence, "art that was Jewish, Bolshevik" or "Masonic," he had decided to "introduce" it to the German people in 1937, as a vestige useful for assessing how far his nation had come.[25] If France was still wallowing in the mire, it was, according to Hitler's logic, because that country was displaying a tremendous weakness. About the Salon d'Automne that Speer described to him as filled with "degenerate art," Hitler simply remarked that "the intellectual soundness of the French people" was of no importance to Germans and that it was in Germany's interest to let France "degenerate."[26]

But was this the result of long, considered reflection, of a "purely rational" decision?[27] Events would show, to the contrary, that Hitler was flying by the seat of his pants. His way of governing left a great deal of latitude to his deputies, to whom he rarely gave precise instructions. The artistic occupation of France was accomplished by means of "bureaucratic decisions"[28] and the individual initiatives of his lieutenants. In the end, despite the ongoing war between his men and his agencies, Hitler felt satisfied with the results.

From the first days of the occupation of France, all and sundry entered the fray, each one assigned to his post: the German embassy, Propaganda-Abteilung Frankreich, Kunstschutz. The best hotels filled up with a new bureaucracy, circulars decreeing the rules of the game proliferated, and the infighting continued in France—just as in Germany. The period following the armistice was conducive to rival projects. Göring, in charge of the Nazi Party's Vierjahresplan, and Walther Funk, minister of economic affairs, fought over exclusive rights to the economic achievements of the new European order. Ribbentrop, as foreign minister, wanted to unite all the planning agencies of greater Europe. And Joseph Goebbels allied himself with the military to take control of the entire propaganda machine.

Beyond the contradictions percolated the Nazi obsession with making art an instrument of propaganda and a diplomatic pawn. Whether dowry or sexual substitute in this "union of France and Germany," whose mutual attraction Jules Romains had loosely located in 1934,[29] art was at the center of the Nazi desire to appropriate France by stealing its masterpieces. That was one way to profitably end an old European cultural war, in which Paris had too often been awarded victory. Only fifteen days after the armistice thus began, in accordance with the law of the jungle, a formidable art-looting operation.

Was this a mere accident of history or a noirish tale of a war economy gone awry? At the Nuremberg trials, such looting seemed like a trifle compared to the homicidal atrocities perpetrated against individuals. It was nonetheless considered a war crime by the international military tribunal, and the circumstances were judged sufficiently telling for the French delegation from the public prosecutor's office to grant it a significant share of attention. The evidence admirably revealed the character of the defendants and the nature of the regimes they had served, in all their contradictions. The seizures carried out by Nazi high officials made the occupiers look like a gang of aesthetes whose internecine wars profited the head bandit, the major beneficiary of what was after all a particularly rich supply of booty. On the French side, the administration vainly resisted, played for time: hobbled in large part, it ran up against German obstinacy and the cowardice of its own government. After the war, its functionaries would look more like weaklings than crooks—but there is proof that some French citizens had committed robbery. This was especially true of the middlemen, who, transformed into "aftermarket" thieves, grudgingly settled for the leftovers, watching thousands of works belonging to dispossessed Jewish collectors slip across the Rhine. In France, as elsewhere, in the rigged game of collaborationist diplomacy, it was the Jews who paid the highest tribute to the vanquisher's greed—and sometimes to that of the corrupt defeated. The situation led all parties to reconsider the definition of "national" collections, taking shelter behind the new laws of racial exclusion.

We begin with an account of these crimes because it will allow us to portray a few of the main players—and because the looting started at the earliest opportunity, even before artistic activities had resumed, and was hidden as much as possible from the public eye.

THE CRIMINAL GANG

Fifteen days after the armistice, on 30 June 1940, Generalfeldmarschall Wilhelm Keitel, supreme commander of the German armed forces, sent a note to General der Artillerie Alfred von Vollard-Bockelberg, military commander of Paris, to announce that Hitler had given the order to "safeguard—in addition to art objects belonging to the French state—art objects and historical documents belonging to individuals, notably Jews."[30] The operation claimed to be merely diplomatic: this measure was not "to constitute an expropriation, but a transfer to the custody of the Germans [of goods that were] to serve as a bargaining chip in peace negotiations." Though the explicit reference to Jewish collections did not augur well, the content of the memo complied with the usual practices of all-out war. In any case, the order Vollard-Bockelberg issued fifteen days later no longer mentioned the ethnicity of the collectors; it was now simply a matter of "safeguarding the art objects in the occupied territory of France" and, to that end, of preventing their circulation or relocation without authorization. In fact, the physical description of any movable object worth more than 100,000 francs that it mandated was the start of an inventory that would facilitate the looting. For the moment, the apparent legalism of the documents, and the fact that the Führer officially entrusted the execution of these measures to the military, left hope that they were only anodyne. The regulations of the German campaign were inspired, in theory, by the Hague Convention, on the laws and customs of war on land, and Franz Graf Wolff-Metternich, head of the Kunstschutz for the occupied zone, could truthfully claim that he was fighting for the defense of art objects of every kind. Appointed by the Oberkommando des Heeres (OKH) on 11 May 1940, this art historian and specialist in medieval architecture was responsible for the conservation of monuments in the Rhineland. He later composed a long detailed report[31] in which he retraced the eventful history of the looting of French collections from the time of his appointment until his dismissal in June 1942. Neither he nor his superior, Brauchitsch, survived the caprices of the leaders of the Nazi Party: Hitler and, in particular, Göring very quickly preferred Alfred Rosenberg instead.

Between Keitel's note on 30 June 1940 and Vollard-Bockelberg's order on 15 July, the Führer began playing one side against the other by allowing Rosenberg, his "delegate overseeing the instruction and the intellectual and doctrinal education of the Nazi Party," to establish a "special general staff" (Einsatzstab Reichsleiters Rosenberg, or ERR), which became the key player in the great pillage. That appointment created rivals: Ribbentrop, his representative and the German ambassador to Vichy France Otto Abetz, and finally Goebbels all scented a lucrative affair. From then on, with Hitler's agreement, a team of archivists, aided by the Gestapo and under Rosenberg's orders, searched libraries and archives in the occupied areas with the intention of discovering "documents of value for Germany." On 17 September 1940, Rosenberg found that his prerogatives had been further expanded in the name of the "methodical" fight "in the realm of ideas" against the Jews and Freemasons and their allies. Works of art belonging to Jewish or Freemason collectors then entered the eye of the storm.

THE BERCHTESGADEN EXPRESS

Abetz grudgingly had to accept the new powers granted to Rosenberg that blocked from that point on the "seizure" of works of art belonging to the French state, French cities, individuals, and Jews, whose most precious objects had been gathered and stored, beginning in July 1940, in the embassy on rue de Lille. For lack of time and means, Abetz's activities remained more modest than those of his rival, though he did have a few impressive depredations to his credit. Among these was the famous collection of Paris modernist paintings, discovered in Bordeaux, from which he hoped to make the largest profit possible, given that the canvases by a Jewish painter such as Camille Pissarro or by too "wildly expressionist" artists such as Georges Braque were supposed to be of interest not to Germany but solely to the French market. Even so, he had to move faster than Rosenberg, who, with the means at his disposal, could at any moment "flood" the market with "degenerate" works. With Ribbentrop's authorization, in early July 1940 Abetz sent Oberstleutnant Hans Speidel, chief of staff of the military command, a list of the names and addresses of fifteen of the most important dealers in Paris, demanding their premises be searched and their collections immediately seized.

Abetz's particularly ruthless action was a source of "shame" even for those in charge of the operation, at least when he gave the order to conduct the seizures by night. In the end, Speidel decided to bar the Geheime Feldpolizei from continuing to work for the ambassador, who then had to request help from a new thief, Carltheo Zeitschel, and the contingent headed by Eberhard Freiherr von Künsberg. The latter had available to him a special commando unit that would eventually extend its looting operations as far as Russia, on the orders of the German foreign ministry (Auswärtiges Amt). The Gruppe Künsberg turned over to Abetz the pieces looted in France from Maurice de Rothschild's residences and from several apartments owned by Jews. In all, between two thousand and three thousand works were sent to Ribbentrop or sold, while the embassy kept about eighty paintings and a few pieces of furniture, including Rothschild's desk, at which Abetz liked to work. By September, however, the Ribbentrop-Abetz faction had lost ground to the Rosenberg-Göring partnership.

In Göring, Abetz found a thief greater than himself who was aboard a locomotive even faster than Abetz's own, according to the rich metaphor the ambassador invented to justify his expediency in France. In 1945, from the depths of the Cherche-Midi prison, Abetz compared himself to the Swiss engineer who, wanting to save the Saint Gotthard express whose brakes had failed, went to meet it with a locomotive. At the moment the locomotive made contact with the express, it had to be going in the same direction and at the same breakneck speed. "Once in place ahead of the train, it could gradually apply its brakes and avoid the catastrophe."[32] Hence Abetz's "tactic" consisted of rushing ahead of his superiors' will: in drafting the first anti-Semitic measures promulgated in the occupied zone, which were approved by Ribbentrop and Reinhard Heydrich, chief of German police; in presenting himself, on 30 July 1940, as a zealous advocate of limiting French cultural influence abroad and as an active defender of Germanic culture and the opening of an Institut allemand in Paris; and, finally, in trying, using his words again, to "avoid the catastrophe," by overtaking the terribly efficient Rosenberg-Göring partnership. In vain, there as elsewhere.

GÖRING'S WHIMS

Beginning in October 1940, the frenzied looting of Jewish property was replaced by systematic seizure. Soon after the military administration was excluded from the game, in November, Göring came to Paris to admire his protégé's first haul. The treasure hunt could begin under the protection of the air force, and anything complementing the collections of the Third Reich and its leader could be spirited away after it was inventoried.

Rosenberg's agency, which entered the fray in October under the direction of Baron Kurt von Behr,[33] began by seeking out collections abandoned in Paris, then in the provinces and in warehouses Because the works had been concealed, often painstakingly so, the operation required a support staff, which the agency hoped to recruit from the French police. But reports complained of their unwillingness, so much so that the ERR had to call in an "external" workforce, shady "informers" who provided the necessary complement to the German agencies' methodical actions. Once the art objects had been brought to the commandeered Jeu de Paume and Louvre museums, they were appraised, photographed, and entered into the record before being packed up. It was then that the inventory, which claimed to be exhaustive, was transformed into a riddle, given the lack of information on the artists and the origins of the pieces. The reports now began lamenting the time spent filling the record books: three between the beginning of operations and April 1943. In all, according to the (less than truthful) report by ERR officer Robert Scholz, a month before the liberation of Paris there were 203 collections comprising 21,903 objects of all kinds, including some 11,000 paintings—the vast majority belonging to Jewish collectors—that were shipped to the Third Reich in hundreds of train cars, departing from the Gare du Nord, between March 1941 and July 1944. The exhibit of recovered "masterpieces" that was held after the war provided a glimpse of the artistic magnitude of many pieces, among which were paintings by masters from every country: Lucas Cranach the Elder, Jean-Honoré Fragonard, Francisco de Goya, Frans Hals, Bartolomé Murillo, Rembrandt, Peter Paul Rubens, Anthony van Dyck, Diego Velázquez, and Jean-Antoine Watteau.[34] The Allies would find crates everywhere: more than five hundred repositories in Bavaria and the Tyrol, in castles, salt mines, mountains, tunnels, schools, convents, presbyteries, and banks, in Germany but also in Austria, Poland, Czechoslovakia, Italy, and Romania.[35]

Even the tremendous scale of that recovery does not accurately convey the extent of the looting. In addition to coveted works sent to Germany, there were the "modern" paintings that were used in France or abroad as currency in acquiring pieces more in keeping with the Nazi aesthetic. There were as well the pieces looted in the last months of the occupation by troops passing through. As for the "decadent rejects," some French dealers rightly wagered that they would one day prove to be very lucrative, and, if need be, they knew how to capitalize on the artistic prerequisites of their interlocutors to palm off on them conventional pieces of mediocre quality. More often, sales or acquisitions took place under threat and at a rate of exchange clearly unfavorable to the French.

For all around the thieves hummed an indispensable intermediary machine, with brokers, experts, and informants. Each group had its own interest in the looting, and each accepted the rules of discretion imposed by the Germans. Informed by all parties, the Göring-Rosenberg faction kept up to date with dealers' and individuals' intentions, ordering its men to make or reply to offers, to buy if necessary, with money from a special account made available to them, or to sell.[36] Then there were the "degenerate" works—impressionist, cubist, fauvist, expressionist, or abstract—that could not be converted into cash. Göring completely defied the Führer's will by sending through Germany a train of impressionist paintings that were to be exchanged or sold abroad. But that operation could not be repeated very often, and the limits of the French market, which had run out of steam by 1943, undoubtedly justified the events of 27 July of that same year.[37]

On that day, Rose Valland, attachée at the Jeu de Paume[38] and the only witness to describe the scene, saw rising up from the terrace of the Tuileries gardens a column of smoke that did not vanish until sundown. According to her account, what went up in flames were paintings marked with the initials "E.K.," *entartete Kunst* (degenerate art), by André Masson, Joán Miró, Francis Picabia, Suzanne Valadon, Paul Klee, Max Ernst, Fernand Léger, Pablo Picasso, Moïse Kisling, Roger de La Fresnaye, Jacqueline Marval, Mané-Katz, and many others. There were five hundred to six hundred in all. Since the start of the looting, they had been kept separate and designated by the Third Reich as liable to be physically eliminated. A letter of 16 April 1943 from Rosenberg to Hitler left in doubt the handling of these rejects. In France, as elsewhere, categories were established by an adjudicative commission similar to that headed by the painter Adolf Ziegler, which had purged the museums of the Third Reich. In Paris, however, the commercial value of the works counted more than their aesthetics. Under these conditions, Walter Borchers of the ERR had no difficulty exacting from Hitler exemptions for the impressionist masterpieces he knew could help fuel the war economy.

Conversely, the works destroyed on 27 July 1943, deemed unlikely to be traded, could not escape destruction on economic grounds. In the case of artworks, as in that of people, the Nazi state demonstrated its desire to instrumentalize its enemies: before being destroyed, they were to serve the machine of the Third Reich, not only its phobias but also its finances. "The excess" destroyed in the gardens at the Jeu de Paume may have been ruthlessly liquidated for "not even" serving the Nazi economy. The men of the ERR fought against the paintings, stabbed and slashed them with knives, tore them to pieces, then transported them in trucks to their funeral pyre.

All that reminds us of the autos-da-fé of books, as well as the destruction of "decadent" paintings from German museums, in Berlin on 20 March 1939, just before the notorious auctioning in Lucerne of modern art purged from public collections, from which the Nazis extracted the largest profit possible. In Berlin, the massacre took place, very sensibly, in the courtyard of the city's main fire station. In Paris, however, the Nazis chose to destroy modern works on the very site where they had been kept, a particularly symbolic place because for years the Musée du Jeu de Paume had been the only venue to promote "foreign" and modern art as well as, in 1937, the genesis of modern and "international" painting, especially the abstract, Dadaist, and surrealist currents, then unknown in France.

The auto-da-fé was judged so significant that it gave rise to various interpretations, some going so far as to question the account furnished by Valland, who was accused by some of the chief perpetrators of the carnage—based on plain statements made to the press (in the 1960s)—of inventing the episode to camouflage French misconduct. In general, however, most refused to call into question the professionalism of that agent of the administration, an exemplary protector of stolen works, who, having unrelentingly spied on the Germans of the ERR, made it possible for the art to be recovered.[39] The events unfolded in a manner so unofficial as to avoid inopportune reactions from the French. The massacre received no publicity because it was regarded as an internal matter decided more in response to money or "space" problems than to an antidecadent policy and because, over time, the ERR had taken on the appearance of a business in the service of high officials.

As it turned out, it was not only the agency's coffers that the pillaging swelled: "a very small percentage" of the hundreds of thousands of works seized enriched Göring's personal collection, as a reward for the role he had played in that hunt for art objects. In his vanity, the art lover claimed that his collection was the largest in Germany, if not in Europe. He had the idea that the rarest pieces were within his reach. His only rival was Hitler: Ribbentrop, an admirer of ancient tapestries, had been left in the dust. Particularly taken with the eighteenth century, Göring was more open than the Führer to some aspects of modern art and often scooped up major pieces, not necessarily neglecting works whose inspiration deviated from official banalities: several of Edgar Degas's dancers; Georges Seurat's *Sleeping Man;* Pierre Bonnard's *Work Table;* Henri Matisse's *Odalisque with Babouches, The Pianist,* and *Checkers Players;* Braque's *Musical Score and Fruit;* as well as Vincent van Gogh's *Langlois Bridge at Arles,* Paul Cézanne's *Bathers,* and, even worse from Hitler's perspective, works by the Jewish artist Pissarro.

Hitler did not have the same audacity, displaying pedestrian, often ethereal tastes, which gave his collections a not very glorious air. In fact, when he asked Hans Posse to round out his collection, which was to be sent to the major museum in Linz, Posse had to admit to the Führer that a number of his acquisitions, often extremely expensive (when Hitler had paid for them), were not up to snuff, particularly all the works of the Munich school that he so prized. Did Rosenberg consider the latter good enough for the Nazi Party? History does not tell us, but we know that those pieces from Hitler's collection less in keeping with the fancies of the two aesthetes Göring and Rosenberg were finally shipped off to embellish the buildings of the Third Reich and the Nazi Party. What is more, in his correspondence, Rosenberg called upon Göring to acknowledge these transfers, as a reproof of the personal appetites of that "friend of the plastic arts": Had not the Nazi Party led the fight against the Jews for twenty years? It was pointless for Rosenberg to treat Göring as if he were a dear friend by having "a little souvenir"—a seascape by the seventeenth-century Dutch painter Jacob Adriaensz. Bellevois—sent to Göring for his birthday, on 11 January 1943.[40] The two men had done battle, and Rosenberg had lost by early November 1940, when Göring came to look at his spoils at the Jeu de Paume and, greatly excited by the sight of the masterpieces there, had the audacity to order Behr and his experts to henceforth take orders only from him, even though they were not supposed to be his subordinates. Hitler simply conceded the Reichsmarschall's authority over the ERR sometime later, thus eclipsing Rosenberg, who had to be satisfied with a letter from Göring giving him to understand that his appointment to the post had created some rivals (Ribbentrop, Goebbels) and that only Göring's authority could put an end to all discussion.

The whims Göring imposed on his entourage, the pomp and circumstances surrounding his birthday each year, suggest the scope of his cruel and immoral childishness. Even in 1944, the Third Reich's setbacks did not prevent him from inviting Nazi high officials to his Karinhall estate on 12 January. They came laden with sumptuous presents carefully specified by Göring himself: ingots from the Balkans, cigars from Holland, and, of course, works of art of great value. Misappropriation of entire train cars filled with all sorts of merchandise acquired on the black market in Europe, withholding from the salaries of German civil servants of money meant to pay for his acquisitions,[41] systematic looting of Jewish collections—the scope of Göring's professional misconduct had no limit. It is true that his greed met with precious little rebuff. Hitler himself only half-heartedly imposed a theoretical restriction on his second in command: French public collections were to be spared, at least until the final victory, when they could no longer serve as a diplomatic pawn.

Moreover, the looting of Jewish collections in France was largely enough to satiate the Führer, who privately railed against his lieutenant's excesses even as he reserved cushy "privileges" for himself. Just as Rosenberg sent the Reichsmarschall, for his birthday in 1943, Bellevois's seascape, in April he dispatched to Hitler, for his birthday, "an album containing photographs of the most precious paintings of the abandoned Jewish collections." In accordance with his orders, these paintings had been "safeguarded, in the occupied territories of the West." The album was to serve as a "complement to the fifty-three most precious works of art that, as a result of that operation, have been added to your collection." Rosenberg hoped thus to procure for Hitler a "brief moment of relaxation before the beautiful art objects that you hold close to your heart," so that they might bring "a ray of joy and beauty into the gravity and grandeur of your present life."[42] The civilized tone camouflaged his gangster-style dealings, for which Zeitschel, echoing Abetz on this subject, found the right word in 1941. Zeitschel had rushed to tell the SS torturer Theodor Dannecker of the departure of the "German Jew at 45, boulevard d'Auteil" who no longer enjoyed the protection of Spain. But Zeitschel was informed too late and complained to his superior, in a letter of 20 June 1941, that he had been unable to act immediately but hoped that there would still be something left "to snatch" (*zu schnappen*).

THE INCORRUPTIBLES

Not all of the German administration adjusted to the scope of the criminal gang's misdeeds, but it had no opportunity to change the rules of the game. Metternich, charged since his installation in Paris, in August 1940, with protecting artworks in France, had tried appealing to the Hague Convention,[43] but he could not prevent the escalation of the looting, which disgusted him and convinced him that his dismissal was more imminent every day. The discussion he had with Göring when the latter came to Paris in February 1941 confirmed Metternich's fears: the Reichsmarschall was going to respond to his integrity as a soldier with increased retaliatory measure. Metternich's men would be corrupted (Hermann Bunjes in particular),[44] and his actions blocked by the activism of those he nicknamed "modern buccaneers." He saw the situation worsen from one day to the next, until he was replaced, in June 1942, by his second in command, Bernhard von Tieschowitz, who likewise, with a few exceptions, could not stay the course of events.

Turned into puppets by the master pillagers, both Metternich and Tieschowitz confined themselves to warning the French administration about planned seizures, particularly when major works in national collections were being eyed. Regarding them, General der Infanterie Alfred Streccius, military commander of France, had ordered that national repositories be plastered with official signs that—in theory—protected them from the pirates.[45] But secret negotiations would get past formal prohibitions. Although the operations that were the most spectacular had occurred between the beginning of the occupation and the end of 1941, the vanquisher's appetite grew progressively as Jewish collections went off to Germany and Franco-German relations became more strained.

The collaborationist press responded with silence or nationalistic triumphalism. In February 1941, *Les nouveaux temps* expressed delight that no French works of art had been sent to Germany. In relation to the villainous laws, that count was accurate. Up to that time, only Jewish collections had made their way across the Rhine. According to

Metternich, the joint response of his agency and the French administration had prevented raids on the museums, but the changing situation made the plans of certain leaders, who saw little reason to wait any longer, more obvious every day. Hence it begins to make sense that Otto Kümmel, director of German museums, placed under Goebbels's authority, was given the task of going, in secret, through French catalogs. On Hitler's orders, all German art objects that had not been returned after the Napoleonic Wars or during World War I were to be acquired in trade deals and become part of the collections in Hitler's future museum at Linz (near his birthplace). Works that supposedly belonged to the Third Reich, however remotely, by virtue of their history or their subject matter, were identified: the list was endless. In September 1940, Kümmel came to France to complete his documentation before providing Goebbels, in early 1941, with two reports totaling about a thousand pages. In all, several thousand works were to be "returned" to Germany following the example of the paintings from Alsatian museums that had been looted immediately, even as works from the army, navy, and aviation museums in Paris, from Malmaison, and from several provincial museums had already disappeared.[46] In late 1941, Goebbels made a promise to Metternich that Germany would wait until the peace treaty was signed to demand its due from France. But it was no use: the attitude of Göring at the least conflicted with these verbal commitments.

After the Jewish collections were exhausted, there was no question but that more looting would follow, only its precise modalities had not yet been determined by the Nazis. The French balked, equivocated, and played for time, but were not always followed by their leaders.

THE SACRIFICIAL *LAMB*

To the occupier's crimes against Jewish collections the various agencies of the French administration responded with stupefied letters or lively protests. It emerges from this rich documentation that no one had enough of a free hand to intervene against the looting as such and that they took a stand only against some of its modalities. The French, being in a position of weakness, resorted to subterfuges, almost always without results, running up against real determination on the Germans' part. Moreover, in the view of some French agencies, once the anti-Jewish laws had been promulgated, the Vichy regime could hope to benefit from the situation.

In the face of the French administration's protests, in particular those of the Vichy Commissariat général aux questions juives, whose own motives were not pure, Germany settled matters, in November 1940, by imposing a new legal apparatus that required total submission from France. Gerhard Utikal, head of the ERR in Berlin, then signed a crushing decree that reminded the French authorities of their subordinate position. In substance, the vanquishers pointed out to France that it was normal that they should receive at least "a small indemnity for the burdensome costs borne and the great sacrifices made by the Third Reich on behalf of the peoples of Europe in the fight against Jewry." They added that Jews were not protected by the Hague Convention because, "for millennia," Jews had considered "all non-Jews to be deprived of all rights." Moreover, the Third Reich was being gracious enough to put up for auction pieces of Jewish property it did not want and to give the proceeds to war orphans and widows in France. As a result, the French state ought to be reasonable enough not to demand more, for, after all, it had not acquired the capacity to dispose of Jewish property "on its own"; rather, "it was the victory of the Third Reich's armies that had given it" that power. It thus had no right to "protest against the measures that the Third Reich, in its capacity as the vanquisher, [enforced] against the Jews."

This position would be repeated every time it was necessary. In November 1941, the ERR general staff responded, yet again, to protests by the Commissariat général aux questions juives by declaring that the Third Reich alone had as a matter of priority the right to dispose of Jewish property and that only a "magnanimous policy" had led it to forgo real estate and other assets and attend "only" to research documents and cultural objects. In addition, the French government had to be aware of "the scope of the major political reform in Europe" and hence was obliged to "explain to the French people that [this was] an extraordinarily considerate measure."[47]

The French sought several times to turn the situation around by drawing on specious legal arguments. The collectors stripped of French nationality had, in the eyes of the law, lost ownership rights to their property, which was thus placed at the French administration's disposal. Because the administration managed that property on behalf of the charity organization Secours national and not on behalf of the state budget, it remained private property and as a result enjoyed the legal protection defined by article 46 of the Hague Convention. The paradox was glaringly obvious: the French wanted control of the proceeds from private property in the name of protecting ownership rights, even though this private property had been stolen from individuals subject to the villainous laws in force in France.

On 14 December 1940, a month after Utikal's decree, the finance minister complained to the Vichy government's general representative to the occupied territories about the assets of the Rothschilds, who had been stripped of their French nationality (in compliance with the law of 23 July 1940). Because of the Germans, he said, the Administration des domaines could not manage the estate as it wished.[48] Somewhat later, that administration, representing French legal authority and in that capacity responsible for ensuring the "management" of Jewish property, claimed the use of the Rothschild family's assets on behalf of Secours national. The author of the note added that the sum total of this estate ought not to be allocated to the state budget but exclusively to Secours national: history, here as elsewhere, would reveal the gaps in the policy. In fact, it was war diplomacy that would profit, when the state decided to offer Francisco Franco the frescoes by José Mariá Sert y Badiá that had decorated one of the Rothschilds' châteaus. By official order, workers camouflaged in a Studebaker from the "prefecture of the Seine" arrived to remove the wood panels frescoed with Chinese subjects that since 1925 had been installed in a gaming room at the château de Laversine.

FRENCH PROPERTY

The situation was all the more ambiguous because, beginning in September 1939, Jewish collectors had entrusted their works to national museums. France could not have released itself from its contract with these collectors except by opposing Keitel's order, of 17 September 1940, which declared illegal any transfer of an artwork to the state that had occurred after the declaration of war in September 1939. Under such conditions, how are we to interpret the argument made by Jérôme Carcopino, minister of national education and youth—and an official who, in other circumstances, attempted to change the direction of German anti-Semitic policy even while rigorously applying the second Statut des Juifs?[49] On 3 June 1941, he explained to Fernand de Brinon, general representative for the French government to the occupied territories, that Germany's seizure of works belonging to Jews—whether or not they had been stripped of French nationality—was irregular, and that that included works in national repositories. It would, moreover, be regrettable if such seizures were to become commonplace and if the works sequestered by the French could not be inventoried. "Some of them," he said, looked to be "first-rate," "worthy of being part of the national collections." A special account, he added, had been made available to the Réunion des musées nationaux for this purpose.[50] Furthermore, what are we to think of the intervention by the vice president of the Conseil des ministres, François Darlan, who, a few days later, pointed out to Brinon the same German misdeeds that "not only prevented the legal liquidation of property placed in sequestration but also were extremely detrimental to Secours national and to the country's artistic patrimony"?[51]

The attitude of Jacques Jaujard, director of the Réunion des musées nationaux and future director general of arts and letters after the liberation, was much less suspect and starkly revealed the limits on the actions of faithful but hamstrung French officials. In the end, in their preoccupation with effectiveness, they confined themselves to protecting only the most prestigious collections belonging to the most "important" Jewish figures. At the start of the occupation, in order to save the collections of Veil-Picard, David-Weill, Bischofsheim, Seligman, Georges Wildenstein, Alphonse Kahn, and Paul Rosenberg, Jaujard proposed to the secretary general of industry and domestic trade that the law of 10 September 1940 be extended to the property of Jews who had not been stripped of French nationality. That law stipulated that provisional administrators be appointed to oversee such property when there was an "economic interest" in not letting it be abandoned.[52] He also suggested entrusting the sequestration of the collections in question to the authority of a commission whose members he determined.[53] In the same vein, he intended to rely on the legislation drafted on 23 June 1941 that would have prohibited the export of pieces dating from before the twentieth century, but the law did not go into effect in the occupied zone.

Jaujard had acquired a reputation as a skillful negotiator, though he had begun his political career by chance: during his travels as an insurance salesman, he happened one day to make an impression on the politician Paul Painlevé, who recruited him to other duties.[54] After distinguishing himself during the evacuation of the Museo del Prado collections threatened by the Spanish Civil War, Jaujard set himself up as the veritable patron saint of France's national museums and put all his energy into defending French property, even if it meant meeting with more than one reversal of fortune at the hands of some other party who, whatever Jaujard did, had the last word.

Under the heading of futile petitions was the German response to his urgent request to do an inventory of works about to be removed. Having been turned down several times, Jaujard must have waited for a propitious moment to "negotiate." That day seemed to have come in October 1940, when the Louvre no longer had enough room to contain the Third Reich's plunder and the occupier demanded the Jeu de Paume, which had the advantage of being autonomous. In the presence of Behr and Bunjes, whom Metternich had brought in, Jaujard handed over this new den in exchange for the promise that he would be able to draw up what came to be known as the Franco-German dual inventory. Those concerned agreed—for the moment—and the inventory began, on the French side, in November, with the arrival of hundreds of crates at the Jeu de Paume under the supervision of Valland, a curator who was attached to the museum's staff. But on the first day, Bunjes arrived to tell her that no French inventory would be done and that he would proceed without her team. He later stated in a report that German scholars were capable of doing it themselves.[55] Thanks to a polite conversation with Behr, Valland managed to remain on site and could thus record, at night and in secret, the information Germans disclosed during the day regarding the works and their destinations. In all other respects, the vanquisher had chalked up another victory. Henceforth soldiers wearing the party's red armband and experts in white smocks could go about their business undisturbed, preparing for All Saints' Day 1940 an exhibition of the plunder, in anticipation of Göring's arrival.[56]

The looting would undoubtedly not have taken the course it did if, on that day, the Reichsmarschall had not lost his head at the sight of the collected masterpieces. But the Third Reich was led by aesthetes ready to sacrifice everything to their refined tastes. Several incidents in particular reveal the eagerness of certain Nazi high officials to loot France before the final victory and probably with Hitler's blessing. First in line was Göring, intoxicated by his initial haul, who wanted to acquire—through exchange or other means—the antependium from the Basel cathedral, Gregor Erhart's *Beautiful German*, a large collection in Rheims of drawings by Cranach, the center panel of the triptych by the Meister der Heiligen Sippe, and so on and so forth; in addition, Heinrich Himmler was interested in the Bayeux Tapestry. Here as elsewhere, Pierre Laval's return to politics as head of the Vichy government in 1942 marked the start of negotiations that were increasingly advantageous for the spoiled children of the Third Reich.

LAVAL NEGOTIATES

French administrative personnel staunchly protected national collections, having taken as much care as possible to hide them away, beginning in August 1939, in the many provincial depositories, once they belonged to the public patrimony. Though it turned out that Pétain, in agreement with the leadership at the fine arts administration, was not inclined to sell off French works, Laval did not hesitate to use them to advantage in his ongoing negotiations with Germany.

In that respect, among the business deals undertaken, that of the *Adoration of the Mystic Lamb* altarpiece was the most edifying.[57] In 1939, Belgium had entrusted that masterpiece by Jan van Eyck to France to protect it from enemy bombardments. It was thus safely stored at the Musée national du château de Pau, until Germany decided to retrieve it. In August 1941, Jaujard notified his superior, Louis Hautecoeur, head of the fine arts administration, that on 6 August Dr. Pfitzner from the Kunstschutz had telephoned his department to announce that a certain Conrad Martin was going to appear at the museum in Pau to claim the altarpiece and return it to Ghent. It was therefore decided that the museum's curator, one Monsieur Molle, ought to be instructed to refuse to hand over the work without a written authorization bearing three signatures: that of the Réunion des musées nationaux, that of Metternich, and that of the burgomaster of Ghent. But on 8 August 1942, Jaujard's assistant, Joseph Billiet,[58] learned, fortuitously, through a telephone conversation, that the *Adoration of the Mystic Lamb* had been handed over to German representatives on 3 August, without anyone being consulted. Upon receiving a visit from the Germans on 1 August, the curator of the museum had not held to the agreement: he had called Vichy, which, forty-eight hours later, authorized him to hand over the Flemish work.

It was Laval[59] alone who made the decision to surrender the altarpiece to the Germans. He gave the order that the office of the minister of national education and youth, to which the fine arts administration reported, should have the curator of the museum follow his instructions, since he was persuaded that Germany would seize the work in any case, whatever France's position. "I need to negotiate," he said in substance, in the presence of his protégé Georges Hilaire. "France as a whole is in a stranglehold. This is no time for bravado."[60] The protests of Charles Rochat, secretary general of the ministry of foreign affairs, did nothing to change his mind. Nor did Pétain's promise to Hautecoeur that he would take things in hand: it was left to Hautecoeur to delegate to his lieutenant the difficult mission of calming the Belgian consul—and of retaining his own job, despite Laval's desire to oust him in favor of Hilaire.[61]

At the same time, negotiations began between Belgium and Germany, as soon as the former became aware of the fate of its property—but in vain. When the Belgians protested to Abel Bonnard, he merely replied, throwing his hands in the air, that France had been defeated. French curators, summoned by Jaujard in November 1942[62] and officially updated on how operations had unfolded since the previous August, could do no more than pass a motion of dissent, which they sent to the minister of national education and youth and which earned the instigator of the meeting a reprimand. In fact, in calling on their support, Jaujard was hoping to obtain what he had managed to extract through negotiations following the exchange of François Boucher's *Diana Emerging from Her Bath,* which had been approved by French high officials. In accordance with Darlan's instructions, that painting had gone to Germany per an agreement reached on 28 April 1941 between Brinon and

Karl Epting, adviser to the German embassy and director of the Institut allemand in Paris. When the Dresden gallery refused to hand over French works dating from the same era, as dictated by the agreement, Boucher's painting was grudgingly returned, though Ribbentrop urged Abetz to continue the search, "there or anywhere else in Germany, for eighteenth-century paintings that could later be exchanged with the administration of French museums for the Boucher."[63]

A combination of favorable circumstances and Jaujard's tenacity had prevailed in that first battle, but the matter of the *Adoration of the Mystic Lamb* did not follow the same course. The protagonists were no longer the same, and the stakes had changed considerably, on both the German and the French sides. Göring's determination was different from Ribbentrop's, and Laval's return, along with Bonnard's arrival on the scene, completely altered an already precarious balance. The "artistic" agreements between Göring and Laval, after his return, defined the new direction the French government's negotiations would take.

THE BASEL ANTEPENDIUM

In December 1942, Göring's representative in Paris[64] let Jaujard know that he wanted to press forward with major exchanges of masterpieces from French museums, the principle of which Laval had accepted following a meeting between the two. The Reichsmarschall had finally found the obliging partner who would allow him to arrive at his ends within a legal framework. On the French side, Laval was acting on his own, backed by Bonnard, his minister of national education and youth, who was well versed in negotiations that did a disservice to France.

A major thinker in intellectual collaborationist circles, Bonnard had dominated salons during the interwar period with his conversational style, wielding words like a bombastic academician. He had been a follower of Charles Maurras before distancing himself from monarchical beliefs in summer 1941, at which time he fully embraced extremism. Considered by the Germans to be the most effective pioneer of a German-French collaboration,[65] he nonetheless remained, because of his age, attached to the values of the land and thus distinguished himself from younger French Fascists, who were quicker to dismiss rural France. For all that, did his background as a Maurrassian bring him closer to the marshal? Pétain in any event opposed his nomination to the post of minister of national education and youth, if only because of the feminine preciosity Bonnard affected.[66] But since the times no longer favored the old traditionalist Pétain's resolutions but rather Laval's inclinations, Bonnard was assigned to the post, which allowed him to keep his eye not only on the education ministry but also on the country's artistic life.

His aesthete's taste and his egotistical attachment to France's national collections, put to the test by collaboration, finally gave way before the vanquisher's demands.

Under pressure from Göring, Bonnard therefore made arrangements to hand over the Basel antependium. A major piece of European goldwork, the frontal had been presented at the beginning of the eleventh century to the Basel cathedral by Henry II of Germany, then purchased in strict accordance with regulations by the Musée du Louvre in the mid-nineteenth century, before being exhibited at the Musée de Cluny. Jaujard fought to have the masterpiece excluded from negotiations. But Bonnard went against his advice. In the report that he submitted about his interview with Göring, in late December 1943, Bonnard was demonstrably impressed by the Nazi leader's selling points: the particular concern of the German army—unlike the Anglo-Americans (presented as looters)—with preserving France's patrimony; the Germanic character of the Basel antependium; the bad faith of the French, who had rushed to overvalue the work as soon as Göring had shown some interest in it; and, finally, the exchanges with Spain to which France had agreed. On this last point, Bonnard went even further, remarking that the objects France had handed over to Franco were of major importance—the crowns of Visigothic kings from the Musée de Cluny, the Iberian bust known as the Lady of Elche—and yet Spain had ultimately refused to turn over, as agreed, the tent Süleyman I had presented to Francis I.

He therefore proposed to offer Göring the frontal and could not even understand the "tone of ultimatum" the Reichsmarschall adopted over "something that was a matter of course."[67] In addition, he accepted on principle sending curators from the Musée du Louvre to Berlin to proceed with the exchange. The representatives[68] would travel with the Basel antependium and a few other coveted works in a special armor-plated railcar that was equipped with an antiaircraft gun and escorted by fighter aircraft, then would be received by Göring in his villa near Berlin. That promised to earn good press coverage.

The board of curators, headed by Jaujard, which had struggled to drag out the negotiations, met on 30 December 1943, against Bonnard's advice. Unanimously, the board decided that nothing was to be done until Jaujard resumed talks with the German administration. The board enjoyed the support of Tieschowitz, at the head of the Kunstschutz in France, and benefited from Kutgens's decision not to give in to Göring's whims. In early 1944, Jaujard was delighted to learn that the exchange of art objects had been called into question because the German pieces that were supposed to be handed over to France—a bust by

Jean-Antoine Houdon and a German primitive painting—belonged to private collections.

Göring therefore made concessions. He proposed the possibility of handing over French prisoners in exchange for the Basel antependium. More plausibly, according to a note of 26 January 1944, he agreed to accept the frontal "as a gift from the French nation as a token of gratitude for the measures taken by the German authorities to assure the protection and preservation of monuments and artworks in France during and after the campaign of 1940." He promised that, should there be military interventions in western Europe, the German army would do everything it could to protect French monuments and, especially, the repositories of the Réunion des musées nationaux.[69] Means of transportation and gasoline would be made available to the agencies so that they could move the protected objects. All these measures would, of course, be announced only after the French government had made the decision to present the Basel antependium to Göring as a gift.

In fact, Göring had already had the satisfaction of putting on display, in early January, *The Beautiful German*, which had been handed over by France, thus silencing the jokes made by his entourage about the resistance of French curators. The latter were reduced to staying the course and accepting the works Germany offered them—Watteau's *Gersaint's Shop Sign*, for example, which Göring was ready to part with in exchange for the Basel frontal. Göring let the French know that, if they did not, and if he met with as much resistance as before, he "still had the intention of restoring the antependium, a typically Germanic piece, to the German patrimony, one way or another."[70]

Subsequent events demonstrated what a point of honor it was for him to come out the winner of this affair, which, as it dragged on, was likely to make him lose face. In early February, he decided that a French delegation would come to "formally" bring the Basel antependium to Germany and that, with journalists, cameramen, and radio broadcasters in attendance, he would personally receive the masterpiece "in the name of the German government." He would thank the Kunstschutz, "perhaps in the form of a letter to Marshal Pétain,"[71] and would announce that the Basel antependium would be placed—after the war—in the center of the Nationalgalerie in Berlin and would bear on its pedestal an inscription reproducing the text of the French law giving it to Germany. In return, Germany would still hand over Watteau's *Shop Sign*.

During this time, the curators balked, thwarting Bonnard's efforts. Eventually, on 25 March 1944, Bonnard informed Göring's henchman Bunjes that he had received authorization from the head of the Vichy government to "follow and conduct" the matter of the Basel frontal himself. Bonnard added that he was happy to do so "because of the personal feelings" that "monsieur le Maréchal d'Empire" inspired in him and that he was honored to represent "the generosity" of his country, just as the Reichsmarschall embodied "all German generosity."[72] Only the liberation would put an end to this interminable negotiation which, like many others, seemed destined to meet with another success for the Nazi high officials favored by French high dignitaries.

The looting highlighted the vanquisher's character, his aesthetic passions, his deceit. Although every previous invasion had given rise to illicit acts, there was no precedent for this level of persistence and bureaucratic trickery. And no defeated nation had had such an opportunity to mount a defense—by simply selling off the possessions of a portion of its citizens. In fact, increasingly, the attacks on Jewish collections and the relentless anti-Semitism appeared not to be just the impulse of a more general desire to rule like a vanquisher. Undoubtedly the occupying force, or at least its leadership, saw France as prey to strip bare, without necessarily waiting for a peace treaty. Yet from the beginning of the occupation, there were also undoubtedly other priorities, including the struggle against the Jews "and their allies," an urgent task to be performed during the war itself. If the looting of collections, carried out as unofficially as possible and with the complicity of a muzzled press,[73] at first affected the least visible part of the French art scene—collectors, the civil service, and the art market—the campaign conducted openly against Jewish artists and Freemasons set the tone for an unprecedented upheaval.

The new rules of the game imposed by the occupier could easily sanction breaks with the past. The villainous laws profoundly transformed a traditionally liberal and cosmopolitan social milieu. For artists, the trauma was particularly severe in that they must have observed the vanquisher's monomaniacal character. The occupiers would demonstrate their effectiveness by presence or by propaganda, but they devoted themselves most readily to flushing out the enemy, responding in that respect to the only clear orders issued by the Führer who, in France as in Germany, "purged" the old order. As for the rest, everyone was astonished at the liberalities of the Nazi regime, though they did not dare believe in them too much. The Third Reich seemed to observe the art scene without wanting to root out anything but its scapegoats, to such an extent that the German presence did not appear to undermine the possibility of continuing "as before." There again, the traumatic shock of defeat and the exiling of many important members of the art scene to the "free" zone or abroad was very quickly replaced by the will to survive; the silence was mostly broken by the first buzz of a cultural scene that rapidly resumed its course after the arrival of occupation troops. Was it not most astonishing to hear the vanquishers themselves demand that the country's artistic activities resume? Only a minority saw that as yet another reason to keep quiet or to flee, so as not to give in to the temptation of underwriting a situation that, in reality, would soon be taken for "normal." But did not the enemy cover his tracks by displaying an extreme courtesy and a Francophilia that was almost always sincere? Most in France were not fooled, but unless they were targeted by the exclusionary laws, they adapted.

Artists were as divided as the rest of the French: they were "collaborators" or "resisters" or simply indifferent to orders from Germany or Vichy. Traditionally in the minority, individualistic, and distrustful of the forces in power, for the most part they proved to be against the exclusion of their comrades but powerless to oppose the state of affairs. History records not so much their demurrals as the effectiveness of an exclusion program that met with active support among a certain number of the French.

NOTES

1. There are countless books on Hitler to consult: the Library of Congress listed fifty-five thousand titles in 1979. The indispensable authors are still Alan Bullock, Joachim Fest, Konrad Heiden, Werner Maser, and John Toland. I refer the reader especially to Marlis Steinert's *Hitler* (Paris: Fayard, 1991), which takes stock of the various theses.
2. For the military history, see especially Hans Umbreit, "Der Kampf um die Vormachtstellung in Westeuropa," in Klaus A. Maier et al., *Die Errichtung der Hegemonie auf dem europäischen Kontinent*, vol. 2 of *Das Deutsche Reich und der Zweite Weltkrieg* (Stuttgart: Deutsche Verlags-Anstalt, 1979).
3. On the armistice, see the issue "Autour de l'armistice de juin 1940," *Revue d'histoire de la Deuxième Guerre mondiale*, June 1951; Hermann Böhme, *Der deutsch-französische Waffenstillstand im Zweiten Weltkrieg*, pt. 1, *Entstehung und Grundlagen des Waffenstillstandes von 1940* (Stuttgart: Deutsche Verlags-Anstalt, 1966); Michel Launay, *L'armistice de 1940* (Paris: Presses Universitaires de France, 1972); Jean-Baptiste Duroselle, *L'abîme, 1939–1945* (Paris: Imprimerie Nationale, 1982), reissued as *Politique étrangère de la France: L'abîme, 1939–1944* (Paris: Editions du Seuil, 1990).
4. At age fifty-one, Georges Huisman left Bordeaux with his family aboard the *Massilia*. Only two professional artists were aboard: Jacqueline Bardin, a sculptor, and Antoinette Sachs, a painter. On the *Massilia*, see Christiane Rimbaud, *L'affaire du Massilia, été 1940* (Paris: Editions du Seuil, 1984).
5. See Joseph Goebbels, *Die Tagebücher von Joseph Goebbels: Sämtliche Fragmente*, pt. 1, *Aufzeichnungen, 1924–1941*, vol. 4, *1.1.1940–8.7.1941*,

ed. Elke Fröhlich on behalf of the Institut für Zeitgeschichte and in conjunction with the Bundesarchiv (Munich: K. G. Saur, 1987), 205.

6. On Hitler's orders, the railway car would become part of Germany's patrimony. It arrived in Berlin on 8 July 1940 and was later destroyed by an Allied bomb attack, probably in Thuringia. Hitler had envisioned exhibiting it inside an enormous cube, designed by Wilhelm Heinrich Kreis, under which a crypt containing the coffins of famous German marshals would have been installed.

7. Directive given to the German press, quoted in Eberhard Jäckel, *Frankreich in Hitlers Europa: Die deutsche Frankreichpolitik im Zweiten Weltkrieg* (Stuttgart: Deutsche Verlags-Anstalt, 1966), 57 n. 46; published in French as *La France dans l'Europe de Hitler*, trans. Denise Meunier (Paris: Fayard, 1968), 87 n. 46.

8. Adolf Hitler, *Monologe im Führer-Hauptquartier 1941–1944: Die Aufzeichnungen Heinrich Heims*, ed. Werner Jochmann (Munich: Wilhelm Heyne, 1982), 115–16; quoted in Steinert, *Hitler* (note 1), 409.

9. During his visit, Hitler, according to Albert Speer, raised the possibility with both his aide-de-camp and Oberstleutnant Hans Speidel (who had welcomed the group at the Opéra) of holding a large parade in Paris to celebrate his victory. He eventually decided against the idea, officially because of the danger of British air attacks, unofficially because they were not "at the end yet." See Albert Speer, *Au coeur du Troisième Reich*, trans. Michel Brottier, 2 vols. (Geneva: Famot, 1974). In English, see Albert Speer, *Inside the Third Reich: Memoirs*, trans. Richard Winston and Clara Winston (New York: Collier, 1981), 172. In addition, in the German archives there is a note from the head of the army's high command, dated 31 August 1940, that mentions Hitler's plan to hold major public displays after the war, with the first and foremost being "a parade of the army in Paris."

    According to Jean Cocteau, six weeks before the defeat of France, Hitler announced to Arno Breker and his wife, "France doesn't want to understand me. I've done everything to help them out. They think I'm a housepainter, a hairdresser's assistant. I don't want anyone to 'smash' Paris. I don't want the French to 'smash' Paris. I don't want the English to 'smash' Paris. I'm the one who will defend Paris. I'll meet you in Paris in six weeks. I won't enter it with generals. I'll enter it with my artists." See Jean Cocteau, *Journal 1942–1945*, ed. Jean Touzot (Paris: Gallimard, 1989), 128.

10. Adolf Hitler, *Mon combat (Mein Kampf)*, trans. Jean Gaudefroy-Demombynes and A. Calmettes (Paris: Nouvelles Editions Latines, 1934; reprint, Paris: Nouvelles Editions Latines, 1982), 30. In English, see Adolf Hitler, *Mein Kampf*, trans. Ralph Manheim (Boston: Houghton Mifflin, 1943), 20.

11. That was at least theoretically the case, though young people were sometimes

admitted without a diploma when their level dictated it. For unknown reasons, Hitler did not insist.

12. On the context of that failure, the reasons for it, and its consequences, more generally, for Hitler's artistic "career," see Hitler, *Mon combat* (note 10); Konrad Heiden, *La jeunesse de Hitler*, trans. Armand Pierhal (Paris: Editions Bernard Grasset, 1940); August Kubizek, *Adolf Hitler, mein Jugendfreund* (Graz: Leopold Stocker, 1953); Jacques Brosse, *Hitler avant Hitler: Essai d'interprétation psychanalytique*, postface by Albert Speer (Paris: Fayard, 1972); Werner Maser, *Naissance du Parti national-socialiste allemand: Les débuts du National-Socialisme, Hitler jusqu'en 1924*, trans. R. Jouan (Paris: Fayard, 1967); Helm Stierlin, *Adolf Hitler: Etude psychologique*, trans. Jeanne Etoré (Paris: Presses Universitaires de France, 1980). On the painter Hitler's "oeuvre" and "artistic career," see J. Sydney Jones, *Hitlers Weg begann in Wien, 1907–1913*, trans. Sylvia Eisenburger (Wiesbaden: Limes, 1980); Billy F. Price, *Adolf Hitler als Maler und Zeichner: Ein Werkkatalog der Ölgemälde, Aquarelle, Zeichnungen und Architekturskizzen* (Zug, Switzerland: Gallant, 1983); Henry Grosshans, *Hitler and the Artists* (New York: Holmes & Meier, 1983); Pierre Milza, *Les fascismes* (Paris: Imprimerie Nationale, 1985); Marc Lambert, *Un peintre nommé Hitler* (Paris: Editions France-Empire & E.C.S., 1986).

Hitler is said to have made about two thousand pieces of art, for the most part watercolors, between 1908 and 1914; two hundred, including many drawings, between 1914 and 1930; and, finally, a few hundred sketches of buildings, up to 1945. Probably 90 percent of his output has disappeared. In the late 1980s, most of the surviving works were divided between the collections of the Galleria degli Uffizi in Florence, the Texas oilman Billy F. Price in Houston, and Henry Thynne, 6th Marquess of Bath, in England, while the Bundesarchiv in Koblenz, Germany, had a few documents relating to them. Copies of his architecture sketches for the entry exam to the Akademie der Bildenden Künste in Vienna were conserved in Munich by August Priesack, who worked for the central archives of the Nationalsozialistische Deutsche Arbeiterpartei (NSDAP)—the Nazi Party—between 1935 and 1939.

13. Marlis Steinert, however, following Franz Jetzinger, Bradley F. Smith, and Werner Maser, puts a salutary damper on Hitler's description in *Mein Kampf* of the poverty that awaited him, noting the inheritances from his father, his mother (who had just died), and his aunt Johanna. See Steinert, *Hitler* (note 1), 45.

14. The largest image Hitler ever painted was probably about twenty-four inches wide. A still life in oil colors of flowers against a red velvet background, it was executed in about 1913 for a friend's uncle, Dr. Doebner, presiding judge of the court of Munich.

15. Subject indexed at the Bundesarchiv in Koblenz, no. N 26/36.

16. Subject indexed at the Bundesarchiv in Koblenz, no. N 26/36.

17. See Camillo Sitte, *Der Städte-Bau nach seinen künstlerischen Grundsätzen: Ein Beitrag zur Lösung moderster Fragen der Architektur und monumentalen Plastik unter besonderer Beziehung auf Wien* (Vienna: Verlag von Carl Graeser, 1889). Published in French as *L'art de bâtir les villes: Notes et réflexions d'un architecte*, trans. Camille Martin (Geneva: Ed. Atar/Paris: H. Laurens, [ca. 1900]).

18. The next day, it was Goebbels's turn to visit the "pearl of civilization"—and to dream of his own personal Trianon. See Goebbels, *Die Tagebücher* (note 5), 225.

19. See Donald J. Bush, *The Streamlined Decade* (New York: George Braziller, 1975).

20. See the analysis of Marc Cluet, who identifies more precisely five architectural orientations of Nazism, in his article, "Idéologie nationale-socialiste et architecture du IIIe Reich," *Revue d'histoire de la Deuxième Guerre mondiale*, April 1981. See also his more recent *L'architecture du IIIe Reich: Origines intellectuelles et visées idéologiques* (Bern: Peter Lang, 1987).

21. Brüchner took out a fifty-mark note and offered it to the old man who, by his refusal, obliged Hitler to then dispatch Breker, who had no more success. See Breker's account of this incident in his memoirs, *Im Strahlungsfeld der Ereignisse: Leben und Wirken eines Künstlers: Porträts, Begegnungen, Schicksale* (Preussisch-Oldendorf, Germany: K. W. Schütz, 1972).

22. But in front of Napoléon Bonaparte's tomb, Hitler conceded to the defeated French the right to recover the ashes of the emperor's son, Napoléon II, Herzog von Reichstadt, which were in Vienna, and decided to have them placed near his father in the Invalides. To which, in December 1940—the ceremony had taken place on 15 December—the popular response was the sharp retort that he could keep the L'Aiglon ("The Eaglet," byname of Napoléon II), for the French preferred to recover their pigs.

23. See Speer, *Au coeur* (note 9), 246–47; Speer, *Inside the Third Reich* (note 9), 171–72.

24. See Speer, *Au coeur* (note 9), 228–29; Speer, *Inside the Third Reich* (note 9), 160.

25. On Hitler's artistic policy, see Adolf Hitler, "Pour un idéal purement artistique," in Adolf Hitler et al., *L'avenir de l'Allemagne* (Paris: Fernand Sorlot, 1936); E. Wernert, *L'art dans le IIIe Reich: Une tentative d'esthétique dirigée* (Paris: Paul Hartmann, 1936); Franz Roh, *"Entartete" Kunst: Kunstbarbarei im Dritten Reich* (Hannover: Fackelträger, 1962); Hildegard Brenner, *Die Kunstpolitik des Nationalsozialismus* (Reinbek: Rowohlt, 1965), published in French as *La politique artistique du national-socialisme*, trans. Lucien Steinberg (Paris: François Maspero, 1980); Lionel Richard,

Le nazisme et la culture (Paris: François Maspero, 1978); Ulrike Aubertin, "La *Grande exposition de l'art allemand:* L'art dégénéré, 1937" (master's thesis, Université Paris-I, 1981); André Combes, Michel Vanoosthuyse, and Isabelle Vodoz, eds., *Nazisme et anti-nazisme dans la littérature et l'art allemands (1920–1945)* (Lille: Presses Universitaires de Lille, 1986); Peter-Klaus Schuster, ed., *Die "Kunststadt" München 1937: Nationalsozialismus und "Entartete Kunst"* (Munich: Prestel, 1987); *Inszenierung der Macht: Ästhetische Faszination im Faschismus* (Berlin: NGBK/Dirk Nischen, 1987); Pierre Milza and Fanette Roche-Pézard, eds., *Art et fascisme: Totalitarisme et résistance au totalitarisme dans les arts en Italie, Allemagne et France des années 30 à la défaite de l'Axe* (Brussels: Editions Complexe, 1989), especially Berthold Hinz, "L'art dans le national-socialisme: Entre dictature et marché," Élodie Vitale, "Le Bauhaus et la République de Weimar: Trois fermetures," Ulrike Aubertin and Annick Lantenois, "La *Grande exposition de l'art allemand* et *L'art dégénéré:* Fondement et symbolique d'une confrontation," and André Gunthert, "La Couleur de l'utopie: La peinture officielle du IIIe Reich"; Jacqueline Lichtenstein and Jean-François Groulier, "'L'art dégénéré' ou la logique des exclusions," *Traverses*, n.s., no. 3 (1992): 61–75. See, finally, the catalogs for the exhibitions of degenerate art that have been mounted in Europe [Munich, 1987; Berlin, 1987, 1992] and the United States [Los Angeles, 1991]. In France, see the catalog for the exhibition held in spring 1993 at the Dunkirk museum, following the first presentation and roundtable "Munich 1937: L'art acclame—l'art diffuse," Goethe Institute, Paris, 5 March–17 May 1989 (organized by Ulrike Aubertin and Annick Lantenois).

26. Speer, *Au coeur* (note 9), 263; Speer, *Inside the Third Reich* (note 9), 184.

27. See Marlis G. Steinert, "La décision en matière de politique étrangère: Un essai sur l'utilisation de théories pour l'étude des relations internationales," in *Enjeux et puissances: Pour une histoire des relations internationales au XXe siècle: Mélanges en l'honneur de Jean-Baptiste Duroselle* (Paris: Publications de la Sorbonne, 1986), 69–82.

28. Steinert, "La décision" (note 27).

29. See Jules Romains, *Le couple France-Allemagne* (Paris: Ernest Flammarion, 1934). At Goebbels's request, Romains was officially invited to Berlin in 1934 and received considerable royalties for the translation and performances of his play *Donogoo-Tonka; ou, Les miracles de la science* (1920). He participated in the Comité France-Allemagne from 1935 to 1938, before denouncing Nazism and the "fifth column" in 1939. See Fred Kupferman, "Diplomatie parallèle et guerre psychologique: Le rôle de la *Ribbentrop Dienststelle* dans les tentatives d'actions sur l'opinion française, 1934–1939," *Relations internationales*, no. 3 (1975): 85.

30. The history of the looting of Jewish collections is partly retraced in Jean

Cassou, ed., *Le pillage par les Allemands des oeuvres d'art et des bibliothèques appartenant à des Juifs en France: Recueil de documents* (Paris: Editions du Centre de Documentation Juive Contemporaine, 1947), which reprints and translates important archival documents. This volume is the source whenever I cite an official text without a particular reference. See, more broadly, the archives of the Centre de documentation juive contemporaine (CDJC), conserved by Vidar Jacobsen; see also the report of the French public prosecutor's office to the Nuremberg tribunal, "Le pillage des oeuvres d'art dans les pays occupés de l'Europe occidentale" (January 1946). After these works were compiled, important documents were added to the record, particularly within the context of the continuing trials at the Haute Cour de Justice. I therefore refer to series 3W conserved at the Archives nationales (AN) and cite the exhibit number whenever necessary. See also archives B 8806 of the Ministère de l'économie et des finances. On the rulings made by the military governor for the occupied French territories, see *Verordnungsblatt für die besetzten französischen Gebiete*, later *Verordungsblatt des Militärbefehlshabers in Frankreich*. See also the account of a witness to the era, Rose Valland, *Le front de l'art: Défense des collections françaises, 1939–1945* (Paris: Librairie Plon, 1961); and the testimony by Captain Flicoteaux, commissaire du gouvernement, reproduced in Otto Abetz's memoirs, *D'une prison* (Paris: Amiot-Dumont, 1949), 218–20. On the question of the theft and removal of works of art, see *Notes et études documentaires*, no. 1109, 4 April 1949, Secrétariat général du gouvernement, série française, CCXXIII *ter;* and, finally, the *Répertoire des biens spoliés en France durant la guerre, 1939–1945*, 8 vols. and 13 supplements (Berlin: Imprimerie Nationale, 1947–50).

In 1964, John Frankenheimer made *The Train*, a film loosely based on one of the last episodes of looting: an action by railway workers to prevent a train of artworks from leaving.

31. This report by Metternich, published by the CDJC, is a very valuable source. Because it was compiled after the defeat of the Third Reich, it requires critical distance in principle, but it seems reliable in style, breadth, and the precision of its information.

32. Abetz, *D'une prison* (note 30), 51.

33. He was posted in France from the beginning to the end of the occupation.

34. See the exhibition catalog *Les chefs-d'oeuvre des collections privées françaises retrouvés en Allemagne par la Commission de récupération artistique et les services alliés: Orangerie des Tuileries, juin–août 1946* (Paris: n.p., 1946), which includes a preface by Albert S. Henraux, chairman of the Commission de récupération artistique (and president of the Société des amis du Louvre). The commission, also overseen by Camille Bloch (Institut de France) and Michel Florisoone (curator at the Musée du Louvre and professor at the Ecole du Louvre), was created on 24 November 1944 and set up at the Jeu de Paume, where the works were brought before being returned to their owners, provided those individuals were still alive and could show proof that the works belonged to them (see the decree of 16 April 1945). The initial deadline for the declaration of stolen goods, 31 December 1947, was extended. The goods not identified in the *Répertoire des biens spoliés* (note 30), compiled in Berlin by the Bureau central des restitutions, were publicly displayed in Paris at the Office des biens et intérêts privés or at the Commission de récupération artistique. In addition, the French state was represented by the customs administration and the state property office (Direction des domaines): the former because the goods had been exported without the export authorization stipulated by the law of June 1941; the latter in instances where stolen works could not be returned to their owners.

In all, by 15 January 1949, 27,854 works recovered in Germany and Austria had been returned, along with 1,736 recovered in France and some 50 recovered elsewhere in Europe. At the same date, 3,000 objects and the contents of 29 crates had still not found their owners and were sold or placed in sequestration.

35. Of about sixteen million works of art looted by the Nazis throughout Europe, most were not recovered. Each country participated in its own way in the return of property. Great Britain moved slowly and cautiously, wanting to make sure that the objects sold belonged to the declared owners; it also regarded purchases made in France by Rhineland museums merely a business matter. The Soviet Union sent back a few meager batches and quickly broke off negotiations. Austria returned a large contingent of works, as did Poland, notably the collections from the Chopin museum in Lyon. Negotiations also took place with Czechoslovakia, where many works had been destroyed in a fire.

Things went differently with the United States, given the major role it played in the recovery. According to recent revelations in the international press, the looting by the Nazis was followed by thefts by U.S. soldiers. The U.S. authorities had arranged to have first access to the most important caches. By the end of 1944, the United States had inventoried eight hundred repositories discovered for the city of Munich alone. In May 1945, on the French side, Rose Valland was denied access to any search area other than her own, which was small. The U.S. organization in charge of the "recovery" of works, placed under the authority of the Office of Strategic Services (OSS), forerunner of the Central Intelligence Agency (CIA), thus had access to the treasures stored in the caves of the Vallée des Merveilles, northeast of Nice, and the Altaussee salt mines, east of the Eagle's Nest (Kehlsteinhaus) and southeast of Salzburg. See, for example, the story of the treasures of the Quedlinburg cathedral, southwest of Magdeburg, in what was East

Germany, which were found at the First National Bank in the small town of Whitewright, Texas, in a safe deposit box under the name of Jack Meador, brother of Lieutenant Joe T. Meador of the Eighty-seventh Armored Field Artillery Battalion of the United States Army, which was charged in 1945 with guarding that area. On this question, see Record Group 226, Records of the Office of Strategic Services (OSS), National Archives, Washington, D.C.

36. On more than one occasion, the works of art were used as liquid assets when matters were "urgent." Hence, the "Bureau Otto," the economic Gestapo charged with controlling the black market, attended to the trafficking in works of art in a way advantageous to itself, even while conducting counterespionage operations linked to the Abwehr, the German military's intelligence organization. See "Verzeichnis der erfassten judischen Kunstammlungen," Centre de documentation juive contemporaine, XIII-45; cited in Pierre Assouline, *L'homme de l'art D.-H. Kahnweiler (1884–1979)* (Paris: Balland, 1988), 372–73.

37. A meeting reportedly took place in Berlin, with Walter Borchers in attendance. He was charged with announcing in Paris the latest decision of the commission: the imminent destruction of rejected works.

38. Before the war, she was assigned to the Musée des écoles étrangères contemporaines, at the Jeu de Paume, run by André Dézarrois.

39. The records constituted, then jealously guarded, by Rose Valland for the Louvre recently have been handed over to the ministry of foreign affairs and are in "the process of being cataloged." They constitute the "fonds OBIP": records of the Office des biens et intérêts privés, charged with recording the theft of private and public property by the Nazi armies in France and with collecting declarations regarding stolen property.

On the bonfire at the Jeu de Paume and the surrounding controversy, I refer to the records temporarily stored in boxes 106 P 48, 577 R 29, 573 R 23; to the notes by Valland (in the form of a journal); and to the note of 23 July 1943 by the head of the security staff at the Réunion des musées nationaux. See also the German inventory with the notation "Vernichtet" (annihilated) across from the names of the works destroyed; and finally, the investigation on the looting in the review *Das Schönste*, in 1962 (May through December issues, passim).

40. See letters from Rosenberg to Göring, 18 June 1942, 11 January 1943; in Cassou, *Le pillage par les Allemands* (note 30), 114 (document 17), 115 (document 18).

41. Speer recounts in his memoirs that, as a member of the Prussian state council (Preußischer Staatsrat) earning six thousand reichsmarks annually, he received a note each year informing him that a large portion of his salary was being withheld for Göring's birthday present. See Speer, *Au coeur* (note 9), 459–60; Speer, *Inside the Third Reich* (note 9), 322.

42. See letter from Rosenberg to Hitler, 16 April 1943, in Cassou, *Le pillage par les Allemands* (note 30), 116 (document 19).

43. The Hague Convention of 18 October 1907 only put in writing a customary law—generally recognized by nations—that banned looting; it did not stipulate legal provisions making it possible to sanction violations. Only the United States had signed, in 1935, the Roerich Pact, which guaranteed the inviolability in times of war of its historical monuments and artistic and scientific institutions.

44. In particular, Hermann Bunjes, who was responsible for the Paris collections, moved closer to Göring, to the point of becoming his most faithful ally.

45. In translation, the text, originally written in German, was formulated as follows: "Order. This building, including all its fixtures and furnishings, is considered a museum and is placed under military protection. The head of the military administration for the region of northwestern France. Signed: Schreiber, lieutenant general."

46. The skimming of works from collections may have stemmed either from real interest or from a desire to expurgate them. See, for example, the policy followed at the Musée de la guerre, related by Sylvie Maignan in her study on its curator, "Un critique d'art parisien: René-Jean, 1879–1951" (master's thesis, Ecole du Louvre, 1979).

47. Correspondence sent from Berlin, 3 November 1941, Haute Cour trial of Jérôme Carcopino, AN, series 3W 122, exhibit 369.

48. In accordance with the law of 5 October 1940, promulgated in Vichy, that assigned to the Administration de l'enregistrement "the management and liquidation of property placed in sequestration as a result of a general security measure." See *Journal officiel*, 23 October 1940. [The *Journal officiel* is the French counterpart of the *Congressional Record* in the United States.—Trans.]

49. After reminding the *recteurs d'académie*—each a university professor appointed by the minister of national education to oversee the schools in a given administrative region, or *académie*—on 7 June 1941 of the students' obligation to display political reserve and the need to respect "the orders of the marshal" (Haute Cour trial of Carcopino, AN, series 3W 121, exhibit 87), Carcopino refused to recommend to teachers a visit to the exhibition *Le Juif et la France* (letter to Paul Sézille, secretary general of the Institut d'études des questions juives, 11 September 1941, Haute Cour trial of Carcopino, AN, series 3W 121, exhibit 96; confirmed by the German report recovered at the Hôtel Majestic in Paris, 10 November 1941, AN, series 3W 121, exhibit 88). See also his proposal not to enforce the policy of exclusion too strictly when it came to the artistic professions (letter to Xavier Vallat, commissaire général aux questions juives, 20 January 1942, AN, series 3W 121, exhibit 95). Conversely, on Carcopino's positions favoring the *numerus*

clausus and the exclusion of Jews, see Claude Singer's exhaustive study, *Vichy, l'université et les Juifs: Les silences et la mémoire* (Paris: Les Belles-Lettres, 1992).

50. Letter sent from the Palais-Royal, 3 June 1941 (copies to Xavier Vallat, commissaire général aux questions juives), Haute Cour trial of Carcopino, AN, series 3W 121, exhibit 83.

51. Note from Darlan to Brinon, Vichy, 10 June 1941, in Valland, *Le front de l'art* (note 30), 244–45.

52. In certain cases only, Jewish dealers were able to keep their property and their businesses. The case of Georges Wildenstein in particular has recently attracted the curiosity of journalists, who have used the archives of the OSS to point out the paradoxes of the Nazis' exclusion policy. Wildenstein's collection, en route to the United States, was reportedly intercepted by the Germans and became the object of a transaction between the art dealer and the occupying forces through the intermediary of Karl Haberstock. Haberstock, a Berlin gallery owner known for his anti-Semitism, took advantage of his semi-official position (he worked for Hitler) to snatch the Wildenstein collection from the clutches of Rosenberg's ERR and to convince Georg Stenger, who was responsible for Jewish affairs, to help "legalize" the French dealer's situation. The "Aryanization" of the collection took place in April 1941. A certain Dequoy (an old friend of Haberstock's), who had previously worked for Wildenstein in New York, sold the works to Haberstock at a "private viewing" at Wildenstein et Cie at 57, rue La Boétie, for the museum in Linz. He deposited the proceeds in a special account abroad; they were returned by the French market only after the war. See "Wildenstein et Cie," the report by the art historian Douglas Cooper, who questioned Haberstock after the war. The report was used by Jonathan Napack in preparing "The Wildenstein Families," *Spy*, October 1991. Much less seriously, see Frank McDonald's novel *Provenance* (Boston: Little, Brown, 1979), which seems to relate the events in its own way.

53. That commission was composed of Gabriel Cognacq, member of the Institut de France, vice president of the Conseil des musées nationaux; François Carnot, president of the Union centrale des arts décoratifs; Albert Henraux, president of the Société des amis du Louvre, president of the Association générale des amis des musées de France; René Dussaud, permanent secretary of the Académie des inscriptions et belles-lettres, curator emeritus of the Musée du Louvre; Jean Jacques Marquet de Vasselot, Paul Vitry, and Charles Boreux, curators emeriti of the Musées nationaux; Jean Robiquet, curator emeritus of the Musée Carnavalet. See the letter of 2 November 1940, in Valland, *Le front de l'art* (note 30), 238–39.

54. Jacques Jaujard, born on 3 December 1895, was secretary to Paul Painlevé in 1922 and principal private secretary (*chef de cabinet*), from 1924 to 1930, of the chair of the Chambre, the chair of the Conseil, and the ministries of finance, and of war. He was named secretary of the Réunion des musées nationaux in 1925, secretary general in 1926, and director of the Réunion des musées nationaux and the Ecole du Louvre in December 1939. After the liberation, he was the originator of many administrative reforms and of a study of legislation on royalties. A member of the Académie des beaux-arts of the Institut de France, he was named a commander of the Légion d'honneur, in July 1946, and was decorated with the Médaille de la Résistance.

55. A vast evacuation plan had been prepared long in advance, to avoid the damages suffered in World War I. Although effective, the drawbacks of such an operation were not anticipated: the deterioration of certain works despite the precautions taken; the necessity of moving telephone and telegraph wires to allow trailers transporting monumental canvases to get through; and so on. See the report of 12 November 1939 on the evacuation of the collections, AN, series F21, 3981.

56. Göring came in civilian clothes, accompanied by his appraiser, Walter Andreas Hofer.

57. For the details of that affair, see Haute Cour trial of Bonnard, AN, series 3W 78, exhibits C5–C10.

58. Joseph Billiet, fellow traveler of the Communist Party, ended his career as curator of the Musée national du château de Malmaison. After the liberation of France, he was director general of fine arts for some time, after Hilaire and before Jaujard.

59. Bonnard, broadly implicated in the affair, was exonerated on that point during his trial at the Haute Cour de Justice. He was reportedly in Paris, not in Vichy (where he remained as little as possible, preferring the collaborationist circles of Paris), on the day the decision was made to hand over the altarpiece. See, in particular, the testimony by Hilaire and Hautecoeur, Haute Cour trial of Bonnard, AN, series 3W 78, exhibits C5–C10.

60. See Hilaire's deposition, Haute Cour trial of Bonnard, AN, series 3W 78, exhibits C5–C10.

61. In this affair, however, it would seem that Hautecoeur had tried to calm things down by encouraging the curators not to protest, as he would be reminded during his deposition on Bonnard's behalf. See Haute Cour trial of Bonnard, AN, series 3W 82, exhibit R26.

62. On 20 November and then again on 26 November 1942. At the session of 20 November, with Jaujard presiding, the following were present: Aubert, Billiet, Bourguignon, Contenot, Devambez, Dorival, Fontaine, Grousset, Lantier, Mauricheau-Beaupré, Merlin, de Montrémy, Pradel, Rey, Rivière, Rouches, Salles, Terrasse, Vaudier, Verlet. The following were excused: Charbonneaux, Deschamps, Ladoué.

After discussion, during which all the curators expressed their support for Jaujard, the committee decided to designate a committee to write a protest. It consisted of Aubert, Billiet, Bourguignon, Fontaine, Rey, and Salles.

During the special session on 26 November, the following were present: Aubert, Billiet, Bourguignon, Charbonneaux, Contenot, Deschamps, Devambez, Dorival, Fontaine, Grousset, Lantier, Ladoué, Mauricheau-Beaupré, Merlin, de Montrémy, Pradel, Rey, Rivière, Rouches, Salles, Terrasse, Vaudier, Vergnet-Ruiz. On a mission in the newly occupied zone: Bazin, Chamson, Huyghe, Stern, Verlet. On sick leave: Dézarrois, Haumont, Parrot.

During that session, only Pierre Ladoué, curator of the Musée national d'art moderne, broke with the committee and refused to sign the collective declaration, judging that taking such a position was not compatible with his official duties, that there was a risk it would be very poorly regarded by the government and would have serious repercussions. He also claimed that he knew from a reliable source that the ministry of foreign affairs was taking care of the matter.

The committee protested as follows: "The decision, which was made above and outside [of the Réunion des musées nationaux], together with the removal itself constituted a grave attack on the honor of the Musées nationaux, which wishes to express the painful emotion they feel about it."

63. See the telegram from Ribbentrop to Abetz, 2 August 1941, in Valland, *Le front de l'art* (note 30), 250–51.

64. Hermann Bunjes, director of the Institut allemand d'histoire de l'art.

65. In cultural matters, he defended "a renewal of the culture of Europe," establishing at the ministry of national education and youth a "Comité de culture franco-européenne" run by a council that he chaired and whose members he named. See Haute Cour, AN, series 3W 77, exhibits B49–B51.

66. Abel Bonnard was born in Poitiers on 19 December 1883. His father, of Corsican origin, was the warden of the prisons in Vienne and died in 1933. Bonnard attended the Lycée Louis-le-Grand and the Lycée Henri-IV, then the Ecole du Louvre. Winner of the first Prix national de poésie in 1906, at age twenty-three, and the Grand prix de littérature from the Académie française in 1925, he was admitted into the Académie française in 1932 by Monsignor Alfred Baudrillart. For his military activities during World War I, he was made a knight of the Légion d'honneur in 1921 and an officer in 1935. Under the occupation, he joined the Conseil municipal of Paris (December 1941), the Vichy Conseil national (November 1941), and the honor committee of the Légion des volontaires français contre le bolchevisme. He was honorary president of the literary branch of Groupe Collaboration, and he participated in the trip to Germany made by French writers, along with Robert Brasillach, Pierre Drieu La Rochelle, Jacques Chardonne, and Marcel Jouhandeau. He was sentenced to death in absentia by the Haute Cour de

Justice. In June 1958, he was incarcerated in La Santé prison in Paris, then temporarily released for health reasons and immediately hospitalized. In July 1959, the request for further information on his case reached the Haute Cour de Justice, while he was leading, according to his file, "a discreet, modest, and solitary existence" in a furnished room on the quai de Passy rented by friends.

On Bonnard, see especially the exhibits for the Haute Cour trial of Bonnard, AN, series 3W 80; Abel Bonnard, *Pensées dans l'action* (Paris: Bernard Grasset, 1941), a collection of articles written between August and December 1940; J. Mièvre, "L'évolution politique d'Abel Bonnard (jusqu'au printemps 1942)," *Revue d'histoire de la Deuxième Guerre mondiale*, October 1977.

67. Haute Cour trial of Bonnard, AN, series 3W 78, exhibit C106.

This goes counter to Hautecoeur's impression that Bonnard made "every effort to defend that important piece," given that he "had too delicate a feeling for art not to refuse the Germans any work in France that was the object of his delectation."

In his belated deposition about Bonnard at the Haute Cour de Justice on 8 June 1959, Hautecoeur was decidedly low-key in his views. He mentioned that he and Bonnard had met at the Lycée Henri-IV, then in Rome at the home of the comte Joseph-Napoléon Primoli, and in Paris salons, before Bonnard was named to the ministry of national education and youth. Their relationship from then on was governed by a "courtesy" that "did not rule out distance," suggesting Bonnard had done nothing to help Hautecoeur when Göring demanded that the latter leave the fine arts administration. Politically, Bonnard appeared to Hautecoeur to be "a poet, an idealist, [who] always considered political questions from such a lofty standpoint that he was sometimes out of touch with the realities." Moreover, Bonnard had "spoken [to him] only once of the danger of Bolshevism and the need to prevent the expansion of Russia." See Haute Cour trial of Bonnard, AN, series 3W 82, exhibit R26.

68. Bonnard had chosen to send to Germany Marcel Aubert, member of the Institut de France, curator in the sculpture department at the Musée du Louvre (Aubert spoke German); Gabriel Cognacq, member of the Institut de France, president of the Comité des musées nationaux; René Huyghe, curator in the paintings department at the Musée du Louvre; and, finally, as an interpreter, a young lycée teacher from Bordeaux, who, by "his affable and open character [would bring]...a very happy element to this group"; see Haute Cour trial of Bonnard, AN, series 3W 82, exhibit C106.

69. In 1939, the Service des monuments historiques and the Réunion des musées nationaux had evacuated the provincial museums. The works from two hundred museums were dispersed to seventy-one repositories, and the law of 10 August 1941 (which included reform of French museums) would allow further transfers of works. On the German side, it was Metternich's Kunstschutz that controlled these repositories; on the French side, it was the administrative staff and young men sent by the unemployment bureau, who sometimes thereby escaped the Service du travail obligatoire (STO), that is, forced labor in Germany.

70. Letter of 27 January 1944, Haute Cour trial of Bonnard, AN, series 3W 78, exhibit C122.

71. Note of 9 February 1944, Haute Cour trial of Bonnard, AN, series, 3W 78, exhibit C130.

72. Letter of 25 March 1944, Haute Cour trial of Bonnard, AN, series 3W 78, exhibit C143. In a new deposition in 1959, Jaujard proved more forgiving than he had been during the trial in 1945, averring that Bonnard had not done anything to "revive" the affair of the Basel antependium. In addition, he credited Bonnard for his attitude toward the young people hired as guards so that they could escape the STO. See AN, series 3W 82, exhibit R28.

73. When the collaborationist press did not remain silent, it responded with fabrications. *Le matin*, for example, certainly raised the issue of robbery, but the looters were "Anglo-Americans" who were raiding "Sicily to enrich their public and private collections," leading readers to fear the worst if those raiders set foot on French soil. See Stéphane Lauzanne, "La dilapidation des meubles du patrimoine national," *Le matin*, 19 October 1943.

CHAPTER TWO

Exclude but Let Them Be

PROPAGANDA

In actuality, the exclusion of Jews and Freemasons in France corresponded to the general orientation of German propaganda, whose goal was to secure that nation by assuring the Third Reich's political, economic, and cultural domination. In accordance with old principles put to the test during previous wars, Germany set out to sap the morale of the indigenous people by bringing them around to the occupier's views and, at the same time, alienating them from the authorities that had previously governed them.[1] In practice, this initial policy was aided by the docility of the Vichy government and its tendency to go the occupying forces one better; but it was undercut by the rivalries between Nazi factions.

There were at least two serious contenders for propaganda turf—namely, Goebbels and Ribbentrop. The military command linked to the Wehrmacht, which oversaw the Propaganda-Staffel Paris, was headed by Major Heinz Schmidtke, a staunch supporter of Goebbels, and headquartered at the Hôtel Majestic, near place de l'Etoile. Schmidtke did not want to depend on the French intelligentsia belonging to the Comité France-Allemagne, which had been formed in the 1930s by his rival Otto Abetz. Abetz, conversely, made use of that committee as an invaluable breeding ground to promote his policy of "cautious disintegration" (*vorsichtige Zersetzung*). A Ribbentrop loyalist and the head of the German embassy on rue de Lille—which oversaw the very effective Institut allemand—Abetz dreamed of turning Goebbels's Propaganda-Abteilung into a straightforward censorship service.[2] This he managed to do, in summer 1942, by broadening the powers of the embassy and the Institut allemand.[3] Abetz's allies, the distinguished Francophiles Karl Epting and Karl Heinz Bremer, held many social events at the institute—where well-known collaborationists came to distract themselves. They also produced a number of militant publications: *Cahiers de l'Institut allemand,*[4] *Deutschland-Frankreich,*[5] and *Die Kunst im Deutschen Reich,* "the most sumptuous review of art in contemporary Germany" (with articles in French, published by the NSDAP), which served up the myths of Nazism with a generously helping of erudition, which had been absent from the organs of the German "popular" press: *Pariser Zeitung*[6] and *Signal.*[7]

The Goebbels-Ribbentrop rivalry undermined the unity of the German initiative, which, if we are to believe the activity reports, quickly ran up against the forces of French inertia and French psychological impulses that did not always correspond to the assumptions of the conqueror. Nevertheless, the propaganda sector employed more than a thousand people throughout France and had considerable financial means at its disposal: ninety million francs a month for the Propaganda-Abteilung Frankreich, and about one hundred million annually for the German embassy, which also had secret funds totaling a billion francs.[8] In June 1940, the Propaganda-Abteilung requisitioned a floor of 52, avenue des Champs-Elysées, which it planned to share with the Propaganda-Staffel Paris. The latter promptly encroached on the Propaganda-Abteilung's territory, by extending its own activities to the provinces. Theoretically, the Propaganda-Abteilung retained the advantage, controlling all information sent to the occupation troops. Through the media and cultural channels, it reorganized, directed, and "shaped" information, either by issuing orders or by censoring anything that was not the Third Reich's official line; finally, it agreed to do "activity assessments" from time to time, which appeared in reports transmitted to the highest echelons, so that the general staff could follow propaganda policy and modify it if need be.[9] Even though, in practice, the program was far from realized, the structures set in place attested to a desire to gradually subject defeated France to official Nazi views.

In December 1940, Propaganda-Abteilung had six distinct agencies (*Fachgruppen*).[10] The Presse-Gruppe monitored print journalism, including even local periodicals published in the subprefectures. From its point of view, Captain von Grote's visit to the news and advertising powerhouse Agence Havas to requisition equipment on the day the German forces entered Paris marked the beginning of German control of a press that would soon prove—save for a few indiscretions—slavishly obedient. The Rundfunk-Gruppe united the various radio stations in the occupied zone into the notorious "Radio-Paris," which answered to the occupying forces.[11] The Aktivpropaganda-Gruppe, which became Kampfpropaganda on 12 April 1944, launched propaganda campaigns in the media or in thematic exhibitions against Freemasons, Jews, or Great Britain.[12] The Film-Gruppe was responsible for controlling the entire French film industry, which was supposed to be merged into a single pan-European framework.[13] The Schrifttum-Gruppe was concerned with book publishing and literary censorship, which was governed by three successive "Otto" lists (after Otto Abetz), the first of which resulted, in November 1940, in the confiscation of a million "degenerate" works.

Finally, the Kultur-Gruppe managed the world of theater, music, variety shows, and the fine arts, beginning its operations in autumn 1940. From the start, the reports that Propaganda-Abteilung submitted, more or less regularly,[14] showed a great deal of optimism toward an art scene intent on moving in the direction of Nazi policy. The official in charge of fine arts reassured the highest authorities by spouting political platitudes and pushing aside any "unpleasant" events. Particularly as of 1941, signs of recovery were obvious to him: the French struggle against "rotten art" as well as the return to the classical tradition of drawing and painting were attested by Matisse's and Maillol's exhibitions at the Galerie Louis Carré and by the great success of the Salon du Dessin et de la Peinture à l'Eau. He was again gratified when Gaston Diehl, on the occasion of his exhibition *À la recherche d'un ordre humain*, spoke of a new phase emerging from the war. After having claimed, on 18 February 1941, that an ever larger group of young French artists was ready to work with Germany, judging from the attitude of some,[15] the writer of the report saw in the establishment of the Ordre des artistes the beginning of fruitful exchanges facilitated by centralization. He also noted that the German authorities were pleased that no one was preoccupied with these artists—at least in appearance. In fact, the situation was much more complex than these self-satisfied reports suggested.[16] At least initially, the wait-and-see attitude of the French did not lead Germany to deploy its war machine. In turn, the Germans' voluntarism—their reliance on voluntary action and volunteers—contributed, oddly enough, to bringing the cultural sector back to life.

IT'S A DEAL

Although German cultural propaganda followed no definitive plan but only general—often empirical—guidelines, its first objective, until summer 1941, was to impose a mask of normality on culture. In fact, the Propaganda-Abteilung had every chance of success, for it revealed only the portion of its assignment likely to be accepted by the vanquished, postponing for a later time its true mission of hegemony. Even while playing to the defeated nation's norms and culture, Nazi Germany still displayed a desire to impose its own, by means of cultural and social events at the Institut allemand, a great deal of Nazi press, bookstores,[17] libraries, schools,[18] concerts, exhibitions of German art,[19] racial censorship, and looting.[20] That lasted at least until early 1943, when the worldwide conflict pushed the Third Reich's cultural voluntarism to the background. Disguised as a patron of the arts, the occupier went so far as to facilitate the return of musicians, dancers, and other performing artists to the occupied zone and promote the distribution of coal and materials to those in the plastic arts.[21] By late 1941, the objective seemed to have been realized. Artistic life was moving into high gear; museums and galleries had reopened to the public,[22] with a series of exhibitions and Salons; even better, the times seemed to encourage novelty and the spirit of enterprise. Galleries and seasonal events multiplied, reinforcing the general feeling. Every new cultural display demonstrated a continuity, a refusal to accept the ambient gloom, a means of escape, of course, but only to mount a greater resistance. That state of mind did not displease the occupier, so long as the French did not exceed certain bounds. Art could just as easily reinforce the order as it could foment unrest.

In practice, the vanquisher did not impose any artistic model on the French, less because of Hitler, who deemed France's artistic "decadence" salutary, than because the French were taking care of the matter themselves. With few exceptions, those in charge of German censorship could count on the indigenous hordes resistant to modernity to do the dirty work. They allowed the Germans to preserve their image in the art world as great Francophiles, possibly even lovers of modern literature and art. Indeed, the local sections (*Staffeln*) of the Propaganda-Abteilung were staffed by curious Sonderführer, specialists who teetered between official orders, fear of being sent to the eastern front, and their "love" of French culture, which led them to establish close ties with "the enemy." The French dealers and artists concerned were often left with good memories of these bashful lovers, who were recruited by the German propaganda ministry (Reichsministerium für Volksaufklärung und Propaganda) from militarized civilians. They were rarely very militant, but they were *Mitläufer*—sympathetic enough toward the Nazi Party not to be suspect—and sufficiently Francophile to deceive their future "collaborators."

After the war, the cultural services agency of the French zone of occupation in Germany hired Lieutenant Gerhard Heller, formerly an official in charge of literary censorship. That attests to the kind of trust Heller had been able to win in France. So too did his appearance on French television, in 1981, which was generally well received.[23] In artistic matters, a certain Dr. Lange also seems to have been respected by the art world: he regularly lamented the overly dogmatic orders he received and later displayed his sincere love of France by opening a "cultural" restaurant in the region of Nîmes after the war. Did the Francophilia of these men rule out all nationalism? Let us note for the moment that harsh orders were softened by the "ecumenical style" of the occupiers and their apparent desire to let the French manage their own affairs.

The occupying authorities could depend on the self-censorship of the art world: they had only to send a message that had already been well understood by the French publishing industry. In September 1940, the authorities had announced to the industry's representatives that they could apply self-censorship, which spared the German administration from looking like the only agent involved in purging the literary scene.[24] The French thus had to understand once and for all that they "retained" their prerogatives, provided they did not publish books written by Jews or Freemasons (or, somewhat later, Communists), or texts hostile to Germany or banned in that country. The Propaganda-Abteilung reserved the right to adjust or change this approach in case of "doubt," on the French side—or the German.

In art as in literature, the deal was struck and then generally respected by the arts sector, which was persuaded that the occupiers came equipped with a rigid plan and would not tolerate any deviation from the rules already in force east of the Rhine. Since these rules were not widely known (even though prior to the war a few reports had informed the French of the "purge" of Germanic art), the French art scene more or less looked the same as ever: varied, figurative, generally traditionalist, but feeling free to borrow (quietly) a great deal from the modernity of the "decadent" art condemned in Germany. That modernity henceforth had to be assessed in terms of the Nazi exclusions that had been decisively displayed at the time of the exhibition of "degenerate art" in Munich in summer 1937.[25] There the organicist conception of Nazi art really took shape, corresponding to the more general desire to purge the social body of its "anomalies." The pure blood of a homogeneous race and a strong community reflected "two thousand years of German culture": the irenic image of race, of a social group or a professional class above suspicion. In contrast, putrid and atomized bodies were the counterpart of the troubling, strange, and questioning works by artists who addressed the individual. Dadaism served as a foil because of its critical force and its derisiveness, abstract art, because it did not inform the Nazi worldview, and expressionism, because it expressed pain and anguish.

Although the artists themselves may have had some illusions about what would come of the "differences" between Goebbels (who supposedly supported expressionism and modern architecture) and Rosenberg (who wanted nothing to do with them), the permanent closure of the Bauhaus, in 1933, despite some of its members' concessions to Nazism, marked the beginning of a coherent official policy in Germany that drew the boundaries of the acceptable.[26] These boundaries did not include any aspect of modernity, as they did in Fascist Italy, but tended to reject outright any representation of the world useless to the Nazi cause. It was therefore in light of a well-defined program that Speer could report to the Führer that works were being displayed in France that would not have been hung from the picture rails of the Third Reich's museums.

They were tolerated in France, however, except for a few works: too "decadent," such works were smuggled in or slipped through the censor's net. In fact, censorship did not deal with formal matters but responded primarily to infringements of the exclusion laws or to anti-German symbols. Picasso and Léger were censored more for their political opinions than for their manners of painting; works by Jean-Louis Forain were the object of censorship because the illustrator had lambasted Germany too much in the past.[27] Vasily Kandinsky was blacklisted because he had belonged to the Bauhaus. All Jewish artists were censored because they were Jewish.[28] On this last point, the occupation authorities counted on the "wisdom" of the French themselves to "purge" an arts sector subject—like society at large—to new laws, French laws. The occupiers had only to verify that the certificates of adherence to the Jewish faith or to Freemasonry were filled out properly and that plans for exhibitions summarily excluded targeted artists.[29] They need only to bring into line all those who had not yet grasped the priority granted to exclusion. Thus, when Lieutenant Lücht and Captain Heinrich Ehmsen of the Propaganda-Staffel Paris repeatedly told Paul Landowski, director of the Ecole des beaux-arts, that his school had to be Aryanized, they expressed astonishment that Jewish life-drawing models were still there and insinuated that some people even claimed that the director himself was Jewish.[30] At that point, one had to increase diplomacy, to accept invitations and in turn ceremoniously invite "the folks at 52,"[31] which Hautecoeur grudgingly took it upon himself to do, hoping thereby to preserve a precarious status quo.

HATRED

With the first villainous laws of October 1940,[32] the welcoming traditions of France were swept away in a few months and replaced with a climate of suspicion and cowardice that sullied a legendary reputation.

France and its capital were doubly humiliated by defeat and submission, yielding to Vichy, which forced the French to support an imported policy whose logic led to carnage. Might the worst have been avoided if every person who carried out the exclusion policy had been aware of the real effects of its implementation? Each, "not knowing," to very different degrees, lent his cooperation to what was only one stop along the appallingly tortuous path to the "Final Solution": from high officials to pencil pushers, police officers to record clerks, Jewish organizations to the average French citizen. Absolute evil may have begun banally, in ignorance of the true meaning of the "special treatment" reserved for the excluded;[33] but the French state's tendency to do the occupier one better, its extensive legislation (sixty laws and decrees in fourteen months), the collusion between the German and French police, and the function of French concentration camps on the road to death, all starkly remind us of the nation's responsibility in setting up the terrifying system.

Of course, only the discourse of the extremists showed its true colors. They did not miss a chance to dehumanize their enemies, though without mentioning their real fate. Curiously, their prose also had a tendency to fall into banality by dint of having served too well, but only after fulfilling its mission of accustoming people to the worst decisions and the worst news. The SS-Obergruppenführer Erich von dem Bach-Zelewski expressed it this way at Nuremberg: "[If] you preach for ten long years that the Slavic peoples constitute an inferior race and that the Jews are subhuman, it will logically follow that people will accept as a natural phenomenon the killing of millions of these human beings."[34]

France was largely inured to the linguistic excesses of an efficient minority. Since 1933, Germany's rulers had placed their cultural policy in the service of the struggle against the "degeneration" of art, by claiming that its decline was the reflection of political anarchy, whose leaders were Jews, Bolsheviks, or Freemasons. In France, the occupation legalized—though it did not invent—a very similar credo that assimilated artistic decadence to the decay of society. The same guilty parties were designated: Jews, Freemasons, Communists, foreigners, or refugees, who were held responsible for all the defeats and all the disillusionments of a diseased society. As in Germany, the hatemongers invoked the Race, the Soil, and the Nation, in the tenacious desire to isolate evil and difference so as to sanitize a society bent on revenge. And as in Germany, France yielded to its old demons, its vengeful narcissism, its fantasy of self-generation,[35] repeating ad infinitum that its blood was pure, that if the French had fallen short, the fault must inevitably lie with the Other. That Other had to be driven out of France. "France for the French" was a very popular and very ambiguous slogan—ambiguous because the foreigner could have the face of the "wog" or that of the vanquisher. The extremist press teemed with anti-Semitic declarations, which defined Jewish art as they defined the Jews, compiled lists of the most famous and tallied all the others, sizing them up and comparing them in the light of Caran d'Ache's caricatures[36] and the canons of "somatic Judaism." The extremists hunted down those, the worst no doubt, still hidden under other names: the Georges Mandels and Pierre Mendès-Frances of the cultural scene. They hurled insults, filth, and denunciations, leaving the moderates to voice their polite grievances against "the foreigners." In the end, they all betrayed the panic of a vanquished people in search of a strong identity.

Lucien Rebatet began the mudslinging in early 1941, succeeding the Swiss art historian François Fosca as the author of a regular column devoted to the fine arts in *Je suis partout*. "French art is in a bad way," the French-style Fascist announced.[37] And, as for France (once again compared to a tree "whose trunk is still robust but whose branches are withering away"[38]), it must first of all "prune its rotted branches." The fine arts must be Aryanized, Jews banned from "every event," and, in particular, it must be explained "without letup why they are being condemned, how their influence has been disastrous to us,"[39] how the Salons have collapsed because of them and those like them, such as Paul Signac, "the sectarian pointillist" and "high-ranking Freemason." Had the situation really been sorted out since the change in regime? Not yet, Rebatet replied. Except for "the absence of the horde of Jews who not long ago paraded the horribly corrupt detritus of expressionism," the Salon des Indépendants of 1941 was just like it had been for years, "only more pitiful."[40] The extremists would fill page after page in this manner, embracing the occupier's racist views and overtaking the Vichy regime on the right. In April 1941, Rebatet, after spending a few weeks at the Hôtel du Parc, seat of the Vichy government, denounced its "imbroglio of weaknesses and contradictions," its resemblance to the ministry of Gaston Doumergue, only "more long-winded but even more defenseless, divided, and unstable."[41] The next year, he attacked the timidity of the "few decrees" printed by the *Journal officiel* and "barely applied."[42] As for the fine arts administration, he took a very dim view of Hautecoeur being named to run it. Rebatet, making a pretense of social consciousness, accused Hautecoeur of doing only as he pleased and forgetting the little people—subordinates, guards denied promotion and dismissed at every opportunity—even as the salaries of museum officials rose noticeably.[43] In addition, Rebatet reproached Hautecoeur for appointing the leftist Jean Cassou, ally of the Front populaire and its "wogs."

Indeed, the representatives of the regime also had to be sized up, assessed in terms of their revolutionary and xenophobic attitude, past and present. They had to be able to boast, like Robert Brasillach, of having been Fascists privately when Fascists were still being insulted, of having been anti-Masonic and anti-Semitic when their fanaticism landed them in prison.[44]

In art as well, a certification of anteriority conferred on extremists the gift of second sight and the right to judge the exclusion laws in force as being still too lax.

MAUCLAIR THE FANATIC

For a long time, the artistic scene had been experiencing a rising resentment against everything that was not certifiably French. Camille Mauclair was now free to vociferate without risking the slightest protest. We need only recall his publications from the 1930s, in which he attacked the "wogs against French art": violence already haunted his words. It remained abstract for a few more years, but it was unleashed by the Statut des Juifs, which was entered into the *Journal officiel* in October 1940, even before the Germans exerted any pressure.

A novelist and poet who had first appeared in symbolist and anarchist circles, torn between dream and action, Mauclair veered toward extremism in the late 1920s.[45] His *Farce de l'art vivant*, published in 1930, was a hybrid work, political lampoon dressed up as a reflection on the history of art. The author prided himself on no longer being an "isolated independent" but now having followers in his crusade against "the man of the avant-garde," "a professional in some sense," like the independent and the "left-winger," "the Jewish dealer," and "the wog artist," and even against—after all, it was still fashionable—the Germanic spirit, which he was not alone in contrasting to a Latin view of things.

The same year, the German collector Wilhelm Uhde's book on Picasso argued that, once the French tradition was exhausted, it ought "to turn to Germany, heir to the Greek genius," which would be "revitalized by the contribution of Jewish genius." Once artists moved beyond a regional and national painting, an "international, European painting" would replace it.[46] His book provided a pretext for Mauclair's attacks. The Ecole de Paris, cosmopolitan in its essence, also served Mauclair as an easy and entertaining target, since its defenders as well as its detractors had long ago established its romantic image. Mauclair had only to exaggerate its features a little to get a rise out of a hidebound and chauvinistic France. Who did not want to hear of sulfurous Montparnasse, where all nations of the world joined together "in the worship of alcohol, cocaine, and the living art of Germans, Polacks, Little Russians, Yankees, Japanese." There were even "niggers and redskins" there, and, among "the whites," "the proportion of Semites [was] about 80 percent, and that of failures [was] nearly equivalent."[47] Although the period when cubists met with Vladimir Lenin and Leon Trotsky was long gone, Mauclair liked to draw his readers' attention to it like a carefully orchestrated carnival act. As a voyeur of the underworld, he invited his readers to the debauch, even while warning "upstanding provincials" of what awaited them in the bowels of the capital and what they would always remember: inverts, morphine addicts, alcoholics, and sex fiends. He provided "an unforgettable vision of the witches' Sabbath, set against a backdrop painted by an international group of borderline psychopaths."[48]

This was a time when almost all "others" were being accused indiscriminately, and national resentment could still sometimes look like buffoonery.

THE END OF EXTREMISM

The scapegoat shifted as extremist diplomacy dictated. When Mauclair decided to publish a new lampoon in 1944, he naturally muted his criticism of Germanness, turning toward an ad hoc pan-Germanism.[49] Three months before the liberation, he still found an outlet for his prose in the sinister *Revivre: Le grand magazine illustré de la race*, the successor to *Le cahier jaune* published by the Institut d'études des questions juives.[50] When Stéphane Galanon questioned him at his home on rue du Cherche-Midi, Mauclair piled up his grievances and his plans: to be done with the "ever more leftist" aspect of art, "to tear to pieces and roast the whole mess in a 'Saint Bartholomew's Day massacre' of Ubu art. Just like Chancellor Hitler did in Germany." It was understood that "art is the only religion we have left."[51] What the extremists had in common was their aesthetic passions: they mixed genres and adopted a much more levelheaded tone when speaking of art than in their political professions of faith. Refusing, like the Nazis, to favor in painting or sculpture anything equivalent to the radicality of Louis-Ferdinand Céline (they liked his style less than his anti-Semitic violence and contempt for society), they were wary of bourgeois academicism but defended solid values in particular. Rebatet, like his fellow ideologues, made a few exceptions: Degas, Maillol, Jean Renoir, Maurice Brianchon, Charles Despiau,[52] a "large sober canvas" by Constant Le Breton, the "pretty delicacy" of Emmanuel de La Villéon's *Quay by the Seine*, the Spaniard Pere Creixams Picó's *Baptism* (if only he had forgone the "purplish-blue color," which reminded Rebatet of "Jewish rot"), and, finally, the true primitive, Henri Rousseau (who also figured in the Communists' dream museum).[53]

A few months before the liberation, the extremists were still conceding nothing—quite the contrary. The team at *Je suis partout* rallied in January 1944 at the Salle Wagram ("free admission and heated room," the invitations announced) around the theme, "We are not cowards." On this occasion, they gave the limelight to Rebatet, who boasted that he was assigned the "last bugle call" because he had "the biggest mouth" in the group.[54] And it was in the name of all the former leftists and all the former rightists, in the name of all the Fascists and all the National Socialists, that he called for revolution by any means, "including the most directly physical means,"[55] while again making the Jews the designated target of a more general battle against the enemy. Even in late July, he reiterated in *Je suis partout* his loyalty to Hitler after rereading *Mein Kampf*, at the same time acknowledging that he did not understand how anyone could find his doctrine "disconcerting." The program Rebatet presented seemed like an echo of the "medicalized" violence of Professor George Montandon's team.

A French emulator of Nazi doctors, Montandon had become famous for practicing "ethnoraciology," the anti-Semitic quackery employed during the occupation to issue certificates of Jewishness or Aryanness—with amounted to death sentences or stays of execution. He was the author of some racist publications, including the notorious *Comment reconnaître et expliquer le Juif?*[56] In April 1944, along with Maurice-Ivan Sicard, Émile Bougère, Jehan Teisseire, and Henri Coston, he signed a booklet titled *Je vous hais*, in which the old obsession with defining "the Jew" historically and scientifically was illustrated in a chapter devoted to art. The major propaganda exhibition *Le Juif et la France* was recalled through five photographs. They showed *The Birthday* by Marc Chagall (spelled "Chazall"), *The Jewess Mae West Seen by Another Jew* (referring to Salvador Dalí, a Catholic and Francoist), a work by Picasso (probably a fake), a statuette by Georges Rouault (a Jew?), and finally another work by Picasso, this one authentic. The text was every bit as violent as the French-language article against "decadent art" that appeared in the Nazi review *Signal*,[57] in which the author referred to the mainstream American press, worn down by anti-European xenophobia. The Nazis were following the example of the December 1941 issue of the major American periodical *Fortune*, which was illustrated with twelve reproductions of paintings by artists "living and working in the United States." Also reproduced in *Signal* was Chagall's *Birthday*, "which had drawn its subjects from the former ghettos," or, as *Fortune* put it, from the "peasant customs of the Russian villages of his childhood."[58]

THE PREWAR PERIOD

Artists had loudly decried the danger before the war but their warnings fell on deaf ears. Given the underlying fear, what good was the appeal made by Jean Lurçat, whose adversaries could then accuse him of associating with the USSR? "Any particular reaction," he warned in 1938, "or any opinion campaign aimed at introducing into our country an extreme nationalism and a rejection of foreigners, will prove to be a harmful activity, dangerous to human progress first and to France second."[59] Speaking against the satirists of the newspaper *Le matin*, who in May 1938 had demanded the removal of the sculpture by the émigré artist Jacques Lipchitz, Lurçat reminded readers that Fernand Cormon, a professor at the Ecole des beaux-arts during World War I, had written in the press that the impressionist school—which Cormon abhorred—was "one aspect of the activity of the German espionage agencies."[60] But, against the Cassandras in their midst, the journalists of *Le matin* retained the advantage of having been the first to attack "the gigantic pile of garbage, supposedly sculpted, placed on the Champs-Elysées." *Prometheus*, the "pile of garbage" in question, was wearing a Phrygian cap and strangling a bird of prey (it has since become famous). It looked to them like a challenge issued to French art whose representatives were "left without commissions," unless it was the joke by a politician seeking to show "the level of barbarism and mindlessness to which Russian 'art' had fallen."[61]

The occupation, after all, legalized a practice that democracy had tolerated as an unavoidable evil. Hatred of the foreigner had established itself in France, taking the rise in immigration as its pretext. Under these conditions, Emmanuel Berl, who was of Jewish descent, announced in 1938 that a statute on foreigners was needed if conflicts between French natives and immigrants were to be avoided. Jean Giraudoux, commissioner of propaganda in the government of Édouard Daladier just before the war, foretold the worst when, in *Pleins pouvoirs*, he described in detail the threats the country faced from that "horde, which are arranging to get their rights as citizens revoked and thus to brave expulsions of every kind, and whose physical constitution, precarious and abnormal, brought them by the thousands to our hospitals, which they overburden."[62] The even more radical Louis Darquier de Pellepoix, municipal councillor of Paris and future commissioner of Jewish issues, began distributing in 1938 a tract qua legislative bill, a veritable Statut des Juifs before its time. So, in reality, there was no way out but to agree with Hitler and proclaim that a policy attains its higher form only if it is racial and then, since one certainly had to remain French, to seek the justification for radical exclusion measures in Jean-Baptiste Colbert and Cardinal de Richelieu. That meant dangerously engaging in a hate competition, one that a little later would lead Xavier Vallat to boast to SS officer Dannecker that, of the two of them, he was the "older anti-Semite." The mudslinging had actually begun before the occupation, suddenly facilitated by the circumstances. Exclusion laws and those who believed in them proliferated, since the risk of being accused of xenophobia had all but vanished.

On the French art scene, there was no dearth of inquisitors, who applauded the persecution while intensifying their onslaught against the victims. Fernand Demeure, Mosdyc, Rebatet, Fritz Vanderpyl, and René Borelly, all loyal contributors to the various media, were ready to serve the cause of might makes right.

AN ORDINARY RACISM

Scholarly works did not have the same impact as the print media, but, being more lasting, they served exclusion in their own way, under the cloak of an erudite and refined detachment. Hence, when Robert Rey published his popular treatise *La peinture moderne, ou l'Art sans métier* in 1941,[63] he protected his reputation as a cultured administrator behind a moderate tone. Although he had been assistant curator at the Musée du Luxembourg, where he had introduced the first naïve art, his audience, fans of the "Que sais-je?" book series, were almost always won over when they saw their own simple ideas about modern art defended. Could the remedies he proposed give rise to even the slightest opposition? It had become a commonplace: art suffered from a lack of craft. Thus, the reader had only to choose whether to remain untroubled or not by the designation of the culprit. For Rey, the foreign scapegoat elicited not hatred but contempt. However much French art had suffered from the cosmopolitanism of the Ecole de Paris—"nearly the entirety" of which comprised "foreign or Semitic painters or sculptors"—"not all of them were without talent," far from it. But they "did not feel," they "did not write" as French people. "Hence the foreignness of their reactions contributed to the confusion of thought." Chagall was impeccable, but in a museum of contemporary ethnography, not as the illustrator of Jean de La Fontaine, "the most Cartesian and the most lucid of our poets."

Rey's ordinary racism had other representatives, with still more official duties. Hautecoeur, designated by Pétain to succeed Huisman (who had departed on the *Massilia* in 1940), never publicly demonstrated his rancor toward foreign artists during the occupation. As a curator, in 1929, he had simply complained of the decadence of contemporary art, corrupted by the presence of foreign critics and artists, both using "a jargon that seems translated from Slavic or Germanic idioms." These foreigners were more susceptible than the French to aesthetic dissertations and took it upon themselves to speak with authority about the French tradition, claiming to reveal to France the virtues and flaws inherent in its "race."[64]

Was he preparing the way, without knowing it, for future acts of barbarism? From June 1940 on, he stood among the ranks of the moderates, barely tolerating the German presence, at bottom completely at odds with the brutal exclusion measures to which his principles could not be reconciled. Conversely, he did his job as a high official, compelled to see the new persecution laws enforced. In this, he was like the entire French administration, which by then looked like a better guarantor of exclusion than of the protection of citizens.

That was probably the intent of the craziest of the plans sent in strictest confidence to the official French authorities between 1940 and 1944. Consider that of one Georges Stéphane K. Comnène, a painter, sculptor, and architect, who in July 1942 proposed that the prefect of Paris place under government authority the "Institut européen pour les questions d'architecture et d'art," which he charged with carrying out a "crusade" against ugliness and decadence. The artist claimed he was descended from the last Corsican king and called for a return to the reign of taste that had been replaced, since 1870, by "the major Jewish art dealers, who discovered and made famous a series of abnormal painters and artists for commercial aims."[65] In the end, the prefecture filed away his proposal, annoyed by the pretensions of this minor nobleman for whom "taste, culture, order, and traditions [were] gifts that princes possessed by blood."[66] But, in the great Vichy tradition, it first ordered a police investigation of his past.[67]

Comnène sent his proposal to the authorities at a time when France had been conducting its exclusion policy for a long time. Laval had just resumed a place within the government, opening still wider the gates of French collaboration with Germany. On the artistic front, he sold off the national collections while granting a favorable hearing, starting at this time, to the request by his trusted man, Hilaire, to exchange his post as secretary general for the civil service at the interior ministry for the directorship of the fine arts administration, to which the faithful Pétainist Hautecoeur was clinging. Laval fired Hautecoeur in spring 1944.[68]

AT THE HEAD OF THE STATE

Hilaire was more modern, more corporatist, and more of a central planner than his predecessor. He had had a curious career path as a radical who entered politics in spite of himself. Although born into a republican family (he was the nephew of Joseph Paganon, Laval's interior minister), he displayed little political ambition, which allowed him to value friends of all stripes, including Rebatet, with whom he crisscrossed Europe before the war, visiting museums and major international exhibitions, without dealing seriously with anything but cultural matters.[69] A defender of a "revolutionary" French painting that regularly "dynamited" the tradition for the better, he took his example from the "new regimes" that had just "proven themselves in Europe" and whose principles could not fail "to influence the future French regime." France would learn to have both a revolutionary painting and a revolutionary regime—from which Jewish artists, with the exception of Pissarro, who proved the rule, and Chagall, who remained a popular image maker, had to be excluded, not for political reasons but strictly on the basis of aesthetic considerations. Naturally, he wrote, in defense of an association only of German artists,

> the paintings of Soutine, Kisling, and other Jewish painters of the Vilnius and Paris schools are tending to disappear from the picture rails of the capital. . . . Jewish painting, like all Jewish arts, is parasitical. It took the Jews to deform and bring into disrepute Cézanne's lesson. . . . Three hundred Jewish painters have grown on French aesthetics like mistletoe on an apple tree. They have disfigured it, arrogantly caricatured it. They have created the misapprehensions of the spurious avant-garde that has deceived Camille Mauclair himself. It is not a political matter to proscribe this debilitating ferment and to prevent freedom from turning into license. It is a matter of hygiene.[70]

Was Hilaire anti-Semitic? Evidently so, based on this document and a few others, which are larded with the usual invectives against the Jews,[71] though he did not make anti-Semitism an obsession, since none of his published texts deals specifically with this question. At the important post he held at the interior ministry, he undoubtedly had to collaborate on Vichy's exclusion policy and to collaborate with the occupier. This is substantiated by a document from June 1942, deposited in the archives of the Haute Cour de Justice. The German officer in charge of the police at the Feldkommandantur found the report by the Direction de la défense in France that placed in doubt the "integrity" of Hilaire and his friend, the police superintendent Brunet, to be "exaggerated." Hilaire had not taken to drink nor had he "gone on a binge with Brunet in Troyes." By contrast, it was "absolutely accurate that Brunet [had] once purchased a pig on the black market destined in part for Prefect Hilaire." Hilaire had attracted attention only once, during an official trip to Paris, when he used his state vehicle to go to the horse races at Longchamp. It was also accurate that he was very ambitious and from a very modest background: his father was a manual laborer and French soldier who had been killed on the battlefield at Verdun. But Hilaire had studied in Germany, spoke German, and had "always been considered to be in favor of the collaboration and a supporter of Laval." In addition, he was "a great enemy of Communism," even if he did not join Jacques Doriot's anti-Communist movement. Finally—and was this not the most important thing?—"he had striven to conform conscientiously to all the regulations."[72] This conclusion would be confirmed in the charges the public prosecutor brought against Hilaire, in 1947. He was the author of a circular, dated 17 August 1942, in which he urged the prefects to support the government's actions on behalf of the *relève*, whereby French citizens volunteered to work in Germany in exchange for the release of French prisoners. He had had mayors dismissed not only for reasons of common law (about 229 of them) but also on the basis of "clearly political" criteria (25), given their "hostile attitude toward the work of national renewal." He had thus committed, during wartime, acts of a nature to be injurious to the national defense.[73]

According to other statements, gathered after the liberation, Hilaire, like almost everyone else, had made exceptions to the rule, and these allowed him to be partly exonerated after the war. He had approached René Bousquet, the Vichy regime's secretary general of the police, in May 1943, asking to have Cassou released,[74] and he took action in support of certain "republican" prefects as well as on behalf of Jewish or Freemason civil servants whom he had protected "as much as possible." Such actions stood in contrast to the time he spent allowing an infernal machine to operate by its murderous rules.[75]

THE LAW OF FUNCTIONS

The fact that there were qualms even at the interior ministry did not at all undermine the efficiency of a system that left very little room for exceptions. This is evidenced by the circumscribed actions of Hautecoeur, who opposed the exclusion measures and was in tears when he had to inform Cassou of his dismissal from the administration.[76] Despite his desire "to mitigate the consequences for the Israelites of an unjust law," Hautecoeur had to confine himself to filling out "laudatory reports on all the Jewish civil servants in his service (except one)," helping them to get to the "free" zone, and securing the retirement of his predecessor, Huisman, while protecting the property at the Gobelins Tapestry Manufactory and continuing to award a few official commissions to Jewish artists.[77] At every level of the government, the new law remained the rule, nearly incontrovertible, and accepted, under protest or not, as long as one remained at one's post. Once that decision had been made, several arguments surfaced to help justify it.

On the artists' side, Landowski recorded in his journal[78] day after day the pangs of a conscience tormented by his decision to remain at his post as director of the Ecole des beaux-arts. As a result of that choice, he felt obliged to join a group of French artists on an official trip to Germany and to enforce the new laws. Starting in August 1940, he watched in disgust as a handful of his colleagues became anti-Semites.[79] Having been forced by a denunciation to prove he was Aryan,[80] he found it all the more difficult to tolerate the persecution and to inform his Jewish staff and professors that they were being "retired," as he was obliged to do.[81] Conversely, he found reassuring the attitude of Georges Desvallières, his colleague at the Institut de France. After speaking out, in November 1940, against anti-Semitic censorship at the Salon d'Automne (of which he was president),[82] Desvallières gave a short speech to the Académie des beaux-arts, telling Emmanuel Pontremoli, a Jewish architect and also a member of the Institut de France, that "Catholics" found all persecution "odious and humiliating," and that, though the church was their "mother," the synagogue remained their "grandmother."[83] As of March 1940, Landowski's wish to resign conflicted with his fear of the risks involved. "What would be good," he wrote a year later,

> is if everyone were to resign. Then France would be in the same chaotic situation. But it's too late. It's no longer possible. If I were to resign on my own, someone would immediately start the rumor that it's because I'm Jewish. . . . If someone asked me to take measures that were too stupid or too ignoble, I would surely find a way to make the necessary gesture. It's already quite enough to have had to let P. M. and B. B. know they were being retired.[84]

To the staff of the Propaganda-Staffel Paris who spoke to him insistently about "the Jewish question" at the Ecole des beaux-arts (which they said they did not want to "settle inhumanely"), he tried to play down the situation: but he was annoyed at even having to hear their insane language.[85] Like many others, he had no precise information about the unfolding tragedy until later. A year after the end of his tenure as director, which he refused to extend in June 1942, he found out, through a friend released from the camps, about the treatment of Russian prisoners, "the systematic annihilation of Polish Jews. Amongst other . . . regular walking skeletons," and the "liquidation" of the Warsaw ghetto. He heard the stupefying figures of a thousand deaths a day and learned of experiments done on Jews and of "women examined like livestock, stripped, their heads and bodies shaven."[86]

THE OUTCASTS

The circulars written in the shadow of officialdom ended in a nightmare for all who could not escape arrest. What is there to add today to the story, told so many times, of the anonymous masses sent to the death camps from France or other countries in Europe, often never to return? Among them were artists, both well known and unknown: Otto Freundlich, deported to Majdanek in Poland in 1943; Abraham-Joseph Berline, arrested in May 1941, interned in Compiègne and Drancy, then sent to Auschwitz, where he died soon after; Jacques Gotko, taken in 1942 as a stateless person, released, then rearrested, sent to Compiègne, Drancy, Majdanek, and finally Auschwitz, where he died of typhus in July 1943; Adolphe Feder, a member of the Resistance, deported in December 1943 to Auschwitz, where he died; Max Jacob, arrested in Saint-Benoît-sur-Loire in February 1944 and sent to Drancy, where he died in March.[87] The list is far longer.

The Nazis' chief objective was the physical, moral, and intellectual destruction of the deportees. The fact that people still spoke, wrote, and drew in the camps simply proves that there were, for some at least, reasons to hope, to bear witness, to be roused,[88] or else to go mad, like Zoran Music. In Dachau, when his fear abated somewhat, he began to draw "as if in a trance.... As if blinded by the haunting expanse of those fields of cadavers.... as if gripped by a fever, with the irresistible need to draw so that such grandiose and tragic beauty would not escape [him]."[89] He had begun to sketch "in secret, in the drawer of [his] lathe. Things seen along the way while going to the factory: the arrival of a convoy: cattle car open: the corpses spill out."[90]

In France itself, even before the occupation, camps were opened to collect undesirable or enemy nationals: Spanish Republicans, then Austrians or Germans, and, after the defeat and the posting of exclusion laws, Jews, Freemasons, opponents of the regime, anti-Nazis. To the circular of 17 September 1939, which set out the practical details for interning all "suspicious, dangerous, or undesirable" foreign refugees, was appended article nineteen of the armistice, which France had, under protest, been forced to accept, and by which it was committed to handing over "on demand, all German nationals designated by the government of the Reich."[91] In the southern zone of France alone, there were numerous internment centers, not only the sadly famous—Gurs, Les Milles, Saint-Sulpice-la-Pointe, Lyon—but also Rivesaltes, Sisteron, Fort-Barraux, Vénissieux, Brens, Collioure, Rieucros: more than a hundred camps in all, gathering up the "enemies" of the day.[92] The internees were hunted down by the German police but also by the French police who, over the course of 1942, increased their collaboration with the vanquisher. That trend is reflected in the pact between the two police forces made on 29 July 1942—recorded and confirmed somewhat later by the Bousquet-Oberg accord. Höherer SS- und Polizeiführer Carl-Albrecht Oberg, chief of the German police in France, required that France help him, "fight preemptively all attacks directed against the security of the Wehrmacht, against the interests of the German people, and against the tranquility of the French people, whether the enemies are Communists, terrorists, enemy agents, saboteurs, or their Jewish, Bolshevik, and Anglo-American straw men, and to do so with all the means placed at their disposal."[93]

The concentration camps in France did not exterminate their prisoners, but they did keep internees crammed together under humiliating conditions—at least until 1942, when French camps were transformed into transit stations for those being deported. It was primarily in these camps, when life still had some semblance of normality, that artists bore witness.

At Les Milles, Max Ernst drew a birdman climbing up a hill and encountering a snake; Hans Bellmer, a portrait of Ernst as a brick mosaic; Max Lingner, the marching of prisoners with stunned looks; Hermann Henry Gowa, marchers with completely blank looks; Éric Isenberger, portraits as effaced as his companions; Peter Lipman-Wulf, the miserable nights in the catacombs. Franz Meyer, who preferred to laugh, proffered a tender view of a repellent little world: the guards, very French; the flag, very French; the sign posted at the entrance, also very French, with the portrait of Pétain wearing a kepi framed by the famous refrain, "Maréchal nous voilà!" (Marshal, here we are!).[94]

Also at Les Milles camp, it was decided that the artists could decorate the walls of their guards' refectory, by inscribing their obsessions of the moment. Some forty artists, more than a few of them anonymous, set to work during autumn 1940, producing peculiar mural paintings such as *Last Supper of Seven Figures at the Feast of the Peoples of the World; Landscape with Ham, Sardines, and Pineapple; Land of Plenty, or, The Camp Guard (the 1000 1000);* and *Procession of Beneficiaries with Giant Sausage, Barrel, and Artichoke.* Were the winds of Pétain's Révolution nationale blowing even there, in a scene depicting labor in the fields?[95] Or more simply, did the continuity of certain traditional themes allow some prisoners to think, in spite of everything, that a "tolerant" regime reigned in the camp?

All resisted in their own ways, sometimes even by finding in the camp a physiognomy adapted to their morbid fantasies. Bellmer, inspired by Charles Baudelaire's "Une charogne" (A carcass), repeatedly said that death could be beautiful, provided one had enough Pernod, and that he was there because he had realized that the Nazis were artists of destruction.[96] Although his attitude remained unique, the situation gave free rein to other extravagant visions, new solidarities, innovative pursuits. Thus, Ernst, Bellmer's barracks mate, devised decalcomanias, colored frottages, and decoupages of poorly baked clay. Unlike most of his friends in captivity, Ernst managed, by an incredible series of events, to leave France for the United States in 1941.

Released in 1939, thanks to the intervention of Albert Sarraut—who had been alerted by Paul Éluard—Ernst hid out in Saint-Martin-d'Ardèche. In May of that year, he was accused by a deaf mute of sending light signals to the enemy. He was thus sent back to Les Milles, where prisoners "placed in danger" by the arrival of the Nazis were crammed onto a train whose destination was at first unknown, then changed a hundred times. It finally arrived at the Saint-Nicolas internment camp, near Nîmes, from which Ernst escaped and returned to Saint-Martin, where he painted *Europe after the Rain*, before attempting to flee the country. An anti-Nazi exile being sought by the Gestapo, he gained his freedom at the very last minute with the help of the Emergency Rescue Committee in Marseilles.[97] Its operations there were directed by Varian Fry, an American journalist and professor who had been sent to France by Eleanor Roosevelt with an envelope containing three thousand dollars of spending money and a list of two hundred refugees under imminent threat of arrest, who were to be expedited to the United States by any means necessary.[98]

EXILE

Picasso and Matisse, like André Gide and André Malraux, refused to leave. Chagall, who was in the greatest danger, decided to go only in May 1941. In the eighteen rooms of the Villa Air-Bel, the Emergency Rescue Committee lodged many aspiring to make the trip, including André Breton, Benjamin Péret, René Char and Tristan Tzara, Victor Serge, and the artists Wifredo Lam, Oscar Dominguez, Victor Brauner, André Masson, and Ernst (an exhibition of Ernst's works was improvised on the grounds). In fact, the list of two hundred key figures to be saved grew considerably longer. In twenty-one months, more than a thousand people were rescued before the committee was banned. But a warning had been given by the "preventive" arrest of tenants at Air-Bel just before Pétain's visit to Marseilles.

At the start of the occupation, no one could say exactly what Germany's policy would be nor could anyone assess the real risks. History has shown that the Germans did not arrest the "moderns," especially if they agreed to do their creative work "in silence." In retrospect, that meant that, in theory at least, all exiles were safe with the exception of Jews and known Communist militants. Those who wanted to leave were more politicized and better informed about the aims of Nazism in Europe. They did not believe it would still be possible to live, think, create, and exhibit freely in France without shame. The painter André Masson boisterously expressed this idea one day on the terrace of a café in Marseilles, after he was taken to task by an admirer of the new France because he refused to stand for the playing of "La Marseillaise." He left the café, shouting that the French ought rather to be made to sing a hymn to submission, for he was convinced that a common soldier would become "a sort of governor maneuvered by the Nazis."

On the Côte d'Azur, at least the occupiers themselves were not yet visible, even though the staff of the French state and its loyalists had in large part installed themselves there. As in the occupied zone, one had to beware of extremists. Rebatet, for example, passed through in August 1941, and sent *Je suis partout* a dispatch of his own invention. At Le Cintra, a café in the old port of Marseilles, there was, he reported, "a Jew in the pink of health, lolling about, planning nonchalantly to spend a pretty penny next door, at Basso's or the Bar du Soleil."[99] That backed up the denunciations of the weekly *Gringoire*, whose headquarters were not far away. It listed its enemies in a shady column that lived up to its name: "Repeat It." And if you dodged the fanatics, there was still the danger of being betrayed by those "nearest and dearest." That was the case for Moïse Kisling (a naturalized French citizen since 1914), who was living on quai de Rive-Neuve in Marseilles. In 1941, he was denounced as a Jew by a model and barely escaped the Vichy police, before leaving for the United States, first crossing the Pyrénées and then heading to Lisbon. But on the Côte d'Azur—whose cultural life, particularly in Marseilles, was greatly invigorated by the many refugees who arrived there between spring and autumn 1940—the call of the open sea was strongest, at least for those who had little time to waste: Jews and political opponents of the regime. The desire to flee an already unbearable climate was spreading, affecting everyone, without distinction or regard for whether there was a real chance of escape. The improvised Salons of the local bourgeoisie and the various charitable organizations made the cities of the Mediterranean coast look like a promised land, but it was an illusion: the French administration proved to be so hostile and discriminatory toward foreigners that they learned to be wary of centers that were welcoming but also served a policing function, such that foreigners risked being sent to prison, to the camps, or back to their country of origin.

PREMONITION, DUTY, AND INNOCENCE

The case of the surrealists created the legend of an exile that was often barely credible but finished well, in New York harbor (then in Greenwich Village), where the adventure, crowned with lasting success, continued.[100] More generally, examples of "successful" exiles contributed to spreading the idea that the Parisian intelligentsia had met up one fine day on the Côte d'Azur, united by a denouement that they had in great part foreseen. In fact, for some of them at least, events had not come out of nowhere—they had already considered fleeing elsewhere for some time. Masson related that "the journey" of the surrealists to America had been decided even before the start of the war, during the summer preceding the invasion, while they were on vacation with Breton in La Baule. The Munich agreement looked like a farce to them and the invasion of Poland seemed imminent. Masson, like the others—and even more resolutely perhaps, since he still had a painful memory of World War I—did not want to see French democracy collapse. He therefore left, telling the world that intellectuals and artists were going into exile on the strength of "premonition" and that future generations would have to recognize the surrealists' gift of clairvoyance. In the eyes of these artists, "Mussolini, Hitler, and Franco were virulent poisons."[101]

Even when artists decided to do their duty by going to war—the painter Jean Hélion, for example, had had the courage to return to Europe from the United States, where he had been living, to "be in on it"[102]—the conditions of the defeat gave notice to some that they should leave to continue the fight elsewhere.[103] The outbreak of hostilities, and especially the occupation, thus led a good portion of the well-known modern artists and writers to cross the Atlantic Ocean. Not all were "resisters," but they were anxious or constrained not to get mixed up with "the evil." Those already mentioned would be joined by Léger, Ossip Zadkine, Chagall, Lipchitz, Amédée Ozenfant, Yves Tanguy, and Roberto Matta (they left from 1939 on), Piet Mondrian (who left in 1938), Dalí (who was in New York after 1939), Man Ray, and Pavel Tchelitchew.

Compared to that glittering exile dressed up as rebellion, the fate meted out to the majority of creative people was disastrous. Once the (minute) possibility of leaving for the United States was ruled out, outcasts or rebels were left with other destinations: Palma de Mallorca (Miró), Portugal and Brazil (Arpad Szenes and Maria Helena Vieira da Silva), and so on. But, when these havens failed, one after the other, those who remained eventually had to find a hiding place in France, preferably in the "free" zone, usually in a village far from the major urban areas, often one recommended by an acquaintance for its welcoming ways and the discretion of its residents. Dieulefit, for example, an old Camisard stronghold accustomed to resistance, saw its population triple, taking in more than a thousand refugees. Pierre Guastalla, Willy Eisenschitz, Étienne-Martin, and Wols were all there, separated to the end by their divergent aesthetic notions: only this involuntary experience[104] and a climate of temporary freedom and mysticism connected them. Their accounts conjure up ecumenical Sundays when peasants and refugees, believers and unbelievers, met at church. Étienne-Martin deepened his knowledge of the Tao, all the while sculpting a monumental Virgin Mary in the sand of the region; Guastalla, a Jew, and Wols, a Protestant, read the Bible, coming in contact with the long-standing faith of Pierre Emmanuel and Emmanuel Mounier, who passed through.

How many of the some five hundred thousand refugees in the "free" zone were artists? We do not have sufficiently accurate figures to hazard a guess.[105] The accounts, statements, and still recent and incomplete history of these provincial centers mention a considerable number of artists who, temporarily at least, preferred to leave the occupied zone and move to the so-called free zone where they could continue to work peacefully, away from the occupier. They did not exhibit there, however, but sent their works to the Salons and galleries of Paris.

The personal accounts discourage hasty generalizations, since each artist had a different reason for fleeing, and each found more or less acceptable ways to survive. The worst conditions were the lot of those who had to hide underground: the Jewish painter Benn (Benejou Rabinowicz) and others, in a cellar; the anti-Nazi German painter Hans Hartung, in the Foreign Legion, after trying, in vain, to join the French army. All were brutally excluded by a nation in a state of shock, withdrawn into itself and blanketed in circulars condemning the new outsiders to ruin.

Wols would draw from his hideous story one of the most eloquent lessons. Expelled from Germany and then from Spain, in 1935, he found refuge in France, before being sent from one camp to another. Once released, he appealed to Fry's committee in 1941, but to no avail. It was too late; the United States was entering the war. Dieulefit eventually took in the human wreck, eaten away by desolation, disgust, and the alcohol he discovered in the camps. Even though he loved "the countryside, the animals, the rivers, the Milky Way," within three years he constructed a formless, teeming, and despairing oeuvre that expunged all conventional points of reference while undermining the last certainties. The ineffaceable image of Wols, who spoke for many others, is undoubtedly a photographic self-portrait of 1944, stamped with the word *apatride* (stateless), in which he is seated, arms crossed, somber and resigned, a question mark on his forehead.[106]

Breton, to whom some of the surrealists still rallied, said that the recent war and the situation it had produced was to be attributed to the monotony of human life in peacetime, to a routine "entirely swathed in velvet," into which a new passion had to be injected at any cost. Was this a poetic version of Pétain's wrath about France's laxity? With panache, as always, the surrealists escaped the "military" battle, preferring verbal violence. Hartung, who volunteered to fight the Nazis—"his own people," as it happened—took this to be an act of impotence. He later begrudged them not for having produced "great speeches" but for not having gone to fight "at the front," since he held action on the ground to be the only true act of political engagement.[107]

In reality, like everyone else, artists were far from sharing a single definition of engagement. The occupation ended up troubling the consciences of a group that was at once marginal, sensitive to the world, and distrustful of all social or political organization. Faced with such vagueness, the Germans ordered that a corporate body that would allow them to keep an eye on that motley population be set up as quickly as possible. They tried to lure into their nets its eminent members, whom they invited to Germany so they might be converted to the Nazi credo and spread it among their peers. In other words, the occupiers set the rules for what they wanted the "engagement" of artists in France to become, obliging them to take a position, to get back in a game in which the "effectiveness" of the protagonists would have no relation to their real political engagement.

NOTES

1. On the ways in which the Third Reich's propaganda was applied, see Jacques Polonski, *La presse, la propagande et l'opinion publique sous l'Occupation* (Paris: Editions du Centre de Documentation Juive Contemporaine, 1946); Élisabeth Dunan, "La Propaganda-Abteilung de France: Tâches et organisation," *Revue d'histoire de la Deuxième Guerre mondiale*, October 1951; Claude Lévy, "L'organisation de la propagande allemande en France," *Revue d'histoire de la Deuxième Guerre mondiale*, October 1966; Hans Umbreit, "Auf dem Weg zur Kontinentalherrschaft," in Bernhard R. Kroener, Rolf-Dieter Müller, and Hans Umbreit, *Organisation und Mobilisierung des deutschen Machtbereichs*, pt. 1, *Kriegsverwaltung, Wirtschaft und personelle Ressourcen, 1939–1941*, vol. 5 of *Das Deutsche Reich und der Zweite Weltkrieg* (Stuttgart: Deutsche Verlags-Anstalt, 1988), esp. 297–308; Laurent Gervereau and Denis Peschanski, eds., *La propagande sous Vichy, 1940–1944*, exh. cat. (Nanterre: Bibliothèque de Documentation Internationale Contemporaine, 1990), esp. Jacques Nobécourt, "L'occupant allemand," 82–91. Finally, on certain questions at least, see the series AJ 40

at the Archives nationales (AN) in Paris and the reports of the Propaganda-Staffel Paris (RW41V221) at the Bundesarchiv-Militärchiv, Freiburg im Breisgau, Germany.

2. Although repeated onslaughts by the embassy made him lose a certain number of prerogatives, Schmidtke, who previously had been in charge of the German press, was alone in retaining his posting in Paris until the end of the occupation, having in the interim attained the rank of *Oberst* (colonel). At first, he had only a few collaborators, but later he commanded between one hundred and two hundred officers supported by a large staff. Supposedly subordinate to the Oberkommando der Wehrmacht (OKW) and hence to the army, he conducted his operation in perfect synchrony with Goebbels and the Nazi Party. After the occupation of the southern zone, Abetz attempted to cut back the activities of the Propaganda-Abteilung Frankreich, pointing out that a reduction in its numbers would free up a large contingent of military forces. Jacques Nobécourt, basing himself on Generalmajor Hasso von Wedel, head of the OKW's Wehrmachtpropaganda-Abteilung, speaks of a reduction in manpower from 1,000 to 380 in July 1944; see Nobécourt, "L'occupant allemand" (note 1), 90. See also Hans Umbreit, *Der Militärbefehlshaber in Frankreich 1940–1944* (Boppard am Rhein: Harald Boldt, 1968).
3. On the Institut allemand, see Eckard Michels, "Das Deutsche Institut in Paris 1940–1944," *Revue d'Allemagne et des pays de langue allemande* 23 (1991).
4. In November 1941, the first issue, on poets and thinkers, of the *Cahiers de l'Institut allemand* appeared under Epting's directorship, with articles or conference papers on Arthur Schopenhauer and Friedrich Nietzsche, Rainer Maria Rilke, Hans Carossa, Erwin Guido Kolbenheyer, workers' poetry, and contemporary German poetry. The six articles were written by Erich Rothacker, Kaspar Pinette, Georg Rabuse, Bruno Meder, W. Albrecht, and Gerhard Funke, respectively.
5. The director was Epting, Bremer was the editor in chief. The first issue, dated 18 April 1942, included articles by Abetz, Epting, Friedrich Sieburg ("Die Sprache als Schicksal"), Édouard Dujardin ("Souvenirs sur Houston Stewart Chamberlain"), Fritz Neubert ("Schiller, Goethe und die französische Klassik"), André Meyer ("Les germanistes français et l'Allemagne"), Ernst Jünger ("Tagebuchblätter aus Frankreich"), Robert Brasillach ("Réflexions d'un prisonnier"), Hellmuth Rademacher ("Die sozialpolitische Arbeit der Militärverwaltung in Paris"), and Georg Rabuse ("La seule France?").
6. *Pariser Zeitung*, whose aim was "the description of German life" and "the explication of German thought," first appeared on 15 June 1941 and ceased publication in August 1944. A German-language newspaper, *Pariser*

Zeitung: Politik, litteratur Handel und Gewerbe, had already appeared in 1838; in the years prior to World War I, there was also the *Pariser Zeitung: Einzige deutsche Zeitung in Frankreich* (created in 1902). Contributors who published articles on the arts between 1941 and 1944 included Paul Strecker, Albert Buesche, Hans Haveman, Martin Raschke, and Wolf Schramm.

7. The French-language German review *Signal*—a supplement to the *Berliner illustrierte Zeitung*—appeared from July 1940 to June 1944.

8. By November 1943, it had already spent three hundred million francs, according to Rudolph Rahn, the adviser in charge of the information office at the embassy. Figures for the Propaganda-Abteilung Frankreich were provided by Generalmajor Hasso von Wedel. See Nobécourt, "L'occupant allemand" (note 1), 90.

9. These reports are held in the Archives nationales (AN), in the subseries of German archives from World War II, AJ 40 1001. On the fine arts ("Bildende Künste") during the period from October 1940 to July 1944, the reports are unfortunately rather thin (when compared to those on theater or literature) and must be read with particular vigilance because the authors filled them with waffle, within the framework of notes intended for the higher authorities of the Third Reich.

10. France was supposed to be divided up and controlled. The Propaganda-Abteilung Frankreich was thus divided into echelons, or *Staffeln*, which received their orders from Paris and were themselves subdivided into branches identical to those of Propaganda-Abteilung. The *Staffeln* reigned supreme in certain cities, in accordance with the territorial divisions made by the occupation army. They oversaw Angers, Bordeaux, Dijon, Paris, and Saint-Germain until 1942, and Lyon beginning in late 1942. The administrative center of each *département* was the target of the propaganda detachment posted there.

11. The group imposed two programs for the use of the French and the occupation troops. Part of the first program consisted of a campaign against British radio, which was enjoying such success that the Germans were led to consider confiscating privately owned sets in spring 1944 and forcing people to listen collectively in special halls.

12. Because its ranks of informers and agitators did not have the anticipated success, they were replaced by information centers that actually served as branches of the police.

13. That initial hard-line policy was amended at the request of the military command, which, in this case as in others, recognized the negative consequences that the annihilation of French cinema would have: it would discourage the sector, foster emigration, and lead to a rebuffing of the Germans.

    On the film industry, see François Garçon, *De Blum à Pétain: Cinéma et société française (1936–1944)* (Paris: Editions du Cerf, 1984); Evelyn

Ehrlich, *Cinema of Paradox: French Filmmaking under the German Occupation* (New York: Columbia Univ. Press, 1985); Jean-Pierre Bertin-Maghit, *Le cinéma sous l'Occupation: Le monde du cinéma français de 1940 à 1946* (Paris: Olivier Orban, 1989).

14. Several times a month at first, then monthly.

15. In a report as late as 30 June 1944, the writer was pleased to note that first-rate artists such as Raoul Dufy (!), Kees van Dongen, Othon Friesz, Henri Louis Bouchard, Charles Despiau, and Paul Belmondo had not, despite external events, lost their positive attitude toward Germany; see AN, AJ 40 1001.

16. See the report of Propaganda-Abteilung Frankreich, *Der Militärbefehlshaber in Frankreich*, from October 1940 to July 1944, AN, AJ 40 1001, subchapter "Bildende Künste."

17. The occupying forces marked their new territory with symbolic gestures. For example, they opened, on the site formerly occupied by the English bookstore Smith on rue de Rivoli, a bookstore for "German soldiers but also Parisians" to visit in their spare time. *Pariser Zeitung* did its share of boasting and announced, in January 1941, that where once "King George and Queen Mary, in sumptuous finery, displayed their coronation smiles, one now sees the portraits of Göring and Brauchitsch." German books stood side by side there with French works: guides, but also historical accounts and "political literature." The "classics"—Hitler's *Mein Kampf* and Alfred Rosenberg's *Der Mythus des 20. Jahrhunderts*—were the most requested books, according to the Nazi daily. Some time later, on 21 April, the cultural occupation gained ground when the Rive Gauche bookstore at 47, boulevard Saint-Michel also became a "Franco-German" bookstore.

18. A school was opened on Île Saint-Louis, at the site of the Musée Mieckiewicz (devoted to Polish art) and the Polish library.

19. The Institut allemand shored up the prestige of German art with *Hans Holbein en son siècle* in autumn 1943, while contemporary German artists were invited to exhibit in French museums and requisitioned galleries. The exhibition of works by sculptor Arno Breker in 1942 at the Orangerie thus followed a more modest exhibition at the Jeu de Paume in 1941, which had assembled works by German soldiers. These works were primarily drawings and watercolors, executed owing to the circumstances, which did not compromise the interest of Parisian critics greedy for these imitative works (portraits, landscapes, war scenes). They were very similar to French works of art hanging in the seasonal Salons.

20. In France, in the area of the fine arts, in addition to the looting of Jewish property already discussed, the Third Reich applied economic pressure through its policy of requisitioning factories and raw materials. Public statues were removed and melted down to provide copper alloys, especially

bronze, provoking protests by the vast majority of mayors. Later, beginning in May 1942, Abel Bonnard actively collaborated in this work, considering it a boon—the opportunity to "reappraise" the "glories" of France. Countering all the "rumors," he attempted to spread the idea that the removals served the French economy exclusively—and the artists, from whom new statues had to be commissioned, this time in stone.

For the list of statues removed and the attitude of France's mayors, see Archives de Paris, series VM 92.

21. See the letter of 13 January 1941, from the director of the Ecole des beaux-arts to Louis Hautecoeur, mentioning the desire expressed by Lieutenant Ehmsen—of the Third Reich's Propaganda-Abteilung—during his visit to the school to "solve as best one can the difficulties that might arise"; see AN, AJ 52 807.

22. See the chronology, this volume, 387–88.

On museum schedules, see Yvon Bizardel (curator at the Musée Galliera), *Sous l'Occupation: Souvenirs d'un conservateur de musée (1940–1944)* (Paris: Calmann-Lévy, 1964). The memoirs of René Huyghe's assistant at the Louvre are very vague and at times inaccurate: Germain Bazin, *Souvenirs de l'exode du Louvre 1940–1945* (Paris: Somogy, 1992).

On the history of the Musée du Jeu de Paume, see Françoise Bonnefoy, ed., *Jeu de Paume, histoire* (Paris: Editions du Jeu de Paume/Réunion des Musées Nationaux, 1991).

23. On the occasion of the publication of his memoirs: Gerhard Heller, with Jean Grand, *Un Allemand à Paris, 1940–1944* (Paris: Editions du Seuil, 1981). Heller was born in Potsdam on 8 November 1909, the son of a minor administrative worker. After joining the Nazi Party and undertaking propaganda activities directed toward foreign countries, he served as a Sonderführer at the Propaganda-Staffel Paris from November 1940 to July 1942 and was then assigned to the literary department of the German embassy until August 1944. After the war, he edited the review *Lancelot* and *Le messager de France*, which published French texts translated into German, before devoting himself to translation. In his memoirs, he cites, among many others, the names "Michel Déon, Pierre Drieu La Rochelle, Julien Green, Jean Orieux, Jean d'Ormesson, Patrick Modiano."

Heller describes himself as truly "disconnecting" from Nazism in 1943. Before that, he had been shocked by the fate in store for the Jews but maintained his "wait-and-see" attitude, according to Jean Paulhan, in 1941 and 1942 at least. Gérard Loiseaux—who has studied the report by Bernhard Payr (of Rosenberg's ESS), *Phönix oder Asche? Frankreichs geistiges Ringen nach dem Zusammenbruch* (Dortmund: Volkschaft, 1942)—makes a less irenic analysis of the "radiant European" presented in Heller's memoirs. Loiseaux calls into doubt Heller's amnesia, reminding us that, unlike Bremer (sent to the Russian front in 1942) or Epting (recalled to Berlin from June 1942 to January 1943), Heller remained at his post in Paris, without interruption, from the beginning to the end of the occupation, to the complete satisfaction of his superiors. See Gérard Loiseaux, *La littérature de la défaite et de la collaboration* (Paris: Publications de la Sorbonne, 1984), esp. 470–83.

24. See text of the convention of 28 September 1940, signed by the Syndicat des éditeurs, reproduced in Heller, *Un Allemand à Paris* (note 23), 213–15.

25. See Ulrike Aubertin, "La *Grande exposition de l'art allemand:* L'art dégénéré, 1937" (master's thesis, Université Paris I–Panthéon Sorbonne, 1981); and Ulrike Aubertin and Annick Lantenois, "La *Grande exposition de l'art allemand* and *L'art dégénéré:* Fondement et symbolique d'une confrontation," in Pierre Milza and Fanette Roche-Pézard, eds., *Art et fascisme: Totalitarisme et résistance au totalitarisme dans les arts en Italie, Allemagne et France des années 30 à la défaite de l'Axe* (Brussels: Editions Complexe, 1989), 139–54.

26. See Élodie Vitale, "Le Bauhaus et la république de Weimar: Trois fermetures," in Pierre Milza and Fanette Roche-Pézard, eds., *Art et fascisme: Totalitarisme et résistance au totalitarisme dans les arts en Italie, Allemagne et France des années 30 à la défaite de l'Axe* (Brussels: Editions Complexe, 1989), 51–75.

27. In March and April 1940, sixty of Forain's patriotic war drawings were exhibited at the Musée des arts décoratifs, during an event on "the war of 1914–1918 according to a few artists." The Société nationale des beaux-arts also decided to pay tribute to Forain during its annual Salon. The Propaganda-Staffel was opposed to it, and the tribute was not paid until 1945. In addition, those works by Forain that seemed to attack Germany were "weeded out" of the looted collections of the Musée de l'armée by the occupying forces.

See Cécile Coutin, "Jean-Louis Forain et la guerre de 1914–1918" (Ph.D. diss., Université Paris IV–Sorbonne, 1986); and Bizardel, *Sous l'Occupation* (note 22).

28. Bizardel mentions another case of censorship, at the time of an exhibition by Entraide des artistes in 1940: German leaders were said to have made "loud protests" upon seeing a painting by Gromaire. See Bizardel, *Sous l'Occupation* (note 22), 68.

29. According to the German formulation, "if no opposition emerge[d] in the two weeks [following] the declaration, the exhibition [could] take place"; reproduced in Bizardel, *Sous l'Occupation* (note 22), 133.

30. In reality, the occupying forces initially demanded that the Jewish students form separate classes, a solution Landowski opposed, on the pretext that there were almost no Jewish students left at the school. See Landowski's unpublished journal, 26 February 1941.

31. Luncheons were held at Lapérouse in May 1941, at La Tour d'Argent in October of the same year, and so forth.

32. The first Statut des Juifs dates from 3 October 1940; the order to prefects in the occupied zone to intern foreign or stateless Jews, from 4 October 1940; the creation of the Commissariat général aux questions juives, from 29 March 1941; the second Statut des Juifs, from 2 June 1941; the university quotas on the number of Jewish admitted, from 21 June 1941; the placement of Jewish property under provisional government administration, from 22 July 1941; the Police aux questions juives, from 19 October 1941; the requirement that all Jews join the Union générale des israélites de France, from 29 November 1941; the law obliging Jews older than six to wear the yellow star, from 29 May 1942; and the prohibition on Jews frequenting public establishments (including exhibition halls), from 8 July 1942.

The first Statut des Juifs barred Jews from a certain number of occupations. In the area that concerns us here, these included posts in the public sector, with a few exceptions for those who, "in literary, scientific, or artistic domains have rendered extraordinary services to the French state" (art. 8).

See the official circulars and models for affidavits that one does not belong to the Jewish "race" sent to art institutions; AN, AJ 53 101, AJ 53 128; and Archives de Paris, VR 32, VR 87.

33. On the condition of Jews in France and the genocide, there is a very large bibliography. See especially Michaël R. Marrus and Robert O. Paxton, *Vichy et les Juifs*, trans. Marguerite Delmotte (Paris: Calmann-Lévy, 1981); Serge Klarsfeld, *Vichy-Auschwitz: Le rôle de Vichy dans la solution finale de la question juive en France, 1943–1944* (Paris: Fayard, 1985); Raul Hilberg, *The Destruction of the European Jews* (Chicago: Quadrangle, 1961). More recent assessments include Philippe Burrin, *Hitler et les Juifs: Genèse d'un génocide* (Paris: Editions du Seuil, 1989); André Kaspi, *Les Juifs pendant l'Occupation* (Paris: Editions du Seuil, 1991); Annette Wieviorka, *Déportation et génocide: Entre la mémoire et l'oubli* (Paris: Plon, 1992); Claude Singer, *Vichy, l'université et les Juifs: Les silences et la mémoire* (Paris: Les Belles Lettres, 1992).

34. Quoted in the foreword to the French translation of *Mein Kampf:* Adolf Hitler, *Mon combat*, trans. J. Gaudefroy-Demombynes and A. Calmettes (Paris: Nouvelles Editions Latines, 1982). [See the testimony of Erich von dem Bach-Zelewski, 7 January 1946, in *Trial of the Major War Criminals before the International Military Tribunal, Nuremberg, 14 November 1945–2 October 1946* (Nuremberg: n.p., 1947–49), 4:494: "If for years, for decades, a doctrine is preached to the effect that the Slav race is an inferior race, that the Jews are not even human beings, then an explosion of this sort is inevitable."—Trans.]

35. That is, "fantasme d'auto-engendrement," to use Léon Poliakov's expression in his works on racism.

36. One of Caran d'Ache's caricatures depicts, in the top part of the drawing (before the French Revolution), a nobleman astride a plowman in the fields; in the bottom part (after the French Revolution), a Jewish financier astride the plowman, plus two "left-wingers."

37. Rebatet was born in Moras-en-Valoire (Drôme) on 15 November 1903, the grandson of the republican Hippolyte Tampucci. He began his career as a film and music critic, contributing to *L'Action française* (under the pseudonym François Vinneuil) from 1929 to 1939. In 1935, his first political articles appeared in *Je suis partout*, to which he had contributed since 1932. He also wrote for *Candide*, *Le jour*, *La revue universelle*, then for *Le petit Parisien* and *Le cri du peuple*. He was the author of *Les décombres* (Paris: Editions Denoël, 1942), *Les deux étendards* (Paris: Gallimard, 1951), *Les épis mûrs* (Paris: Gallimard, 1954), and *Une histoire de la musique* (Paris: Robert Laffont/Raymond Bourgine, 1969), which is still widely read. After the war, he was on the editorial staff of *Dimanche-matin* and an occasional editor for *Le crapouillot* and *Les écrits de Paris;* under his pseudonym, he also worked as a film critic for *Le spectacle du monde*.

38. The metaphor was used by Pétain and by all the admirers of the Révolution nationale. Abel Bonnard, not yet minister of national education and youth, used it on 14 February 1941 in *Je suis partout*, launching an appeal to "replant [ourselves] in our soil," "to become once again French like trees, not through an overly precise idea of our country, but through a rising of our sap." See Abel Bonnard, "France!" *Je suis partout*, 14 February 1941, 1.

39. Lucien Rebatet, "Entre le Juif et le pompier," *Je suis partout*, 14 February 1941, 7.

40. Lucien Rebatet, "Au Salon des Indépendants," *Je suis partout*, 21 March 1941, 7.

41. Lucien Rebatet, "La fin d'un monde: Ce que j'ai vu à Vichy," *Je suis partout*, 4 April 1941, 1.

42. Lucien Rebatet, "L'étoile jaune," *Je suis partout*, 6 June 1942, 1.

43. Their salaries had risen from thirty thousand to sixty thousand francs, as opposed to that of the 950 guards, which had not increased since 1937. See Lucien Rebatet, "Désordre des Beaux-Arts," *Je suis partout*, 14 March 1941.

44. See Robert Brasillach, "Nous, nous continuons," *Je suis partout*, 2 June 1941, 1.

45. Camille Mauclair (1872–1945) was the author of the novels *Le soleil des morts* (Paris: Paul Ollendorff, 1898), *L'ennemi des rêves* (Paris: Paul Ollendorff, 1899), and *La ville lumière* (Paris: Librairie Paul Ollendorff, 1904) and the nonfiction works *Princes de l'esprit* (Paris: Albin Michel, 1920), *Servitude et grandeur littéraires* (Paris: Librairie Ollendorff, 1922), and

De Jérusalem à Istanbul (Paris: Bernard Grasset, 1939). *De Jérusalem à Istanbul* was the last of eight books in his "Mediterranean cycle." He contributed to *Le Figaro* as well as to *L'ami du peuple* before the war. After his death, he was succeeded by one of his rivals: Paul Biehler, a painter and journalist, author of *La civilisation en clandestinité, L'archevêque au Sabbat,* and other works. In May 1936, Mauclair was fired from the special consultative commission for state acquisitions (one of thirty-nine members) by Georges Huisman, director general of the fine arts administration.

46. Camille Mauclair, *La farce de l'art vivant II: Les métèques contre l'art français* (Paris: Editions de la Nouvelle Revue Critique, 1930), 108.

47. Mauclair, *La farce* (note 46), 41.

48. Mauclair, *La farce* (note 46), 42.

49. Under the occupation, he also gave precedence to a more strictly political criticism. See, for example, his "Pourquoi l'Angleterre est enjuivée," *Le matin,* 16 November 1943.

50. *Le cahier jaune,* a monthly review, appeared from November 1941 to March 1943. Contributors included Paul Sézille, secretary general of the Institut d'études des questions juives, Robert Denoël, Charles Laville, Marcel Denys, Laurent Viguier, Maurice de Bonnières, Jean Dauvillier, Luc-Cyl, André Chaumet, Louis Dumaine, Jean Drault, and Jean-Hérold Paquis. *Revivre: Le grand magazine illustré de la race,* which succeeded it, was published until July 1944 and was also violently anti-Semitic but pretended to be open to less monomaniacal issues. Contributors included Élisabeth Lebret, André Roy, Louis Walther, and Jean Ajalbert of the Académie Goncourt.

51. Stéphane Galanon, "Les mystères de l'art vivant," *Revivre,* 5 May 1944, illustrated by reproductions of works by Picasso, Chagall, and Louis Marcoussis.

52. See Lucien Rebatet, "L'académie de la dissidence, ou La trahison prosaïque," *Je suis partout,* 10 March 1944, 1.

53. See Rebatet, "Au Salon" (note 40), 7.

54. At the Salle Wagram on 15 January (from 3:00 to 5:00 P.M.), the speakers were Pierre-Antoine Cousteau, Claude Jeantet, Alain Laubreaux, Henri Lèbre, Charles Lesca, Ralph Soupault (a satirical cartoonist), and Pierre Villette.

55. See Lucien Rebatet, "La réunion de Wagram," *Je suis partout,* 7 January 1944, 2.

56. George Montandon, *Comment reconnaître et expliquer le Juif?* (Paris: Nouvelles Editions Françaises, 1940).

57. Published in June 1942.

58. "The Great Flight of Culture: A Portfolio," *Fortune,* December 1941, 106. See also *The American Mercury,* whose sulfurous pages were plagiarized by the Third Reich's propaganda machine. Thomas Craven wrote "a plea for robust, living culture" in which he attacked the decadence of museums. This time, his whipping boy was "a played-out Europeanism," which had imposed a decadent and imported art on a "plain" American public, while scorning "all native artists who perform with originality and a knowledge of American values." See Thomas Craven, "Our Decadent Art Museums," *American Mercury*, December 1941, 682, 683, 687, 684.

59. Jean Lurçat, *Peintres et sculpteurs de la Maison de la culture*, no. 7 (July 1938).

60. Lurçat, *Peintres et sculpteurs* (note 59).

61. See *Le matin* throughout May 1938. A petition was signed by only a small number of personalities but obtained the support of the Association des anciens élèves de l'Ecole des beaux-arts.

62. Jean Giraudoux, *Pleins pouvoirs* (Paris: Gallimard, 1939), quoted in Léon Poliakov, Christian Delacampagne, and Patrick Girard, *Le racisme* (Paris: Seghers, 1976), 92–93.

63. Robert Rey, *La peinture moderne, ou L'art sans métier* (Paris: Presses Universitaires de France, 1941).

64. See Louis Hautecoeur, *Considérations sur l'art d'aujourd'hui* (Paris: Librairie de France, 1929), 71.

65. Letter of 17 July 1942 from Georges Stéphane K. Comnène, founder and secretary general of the Institut européen pour les questions d'architecture et d'art; Archives de Paris, series VR 29.

66. See the "note d'information" by the prefecture of the department of the Seine, 4 August 1942; Archives de Paris, series VR 29.

67. Results of the investigation: Comnène was Egyptian and had studied at the Ecole des sciences politiques before launching a career in journalism as a Paris correspondent for several Egyptian and Greek newspapers. He had always indulged his taste for the arts, rapidly exhibiting in Paris Salons and abroad. After the death of King Fu'ad of Egypt, he designed a palace in memory of the sovereign on a commission from the Egyptian government. Possessed of a small fortune, he was at the time restoring paintings by masters that were entrusted to him by major Parisian antiquarians. He had never attracted notice by illicit political conduct, but the minor functionary charged with writing this report for Vichy warned the authorities that the entire branch of the Comnène family established in Corsica had always "displayed its illustrious origins with a certain boastfulness."

68. Hilaire was named secretary general of the fine arts administration on 19 March 1944. Born on 24 December 1900, he earned a *licence* (bachelor's degree) in law and letters and, prior to the war, contributed to *La dépêche de Toulouse*, *Le petit parisien*, and *La revue des beaux-arts*. He began his administrative career in 1924. Deputy head of the Laval cabinet in 1931, he was subprefect of Pontoise in 1935, then prefect of Aube in 1940, then assistant prefect to the prefect representative at the interior ministry in the occupied territories. In April 1942, he became secretary general for the administration of the interior ministry.

69. See the deposition by Lucien Rebatet, 7 November 1945, Haute Cour trial of Georges Hilaire, AN, series 3W 195, exhibit II 97.

70. Georges Hilaire, "La fausse liberté" (undated typescript from his files, apparently unpublished), Haute Cour trial of Georges Hilaire, AN, series 3W 195, seal no. 1.

71. See Georges Hilaire, "Renaissance du mélodrame" (on Michel Daxiat's *Pirates de Paris*), and Georges Hilaire, "Le langage du film," Haute Cour trial of Georges Hilaire, AN, series 3W 195, seal no. 1.

72. See Haute Cour trial of Georges Hilaire, AN, series 3W 195, exhibit II 139 (original text), exhibit II 138 (French translation).

73. In terms of the municipal councils, of a total of about 605 notices of reduction of staff, death, or resignation, 22 were the result of opposition to "the work of national renewal." In addition, 131 notices of dismissal gave "very vague" reasons. See the charges against Georges Hilaire, 5 February 1947, Haute Cour trial of Georges Hilaire, AN, series 3W 195, exhibit submitted after the conclusion of the trial, no. 5.

74. See Haute Cour trial of Georges Hilaire, AN, series 3W 195, exhibit II 83 (note from Hilaire to René Bousquet, Vichy, 28 May 1943); exhibit II 84 (letter from René Bousquet to Hilaire, Vichy, 26 June 1943); exhibit II 82 (letter from Jean Cassou in support of Hilaire, 25 November 1944).

75. See Haute Cour trial of Georges Hilaire, AN, series 3W 195, exhibit II 9 (deposition by Monique Morany, private secretary to Hilaire from November 1941 to December 1943, minutes of 15 February 1945); exhibit II 11 (deposition by Élisabeth Courtois, private secretary to Hilaire from 1 March to 15 August 1944, minutes of 22 March 1945); exhibit II 64 (deposition by Paul Flandin, editor at the delegation of the interior ministry beginning March 1942, later secretary to Hilaire, minutes of 2 May 1945); exhibit II 113 (deposition by Otto Abetz, German ambassador, minutes of 7 December 1945); exhibit after voluntary appearance, no. 7 (letter by André-Louis Dubois, civil servant dismissed in August 1940, subsequent to the evidence recorded by the *commissions rogatoires* of 1944–45, 18 January 1955).

76. Interview with Jean Cassou, 3 May 1983, in Laurence Bertrand Dorléac, "Art, culture et société: L'exemple des arts plastiques à Paris entre 1940 et 1944" (habilitation thesis, Institut d'études politiques de Paris, 1990), 2:429.

77. See the memoirs of Louis Hautecoeur, *Les beaux-arts en France, passé et avenir* (Paris: Editions A. & J. Picard, 1948). On purchases from Jewish artists, see the inventory book of acquisitions by the French state, in which the names of certain Jewish artists—Michel Kikoïne, for example—can be found until May 1943. The state purchased his *Village Entrance* (painting) on 28 December 1940 (destined for the labor ministry, decree of 11 May

1942), his *Bouquet in a Landscape* (painting) on 6 December 1941 (destined for the labor ministry, decree of 11 May 1942), and his *Autumn* (painting) on 11 May 1943 (destined for the Musée des Augustins in Toulouse, note of 8 May 1943). The purchasing board acquired a series of drawings from Mané-Katz on 23 January 1941 (destination unknown).

78. Mme Françoise Landowski allowed me access to this as-yet-unpublished journal, a valuable source for the historian, in which the sculptor appears particularly honest, commenting precisely on the state of the art scene and on his own choices.

On Paul Landowski and his work, see especially works by Michèle Lefrançois, curator of the Musée Landowski in Boulogne-Billancourt, such as Bruno Foucart, Michèle Lefrançois, and Gérard Caillet, *Landowski* (Paris: Editions Van Wilder, 1989).

79. Paul Landowski, unpublished journal, 24 August 1940 and 24 May 1941.

80. Paul Landowski, who was Polish, was alerted by René Jaudon about the investigation concerning him (conducted by Alexandre Umbdenstock) in September 1940. See Landowski's unpublished journal, September 1940, 24 March 1941, 19 May 1941, and 18 May 1944.

81. Paul Landowski, unpublished journal, 2 October 1940.

82. Desvallières sent a note to several of his comrades on 12 November 1940, just after the intervention of the German officer Schnurr, who was sent to remove all works by Jewish artists. According to the memoirs of Yvon Bizardel, curator of the Musée Galliera, Schnurr deplored the presence of the portrait of Mademoiselle Desvallières by her father. Desvallières's note was formulated as follows:

> Dear colleague, dear comrade,
> Today we were visited by the representative of the Propaganda Staffel, who came to inspect our exhibition. Following that visit, our comrades of the Jewish race were ousted for reasons of a political nature. I cannot tell you how much the members of the bureau, and its president first and foremost, have suffered as a result of that situation, which is inconsistent with our traditional liberalism. Once again, believe in the sincerity of our feelings of camaraderie and friendship.

For the French original of this note, see Bizardel, *Sous l'Occupation* (note 22), 62.

83. Paul Landowski, unpublished journal, 19 October 1940. On 14 October 1941, Landowski learned from Jérôme Carcopino that Pontremoli could not be placed in the "exceptional category" and thus avoid exclusion, because Carcopino had to "help out... younger Israelites"; see Paul Landowski, unpublished journal, 14 October 1941.

84. Paul Landowski, unpublished journal, 6 March 1941.

85. Paul Landowski, unpublished journal, 19 May 1941.

86. Paul Landowski, unpublished journal, 16 May 1943.

87. On the final days of Max Jacob's life, see the very complete account by the man who remained his friend to the end: Pierre Andreu, *Max Jacob* (Paris: Wesmael-Charlier, 1962).

88. I am thinking of works by Isis Kischka, Boris Taslitzky, René Baumer, Avigdor Arikha, Walter Spitzer, Dorothée de Ripper, Mania Mavro, Maryan S. Maryan, Anna Staritsky, France Audoul, and Maurice de La Pintière.

89. Giuseppe Mazzariol, *Music* (Milan: Electa, 1980), 26, 27.

90. Mazzariol, *Music* (note 89), 24, 26.

91. See article 19, paragraph 2, of the armistice convention of 22 June 1940; and Barbara Vormeier, "La situation des réfugiés en provenance d'Allemagne: Septembre 1939–juillet 1942," in *Les camps en Provence: Exil, internement, déportation, 1933–1944* (Aix-en-Provence: Editions Alinéa & L.L.C.G., 1984).

92. See Patrick Pentsch's map in Jacques Grandjonc and Theresia Grundtner, *Zone d'ombres, 1933–1944: Exil et internement d'Allemands et d'Autrichiens dans le sud-est de la France* (Aix-en-Provence: Editions Alinéa, 1990), 203. On the French camps, and on the exiles more generally, see also *Les camps en Provence: Exil, internement, déportation, 1933–1944* (Aix-en-Provence: Editions Alinéa & L.L.C.G., 1984); Karel Bartosek, René Gallissot, and Denis Peschanski, eds., *De l'exil à la résistance: Réfugiés et immigrés d'Europe Centrale en France, 1933–1945* (Saint-Denis: Presses Universitaires de Vincennes/Paris: Arcantère, 1989); Anne Grynberg, *Les camps de la honte: Les internés juifs des camps français (1939–1944)* (Paris: Editions La Découverte, 1991); Maurice Rajsfus, *Drancy: Un camp de concentration très ordinaire, 1941–1944* (Levallois-Perret: Editions Manya, 1991); Albrecht Betz, *Exil et engagement: Les intellectuels allemands et la France, 1930–1940*, trans. Pierre Rusch (Paris: Editions Gallimard, 1991).

93. Excerpt from a letter from Carl-Albrecht Oberg, 4 May 1943, relating to the Bousquet-Oberg accords of 16 April 1943, Bonn, Politisches Archiv, Auswärtiges Amt, Series Inland II g. 81; quoted, in French, in Grandjonc and Grundtner, *Zone d'ombres* (note 92), 202 n. 27.

94. See the reproduction of these works in André Fontaine, *Le camp d'étrangers des Milles 1939–1943 (Aix-en-Provence)* (Aix-en-Provence: Edisud, 1989). On the immigration and the works created by artists in exile in France, see also Heidrun Schröder-Kehler, "Deutsche Künstler im französischen Exil," in *Widerstand statt Anpassung: Deutsche Kunst im Widerstand gegen den Faschismus 1933–1945* (Berlin: Elefanten, 1980); and *Emigrés français en Allemagne, émigrés allemands en France, 1685–1945*, exh. cat. (Paris: Institut Goethe, 1983). Finally, see Emmanuelle Foster, "Les artistes peintres et graveurs allemands en exil à Paris: 1933–1939" (Ph.D.

diss., Université Paris I–Panthéon Sorbonne, 1990); Pierre Milza and Denis Peschanski, eds., *Exils et migration: Italiens et Espagnols en France, 1938–1946* (Paris: Editions L'Harmattan, 1994).

95. See André Fontaine, "Les peintures murales des Milles (automne 1940)," in *Les camps en Provence: Exil, internement, déportation, 1933–1944* (Aix-en-Provence: Editions Alinéa & L.L.C.G., 1984).

96. Fontaine, "Les peintures murales" (note 95).

97. On Marseilles, see especially the detailed study by Jean-Michel Guiraud, *La vie intellectuelle et artistique à Marseille à l'époque de Vichy et sous l'Occupation, 1940–1944* (Marseilles: C.R.D.P, 1987); André Breton, "Le jeu de Marseille," *VVV*, nos. 2–3 (March 1943); Claude Lévi-Strauss, *Tristes tropiques* (Paris: Plon, 1955); Pierre Guiral, ed., "La Provence pendant la guerre," *Revue d'histoire de la Deuxième Guerre mondiale*, Special issue, January 1979; Peggy Guggenheim, *Out of This Century: Confessions of an Art Addict* (New York: Anchor, 1980); Agnès Angliviel de La Beaumelle, "La dispersion des surréalistes: Marseille," in *Paris 1937–Paris 1957: Créations en France*, exh. cat. (Paris: Centre Georges Pompidou, 1981), 82–86; Daniel Bénédite, *La filière marseillaise: Un chemin vers la Liberté sous l'Occupation* (Paris: Editions Clancier Guénaud, 1984); Georges Raillard, "Marseille: Passage du surréalisme," in *La planète affolée: Surréalisme, dispersion et influences, 1938–1947*, exh. cat. (Marseilles: Direction des Musées de Marseille/Editions Flammarion, 1986).

98. On exile to the United States and elsewhere, see the memoirs of Jean Hélion, *They Shall Not Have Me (Ils ne m'auront pas): The Capture, Forced Labor, and Escape of a French Prisoner of War* (New York: E. P. Dutton, 1943); Ossip Zadkine, *Le maillet et le ciseau: Souvenirs de ma vie* (Paris: Editions Albin Michel, 1968); André Breton, *Martinique, charmeuse de serpents* (Paris: Jean-Jacques Pauvert, 1972); André Masson, *Vagabond du surréalisme*, ed. Gilbert Brownstone (Paris: Editions Saint-Germain-des-Prés, 1975); Suzanne Blum, *Vivre sans la patrie 1940–1945* (Paris: Plon, 1975).

99. Lucien Rebatet, "Marseille la Juive: Choses vues," *Je suis partout*, 30 August 1941, 1.

100. There were a number of surrealist events, including those by Pierre Matisse, who exhibited Léger, Yves Tanguy, Piet Mondrian, Lipchitz, Ossip Zadkine, Chagall, and Pavel Tchelitchew. See Stephanie Barron, with Sabine Eckmann, *Exiles and Emigrés: The Flight of European Artists from Hitler*, exh. cat. (Los Angeles: Los Angeles County Museum of Art, 1997).

101. See Barron, *Exiles and Emigrés* (note 100); and Michelle Michel, *Exposition résistance, déportation: Création dans le bruit des armes*, exh. cat. (Paris: Chancellerie de l'Ordre de la Libération, 1980). On Masson, see the work of Françoise Will-Levaillant, including André Masson, *Le rebelle du surréalisme: Ecrits*, ed. Françoise Will-Levaillant (Paris: Hermann, 1976).

102. Hélion left New York to defend free Europe, after his escape from a camp in Pomerania. See his memoirs, *They Shall Not Have Me* (note 98), which were written in the United States and were a great success there.

103. André Breton published a review with Marcel Duchamp and Max Ernst and broadcast messages to the French over Voice of America.

104. See Valérie-Anne Sircoulomb, "Les artistes réfugiés à Dieulefit durant la Seconde Guerre mondiale" (master's thesis, Université de Lyon II–Louis Lumière, 1989).

105. See the figures in Henri Michel, *Vichy, année 40* (Paris: Robert Laffont, 1966), 93.

For varying lengths of time, Hans Arp, Sophie Taeuber-Arp, and Alberto Magnelli were in Grasse, Sonia Delaunay and Robert Delaunay in Mougins. In the vicinity were François Stahly and Ferdinand Springer; Jacques Villon was in Tarn; Chaïm Soutine in Touraine (until his death in 1943); André Marchand, Francis Tailleux, and Tal-Coat in the vicinity of Aix-en-Provence; Jacques Lipchitz in Toulouse; Victor Brauner in Perpignan, Le Cannet Plage, and the Pyrénées-Orientales (Saint-Féliu-d'Amont); Hans Bellmer in Toulouse.

See the very useful chronology compiled by Agnès Angliviel de La Beaumelle and Claude Laugier, "La dispersion des artistes—chronologie," in *Paris 1937–Paris 1957: Créations en France*, exh. cat. (Paris: Centre Georges Pompidou, 1981), 86. See also Claude Laugier, "Le groupe de Grasse," in *Paris 1937–Paris 1957: Créations en France*, exh. cat. (Paris: Centre Georges Pompidou, 1981), 92–95.

106. See the texts by Henri-Pierre Roché, Werner Haftmann, and Jean-Paul Sartre, in *Wols en personne: Aquarelles et dessins* (Paris: Delpire, 1963); Laszlo Glozer, *Wols photographe*, exh. cat. (Paris: Centre Georges Pompidou, 1980), 110, no. 197; and Claire van Damme, "Le bateau ivre: Biographie critique et documentée de l'artiste Wols (1913–1951)," in *Wols, sa vie*, exh. cat. (Paris: Goethe-Institut, 1986).

107. See the interview with Hans Hartung, 18 February 1981, in Bertrand Dorléac, "Art, culture et société" (note 76), 522–37.

CHAPTER THREE

The Art of Diplomacy

THE WEIMAR PILGRIMS

In November 1941, an official tour of Germany by a group of French painters and sculptors roused the art sector, which was still having a hard time assessing the terms of its "collaboration" with or "resistance" to the new state of affairs. Their colleagues' trip as guests of the Third Reich stirred consciences, and if a few artists were envious of those who went, most of those who remained in France vaguely felt the gravity of the gesture and were relieved that they had not participated.

The passion that surrounds the subject even now demonstrates the symbolic value attached to accepting the Germans' invitation, yet it has often been pointed out that the majority of the Weimar pilgrims entered into the collaboration quite lightly.[1] For a few kilos of coal, the pride of representing French art, and, for some at least, what they thought was a chance to bring about the release of prisoners, these artists agreed to take part, generally believing they were going not on a political mission but on a straightforward educational journey. The most clear-sighted among them were stripped of their illusions when they arrived at the train station and found themselves surrounded by paparazzi.

Brought together in the group photographs are a cluster of well-known artists—all members of the Académie des beaux-arts or sure to be admitted to it, all disappointed with modernity or militant traditionalists, all less famous for their political convictions than for their "professional success." Of the sculptors crowded onto the station platform,[2] the eldest was Charles Despiau, the most respected sculptor in France after Maillol, in whose footsteps he was following. Despiau had built up a reputation as a sensitive soul fostered in his early days by the master

Auguste Rodin. The sixty-seven-year-old artist may have had esteem heaped upon him, but he was hard up and would happily have gone anywhere for a few extra kilos of hard coal. Soon after, he signed his name to a monograph glorifying the Third Reich's sculptor, Arno Breker.[3]

At his own request, Despiau was accompanied by his student Paul Belmondo, fledgling leader of sculpture in France, future member of the Académie des beaux-arts and designer of medals for the celebrities of the Fifth Republic, from de Gaulle to Michel Droit to Maurice Druon. At the time, he was preparing to decorate the Autoroute de l'Ouest in a neoclassical manner in keeping with the European fashion of the moment.[4]

At age sixty-six, Henri Louis Bouchard had accrued official duties but had not achieved the popularity of Despiau or Maillol.[5] A member of the Institut de France since 1933, he played an active role in the plan for a new artists corporation—which, pressured by the occupying forces,[6] he was trying to get the Académie des beaux-arts to oversee—while continuing a career noted for war memorials. Passionately interested in the traditions of Burgundy, he contributed to the tastes of the time a social art glorifying rural life in statues of diggers or plowmen, when he was not devoting himself to the dukes of Burgundy, whom he depicted realistically, with the certainty of pleasing the majority of the public. This was also the agenda of Louis Lejeune, winner of the Prix de Rome, whom Bouchard had just imposed on the Institut de France.[7]

At their side, Paul Landowski seethed at being in such bad company.[8] But he was sure that, with this trip, he could secure the release of young artists imprisoned in Germany. At age sixty-six, he was accumulating honors and official duties, from director of the Ecole des beaux-arts to member of the Académie des beaux-arts to president of the new artists corporation. He was apparently the paragon of an official artist, living on public commissions and carving busts of those in power—the French president Alexandre Millerand and Marshal Pétain (before the occupation). Yet he really had his heart set on only one thing: to complete and have installed his giant temple to the glory of human history, which combined all the ingredients of a humanistic socialism à la Henri Barbusse with a pan-Europeanism à la Romain Rolland.[9] Like the other travelers no doubt, Landowski had heard about the plan for the journey in June (through Bouchard), a few months before the occupier issued all the invitations. It was only at the last minute, in October,[10] that Schnurr and Ehmsen, of the Propaganda-Staffel Paris, urged him to accept, promising him in return a "large release of prisoners." As director of the Ecole des beaux-arts—which had a number of students imprisoned in Germany—he agreed, tormented by doubt and knowing in advance that someday he would have "an unyielding group" against him, including friends of his opposed to Nazism and hostile to any "respectable" contact with the Germans.[11] Up to that time, the Germans had proved courteous and cooperative. Landowski knew well enough that the release of prisoners depended on the army, "perhaps more directly on Hitler himself";[12] even so, the assurances of the Paris propaganda office put his mind at ease about the fate of those on the list he had drawn up based on information provided by his colleagues from each of the artists' organizations. The director of the fine arts administration himself, Louis Hautecoeur, advised him to accept. On 27 October, the issue of the trip was also debated in the committee of French artists to which he belonged: the traditionalist little society decided unanimously to endorse the tour "not only for the sake of the prisoners but also for the prestige of French art."[13]

The following day, Schnurr invited the travelers to tea on the terrace of 52, avenue des Champs-Elysées, headquarters of the Propaganda-Staffel Paris. They gathered in the company of the publisher Flammarion, and Landowski unsparingly sketched the assembly "at the little tables, sipping." There were his sculpture colleagues: Belmondo, with his "seductive black eyes. Always smiling. Bouchard, nothing but dry little features, thin mouth, not an atom of sensuality, jacket tight, worn.... Despiau, his head atop a skinny neck [emerging] from his collar like a turtle's head from its shell... [smiling] continually silently and smugly... deaf, which allowed him to always seem like he had just landed there from the moon."[14] There were also the painters, whom Landowski knew less well: Raymond-Jean Legueult, "half-grown," with a "rather silly expression"; André Derain, an "enormous, strapping fellow" with "power" and a very intelligent air; Maurice de Vlaminck, a "rich and formerly red-headed hooligan, stubborn as a peasant"; Kees van Dongen, an old clown with a long pink face, framed by a long white beard, and with a sensual mouth; Othon Friesz, "a nice boy, kind and red-faced," with a round face, round eyes, round nose.[15]

Two days later, the travelers gathered en masse on the platform of the Gare de l'Est (see p. XIV). Mixed in with the sculptors already mentioned were the painters. Roland Oudot,[16] Legueult,[17] and André Dunoyer de Segonzac[18] were all representatives of the programs of poetic realism and figurative landscape, incarnating to perfection the proprieties of the most popular painting of the interwar period. But among those about to cross the Rhine were other painters equally hostile toward modernity, for the most part, but by virtue of a very different past. Disappointed by the radical ventures they had been part of in the early years of the century, they were fauves who had repented their extravagance with color and gone back to the earth tones of the return

Pls. 20–22

to order or to easy society portraits. So it was that van Dongen, adapting brilliantly, confounded his early reputation as a rebel: in 1913, one of his works had been judged "obscene" and withdrawn from the Salon d'Automne at the request of the prefect of police.[19] Friesz[20] counted for Pls. 18, 19 less in this story than Derain and Vlaminck, two key figures in the fauve movement. Like them, however, he had changed tack when the French fell prey to the post–World War I backlash that delivered a mortal blow to riotous palettes. In the end, Vlaminck and Derain had the remarkable privilege of having their early paintings sold off as "degenerate art" by the Third Reich in Lucerne in 1939 and their later work held up as exemplifying French excellence. Their recent pieces met the criteria in force after the occupation, and their celebrity guaranteed the artists' journey to Germany a good deal of its renown.

What did it matter that, before the war, Derain had joined the committee supporting artists persecuted by Nazism, which had rallied to the cause of the German painter Otto Freundlich?[21] The Nazi authorities seemed to have wiped the slate clean: they were prepared to tolerate paradox and to break with their monolithic doctrine in favor of the *pure present.* After all, Göring had been known to be thoroughly infatuated with Matisse, Pissarro, or van Gogh. What did the tumultuous past of certain of the travelers matter, since they had repented in their works and in their sensational declarations? When the Nazis invited them to Germany, the undreamed-of opportunity arose not only to exact the greatest penance from them but also to make them pay homage to the Nazi model. In the eyes of the organizers, the virtue of the journey lay in the publicity they could expect: the onslaught that had begun at the train station would continue in Germany.

Derain was undoubtedly among those most troubled to be visiting the enemy. At least that is what emerges from the statements of those who knew him and who invite us to look closely at the defense plea found after his death in Chambourcy.[22] The painter's appeal would then serve not only to exonerate him in the eyes of history but also, quite simply, to describe how an artist could have gotten caught in the occupier's snares. In reality, before his house was looted and he was invited to take the trip, the war had had no hold on the painter, who spent his dreary sixtieth year inside his bourgeois home, except for a few visits designed to distract him from a settled existence that his newly sober art did nothing to disrupt. There was of course his return to sculpture in autumn 1938, when he modeled the clay discovered under an old fir tree uprooted by a violent storm, happily plunging his hands into his native soil and forming from it small pieces inspired by the archaic forms in his imaginary museum, from Cypriot idols to African statues. There were as well the elegant and primitive illustrations of the adventures of François Rabelais's Pantagruel, commissioned by the Geneva publisher Albert Skira. But, in contrast to these rediscovered naïvetés, Derain's painting was bogged down in conformism and monotony, as the artist himself admitted in his way. There was no mystery left in the boredom and conventionality of his painting, which now aspired to be "classical" at all costs. One has only to look at his portrait of himself surrounded by his family in 1939.[23] Just before the exodus from occupied France, Derain depicted himself as an anxious bourgeois man, facing an easel lost in a cozy parlor that betrayed his growing unease about an existence without real purpose. All and all, more than painting he probably preferred women, good wine, and the inner workings of his small-scale models: airplanes and tanks. Fragile, he now lived apart from the artistic community, seeing almost no one anymore, except for Braque, Balthus, the Bulgarian painter Georges Papazoff, and, just prior to leaving for Germany, Vlaminck, with whom he was reconciled after years of estrangement.

The German occupation began for Derain with exile in the provinces, the looting and requisitioning of his house in Chambourcy in November 1940, and a summons before the Nazi authorities, who promptly told him of the artists' journey and of the possibility of reclaiming his property if he went. Over the next year, they increased their pressure on him, finally compelling him to "pack his bags" in autumn 1941.[24] The painter Constant Le Breton, it is said, then provided him with the names of artists imprisoned in Germany (including members of the Société des artistes indépendants and some of the youngest students at the Ecole des beaux-arts). Derain took along four copies, promising himself to "deliver [them] when the opportunity arose."[25] But his memoir says nothing of such opportunities, which no doubt never occurred during a "long, very boring" tour, in the course of which he was "very cold" and often remained shut up in his hotel room.[26] When he was able to reclaim his house in Chambourcy—only in December 1944, after the liberation—and he learned for certain that the Germans had promised a mass release of prisoners only to convince the French artists to go on the tour, he lost the only justifications he had had for compromising himself. Forced to retreat to the studio on rue d'Assas that he shared with Léopold-Lévy (in Turkey since 1936) or the bourgeois apartment at 20, rue de Varenne that he rented from a Jewish landlord who had sought refuge in the "free" zone, he was left with nothing but remorse for not having been among the French who were content to ignore the Germans. At least he could still boast that he had refused to make any new deals with the enemy and had declined the offer he received between 1940 and 1941 to paint the Ribbentrop children.

In the meantime, his trip to Germany had begun to trouble his conscience—and those of his colleagues, no doubt. Had shame overcome the group of travelers in the course of their visit? There had been, for some, pangs of patriotic remorse from the first day, when, in Munich, a young member of the Nazi Party had forced them to listen to a revanchist speech that portrayed the current war as a natural prolongation of World War I. Schnurr and Ehmsen, accustomed to the civilized tone of collaboration in Paris, had even bewailed this introduction of matters too intense for their taste and complacently promised themselves to make the rest of the trip less violently "political," if at all possible. But how could anyone forget current events when face to face with Hitler's watercolored architectural models or Nazi ceremonies, when confronted with Josef Thorak's monumental and martial sculptures or, in Breker's studio, with the photographers and journalists come to "cover" the French artists' arrival? Encounters with imprisoned compatriots reminded the pilgrims of what was at stake on that trip, of the ambiguity of their situation, cruelly made still more evident when their detained comrades asked for a little space to go home with them in their luggage...

Yet the trip had its pleasures—visits to prestigious national collections (in particular those with works by Albrecht Dürer), historic sites, spacious and "modern" exhibition halls, plus the discovery of Germany, where most had never been: Munich, Nuremberg, Dresden, Berlin, Düsseldorf. Landowski admitted that a "certain feeling of curiosity was certainly not absent" from his decision to make the trip and that he ended it satisfied from that standpoint.[27] He was bitter about having been pressured into undertaking it but was ultimately rather confident about the future. He was not at all persuaded that the Germans would be the victors, especially as he had met along the way a few artists hostile to the regime.

But those encounters were the exception during a trip designed in its slightest details to be convincing. Witnesses remembered the tact with which the Germans were able to hold the attention of their guests and keep them close by. They did not want the travelers wandering about on their own. Hence the famous evening, when, to flatter the reputation of the French, the Germans arranged to have hand-picked prostitutes waiting for their guests. Indeed, the travelers were the object of meticulous precautions, which certain German leaders had quite particularly insisted on. Afraid of bombings, they had even considered calling off the trip altogether. Yet Goebbels had been obdurate: Germany needed the raucous contributions of French writers, actors, and artists. The Franco-German collaboration could only emerge the stronger for it; likewise the Third Reich, which had taken the initiative in the matter. History proved Goebbels right in the end, for the journey came off without a hitch; and, once they had returned to France, certain guests shared—officially at least—good memories with a press prepared to print a selection of their "impressions of Germany."

It was the Parisian newspaper *Comoedia* that got the best scoops, having been avidly interested, for some time, in the writers' trip to Weimar, the literary equivalent of that made by the artists. In early November, André Fraigneau had reported the excitement of the European writers, himself included, in the audience at the little theater in Weimar where German actors were performing Johann Wolfgang von Goethe's *Iphigenie auf Tauris*. All that reminded him of Paris, but only because of Herbert von Karajan's surprising version of Richard Wagner's *Tristan und Isolde*. The young Walter Grüntzig, who was playing Orestes, reassured Fraigneau that he liked an antinaturalist, nonpathetic, and nonexpressionist art. That was all the minor French writer needed to identify a chaste and economical tradition and, better still, to delight in the "new classicism of the young Germans" that corresponded to the French style. Here was "an involuntary, natural, and seemingly familial rapprochement between the geniuses of these two peoples."[28] At the time, his reminiscences appeared on the same page as a review of the art exhibition in Munich that provides a glimpse of German "classicism" in painting: the eye moves across a selection of pitiable daubs and stops at the obstinate expression of Peter Baumgartner's *Little Peasant* and the satisfied grimace of Sepp Hilz's *Laborers*. The pilgrims had their fill of German works during their two-week excursion,[29] which took them to museums, academies, and artists' studios. They did not necessarily find them to their taste, but they came back to France forced into an overall positive assessment—at least in the case of those who had agreed to take their "collaboration" a step further. Pl. 5

Before crossing the Rhine, Despiau had worn himself out working on his *Apollo*. He returned "looking hale" and confided to Maximilien Gauthier that the adventure had done him the greatest good.[30] Of course, he assessed the differences that distinguished the artists of the two countries: the Germans were more attached to line than to color, to the public sphere more than to the private. But should not each nation cultivate its genius? Despiau felt "profoundly French" but hoped for the advent of a Europe that would admit "its qualities and its faults." Politics? Not really his line, noted his colleague Dunoyer de Segonzac, who recognized, as did his comrades, that at least the German state was "passionately" interested in artists and that "a powerful impetus" backed their efforts. The decent Gauthier tried to help him out, making an insinuation about "the excess of organization." But Dunoyer de Segonzac did not see a hint of a flaw in that, for the greatest artists knew very well how to escape by becoming "magnificent pariahs." Van Gogh would always be van Gogh; all the others could at least feel they had support.

Did French artists seem unable to muster the requisite enthusiasm? Bernard Poissonnier was set to work to straighten matters out by educating the average Frenchman: in Munich, people walked around like "pygmies among athletes," and artists were staggering under the workload. France therefore needed to learn from the example of Nazi artistic policy, to take note of the Third Reich's progress and the speed of its reforms: a forward-looking decree stipulating that between 2 and 10 percent of the budget for constructing a public building be spent on works of art; the development of education; the creation of fine arts academies in regional centers as well as schools for the decorative arts; the abundant supply of scholarships; the construction of complexes of spacious and comfortable studios at very low rents;...[31] The catalog went on and on, slick as a German circular and repeated again and again by the French journalists trained to parrot it back.

Bouchard did not need to be called to order to describe in detail "the almost magical life" of "children cherished by the [German] nation" in *L'illustration*, ever at the service of the occupying forces. In this instance, the worth of his brief piece also lay in its pictures: from the Führer's palace in Munich to the planned communities set aside for artists, from the photograph of the pilgrims around Breker's dinner table to Breker's own works, the sculptor's prose advanced inexorably toward the heralded next step, more important still: the exhibition of works by the Third Reich's favorite the next spring, at the Orangerie in the Tuileries gardens. The second round of recollections would arrive just in time to reinforce the impact of that event: Despiau's naïve account, a bit less fresh, would ultimately shock the art world, by referring to the monograph on Breker that he had just put his name to for Flammarion as a tribute to their long-standing friendship.[32]

Certainly, Breker's personality had been the heart of collaboration operations. Since the trip, which had succeeded in large part thanks to his presence, most of the pilgrims had remained ambivalent about the gigantic scale of his art, but those who knew him were, in the end, bound by the friendships Breker established during his long stay in Paris in the 1920s. The trip had sent a tremor through the art scene; Breker's exhibition at the Orangerie in May 1942 shook it up definitively. The aesthetical-political quarrels began at that time never to subside, for no one, whether on the French or the German side, could ignore the political stakes of such an exhibition: the most important event of the cultural collaboration, it occurred just as Laval returned to the government and some time before the decisive shift in the worldwide conflict, which relegated German cultural voluntarism to the background.

THE NAZI MODEL

Arno Breker's giants at the Orangerie in the Tuileries gardens in May 1942 were much more than a grandiloquent body of work mimicking Greco-Roman antiquity. They were Nazi fantasies in Paris—the much talked-about Übermensch and his sanitized female companion, the world of men at last wrested from its humanity. The display was acclaimed by corrupt Parisian high society—political, financial, literary, and artistic. It was well and good for Simone de Beauvoir to reassure herself, recounting in her memoirs that "almost the entire French intelligentsia" had snubbed the exhibition by the Third Reich's favorite.[33] But in reality a large crowd showed up;[34] even some of Breker's detractors came to get a close look at the enemy's statues. The event might easily have passed for a demonstration of force on Germany's part. And yet the reality was even more bitter: defeated France, in the person of Jacques Benoist-Méchin, had taken the initiative for what would become one of the most stinging affronts of the entire occupation. The artistic collaboration brilliantly begun at the time of the trip to Germany triumphed with this exhibition, officially supported by the pilgrims of the previous year and by many others, almost all sure that the Germans' victory would last forever. Breker was at the apogee of his dual career, as official artist and as an "old Parisian" who had long worked for Franco-German reconciliation.[35]

GENESIS OF AN OFFICIAL ARTIST

Breker's life as an artist began in 1909 in Elberfeld, in the Rhineland, where he was born into that milieu: his father was a stonecutter who gave him his first lessons. He later spent five years at the Kunstakademie Düsseldorf, trying his hand at cubism, giving up life studies, and even going to the Bauhaus, where the methods of Klee and Walter Gropius put him off modernity for good, though he had once believed it necessary for the reconstruction of a Europe destroyed by the war. He had thus reconsidered, mulling over the lessons of the Munich-based sculptor Adolf von Hildebrand, meditating on Greek and Roman works and the more recent pieces by French sculptors, which he came across in the little museum in Elberfeld. He left for Paris in 1927 to more closely study the old masters, Antoine Bourdelle and Rodin (whose *Bronze Age* he had admired at the museum in Düsseldorf in 1915), but also more contemporary sculptors, Despiau, who gave him a few lessons, and Maillol.[36]

He moved to the area near the Vallée de Chevreuse, which reminded him of the landscape of the Wuppertal, then to avenue d'Orléans in Paris, thereby bringing himself closer to the bohemia of Montparnasse and to all his artist friends. He left them with regret in 1933, after being awarded the Rom-Preis by the Prussian culture ministry.

He then made his initiatory journey of discovering monumental antiquity, which culminated in Florence, before the *David* of Michelangelo, who had planted his "victorious youth" in front of the dark walls of the Palazzo Vecchio. Breker lingered there, struck by its beauty, but also to hear, "like a mystic call, like an order," something that told him never to labor "for profit and rich people or to sculpt objects made to pass venally from hand to hand or to work for jealous collectors" but instead to "labor for art, for the public forum, for the people, for the world."[37] There was a gulf between the values of the young Florentine republic that Michelangelo had incarnated and those of National Socialism to which Breker preferred to close his eyes, his mind clouded by his excitement over the perfection of the model, the citizen-warrior vibrating with "force" and "passion." Michelangelo and his contemporaries had resorted to a protean antiquity to illustrate a timeless project without abandoning innovation. The sixteenth century had discovered the perfection and complexity of the human body by stripping it bare; the twentieth did the same to matter. Breker was therefore four centuries behind, but he had the copyist's intuition that the time had come for a return to the *past of the past.* It had been a thousand years since nudes were exhibited in the public square in Germany. The republic was no longer the order of the day; in its place stood a totalitarian regime that was already mistreating bodies.

A bit of erudition and a critical mind were needed to grasp the extent to which the artist aped tradition while deflecting it just enough so that it could serve barbarism and the depiction of an Übermensch. The course of events seems merely to have held in check since Johann Joachim Winckelmann Germany's love of antiquity, a love that was reactivated by the Third Reich's Nietzschean propensity to embrace past glories. Thorak had seduced the regime before Breker, whose art was less verist and more subtle. Hitler sized up French moderation and in the end seemed to prefer neoclassicism, which evoked more explicitly a glorious history. For the Third Reich had reached that point: on one hand, consigning to flames "the bad spirit" of the past, continually privileging immediate action "as if nothing had existed before it";[38] on the other, venerating the classical model that conferred a sacred but dead culture on Germany. To succeed at incarnating the Nazi absolute and set himself up as a true artist, not a mere copyist, Breker had to force his line just enough to leave the humanist tradition behind and illustrate the famous mutant of *Mein Kampf*. A few centimeters too many and a maniacal precision brought to bear on certain elements (muscles, veins, distensions of the skin) were to assure him a career as a model illustrator in the service of the regime's architecture. Grandiloquent, sure to impress the human mob always smaller than his titans, obsessed with detail, Breker earned the approval of those who believed in the veracity of his statues, as if they had seen photographs enlarged and in three dimensions. Pl. 1

Between his early pieces and the first works that would serve the Third Reich, Breker had wandered from master to master. France offered him lyricism and human imperfection with Rodin, femininity and sensitivity with Maillol and Despiau; almost no one but Bourdelle could point the way toward grandiloquence. Breker's fascination with the monumental finally prevailed, though he was not unwilling to do intimate portraits that allowed him to express a less heroic sensibility in associating with celebrities.[39] He then sculpted a few nudes in the Rodinesque manner before smoothing out his works little by little until he obliterated, after his time in Rome, any roughness in the material.

IN THE SERVICE OF THE THIRD REICH

Breker's political allegiance to Nazism came about less rapidly than his aesthetic choices. It even appears that the sculptor would have returned to Paris in 1934, if French immigration policy had allowed him to live and work there legally. Goebbels's visit to the Accademia Tedesca in Rome in November 1933 introduced Breker to the Nazi cultural project: the state was inviting all its expatriate artists to return to the fold. Breker left for Berlin the next year and was met with attacks in the National Socialist press, which accused his Greek wife of being Jewish. The campaign against her, a model who had posed for Maillol and Picasso, did not frighten him, however. He even turned down the only commission offered by the culture ministry: a bust of Hitler, poorly remunerated (six hundred marks).[40]

He then came to respect the harsh laws governing the position of official artist. For example, while serving on the panel of judges named by the propaganda ministry, he is said to have tried, in vain, to defend works judged "degenerate" by Ziegler, the mediocre painter who had been made head of the Reichskammer der Bildenden Künste. On that occasion, neither the last student protest march nor Breker's indignation had had any effect, for Goebbels favored the strongest censorship. Breker's wanderings in the desert seemed to be over as of the 1936 Olympic Games, when he was singled out for his two statues of more than three meters high: a Victory bearing an olive branch and a decathlete modeled on the champion Gustav Stührk. In an act of diplomacy, Hitler refused to award him the gold medal, conferring it on Italy, which had been less fortunate than Germany on the sports field. The artist had to be satisfied with second place and a few words from the Führer, who, when they were introduced, asked Breker whether he was really the one who worked from the Greeks. To which Breker, already stung by the press, which accused him of being content to copy the ancients, replied that he worked "from nature." Goebbels promptly commissioned a portrait of himself as well as a colossal Prometheus to decorate his ministry.

It was still too little for this young star, who was champing at the bit, pressing Speer to see him. The latter, who was handing out commissions left and right, finally summoned Breker to show him the model for the courtyard of the new chancellery and invite him to decorate it. On the bus that took him back home, Breker sketched two very simple designs, a man holding a torch, and a second man holding a sword: *The Party* and *The Wehrmacht.* They would thrill the Führer, who was now inclined to entrust to Breker his famous triumphal arch, which Hitler had designed just after being wounded for the first time, during World War I. The renovation of Greater Berlin was finally within Breker's purview. He thus went on to decorate the enormous fountain planned for the new north-south axis with a six-meter-tall Apollo driving a quadriga, accompanied by his nymphs, surrounded by popular athletes, this time in the guises of the thinker, the chosen one, the active man, and the wounded warrior. Breker now became the head of state's darling, taken care of at government expense, untouchable, even within the NSDAP, torn apart by internal rivalries, but at the beck and call of the Führer. The next important stage for Breker would be the famous trip to Paris with Hitler, just after the Franco-German armistice.

Throughout his life, Breker described that journey as an event marking the start of his complicity with "the Führer," and as the justification for everything that followed, as if the chancellor's aesthetic pleasure made up for his old demons. As the sculptor saw it, even if he had gotten lost in politics, at least there was this as an extenuating circumstance: he had remained an artist to the end. Speer and Giesler had made an impromptu visit to Breker's home, refusing to give him any explanation but telling him to follow them. Breker then waited at a small village school, before finally leaving for Hitler's headquarters. There the Führer was waiting for "his artists," his helmet "pushed down over his eyes" and hiding "his tanned face," wearing "a simple uniform, without decoration, short boots coming only to the calves... looking like an ordinary soldier." On a bright summer morning, in the four-engine beige aircraft piloted by Hans Baur, Breker contemplated a deserted landscape, where the only living things were animals in the pastures. Everything in Breker's account betrays his feeling of childish pride at becoming a favorite of a leader who fascinated him then and who would fascinate him always. From that time on, the Führer's political rationale justifying the occupation was beside the point: the bashful lover of France now succumbed to the charms of "national pride," and the "moral burden" of the vanquisher's reign did not interfere with Breker's vanity at serving as a guide to Hitler, who had supposedly come not as a warrior but as an aesthete.[41]

After that journey in June 1940, summer went well for Breker, who devoted the end of the season to restoring a castle and an eighteenth-century house in the eastern part of Germany, in Oderbruch, out in the countryside, far from the bombing that threatened to destroy his Berlin studio. Speer gave Breker the idea of also having a studio annex built near Wriezen, where the sculptor could leave the bas-reliefs for the great arch in Berlin, and where he would also have available a plasterworks run by French prisoners, masters in the material, whom Breker had known during his stay in Paris before the war.

THE DEFEAT BEFORE THE DEFEAT

This forced "collaboration" with Germany was freely accepted in Paris by Jacques Benoist-Méchin, a minister in the new government and the first to dash off to Berlin, just after the defeat, to invite Breker, his old friend since 1925, to come exhibit as soon as possible. In fact, Benoist-Méchin's career as a mediator had begun before his appointment by Vichy: possessing an excellent knowledge of German language and culture, he had endeavored to spur the still hesitant efforts of Franco-German rapprochement, without having been deputed by his country. Since that time, as Breker liked to tell it, Benoist-Méchin, who had attracted notice as a writer and composer, enjoyed a "quasi-mythical renown."[42] Let us add to the hagiography that he was an interpreter for the interallied general staff during the occupation of the Ruhr in 1923, editor in chief of *Le quotidien* and then of *L'Europe nouvelle*, two years later, before dedicating himself to a career as a historian, which included writing a *Histoire de l'armée allemande* in six volumes, the first of which appeared in 1936 and was quickly translated into German. When the war broke out, he had already amply demonstrated his love for Germany and his admiration for Hitler, by trying to "popularize" *Mein Kampf* in France.[43] In short, Benoist-Méchin was one of those men who, against a French public hostile to Germany, advocated a reconciliation between the two countries, using culture—reputed to be neutral—to political ends.

The genesis of that "better understanding" between France and

Germany has been retraced by Fred Kupferman. Its architects were not all staunch Nazis, only sorry imitators. There was, of course, the stance taken by the young intellectuals in the Parti radical who subscribed to extremism: Alfred Fabre-Luce along with Jean Luchaire, who organized the Sohlbergkreis after a gathering of German and French youth in the Black Forest, in 1930, in concert with his German counterpart, Otto Abetz, a drawing teacher and future ambassador to Paris. Not all the "reconcilers" had the scruples of Marc Sangnier's *ajistes* (youth hostelers), who were in contact with German *Wandervogel* groups but ceased their activities after the Nazis came to power. After 30 January 1933, some even entered, more or less consciously, the minefields of psychological warfare, which the Nazis would make into a favorite weapon. Indeed, the Dienststelle Ribbentrop, a propaganda committee in France, worked toward creating an acceptable, even appealing, image of the new Germany, focusing its strategy in part on establishing relations between organizations for veterans and young people on both sides of the Rhine. From this moment on, Ribbentrop and Abetz put to the test the effectiveness of their tandem setup, early on flouting Goebbels by successfully reestablishing the Deutsch-Französische Gesellschaft on 25 October 1935. Goebbels, for lack of a better alternative, had ordered that organization disbanded in July 1934, because it had been seriously compromised by the counterpropaganda of anti-Nazi German émigrés in France. A year later, Abetz chalked up another victory, creating the Comité France-Allemagne at the Hôtel George V on 22 November 1935. Thanks to that committee, the Nazi version of events would gain ground. To this contemporary Germany, crudely disguised as a lamb, some adhered out of "ex-serviceman" pacifism, preferring to remain blind to the nature of the Nazi regime rather than risk a new war. Others supported it out of real sympathy for the Third Reich's plans. Consider that, until at least 1938, the desire for peace was so strong that André Weil-Curiel, a young lawyer who was a socialist, a Freemason, and a Jew, belonged to the committee; while in 1937, Léon Blum, who maintained a relationship with the group, renewed the subsidy that it had been granted up to that point to cover the costs of receiving German guests. Blum then invited the committee's members to lunch at the ministry of foreign affairs, at quai d'Orsay, and there was even a rumor that Ribbentrop had gone so far as to have young Jews invited in by the Hitler-Jugend to attest the pro-Semitism of the new Germany.

Benoist-Méchin, at age thirty-four, did not join the Comité France-Allemagne by mistake. He was attracted by a strong and dynamic Germany, which he admired more than an aged France where life seemed to have "stopped... half a century ago."[44] He thus called for "a purity cure"[45] that he undoubtedly believed already achieved in the resolutely youthful and virile work of his friend Breker. Head of the diplomatic service for French prisoners of war in Berlin (from November 1940 to February 1941), he became secretary general attached to the vice president of the Conseil d'Etat, responsible for Franco-German relations, when the Darlan government was formed; he later assumed the post of secretary of state. Considered an ideological and independent state collaborator, Benoist-Méchin was sentenced to death after the war—the sentence was commuted in 1953—for having clung to the manias of the Parisian extremists. He had been ready to cover up the machinations of the fascist Parti populaire français[46] led by Jacques Doriot, who, like Benoist-Méchin, had belonged to the Comité France-Allemagne before the war. He then found a place on the central committee of the "Légion tricolore," created by Laval in July 1942—on Benoist-Méchin's recommendation—to allow Frenchmen, in French uniform, to fight against Bolshevism and its allies.[47] He resigned in September 1942, after his plan for rapprochement with Germany failed and a few months after the debut of the Breker exhibition. In the end, Benoist-Méchin judged Laval too spineless to defend his totalitarian aims.

RACKING UP FAVORS

In reality, when Benoist-Méchin met with him in Berlin at the start of the occupation, Breker had expressed reservations about going to Paris to exhibit under the noses of his peers. It was only after reflection—and discussions in high places—that he accepted the deal, and only provided his conditions were met. He demanded the release of Eugène Rudier, the famous founder for Rodin and other French masters, who was languishing in the Fresnes prison, outside Paris, because he refused to turn his foundry into an armaments factory. Rudier was the only one who had truly mastered the technique of sandblasting, and he had a team of assistants whom Breker did not want to do without. The message sent to the prisoner initially met with a negative response. But Speer's energetic intervention, through the Propaganda-Staffel Paris, sufficed to persuade the artisan to agree to a collaboration that was to take him to Berlin to sort out working methods with Breker. In the end, the sixty to eighty metric tons of bronze needed for the operation did not even come from Germany: Rudier confided to the artist that he preferred his own materials (which he had not declared during the requisitions). He ultimately proved tractable, once allowed to reclaim his studio, and took seriously his new career in service of the Third Reich. It was also Rudier who "processed" the French statues that the occupier ordered removed and melted down for the benefit of the German economy or certain Nazi high dignitaries. Göring in particular yearned to acquire a *Diane d'Anet* after Jean Goujon. For Rudier then, Breker's commission was only a first stage in his life as a functionary of the Third Reich.

Little by little, Breker broke down all resistance, deploying his old Parisian patriotism and the "helping hands" he could call on in the German administration to facilitate the release of one person or improve the situation of another. So Editions Flammarion, which was to publish his monograph, was threatened with closure when it was learned that Mme Flammarion was of Jewish extraction? Breker went to see Helmuth Knochen of the Gestapo and had her name crossed off the list of suspects. So the attendants at the Orangerie balked at the task of moving his colossi? The artist immediately had cigarettes, a rare commodity in France, taken to them. He knew how to find a quick solution to every problem. His difficulties began only when he was forced to leave the easy terrain of the social world.

Having chosen Hôtel Ritz as his headquarters (until he took over, with the help of Ambassador Abetz, Helena Rubinstein's "Aryanized" apartment on Île Saint-Louis),[48] Breker held court at the luxury hotel, giving his old friends a taste of what he considered to be the continuation of sincere friendship. He also took himself to be an "official" without precise duties, who could play, in excellent Rhenish, his role of a mediator attached by tradition to French culture. He liked as well to observe that the German cultural representatives in Paris had not hesitated to throw their lot in with foreign women. Abetz had married a Frenchwoman, Epting a Swiss, Ernst Achenbach—an adviser at the embassy—an American, and Breker himself a Greek. Thus it seemed to him that the world gathered together in peace at his Ritz salons, where he could in complete confidence win over cultivated—or unpolished—French men and women. Maillol heard *The Goldberg Variations* for the first time at Breker's exhibition, where the famous pianists Wilhelm Kempff and Alfred Cortot and the soprano Germaine Lubin all performed for the benefit of the impoverished people of Paris.

Even Le Corbusier agreed to meet the artist, though discreetly this time, at the renowned Joséphine bistro on rue du Cherche-Midi, on a day when it was closed. Over lunch, the architect welcomed the sculptor, who was resolved to win his confidence. Breker congratulated Le Corbusier for his plans to build major arteries and to open up the urban cores. They discussed using concrete, steel, and glass exclusively: even though he would claim after the war that the Third Reich had intended to practice a functionalist architecture, Breker was leery, and he communicated his reservations to the modernist, who replied sarcastically that he was striving toward pharaonic work, since cut stonework seemed outmoded to him. This was a jab at the Third Reich's obsession with making the colossal effort of the master builders visible at all cost. When used across the Rhine, concrete, a fluid and malleable material, was immediately "moralized" and handed over to history: covered with stone, if need be ostentatiously reworked. Hence the lunch ended without a consensus: the two men agreed only that one should trigger "constant sensations"[49] in the objectified masses.

ON THE HONORARY COMMITTEE

As with the artists' journey of the previous year, the success of the exhibition at the Orangerie depended on the media support provided by the Germans—and the French. But, above all, it was the event's official character that conferred on it an extraordinary importance. Up to now, the state's leaders had stood somewhat apart from the artistic life of Paris. By holding a luncheon for Breker at the French prime minister's official residence, the Hôtel Matignon, Laval, newly returned to the Vichy government, gave the exhibition its true political dimension. It then became impossible to believe that art could escape the complications of the collaboration. The major collaborationists would show up more or less everywhere at the many festivities held for the event. More than ninety journalists crowded into the basement of the Lido cabaret on the day of the press conference given by Breker. The sculptor may have faced almost universal hostility, but the loyalists of the collaboration boisterously summoned Parisians to the Orangerie. The example would be set by the many guests present at the preview on 15 May, where old social habits generally managed to quell the uneasiness the visitors experienced beneath the colossal statues that they had to tip their heads back to see. All in all, it was much like 1937, at the time of the Exposition internationale des arts et techniques dans la vie moderne, when the esplanade of the Trocadéro had the air of an ancient amphitheater in which Soviet and Nazi titans faced off. The Parisian crowds had liked the pompous style of the European pavilions, even though they were often alarmed by the disproportion of Hitler's (and Stalin's) statues. The colossi were back in Paris, and the viewers were now in a poor position to grasp their good qualities—or their flaws.

The exhibition at the Orangerie was the occasion for much astonishment. There were many statues of men and only a few of women: the Third Reich showed its virile colors, which could be seductive. Hence Jean Cocteau stood stock-still before *The Wounded Warrior*, in which he thought he recognized the champion cyclist André Leduc—a detail confirmed by the artist, who had used a photograph taken during Leduc's fall on the sixteenth stage of the Tour de France in 1930.[50] Breker's love of

Pls. 2, 4

France knew no limits, as witnessed as well by the fame of the members of the honorary committee. Cogs in the machine, the Weimar pilgrims Pl. 3 had had to respond to the call. They were joined by the aged Maillol, who came to Paris especially at Breker's request. Lieutenant Heller, in charge of literary censorship, was given the mission of escorting the old master, who is said to have confided to him during the trip his misgivings about the grandiloquence of the work he was coming to celebrate.[51] Without a doubt rather critical of Breker's art, he would soon have interests of his own to put forward. He chose to declare publicly to Gaston Diehl that Breker had finally found "an art rightly his," "truly German," whose "definitive and clear" expression corresponded perfectly to modern Germany.[52] Securing the release of his young model Dina Vierny, a Jew and a resister, with whom he had fallen in love,[53] cost him dearly in terms of compromises. He posed for Breker soon after, complaining to his friends about the sculptor's obsession with detail: Breker even had him pose again to complete his warts.[54] And Maillol accepted a major commission from Germany in 1944, for which he was paid, according to the sculptor himself, the sum of 100,000 marks; according to other sources, however, it was a simple request that was never followed up.[55]

On the honorary committee of the Breker exhibition in 1942, the old master was in good company, and everyone had fine reasons for participating. There were government officials such as the extremist Abel Bonnard, who was minister of national education and youth, and Louis Hautecoeur, secretary general of fine arts; the writers Robert Brasillach, Jacques Chardonne, René Delange, and Pierre Drieu La Rochelle; and, finally, the architects Jacques Greber, Auguste Perret, and Jean Walter. On the day of the preview, it was the chairman of the honorary com- Pl. 4 mittee, Abel Bonnard, who represented the French government and formally renewed cultural relations, which were supposed to overcome every other kind. A good loyalist to the German cause, he was bursting with servile lyricism, using to his advantage the commonplaces of Nazi literature, hailing "the sculptor of heroes" sprung from "a coherent society," the "sublime inhabitants of marble or bronze" who were no less necessary than "their common inhabitants of flesh."[56] For what would fire the imagination most was the perfection of a model come to replace small, sick humanity.

As Cocteau wrote several days later for the front page of *Comoedia*,[57] these "beings" had arrived one night in spring on the place de la Concorde with the terrible strides of the Vénus d'Ille,[58] lacking nothing but speech. But everyone in turn made these living statues speak at every possible opportunity, including their true mentor, Adolf Hitler. The talent of that "leader of men" and "commander of armies" who was also a passionate lover of architecture was hailed by Benoist-Méchin, when he spoke, after Bonnard, at the opening of the exhibition.[59] Breker's statues had come to Paris as diplomats, in that "harsh intermediate period," to bring peace between the two nations. They were very athletic to be sure, a bit warlike certainly; but in the hope expressed by Jacques Roujon, director of *Le petit Parisien*, at a reception held by the newspaper, the French could reassure themselves by simply seeing these statues as harbingers of a future world, where action could and ought to remain "the sister of dreams."[60]

COCTEAU'S SALUTE

For all those whom they did not frighten, Breker's giant statues were "truer than the true." That was what Cocteau liked about the artist—his taste for detail and relief, his veins and muscles, which Cocteau contrasted to the "boring volumes of his masters." When Chardonne called him on 6 May to recommend that he pay tribute to the German sculptor "in the name of the Laval government," Cocteau, who had met with Breker at Le Boeuf sur le Toit in 1925, still balked, even though he knew he owed Breker for a "service"—probably an attempt to protect Jean Marais after his dispute with Alain Laubreaux, theater critic at *Je suis partout*.[61] At a time when Cocteau was feeling "insulted" by the pro-German French press—*Je suis partout* in particular—over the issue of his "invert theater,"[62] the artist of the Third Reich suggested that Cocteau should call him on a special telephone line to Berlin should something happen to him or to Picasso, who were in danger in Paris. Cocteau had found Breker's sculpture mediocre—had not he called for "the brand new"?[63] But in his journal, Cocteau admitted that at the Orangerie he had discovered he loved it with a passion and that the artist had "an almost sensual taste for detail and for the human." Sacha Guitry accompanied him, not about to miss a social event, but mocked Germany and the Germans the entire time: he may well have told Cocteau that if the colossi "had an erection, no one would be able to move."[64] Cocteau returned, contemplative, to the closed Orangerie on 18 May, without his mocking companion and in the company of the artist and his wife.

This day ended for him at the home of Paul Morand, in the company of the Brekers and Cortot, to whom Pétain had just given the assignment "to reorganize music in France." There was much discussion of artistic matters, interlarded with political gossip: Göring's caprices; the wrangling of the German bureaucrats in Paris versus the conduct of those Hitler had sent east; the informed visit of the Führer and his love for France, which "did not want to understand him" before the war, taking him for a housepainter or a hairdresser's assistant; Hitler's wish that no one should "break" the capital, which he would defend at all costs against the English, the French, and the rest. By the end of dinner, Cocteau's mind was made up: Breker had gotten lucky too soon, and it was his bad luck. His range was too narrow and had pushed him into the jaws of the beast. Cocteau's judgment was as incisive as always, but it did not have any effect on his frantic optimism, which had led him to compare the large German billboards in Paris to scissors in the stomach of an ostrich—an animal that can reputedly digest anything. He was friends with Éluard[65] and Picasso at the same time; surrounded by yellow stars, he took part, with Picasso, in Chaïm Soutine's very private funeral procession[66] and he also fraternized with the enemy—the game of seduction always prevailing over the rest, grounded in a dandy masochism that made him love to be "attacked by all, free (?) and penniless."[67]

Like Marais and his friend Karl Münch,[68] Cocteau would probably have preferred to love a defeated Breker. But that did not prevent him from meeting the sculptor at the Orangerie the very next day, again after closing, this time to introduce Marais to Breker, since the actor was "the same 'type' as his sculptures."[69] In exchange, two days later, Breker threatened to call Berlin if Marais did not have his travel pass before noon the next day. Nothing happened without protection—or without love. Fundamentally, the relationship between Cocteau and Marais was like that between Hitler and Breker. The Führer advised the sculptor to drive slowly on the roads and to telephone him regularly. Breker, as he himself said, was "an adopted son" for Hitler—"like Jeannot [that is, Marais]" was for Cocteau—and France would never meet with "a man as sensitive [as Hitler]." As for "the Jewish question," Breker was categorical: he mirrored the Führer. "No possible exception." It was a "duel to the death." Thus, on 29 May, after a private lunch with the sculptor on the Champs-Elysées, Cocteau came to understand, this time with sadness, that the sculptor had remained in Paris after his exhibition to "take stock of things and to give an accounting to his leader."[70]

Indeed, Cocteau dreamed of a world devoid of political commitments. Ready to go to the reception organized in Breker's honor by Lücht—head of the Kultur-Gruppe of the Propaganda-Staffel Paris—at the cabaret L'Aiglon on 22 May, he was furious to learn that the event was canceled because of the unwillingness of the politicians. It would have been so simple, he thought, to welcome Breker as an artist and not as "the friend of the Führer." In short, Cocteau was the only one to defend with such naïveté the apolitical virtues of cultural neutrality, when the trend was toward the repoliticization of a collaboration dominated by extremists.

PARISIAN HIGH SOCIETY

In Paris throughout the month of May, reception followed reception in honor of Breker, and everyone who went spoke his piece without letting slip a hint of the disdain the sculptor himself had so feared: Alphonse de Châteaubriant, at a lunch given by the journal *La gerbe;* Brasillach and Pierre d'Espezel, at the matinee performance at the Théâtre des Arts-Hébertot and the restaurant Lapérouse; Pierre Benoit, at the restaurant Ledoyen; and Benoist-Méchin, once again, at a banquet for the Third Reich's artisan and the workers who had collaborated on the event. After all, as the driving force behind the exhibition, Benoist-Méchin was now receiving recognition for the show, which he closely followed as his handiwork. Finally, Georges Grappe, curator of the Musée Rodin, welcomed Breker, thereby also crowning with success the largely literary Groupe collaboration, for which he headed the plastic arts branch.[71] In 1942, that group had not yet entered its radical phase and was content to stick to its initial goal: to reconcile France and Germany, by "doing propaganda work on cultural subjects," apart from all politics, in line with the Comité France-Allemagne. Later, it hardened its positions and its methods, so that by its final phase, after 1943, the group had turned into a gateway to paramilitary and extremist organizations.[72]

Two hundred people attended the affair at the Musée Rodin, which may be considered the only notable success for the plastic arts branch of a group that had trouble convincing the masses.[73] Despiau, Landowski, Vlaminck, and Dunoyer de Segonzac—all present at the event, all members of the Arno Breker honorary committee, after having gone to Germany the previous year—were to be transformed into official advocates of the group, merely by being there. They would have to explain themselves after France's liberation: they responded to their accusers by saying that they had been signed up automatically, against their wishes. That turned out to be a common practice for this marginal organization, whose real size remains a mystery. The 260,000 index cards found at Gestapo headquarters on rue des Saussaies in 1945 corresponded in any event to the de facto membership records of visitors who were not necessarily supporters but who had attended, at least once, the group's lectures, thus leaving behind a signature and even an address.[74]

That was not enough to make all those present staunch Nazi sympathizers, but it was certainly enough to show that they were increasingly enmeshed in the occupier's nets. Its success was complete on 19 May, when the Third Reich's favorite entered the Hôtel Matignon for the luncheon in his honor hosted by Laval, who had just recently learned of the solid friendship between the artist and the German chancellor and had promptly decided to "make everyone forget the indifference that he had shown him [Breker] up to that time."[75] The political world was consigned to the periphery of the exhibition: At Hitler's request, Göring and Speer appeared, "for reasons of security," not at the preview but a few days later, incognito. On the French side, Pétain likewise declined to show up, also officially for reasons of security and for motives "of a political nature." He did send a few words in his own hand to the artist, congratulating him on his work, of which he had had a glimpse thanks to the monograph[76] signed by Despiau and published by Flammarion.[77] But when Breker offered him one of his heroic statues as a gift, Pétain assured him that it was admirable but that he preferred an antique Grace. The artist, when told this by his close friends, naturally interpreted it as a demonstration of the immoderate—and very French—love that Pétain had for women.

It was therefore Laval, newly returned to public affairs, who threw wide the doors of artistic and political collaboration, by thanking Breker for his exhibition, a gesture that did not escape "anyone" and that "profoundly" affected the Parisians.[78] His words were laudatory but put heavy emphasis on Germany's debt to France in artistic matters. To hear him talk, what Houdon, Clodion, Jean-Baptiste Pigalle, François Lemoyne, and Étienne-Maurice Falconet had imparted to Germany was now being returned to France with an "ardent and singular originality." It was "with all the dynamism of Rude and all the inspiration of David d'Angers" that Breker approached monumental sculpture in the present day. The artist thus was indebted to French genius for his appearance at the Orangerie, a meager satisfaction and, in any case, the only one conceded by Laval, who never wasted an opportunity to hail the slightest expression of faith in the future of "good relations between France and Germany." The festivities went on, right up to the departure of the artist, who was instructed by Fernand de Brinon, the Vichy ambassador in Paris, "not to be too modest" with Hitler when he met with him and "to describe to him the welcome that the artists of Paris" had given him "spontaneously and as a result of their taste for the beautiful."[79]

Indeed, during that last "intimate" reception given by the ambassador on 3 June 1942, proof was provided, if any was needed, of the eclecticism of the "Breker network," which represented a broad cross section of the collaboration. The sculptor's farewell celebration was, of course, attended by his artist friends: Friesz, Derain, Despiau, and Dunoyer de Segonzac. But also at the reception were the usual officials, such as Hautecoeur and Germans from the general staff (Abetz, Humm, Soehring, Waldthausen, and Carltheo Zeitschel); show-business personalities such as Arletty; men of letters such as Brasillach and Cocteau; the critic André Salmon; the industrialist Dubonnet; and the extremist

Marcel Déat.[80] Until the end of his trip, then, Parisian high society ("Tout-Paris"), like Cocteau's "fatherland of poets," assured Breker of its loyal friendship,[81] scoffing at borders and trusting only in the still-civilized rules of the social world, in wartime as in peacetime. The episode ended in joy and augured well for the many "services" that each side would continue to render the other. Breker thanked France in his own way by opening its eyes: he arranged for his master Maillol to be officially rewarded for his talent. Brinon thus announced on 3 June that Breker's wishes would be granted. With Pétain's approval and on Laval's orders, "Maillol's beautiful statue representing French aviation" would quickly find a place worthy of it in Toulouse, which had heretofore balked at finding a site.[82] In addition, since the new French state had "the aim of restoring men and things to their rightful places," Laval decided to bear witness to his "high esteem" for Maillol's art by giving him a special commission.[83]

THE FIANCÉE OF THE COLOSSUS

It was surprising to see Maillol's "timeless" and "sensual" work being appropriated by politicians, who had come there to force the hand of the reigning powers whom they judged too timorous. The presence of Brinon and Abetz, like the role of Benoist-Méchin in organizing the Breker exhibition, could in fact be traced back to the genealogy of the collaboration. The three men had in common their long experience with Franco-German "reconciliation" and their battles at the Comité France-Allemagne.

Brinon, who proclaimed Maillol's triumph, was undoubtedly the most extreme of the French participants. Foreign policy editor at *L'information* in the 1930s, Brinon distinguished himself, in November 1933, by publishing in *Le matin* the first interview with Hitler by a French journalist, and he quickly became a privileged interlocutor of the Nazi regime. The German translation of his book *France-Allemagne, 1918–1934* appeared in 1934 with a preface by Friedrich Grimm, a university professor who became one of the driving forces of Nazi propaganda in France. Imposed by Germany as general delegate to the government of occupied France, Brinon remained in power to the end, even picking up the title of secretary general in September 1942. That granted him new proximity to the Vichy regime, since he now attended certain ministry councils. He was the founder of the Légion des volontaires français contre le bolchevisme, which he attempted to make official in August 1941. Seeking the overthrow of the Laval government in favor of a government of extremists in July 1944, present as well at the talks at Ribbentrop's residence in Steinort (Sztynort, Poland) when

French extremist leaders met with Hitler, he constructed with Ribbentrop a plan to have Doriot seize power and attempted, in vain, to get Pétain to accept it. Brinon, counted among the early apostles of radical collaboration, was sentenced to death after the war and was executed by firing squad on 15 April 1947.[84] His role as Vichy's ambassador in Paris placed him at the center of events in the Parisian collaboration, where culture occupied a privileged place. In terms of the events that interest us here, he naturally found himself close to Breker in May 1942, with a ringside seat at the reception given by Grappe at the Musée Rodin on 22 May.

On the evening of 3 June, he was undoubtedly a bit forward in announcing the French government's sincere interest in Maillol. But was that not a constant of collaboration diplomacy—to speak in the name of the leaders, in an effort to trigger retroactively a decision already made for them. In this instance, Brinon was not taking much of a risk in asking the government to make a gesture in support of a body of work already widely recognized in France. At the last minute, Benoist-Méchin managed to compel Laval to show a minimal regard for Breker; Maillol won votes in high places even more easily, as attested somewhat later by a visit to the sculptor's studio by the Vichy general commissioner of sports.

The Franco-German reconciliation thus set up a morganatic marriage between one of Breker's colossi and one of Maillol's *Three Graces*. Breker had come to France to draw on the famous reservoir of "little women of Paris," and undoubtedly even more on the generous curves of Maillol's matrons. In this, he unfailingly acted like one of the Third Reich's "gardeners," who saw France as one of the "new Europe's kitchen plots." In art as in other areas, France played its role as the submissive woman: witness the neoclassical consensus formed around Maillol and Breker, under the auspices of the regimes in place. In June 1942, Cocteau, with his razor-sharp wit, confused the issue by characterizing Maillol as a "Germanic Frenchman" and his friend Breker as a "German of France."[85] This perfidiously recalled that the master of Banyuls-sur-Mer had seduced collectors from across the Rhine, even before the French, during a career that had not gone as smoothly as the Rhinelander's.

In the late nineteenth century, Aristide Maillol, who grew up motherless in Banyuls-sur-Mer, had experienced the pain of failing the entrance examination for the Ecole des beaux-arts. But he was ultimately able to work in the academy studios of Jean-Léon Gérôme and Alexandre Cabanel. He did not find his place in Paris, however, where he led an impoverished life,[86] despite the aid of a few friends and the provisions sent by his family from Roussillon. He missed the outdoors, and his unsociability did not help his difficult beginnings. The situation was worsened by his fragile health, which regularly sent him to the hospital. At the time, Paul Gauguin and the group of artists known as the Nabis (Paul Sérusier, Maurice Denis, Pierre Bonnard, Edouard Vuillard, and others) particularly interested him, and he moved toward a decorative, rather vapid art, populated by gardens and figures who were usually female, an art that was a less vivid echo of his comrades' experiments. His poor eyesight forced him to abandon tapestry for sculpture, and his first major piece, *The Mediterranean*—exhibited at the Salon d'Automne in 1905—was among his sculptures of women that alluded, at least in scale, to Rodin's *Thinker* and Michelangelo's *Night*. During the same period, he met Harry Graf Kessler, a German diplomat and patron of the arts, who three years later took Maillol to visit Greece in the company of the Austrian poet Hugo von Hofmannsthal and would eventually invite Maillol to illustrate Virgil's *Eclogues*. Thanks to this protector, Germany came to know Maillol as the modeler of archaic and natural women, and this well before France, which was smitten only when it entered into economic crisis. Deprived of sure values, the French were inclined to reassure themselves with the rounded forms of femininity. In the interim, Maillol had to endure the contempt of his colleagues, as well as Léon Daudet's accusation, printed in *L'Action française* just before World War I, that he was nothing less than a spy in the service of the enemy and "boche art."[87] Unfortunately for Maillol, in 1914 a telegram from his friend Kessler instructing him to bury his statues in anticipation of the war was intercepted, which put Maillol in the foreigner's camp. The incident was to be elided by his growing success during the interwar period, which saw the taste for antiquity come back in fashion and invited the art scene to heap honors and commissions on the sculptor.

MAILLOL'S GRACES

At the outbreak of World War II, Maillol, age seventy-eight, incarnated French excellence in sculpture in the eyes of the art world and art lovers. He thus succeeded Rodin and Bourdelle in that role, serving as the mentor for the younger generation of "classical modern" artists. But history brought new currency to old suspicions: Maillol seemed to be consorting with Germany once again, this time from a better position, at the side of a vanquisher likely to impose the canons of classical antiquity on Europe as a whole, which was already convinced of the exemplarity of the model. If Breker gave the most well-informed beholders the impression that he was copying a thousand-year-old lesson, just adding a few extra centimeters and a quasi-photographic precision, Maillol mimed to perfection the *Esquiline Venus* from the first century B.C.: the thickset body, the high pelvis, the full forms, and the small, widely separated breasts. He too added a few centimeters, not in height but in width, which gave his women an increasingly less triumphant but more "authentic" appearance. In fact, though the female nude was a rarity in the classical world—the nude was reserved for the Spartans and other men—the history of art had since largely made up for it, especially in painting. When Maillol was tirelessly making his nudes, his favorite subject was already well worn from overuse. And it was not long before art lovers of the postwar period, disencumbered of the fantasies of a nostalgic society turned toward its childhood, were struck by that fact. But during the occupation, though French women had begun to prefer the slenderness of movie stars, Maillol's "plump and wholesome" biddies still pleased and reassured. Their nonchalant poses referred back to "Mother Earth"[88] by judiciously recalling the reactionary values of the moment, while answering the timorous expectations of the French—and of the Germans. Epting, director of the Institut allemand, even suggested that the sculptor's sensuality was not French per se but rather southern, Provençal, and pagan, and could just as well be German.[89]

So Maillol was European and agreeable to all, neo-Greek in Roussillon and chauvinistically French in Paris: "A lady is never too elegant,"[90] he told beginners in front of their models. Whereas Breker found his models among athletes, the old master had some trouble convincing the young peasant women of Banyuls-sur-Mer that they could pose for him without losing their honor. A young working-class woman he married in the late nineteenth century served as a model early on. His last model was Dina Vierny, whom Maillol chose in part to avoid Parisian women too sophisticated for his taste, and she later devoted herself to defending his work. A Russian Jew, she was to incarnate provincial France, which at that very moment was busy eliminating all diversity. Once again, art fed on paradoxes, yet without transgressing the prohibitions in force. Quite the contrary. When the Gestapo arrested Vierny, she was released thanks to the intervention of Breker, so that his old friend Maillol would still have a taste for life and for fashioning a few last generous women, who might agreeably serve as the counterparts to his Germanic colossi. That was how things stood before the party on 3 June marking Breker's departure for Germany. The task at hand was to reconstitute an inseparable and complementary couple, divided by the war but brought back together by the collaboration. As everyone had noticed on visiting the Orangerie, Breker did not like to sculpt women and imposed virile and glacial canons on them when he did. France preferred the rounder and more welcoming femininity of Maillol's *Graces*, and Maillol had no taste for depicting men. The division of labor appeared equitable, if one was obliging enough to admit that the vanquisher was offering its eternal warrior, while the vanquished offered its eternal peasant woman. So, before returning to his country, Breker asked France to take care of old Maillol, who had welcomed the government's admiration. In May 1943, Maillol received a visit from Colonel Joseph Pascot, a former Roussillon rugby player then acting as Vichy general commissioner of sports, come to order a statue of an athlete for a sports center. He had failed to grasp the lesson previously given. As Claude Roy reported,[91] the project undoubtedly was pleasing to Maillol, who accepted but never completed the project: devoting himself exclusively to his female works, Maillol never departed from the division of labor and the one genre that had brought him such success until then. He died on 16 September 1944, in a car accident that spared him the ordeal of the purge. Given a little time, would the old sculptor have embodied the horizon of expectation of the French people and of their government as well? The story ended brutally without providing an answer—in the tacit agreement between a Grace and a colossus, which warded off the dark reality by captivating the eyes of the distraught masses.

NOTES

1. For the recollections of the artists and art world personalities who participated in the trip to Germany or who were witnesses to it, see volume 2 of Laurence Bertrand Dorléac, "Art, culture et société: L'exemple des arts plastiques à Paris entre 1940 et 1944" (habilitation thesis, Institut d'études politiques de Paris, 1990).
2. The list of travelers is rarely given accurately. Because the event has been recounted at every possible opportunity, there have been many slip-ups in the telling and the writing: Édouard Pignon, quoted by André Halimi in *Chantons sous l'Occupation* (Paris: Olivier Orban, 1976), has Maillol leave for Germany; Germain Bazin, in his *Souvenirs de l'exode du Louvre 1940–1945*, includes Jacques Despierre; Véronique Julia, who compiled the chronology that appears in Daniel Lindenberg, *Les années souterraines (1937–1947)* (Paris: Editions La Découverte, 1990), lists Maurice Brianchon; and so on.
3. Despiau was born in Mont-de-Marsan on 4 November 1874 and died in Paris on 28 October 1946. He studied with Hector Joseph Lemaire at the Ecole nationale des arts décoratifs, then with Louis-Ernest Barrias at the Ecole des beaux-arts. He exhibited for the first time at the Salon des Artistes Français in 1898, then at the Salon de la Société Nationale des Beaux-Arts, alongside Bourdelle, Camille Claudel, and Lucien Schnegg.

4. Belmondo was born in Algiers on 8 August 1898 and died in Ivry-sur-Seine on 1 January 1982. He was the student of Jean-Marie Boucher at the Ecole des beaux-arts and won the Prix Blumenthal in 1926. He did a bust of Louis Hautecoeur, secretary general of the fine arts administration under the occupation. A professor at the Ecole des beaux-arts as of 1952, he was admitted to the Académie des beaux-arts of the Institut de France on 17 February 1960.
5. Bouchard was born in Dijon on 13 December 1875 and died in Paris on 30 November 1960. He was Louis-Ernest Barrias's student at the Ecole des beaux-arts and won the Prix de Rome in 1901. He received the medal of honor from the Société nationale des beaux-arts in 1925 and was a member of the jury for the Exposition internationale des arts et techniques dans la vie moderne, held in Paris in 1937. He was a professor at the Ecole des beaux-arts from 1929 to 1945.
6. See the reports of the Propaganda-Abteilung Frankreich, Archives nationales (AN), AJ 40 1001, subchapter "Bildende Künste."
7. Lejeune was born on 22 January 1884 in Livet-sur-Authou (near Brionne) and died on 7 April 1969 in Paris. He received the Prix de Rome in 1911 and a few Salon prizes. He was admitted to the Académie des beaux-arts of the Institut de France in 1941.
8. In fact, Landowski hid from photographers throughout the trip and therefore does not appear in this first photograph.

   Landowski was born in Paris on 1 June 1875 and died in Boulogne-Billancourt in April 1961. The sculptor exhibited for the first time in 1906 at the Salon des Artistes Français and received his first medal for *Les fils de Caïn*. He is the author of *Peut-on enseigner les beaux-arts?* (Paris: Editions Baudinière, 1943). There is a museum dedicated to him in Boulogne-Billancourt.
9. See Bruno Foucart, Michèle Lefrançois, and Gérard Caillet, *Landowski* (Paris: Editions Van Wilder, 1989), esp. Lefrançois's text, "C'est en touchant le sol qu'Antée, fils de la terre, retrouvait sa puissance," 9–18.
10. On about 25 October, Landowski was invited to take the trip, which began a few days later. See Paul Landowski, unpublished journal, 25 October 1941. On that trip more generally, see the entries dated 7 June 1941, 26, 27, 28 October 1941, 17–20 November 1941, 22 November 1941, 9 December 1941, October 1945, 5 April 1946.
11. Paul Landowski, unpublished journal, 25 October 1941.
12. Paul Landowski, unpublished journal, 28 October 1941.
13. Paul Landowski, unpublished journal, 27 October 1941.
14. Paul Landowski, unpublished journal, 28 October 1941.
15. Paul Landowski, unpublished journal, 28 October 1941.
16. Oudot was born in Paris on 29 July 1897 and died there on 17 July 1981. He took classes at the Ecole nationale des arts décoratifs, before working on

sets for the Ballets Russes until the death of Léon Bakst, its innovative chief set designer, in 1924.

17. Legueult was born in Paris on 10 May 1898 and died there in July 1971. He was a student at the Ecole nationale des arts décoratifs, where he was appointed professor in 1925, before moving to the Ecole des beaux-arts in 1952.

18. Dunoyer de Segonzac was born on 7 July 1884 in Boussy-Saint-Antoine and died in Paris on 17 September 1974. He received the Carnegie Prize in 1933 and the grand prize for painting at the Venice Biennial in 1934.

19. Van Dongen was born on 26 January 1877 near Rotterdam, became a naturalized French citizen in 1929, and died in Monaco on 28 May 1968. He studied at the Academie van Beeldende Kunsten in Rotterdam, where he was the student of Jan Striening and Johannes Gerardus Heyberg. He settled in Paris permanently in 1900 and, starting in 1901, contributed to illustrated publications: *Le rire*, *Gil Blas*, *La revue blanche*, and *L'assiette au beurre*. He exhibited at the Salon des Indépendants beginning in 1904, at which time he became associated with André Derain and Maurice de Vlaminck. The first exhibition of his work was held in 1904 at Ambroise Vollard's gallery in Paris. He contracted for the exhibition of his works first with Daniel-Henry Kahnweiler in 1907, then with the firm Bernheim-Jeune in 1908.

20. Friesz was born in Le Havre on 6 February 1879 and died in Paris on 10 January 1949. He enrolled at the Ecole des beaux-arts in Paris, where he was the student of Léon Bonnat, who discouraged him and whom Friesz liked less than his former teacher in Le Havre, the painter Charles Lhuillier. He received the Carnegie Prize in 1925.

21. Freundlich (b. 10 July 1878, Stolp, Pomerania [now Słupsk, Poland]; d. 9 March 1943, Lublin-Majdanek, Poland) was a German painter and sculptor, a pioneer in abstract art, who spent much of his artistic career in France. One of his sculptures appeared on the cover of the catalog for the Nazi exhibition on "degenerate art," held in Munich in 1937.

The anti-Nazi committee in his support collected the signatures of Adler, Hans Arp, Georges Braque, Jean Cassou, Léo Charles, André Derain, Paul Dermée, Max Ernst, Anne Gacon, Albert Gleizes, Auguste Herbin, Max Jacob, Oskar Kokoschka, Fernand Léger, Jacques Lipchitz, Pablo Picasso, Read, Sophie Taeuber-Arp, Wilhelm Uhde, and Paul Westheim, among others.

22. See Pierre Cabanne, *André Derain* (Paris: Somogy, 1990), 109–10. On Derain more generally, see Jane Lee, *Derain*, exh. cat. (Oxford: Phaidon, 1990); Michel Hoog, *Un certain Derain*, exh. cat. (Paris: Réunion des Musées Nationaux, 1991); Michel Kellermann, *André Derain: Catalogue raisonné de l'oeuvre peint*, 3 vols. (Paris: Editions Galerie Schmit, 1992–99).

23. André Derain, *The Painter and His Family*, ca. 1939, oil on canvas, 176.5 × 123.8 cm, Tate Collection, London.

24. According to Derain's still-unpublished journal, the residents of his village had in the meantime informed him that they had heard the occupiers were going to shoot him because he was Jewish and had done "obscene drawings depicting Hitler." After more than sixty soldiers had occupied his home, the village baker gave Derain asylum.

The police came to interrogate him on 20 December 1940, asking him if he was Jewish. The next summer, one of his former models from the 1920s paid him a visit on behalf of the Third Reich's official sculptor, Arno Breker, whom he did not know.

25. An unsigned document, probably composed by a few of the trip's participants, clearly records this time the travelers' agreement to go, in exchange for the "formal promise that a very large number of artists being held as prisoners of war will be released." Lists containing about three hundred names of artists from the different salons were submitted to Paul Landowski, director of the Ecole des beaux-arts, who supposedly "transmitted" them (private archives; and in AN, Z6 NL. 1678, dossier Othon Friesz).

26. His letter to his wife, Alice, sent from Vienna on 4 November, gives a more cheerful picture of the journey, which was tiring—given the many visits and receptions—and cold, since it was snowing in Munich and raining in Vienna. Derain speaks of a sumptuous welcome and of "very interesting things." He mentions the visit to the studio of Arno Breker, who had "two magnificent live horses as models, as well as an organ" that reminded Derain of his own instrument in his (requisitioned) house. He also said he had discovered "remarkable" German works in an exhibition of drawings done during the Russian campaign. See the handwritten letter, private archives, cited above.

27. Paul Landowski, unpublished journal, 17–20 November 1941, written after his return.

28. André Fraigneau, "Le voyage en Allemagne des écrivains français: *Iphigénie* à Weimar," *Comoedia*, 8 November 1941, 9.

29. That trip ended on 16 November. They were in Vienna, Austria, on 4 November, after being received in Munich.

30. Maximilien Gauthier, "Impressions d'Allemagne," *Comoedia*, 29 November 1941, 9.

31. See Bernard Poissonnier, "Peintres et sculpteurs français en Allemagne," *Comoedia*, 22 November 1941, 9.

32. Ten thousand copies were printed, of which eighty-seven hundred were sold. The book was recommended by German propaganda in December 1942. Despiau, at Breker's side, did a book signing in May at the Rive-Gauche bookstore on place de la Sorbonne.

33. See Simone de Beauvoir, *La force de l'âge* (Paris: Gallimard, 1960), 2:588.

34. Breker and his hagiographers spoke of eighty thousand visitors.

35. On Breker and his work, see Charles Despiau, *Arno Breker* (Paris:

Flammarion, 1942); Arno Breker, *Paris, Hitler et moi* (Paris: Presses de la Cité, 1970); Arno Breker, *Im Strahlungsfeld der Ereignisse: Leben und Wirken eines Künstlers Porträts, Begegnungen, Schicksale* (Preußisch-Oldendorf: Verlag K. W. Schütz, 1972); Michel Marmin and José Manuel Infiesta, *Arno Breker: El Miguel-Angel del siglo XX, le Michel-Ange du XXeme siècle* (Barcelona: Ediciones de Nuevo Arte Thor, 1976); Bernard Noël, *Arno Breker et l'art officiel* (Paris: Jacques Damase, 1981); Arno Breker, *Arno Breker: The Collected Writings*, trans. Benjiman D. Webb and Lynne Kvinnesland (New York: West-Art, 1990); Alain Rubens, "Arno Breker, sculpteur du IIIe Reich," *A, les aventures de l'art*, April 1991, 40–45, 96; Klaus Staeck, ed., *Nazi-Kunst ins Museum?* (Göttingen: Steidl, 1988). See, finally, the documentary short film *Arno Breker—Harte Zeit, starke Kunst* (Berlin: Riefenstahl-Film/Kulturfilm-Institut, 1944), 13 min., 35 mm, directed by Hans Cürlis and Arnold Fanck, produced by Leni Riefenstahl and Hans Cürlis.

36. During a first trip, in 1924, Breker paid a visit to Daniel-Henry Kahnweiler on rue d'Astorg, without success. A few years later, he obtained support from the German-Jewish art dealer Alfred Flechtheim. See Pierre Assouline, *L'homme de l'art: D.-H. Kahnweiler (1884–1979)* (Paris: Balland, 1988), 377.

37. Quoted in Despiau, *Arno Breker* (note 35), 43–44.

38. On this question, see the remarkable works by Éric Michaud. See also Max Picard, *L'homme du néant*, trans. Jean Rousset (Neuchâtel: Editions de la Baconnière, 1947). On the Nazis' taste for classical antiquity, see P. Villard, "Antiquité et *Weltanschauung* hitlérienne," *Revue d'histoire de la Deuxième Guerre mondiale*, October 1972; Alfred Rosenberg, *Tradition und Gegenwart: Reden und Aufsätze 1936–1940*, ed. Karlheinz Rüdiger (Munich: Franz Eher Nachf., 1941).

39. He continued to do intimate portraits after the war, to the point of devoting himself to them almost exclusively. During his career, he made busts of more than three hundred personalities, including Aristide Maillol, Serge Lifar (1941–42), Jean Marais, Céline, Alfred Cortot (1942), Henry de Montherlant (posthumously, at Louis Pauwels's request), Jeanne Castel, Katia Granoff, Max Liebermann (1934), Abel Bonnard, Philippe Henriot, Robert Valençay (1931), André Dunoyer de Segonzac, Salvador Dalí (1976), Félix Houphouët-Boigny (1972), Léopold Sédar Senghor (1978), Albert Speer (1940), Cosima Wagner (1978, at the request of the municipality of Bayreuth), Wieland Wagner, Richard Wagner, Franz Liszt, Ernst Fuchs (1974), Wilhelm Kempff, Ezra Pound (1967), Heinrich Heine (1930 and 1980), Peter and Irene Ludwig, Marcel Pagnol, Paul Morand, Anwar el-Sadat, Sultan Muhammad V, and Jacques Benoist-Méchin.

40. After Hitler's visit to Paris in 1940, Breker proposed that the Führer pose for him. Hitler refused, replying that Breker could not do better than he had already done. Breker would make three busts and one bas-relief of Hitler, always from a photograph. See Marmin and Infiesta, *Arno Breker* (note 35), 60.

41. On the account of this trip, see Breker, *Paris, Hitler et moi* (note 35).

42. Breker, *Paris, Hitler et moi* (note 35), 133.

43. See Henry Rousso, *La collaboration* (Paris: M.A. Editions, 1987).

44. Jacques Benoist-Méchin, *La moisson de quarante: Journal d'un prisonnier de guerre* (Paris: Editions Albin Michel, 1941), 105.

45. Benoist-Méchin, *La moisson de quarante* (note 44), 50–51.

46. See Pascal Ory, *Les collaborateurs 1940–1945* (Paris: Editions du Seuil, 1976; reprint, 1980), 39.

47. As secrétaire d'Etat de la vice-présidence du Conseil (junior minister to the prime minister), Benoist-Méchin again played a particularly compromising role while transmitting, as if they had come from Hitler, the diplomatic wishes of his counterpart, Abetz. In early 1942, he proposed that France go to war against the Allied powers, in exchange for a "profound modification" of its relationship with Germany. Although discussed in Vichy, that "new" peace was never concluded because Hitler had no desire to better France's fate. Benoist-Méchin thus made a great effort, in vain, to obtain a response from Abetz to the (more reserved) French proposals. He saw only too late that he had led France up a humiliating blind alley. Abetz was gradually marginalized by Ribbentrop. This outcome followed the failure of the meeting between the French prime minister François Darlan and Hitler on 13 May 1941—which was the prelude to the notorious Paris Protocols. See Eberhard Jäckel, *La France dans l'Europe de Hitler*, trans. Denise Meunier (Paris: Fayard, 1968); and Robert O. Paxton, *La France de Vichy, 1940–1944*, trans. Claude Bertrand (Paris: Editions du Seuil, 1973).

48. The report concerning the Rubinstein apartment at 24, quai de Béthune, stated that Abetz considered "the visits of Professor Breker to Paris very important." See the retranscription of the document in Yvon Bizardel, *Sous l'Occupation: Souvenirs d'un conservateur de musée (1940–1944)* (Paris: Calmann-Lévy, 1964), 157–58.

49. Laurence Bertrand Dorléac, *Histoire de l'art, Paris 1940–1944: Ordre national, traditions et modernités* (Paris: Publications de la Sorbonne, 1986), 98 n. 15. Le Corbusier, quoted in Éric Michaud, "Art, propagande, publicité autour de Paris, 1937," in *L'art face à la crise: 1929–1939* (Saint-Étienne: Centre Interdisciplinaire d'Etude & de Recherches sur l'Expression Contemporaine, Université de Saint-Étienne, 1980), 85.

50. See Jean Cocteau, *Journal 1942–1945*, ed. Jean Touzot (Paris: Gallimard, 1989), 664.

51. See Gerhard Heller, with Jean Grand, *Un Allemand à Paris, 1940–1944* (Paris: Editions du Seuil, 1981), 123–25.

52. See Gaston Diehl, "Le scandale de Toulouse" (interview with Aristide Maillol), *Comoedia*, 30 May 1942, 6.
53. See Breker, *Paris, Hitler et moi* (note 35), 227 f.; Michel Bouille, *Maillol, la femme toujours recommencée* (Paris: Editions Eole, 1989), 64, 66. On Dina Vierny, see *Le matin*, 24 April 1943, and *La semaine*, 3 July 1943; cited in Bouille, *Maillol* (this note), 64 n. 5.
54. To make the bust of Maillol, Breker drove from Berlin to Banyuls-sur-Mer in 1943, accompanied by his wife and by Dr. Lange, detached by the Propaganda Staffel. They stopped in Alsace, in Mulhouse, at the home of Epple, director of Editions Braun, which planned to publish a work on Breker in the series "Artistes de tous les temps." Once the bust was finished, Maillol wanted to leave for Paris to find his model, who was supposed to be released through Breker's intervention. On Breker's portrait of Maillol, see also Henri Frère, *Conversations de Maillol* (Geneva: Pierre Cailler, 1956). See reproductions of the work in Arno Breker, *Bildnisse unserer Epoche = Visages de notre époque = Portraits of Our Epoch* (Dorheim, Hesse: Podzun-Verlag, 1972).
55. See Arno Breker, interview by Laurence Bertrand Dorléac, 16 April 1980, Düsseldorf, in Bertrand Dorléac, "Art, culture et société" (note 1), 2:396–97. At issue was a statue designed for the renovation of Berlin, which was to have been placed in the Berliner Forst Grunewald. See the different versions, in terms of outcome, in Bouille, *Maillol* (note 53), 70; and Frère, *Conversations de Maillol* (note 54).
56. Abel Bonnard, "Discours prononcé . . . à l'inauguration de l'exposition Arno Breker à l'Orangerie des Tuileries, le 15 mai 1942," in *Exposition Arno Breker à l'Orangerie des Tuileries, Paris, mai–juillet 1942: Discours et allocutions* (Paris: E. Desfossés-Néogravure, Imprimeurs, 1943), 5. [The speech is posted at http://abelbonnard.free.fr/breker.htm (17 August 2007).]
57. Jean Cocteau, "Salut à Breker," *Comoedia*, 23 May 1942, 1.
58. The text ran as follows:

> I salute you, Breker. I salute you from the great fatherland of poets, a fatherland where fatherlands do not exist, except insofar as everyone brings to it the treasure of national labor. I salute you because you rehabilitate the thousand reliefs whereof a tree composes its grandeur. Because you regard your models as trees and because, far from conforming to volumes, you endow your bronzes and your plasters with a delicate sap that twists the Achilles' shield of their knees, that makes the river system of their veins pound, that twines the honeysuckle of their hair. Because you are inventing a new trap in which aestheticism, enemy of enigmas, will be caught. Because you return the right to life to the mysterious statues in our public gardens. Because, by the light of

> the moon, the true sun of statuary, I imagine your beings arriving one night in spring on place de La Concorde, with the terrible strides of the Vénus d'Isle [*sic*]. Because the great hand of Michelangelo's *David* has shown you the way. Because, in the great fatherland in which we are compatriots, you speak to us of France.

Cocteau, "Salut à Breker" (note 57), 1. ["La Vénus d'Ille" (1837) is the title of a short fantastical tale by Prosper Mérimée in which a bronze statue comes to life.—Trans.]

59. Jacques Benoist-Méchin, "Discours…à l'inauguration de l'exposition Arno Breker à l'Orangerie des Tuileries, le 15 mai 1942," in *Exposition Arno Breker à l'Orangerie des Tuileries, Paris, mai–juillet 1942: Discours et allocutions* (Paris: E. Desfossés-Néogravure, Imprimeurs, 1943), 7–9.

60. Jacques Roujon, speech at the reception for Arno Breker, *Le petit Parisien*, 23 May 1942, 1. [He was alluding to Charles Baudelaire's poem "Reniement de Saint Pierre": "Certes, je sortirai, quant à moi, satisfait / D'un monde où l'acton n'est pas la soeur du rêve" (As for me, I shall surely depart content / From a world where action is not the sister of dreams).—Trans.]

61. See Cocteau, *Journal* (note 50), 112.

62. See Serge Added, *Le théâtre dans les années-Vichy, 1940–1944* (Paris: Editions Ramsay, 1992), 43–44.

63. See Cocteau, cursing the revival of the classics in theater and yearning to "rediscover the fire that moves and jostles the shadows," in Jean Cocteau, "Adresse aux jeunes écrivains," *La gerbe*, 3 December 1940. Let us not forget that in 1940 Cocteau had had to beg French authorities to allow his play *Les parents terribles* to be performed again. His request was, moreover, the subject of a garbled note to the minister of national education, Albert Sarraut. The author of the note (on the instructions of the censor, who opposed the revival of *Les parents terribles*) emphasized, on one hand, Cocteau's insistence that his play be performed again (to alleviate his dire economic situation) and his desire to make all the requested modifications to his work; and, on the other, the scandalous character of the play, which did not much "conform to the idea of the French family that we would like to spread throughout the world today." He did not want "the historians of French civilization" to someday be able "to reproach the Parisians of 1940 for having preferred new performances of *Les parents terribles* to the revival of a cycle by Corneille or Racine." He therefore agreed to the revival of Cocteau's play only on the condition that its "odor of delicate rot" be "attenuated" and that "the shocking aspect, bordering on the incestuous, of the overly tender relations between a hysterical mother and a slightly 'loony' son" be banished from the stage. Unsigned note, Palais de Chaillot, to Albert Sarraut, 7 May 1940, AN, F21.

64. Cocteau, *Journal* (note 50), 125.

65. In his letter of 2 July 1942, Éluard lectured him as follows:

> My dear Cocteau,
> Freud, Kafka, and Chaplin are banned by the same people who honor Breker. We considered you among the banned. How wrong you were suddenly to show up among the censors! The best of those who admire and who love you were painfully surprised.
> Restore our trust. Nothing must separate us.
> Yours,
> Paul Éluard

When Cocteau got wind of Éluard's reaction, on 22 June, from Marie-Laure de Noailles, he wrote: "Even him! What foolishness! He could not even understand the complex feelings that impelled me to write it. After that, how can you expect me to believe that his poems have shadings, under-currents, roots. Once and for all, I must get used to being incomprehensible, to living alone, to living quarantined." Letter reproduced in Cocteau, *Journal* (note 50), 174. For Cocteau's reaction to his friend's revolt, see Cocteau, *Journal* (note 50), 162–63.

66. In August 1943, Soutine died of a stomach ulcer, after being rushed from Champigny-sur-Veude in Touraine—where he had been in hiding with his girlfriend—to a Parisian clinic.

67. Cocteau, *Journal* (note 50), 132.

68. Karl Münch hosted the program "L'heure du soldat" on Radio-Paris (which was run by the Germans and their French collaborators during the occupation) while passing himself off to Marais as an intelligence agent.

69. Cocteau, *Journal* (note 50), 130.

70. Cocteau, *Journal* (note 50), 138.

71. To celebrate the event, a sumptuous reception was held at the Hôtel Ritz on 14 May 1942 at 8:00 P.M. For the guest list, see Haute Cour trial of Jacques Benoist-Méchin, AN, series 3W 63, seal 1, dossier 9.

The following were invited, in order of importance (names are generally followed by a handwritten *v* or *oui*, or by a *non*): Professor Arno Breker; Ambassador Abetz *v;* SS-Brigadeführer Generalmajor Oberg *v;* Minister Schleier *v;* Monsieur Neuendorf *non;* Professor Kreiss *v;* Doctor Hoffmann *v;* Minister Rahn *v;* Reichsamtsleiter Dr. Kruger *v;* Oberstleutnant Schmidtke *non;* General Konsul Knothe *oui;* Oberstleutnant Von During *non;* Doctor Haberstock; Epting *oui;* Schneider (Kunst-Dienst) *oui;* Leutnant Lücht *oui;* Ehmsen *oui;* Sonderführer Lange *oui;* Rudier.

Another list of personalities who had accepted followed: Benoist-Méchin, de Grosville, Châteaubriant, Jacques Greber, Jacques Chardonne,

Legueult, Landowski, Knothe, Bouchard, Louis Hautecoeur, Jean-Claude Dondel, Friesz, Dunoyer de Segonzac, Brasillach, Despiau, Oudot, Neuendorf (crossed out), Epting, Gabriel Cognacq, Kruger, Prof. Schneider, Dr. Hoffmann, Abetz, Oberg, and so on.

Then there was a list of those who had refused: Schaumburg, von Stülpnagel, Auguste Perret, Oberst Koszmann, Neuendorf, During, Schmidtke.

72. Groupe collaboration formed just after Pétain's meeting with Hitler at Montoire-sur-le-Loir, at the initiative of Alphonse de Châteaubriant (who had just founded *La gerbe*). It was made up of the hard-core pro-Nazis from the Comité France-Allemagne. See Catherine Brice, "Le groupe 'Collaboration' 1940–1944" (master's thesis, Université Paris I–Panthéon Sorbonne, 1977–78).

At the head of the group: Ernest Fornairon, secretary general; Jean Weiland, vice president (general director as of 1941); René Pichard du Sage, vice president. Heading the branches that operated in Paris (the group was active throughout France): P. Parme and J. Maillot, economic and social branch; Professor Le Fur, André Jacquemont, Georges Claude, and Professor Fourneau, scientific branch; Abel Bonnard, Paul Courant, and René Pichard du Sage (curator of the Versailles library), literary branch; Jean Sarment, theater branch; Alfred Bachelet, Max d'Ollone (director of the Opéra-Comique), and Florent Schmitt, music branch; Georges Grappe, plastic arts branch. There was also a youth branch (JEN).

The group had several organs of the press: *Les cahiers franco-allemands* (which had served the cause of the Comité France-Allemagne), Châteaubriant's *La gerbe*, and the bulletin *Collaboration*. Its views were also expressed in lectures (at least twenty in Paris) and in radio "chats."

73. Brice, "Le groupe 'Collaboration'" (note 72).

74. Brice, "Le groupe 'Collaboration'" (note 72).

75. See Jacques Benoist-Méchin, *De la défaite au désastre*, vol. 2, *L'espoir trahi, avril–novembre 1942* (Paris: Albin Michel, 1985), 82.

76. See the letter from Pétain to Breker, Vichy, 23 June 1942: "Maestro, I have received the very beautiful document you were considerate enough to bestow on me. I was therefore able to take stock of how deserving you are of the praise that has been directed at you. I appreciate your art and congratulate you. Sincerely yours." See Haute Cour trial of Philippe Pétain, AN, series 3W 294, seal 62, exhibit A25.

77. The critic Gaston Diehl paid tribute to Despiau as a sculptor—and as a writer—in an issue of the Italian legislative record, *Il tempo* (17 December 1942). But Despiau, who knew Breker well, certainly had not written the monograph but merely signed his name to it; he also did a book signing on Saturday, 30 May 1942, at the Rive-Gauche bookstore on place de la Sorbonne, alongside Breker.

The distribution of the book was very carefully planned. It was undertaken by the traditional channels but also targeted the government and social spheres. In addition, Editions Flammarion was given responsibility for circulating the texts of the short speeches given in Breker's honor.

See, for example, the letter from Patris d'Uckerman, for the Flammarion publishing house, to de Grosville, attaché to the cabinet of Benoist-Méchin, 16 June 1942; and the thank-you letter from Benoist-Méchin to d'Uckerman, 17 June 1942; AN, series 3W 63, seal 1, dossier 9.

78. Pierre Laval, "Allocution prononcée... au déjeuner offert à l'Hôtel Matignon, le 19 mai 1942," in *Exposition Arno Breker à l'Orangerie des Tuileries, Paris, mai–juillet 1942: Discours et allocutions* (Paris: E. Desfossés-Néogravure, Imprimeurs, 1943), 11–12.

On the German side, the following were invited to the official luncheon: Breker and his wife; Speer and his wife; Abetz and his wife; the generals von Stülpnagel and Schaumburg; the minister Schleier; the professors Kreiss, Wolters, and Kempff. On the French side: Benoist-Méchin and his wife, Fernand de Brinon, Bonnard, Marcel Déat, François Lehideux, the rear-admiral de Rivoyre, Magny, the admiral Bard, Trochu, Hautecoeur, and Cortot.

For the list, see Haute Cour trial of Jacques Benoist-Méchin, AN, series 3W 63, seal 1, dossier 9.

79. See the archives of Fernand de Brinon, Vichy representative to German-occupied French territories, AN, 411 AP3 (ceremony).

80. In his memoirs, Déat recounts Breker's success in Paris; his meeting at Brinon's home with Maillol and "a good roomful of very Parisian personalities"; his drive to the home of the German sculptor with Otto Abetz; and so on. See Marcel Déat, *Mémoires politiques*, ed. Laurent Theis (Paris: Denoël, 1989), 775–76, 918.

81. Also invited were Lucien Lelong; Jean Luchaire and his wife; Raymond Lopez and his wife; the vicomte and vicomtesse de Foy, "etc., etc."; see the archives of Fernand de Brinon, AN, 411 AP3 (ceremony).

82. See Diehl, "Le scandale" (note 52), 1, 6.

83. See the typewritten sheet titled "Arno Breker (Réception du 3 juin 1942)," archives of Fernand de Brinon, AN, 411 AP3 (ceremony).

84. He presented himself to the U.S. authorities on 8 May 1945, after being turned away successively by the Swiss and the Germans.

85. Cocteau, *Journal* (note 50), 141.

86. On average, Maillol had less than 2 francs a day at his disposal; during the same period, the daily wages of a Parisian worker were about 5.25 francs. See Bouille, *Maillol* (note 53), 20.

87. Léon Daudet, "L'art boche," *L'Action française*, 6 January 1915.

88. *Maurice Denis*, exh. cat. (Paris: Galerie Louis Carré, 1941).

89. Karl Epting, *Réflexions d'un vaincu: Au Cherche-Midi à l'heure française...*, trans. Jean Carrère (Bourg-en-Bresse: Editions E. T. L., 1953), 146.

90. See Jean Osouf, interview by Laurence Bertrand Dorléac, 3 May 1980, Paris, in Bertrand Dorléac, "Art, culture et société" (note 1), 2:612.

91. See Claude Roy, "Maillol devant la caméra," *Comoedia*, 29 May 1943, 1, 6.

CHAPTER FOUR

The Marshal ad Infinitum

CONVINCING FRANCE

Since the 1930s, Germany had been demonstrating that it was possible to "edify" the mob through works of art (which had the enormous advantage of supposedly not being made to convince) in addition to the traditional tools of propaganda—grand ceremonies and the media: radio, film, photography, posters, graphic design. Some weapons were certainly more effective than others, though each ultimately played a role suited to its measure, relentlessly bombarding hearts and consciences at every moment of an existence increasingly suffused by the social diktat. In this new age of the masses, propaganda had forged weapons that were all the more redoubtable for being as yet unrecognized. The initial formulas had been tested by the Soviets: schematization, repetition, series, edifying colors, edifying forms, edifying messages.[1] France followed in the footsteps of the pioneers, as a moderate consumer of "messages" aimed at the masses but still confined to the realm of industrial advertising or functionalist projects. After the defeat, Vichy, capitalizing on economic scarcity, controlled the display of posters and billboards and reserved public wall space for propaganda alone. Did it have any other choice than to extend the first "modern" lessons to politics? It adapted them to French tastes, seeking inspiration when necessary from theories that were duly imported, then taken up by slavish followers.[2]

The lesson was summed up in a few idées fixes. Truth in its pure state was dangerous to handle. To change an already-existing opinion, it was better to work gradually than to strike head-on and undoubtedly provoke the "subjects'" resistance. Subjects had to be allowed "some place for reflection," yet they should not be allowed to think that a "ready-made" argument was being foisted on them. And, finally, it was obligatory that an easily accessible truth be presented to them. On this last point, the significant place granted to the visual was the result of Goebbels's own words. Refusing to require "the slightest effort" from his audience, he paid particular attention to the length of a message, the typographic presentation, the presence of images and numbers, and "the most striking and most eloquent" expressions of the "facts of public life."

Although the French state had not fully developed a visual propaganda policy, it was not reluctant to intervene frequently. In the midst of disorder, it was always ready to exert its influence, while leaving the most radical—and hateful—registers to the occupier and the extremists. The situation proved particularly ambiguous in that the occupying forces were careful not to distinguish their actions from official campaigns originating in Vichy. Hence, the occupier's major propaganda exhibitions, beginning in autumn 1940, employed collaborators, as a pledge of "Frenchness."[3] The organizers made generous use of methods recalling the Third Reich's massive investment in Germany since 1933. They utilized, at least in part, exhibitions that had already occurred in Munich, Berlin, and Rome. The second exhibition in particular—*Le Juif et la France*—held in September 1941, under the auspices of the Institut d'études des questions juives, demonstrated that Goebbels's directives, privileging the brutal impact of image and text, had now reached France. In formal terms, the devices were reminiscent of the skillful compositions of El Lissitzky in the service of the Russian Revolution in the 1920s, but on this occasion the glorification of model workers was replaced by the denunciation of bad Europeans, said to be present everywhere, especially in liberal and cultural circles, where their influence could supposedly be quantified: it was announced that 40 percent of artists were corrupt![4]

The exhibition debuted on 6 September at the Palais Berlitz on the boulevard des Italiens,[5] "in the busiest district of Paris,"[6] where the general public was invited to discover "the racial characteristics of the Jews"—in reality, to drop all resistance to the fate reserved for that group. There, everything hit the viewer in the gut. But, because mere caricature might have tipped the demonstration into farce, the massive presence of photographs, inevitably "objective" in the public's mind, reestablished the "truth." Although René Péron's poster announcing the exhibition drew on the conventions of the street fair,[7] it was described by journalists in all seriousness as "a great allegorical composition representing a kind of long-bearded vampire with thick lips and a hooked nose, whose gaunt fingers, resembling the talons of a bird of prey clutch a globe of the world."[8] The caricaturist had opted for a cross between Mephistopheles and an Epinal image of the wandering Jew, for a cinematographic or advertising style crossed with an expressionism whose excesses suited a haunted house ride: per the conventions of the genre, nothing should be left to chance, particularly not the text, when it came to producing revulsion. But who noticed that the tortured typography of "LE JUIF," where each stroke ended with a flamelike flourish, stood in stark contrast to the squareness of "FRANCE," whose characters were staunchly aligned at the base of the globe? In the production of hatred, however, nothing was gratuitous, and every medium deployed in the exhibition did its part to create the impression of cool "objectivity," whether photographs, montages, dioramas, or "historical" fresco, and to provide its share of "entertainment," whether caricatures or an enormous sculpted bust ("the Israelite facies"). Of all the paraphernalia enlisted to convince, the life-size black-and-white portraits, set up like silhouettes at a shooting gallery, likely awakened the strongest feelings.[9]

What proportion of the French managed to shake off the morbid fascination of a spectacle addressed more to the subconscious than to their intelligence? To what degree did they have the capacity to grasp how much that clearly marked route owed to the elementary experiments already done by the Nazis? How much, finally, were the attendance figures announced in *L'illustration*—eighteen thousand visitors in five days—to be taken seriously? France balked no doubt, just as Jérôme Carcopino, the Vichy minister in charge of national education and youth, balked when the occupier demanded that schoolchildren be sent on that haunted house ride.

Nevertheless, propaganda, more or less violent depending on who commissioned it, was spread across the walls, without anyone knowing clearly how much of it was to be attributed to the French government. The regime showed itself voluntarist in this matter, as no government had been up to then, but with an ambiguity that related to its tortuous political course. Despite a desire for unprecedented centralization (compared to the situation during World War I), the propaganda administration often changed its name and its director, following closely on struggles for power. Denis Peschanski has identified at least four periods, each corresponding to a different strategy for controlling French society.[10] During the first phase, Pétain, who saw propaganda as a way to consolidate his power and bolster his image, appointed the press baron Jean Prouvost as its head, but Prouvost resigned in July 1940, unable to stop the internecine quarrels or the anarchy of the information services. The second phase came in August 1941, with Paul Marion and his project

his instructions. He inevitably appears in them with bright, piercing eyes, without glasses, looking his best.

Ménétrel advised him to agree to a few exceptions, maintaining the contrary view that photography could not replace the artist's gesture and lacked "soul." Pétain thus met with at least a few candidates for the post of official artist, without officially choosing one of them over the others. In reality, the marshal's apparently eclectic policy, thought out or not, seemed singularly lacking in audacity, as he did not choose any definitive style. The true originality of the regime certainly did not lie in form, which was not very unified, but in the repetition of the major subject: Pétain himself, the famous victor of Verdun, father, grandfather, savior, martyr, who ultimately became a style in himself. In all, three registers in particular served to fix his image in his people's consciousnesses, simultaneously penetrating the public and private spheres: the first was photographic realism, the second was symbolism, and the last was the naïve and popular style.

These three genres drew not only from the fount of age-old traditions but also from that of a nascent modernism, giving the regime a multifaceted image. Whether by chance or not, the three artists closest to the marshal each worked in one of the favored registers. François Cogné, Robert Lallemant, and Gérard Ambroselli were all to some degree mavericks, on the fringes of the institutions of the fine arts but close to the tendencies on display at the time in the traditional Salons.

The first, Cogné, immortalized the marshal by sculpting his bust in the manner of virtuosos in love with realism. It gave viewers the impression that they were standing in front of a stereoscopic image, that is, before the marshal himself. The second, Lallemant, confined himself to the symbolic attributes associated with the head of state, particularly the two-headed ax, the so-called *francisque*, which he used as a significant but decorative motif, functionalizing it as he had learned to do from the moderns. Finally, the third, Ambroselli, was in charge of the ingenuous, folkloric, and retrograde version of the regime, inserting the marshal into the popular playfulness of Epinal images.

FROM PÉTAIN TO MANDEL

François Cogné[18] sculpted the photographically accurate bust of the marshal that, it was said, was to replace Marianne, symbol of the French republic, in the city halls and schools of France. At least initially, the mass-produced busts were seemingly not intended just as diplomatic or civic gifts: evidence is scanty, but it appears that the decision to remove Marianne was left up to the individual and that the allegorical figure of
Pl. 14 France often coexisted with a portrait of the Vichy head of state.[19] In

April 1941, the weekly review *Beaux-arts* headlined Cogné's bad luck: having avoided the ordeal of a competition and the academic circuits of officialdom, he was paying the price for an about-face at the highest level.[20] The journalists deduced that the marshal had not appreciated "so much publicity" and so announced that he was opposed to his bust being placed in every city hall, though this did not settle the matter. Was his action a rejection based on aesthetics, or was there a desire that "the memory of Marianne not vanish completely"? The reader is left unsatisfied, without access to all the evidence in a complex case.[21]

On 22 October 1940, the marshal did indeed authorize Cogné to have his sculpture produced so that it could become "the official bust,"[22] and he assigned the minister of public education and youth the task of working out the practical questions with the artist.[23] But Cogné quickly met with reluctance on the part of the fine arts administration, which balked at satisfying the desire of an ambitious maverick who had sidestepped the traditional rules governing public commissions, namely, selection by competition and the ceding of reproduction rights to the state. Economic uncertainties exacerbated the power struggle. Which agency—propaganda or fine arts—was going to pay the cost (about twenty million francs) for a large operation whose aim, at least in theory, was to distribute some 200,000 busts throughout France?[24] Richard, an adviser who was a staunch supporter of the fine arts administration, explained its verdict in a report of 28 March 1941: he noted that state commissions to artists were traditionally preceded by a competition and that the terms of the anticipated contract between the Réunion des musées nationaux and the artist assigned reproduction rights to the artist and, thereby, "significant sums of money, whereas other artists [were] in a very precarious situation." He therefore suggested setting aside a percentage of the profits from sales by national museums for "charitable assistance to artists" to be designated by the head of state.

Did Pétain bow to the reservations expressed by the art world, caught in the snare of "tradition"? Was he afraid he would be accused of being involved in an overly commercial enterprise with an artist ill regarded by the traditional art world? It was after Richard's report that his initial plan seems to have been abandoned, in favor of a more flexible solution that allowed local leaders to choose whether to order Cogné's famous bust of the marshal.[25] Nothing in his statue's manner could have displeased Pétain, who was depicted at his best, with virtuosity and sobriety, bareheaded, in his uniform from Verdun, with the single military medal he liked to sport in his official portraits.[26] Pétain had known the artist for a long time, and the latter had already depicted him in a very similar manner some ten years earlier. Cogné had undoubtedly asked to do a bust of Pétain in the late 1920s, before having a soldier named Leconte pose as the World War I veteran who would accompany him.[27] That tribute to victory and to the ordinary soldier captivated him so much that, in his revised will and testament of 1938, he granted permission for a monument in his memory to be erected in Verdun, as the municipality had long urged him to do.[28] On 21 January 1936, the marshal also decorated Cogné with the necklet of a commander of the Légion d'honneur.[29]

At the start of the occupation, Cogné, age sixty-four, had just sculpted Louis Hubert Gonzalve Lyautey[30] and François Darlan. He seemed crowned with official success even though his career did not have the same luster as those of his colleagues, who had been admitted to the Académie des beaux-arts or were sure to be so. Actually, he had mostly made a name for himself the hard way: his people were miners and blast furnace workers in Aveyron, and the decline of the region in the 1880s had obliged his family to move to Paris. There, he had not tried for the prestigious Académie des beaux-arts competition that would have made him eligible for the Prix de Rome. But he was one of the first to attend the new Ecole Boulle, created by the municipality to prepare students for careers in art. He placed second in sculpture in the entrance exam and graduated four years later, ready to respond to invitations to tender bids, which were not scarce, in that end of the century boom in architectural building. He thus went through the ordeals reserved for official apprentices, doing both institutional and private commissions: from a church (Saint-Bernard de la Chapelle) to a wedding hall (both in the 18th arrondissement), from the Pavillon de l'Indochine (at the Exposition universelle et internationale de Paris of 1900) to the interior decor of the auditorium of the Fémina theater—inaugurated in 1907—for which he sculpted, in the frieze, the faces of the celebrities of the day: Sarah Bernhardt, Constant Coquelin, and Yvette Guilbert. Thanks to his master Denys Puech,[31] his work was accepted by the Salon des Artistes Français, where he won the medal of honor in 1909 for his *Gypsy Woman*. The next year, he exhibited *Secret*, a female nude with a rounded belly. At age thirty, his success seemed assured, bolstered by his series of satirical masks of celebrities signed *Nogec* and reproduced in the review *L'assiette au beurre*. His purchase of a piece of property in 1911 attests to the affluence he had achieved by the time the war broke out (he would be wounded in the course of it).

Immediately after World War I, Cogné began a new official career. Having caricatured great men, he now undertook an extended series of busts glorifying them. Since his considerable charm and his sophistication allowed him to approach them easily, public figures were constantly visiting his studio on rue de Villersexel, where he immortalized the living and the dead: soldiers (Robert-Georges Nivelle; Joseph-Jacques-Césaire Joffre; Ferdinand Foch; Lyautey, clearly his favorite[32]); politicians and statesmen (Georges Clemenceau, Aristide Briand, Louis Barthou, Joseph Caillaux, Pétain, Paul Ramadier, the Spanish king Alfonso XIII); religious figures (Pius XII); administrators and architects (Paul Léon, director of fine arts; Henri Paté, high commissioner of sports; Georges-Eugène, Baron Haussmann); aviators (René Fonck, Maurice Boyau, Georges Guynemer); writers (Robert de Flers, Roland Dorgelès); stars (Maurice Chevalier, Gaby Morlay). In 1927, he said he was completing his thirtieth bust, which was of Clemenceau.

World War I also drastically altered the closed field of artistic officialdom. The demand for war memorials gave work to architects and sculptors, particularly since municipalities often preferred "custom-made work" by local personalities to mass-produced monuments.[33] In his depictions of celebrities and athletes,[34] Cogné had demonstrated that he excelled in the art of fidelity to his models. In 1920, in response to a request from the city hall of Saint-Germain-sur-Morin, where he had his secondary residence, he built a monument, measuring about nine feet by six feet, that depicted the villagers embracing one of their dying children. Then, in the same edifying style dictated by the commissions themselves, he designed a commemorative monument for Nangis; two proud World War I soldiers, one for Champagne-sur-Seine (in stone), the other for Lamarche in Vosges (in bronze); a "history lesson" for the main courtyard of the Lycée Carnot in Paris (1921); and a monument for Dombasle-sur-Meurthe (1925), a replica of the Lycée Carnot piece. Like his colleagues solicited from all sides, he turned a profit on pieces that could be modified only slightly to make them serve again for new commemorations. He thus dotted France with his monuments to the dead and his statues of famous men, of which the most familiar, located on the Champs-Elysées, depicts Clemenceau striding forward on a boulder from Fontainebleau.

Less than ten years later, the demand for official art gave Cogné an active role in the incarnation of the new French state. He had known the marshal well before the war and executed a bust of him in 1940, though it is not clear exactly how the sculptor proceeded. Perhaps, as for his bust of Pius XI, he took photographs, wrote down measurements, and hastily drew a few sketches during an initial sitting; then, alone in his studio, he roughed out a bust in modeling clay, in anticipation of a second sitting, during which he may have corrected his work, in order to complete the bust the next day.[35] Did Cogné work by taking as his starting point the bust of the marshal that he had already made or did he have Pétain pose again?

With or without his model before him, Cogné engraved and sculpted the marshal in his realist and almost photographic style, portraying him Pl. 12 at bust- or full-length, in military uniform, alive in every detail, looking only slightly younger than he was, only slightly glorified. The critic Arsène Alexandre characterized the artist as an innovator who, like James Abbott McNeill Whistler, liked to laboriously efface "the traces of labor." In Cogné's art, contemporaries would appear "as they were, neither more nor less."[36] On 16 May 1942, *L'illustration* devoted its front page to him, on the occasion of his exhibition at the most recent Salon des Artistes Français.

Did the town of Cusset, where his busts were manufactured, serve as a sanctuary for "young fugitives from Germany or threatened by the STO [Service du travail obligatoire]," as Marc-André Fabre argued in 1952?[37] In any case, the artist's later work seems to vouch for his conduct under the occupation. Like almost all Vichy officials, Cogné confined himself to "serving" the marshal as he had served other heads of state, without compromising with Nazism. As a result, after the war, he had the right to decorate with a bronze medallion a monument to Georges Mandel erected along Route National 7, just south of Fontainebleau, where the former interior minister had been murdered by the Vichy paramilitary unit Milice française. It is thus not surprising that on 7 July 1946, at the inauguration of the monument, Cogné could be found next to former prisoners of war and fifteen French ministers, including Paul Reynaud and Léon Blum. And on 18 September 1947, he was in Fontainebleau, inaugurating his "milestones on the road to freedom," for which he had produced a model in the shape of a torch. His design was chosen by général d'armée Alphonse-Pierre Juin to mark the path taken by Major General George S. Patton's United States Third Army between June 1944 and January 1945. Unsurprisingly, Cogné devoted his final days to military figures: Marie-Pierre Koenig, Jacques-Philippe Leclerc, Winston Churchill, and Juin. In short, his career ended very differently than that of Robert Lallemant, who preferred adventure, travel, and industry to the well-trod official trajectories.

THE MODERN AND THE ANCIENT

Lallemant's mission consisted of setting up the Service artistique du Maréchal. Did the head of state want yet again to be sure that the image of power would not deviate from his vision? In any event, he wanted to control at least part of the propaganda related to him meant for internal and external consumption: all the decorative or utilitarian objects distributed as gifts, in France and abroad, henceforth bore his mark—his portrait or his new symbol, the *francisque*. With this new department attached solely to his person, he invented an institution on the fringes of the traditional artistic organizations and broke with republican norms that had never fostered such an autocratic imagery.

Chosen as its head was the brother-in-law of the faithful Dr. Ménétrel, Robert Lallemant, who had always led a private life, without any involvement in politics.[38] Though his career had not predisposed him to take on such responsibilities—particularly since he had abandoned decorative art in favor of industrial work several years earlier—the former modernist designer agreed, primarily out of friendship, to follow his traditionalist impulses without abjuring his old functionalist convictions. In many respects, he belonged to the generation of artists who had taken stock of the evolution in government authority, which had long placed the applied arts in the service of industry.[39]

After leaving the Ecole des beaux-arts in Dijon, Lallemant turned to ceramics. But rather than conforming to the profile of a traditional potter, he took on that of a man fascinated by modernity. As one of his female admirers said,[40] there was something "of the tie rod, the screw thread, the engine, the rail," and even the artillery shell in his decorative work, which found a place in homes least resistant to recent advancements. His tastes were those of his friends in the Union des artistes modernes, with whom he exhibited in the early 1930s: function, industry, speed, the polished angles of cubism—but also African art and the primitive arts that were part of the new panoply marking the modern man.[41] These propensities remained with him until his accidental death in the mountains on 8 March 1954. Before then, he had abandoned ceramics in 1933 and left behind his kilns—though he kept his contacts in artistic circles—to join the family business of his father-in-law, Célestin D. Montcocol, who had played a role in the construction of the Paris metro at the start of the century.

The marshal's chosen official was not a quiet craftsman but rather a manic productivist, an athletic man in his forties, and an ardent seafarer. A volunteer in the navy, he arrived in Vichy only in August 1942, after being discharged in April by the French admiralty, which ordered an album of photographs from him. Lallemant actually remained in Vichy for little more than a year, dying to take to the open seas again, where different missions and different boats awaited him: he served on at least seven before the liberation. During that year, he had time enough, barely, to set up the Service artistique du Maréchal, and he declined the directorship of the Sèvres porcelain factory, which was too servile to the occupier's whims for Lallemant's taste. He did not as much as see the exhibition of the agency's works and had already left Vichy when a press campaign launched "marshal art." He had simply contacted a certain number of artists and developed a few models to be mass-produced in all sorts of media: silver or precious materials (from Puiforcat or from Degroote for the jewelry), glass (from Baccarat), iron, ceramic—and even plastic, such as the paperweight with the marshal's image that he arranged to have made at the Ecole nationale in Oyonnax.[42] If we are to judge by the list of artists who exhibited in May 1944 under the banner of the Service artistique du Maréchal, Lallemant had invited to the table more or less traditionalist artisans, all reputed for their expertise: Albert Decaris (a vase and a box), André Lavrillier (a medal and a stamp), Henri Dropsy (a small plate and a brooch), Cogné (a medal), Jean Picart Le Doux (a matchbox and a propaganda message), and himself (a paperweight and a drinking glass with the *francisque*).

After Lallemant's departure, it was not until spring 1944 that the marshal's artistic propaganda policy entered a new phase, just as the head of state was leaving Vichy to go into exile in Germany, on 7 May. The next day, Abel Bonnard, minister of national education and youth, opened the annual Salon de l'Imagerie Française at the Louvre. Rather than hosting unofficial propaganda by isolated artists, as it did every year, in 1944 the Salon to some extent celebrated the institutionalization of marshal art, in a room reserved for the Service artistique du Maréchal.[43] The display of objects of all kinds was not a revelation, but the works were strictly in keeping with the propagandist art placed in the service of the regime since its beginnings—formally eclectic, but effective in their message, most were decorated with the *francisque*, the colors of France, and the words of its leader. Unquestionably, the item that was most surprising came from the "marshal's tapestry workshop," which might have been expected to produce a justificatory image. But, for the first piece to come out of the Creusois workshop in Felletin, the designated artist, Jean-Denis Malclès, preferred the traditional and highly prized genre of the still life, combined with the reasonably modern style of the followers of Matisse and Picasso. Unless one associates this hymn to nature with the inevitable "return to the land," it is impossible to find the slightest direct allusion to the regime in its playful assemblage of flowers and grape clusters. The work referred in particular to the shows at the Salons and Parisian galleries open to art in the modern tradition, the result of a skillful compromise between classical traditions and the modern achievements of the early part of the century, which undoubtedly did not meet with unanimous approval, although it pleased an increasingly large public.

Was this so different from the program of the Service artistique du Maréchal, announced the previous month by the press attaché in Pétain's civil cabinet? The terms of the project were sufficiently vague as to exclude only art that did not serve "France"—and hence its leader.

In keeping with the formulas of the official rhetoric—which advocated moralism, nationalism, and a break with the immediate past—war was declared on "the excesses of anarchy" and on the "cold abstractions" that resulted from them, though a certain freedom remained in play. The solution lay in a return to the sources of "national genius, borrowing nothing from others," and in the "restoration of a strong regime." Not Germany but an old "French Europe" was invited to the banquet of rebirth, since the "invincible appeal" of the French language and of French arts was irresistible to other countries. And because it was impossible, in spite of everything, to draw on the marshal's words of wisdom in matters of art—he never spoke of it in public—the cultural lesson was to be drawn from his mother tongue, which he had done his utmost to defend when it was "attacked from the outside and undermined from the inside." The marshal had revived it well, "in a style sharp and pure as a sword's edge: it can be moving and achieve the sublime, while remaining clear." What was wished for was that the person of Pétain would be sufficient to fire up generations of artists, who would celebrate less "his glory and his merits" than "these eternal truths," by "grounding new masterpieces... in the old themes of nation, family, and work." All quite natural, until you got to the end of the program, where you could make out the fingerprints of the modernist (and once more seaborne) Lallemant. The Service artistique may well have relied on the usual assistance of artisans, draftsmen, painters, sculptors, and engravers, but it was more comfortable evoking "French industry, which has made itself the propagator of our country's genius throughout Europe." It sought "to get away from traditional conformism," just as "crystal and porcelain, in response to new ideas, embrace new forms."

Curiously enough, then, the technocratic and modern version of a regime officially oriented toward the past showed through. The manifesto of 1934 by the Union des artistes modernes, to which Lallemant had subscribed, was presented in terms of a Révolution nationale, whose loyalists obviously rejected neither progress nor the machine—"that blight" held responsible for every evil—nor intensive production nor rationalization.[44] Hence the impressive mass production of objects bearing the state's coat of arms might seem less anachronistic. Yet the Service artistique du Maréchal did not brilliantly demonstrate the regime's intention to fully rationalize its artistic propaganda. On the contrary: the very personality of Lallemant, who fled at the first opportunity, as well as the rudimentary nature of his organization and of its development, quickly brought to light the project's flaws. Even so, there was a real desire to intensify and systematize a propaganda practice that remained in its embryonic state until the defeat.

Did the modern side of marshal art embody a particular orientation within the regime, different from Pétain's own? The choices he made himself lead us to think that he was not especially resistant to the rationalization of images, at least when it concerned serial images expected to serve his ends. So if the old marshal is more readily associated with the obsolescence of small local craft industry and with childlike images, it is undoubtedly because mass-produced items of that kind inundated France more than any other form of propaganda and because they incarnated to perfection the dominant image of the regime and its lies.

THE NAÏVE STYLE

Gérard Ambroselli produced the best-known of this "naïve" imagery. He refashioned the history of France in an album that became known during the occupation for illustrating the official creed in clear and simplified lines, in the minor key of the Epinal print. The album's images moved from an everyday and familiar view of the old leader to heroic
Pls. 6, 7 scenes from his military life. Viewers may not know the artist's name, but everyone is familiar with Ambroselli's giant marshal, who has just stepped out of a fairy tale, his baby face serene and familiar, his left arm covered with stars, his light gray uniform standing out against the blacks of the war and of villages burned by "the traitors," his little French loyalists crossing wheat fields and vineyards to gather behind their savior.

After the demobilization of July 1940, général de brigade Jean-Marie-Gabriel de Lattre de Tassigny, whose trust Ambroselli had earned, urged him to come to the Hôtel du Parc in Vichy. There, later in 1940, Ambroselli was introduced to Pétain, who asked the artist, as he always did when he met one, what he knew how to do. While working for de Lattre, chief of the general staff, Ambroselli had exhumed the imagery of Epinal (laid to rest at the end of the nineteenth century). His images, manufactured with the help of Louis Joseph Soulas using traditional wood-engraving processes, were supposed to raise the morale of de Lattre's troops by honoring the heroes of the Armée d'Alsace. Printed in black and white, massive quantities were sent to Alsatian schools to be colored by the pupils. In line with Vichy's folklore policy[45] and the cult of the marshal, Pétain offered to have Ambroselli continue in his service and allocated him some funds so that he could open a small factory to his liking. Ménétrel was to keep an eye on things, while Jacques Bleck, who had been Pétain's driver during World War I, before representing a large fabric firm, was to oversee its management. On the evening of his meeting with the head of state, Ambroselli began by drawing a wounded soldier from 1940, picked up by the World War I veteran in front of a tattered flag. This drawing was to serve as a prototype for the advertisement for the Légion française des combattants, which was created shortly thereafter. Ambroselli then did a portrait of the marshal and a series of images engraved on wood by a professional[46] and stenciled by the villagers of the region: a cleaning woman who ran the workshop, young adolescents who developed a knack for the work, as well as housewives anxious to earn a little money. Indeed, the business turned out to be most profitable, to the point of supporting households while yielding real profits, as attested by the receipts of the Boutique de l'Imagerie Française opened in Vichy. Behind the charming light-blue storefront spangled with stars and *francisques*, the art lover could acquire at reasonable prices the album of prints of the marshal as well as nicely prepared series of traditional images designed to brighten up thatched cottages, including "Fables," "Fine Crafts in France," "Maxims and Sayings," and "Patron Saints."

In November 1942, however, after the occupation of the southern zone and de Lattre's escape to North Africa, which gave his close friend Ambroselli reason to worry, the marshal's image maker was to cease almost all activity, save for printing a few images of the Virgin. The next year he joined an armored division in Algiers. Two years later, he landed in Provence, went up the Rhône valley, entered Alsace, and liberated Colmar, before rejoining de Lattre's army. The general rehired him, this time to manufacture topical images to stick up on the walls of liberated cities.[47] While serving in de Lattre's Armée d'Alsace, before the defeat, Ambroselli had begun to represent Nazism as a wolf covered with swastikas. He now reestablished his ties with the French republic, by drawing, without a change in style, famous French military men from history: Louis-Lazare Hoche; Jean-Baptiste Kléber; Henri de La Tour d'Auvergne, vicomte de Turenne; Sébastien Le Prestre de Vauban—and de Lattre, of course. When Ambroselli asked de Lattre how many portraits of him to reproduce, the general responded that he wanted five tons of them. Ambroselli's career, though not over, had to adapt to new circumstances. His imagery did not weather liberation with the same success it had enjoyed during the occupation, though the artist did print a few more engravings. Ultimately, he accepted other commissions and moved on to sculpture. In 1990, he produced a monumental Jesus Christ, in a photo-realist style, for a small Alsatian church.

VICHY SPECIALTIES

Like most of the artists who served the regime, Ambroselli had not seen any Germans and believed, at the time, that in serving the marshal he was serving the country. An intransigent Catholic and a traditionalist, he was different from both Cogné and the modernist Lallemant. In the end, each of the three had his own character, his own way of serving his leader, his own way of believing in France. Two of the three were soldiers, however, and they all shared an ability to charm Pétain with their loyalty and with a career successfully learned "on the job," far from the academic aristocracy. In fact, the marshal, who might have recruited more conformist and steady individuals, preferred to rely on chance encounters and relationships, watched over by his trusted Ménétrel. He could also count on the impromptu aid of all their rivals within officialdom (a good hundred or so), among whom it is difficult to distinguish the ingrained propensity to serve whatever regime was in power from sincere loyalty to the Vichy regime.[48] Although it would be impossible to find in that little constellation of stars a common style and identity, roughly speaking the artists fell into the three categories already mentioned (in relation to the marshal's three favorite artists), whose many variants were on display during the traditional Salons, at the Hôtel du Parc, and above all at the influential Salon de l'Imagerie Française. Run by some six hundred small craftsmen, devout and often knowledgeable about the cause of folklore championed by the marshal[49]—in whose honor the first competition was held, in 1941—the Salon de l'Imagerie Française was able to exhume the old means of edifying: the fashionable traditional symbols from the Middle Ages, two-dimensional spaces, broad gestures, blank areas, the grandeur of coded subjects, the legible and nostalgic imagery of Epinal, and, to a lesser degree, more "modern" treatments of archaic themes. Although the marshal took pride of place, other saints (Joan of Arc, for example), martyrs, and popular historical figures came to sanctify his divinity in the diverting style of the propaganda of yesteryear. Its defenders easily convinced various official administrations of the efficacy of friendly, peaceable, mass-produced little images, which were liable to quietly work their way into people's imaginations by reminding them of the old days through illustrations in official papers, documents, regulations, and corporatist propaganda,[50] but also on diplomas and awards dispensed by the French state. This avalanche found an echo in the fables and popular songs that reached the French people with even greater ease.

Indeed, the strengths of the marshal style were its eclecticism and its ability to use every distribution network, every medium, and every material. In its way, Vichy was an innovator. It diffused its image throughout France, in its shops and information centers, supported by a resurgence of trade and by its faithful agents, including Secours national and the Chantiers de la jeunesse and other youth movements. Furthermore, although propaganda had previously been limited to elementary diplomatic maneuvers—gifts to chiefs of state, a few honors granted to exceptional citizens—Vichy became a formidable producer of all sorts of objects meant not only to regale its foreign friends but also to shower the French people in its service with awards, commensurate with their actions and their importance. For deserving subjects, there were Sèvres vases of all sizes decorated with the *francisque* and with stars (especially those by Lallemant); the marshal's portrait, quota- Pl. 9 tions from him, and medallions in biscuit; and busts of the French leader in terra-cotta or, more precious, in Sèvres biscuit (especially those by Cogné). Finally, for all and sundry, there were ashtrays, medals, minuscule busts, portraits on frosted glass, penknives, photographs, vignettes, or the famous album of twelve prints by Ambroselli.

In return, there were the countless gifts sent from all over France to pay tribute to the marshal that ended up in the cellars of the Hôtel du Parc. It was as if the regime's propaganda had awakened every artisan—supposedly spontaneously—each proud to belong to the greater nation as well as to his region, his village, his trade, or even his brotherhood. The inventory of these gifts reveals not the generosity of indi- Pls. 15–17 viduals acting in isolation (this was rather rare) but the voluntarism of municipalities, professional and trade organizations, managers of work projects, groups effectively under state control, and religious and educational institutions. All sent the marshal their local specialties: canes, kepis, wine, boxes of cookies or candies, decorative objects, jewelry, tapestries, embroidered handkerchiefs, and so on. In this hodgepodge produced by official artists as well as by all the "anonymous" makers, the fragmented image of the regime corresponded to the aspirations of each.

Emulators of the photographic style were the architects of a message that was modern, direct, and apparently realistic (after retouching). From simple black-and-white photography to the most "lifelike" stereoscopic reproduction (a "remarkable French invention"),[51] from stylized sculpture by the virtuoso to coins carved from seashells, the genre prospered by imposing on the country the misleading image of a perfectly "cast" leader, still young and with a piercing gaze. The censored proofs or, some years later, a few television close-ups, would have jeopardized that image in short order.

The symbolic style gave rise to all sorts of variations, especially of the *francisque*, the famous ax chosen by the marshal to embody the regime: the ancient weapon of the Germans but equally the Franks, as ambiguous as its mentor. Pétain began by prohibiting anyone from depicting or wearing it without observing certain merit-based rules,[52] but he still encouraged the widespread, decorative, and massive use of the simple sign, reminiscent of the lyric form of the cross. Hence, the *francisque* Pl. 8

adorned every object possible, even those famous escutcheons embroidered on white grounds, which revived the vogue for heraldry.[53]

The regime's naïve style ultimately fostered a childish familiarity with the leader, who was reduced to the status of a toy soldier manhandled by clumsy but pious hands. There was apparently a world of difference between this naïveté of technique and the authority of the huge depictions of the marshal exhibited during important official ceremonies. Consider, for example, the portrait unfurled on 8 May 1944, for the festival in Lyon in honor of Joan of Arc. Philippe Henriot, flanked by a group of militiamen, delivered a fierce speech in front of this image, which was more than sixteen feet tall, framed like a painting, and surrounded by a play of tricolor flags, gammas, and *francisques*. Between a movie still and a silk screen, even now the image no longer belongs to the dark years but brings to mind the "modern" images of Benito Mussolini disseminated in Fascist Italy[54] as well as a French version of the pop art to come. With its large areas of solid color, its strong shadows, and its sleekness, it no doubt had a better chance than Ambroselli's childlike little scenes of complying with the radical style of the Fascist French orator Henriot and with the liberties taken by all who, like him, sought to shake up the image of a judicious and out-of-date national revolution. The Revolution nationale in fact embraced various causes, various representations, various artists.

The absence of famous names might suggest that an artist had to be "in need" before he joined the ranks of the Révolution nationale and perhaps had to believe that at least his chances of becoming part of history thereby increased tenfold. As it turned out, that was not at all the case. But the artists were not really blamed for their actions: the postwar purge, as we will see, punished only "the collaborators." Those who had begun their careers in the service of democracy continued them altogether naturally, while others faced, on occasion, a few retaliatory measures without major consequences. One result was the metamorphosis of an outmoded style. Of the genres in force under the occupation, only what was still consistent with the messages of the democratic state would persist into the future. It is not that political propaganda disappeared: on the contrary, it became more systematic, more subtle, more effective perhaps. Of the three styles practiced under Vichy, the new French Republic chose the (photo-)realist mode, disregarding the other two. Lallemant, who had a modern vision, was content to plaster the symbols of power onto geometric forms that, once the regime had fallen, no longer had anything official about them. As for Ambroselli's Epinal imagery, it no longer had a place within a France oriented toward modernity.

Only the "precision" of photographic "realism," with its academic variants and its host of "artistic" effects (recall the posters that secured President François Mitterrand's victory: his face superimposed on a tranquil small-town France), still had its place. We need only consider the Cogné-style busts—usually manufactured by virtuosos of the Institut de France—with which officialdom continued to be smitten after the war. There was therefore a great deal of continuity, with the exception of certain "Vichy specialties," which were packed away in storerooms of historical museums and collections of secondhand dealers.

Marshal art was not very different from the art realized under other regimes. It only added the figure of Pétain and the emblems of his Révolution nationale to the same old styles.[55] That was precious little by the Pl. 11
standards of a market repelled by the frenzied productivism of Vichy, which transformed every official piece into a vulgar industrial object. All the same, for four years, that which later became a weakness, and rapidly so, was the strength of a regime oriented toward the production of a propaganda for the masses and of mass-produced propaganda.

THE LAW OF SERIES

In terms of propaganda, stamps had a tremendous capacity for distribution. At a time when a French citizen's every movement was being watched, the postal system set the French leader in motion over and over again, by devoting more than six billion stamps to his person:[56] seventeen series to his glory and his favorite themes. This was one of the best propaganda operations, and it was not undermined by the modesty of its format—although the stamps were sometimes transformed into giant posters, as for the Exposition des artisans français at the Palais de Pl. 13
la porte de Versailles in October 1942. Every household in France inevitably engaged in philately, a repetitive and anodyne act of allegiance, despite the fact that it broke the rules for the use of French postage stamps. Indeed, though no modern constitutional statute governed the production of stamps depicting a head of state, custom dictated that a likeness not be issued until after his death. Pétain thus joined the only other exception to the rule: Napoléon III.

At the start of the regime, the most eloquent images from among a hundred models devoted to the cult of the marshal were selected by means of a competition. Oddly enough, these images respected the continuity of the genre: the subject was certainly different, but the stamps conserved their usual academic and virtuoso style, which the artists generally had learned while at the Ecole française de Rome. In fact, when *Le monde des philatélistes* placed a stamp honoring Marshal Pétain side by side with one of General de Gaulle,[57] the resemblance was striking, the elementary design identical. Both heads of state, one in military uniform and kepi, one in civilian clothes and bareheaded, are accompanied by their symbolic attributes, the *francisque* and the cross of Lorraine, respectively. That exercise deliberately recalled the imperatives of official art, identical under Vichy and under the French Republic. In this case as elsewhere, differences could be perceived by the persistent observer, but only in the details.

In addition to the inevitable presence of the leader that attested, once again, to the autocratic aims of the new regime, the accompanying inscriptions conferred on the subjects very different political attitudes. Hence, the words *Postes françaises* or *Etat français* appeared below the portraits of the marshal, above the "muscular" motto *Travail, Famille, Patrie* of 1943, while the phrase *République française* was de Gaulle's watchword. But here, as in other cases, the voluntarism of the Vichy regime was sometimes undermined by contradiction as far as "change" was concerned. Classic stamps from the prewar period—Iris, Mercury, The Sower, and Peace—were still issued with the old legend of *République française.*

During these four years, the state's issuance of stamps responded to events, even though two-thirds of new stamps were regularly devoted to the traditional official subjects valued in a democracy. Marshal art
Graph 4 took up the last third, and a bar graph of the series of stamps issued makes clear the persistence of the head of state's image until 1943. If we add up the series dealing with the propagandistic themes of the regime fashioned in the marshal's image, we find that the year 1941, caught up in the euphoria of the regime, holds the record. Yet continuity was assured by the postage stamp artists, who, with the exception of a few new recruits, did not change. They were likewise in the best position upon liberation to ensure a continuation to which no one would object, since the genre itself was destined to accommodate the most varied allegiances. Feigned or not, the commitment of the artists seemed to have more to do with the practice of a certain style than with the subject treated. The advantages of official status, the earnings from a valued specialization, the assurance of never being without commissions were undoubtedly in their eyes well worth the price of having an agenda that was at once very restrained and quite fantastic imposed on them. Consider the case of Jules Piel, winner of the Prix de Rome in 1910, who produced a number of illustrations for banknotes and, in 1936, the engraving of a stamp designed by René Grégoire depicting the socialist Jean Jaurès addressing the Chambre des députés. He drew and then engraved the figure of the marshal in 1940 and in 1941; but that did not prevent him from producing a stamp of the anarchist thinker Pierre-Joseph Proudhon

in 1948, then a Marianne after a design by Louis-Charles Muller in 1955. Similarly, in 1941 Pierre Gandon, a painter and the winner of the Prix de Rome in 1921, paid an academic tribute to the head of state; but it was forgotten much more quickly than his Marianne on the barricades of 1945 and his Marianne as Liberté of 1982, issued in vast quantities to embody a classic and unifying variant of the French Republic inspired by Eugène Delacroix's *Liberty Leading the People*. The latter stamp has only recently been dethroned in favor of Louis Briat's computerized image of a more "dynamic" France.[58]

It is thus not the list of artists chosen by the regime that reveals Vichy's specialties but the unique way their works were instrumentalized. In the same way, the public toward whom the propaganda was directed was used to having certain "civic" messages imposed on it—but within certain quantitative limits, which were largely exceeded by Vichy. At least the adults could resist the onslaught—if they understood it as such. But the young, a "fresh and malleable mass," were subjected, more dangerously, to an efficiently executed propaganda campaign, by turns cajoling and constraining.

TARGETING THE YOUNG

Of all the groups within the French population, it was undoubtedly the young—schoolchildren included—that those in charge of propaganda targeted as their first priority. In charge was Pétain, who had long been persuaded that political change depended on a revolution of the social environment. After years of raging against a teaching staff that was "secularist," antifascist, and pacifist, he could finally announce, as part of his Révolution nationale of July 1940, a reform of the school system and a purge of teachers. The normal schools for teacher training were eliminated on 18 September, and during the second half of 1940, more than twenty teachers were dismissed every day. In 1941, four million students of all ages and their 130,000 instructors were supposed to submit to an unprecedented set of directives: salute the flag weekly in the schoolyard (the occupier had little taste for this); sing in chorus the famous "Maréchal, nous voilà!" every day before classes; have the school curriculum reviewed and corrected by "revolutionary" commissions; participate in physical education classes, obligatory despite the privations of wartime; read the copious literature devoted to convincing the young—and their parents—of the merits of the Révolution nationale; and finally, of course, demonstrate allegiance to Pétain, whose omnipresent image, preferably tacked to pupils' desks, reminded them at every instant that a sacred figure protected the schoolchildren of France.

Even in the school supplies sector, that reassuring figure of the leader stood permanent guard against the anonymity of power, covering notebooks, penholders, and prizes. To all this, the teachers, who were usually loyal to the democratic French Republic, responded by dragging their feet as long as they could—when they did not turn to the Resistance—by conscientiously overlooking the little ceremonies glorifying the marshal that had been imposed. As for the young targets, could the program seriously appeal to a population rather resistant to the "joys of exertion"? They were more likely to appreciate the rewards in kind that their affection for the old leader sometimes brought them. Hence, on behalf of the Inspection générale de l'enseignement primaire, Chattelun spread some good news in his note of 17 March 1941: the head of the propaganda service at Entraide d'hiver du Maréchal had just informed him that awards would be bestowed on the fifteen hundred students from the *département* Seine who distinguished themselves in the sale of Pétain's portrait. They would earn a large image of the head of state; in addition, "a kilogram of dates" would go to "each of the best 375 salesmen among the pupils."[59] That was better, all in all, than the supplementary rations of casein crackers distributed to those who accompanied an adult to a public rally in support of the marshal.

Operations began in winter 1940, within the framework of the campaign run by Entraide d'hiver, and the marshal's cabinet ministers were delighted with the success of the "postcards of Marshal Pétain" that schools requested in growing numbers. In November 1941, the prefecture of the Seine sent out a note that encouraged directors of professional, primary, and nursery schools to raise funds from students and staff members: the image of the marshal (engraved by Gandon) was being put up for sale to benefit Secours national, which would redistribute the proceeds to prisoners of war and their families. The idea was to "emphasize the highly helpful character of the fundraiser," while touting the "artistic quality" of the portrait, which deserved to "occupy the place of honor in every school."[60] The marshal would be ever vigilant. The minister of national education and youth, Jérôme Carcopino, emphasized that young people had to be invited to participate in the national effort being implemented by Secours national, the Red Cross, and committees aiding the families of prisoners. It was up to every classroom to assume responsibility for the relief of unfortunate prisoners and refugees, by collecting everything it could for care packages.

On 18 March 1942, Carcopino wrote to school inspectors, inviting them to intensify the effort, by setting up fundraisers in schools that had not yet had the opportunity to sell Gandon's image. Students in any institution that collected more than one hundred francs for the fund would receive a print on China paper of the work in question.[61] Previously,

Carcopino had announced that altogether the sale of portraits, plaques, and objects devoted to the head of state's glory had reached, as of 15 October 1941, the tidy sum of 16,846,000 francs.[62]

It was decidedly easier to convince the young by combining brainwashing with entertainment: instructions focused most on classes in drawing or handicrafts, and teachers put on the agenda the themes of the moment, particularly the figure of the marshal, who—along with the "image makers of France" album by Ambroselli[63]—served all the children in France as a model for their coloring beginning in 1941. And since nothing or almost nothing could be left to chance in this first "guided" exercise, any symbolic license was forestalled: text in the margins gave strict instructions for rendering the "true" color of history. Youngsters had to associate the marshal's life with the French flag, which was supposed to inspire "more than liking—devotion, as they inscribed in its folds the very pure blue, the explosive red. They [would] set off the white."

Once educated in the "true" image of their leader, young people of all ages were invited to celebrate his "legendary figure."[64] Thus the subject was mass-produced without necessarily glorifying the model, whose physiognomy was not yet "fixed": inspiration came more from the puppet Punch than from official portraits. The marshal often took on the air of a street urchin, systematically rejuvenated and covered with symbolic attributes cherished by children: medals, kepi, officer's stripes. What did it matter? At Christmastime in 1940, Vichy was delighted to receive nearly two million drawings, the "best" of which were exhibited at the Grand casino de Vichy, and every child was sent a postcard bearing the grandfather's image, plus a short message "in his hand." The next year, 1,440 privileged individuals were invited to come in person to present the head of state with their good wishes. In this merit contest, did the judges separate the wheat from the chaff? As a last resort, the media reinforced the meaning of these repeated tributes. The press gushed over the children's exhibition in January 1942, first at the Musée Galliera, then at the Musée Cognacq-Jay.[65] Some months later, it was similarly delighted with the exhibition contest on "youth festivals in the France of tomorrow," which was open to young people aged fifteen to twenty-one, who were called this time to "joy and exertion."[66] Henri d'Amfreville—a Sunday painter and head of the art bureau of the general secretariat of youth,[67] responsible for showing the youngsters' works—established firm connections between his "revolutionary" pedagogical project and the return to national order. His language bordered on esoteric and soppy gibberish: it was in fact the children who were to educate the adults, since they were far "beyond men in their feelings," not yet corrupted by clever reasoning but still instinctual, having nothing to do with "the prestige of History" but going straight to the marshal, guided by a "secret affinity" and by "the call of blood ties." He read out sincere little passages written on the backs of the children's pictures: one from six prodigies who merely signed their names in a column, professing that they were "too little" to draw as yet but surely not to give a "great big" hug to the marshal; another from the child who said that his work was not yet finished but that did not keep him from loving "his marshal." And because it was necessary to make sense of such divine spontaneity, d'Amfreville ranked the young novices by region, capitalizing on Pétain's revival of the provinces, by evoking, as always, the harmful influence of the city and modernization on young minds. The urban youth of France were seduced by the mere "copy," by "store windows and their piles of illustrated propaganda," by everything that "the little people in the country"[68]—less wicked, less superficial, more concrete—would manage to escape for a while longer.

ON YOUR MARK

For there it was: abstraction, they said, that is what is failing France, in art as elsewhere, and first and foremost in the schools, where the excesses of a "sit-down pedagogy" had stuffed minds "without reaching souls"[69]—or bodies. Education no longer toughened up these young people, spoiled by a verbalism that no longer took its cue from reality. How, under such conditions, could matter not have taken its revenge during the defeat, a state of affairs now requiring that control be reexerted over man as a whole: body, mind, and character? Thus Rabelais was called to the rescue of a stupefied and sprawling youth, to recommend playing ball and tennis in the morning; horse riding, spear throwing, javelin throwing, ax throwing, shooting, jumping, wrestling, swimming, and rock climbing in the afternoon. So was Michel de Montaigne, with his "hale and hearty" boy, inured to sweat, cold, wind, and sun, and to all the dangers he would need to defy. Then there was Jean-Jacques Rousseau, who dragged his Émile through the countryside in any weather, barefoot and bareheaded, convinced it was better not to teach at all than to teach too much.[70] And finally, closer to the present, Henri Bergson, for whom man was not pure intelligence but an active being.[71]

Armed with these lessons for the edification of depraved youth, those responsible for French reform had only to update a program to which the Front populaire had already given renewed popularity. In this case as elsewhere, the continuity is strikingly apparent, even though Vichy, through its excesses, ultimately proved unique.[72] The defeat allowed the later regime to accuse its predecessors of bequeathing it an army of incompetents and rejects. In 1918, 26 percent of eligible men in France were unfit for military service versus 27 percent in Germany; in 1938, it was 33 percent versus 17 percent. Jean Borotra, a graduate of the Ecole polytechnique and former tennis champion, served Vichy as the first general commissioner of sports between 13 July 1940 and 18 April 1942. He had ample opportunity to conduct an unprecedented fitness policy that would obliterate the memory of the terrible decline of bodies. He was in charge of a budget of nearly two billion francs to develop facilities (compared to fifty million francs in 1939 for fitness policy as a whole). Less authoritarian than his successor, Colonel Pascot, Borotra could run with the hare and hunt with the hounds. At times he even looked to the past: in Paris on 5 October 1941, he went so far as to celebrate the memory of Léo Lagrange, who had been in charge of fitness policy under Léon Blum and who died on the battlefield in a village in Aisne on 9 June 1940. With him, athletic events took on the ostentation of grand patriotic celebrations where the national anthem and French flags were everywhere apparent. Ultimately, Borotra alarmed the Germans who, suspecting him of Anglophilia, impeded his reforms and ended up arresting him, six months after his dismissal on 18 April 1942. Nonetheless, despite opposition from the church, which was hostile to the glorification of the body, and from the Académie de médecine and parents alarmed by the exertions forced on underfed young people living on starvation rations of 1,800 calories a day or less, Borotra achieved his goal,[73] increasing the number of athletic organizations, records, sportsmen—and sportswomen. Paradoxically, at a time when the new status of women confined them to the joys of home and family, the younger generation of girls took advantage of their temporary freedom to disport themselves in nature. Indeed, it was outdoor sports that had the most success, less in response to the old marshal's famed call to return to the land than to the recent discovery of skiing, mountaineering, kayaking, and scuba diving.

Malnourished, shivering in makeshift garments, the French, young and not so young, had never subjected their bodies to so much use. Jean-Louis Gay-Lescot described admirably the gap in understanding that opened in 1940 between the official proponents of sports activity and the masses of sportsmen. For the officials, sports were a means to maintain order and hierarchy, to obscure social conflicts and religious differences, to train the young people to be not so much "athletic" as "rustic." The masses, in need of distractions, saw sports—along with shows and art exhibitions—as an effective way to lighten the morose atmosphere. This conjuration against fate was facilitated by the government's own policy, which showed all the ambiguity of a regime that dispensed venom and antivenom by turns—but primarily venom after April 1942, when Pascot's reign put an end to Borotra's popularity.

Under such conditions, it is not surprising to find artists ready to compete, if not in stadiums, then at least in the decoration thereof. Often largely insensitive to the regime's true motivations, those concerned benefited from its official information policy and from its broad recruitment of makers of posters, plaques, medals, trophies, sculptures, and vignettes. In 1941, the new Serment de l'athlète, or athlete's oath, provided an opportunity to launch a poster competition, which was won by Bernard Villemot, Jean A. Mercier, and Pellos. Were the posters Pétainist or just naïve? What was true of the subject was also true of the depictions: you had to be very sharp to find a difference between the "Front populaire" style of sports imagery and the new regime's still-benign variety. It is therefore not surprising that, the next year, the Salon de l'Imagerie Française adopted a popular theme that was broadly treated in the mode of the Epinal image or with high-spirited, breezy naïveté. Between May and July 1942, the many products of the "sports trophy grand prix" were exhibited at the Louvre's Pavillon de Marsan. There was an endless stream, from medals to pictures, posters, programs, souvenirs, diplomas, scarves, signs, animated cartoons, and postcards. Gilbert Poillerat, Roger Bezombes, and Marcel Gili were among a long list of artists who displayed their modest tributes to exertion there.

Earlier, in February 1942, at Vichy's town hall, during a major exhibition titled *L'art et le sport*, Borotra and Carcopino had sanctioned the official willingness to unite two inextricable genres, a willingness reaffirmed the following year by a lecture cycle at the Sorbonne designed to scientifically warrant the validity of a program seeking to revive ancient traditions, combine strength with beauty, and assure the permanence of an old idea reactivated by a situation that now benefited the aesthetes. At Vichy, it was not merely minor artists who exhibited, as at the Salon de l'Imagerie Française, but also a constellation of regulars from the more or less traditional Parisian Salons: Dunoyer de Segonzac, Vlaminck, Belmondo, Yves Alix, Luc-Albert Moreau, Raymond Gid, André Jacquemin, La Patellière, Jean-Emile Laboureur, Alexandre Savignac, and Hubert Yencesse, but also Raoul Dufy, Jacques Villon, Edouard Goerg, Marcel Gromaire, Charles Walch, François Desnoyer, and André Lhote. This shows the popularity sports enjoyed with artists—and with a public catered to by the official media and the mainstream press, which often amounted to the same thing.

Jean Giraudoux, who ultimately signed his name to the preface of the album in honor of the marshal produced for the February exhibition in Vichy, had staked out his position the previous year. Since he liked to tally art reviews and gymnasts, he deduced from them that nations with the highest percentage of the first—Finland and Germany—were also those who enjoyed the most advantageous percentage of athletes. That gave him an opportunity to flatter the occupying forces and to humiliate the French, whose reputation as idlers was already made. But, above all, it gave him an opportunity to point a finger at his own people and to reserve the largest share of his bile for his own community: intellectuals were "the head of the nation," and "there [was] no reason for that head to be ugly,"[74] he snickered. Texts abound that, in this vein, vaunt the merits of physical exertion immediately followed by moral recovery. As for illustrations, the entire French press fell in line with the athletic iconography of totalitarian countries. Even reviews with cultural pretensions subjected their readers to the exemplarity of a well-built body, preferably in motion. Agrarian France now had its landscape of the body, its "beautiful human atlas," and was ready to take Henry de Montherlant at his word: in 1940, the writer had compiled his "reverent collection of young French bodies,"[75] preparing the way for the future.

That is how it had been since the defeat: in the final analysis, it was still possible to immediately grasp that the runner, knee to the ground and on his mark, in Dunoyer de Segonzac's classic drawing—reproduced on the front page of a weekly newspaper—was also France, still fighting anywhere the vanquisher conceded one last space for revenge. Of course, this was far from Breker's Nazi Übermensch, modeled on the very athletic Gustav Stührk. Here as elsewhere, France remained modest and reconciled with difficulty its agrarian image, weakened by rationing, and its athletic, hygienic, and triumphant double. In the same way, it was surprising to see artists convene on the sports fields, when in the popular imagination they belonged to the dissipated ranks of the revelers. Indeed, the art world, universally attacked for its vices, was to be reformed from top to bottom. After all, the first to respond to the regime's call for contributions had showed its goodwill by rejoining at last the suffering body of the nation. It was a step on the path toward the militarization desired by the regime, which was betting on the raised awareness of a cantankerous sector, accustomed to marginality—and discomfort.

THE FINE ARTS ADMINISTRATION

Every ministry and every department—sports, youth, propaganda, the Service artistique du Maréchal, the City of Paris,[76] in short, all the rivals of the fine arts administration (under the supervision of six successive ministers of national education and youth)[77]—endeavored to seduce a population that was recalcitrant by nature. To fine arts fell the principal effort and the charge to serve by calling on their ranks to rebuild, like everyone else. Louis Hautecoeur, at its head from July 1940 to April 1944, was a loyal Pétainist and did not feel he was espousing an extravagant cause. An academic and museum curator,[78] he was among the staunch traditionalists who had not waited for the Révolution nationale to embrace its program of "reform." Although his duties as an administrator did not make him a member of government compelled to adopt a "political" (as opposed to a "technical") posture, he felt in tune with the regime, at least with its "patriotic" Pétainist side. He was hostile toward Laval, who in 1941 tried to undermine his program by imposing the Laval loyalist Georges Hilaire in Hautecoeur's place. Especially from the time of Laval's return to power in spring 1942, Hautecoeur was hampered by that threat and by the preeminence of Abel Bonnard, installed, against the marshal's recommendation, at the ministry of national education and youth, which oversaw the fine arts administration.[79]

We have seen how Laval and his men replaced defense of France's patrimony with a policy of active collaboration, selling off collections at bargain basement prices and encouraging events sponsored by the occupier, the Breker exhibition in particular. Between his appointment and his dismissal in April 1944, however, Hautecoeur more or less succeeded in following the course he himself had set. His principal aims were to defend the national collections; acquire works of art; reform the museums and factories; strengthen the administration's power, especially outside of Paris;[80] get rid of the existing Conseil supérieur des beaux-arts, which was too modernist for his taste; and similarly reform the education of curators[81]—and artists.[82] All this was carried out by civil servants already in place before the occupation and who, Hautecoeur was pleased to see, remained at their posts, with not a single one "crossing the border."[83]

In his methods and choices, he remained true to the tradition of the cultural agencies to which he had been close. In 1937 particularly, when he was named to lead the artistic organization of the Exposition internationale des arts et techniques dans la vie moderne, he championed an unoriginal program, intending to give the work to those most poverty-stricken, despite a brittle certainty that the arts sector would never really forgive him.[84] He was regularly reproached for being too conciliatory toward "the cubists" and for behaving like an ethnologist rather than a decision maker or a man of taste.[85] Belying such criticisms, in terms of state commissions he was guided by common sense, which had led to official France falling behind on contemporary art. It is instructive that at the time of the preparations for the Exposition internationale of 1937, he stinted with the commission granted to Robert and Sonia

Delaunay and Félix Aublet for the decoration of the transportation pavilions. The artists were to receive 132,000 francs, but Hautecoeur asked that their fee be reduced: it was unfair, he said, for the price per square meter (between 475 and 692 francs) of an "entirely geometric" design with "very large zones" covered with "flat colors" to be on par with that for designs with "figures."[86]

In fact, Hautecoeur personified the reactionary version of the French administration. At the time of the Front populaire and the reign of Georges Huisman, the administration had distinguished itself by its unusual voluntarism in the fine arts, concurrently endorsing "independent" and "modern" art, endeavoring to "popularize" culture (no doubt less effectively than the private sector), and modernizing the education program and museum operations.[87] In that domain, Hautecoeur, who was fundamentally elitist, broke with the "Marxian" tone of his predecessor Huisman, who declared in 1937 that "after creating the museums for the elite in the eighteenth century and for the bourgeoisie in the nineteenth, it was now necessary to undertake the organization of museums for the common people, who know nothing of them."[88] In the midst of the Front populaire, Huisman was swept up in a wave of enthusiasm and impelled, at the highest level, by Blum, Jean Zay, and Jean Cassou, to push forward the Delaunays' modern projects and the pavilion of the Union des artistes modernes, whose spare style irritated traditionalists such as Hautecoeur.

More than his predecessor, Hautecoeur, who would be admitted to the Académie des beaux-arts in 1952 (and would become its permanent secretary),[89] privileged a middle-of-the-road, figurative art handled in a learned but timorous manner, which generally meant landscapes, still lifes, or portraits, the majority by artists for the most part forgotten by history—all the while appealing for support for a more "edifying" art. Pierre Ladoué, chief curator of the Département d'art moderne and inspector general of fine arts, hastened to provide that support: "In the year of war 1942," he called for works "executed with funds from the masses" (large-scale public commissions) to be used for "the intellectual development of the masses" and to elicit "loftier thoughts than the thoughts making up ordinary life."[90]

Although the state's purchasing commission clearly privileged mural decorations, especially as of 1942, in practice very few large-scale commissions answered the didactic aims of these leaders and of a good many critics. In 1943, a campaign conducted by Marcel Raval had vainly promoted Porte Maillot, a monumental housing complex endorsed by Auguste Perret and Aristide Maillol. Was the failure due to lack of time or of financing or to the spinelessness of decision makers?

The only monumental project seriously developed was a Greco-Roman complex designed for the Autoroute de l'Ouest, reminiscent of the pomp of the Exposition internationale of 1937 or of Speer and Breker's plans for the new Berlin, only less colossal. Some, always on the lookout for the "failures" of the Révolution nationale, found that design regrettable in advance.[91]

The state's purchasing commission enjoyed an appreciably higher Graph 1 budget in 1940, but its subsequent allocation gradually declined until 1945.[92] The commission, considerably restricted at Hautecoeur's own request,[93] gave a lower priority to ambitious projects—the artists and the works that it felt must become part of the national collections at any cost—than to those that "needed" it most. A crisis program largely begun in 1937, it was fondly remembered by all those, of various artistic persuasions, who had benefited from it, at the expense of the more "radical" currents, which the collegial commissions—even tempered by a few modernist decision makers—did not want to encourage. Of the many works acquired and commissioned under the occupation, how many would be remembered in history for their importance? Against a few minor pieces by Pierre Bonnard, Albert Marquet, and Matisse,[94] how many outdated acquisitions would be left in storage? The latter included religious works (more numerous than usual), Joan of Arcs (from Maxime Real del Sarte's to Henri Louis Bouchard's), minor personages from the provinces, murals celebrating the marshal, and scenes of military life.[95] Save for a fairly limited number of novelties, the acquisitions as a whole corresponded to an already well-established majority taste. The state, like the public, preferred landscapes most of all, followed by decorations, Graphs 2, 3 portraits, and still lifes.

PORTRAIT OF AN AVERAGE ARTIST

To compose a profile of the artist best situated under the occupation to receive the top commissions, it would be necessary to consider the lessons of the Exposition internationale of 1937. The most likely winner was a man, since women represented only 15 percent of those chosen (the same proportion as their representation in the art world); women were paid fairly, but never above the amount reserved for the "greats," which they were not.[96] The winner was a mature man, inevitably over the age of forty, and preferably over sixty. He was a Parisian, usually living on the Left Bank, in the 5th, 7th, 14th, or 15th arrondissement. Finally, he was a painter rather than a sculptor, who had less luck on the market.

As was the case before the war, in its choices the state's purchasing commission followed rather faithfully the division of genres among the different Salons then in existence, which were held in succession at the Palais de Tokyo—an uncomfortable venue where, teeth sharpened, the art world gathered each season before artworks that were, however, almost never more surprising than those of the previous season.[97] That was all the more true when the same artists exhibited at two or three different Salons. The Salon des Indépendants was open to all without restrictions, which gave it a certain eclecticism, often merely quaint, but sometimes freer. The more structured Salon des Tuileries and Salon d'Automne attracted even the most moderate representatives of the "modern tradition." Finally, the Salons held by the Société nationale des beaux-arts and by the Société des artistes français, the most academic and homogeneous, championed large erudite contrivances and resolutely opposed any "adventures," at least on their own walls. That did not prevent those among its members willing to risk their hard-line reputations from going elsewhere to present their concessions to "fashion" and the market. Indeed, academicism was in the process of changing fantasies, not only in the world of art lovers but also among a broader public. That public, which had barely been aware of the freedom of the *années folles*—the "crazy years" between the two wars—had been undergoing an evolution, ever since it had been invited to the first high mass of living art in 1937.[98] "The masters of independent art" who exhibited at the time, though remaining moderate enough, offered them more color, more emotion, more personal feeling than the rigid and cold academic canvases in large formats, whose erudite subjects went past the public without touching it. If that public continued to be hesitant about the "modern tradition"—especially in contemporary sculpture (still neoantique)—it was at least accustomed to new forms dressed up to fit the tastes of the time and what was said to be "the French spirit." The art world generally seemed won over to the lessons of the avant-garde from the early part of the century: absence of perspective, idiosyncratic deformation of reality, colors applied uniformly at the expense of local tones. This allowed it to understand and appreciate an unexceptional painting with the appearance of compromise, that looked postimpressionist or postcubist in form. Edouard Vuillard, Pierre Bonnard, Braque, and Matisse served as masters, venerated (except by academicians) and imitated by a crowd of followers much less gifted than they.

Was this lucidity on the part of the art world? Even in the years blamed for the most radical works (which, however, almost never hung in the Salons and museums), there were complaints about the monotony and the disarray and calls for something "new"—which would look like the old. There was an appreciation for all those who most explicitly evoked the established traditions while knowing to give to commonplaces the effect of the new. But the Salons and the inventories of art dealers overflowed in vain: quantity produced neither quality—nor novelty.

THE MARKETPLACE

An avant-garde, abstract, surrealist, or "deformative" artist undoubtedly had some chance of finding solid support from a particularly intrepid dealer, from Galerie Jeanne-Bucher, Galerie Jeanne Castel, Galerie Alfred Poyet, the little Resistance gallery L'esquisse, Galerie de Berri, or Galerie de France. René Drouin and Louis Carré, with their far greater financial assets, regularly demonstrated that fact.[99] Nonetheless, the insular private market proved to be as cautious as Salon organizers, though there were a few exceptions: it had no qualms about circulating Picassos or works by Jewish artists, sure that there was a demand for them.

What was really in fashion, however, was the "decorative," the consoling, the safe asset. For those who had gotten rich on the black market and for most buyers, art was supposed to procure the enjoyment of a charming sight and at the same time the assurance of a worthwhile investment. In these times of economic crisis and fear of devaluation, the completely unregulated art market was thriving. It was radically transformed, however, by the exclusion laws that forced Jewish dealers to cease operations. Their galleries were to be entrusted to fronts, requisitioned, or sold off at bargain basement prices. Here as elsewhere, the occupier's policy reigned: the "Aryanization" of businesses demanded the forcible displacing of Jews and replacing them as needed with provisional administrators won over to the vanquisher's cause. Every economic and political benefit was then conceivable.[100]

Thus the Galerie Bernheim-Jeune, sequestered and sold to Louis Darquier de Pellepoix's principal private secretary for two million francs—it was worth fifteen million, according to appraisers' estimates[101]—now exhibited military works by ordinary German soldiers. The Galerie Paul Rosenberg passed into Octave Duchez's hands, and Galerie Wildenstein into Roger Dequoy's.[102] This last case, which the press, intrigued by its paradoxes, revived some time ago, remains an ambiguous and atypical example. Georges Wildenstein himself asked his employee to take care of his affairs, without balking, according to Jonathan Napack, at accommodating the occupying forces. The documents Napack discovered in American archives in the 1990s indicate that Dequoy did not hesitate either to hand over the gallery's files to the Nazi authorities or to let them avail themselves of the premises or to buy back works from Jewish collectors so as to resell them to the authorities.[103]

Also attesting to the contradictions of the time, the interview granted to Hervé Le Boterf by the dealer Emmanuel David threw light on a practice already encountered, linked to the propensity of certain officials at the Propaganda-Staffel Paris to intervene in behalf of their "good outcasts." Without asking for the compensation stipulated in the previous case, Dr. Lange saved David—who, in 1942, came to open a gallery on rue du Faubourg Saint-Honoré—from the Gestapo's clutches. "Young, blond, handsome, in a purple velvet dressing gown,"[104] Lange received David as a man of the world, simply pointing out to him that his new identity papers and a certificate of Aryanness awaited him at Gestapo headquarters. Lange also protected David when necessary.[105] The "bashful lovers" posted in Paris remained oddly at the disposal of their "obligees," even at the galleries, where they usually came, dressed in civilian clothes, as honest and passionate buyers. When asked whether dealers knowingly sold them works at the time, the most lucid answered that the German buyers knew to blend in with the most respectable collectors or to have French brokers, who did not always reveal their clients, buy in their place.

With life in Paris dangerous from every standpoint, the majority of art dealers, like Daniel-Henry Kahnweiler, preferred to retire to the provinces or to "paradise in the shadow of the crematoriums," as he put it. Pierre Assouline has masterfully recounted his fate in exile in the interior of France. He fit the profile of the ideal gallows bird: a German Jew who had gone over to "the enemy" and a major defender of "degenerate" art. Steeped in German culture, and with no particular interest in Judaism, he made a pragmatic choice in 1936, when the extreme right attacked the Jews: he would be on the side of those who considered him "no different from them, the leftist parties, the Front populaire."[106]

Thanks to chance and his protectors in the Limousin and then in the *département* Lot, he survived the war. At age fifty-six, he took advantage of the situation to read, at the municipal library, learned works on the origins of Christianity, Europe, and the Limousin, among them poems by a medieval troubadour, Bertrand de Born. He also spent his time writing, meditating, and taking stock of questions close to his heart: modern art and Juan Gris, but also the disappointing incoherence of history and men. Only books could really console him about the course of things by "breaking the isolation." They were the only things capable of uniting him with "humanity, the whole, God."[107] In his refuge in the Limousin, his spirits were lightened by a friendly colony of intellectuals in transit who, from time to time, brought fresh news of the capital. Among his guests were Elie Lascaux and his family, Raymond Queneau and his family, the writer Georges Limbour, the master of the arts and popular traditions Georges-Henri Rivière, the painters Suzanne Roger and André Gustave Beaudin whom he had defended, and a few others, including Michel Leiris and his wife, Louise, Kahnweiler's sister-in-law, who had purchased his "Aryanized" gallery[108] and regularly gave him news of "his artist" Picasso.

His province was, in short, not the exile market, which, like the Paris market, was thriving. Far from the occupied capital, galleries remained open, and vocations were conceived as circumstances allowed. Cities on the Côte d'Azur experienced an upturn in activity. Maurice Laffaille, originally an interior designer, recounts in his memoirs how he built his business on his love of art. He exhibited on one of the main thoroughfares of Nice works by Bonnard, Vlaminck, Derain, Dufy, and even Picasso.[109] He remembers having been "allied" with "sellers"[110] and with dealers, "Aryan" and Jewish, who could no longer practice their professions legally, with an Italian who paid him in tobacco, and with personalities from the worlds of art, literature, and show business who came to visit him: Katia Granoff; Anna (or Hanka) Zborowska, wife of the major collector of works by Chaïm Soutine and Amedeo Modigliani; Georges Huisman, former head of the fine arts administration; Francis Carco; René Gimpel; and Charles Trenet.

But it was in Paris that works moved with the greatest success, while the number of exhibition spaces did not fall. Once activities truly resumed, in 1942, the press mentioned some seventy gallery names every week just in the capital. The crisis favored the art economy, which was opening up to newcomers. The Galerie de France, for example, launched in February 1942, gave as its mission "to defend energetically the young masters of independent art" and soon attracted the Jeunes peintres de tradition française—who were moving toward abstractionism—and their new admirers. Yet the success of places older or "richer" in prestigious collections proved to be more certain. Thus, people flocked to previews at the gallery belonging to Louis Carré, who had salvaged the premises of his exiled colleague André Weil, on avenue Matignon, and who promoted recognized artists—Maurice Denis, Dufy, Matisse, Georges Rouault, Vuillard—as well as those less "secure," such as Oscar Dominguez, or Villon, whom he added to his team by buying up everything he produced.[111]

People also were eager to visit the very powerful Galerie Charpentier, which exhibited the more "moderate" artists. Or, for a select group of art lovers, there was the gallery of Martin Fabiani, a big-time gambler, publisher, and dealer newly arrived in the art market, armed with a powerful war machine, the estate of Ambroise Vollard. At Vollard's request, Fabiani had taken over the gallery on avenue Matignon from a Jewish colleague he had met in Nice. The latter went into exile in the United States and, after the war, Fabiani returned the exile's property, "not without a touch of melancholy."[112] Unfortunately for the historian, in his memoirs, which exhibit a mixture of cynicism and embitterment, Fabiani passes quickly over his first successes during the occupation. It is possible to glean from them that he had encountered poverty-stricken artists whose disposition changed as soon as peace returned. That was particularly true of Matisse, whose about-face Fabiani dates from the arrival of the Americans "with their pockets full of dollars."[113]

Galerie René Drouin, which opened just before the war in the posh locale of the place Vendôme, was likewise prestigious in its way, accurately reflecting the ambient mood of eclecticism, oscillating between traditional shows and exhibitions of newer artists—from the painter Emili Grau Sala (presented by Jean-Marc Campagne), for example, to *Maîtres et petits maîtres du XIXe* and *Le portrait français*. The portrait was, in fact, very much in vogue (the exhibition was introduced by the academicians Louis Hourticq and Louis Réau). As of 1943, and on the advice of enlightened art lovers Gildo Caputo, Jean Paulhan, and Francis Ponge, the gallery proceeded to present Jean Fautrier, then nudes by Matisse, Dufy, and Vlaminck—but also, for the first time, Jean Dubuffet, sometime later exhibited there with Dora Maar, Bernard Lorjou, and some of the Jeunes peintres de tradition française. Drouin gradually revived the modernist project (oriented toward surrealism) that had been set out in 1939 by Leo Castelli,[114] future pope of the New York avant-garde and husband of Ileana Sonnabend, whose parents financed the costly debut of their son-in-law at a gallery a few steps from the Hôtel Ritz. Drouin also remained true to his early work as an interior decorator and designer of glass and steel furniture, close to the modern spirit of the Union des artistes modernes and Le Corbusier.

The commercial art scene reflected an evolving landscape. The codes of modernity, such as those now perfectly internalized by a good minority of art lovers, were being popularized, profoundly revolutionizing mental representations. But this did not give the average Frenchman the desire to cross the thresholds of the closed and silent temples of art. One has only to take up the studies by Raymonde Moulin or Pierre Bourdieu to recognize that a formidable chasm would long separate propositions made to the public (including those concerning museums) and the public's capacity to respond to them.[115]

Had the lessons the Front populaire tried to impose been without effect? Not for lack of trying. It sponsored not only the Exposition internationale of 1937 and its art exhibitions, *Les chefs-d'oeuvre de l'art français*, but also, though they did not concern modern art, the first major "pedagogical" exhibition, which was devoted to van Gogh, the first international congress of museology at the Ecole du Louvre, the very dynamic Association populaire des amis des musées,[116] and the evening opening of the Musée du Louvre, which considerably increased the number of visitors (to about 400,000 in 1937).

But one must not overlook the imperceptible changes that occurred during the occupation, when the vacuity of the time sent the least informed collectors toward the private stocks of the educated elite. Financial opportunism and the new sociological shifts may also account for the turmoil in the salesrooms, which were traditionally more open than the galleries. People flocked to the Hôtel Drouot to buy "still lifes, and more specifically bouquets of flowers, whatever their date; landscapes, in particular impressionist and eighteenth-century Italian landscapes."[117] A thirst for nature was not inconsistent with either the state's purchases or the chief successes of the art scene—namely, the major exhibitions at the Musée de l'Orangerie of landscape works by Claude Monet and Rodin in 1940 and by Berthe Morisot (introduced by Paul Valéry) in 1941, despite the calling into question of impressionism, which was often blamed for dragging painting toward a culpable laxity. Then there was *Le paysage français de Corot à nos jours* at the Galerie Charpentier in June 1942, described as 293 works by landscape artists with a "character in profound harmony with the soil."[118] The bucolic effusions continued in the auction rooms, where the selling price of landscapes by Manet topped 400,000 francs, closely followed by those of Pissarro—though one of the highest bids was for a *Portrait of a Young Woman* by Jean-Marc Nattier, which sold for 780,000 francs in 1943.

During the single year of 1941/1942, two million objects passed through the Hôtel Drouot. There works by Modigliani, Chagall, Léger, and Picasso went for bargain basement prices (but not those by Bonnard, Braque, or Matisse, considered a "safe" modernity and already very expensive); whereas those by the French "Aryan" painters, especially when they conformed to the tastes of the time, saw returns beyond their usual value. A *Portrait of the Artist* by Picasso was worth 3,400 francs, the same as a simple drawing by Maillol (1941). A *Still Life* by Fernand Léger fetched 5,650 francs, while the same subject by Fautrier sold for 1,500 francs (1941), much less than a somber *Village* by the new-style Vlaminck, which easily brought 55,000 francs.

Moreover, an attentive visitor who took a stroll through Paris would have had the impression that he was seeing an enormous Vlaminck exhibition, disseminated more or less everywhere. Vlaminck's success was similar to that of his friends and many followers, who like him were disappointed with fauvism. Derain, Friesz, and van Dongen were appreciated all the more for having renounced their intention to shock. In fact, had you asked the art world what ought to replace the contemporary chaos, it might have pondered—like Gaston Diehl, in regard to the exhibition *Peintres du Ier Empire*[119]—the "subtle correspondences" with the age of Napoléon, "confined like it to a certain Spartan rigor, a severe orderliness, a need for cohesion."[120]

The less theoretical reality revealed an admirable continuity. Artists painted soothing landscapes, sensitive portraits, the order of an old rural world, humane, peaceful, barely jostled by modernity. It was "just like before," when the crisis of the 1930s came crashing down on Europe, leaving artists even more at a loss than usual.

MUTUAL AID

In 1937, Valéry wondered how artists had been able to live thus far, before answering that they had made the best of their condition, thanks to the imprecision of the "economic mechanism." His liberalism led him to prefer that artists face the difficulty of an existence in freedom rather than the certainties of civil servants in totalitarian countries. And those concerned seemed to concede he was right, though they regularly complained of their wretched fate, while dreaming of a reconciliation of art and society that would necessarily involve an improvement in their material circumstances. The Exposition internationale of 1937 had momentarily ameliorated the condition of French artists, by greatly increasing the commissions for the most famous and for all those who "needed" them.[121] In the same way, the broader allocation of decorative and artistic works for public construction projects (the precursor of the 1 percent allocation) under Jean Zay held happier prospects for artists. Still, that situation seemed to be the exception, especially when compared to the years of economic crisis that began in 1929/1930, when a third of the galleries were forced to close, breaking their contracts (never put in writing) with artists, while the state reduced the number of its commissions.[122] When war broke out, artists were still living on the margins of civil society, among prostitutes and tramps. Of course, since 1934 the government had been allocating unemployment benefits to them, but only fourteen francs a day, a sum that was further reduced when they sold a work and decided to declare it. Each artist's situation therefore depended primarily on his personal fortune and success in selling his work. Some made out easily, particularly the most official or the most conventional, who were certain to receive regular commissions from the state or the municipalities. Others, and not always lesser artists, merely survived, as attested in the letters of recommendation that regularly drew the attention of the relevant authorities, charged with setting aside commissions or subsidies.[123] These commissions did not always materialize, leaving the less fortunate artists facing ruin or constrained to do menial tasks that kept them from their creative work. Under such conditions, the most politically active called on their comrades to boycott the system, which did not inspire confidence in a population reputed to be asocial. In this, artists were much like "intellectuals," of whom Edmond Humeau drew a dark portrait during the occupation, fiercely attacking the psychology of the "unemployed intellectual": individualistic, paranoid, afraid of being "inferiorized" by the work assigned him.[124] The time had come to make this group participate in "a work of national interest," on intellectual and artistic works projects in particular, under which artists were to catalog, inventory, and reproduce France's patrimony, in museums, libraries, and rural areas.[125] The war did not help things at all by increasing tenfold the fragility of a population already in an unstable situation. A charitable movement had responded to the suffering of World War I by providing active aid to mobilized artists as well as to their families. In all, 2.5 million francs were distributed over four years. This, along with a great deal of ingenuity, had allowed them, most of the time, to withstand the worst.[126]

In 1939, artists went off to fight like everyone else, before returning with a plan to "start again"—no matter what. But, even aside from the Jewish artists in danger, the occupation brought its share of daily miseries. Even though the Direction générale des beaux-arts had a larger budget than usual at its disposal and the City of Paris displayed some initiative,[127] even though the fashion of the day favored the decoration of public places (very poorly remunerated, however)[128] and the private market was thriving, many still needed help. A charity movement, emerging amid hostility, took charge, setting "as its goal the moral and material care of artists (painters, sculptors, engravers, draftsmen, decorators, designers) in the exercise of their profession."[129]

Entraide des artistes[130] kept itself at equal distance from governmental whims (though the state subsidized it, as did the City of Paris) and the extreme individualism of the art sector (though every artists' society helped it along by making contributions commensurate with its size). The small organization, governed by the law of 1901, demonstrated its effectiveness after a fashion, providing a clothing exchange,[131] a dining hall, medical care, lectures, exhibition-auctions,[132] and promotional material at its headquarters in part of the beautiful mansion at 9, rue Berryer, bequeathed by Baronness Adèle de Rothschild to the French state in 1922. The group was overseen by a committee of representatives from the art world, presided over by Anatole de Monzie, the talkative French finance minister who prided himself on loving the arts. He had "radicalizing, even socialist tendencies, but was very independent by nature,"[133] according to Gisèle and Serge Berstein. Monzie, who had made his mark by defending an alliance with Mussolini, was the puppet Entraide needed to get the state to agree to its allocations. In reality, things were run by the painter Maurice Guy-Loë. Having succeeded the poet Paul-Louis Garnier,[134] he started his career as a philanthropist before having other successes: opening the first retirement home for artists in 1944 and instituting the first laws granting them full social benefits, in 1964, 1977, and 1986.[135]

To the detriment of his career as a painter, Guy-Loë devoted his life to improving the lot of his comrades, convinced that it was necessary at all cost to compensate for the lack of social programs, but without engaging in orthodox political activity. In a sector prone to infighting and deeply marked by the initiatives of the Communist Party, he brought all sides together, reaping the benefits of a first social effort carried out in the 1920s and 1930s by relatively political corporate associations, particularly the Confédération des travailleurs intellectuels, which fought against intellectual unemployment. In the late 1930s, the Communist Party and the Confédération générale du travail above all, through the Maison de la culture, set forth a long list of demands. But in practice, the debate of principles still occupied the protagonists to a greater degree, and they relegated immediate demands to the background.[136]

Entraide des artistes took up the torch, confining itself to concrete resolutions.[137] Under the occupation, it had fewer members to call on, but it had networks of sympathizers that, at least partly, broke down French and German resistance. In addition to the usual hardships, there was the lack of materials, which had to be obtained without paying high black market prices and by making do with the "services" overseen by the Nazi authorities, who, after much shilly-shallying, had empowered Entraide to distribute the necessary products: paints, canvas, brushes, cardboard, gasoline, wood, glue, paper, plaster, and charcoal. In all, about 350,000 francs were distributed to artists in the form of services and various vouchers, plus another four million before the liberation in the form of state commissions. Indeed, in some respects the organization served as the intermediary between government institutions and the artists concerned. The latter, though not accurately counted, were known generally through artists' societies, to which they contributed and which regularly exhibited their works at Salons.[138] A number of them inevitably slipped through the traditional information networks but relatively few, given the real representativeness of the societies and associations that together commanded the organization.[139] This was quickly noticed in the higher echelons of the regime, especially when it was learned that Entraide was in the process of setting up a directory, as exhaustive as possible, which listed about fourteen thousand names.[140]

The leaders of the organization, headed by Guy-Loë, conceived of this first documentation of the art sector in full awareness of the risks involved during a period of extreme normalization, on the French side—and on the German. Hence they were not surprised that, throughout the occupation, they had to protect their free agency by resisting pressures that were not long in coming: in late 1940, the state threatened to turn Entraide into a corporation.

THE CORPORATION PLAN[141]

When Pétain replaced the universalist republican motto "Liberté, Egalité, Fraternité" (Liberty, Equality, Fraternity) with his "Travail, Famille, Patrie" (Work, Family, Nation), he asserted the primacy of three societies—professional, familial, and national—and of their respective institutions—corporation, home, and state. In the case of the corporation, history long ago proved Claude Mauriac right: in his doctoral thesis, submitted to the faculty of law at Bordeaux in 1941, he warned readers of the existence of a manifold corporatism. His moderate definition has the merit of clarity: corporatism is a "mode of organization of the profession that grounds society in natural groups of individuals, united by the same function, and receiving statutory allocations of an economic and social nature, as well as public representation in the political and administrative organs of the nation, or at the very least alongside them."[142] The Vichy corporation plan fit the mold completely, even as it drew inspiration eclectically from old experiments and doctrines and from the contemporary example of authoritarian and Fascist regimes: Italian, German, Spanish, Hungarian.[143] In many respects, it is clear that the plan for an arts corporation could have been conceived only in that extreme situation, in which a defeated France had embarked on a quest for a strong social bond and a golden age. In art as elsewhere, the dominant discourse was dedicated to the description of evil. Here and there, decadence and imported liberalism were set up in opposition to the return to traditional values: order, selectivity, and a national dimension. And whether it was art or society in question, the obligatory reference to the past evoked the superiority of Roman antiquity, the Middle Ages, and the centuries prior to the French Revolution.

In terms of achievements, it cannot be overestimated how pleased the government was to "fly by the seat of its pants," as Jean-Pierre Azéma has shown. This was particularly the case when it came to giving concrete form to that vast corporation plan, which was to fight "state control" and "individualism," in other words, to simultaneously curb social conflicts and free-market competition. After the government's success in forming the Ordre des médecins in October 1940, the law of 2 December established the Corporation paysanne in an apparently auspicious sector. It did not factor in individualist identity: those concerned balked as soon as the organization moved in the direction of becoming a state instrument responsible for distribution and collection.[144] In reality, behind the prolix discourse on the benefits of corporatism, vigorous divergent interests persisted, and only the government had solid reasons for bringing them together under a single banner. As for the artists, they were linked to artisans, the big winners on the official ideological awards list for representing a deeply rooted France. On 1 May 1941, the marshal once more paid tribute to that France, saluting the many efforts by protocorporations that merely awaited legal recognition.[145] Inspired by the anonymous creators of medieval masterpieces, the defenders of an arts corporation prepared to wage their final battle, which would put an end to the egotism of the modern creator, who had been smitten with freedom since the French Revolution. Had not that revolution given birth to the principle of equality among men, to the individualism born of the dissolution of natural communities, and to free enterprise, so many "evil agents of the venture" combated, in the nineteenth century, by René La Tour du Pin,[146] a social Catholic and founder of the charitable organization Oeuvre des Cercles catholiques ouvriers, who conceived of the corporation as the major instrument of the "counterrevolution."

The Vichy regime similarly sounded the call for a return to the "natural" order and to that golden age of art education when a young man destined for a career in the arts went to live with a master, his parents or guardian having signed an apprenticeship contract in the presence of a notary. Thus, as was reported by Hautecoeur, Pierre Mignard had promised Jean de La Borde to "show and teach him over the course and span of five consecutive years . . . that art of painting and everything involved in it."[147] It was a reasonable and well-trod path, which Jacques-Louis David had supposedly abandoned by distancing himself from his students and by fighting the Académie royale de peinture et de sculpture. What had been forgotten was that, well before the French Revolution, artists had loudly begun to consider the matter, so much so that their "dissertations" had given rise to a critique and a reform of artistic practices based on studies from nature, in other words, on lessons that the traditional guilds had been unable to dispense. At the same time, the guilds had found themselves called into question. It was against these guilds, challenged by the Italians during the Renaissance and somewhat later in France and the rest of Europe, that the Académie royale de peinture et de sculpture was founded,[148] out of a desire on the part of artists to have their work distinguished from what were called the "mechanical arts." The French Revolution inaugurated the decline of a cultural era during which artists appealed to society, to patrons of the arts, and to the public. Though it would be necessary to moderate the speed of that evolution, it was now from his profound solitude that the artist created, responding only to the constraints of creativity itself and not necessarily taking into account the economic, moral, or aesthetic conventions of the time—except perhaps to oppose them. That way of life opened the way for a freedom of action and a questioning of norms that was becoming intolerable in June 1940, when the dominant plan was to rectify France's mistakes by fighting the disorder of institutions and of intellects.

The conditions for putting an end to the exceptional status of the free creative artist—or rather to his lack of economic and social status—had never come together to such an extent. The governmental initiative, the trend toward a return to order, and German pressure seemed to have gotten the better of artistic individualism and social rebellion, which was assumed, wrongly, to inevitably go hand in hand with political revolt. As of October 1940, the specialized press expressed delight over the plan for a professional organization. Pierre Imbourg, who had cut his teeth before the war at *L'oeuvre*, *Paris-Soir*, and *Paris-Midi*, was now the director of the largest art review, *Beaux-arts*,[149] and he gave carte blanche to the authorities in terms that were at odds with the review's political moderation before the occupation. According to him, artists would never dare "raise their voices," and it was therefore up to the government to set aside for them a "nice place in the commonwealth," in other words, to impose it on them without asking for their opinion. There was no dearth of good precedents, both historical and contemporary, as provided by "the totalitarian regimes."[150]

The secretary general of fine arts, Louis Hautecoeur, was given formal notice to constitute a corporation for the graphic and plastic arts, without anyone having solicited the opinion of the interested parties.[151] He was very busy at the time implementing the Ordre des architectes, which came into being on 31 December 1940, thereby fulfilling Hautecoeur's long-held wish. Its case was not difficult to argue: architecture was a liberal profession practiced by creative people with an obvious responsibility toward their clientele. At the risk of injustice, Hautecoeur expelled from its ranks architects "with no preparation or conscience." The majority, however, saw the corporation as a way to keep the crisis in check by spurring an increase in public and private commissions.[152] But what would become of these selection criteria, largely technical in nature, when it came to the art scene? What kind of aesthetic certificate would be issued and under what conditions? These were the concerns raised by those who initially opposed the project, even as it was becoming official, and they also weighed on Hautecoeur: despite his traditionalism, he quickly grasped the difficulties of introducing a restrictive system, as well as the risks of having his power over the "sector" undermined.

Though no one had taken very seriously the first federation of artists set up in autumn 1940, at the headquarters of Entraide des artistes,[153] the little art world became worried when there was serious talk of turning it into a corporation under the pressure exerted by Germany through Fernand de Brinon.[154] Geographical distance complicated matters: Hautecoeur, in residence in Vichy, complained that he was not being kept adequately informed of what was afoot in Paris.[155] The heads of the various societies discussed their lot and, knowing that things would go forward in any case, responded to summons to the planning committees for the corporation formed by Hautecoeur, who hoped to do the occupying forces one better. Although some balked, artists more often were flattered that, for once, the state had invited them to negotiate their social status. Officially, two committees were to be created in succession: a study committee to present the preliminary proposals, followed by a professional committee to organize the artistic professions for good. The plan did not factor in a final intervention by the higher echelons of government, which would make an already very restrictive plan even more rigid before it even got to Vichy.

UNDER STUDY

Given the complexity of applying the organization law of 16 August 1940 to the art world, some time after it had been applied to show business, the study committee in charge of graphic and plastic arts was set up in accordance with the decree of 17 February 1941. Headed by the sculptor Paul Landowski, a member of the Institut de France and director of the Ecole des beaux-arts, it brought together ten or so key figures. All were members of the Académie des beaux-arts or committed to the conservative aesthetic values that supposedly represented the art world, although only three representatives of the traditional Salons were present, which annoyed those rejected. Advice was to be taken only from the largest professional groups, which left the erroneous impression that all artists must have felt more or less affiliated with them. In fact, the art scene was extremely diverse, teeming with societies and Salons. As of 17 February 1941, the recruited members of the study committee had two months to plan for the future of the profession. They handed in their report late, and the corporation's organization program was not drawn up until after 24 May 1941.[156] The recruits, even those most dedicated to the task, stumbled over political and legal problems for which their vocation had not necessarily prepared them. Their first headache had to do with the corporation's identity. Who would be part of the Ordre des artistes and on the basis of what criteria? To decide these questions, they had to establish a coherent definition of "artist" and "work of art." They all firmly believed that artists were different from mere artisans—but then what? How could they establish a definitive rule that would determine the value of an original creation? The debate necessarily echoed the credo of the moment on the status of contemporary work accused of violating age-old traditions, on the fine craftsmanship that was being lost, on the excesses that revealed the moral crisis, and on the increasing number of artists. If we focus solely on the minutes of the study committee meetings, it emerges that participants were urged to act rather than discuss, as if the consensus regarding the modalities of the crisis was enough to make words superfluous. The study committee's president, Paul Landowski, was there to preserve harmony and could call his colleagues to order when they embarked on "aesthetic discussions" or those too general for his taste.[157] After all, he was acquainted with the other side of that sort of debate, which had flourished especially during the Front populaire. The war had considerably diminished the infighting; it was not a question of returning to the battle but of imposing the guidelines necessary for the reorganization of a profession where liberalism was proliferating unchecked.

The conditions for entry into the Ordre des artistes looked to be more liberal then some had hoped. The old conservatives from the Société des artistes français had wanted membership solely by society—which would have excluded the large number of artists outside the ranks of the professional organizations—but the study committee decided in favor of individual memberships. Besides, admission was not easy. It was to be determined by the order's regional councils, and it required that they judge works of art worthy according to criteria that were necessarily arbitrary. Later revised in the higher echelons, the initial plan called for entry to be reserved for those holding a degree from an art school recognized by the state or for those who had "practiced their art in actuality or manifestly" for "three consecutive years." Concerns were raised about the attitude of the very influential Henri Louis Bouchard, a member of the Institut de France. He was intent on carving out, brutally, the best place for the Académie des beaux-arts, for which he obtained an institution by "sovereign *jurande*"[158] that could, as a last resort, rule on a candidacy. The situation made more apparent the old quarrels within the Institut de France: Bouchard shocked his colleagues and fellow members Denis, Desvallières, and Landowski, who all insisted that the admittance of artists to the order take place "under very liberal conditions and with the greatest spirit of understanding so that the artist's freedom and personality shall in no case be fettered."[159] That amounted to demonstrating, in theory at least, a great tolerance, even though they accepted or defended less ecumenical measures as well.

Of all the artists, foreigners seemed the most threatened by the envisioned recruitment policy. For decorative artists, Maurice Dufrène proposed that foreign nationals be chosen by their respective countries, which disqualified a good portion of those who had come to France fleeing hostile governments. The profession thus aspired to be founded on an "affectionate and charitable understanding by all"[160]—but with the exception of expatriates and all those who no longer enjoyed their civil rights. From the first corporative principles it laid down, the French art scene had never been so at odds with its hospitable traditions, its members forced to load up on certificates, including those attesting to their "upstanding life and morals,"[161] which made more than one artist snicker.

In fact, the prerogatives envisioned for the Ordre des artistes were very broad, extending even to the criticism of art as practiced by "unqualified writers," who were held responsible for the change in mentalities.[162] Here too, the definition became so vague that it authorized the worst abuses, at least in theory. By claiming the right to look over critical writings, the order's council was guaranteed a higher level of censorship, which it further increased by holding sway over art competitions and exhibitions. By regulating even the price of works of art in galleries, the order would overthrow the previous liberal system. Finally, by making the corporation the guardian of the "archives of contemporary art," it was guaranteed control over artistic traditions and, ultimately, over a history of art that some would inevitably see turned upside down. Offered in exchange was the promise of a retirement system and minimal protection that sounded like a novelty to a population deprived of rights. Was it worth the price of captious regulations? Those concerned might, in a pinch, agree to take an oath to practice their art "in good conscience"—all the more so as it was not stated in what that consisted, though the stipulated disciplinary penalties were good reason to worry.

In late 1941, the painter Jean Bazaine mounted the battlements alone, in *La nouvelle revue française*, directed by Pierre Drieu La Rochelle, who shut his eyes. Bazaine scoffed at the public institutions of the past, before attacking the authorities then in power with a verve that would earn him a few words with the French authorities. Even though the personalist wanted a reconciliation between art and the general public, he hoped for a reunion safe from the firm hand of the state and from those "men of the awful right wing" wanting to purge France of the "Judeo-Marxist breasts and tricolor buttocks of which [artists] were so shamefully fond."[163] Joining his revolt, but through official channels, were the students at the art schools, who had trouble tolerating the desire to reform the sector, complaining, even in 1943, to Lallemant in Vichy, that the corporation ran the risk of "interfering with the blossoming of young talents."[164] Such responses may have remained isolated, but they undoubtedly had their effect on the rank and file: even those on the organizing committees balked. Bazaine, who was not on any of the committees, had the opportunity to get an advance look at the preliminary by-laws of the Ordre des artistes thanks to his poet friend Jean Follain, who got them from his father-in-law, Maurice Denis. That summer, Denis had fled the hornet's nest surrounding the order, whose presidency had been foisted on him after he agreed to participate in the sessions of the professional committee in charge of the initial plan for setting up and administering the order. Though the first "study committee" had still operated as a roundtable, the succeeding "organizing committee" took on a distinctly more serious cast, of which the former Nabi was wary, to the point of rebellion.

THE ARTISTS' BUREAUS

After reflection, seeing that the initial plan for the Ordre des artistes had ultimately been made much more rigid in the higher echelons—especially regarding the artists' societies, whose powers were considerably fettered—Denis flatly refused his appointment as president of the order, which had been announced in the *Journal officiel.* On 5 August 1941, he expressed astonishment to Hautecoeur that he had been chosen against his will. A worse blunder could not have been made, given that his experience at the meetings he had been attending had confirmed his "preference for the rule of freedom, for the freedom of art organizations."[165] The first rebuff thus came from a believer in the establishment who ought to have aroused wariness: an academician, the old royalist had already shown his independence of mind in the past. Aesthetically, he considered Édouard Manet a "great classical artist" and was opposed to the disappointing plan for the Musée du Trocadéro supported by the Institut de France; politically, he felt it his patriotic duty to drop Charles Maurras. He recorded his disgust in July 1940 in his journal: he could resign himself neither "to seeing the victorious enemy everywhere, nor to submitting to [its] orders, nor to hearing [its] praises from French friends who [had] no further reaction against it."[166] Curious about what had occurred in totalitarian countries prior to the war, he had insisted during the first preliminary meetings for the order that they find out what had been done there on the subject of artists' organizations. At the same time, he wanted the corporation to remain "strictly French," undoubtedly as much to keep out the occupying forces, which heavily endorsed the establishment of the order, as to hold foreign artists at bay on principle.

That first resignation, spectacular because of the old painter's notoriety, was followed some months later, on 25 October 1941, by the much less brilliant appointment of Jean Dupas, a painter and a member of the Institut de France. He at first sought to extricate himself out of modesty, before reluctantly agreeing to give it "a try." His agreement in principle was marked by his anguish at having to bear such a heavy responsibility, one that would ultimately keep him from his own work. Less than a year later, he put an end to an experiment punctuated by absenteeism, citing his lack of "qualifications." He handed over the reins to his colleague, the sculptor Paul Landowski, a man to be trusted with official duties, but who likewise increasingly balked at wasting time away from his studio. More than a year and a half after the start of the operation to militarize the arts, he took over a corporation still in the planning stages. Indeed, the professional committee was still hesitating over whether to call it an "order" or a "corporation": the latter sounded less directive than the former.[167]

The Comité d'organisation professionnelle des arts graphiques et plastiques conformed to the model of all the other professional organizations and, in accordance with the law of 16 August 1940, was to respond in its way to the program set up for all branches of industrial and commercial activity. It was to draw up production and manufacturing schedules; plan for the acquisition and distribution of raw materials; establish general rules of operation while ensuring the qualifications of staff and workers; and regulate competition.[168]

Like the study committee, the professional committee still did not have its own headquarters and met at the offices of the general secretariat of fine arts. Denis had resigned; Marcel Temporal was no longer there; Landowski, Dufrène, Richard, and Vincent Poli remained faithfully at their posts, while Pierre-Victor Dautel, Laborie, Jacques Beltrand, Dupas, and Pierre Ladoué had joined. Desvallières and Bouchard no longer belonged to the core group but were busy with the specialized bureaus that were coming on the scene, as a mainspring for the Ordre des artistes being formed. By decree, these bureaus brought together a team of representatives from different artistic professions: eight painters, eight sculptors, six engravers, four medal engravers, and eight decorative artists. They were all handpicked and perfectly integrated into French artistic life, even those who were not members of the

Institut de France: only André Lhote, at the painters' bureau, betrayed a little the very traditionalist public image of the groups.[169]

The rank and file still seemed enthusiastic, but their leaders were running out of steam. A large number of artists had already agreed to join the corporation, but even so the work did not advance any faster, and for good reason. Meetings were not convened on time, as the decorative artist Maurice Dufrène complained on behalf of his comrades on 4 July 1942. A month later, Landowski, standing in yet again for the order's absent president Dupas, raised morale by paying tribute to the marshal's regime—which, as it happened, had not facilitated the task of the corporation of the arts.

Lacking the financial means to complete their undertaking, Pierre-Paul Montagnac and Landowski had suggested that the order be allocated a subsidy by the traditional Salons and the Vichy government. Their request was opposed by the finance minister, who argued that all the other organizing committees had bankrolled their own needs without appealing to the state.[170] In fact, the law of 16 August 1940 stipulated that a corporation's expenses be covered by contributions from members, a system that the Ordre des artistes had not yet successfully set up. Landowski had attempted a "briefing on German methods of art organization," in which he focused on the collection of contributions;[171] but at the higher echelons everything seemed to run counter to the smooth operation of the enterprise. In July 1943, the finance minister dispatched a message to the head of national education and youth to alert him that the professional committee did not have the right to impose on its members dues to be used to cover part of its administrative expenses. For that matter, the committee did not in his opinion have a status that allowed it to collect any financial contributions whatsoever.

Lacking a fixed work schedule, artists were plagued by their old economic headaches. The law of 4 September 1942 again raised the issue of the artist's singular position. Historical examples were not lacking: had not Henri Rousseau's hours as a municipal employee overridden his "artistic" schedule? An artist was considered an independent contractor who was supposed to work more than thirty hours a week or else apply for unemployment. But how could an artist decide, except in "good faith," whether he had really worked a sufficient number of hours? And at what point could he consider himself on vacation? The case of Georges Lepape was instructive. Arrested by the police in 1942, he was unable to prove he had a steady job at which he worked more than thirty hours a week, and he therefore requested that a certificate of his qualifications as an "artistic painter" be delivered to him. To top if off, Robert Pougheon remarked, an unemployed artist was in fact merely an artist who did not sell his works, not one who had stopped working. But the law of September 1942 did not allow for any bending of the rules: an artist on unemployment, like any other citizen, could be useful and his expertise requisitioned by mandate.

To the higher echelons, the singularity of the art sector was an annoyance; the pace of the corporation's organization process was a disaster; the artists responsible for the corporative proceedings were running out of steam for lack of funds; and those who were not participating made fun of the project, hoping it would fall short. When Hautecoeur's successor, Georges Hilaire, took up the torch in April 1944, he spoke of the corporation as if the idea had just been raised. Nearly four years had not sufficed to militarize the art world. By contrast, Hilaire's campaign, launched in due form in July, seemed to rouse a weary sector grown used to the idea of having a social status mirroring that of all the French—or nearly all—imposed on it. Many things suggested that with a little time the Ordre des artistes would be viable.[172] Hilaire knew the art sector well, from the inside, unlike Hautecoeur, whose haughtier personality had ultimately alienated him from his subordinates. Hilaire was less an arbiter of good taste, more modern, less an "administrator," more interventionist, but also more diplomatic. Was he responding to the demands of Laval, who had supported him for years? No, the head of the government simply trusted in him, without having a plan for the arts drawn up. In any case, we know nothing of Laval's tastes except that he said he passionately loved blue and that he "wanted to live in blue: blue wallpaper, blue curtains, blue suits"[173]—and that he had likewise distinguished himself by signing, in August 1935, a legal decree that reduced the hours when museums were open, eliciting a protest from the left.

Laval's man, as Hautecoeur faulted him to his face, was content to reiterate, word for word, Hautecoeur's programs for reform,[174] while being careful not to offend the interested parties. In July 1944, he sent a personal letter to about a hundred artists, architects, musicians, and writers on art, representatives of the different currents of French art: Perret and Michel Roux-Spitz in architecture; Matisse, Braque, Lhote, Gromaire, and Maurice Estève in painting; Cassandre for the poster designers; Jacques Copeau, Charles Dullin, and Pierre Fresnay on the theater side; and Arthur Honegger on music.[175] He invited them to be part of his new "active and useful council," to be at the head of an ambitious reform program that addressed everyone's concerns: safeguarding and enhancing monuments and sites of interest; elaborating urban development policy; teaching the arts and reeducating the public's taste; holding exhibitions; promoting state commissions; presenting public collections; considering the status of shows; exerting influence

Table 1

abroad; fostering artisans and popular art; and organizing corporative and social groups.[176] Serge Added has pointed out that, in the original proofs of an interview given by Hilaire, the term *censure* (censorship) was altered—one way of pushing through a project that was oriented toward more pronounced state intervention than under Hautecoeur.[177] Yet the project was open to contemporary design, as attested by at least part of the list of those on his "active council."

Five months away from liberation, there remained just enough time for that first public relations operation—which came too late to bring French artists to heel as the architects, doctors, and lawyers had been. The actions of the leaders of the corporation and of fine arts had certainly not facilitated setting up the project. Like Hautecoeur, Landowski, in charge of the Ordre des artistes, cared mainly about the educational reforms instituted at the Ecole des beaux-arts since October 1940. A new preparatory course of study was created based on manual workmanship, and all young artists were to take it, whether they went on to specialize in architecture, painting, or sculpture.[178] As for the rest, Landowski had said, as far back as 1940, that he was rather "amused" by the turn that events might take, seeing therein a new area of discord between the different Salons, which, to his great regret, were not about to disappear after all. Along the way, he grew impatient, mocking all sides for their inertia, including Hautecoeur—who, said Landowski, ended up "taking himself seriously," "having come out of the Ecole normale a historian"—and his replacement, Paul Tournon, who was supposed to complete his educational reform.[179] In fact, Landowski was engrossed in his studio[180] and increasingly disengaged from the corporation project. But he plainly recognized the positive role of Entraide des artistes, "an independent organization" founded by artists and a few art lovers, "an extension of the Fraternité des artistes, which the Académie [des beaux-arts] founded in 1914–1918." In hard times, the Entraide had been able to palliate the state's failings.[181] That was essentially the position of many artists who, sometimes for different reasons, had not managed to reconcile the artist's indispensable individualism and the hunger for social change that had been raging everywhere, even in their own ranks, since the 1930s.

NOTES

1. See Igor Golomstock, *Totalitarian Art in the Soviet Union, the Third Reich, Fascist Italy, and the People's Republic of China*, trans. Robert Chandler (London: Collins Harvill, 1990); translated into French as *L'art totalitaire: Union soviétique, IIIe Reich, Italie fasciste, Chine*, trans. Michèle Levy-Bram (Paris: Editions Carré, 1991).

2. On propaganda in France, there are numerous archives, many not yet in the public domain. I have consulted series 2AG (Etat français) at the Archives nationales (AN); the holdings of the Centre des archives contemporaines at the AN; the iconographic collection Q MAT at the Département des estampes et de la photographie at the Bibliothèque nationale de France; and auction catalogs focused on works from the years of the occupation, particularly the sales catalog *Seconde Guerre mondiale: 30000 documents... etc.* (auctioneers Jacques Lenormand, Patrick Dayen, and Richard Morand), Paris, Drouot Richelieu, 19 and 20 July 1990. See also the significant holdings of the Musée d'histoire contemporaine of the Bibliothèque de documentation internationale contemporaine (BDIC). In terms of publications, see especially Laurent Gervereau and Denis Peschanski, eds., *La propagande sous Vichy, 1940–1944*, exh. cat. (Nanterre: Bibliothèque de Documentation Internationale Contemporaine, 1990); Laurent Gervereau, *La propagande par l'affiche* (Paris: Editions Syros-Alternatives, 1991); Jacques Polonski, *La presse, la propagande et l'opinion publique sous l'Occupation* (Paris: Editions du Centre de Documentation Juive Contemporaine, 1946); René Jean, "L'art de Vichy," *Arts de France*, no. 7 (1946): 65–68; Jean-Marie Domenach, *La propagande politique* (Paris: Presses Universitaires de France, 1950); Jacques Ellul, *Histoire de la propagande* (Paris: Presses Universitaires de France, 1967); Philippe Amaury, *Les deux premières expériences d'un "ministère de l'information" en France* (Paris: Librairie Générale de Droit et de Jurisprudence, 1969); Stéphane Marchetti, *Images d'une certaine France: Affiches 1939–1945* (Lausanne: Edita, 1982); Denis Peschanski et al., *Images de la France de Vichy, 1940–1944: Images asservies et images rebelles* (Paris: La Documentation Française, 1988); Dominique Rossignol, *Histoire de la propagande en France de 1940 à 1944: L'utopie Pétain* (Paris: Presses Universitaires de France, 1991).
3. The monthlong *Exposition maçonnique* was held in October 1940 at the Petit Palais. Later came the *Exposition de la France européenne*, which was on display for much longer, from 31 May to 31 October 1941, at the Grand Palais; it was promoted by Jacques de Lesdain, director of *L'illustration*, on the orders of the occupying forces. After a violent denunciation of Freemasonry throughout history, the operation sought to establish the idea of an agricultural France, breadbasket of the new Europe. In September 1941, the exhibition *Le Juif et la France* prepared the way for an increasingly terrifying persecution. Then the exhibition *Le bolchevisme contre l'Europe*, organized by Paul Chack and Louis-Charles Lecoc (who had founded the Comité d'action antibolchevique in July 1941) in conjunction with the occupying forces, opened in March 1942, this time insisting on the complicity between Judaism and Communism. The cycle ended in April 1942, with a second installment of *Exposition de la France européenne*.

4. See Robert de Beauplan on the exhibition *Le Juif et la France*, *L'illustration*, 6 September 1941.
5. Although it was placed under the aegis of the Institut d'études des questions juives, the exhibition was organized by the information branch of the German embassy, in collaboration with the Paris bureau of the Sicherheitsdienst (the intelligence arm of the SS), which ensured that Otto Abetz would get credit for the event.
6. See the translation of the note by Otto Abetz, dated 5 September 1941, found in the archives of the German embassy in Paris, in Polonski, *La presse* (note 2), 118.
7. René Péron worked primarily for the movie industry and continued his activities after the liberation. He created a show bill for the film *Les visiteurs du soir* (*The Devil's Envoys*) in 1942. The other poster for *Le Juif et la France* was signed by Michel Jacquot, who also lent a helping hand to the Comité d'action antibolchevique. See Claude Menges, "Les affiches de spectacles à Paris de 1936 à 1946" (Ph.D. thesis [nouveau régime], Université Paris I–Panthéon Sorbonne, 1991).
8. See Robert de Beauplan, "L'exposition antijuive," *L'illustration*, 6 September 1941, 59.
9. The subject's name appeared at the bottom of the portrait, while the silhouette had stamped across it the nationality of each subject followed by a question mark and "non!! juif!" (No!! Jew!).
10. See Denis Peschanski, "Encadrer ou contrôler?" in Laurent Gervereau and Denis Peschanski, eds., *La propagande sous Vichy, 1940–1944*, exh. cat. (Nanterre: Bibliothèque de Documentation Internationale Contemporaine, 1990), 10–31.
11. On this subject, it seems to me that Dominique Rossignol's conclusions underestimate the Vichy regime's propensity for lies—by omission.
12. The Equipe Alain-Fournier was formed in 1940 by Jean Demachy and Géraud de la Garde de Saignes in Lyon, who were soon joined by Philippe H. Noyer, Joël Bellon, and Veyron La Croix, then Pierre Prud'hon, D. Baron, Sagn, Hubert Gaillard, Bernard Aldebert, P. Kaïser, and M. Takizawa. Sixty-two posters were designed up to April 1944, of which the most famous and widely disseminated was the first: Noyer's *Révolution nationale*, which depicts the chief of state full-face, wearing a kepi, in sepia tones, with the tricolor French flag waving behind his head.

    Poster artists adapted to the economic restrictions that were strangling industrial advertising by turning to show business and propaganda. They rarely placed themselves in service of Nazi propaganda, more often working for the Vichy regime, while often continuing to do show bills. On the Nazi side there were René Péron and Jeanne Castel, for example, who nonetheless did posters for the film *L'éternel retour* (1943; *Love Eternal*), written by Jean Cocteau.

On the question of posters, see Gervereau, *La propagande par l'affiche* (note 2).

13. With a few rare exceptions, including R. Vachet's anti-Semitic poster for the Révolution nationale's propaganda center in Avignon.

14. Another academic, Jean Baudry, monitored French work abroad, folklore, and artistic and literary propaganda related to Pétain, and thus censorship of the marshal's image.

15. Images that did not suit him were censored: a postage stamp (issued in 1941) by the philatelic artist Jean Vital Prost was quickly withdrawn from sale and a photograph, likewise too "realistic," showing the marshal looking anxious and old, was marked "strictly prohibited." The latter is reproduced in Thérèse Blondet, "La photographie," in Laurent Gervereau and Denis Peschanski, eds., *La propagande sous Vichy, 1940–1944*, exh. cat. (Nanterre: Bibliothèque de Documentation Internationale Contemporaine, 1990), 158 (no. 2).

16. See the statement of Paul-Pierre Lemagny in Raymond Duxin, Pierre de Lizeray, and Adalbert Vitalyos, *Ceux qui créent nos timbres*, Etude no. 9 by *Le monde des philatélistes* (Paris: Imp. du "Monde," 1955).

17. Germaine Lelièvre, in her work on François Cogné, likewise noted this in Captain Bonhomme's papers, AN, series 2AG 15 ff.

18. I am indebted to Germaine Lelièvre, who has been working on the sculptor for several years, for valuable information, some of which has been published in the bulletin of the scholarly association Greha.

19. Note that a sculpted bust of Marianne still surmounted a photographic portrait of Pétain in the conference room at Paris's city hall on 5 January 1942; see Laurent Gervereau, "Y a-t-il un 'style Vichy'?" in Laurent Gervereau and Denis Peschanski, eds., *La propagande sous Vichy, 1940–1944*, exh. cat. (Nanterre: Bibliothèque de Documentation Internationale Contemporaine, 1990), 144 (no. 1).

20. See *Beaux-arts*, 18 April 1941; and *Beaux-arts*, 4 April 1941, which reported the art sector's wariness upon the announcement of the commission granted to Cogné.

21. See AN, series F21 6975, analyzed by Germaine Lelièvre.

22. "Along with the reduction of the monument that he [had] executed for Verdun." See a note written in Vichy, dated 22 October 1940 and signed by Pétain, in which the marshal authorized Cogné to "produce [*éditer*]" his bust and to come to an agreement with his minister of public education and youth "for all reproductions to be executed"—which the artist hastened to do (AN, series F21 6975, brought to my attention by Germaine Lelièvre).

Ever tactful, Cogné had written to Dr. Bernard Ménétrel, the marshal's secretary, from Casablanca on 21 August 1940. He had met Ménétrel's father in Pétain's office before the war and knew through a friend that the doctor, in his father's footsteps, continued to be fully occupied with the leader, to whom Cogné of course expressed his affection again and sent his "wishes for the good health necessary for the enormous labor to which he [had] devoted [himself] for the revival of a better France." Finally, Cogné announced that he was coming to Vichy in September. On 13 September, Ménétrel promised him a series of meetings, with Pétain, of course, but also with Laval, Darlan, and Marcel Peyrouton, as well as the permits necessary for his trip. In a letter of 21 September 1940, Cogné warmly thanked him, while suggesting he could do a bust of his father in bronze...; see AN, series 3W 291, item 44.

23. The deputy inspector general Louis Lavalle took care of the matter.

24. A study of the cost to produce the bust (in three different sizes) submitted by Velten, the head of the casting workshop of the Réunion des musées nationaux, and a draft contract between the management of the Réunion des musées nationaux, the Ecole du Louvre, and Cogné were put forward in March 1941.

25. These busts were cast in Cusset by the Fargette ceramics firm and produced by Vuitton and Vuitton. See the copies held by the Musée d'histoire contemporaine; and the illustration in Denis Peschanski, "Encadrer ou contrôler?" in Laurent Gervereau and Denis Peschanski, eds., *La propagande sous Vichy, 1940–1944*, exh. cat. (Nanterre: Bibliothèque de Documentation Internationale Contemporaine, 1990), 10 (no. 1).

26. See the reproduction of Cogné's bust of Pétain that appears on the front page of *L'illustration*, 26 April 1941, along with an autograph by the head of state, who, as the publisher explains, had refused to have an issue devoted to him. See also the photograph of Cogné next to the scale model for the full-length statue of the marshal exhibited at the Salon des Artistes Français in April 1942 in Peschanski et al., *Images de la France* (note 2), 146. Reference is made to that full-length statue, exhibited at the Salon des Artistes Français, in *L'illustration*, 16 May 1942.

In addition, général de division Charles Brécard, grand chancellor of the Légion d'honneur, unveiled a statue of the marshal by Cogné on 1 May 1943, on the occasion of the feast of Saint Philip the Apostle, Pétain's patron saint.

27. According to Bonhomme's notebooks, the artist saw the marshal several times in 1940, on 12 and 20 June, and on 1 and 2 December.

28. On 2 February 1929, *L'illustration* published a photo of Cogné's first bust of Pétain. See Bonhomme's diary; the municipal archives of Verdun; and, on the marshal's will, Herbert R. Lottman, *Pétain*, trans. Béatrice Vierne (Paris: Editions du Seuil, 1984).

29. Moreover, according to his close friends, Pétain told Cogné that he was not awarding the artist just any ribbon but rather the marshal's very own, which he had worn in Verdun and had almost given to Paul Valéry.

30. The statue was unveiled in Casablanca in November 1938. See *L'illustration*, 5 November 1938.
31. Puech was awarded the Prix de Rome in sculpture in 1884 and also won the grand prize at the Exposition universelle et internationale de Paris of 1900.
32. Cogné sculpted Lyautey four times, in 1922, 1932, 1934, and 1938.
33. The law of 25 October 1919 stipulated a subsidy to communes for commemorations. The financing law of 31 July 1920 established a very complicated method for calculating these subsidies, which took into account the relation between the number of combatants born or residing in the commune and the number of residents of the commune "determined by the census of 1911, and in inverse proportion to the per capita municipal tax for the year in which the subsidy was granted." See "Le monument aux morts de Saint-Germain-sur-Morin et son sculpteur François Cogné," *Greha*, October 1990, 5 (memo no. 17).
34. See his series of reinforced plaster casts, the original models for which are housed in the storerooms of the Musée Picasso in Antibes.
35. See Léon Cogné, "Comment j'ai fait le buste du Saint-Père," *L'illustration*, 14 October 1922, 358–63.
36. Arsène Alexandre, "Un sculpteur nouveau: François Cogné," *Journal de l'Aveyron*, 23 December 1923, 1.
37. Quoted in "Le monument aux morts" (note 33), 14 (memo no. 17).
38. On Robert Lallemant and his work, see *Les années UAM, 1929–1958*, exh. cat. (Paris: Musée des Arts Décoratifs, 1988), 204–5 (catalog entry by Chantal Bizot); "Un maître potier: Lallemant," *ABC décor: Antiquités, beaux-arts, curiosités*, no. 219, April 1983; and the archives of Mme Robert Lallemant.
39. See Pierre Vaisse, "La Troisième République et les peintres: Recherches sur les rapports des pouvoirs publics et de la peinture en France de 1870 à 1914," 3 vols. (Ph.D. diss., Université Paris IV–Paris Sorbonne, 1980).
40. "Un maître potier: Lallemant" (note 38).
41. See Herman Lebovics's analysis in his "Donner à voir l'Empire colonial: L'exposition coloniale internationale de Paris en 1931," *Gradhiva*, no. 7 (1989/1990): 18–28.
42. The production of the remaining works fell to the firms Canale (cast iron), Draeger Frères (cigarette boxes and plaques), and Coquemer (fold-out calendars), and to the Administration des monnaies et médailles.
43. See, at the Bibliothèque nationale, the press file under the shelf mark Yd2 1843 (27) 4°, as well as the photographic coverage of the event under shelf mark EST.Q.Mat.
44. See the Union des artistes modernes (UAM) manifesto of 1934; reprinted in *Les années UAM* (note 38), 37–66.

45. On this subject, see Christian Faure, *Le projet culturel de Vichy: Folklore et Révolution nationale, 1940–1944* (Lyon: Presses Universitaires de Lyon/ Centre Régional de Publication de Lyon, 1989).

46. Jules Léon Perrichon, a student of Paul César Helleu and the chief engraver of marshal imagery.

47. Ambroselli has reported that de Lattre, who had arrived in Colmar a few days after the city was liberated in February, asked him to go see the Isenheim Altarpiece, which they visited in its cramped haven, pressing their chests against the chest of Christ. De Lattre also asked for news of Frédéric-Auguste Bartholdi's bronze monument to général de division Jean Rapp and, learning that it had been shattered, ordered that it be restored (which the founder Eugène Rudier did) and set back in its place in Colmar for the ceremonies held on 14 July. Gérard Ambroselli, interview by Laurence Bertrand Dorléac, 13 December 1990.

48. The following is by no means an exhaustive list and excludes the poster artists already mentioned: Clément Rousseau, Lucien Bazor, Berthe Bonnefous de Randan, Bouchard, René Cottet, Ambroselli, Lallemant, Robert Coutre, Henri Dropsy, Raoul Benard, Castelain, Eugène-Baptiste Doumenc, E. Veron, Thommeret, Raffo, Patraud, Leduc, Jean Sève, Maurice Roumier, Louis Gautier, Michel Dufayet, Maria Brun, Roullet-Renoleau, Th. Correia, Otinelly, de Nune, Pierre Turin, Maurice Delannoy, François Angeli, Léonce Alloy, Charles Breton, Mouroux, Henri Vergé-Sarrat, Gérard Cochet, Cogné, Louis Joseph Soulas, Parvilliers, Gaudin, Michel Ciry, Simont, Le Breton, Léon Drivier, Georges-Léo Degorce, Sogno, André-Louis Dubois, Méteigner, Jacquemin, Dufour, Dusnel, Charles Mazelin (b. 1882; Salon des Artistes Français, Prix de Rome in 1908, Grand prix de l'Art philatélique in 1951), Jean Bouchaud (b. 1891; Salon des Artistes Français, grand prize at the Exposition internationale of 1937), Lucien Jonas (b. 1880; Salon des Artistes Français, runner-up for the Prix de Rome), Paul Charlemagne (b. 1892; Salon d'Automne, Salon des Indépendants, Salon des Tuileries), Paul-Pierre Lemagny (b. 1905; Prix de Rome in 1934, Académie des beaux-arts in 1949), Jean Eugène Bersier (b. 1895; Salon de la Société Nationale des Beaux-Arts, Salon des Tuileries, Salon d'Automne, Salon des Indépendants; during the occupation, belonged to the Front national des arts), Jules Piel (b. 1882; Prix de Rome in 1910, Salon des Artistes Français), Pierre Gandon (b. 1899; Prix de Rome in 1922), Albert Decaris (b. 1901, Prix de Rome in 1919).

    Conversely, some artists were reluctant to serve the forces in power: Henry de Waroquier, Edmond Céria, and Jean-Gabriel Daragnès, for example, who were assigned by René Héron de Villefosse, curator at the Musée du Petit Palais, to illustrate the deluxe album that was to pay tribute to Pétain on the "second anniversary of his assumption of power." Among authors, Cardinal Alfred Baudrillart, Henry de Montherlant, René

Benjamin, and Hautecoeur did not answer the call either, unlike Paul Valéry (of the Académie française), the Dominican friar Antonin-Gilbert Sertillanges (of the Académie des sciences morales et politiques), Henry Bordeaux (of the Académie française), Pierre Champion (of the Académie des sciences morales et politiques), général d'armée Julien Dufieux, général de division Bernard Serrigny, Abel Bonnard (of the Académie française), Jean-Louis Vaudoyer, André Chaumeix (of the Académie française), and Georges Suarez. Their respective texts were illustrated by engravings of Cottet, Jacquemin, Degorce, Dufour, Soulas, Cochet, Vergé-Sarrat, Lemagny, and Ciry.

See the report of Georges-André Masson, inspector general of fine arts for the City of Paris, 22 April 1941; and Héron de Villefosse's letter to Georges-André Masson, 17 June 1942; both in Archives de Paris, series VR art. 28. The City of Paris devoted a budget of 150,000 francs to the event, of which the sum of 5,000 francs was allocated to each of the artists and 2,500 francs to each author. The work was produced by the Ecole Estienne in Paris. See decree issued by the prefect of the Seine, 3 June 1942, Archives de Paris, series VR art. 28.

49. The Salon de l'Imagerie Française was founded in 1940 and placed under the patronage of the fine arts administration and the City of Paris. Under the occupation, it was run by Paul Lavalley (founding president), Robert Bonfils and André Foy (vice presidents), Guy Dollian (treasurer), Paul Bony, Paul Charlemagne, Lucien Coutaud, Maurice Frédéric, Jean-Denis Malclès, Paule Ingrand, Marthe Lebasque, Pauline Peugniez, Rémy Hétreau, Jacques Le Chevallier, Jean Picart Le Doux, and Raymond Templier. Charles Walch and Yves Alix left along the way. Gustave Singier, Georges-Henri Rivière, and Louis Chéronnet also participated in some of its activities. The Salon, which took place annually at the Musée Galliera, then at the Musée des arts décoratifs, was divided into sections: light, popular, scholastic, and religious images; toys; signs; marionettes; books; cartoons; souvenir objects; ceramics; fabrics; show bills; and a retrospective organized by Georges-Henri Rivière. Nearly a thousand objects were exhibited there each year, produced by some six hundred participants, a number that grew over the course of the occupation. A certain number of exhibitions, retrospectives, and competitions were also organized on the themes of sports, religion, the marshal, and the professions.

50. Georges-Henri Rivière, who served as artistic adviser of sorts to the young Corporation paysanne, recommended the chair of the Salon de l'Imagerie Française to the director of the Union générale des syndicats agricoles, with a view to offering the union assistance from the Salon's image makers. Several themes were considered: a label with the *francisque* and the Gallic cock; images by schoolchildren on the theme "You will be a peasant";

the Corporation paysanne as an "instrument of the peasant's freedom and security"; and the marshal handing the Corporation paysanne's charter over to peasants. Of note is Lucien Lautrec's participation on a project that created displays on the theme "State control and trusts." See AN, series F10 5052; and also Faure, *Le projet culturel de Vichy* (note 45). On painting and the rural world, see Héliane Bernard, "La terre et ses mythes: Voyage au centre de l'image: Le thème rural dans la peinture française, 1920–1955" (Ph.D. thesis, Université de Lyon II, 1988). On the Corporation paysanne, see Isabel Boussard, *Vichy et la Corporation paysanne* (Paris: Presses de la Fondation Nationale des Sciences Politiques, 1980).

51. The press campaign accompanying the sale of stereoscopic photographs by Secours national credited France with their invention.

52. See the law of 16 October 1941. Its reproduction as a decoration in certain sizes was henceforth prohibited; it could no longer be depicted in relief, only against a solid, decorative background, even though at the time the relief was becoming a procedure often used to represent the regime. See AN, series AJ 53 101.

53. See as well the numerous little embroidered escutcheons; the postage stamps with the coats of arms of French cities; the competition at the Ecole des beaux-arts on the theme of a tapestry bearing France's coat of arms; the publications showing the coats of arms of provinces and new corporations; and finally, the modification of coats of arms of eighty communes of the prefecture of the Seine.

54. See, for example, the propaganda billboard bearing Mussolini's face and the slogan "Per lui per l'Italia si!" (For him, for Italy, yes!) photographed in Valle d'Aosta in 1934; reproduced in Gervereau and Peschanski, *La propagande sous Vichy* (note 2), 250. On the French side, see also the "modernized" Pétain on the infamous poster that thanked the French legionnaires who had joined the German crusade against the Bolshevik peril; or, on the same theme, the enormous poster of Pétain hung behind Vichy minister Joseph Darnand at a meeting related to the Service d'ordre légionnaire at the amphitheater in Cimez, near Nice (n.d.), reproduced in Peschanski et al., *Images de la France* (note 2), 174–75.

55. For reports on the auctions devoted to that aspect of official art, see especially Alice Sedar's articles in *Le monde*. In 1990, it was possible to acquire, at the Parisian shopping emporium Le Louvre des antiquaires, a small Pétain tapestry for 2,800 francs, a medal designed by Pierre Turin for 1,500 francs, and a *francisque* for between 400 and 1,500 francs—all much less, in short, than the plaque of "Boulevard Maréchal-Pétain," which the dealer would not part with for less than 5,800 francs.

56. Between 1941 and 1944. About half depicted the head of state bareheaded and against a brown background. The 1.50 franc stamp, designed by Bersier and engraved by Piel, depicted the marshal full-face, in military uniform, wearing a kepi, and looking markedly younger than he actually was.

57. See the dossier "Pétain" presented by Jacques Sidos and Dominique Buffier in *Le monde des philatélistes*, November 1989, 35–39.

58. Issued from 1990 to 1996. See Louis Briat, interview by Pierre Jullien, in "De la *Marianne* de Briat," *Le monde des philatélistes*, January 1990, 48.

59. Document, sold at auction, 19–20 June 1990; see *Seconde Guerre mondiale* (note 2).

60. Note of 10 November 1941, sold at auction, 19–20 June 1990; see *Seconde Guerre mondiale* (note 2). Two versions circulated, an ordinary print and a "deluxe" print.

61. Document, sold at auction, 19–20 June 1990; see *Seconde Guerre mondiale* (note 2).

62. Note of 15 October 1941, sold at auction, 19–20 June 1990; see *Seconde Guerre mondiale* (note 2).

63. Printed in Limoges.

64. In the words of the journalist R. de C., *Beaux-arts*, 6 February 1942, 9.

65. Organized by the municipality of Paris, the exhibition *Hommages au Maréchal*, consisting of drawings by Parisian schoolchildren, was opened in Vichy on 10 July 1942 by Pétain. He warmly congratulated the sixteen winners, who had come from Paris to present their works.

66. Prizes were awarded at the end of the event, by a jury under the authority of Auguste Perret, president of the Ordre des architectes.

67. Born in 1906, Henri d'Amfreville had earned a law degree and also called himself a writer.

68. Henri d'Amfreville, "Vers un retour à un art de tradition populaire: En marge de l'exposition de dessins d'enfants en hommage au Maréchal," *Comoedia*, 31 January 1942, 1.

69. Roger Vercel, "Un programme d'éducation générale pour refaire la France," in *Disciplines d'action* (Vichy and Paris: Commissariat Général à l'Education Générale & aux Sports, [1941]), 4–8.

70. On Rabelais, Montaigne, and Rousseau, see Vercel, "Un programme" (note 69).

71. Official instructions, 1 June 1941.

72. For Vichy's sports policy, see the works of Jean-Louis Gay-Lescot, in particular his doctoral thesis, "L'éducation générale et sportive de l'Etat français de Vichy (1940–1944)" (Ph.D. diss., Université Michel de Montaigne–Bordeaux III, 1988); and his essay "La politique sportive de Vichy," in Jean-Pierre Rioux, ed., *La vie culturelle sous Vichy* (Brussels: Editions Complexe, 1990), 83–115.

73. Jean-Pierre Rioux, "Survivre," *L'histoire*, no. 80 (1985): 87.

74. Jean Giraudoux, "L'art et le sport au stade Roland-Garros," *Comoedia*, 5 July 1941, 1.

75. See André Fraigneau, review of Henry de Montherlant's *Paysage des Olympiques* (Paris: Grasset, 1940), *La gerbe*, 22 May 1941, 7.

76. The City of Paris, which had its own board for purchasing and commissioning works of art, was considered by the fine arts administration to be "a state within the state," in the words of Hautecoeur, who, as of the occupation, wanted to restrict its leaders—Pierre Darras and, after his dismissal, Georges-André Masson—to "coordination." In the Paris region, the prefect of the Seine allocated funds from the city budget to underwrite intellectual and artistic public works projects: seventy public sculptures and murals in two years. See the law of 4 June 1941, which stipulated that five million francs would be set aside for unemployed intellectuals, artists, and musicians, with half of that sum devoted to artists. Masson, inspector general of fine arts for the City of Paris, set up a program to aid artists, with many purchases, commissions, exhibitions, publications, and competitions, on various themes: *Nouveaux tableaux de Paris, Paris qui disparaît, Partant pour la banlieue, Art et ingéniosité, Madeleine-Bastille, Le centenaire de la naissance de Mallarmé.* His board brought together individuals with tastes as conservative as those on the state purchasing commissions.

    See Archives de Paris, series VR arts. 29, 80, 87, 115.

77. Albert Rivaud, 16 June to 12 July 1940; Émile Mireaux,12 July to 6 September 1940; Georges Ripert, 6 September to 13 December 1940; Jacques Chevalier, 13 December 1940 to 23 February 1941; Jérôme Carcopino, 24 February 1941 to 18 April 1942; and Abel Bonnard, 18 April 1942 to 20 August 1944, the end of the Vichy regime.

78. Born on 11 June 1884, a graduate of the Ecole normale supérieure, an *agrégé* in history, a member of the Ecole française de Rome, a doctor of philosophy, and a lycée teacher, Louis Hautecoeur began his university teaching career in France in art history in Caen in 1919 (where he remained until 1921). In 1919, he was appointed to the information committee of the Paris Peace Conference. He was a professor at the Ecole du Louvre as of 1920 and at the Ecole des beaux-arts as of 1923, where he taught architecture. He was hired as a curator by the Musée du Louvre in 1920 and by the Musée du Luxembourg in 1928. From 1927 to 1930, he was director of fine arts in Egypt and, in 1937, director of works of art for the Exposition internationale. He was named director general of fine arts on 21 July 1940 and served as secretary general of fine arts from 24 February 1941 to 1 January 1944.

79. According to his autobiography, up to his departure from fine arts, Hautecoeur suffered harassment by Laval and his men, who were supported by Göring: he was refused a passport for Geneva in May 1943; use of gasoline was restricted for the fine arts department; and so on. See Louis Hautecoeur, *Les beaux-arts en France, passé et avenir* (Paris: Editions A. & J. Picard, 1948).

80. On the reform of museums, see, in the *Journal officiel*, the law of 10 August 1941, which made the distinction between an administrative council and a technical council (composed of artists, art lovers, and representatives of higher education). It also made provisions for the advancement of curators; the creation of positions for assistants; the evaluation of twenty museums; and the placement of other museums under state control instead of only departments and municipalities.

81. The advanced degree granted by the Ecole du Louvre was overhauled in June 1941. To give a scientific character to the school, which was attracting many dilettante auditors, two categories of students were henceforth distinguished: the registered students and the auditors.

82. On the Ecole des beaux-arts and the Ecole nationale supérieure des arts décoratifs, see AN, series AJ 52 and AJ 53, now fairly complete, since the deposit of new items in AJ 52 in 1983. For the operation of the fine arts administration more generally, see the same archives. At the beginning of 1940, an "agency for education, art works, and spectacles," headed by Allirol (a member of the administration since the 1930s), included a bureau of education, manufacture, and government property; a bureau of works of art, museums (no longer included in 1944), and exhibitions, directed by Vincent Poli; and, finally, a bureau of music, spectacles, and art activities abroad. See the *Guide périodique de l'administration française;* and Luce Namer, "La politique artistique du gouvernement de Vichy" (D.E.A. [*diplôme d'études approfondies*] thesis, Institut d'études politiques de Paris, 1983).

83. Hautecoeur, *Les beaux-arts* (note 79), 8. The assistant director of fine arts, Léon Lamblin, remained at his post from the beginning to the end of the occupation.

84. On the Exposition internationale of 1937, see Stéphane Sinclair, "Les arts de l'intérieur de l'Exposition internationale des arts et techniques appliquées à la vie moderne de Paris, 1937" (thesis, Ecole nationale des chartes, 1988); see also *L'art face à la crise, 1929–1939: Actes du 4e Colloque d'histoire de l'art contemporain tenu à Saint-Étienne, les 22, 23, 24 et 25 mars 1979*...(Saint-Étienne: Centre Interdisciplinaire d'Etude & de Recherches sur l'Expression Contemporaine, 1980); and *Paris 1937, l'art indépendant*, exh. cat. (Paris: Musée d'Art Moderne de la Ville de Paris, 1987).

85. As the personal journals of artists hostile to modern art attest.

86. See Louis Hautecoeur to Edmond Labbé, 27 January 1937, AN, series F12 12194 (3). Quoted in Sinclair, "Les arts de l'intérieur" (note 84), 193–94.

87. Here, Hautecoeur's personality should be compared to those of the directors of museum involved in the progressive battle: Georges-Henri Rivière, Jacques Soustelle, and Agnès Humbert for the Musée des arts et traditions populaires; Madeleine Rousseau, official representative of the Musée du Luxembourg; André Dézarrois, curator of the collections of the Musée des

écoles étrangères contemporaines at the Jeu de Paume; and Jean Cassou.

88. Georges Huisman, "Nouveaux rapports de l'art et de l'état," *Europe: Revue littéraire mensuelle,* June 1937, 160; quoted in Pascal Ory, "La politique culturelle du Front populaire (1935–1938)" (Ph.D. diss., Université Paris X–Nanterre, 1990), 534.

89. From 1955 to 1964.

90. Pierre Ladoué, "L'art vivant: Les achats et commandes de l'Etat aux artistes en 1942," *Revue des beaux-arts de France,* April–May 1943.

91. In France, Belmondo signed on for *Apollo* (two monumental groups) and Félix Joffre for *Diana;* while Henri Lagriffoul, Grattesat, Gaston Cadenat, and Petit produced four nymphs; Henri Valette, Jean Corin, and Raymond Corbin did the *Hunting Scenes* (bas-reliefs); Gaston Dumont, coats of arms; René Debarre, *Child with Fish* (fountain motif); Ottavry, Firmin Marcelin Michelet, Auguste Biaggi, Georges Ridet, and Constant-Brûlé, monumental ornate vases; and, finally, Georges Halbout, four keystones.

92. About ten million francs were set aside for commissions in 1942 and 1943. See AN, series F21; the figures cited in Maximilien Gauthier, "Le courage du choix: À propos du budget des Beaux-Arts," *Beaux-arts,* 5–12 September 1941, 8; and Hautecoeur, *Les beaux-arts* (note 79). During the prewar years, the fine arts administration's budget dropped sharply in 1936, before rising again in 1937, and doubling in 1939. It represented 3 percent of the overall budget of the ministry of national education and youth between 1935 and 1938, 6 percent in 1939, and 5 percent in 1940. See Service national des statistiques, Direction de la statistique générale, *Annuaire statistique abrégé* 1 (1943): 152.

In 1942, 241 artists in Paris or in the provinces were affected by the state's policy for acquiring works of art. See Ladoué, "L'art vivant" (note 90). See also AN, series F21, for the sums allocated to artists, under the heading of "secours" (aid), generally between two hundred and fifteen hundred francs per person.

93. Whereas the purchasing commission had been voluntarily broadened by Huisman to include a few individuals who were progressive, at least in terms of their aesthetic choices (André Dézarrois, Cassou, and Rivière), Hautecoeur restricted its composition. It brought together the head of the Bureau des travaux d'art, the director of the Réunion des musées nationaux, the curator of the Musée national d'art moderne, the curator responsible for provincial museums, the president of La société des amis du Louvre, and the administrator of Mobilier national (who was likewise director of the national factories). Ladoué was assigned to deal with the artists; Raymond Cogniat, an inspector, to visit provincial studios; Albert Laprade, to visit studios in Paris. Also on that commission were Darras, director of fine arts for the City of Paris, then his successor, Masson, as well as representatives from the Commissariat général aux sports, two painters, two sculptors, and two decorative artists.

Once works of art were acquired by the commission, they were dispatched to various French museums, to Mobilier national, or to public institutions: ministries, prefectures, subprefectures, city halls, courts of justice, embassies, university departments, lycées, elementary schools, conservatories, churches, hospitals, and châteaus. On the fine arts administration before the war and on the Conseil supérieur des beaux-arts, which was specifically eliminated in July 1940 (under the law of 12 July 1940 against advisory organizations), see Marie-Claude Genet-Delacroix, *Art et Etat sous la IIIe République: Le système des beaux-arts, 1870–1940* (Paris: Publications de la Sorbonne, 1992).

94. Under the occupation, the state acquired several works by Pierre Bonnard: *Landscape* (painting), in November 1940 (destination, Musée Toulouse-Lautrec d'Albi); a watercolor, in February 1941 (destination unknown); another watercolor, in March 1941 (destination, Musée Toulouse-Lautrec d'Albi); and *Women and Children* (painting), in September 1941 (destination, Musée national d'art moderne). It also acquired two works by Marquet, *View of Rotterdam* (painting) and *View of the Seine in La Frette* (painting), in October 1940 (destination, Musée national d'art moderne). And several works by Matisse: two drawings, *Still Life with Fruit and Vase* and *Woman's Head*, in December 1941 (destination, Musée national d'art moderne); and *Interior at Ciboure* (painting), in October 1941 (destination, Musée Toulouse-Lautrec d'Albi).

95. A voluntarist purchasing movement privileged, especially in 1940, the series of drawings done in the armed forces by mobilized artists.

96. On the life of a female painter under the occupation, see Jacqueline Gaussen-Salmon, *Une prière dans la nuit: Journal d'une femme peintre sous l'Occupation*, ed. Frédéric Gaussen (Paris: Payot, 1992).

97. Other Salons that took place under the occupation were the Salon de l'Imagerie Française (for artisanal works), the Salon d'Hiver, the Salon de l'Union des Femmes Peintres et Sculpteurs, the Salon des Humoristes, the Salon des Anciens Combattants, the Salon des Moins de Trente Ans (supposed to redraw the map of artistic trends), and the Salon du Dessin et de la Peinture à l'Eau, which took place in summer, for the first time in 1941, initially to keep the occupying forces from requisitioning the Palais de Tokyo during the summer vacation period.

98. See Éric Michaud, "Art, propagande, publicité autour de Paris—1937," in *L'art face à la crise, 1929–1939: Actes du 4e Colloque d'histoire de l'art contemporain tenu à Saint-Étienne, les 22, 23, 24 et 25 mars 1979*... (Saint-Étienne: Centre Interdisciplinaire d'Etude & de Recherches sur l'Expression Contemporaine, 1980).

99. See entries for the artists these dealers defended in the chronology, this volume, 378–408.

100. On economic Aryanization, see Joseph Billig, *Le Commissariat général aux questions juives (1941–1944)*, 3 vols. (Paris: Editions du Centre, 1955–60); Henry Rousso, "L'aryanisation économique: Vichy, l'occupant et la spoliation des Juifs," *Yod*, no. 15–16 (1982); Martine Soëte, "L'aryanisation économique: Commissaires-gérants et administrateurs provisoires, Vichy, 1940–1944," (master's thesis, Université Paris I–Panthéon Sorbonne, 1986); and finally, the recent overview by Claire Andrieu, "Le mythe de la banque juive et les réalités de l'aryanisation," in André Kaspi, Annie Kriegel, and Annette Wieviorka, eds., "Les Juifs de France dans la Seconde Guerre mondiale," special issue, *Pardès*, no. 16 (1992).

101. See the underground *L'art français*, no. 5 (1944).

102. The auditor was unable to assess a huge inventory. The sum total of 9,654,455.65 francs did not account for the real value of the works in stock at the Galerie Wildenstein. See the Wildenstein dossier, AN, series AJ 40 610; quoted in Pierre Assouline, *L'homme de l'art: D.-H. Kahnweiler (1884–1979)* (Paris: Balland, 1988), 371.

103. See the account give by Jonathan Napack, "The Wildenstein Family: The Secret Lives of the Dealers Who Run the Masterpiece Market," *SPY*, October 1991.

104. See the remarks in Emmanuel David, *Le métier de marchand de tableaux: Entretiens avec Hervé Le Boterf* (Paris: Editions France-Empire, 1978), 84.

105. Misinformed Gestapo agents took David to the Drancy concentration camp, where he remained only briefly, since he had been able to alert his protector beforehand; see David, *Le métier de marchand* (note 104), 87. On his career as an art dealer under the occupation, and on the role of the German painter Paul Strecker (whom David had known since before the war) in David's run-ins with the Gestapo, see David, *Le métier de marchand* (note 104), 77–91.

106. Daniel-Henry Kahnweiler to Max Jacob, 27 November 1936, in Isabelle Monod-Fontaine and Claude Laugier, with Sylvie Warnier, *Daniel-Henry Kahnweiler, marchand, éditeur, écrivain*, exh. cat. (Paris: Centre Georges Pompidou, 1984), 150; quoted in Assouline, *L'homme de l'art* (note 102), 368.

107. Daniel-Henry Kahnweiler to Marcel Moré, 20 July 1940, in P. G. Persin archives; quoted in Assouline, *L'homme de l'art* (note 102), 364.

108. Some twenty years earlier, Kahnweiler, as a German-born collector, had had the contents of his Paris gallery (fifteen hundred items) sequestered and, in 1921, sold for a pittance: 909,000 francs, hardly more than the value of a single painting by Eugène Delacroix, *The Death of Sardanapalus*. Under the occupation, an anonymous letter pointing out Louise Leiris's family relationship to Kahnweiler was sent to the Commissariat général aux questions juives, almost scuttling the transaction. The sale was finally recorded on

16 July 1941. The Galerie Simon possessed capital of 240,000 francs, and Louise Leiris purchased it without a ground lease for 73,460 francs; see Archives du Registre de commerce; quoted in Assouline, *L'homme de l'art* (note 102), 373–74.

109. Picasso's works supposedly riled an old woman, who threatened to report the dealer to Pétain, holding the dealer and the painter responsible for the defeat of France. See Maurice Laffaille, *Chronique d'une galerie de tableaux sous l'Occupation* (Paris: Editions Galerie Fanny Guillon-Laffaille & Marval, 1988), 32.

110. Especially as the situation became more and more dangerous and Jews who had taken refuge in coastal cities had to sell their possessions and flee to remote villages.

111. Jean Bazaine had introduced Carré to Villon, whose work Carré liked so much that he asked him to produce more. The dealer had electricity installed at Villon's studio, but the painter was not happy with it. Jean Bazaine, interview by Laurence Bertrand Dorléac, March 1992, Clamart.

112. Martin Fabiani, *Quand j'étais marchand de tableaux* (Paris: Julliard, 1976), 137.

113. Fabiani, *Quand j'étais marchand* (note 112), 137.

114. Gildo Caputo, who was close to the parties involved, considered Drouin's initially confused position under the occupation to be a result of the harmful influence of a certain Paul Maratier, a major collaborator. Only the influence of Drouin's friends finally convinced him to drop Maratier. Still, it was Maratier who led Drouin to discover the paintings of the Jeunes peintres de tradition française. Also according to Caputo, during the occupation years Maratier signed his name to the arts column in *Comoedia* while using Caputo as a ghostwriter. Called in by the publication's director, who had discovered their deceit, Caputo was hired in Maratier's place. Caputo then wrote a number of articles, only one of which was censored, against the Ecole des beaux-arts and the Prix de Rome. See Gildo Caputo, interview by Laurence Bertrand Dorléac, Paris, 1 April 1981, in Laurence Bertrand Dorléac, *Histoire de l'art, Paris 1940–1944: Ordre national, traditions et modernités* (Paris: Publications de la Sorbonne, 1986), 357–62; the interview is reprinted in Laurence Bertrand Dorléac, "Gildo Caputo: Interview—Les années sombres/The Dark Years," *Cimaise*, no. 205 (1990): 61–63.

115. See Pierre Bourdieu and Alain Darbel, *L'amour de l'art, les musées et leur public* (Paris: Editions de Minuit, 1966); Raymonde Moulin, *Le marché de la peinture en France* (Paris: Editions de Minuit, 1967; 2nd ed., Paris: Editions de Minuit, 1967); and Raymonde Moulin, with Pascaline Costa, *L'artiste, l'institution et le marché* (Paris: Flammarion, 1992).

116. The Association populaire des amis des musées (APAM), which was run by the non-Communist wing of the progressive movement, played a leading role in the world of associations. In 1937, members included Léo Lagrange, Jean Zay, Romain Rolland, René Belin, Pierre Bonnard, Albert Demangeon, Marc Sangnier, and Michel Leiris. To reach the widest possible audience, APAM organized lectures and traveling exhibitions, and even went into factories.

117. Moulin, *Le marché de la peinture* (2nd ed.), 40–41. See the catalogs for the Hôtel Drouot, which resumed its auctions in autumn 1940. See also the results of sales in the provinces, particularly in Aix-en-Provence, where the Belval collection was sold during the occupation, in 1942, attracting many art lovers and dealers.

118. See Jean-Marc Campagne's preface in *Le paysage français de Corot à nos jours*, exh. cat. (Paris: Galerie Charpentier, 1942).

119. At the Galerie René Drouin, in 1942.

120. Gaston Diehl, "Présence des maîtres," *Aujourd'hui*, 15 January 1942, 2.

121. In all, 464 painters, 577 sculptors, and 336 decorative artists produced work for the Exposition internationale. See the statement by Jean Locquin, AN, series F60 964; quoted in Ory, "La politique culturelle" (note 88), 585.

122. Hautecoeur, *Les beaux-arts* (note 79), 148.

123. Regarding the Direction générale des beaux-arts, see AN, series F21; concerning the aid granted by the City of Paris, see Archives de Paris, VR art. 29.

124. Edmond Humeau, "Le chômage intellectuel," *Chantiers*, 1 October 1941; and Edmond Humeau, "Un problème d'Etat—l'avenir des intellectuels," *Chantiers*, 10 and 25 December 1943. The author, head of the Service des chantiers intellectuels et artistiques under the occupation, was a devotee of the review *Esprit*. In 1943, the City of Paris awarded him—along with about a hundred key figures from the art world—a "Beaux-Arts" medal for his actions in support of the struggle against the unemployment of intellectuals and artists. On his actions related to the City of Paris, see the Archives de Paris, VR arts. 32, 165.

125. Consider, for example, the activities of Jean Amblard, who was assigned by Georges-Henri Rivière, on behalf of the Chantier d'intellectuels associated with the Musée des arts et traditions populaires, to "depict" the life of peasants from his village Montcheneix. He accomplished the task while also undertaking activities for the Resistance, as part of the Front national des arts and the 126th régiment d'infanterie. He took part, as a painter for the armed forces, in the liberation of Alsace with the 5th armored division, before being gravely wounded subsequent to the taking of Colmar. A militant in the Communist Party beginning in 1934, he was one of the party's official artists. In 1946, Robert Rey commissioned from Amblard a mural measuring 150 square meters, or about 180 square yards, glorifying the heroes of the maquis; it was to be installed in the city hall at Saint-Denis.

See the texts by Auguste Gillot, Paul Éluard, Elsa Triolet, and Jacques Gaucheron in *Les maquis de France: Peintures de Jean Amblard, mairie de Saint-Denis* (Paris: Editions du Cercle d'Art, 1951); *Vingt dessins de Jean Amblard, peintre en ethnologie, combattant des maquis d'Auvergne...* (Saint-Denis: Musée d'Art & d'Histoire de la Ville de Saint-Denis, 1982); and Héliane Bernard, "Jean Amblard: Salarié du Musée national des arts et traditions populaires, peintre du monde artisanal (1943–1944)," Bulletin du Centre Pierre Léon, no. 3–4 (1984).

See also Georges-Henri Rivière, interview by Laurence Bertrand Dorléac, 2 October 1982, Paris, in Laurence Bertrand Dorléac, "Art, culture et société: L'exemple des arts plastiques à Paris entre 1940 et 1944" (habilitation thesis, Institut d'études politiques de Paris, 1990), 2:640–52.

126. See Philippe Vatin, "Fonction des arts graphiques en France pendant la Grande Guerre" (master's thesis, Université Paris I–Panthéon Sorbonne, 1985).

127. Masson, inspector general of fine arts for the City of Paris, set up an aid program for artists, increasing purchases, commissions, exhibitions, publications, and competitions. In December 1941, its board included key individuals whose tastes, for the most part, were conservative: Pierre Revilliod, general secretary; Réne Héron de Villefosse, assistant curator at the Musée du Petit Palais; François Léon Boucher, curator at the Musée Cognacq-Jay; Yvon Bizardel, curator of the Musée Galliera; Max Terrier, assistant curator at the Musée Carnavalet; Georges Contenot, former president of the municipal council; Paul-Louis Garnier, representative from Entraide des artistes; Jacques Beltrand, painter and engraver; Jean-Gabriel Daragnès, painter and engraver; and Pierre Darras, director emeritus of fine arts for the City of Paris.

Under the law passed on 4 June 1941, five million francs (from the budget of the City of Paris and the *département* Seine) were set aside for unemployed intellectuals, artists, and musicians, with half reserved for painters, sculptors, engravers, draftsmen, and ceramists. Each received on average twenty-five hundred francs. A privileged few (including many official artists) received more than ten thousand francs (in 1942: Mme Chadel, Brochard, Dupré, Eugène Louis Corneau, Edmond Heuzé, Luigi Corbellini, Émile Bouneau, André Léon Galtié, Delzers, Louis Lejeune, Émile Henri Feltesse, Munier, Gabriel-Antoine Barlangue, Henri-Lucien Cheffer, Cosson, François Quelvée, Charles Mazelin, Maurice Dufrène, Pierre Gandon, Serres, René Cottet, Félix Benneteau, Georges d'Espagnat, Jean Eugène Bersier, Henri Vergé-Sarrat, Gérard-Paul Cochet, Robert Jeannisson, Pierre-Marie Poisson, Georges-Léo Degorce, Rispal, Alfred Bachelet, Reddet, Claude Venard, André Planson, Fernand Herbo, André Civet, Henri Jannot, Estève, Mazurier, Paul-Albert Moras, Peyret, Girondeau, Paul Vincent, Louis Pierre

Rigal, Devoncoux, Francis Gruber, Émile Gaudissard, Pierre Traverse, Philippe Leclerc).

See Archives de Paris, series VR arts. 29, 80, 87, 115.

128. A fresco was remunerated at 1,000 francs per square meter, the same amount as in 1935, according to the underground *L'art français*, no. 2 (1942). In December 1935, the state was paying 18,000 francs per square meter for sculpture, 6,000 francs for painting; in February 1936, 5,000 francs per square meter for sculpture in bas-relief, 8,500 francs for sculpture in high relief.

129. First article of the by-laws of Entraide des artistes, private archives.

130. Initially known as the Fédération des artistes, it then became the Fédération d'aide aux artistes, Aide aux artistes, Entraide des artistes, and, finally, Entraide.

131. Cognacq-Jay, who was in charge of Entraide d'hiver du Maréchal and director of La Samaritaine, accepted clothing vouchers issued by Entraide des artistes.

132. In 1940, Entraide des artistes organized the first exhibition to be held at the Orangerie in the Tuileries gardens after the armistice; the same year, it organized the exhibition *Centenaire Monet-Rodin* (which brought in 275,000 francs). In 1944, at the Galerie Charpentier, the sale of about a hundred works donated by benefactors, directed by Etienne Ader, brought in more than two million francs. Works by Maurice Utrillo, Renoir, van Dongen, Vlaminck, Derain, Legueult, Oudot, and Planson were sold.

133. See Gisèle Berstein and Serge Berstein, *La Troisième République* (Paris: M. A. Editions, 1987), 213.

134. Upon Garnier's death, in 1941.

135. The law of 1964 established medical insurance; that of 1977 applied a system of social insurance almost identical to that of the ordinary wage laborer (Code de la Sécurité Sociale L.613); and that of 1986 granted artists all the rights of wage laborers, including daily indemnities.

136. On 20 January 1938, at the Congrès des chômeurs de la région parisienne of the Confédération générale du travail (CGT), a list of demands by artists and artisans was defended that stipulated some ten measures: a rise in unemployment benefits; daily deductions for benefits and heating allowance; state vouchers for materials; the establishment of a supervisory committee to defend unemployed persons in trouble; minimal representation of the unemployed during seasonal Salons and in the artists' societies; and free entry at all times to museums and exhibitions for the unemployed. In return, works by the unemployed would be donated to various groups and the state as a function of their support. See the journal *Peintres et sculpteurs de la Maison de la culture*, February 1938.

137. Before the war, Maurice Guy-Loë was president of the Association Florence-

Blumenthal, created by an American patron of the arts to award stipends to young artists. He was also a member of Porza—an international association whose aim was to foster enlightened intellectual and artistic exchange at residential retreats across Europe (see the notice by Jacques Viénot, in *Ce temps ci* 1 [1928]: 20)—which was presided over by Anatole de Monzie and supported by Jean-Richard Bloch, Le Corbusier, Georges Duhamel, André Maurois, Louis Jouvet, and many others.

138. With the goal of obtaining commissions for them, Entraide's board, composed of representatives who were more or less traditionalist (Lejeune, Raoul Lamourdedieu, Binon, Montagnac, Georges d'Espagnat, and Maurice Dufrène), proposed names of artists to the Commissariat à la lutte contre le chômage.

139. Entraide des artistes brought together the Société des artistes français (Albert Tournaire, Chataigneau), Société du Salon d'automne (Guy-Loë, Montagnac, Georges d'Espagnat, Pierre Ladureau, Gustave Louis Jaulmes), Société des indépendants (Charles André Igounet de Villers, Jean-Louis Lefort), Société nationale des beaux-arts (Pierre Prunier, Marius-Léon Cladel), Société du Salon d'hiver (Étienne Corpet), Union des femmes peintres et sculpteurs (Mme Camax-Zoegger), Société du Salon des Tuileries (Auguste Perret, Henraux), Société des indépendants (Félicien Cacan), Société de l'Ecole française (Dupati de Clam), and Société de la Samothrace (Réni-Mel). The Société du Salon de l'imagerie française, Société du Salon des surindépendants, Société des dessinateurs humoristes, Société des anciens lauréats de la Fondation américaine, Société des artistes décorateurs, and Société des peintres-graveurs français, as well as about ten other societies, were also affiliated with Entraide. When it was created in 1939, the following key individuals formed a bureau that was to meet regularly: Beltrand, Bessard, Bonnier, Cacan, Cladel, Chataigneau, Gabriel Cognacq, David-Weill, Despiau, Paul-Louis Garnier, Paul Graf, Lucien-Victor Guirand de Scévola, Albert Henraux, Huisman, Landowski, Masbau, Montagnac, Perret, Rey, Sainte-Lagüe, Saint-Prix, Sommier, and Wildenstein.

140. The computerization of the directory of the profession did not take place until 1979. The figures remained approximate, often inflated by the art sector, which complained of an excess of members.

The 1943 *Annuaire statistique abrégé* (note 92) gave the figure of 49,800 people engaged in "letters and arts" (thus including writers) in 1936; Guy-Loë, in 1936, listed 5,850 artists, painters, or engravers and 950 sculptors in the Paris region; in a note of 25 March 1936, Giudicelli adopted the statistics communicated by the police prefecture, which probably corresponded to the number of artists declared unemployed: 883 painters and miniaturists, 317 sculptors, 480 decorative artists, 218 draftsmen, and 77 engravers and lithographers.

141. On this project, see Laurence Bertrand Dorléac, "L'Ordre des artistes et l'utopie corporatiste: Les tentatives de régir la scène artistique française, juin 1940–août 1944," *Revue d'histoire moderne et contemporaine* 37 (1990). The issue is treated more exhaustively in Bertrand Dorléac, "Art, culture et société" (note 125), vol. 4, supplement 1: "Comment le gouvernement s'y est pris pour mettre en oeuvre la corporation des arts graphiques et plastiques."

142. Claude Mauriac, "La corporation dans l'Etat" (Ph.D. diss., Faculté de Droit, Université de Bordeaux, 1941), 10.

143. On this subject, a large body of militant and scholarly literature appeared at the time: more than a hundred titles between 1940 and 1944.

144. See Isabel Boussard, ed., *Vichy et la corporation paysanne* (Paris: Presses de la Fondation Nationale des Sciences Politiques, 1980).

145. See Maurice Bouvier-Ajam, *L'Etat français sera corporatif: Extraits des messages et écrits du maréchal Pétain en 1940, 1941 et 1942 reliés et brièvement commentés* (Le Mans: Editions "CEP," 1943), 7.

146. See Claude-Joseph Gignoux, *La Tour du Pin* (Le Mans: Editions "CEP," 1944), 7.

147. See Louis Hautecoeur, *Considérations sur l'art d'aujourd'hui* (Paris: Librairie de France, 1929), 66–67.

148. On the first academies, see Frances Yates, *The French Academies of the Sixteenth Century* (London: Warburg Institute, 1947).

149. After the war, Pierre Imbourg worked as a journalist at *Les nouvelles littéraires* and *Une semaine de Paris;* he also served as editor in chief at *La gazette de l'Hôtel Drouot* and director of *Journal de l'amateur d'art.*

150. See Pierre Imbourg, "Pour être fort, soyez unis: Un projet de Fédération des artistes est actuellement à l'étude," *Beaux-arts*, October 1940.

151. The bulk of the archives on the corporation plan, recently discovered in a wine cellar, is now being cataloged by the contemporary section of the Archives nationales.

152. On issues related to architecture, see Rémi Baudouï, "Planification territoriale et reconstruction 1940–1946," 2 vols. (Ph.D. diss., Université Paris XII–Val-de-Marne, 1984); Rémi Baudouï, "L'architecture en France des années 1930 aux années 1940: Conflits 'idéologiques' et continuités formelles de la crise à la Libération," in Pierre Milza and Fanette Roche-Pézard, eds., *Art et fascisme: Totalitarisme et résistance au totalitarisme dans les arts en Italie, Allemagne et France des années 30 à la défaite de l'Axe* (Brussels: Editions Complexe, 1989); and Frédérique Boucher and Danièle Voldman, "Les architectes sous l'Occupation" (research report, Institut d'histoire du temps présent, Paris, 1992).

153. In November 1941, its bureau was reportedly composed of Desvallières (president); Montagnac, Charles André Igounet de Villers, Bouchard, Viret, Guiard, Raymond Subes, and Despiau (vice presidents); Raoul

Lamourdedieu (secretary general); Bouchery (assistant secretary general); and Legrand (treasurer).

154. A note from the legal council of Entraide des artistes to Anatole de Monzie, 15 March 1941, mentions that the German army officer Heinrich Ehmsen had directed that the group's by-laws be reworked in accordance with de Brinon's "[authoritarian]" directives, while Hautecoeur had just constituted an organization committee to set up the Ordre des artistes. The author of the note remarked that this put the leaders of Entraide in an embarrassing situation: disobey either the French government or the German directives; private archives.

On the Germans' desire to see the French art sector rigidly reorganized through a reliance on certain key individuals, particularly Henri Louis Bouchard and Marcel Temporal, see the reports of the Propaganda-Abteilung Frankreich, "Bildende Künste," 7 January 1941, 3 February 1941, 25 February 1941, and 26 March 1941.

See also the unpublished journal of Paul Landowski, entry of 12 October 1940, in which he discusses the Germans' request to Chataigneau (head of the Fédération des artistes) that "these countless societies" disappear and that all Jews be excluded from them.

Of note is the pressure the Germans applied to impose Bouchard as president of the Fédération des artistes.

155. The secretary general shuttled between Paris (where he entrusted the administration to Léon Lamblin) and Vichy, seat of the government, where the fine arts administration had modest offices: his own, he complained, was a small bedroom where he received visitors "between the bed and a bidet." See Hautecoeur, *Les beaux-arts* (note 79), 20.

156. The minutes of seven meetings of the study committee, up to June 1941, are at the Archives nationales (AN).

157. See the minutes of the study committee meeting, 10 May 1941, AN.

158. [*Jurande:* Under the ancien régime, a professional group founded on an oath made by all its members to one another and enjoying a great deal of autonomy.—Trans.]

159. Minutes of the study committee meeting, 10 May 1941, AN. Later, in 1943, Landowski would not find more realistic the desire of his comrades to have the Académie des beaux-arts intervene directly, through the coordination committee of the Ecole nationale supérieure des arts décoratifs and the Ecole des beaux-arts. He remarked that "those people are forgetting that the Académie des beaux-arts has not been officially concerned with teaching for the last century and a half"; Paul Landowski, unpublished journal, 29 May 1943.

160. In the words of Desvallières, minutes of the study committee meeting, 2 May 1941, AN.

161. See Dufrène's proposal regarding the Ordre des artistes décorateurs, 3 July 1941, AN.

162. Desvallières was the one who protested most vigorously, invoking Manet, against the general opinion favoring strict regulation. See Paul Landowski, unpublished journal, 13 June 1941.

163. Jean Bazaine, "Masques corporatifs," *La nouvelle revue française*, December 1941, 710.

164. According to the remarks reported by Paul Landowski, unpublished journal, 10 May 1943.

165. See the letter from Maurice Denis to Louis Hautecoeur, AN.

166. Maurice Denis, *Journal* (Paris: La Colombe, Editions du Vieux-Colombier, 1957–59), 3:220.

167. See the minutes of the study committee meeting, 23 January 1942, AN.

168. See the decree of 7 July 1941, establishing the Comité d'organisation professionnelle des arts graphiques et plastiques.

169. In March and April 1942, the following artists were selected. Painters' bureau: Hugues de Beaumont, Edmond Céria, Roger Chapelain-Midy, Paul Charlemagne, Georges Desvallières (member of the Institut de France), Lucien-Victor Guirand de Scévola, André Lhote, Robert Pougheon. Sculptors' bureau: Paul Belmondo, Henri Louis Bouchard (member of the Institut de France), Léon Drivier, Charles Despiau, Marcel Gaumont, Alfred Auguste Janniot, Louis Lejeune (member of the Institut de France), Paul Niclausse. Engravers' bureau: André Dauchez (member of the Institut de France), André Dunoyer de Segonzac, Pierre Gandon, Robert Lotiron, Louis Joseph Soulas, Henry de Waroquier. Medal engravers' bureau: Claude Mascaux, Louis-Charles Muller, André Rivaud, Pierre Turin. Decorators' bureau: Jacques Adnet, Louis Barillet, André Domin, Jean Dunand, René Kieffer, Jean Luce, Pierre-Paul Montagnac, Raymond Subes.

170. See the note from Vincent Poli, head of the Bureau des travaux d'art, musées et expositions, to the head of the Service administratif et financier du 3e bureau, 16 April 1942. The response was signed on behalf of the minister by Dagnicourt, assistant director in charge of managing the budget office in Paris, AN.

171. See the minutes of the meeting of the Comité d'organisation professionnelle des arts graphiques et plastiques, 6 February 1942, AN. See also Paul Landowski, unpublished journal, 17 and 20 November 1941 (during his trip to Germany).

172. The responses noted by André Fougeron provide proof of this. They come not only from artists known for their conservatism but also from personalities close to progressive circles or to the Communist Party.

173. See Georges Hilaire, writing under the pseudonym Julien Clermont, *L'homme qu'il fallait tuer: Pierre Laval* (Paris: Actes des Apôtres, Charles de Jonquières, 1949), 308.

174. See Hautecoeur, *Les beaux-arts* (note 79), 328–30.

175. The list was composed of the following key individuals. Painters and draftsmen: Pierre Bonnard, Matisse, Jean Puy, Georges Rouault, Braque, Derain, Friesz, Dufy, Henri Charles Manguin, Dunoyer de Segonzac, Jean-Gabriel Goulinat, Gus Bofa, Lhote, Gromaire, Waroquier, Durey, Brianchon, Adrien-Pierre Bagarry, Wild, Bersier, Guy-Loë, Jean Claude Aujame, Legueult, Berthommé Saint-André, André Marchand, Estève, Germain Delatousche. Arts journalists: Bernard Champigneulle, Pierre du Colombier, Jean-Marc Campagne, Émile Vuillermoz, Diehl, Viénot. Sculptors: Maillol, Despiau, Drivier, Niclausse, Yencesse, Jean Osouf, Marcel-Antoine Gimond, Robert Couturier. Engravers: Decaris, André Jacquemin, etc. Decorative artists: Jacques Adnet, Lurçat, Bouilhet, Mme Maumel, Lallemant. Art publishers and advertisers: Paul Peignot, Daragnès. Craftsmen and popular artists: Chéronnet, Duchartre. Set decorators: André Dignimont, Oudot, Touchagues. Photographers: Boudot-Lamotte. Actors: Barsacq, Marchat. Architects: Albert Laprade, Eugène Beaudouin, Moreux, Roux-Spitz, Henri Pacon, Barbe. Urban developers and protectors of monuments: de Ségogne, Pillement, Héron de Villefosse, Pierre d'Espezel, Marcel Raval, Wanecq. Musicians: André Cluytens, Ludwig Beck, etc.

176. See excerpts from this program and a sample of the correspondence from Hilaire sent in July 1944 to about a hundred personalities from the art scene in volume 3 of Bertrand Dorléac, "Art, culture et société" (note 125).

177. See Serge Added, *Le théâtre dans les années Vichy, 1940–1944* (Paris: Editions Ramsay, 1992), 35–36.

178. See Paul Landowski, unpublished journal, 12 October 1940. Along the same lines, Landowski was an advocate of a single order for artists and architects, opposing Hautecoeur, who insisted the two groups be separate; see Paul Landowski, unpublished journal, 13 June 1941. That reform was on the table until late 1943.

179. Paul Tournon, born in 1881, was an architect much taken with sacred art He built the Eglise du Saint-Esprit on avenue Daumesnil in Paris and the Vatican pavilion at the Exposition internationale in 1937.

180. Paul Landowski, unpublished journal, 26 May 1943.

181. Paul Landowski, unpublished journal, 2 June 1943.

CHAPTER FIVE

Eternal Return

ART FOR ALL

For too long, art had locked itself away in its ivory tower, besotted with its own greatness and contemptuous of a nation of ignoramuses who always lagged behind its advances. In the midst of reconstruction, art was to be driven out of its seclusion; artists had to be reminded of their social and redemptive mission, as everyone agreed that "art for all" should not be a diversion but rather a spur that roused sluggish minds and spirits. The past was teeming with edifying examples. Indeed, on 14 December 1941, Robert Leforestier, a Pétainist from the first, appealed to skeptics by telling them the touching tale of van Eyck's *Adoration of the Mystic Lamb* carried in triumph for several days by the people of Ghent and "then venerated as a new deity."[1] Artists were invited to be more modest and more devout, to at long last take to the streets and meet the jubilant crowds burning to resacralize art. They had to occupy the common ground between the marshal's Révolution nationale and the altruistic project of the French "new artist."

In the ranks of officialdom, the point of view held by Hautecoeur was close to the general sentiment: every critique of art corresponded to a judgment on French society and the upheavals it had gone through. For him, placing art in the service of the community meant giving up the hope of a golden age assured by the progress of technology and the dream of an "elysian existence entirely devoted to playing cards [*belote*] and angling."[2] This was a very common image of France, shared even by the occupation troops, who were reassured by the "harmless joys" of card games played at the bistro.[3] On the French side, it did not take a genius to make out the shadow of the Front populaire and its social achievements, the contempt for the masses enervated by leisure time, always accompanied by the standard attack on the mores of the Third Republic. In 1940, Hautecoeur was a happy civil servant: he agreed with "everything behind" the regime, and he had never had so many means to combat artistic modernity and to put in its place an old-style art, whose "true role" was to "elevate spirits" and "create a state of mind."

Like Pétain, Hautecoeur was quickly left behind by those more extreme than he. They invoked the Révolution nationale, all the while declaring that French culture had to fall in line, to learn from the example of totalitarian countries, especially Germany. The Third Reich was obsessed with the question of art, and the number of visitors to the state museum in Berlin was four times higher than the number visiting the Musée du Louvre.[4] Though the far right had largely balked at the initiatives of the Front populaire in cultural matters, mocking its "schoolmasterly" tendencies and its "advertising methods," the time had come for an about-face that required both co-opting and moving beyond the Révolution nationale. On the margins of the regime, therefore, publications that pledged allegiance to the old chief of state—while adding muscle to his remarks—were thriving. For instance, René Borelly, in his *Atalante: Revue d'art et de culture*,[5] first issued in December 1941, defended a radical conception of art for all, an art freed from "the foreign blight," without setting out its canons. He provided only a bombastic and approximate formula, contrasting it to "decadent art," regarded as a reflection of the nation's "intellectual and moral anarchy." His art of the new age, which was supposed to illustrate the virtues of the day—courage, energy, physical and moral health—was to act on an "amorphous mass," on all "persons, even the most unpolished," on the general public of the "uninitiated," to whom Rebatet as well wanted to provide an "artistic education." In the August 1941 issue of *Beaux-arts*, Rebatet lamented the ignorance and indifference of the French on the subject, then proposed a solution. His reform was simple: privilege "art masterpieces," he said, and discard "horrid bourgeois academicism"; take Germany as an example; educate "the French eye, and thus work for the beautification of their daily lives and of their country."[6]

In the same vein, Abel Bonnard broke all records for lyricism when, inaugurating the exhibition of Breker's works in 1942, he reminded the French that it was up to them alone to "wash away" their troubles with "higher activities," by fostering works by the fervent proponents of this union that was finally being established. "From this firebox of the mind" was "to shoot forth the spark of the arts." At a time when nourishment of the body was severely restricted, art would offer itself to all French people as the "only unbounded banquet...the repast of nectar and ambrosia that gives comfort to men." "Let France rise above all material sufferings," he said, and "engage with greater inspiration than ever before in those arts that have been its glory."[7] In a nod to the Breker exhibition, deemed exemplary, he asked France to uphold with a bloody arm "the torch that is never extinguished."

In fact, the most troubling aspect of this was that the supporters of the regime seemed to be responding, like an echo, to all who, since the late 1910s, had wanted to reconcile art and the general public. Without a doubt, the ideological ingredients and the aesthetic variants made the difference between discourses with a totalitarian aim and other discourses. But, thanks to the atmosphere of the time, one had to be very sharp to distinguish among the different positions—often laid out in the same media—which ultimately converged on the essential points: the reconciliation of art and the public, and the instrumentalization of art in the service of a revolution of society and humanity. The demand for an "art for all"—traditionally formulated and tried out by the left, under the Front populaire in particular[8]—thus finally moved into the right-wing camp in power, and it was not unusual to see former militants from 1936 defend old socialist convictions within the new frameworks of the Vichy regime.

Hence, Lucien Lautrec, who had begun his life as an artist by decorating youth hostels, now contributed to *Le rouge et le bleu: Revue de la pensée socialiste française*, directed by Charles Spinasse, a former Front populaire minister who had been won over to the battle against communism and liberalism. There Lautrec reported on his activities as part of Jeune France, an organization placed under the aegis of the state. The group's aim was to decentralize French society through the widest possible diffusion of a "living culture," far removed from the "coteries of the Salon or the cafés, wherever the popular virtues were less severely compromised." Close to the young modern painters "of the French Tradition," he seemed disconcerted by the problem of his pedagogical mission among young people, most of them unemployed, who, "especially in the major urban centers, were responsive to the spectacle of the surfaces of life as it was constituted by illustrated propaganda, commercial industrial production, cinema, advertising, etc." Young people had accepted the norms of that spectacle and tended to imitate them, since such norms represented their "ideal of perfection." An apostle of "authenticity" who had turned to pedagogy, Lautrec offset this pessimistic assessment of modern conformism with a call for the patience and will to undertake "a real cleanup operation."[9]

More elitist than his colleague, Jean Bazaine had also worked for the Front populaire by decorating one of the first youth hostels, after signing Emmanuel Mounier's personalist manifesto in 1934. A member of Jeune France as well, he wavered between voluntarist positions stemming from his desire for immediate action and the more critical attitude of a scholar and a painter ultimately less devoted to any social project than to the problems that painting raised for him. He wondered, without reaching a conclusion, what art was to become "in this passionate search for a collective ideal," knowing that the artist's isolation was a long-standing issue but that the temptation to add one's stone "to a great collective work" had rarely been so strong. It could "become, depending on the case, a strength or a weakness, revivifying or asphyxiating."[10] In the meantime, his work supported the unfolding events without responding to official slogans. It remained within the narrower scope of a painter's studio or a laboratory.

FOR A GRAND DESIGN, A LARGE FORMAT

Art was still fitted to the dimensions of the bourgeois sitting room at a time when many were hoping to see it take to the streets. What people saw was the same old failure, especially in the case of painting, whose insularity scandalized all those who believed, like Maurice Denis, that it ought to render a "service" and bear "witness," as it had done in the past. In 1935, the old royalist Nabi was smitten with the Fascist revolution's exhibition in Rome: "a good present-day example of art, education, and propaganda, of a partisan art." Moreover, though he had probably never imagined giving up his old intimist obsessions, he saw things clearly when he took note of "the systematic use of new means to move and excite a public, without calling on painters."[11] His political adversaries, who opposed the fledgling totalitarian regimes that were putting the effects of gigantism to the test, were arriving at nearly the same conclusions.

In the 1920s, Fernand Léger, drawn to the Communist Party, was not the only leftist to raise the problem of the social role of art. The Front populaire would encourage him in that arena by providing mass industrial society with a more appealing image and by indulging the demands of artists who aspired to be associated with an ambitious policy of public works projects. Nearly ten years after the crisis of 1929, which had largely affected the art economy by convincing that sector of its fatal isolation, the Exposition internationale of 1937, though it marginalized many talents, also inspired others to put away their easels, to see larger, to learn to work in teams. In the end, artists sent the world messages that probably never would have been gotten by means of works of traditional dimensions. Visitors to the exposition would invariably remember the large frescoes in the pavilions and the gigantic neoclassical sculptures, almost ubiquitous, especially on the part of the Germans and the Soviets, but quickly forgot the exhibition of works by the masters of independent art, which simply looked like an excellent seasonal Salon.

In 1940, though the Révolution nationale had set the stage for a policy of artistic monumentality, the regime seemed instead to be banking on the first mass-produced representations of Pétain and the symbols of his power, often of modest size, matching his soft revolution. Of course, a few monumental works were envisioned, but no one set aside the funds needed for a spectacular policy. The men of the regime fastened on declarations of principle, which were very quickly taken up by the advocates of gigantism. Among the extremists, René Borelly called for a German-style program: the new regime ought to construct "expressways, works of art, gigantic stadiums," and these would have to be adorned with "grandiose monuments" that would respond to "the general rise in the standard of living," leaving an impression "more lasting than what is merely charming."[12] Here painting again lost ground to sculpture in particular, which was better equipped to express nobility and heroism—emotions no longer to be confounded with the more "ordinary" sentiments of joy or "maternal feeling," for which "the human scale" would suffice.[13]

In 1943, Pierre Velut, assistant secretary of the Confédération de l'éducation, drove the point home by announcing the ouster of painting. It was, he said, an individualistic and complex genre, unlike—"possibly"—sculpture but especially architecture and cinema. Indeed, for some of the men of the regime, modernity had its good points. One had only to bring to heel the mechanization that had run amok "in the feeble hands of the bourgeoisie" for it to quickly become "a docile slave," "kept under control by an iron fist."[14] Of course, this was not the first time that painting had appeared under the heading of outdated things, even as its detractors reproached it for no longer being human and for being too modern, as a result of systematization and abstraction. Had not painters dug their own graves by announcing painting's decadence, its futility, its absence of craftsmanship—of fine craftsmanship?

THE BEAUTIFUL WORK

To sway the public, it was said, familiar works had to be produced. Rather than license and color, drawing was back in fashion. Hautecoeur (followed by school principals) established a reform of fine arts education that, in contrast to what had been proposed under the reign of his predecessor, involved better training in the French tradition as well as a stringent selection process by which all students who were already at the Ecole des beaux-arts but showed no real chance of winning the Prix de Rome were channeled toward the (despised) decorative arts.[15] "Craftsmanship was the condition for art," said Hautecoeur in 1929, waxing nostalgic for those happy days when the young artist was above all a craftsman listening to his master, part of a studio, mastering his technique a little more each day, until he was finally able to elide even the difficulties of the undertaking.[16] Indeed, what was horrifying about the modern artist, in addition to his deformations of reality, was the presence in his work of his doubts and efforts, which were interpreted as weaknesses. His humility itself appeared to be a feint: he was suspected of believing, much too soon, that he was emancipated.

Valéry, a patron of the impressionists, was invoked by the extremists, who were smitten with his *Pièces sur l'art.* In this work, he lamented that, in an age of precision and applied science, the arts suffered from "such laxities" and delighted "in games of inadequacy and easy solutions." A tendency toward asceticism was favorably observed by the occupying forces in the reports of the Propaganda-Abteilung Frankreich, which made much of the return to order in France.[17] There as elsewhere, the art world was moving, without necessarily knowing it, in the direction of the marshal's epigrams—in this case, from a speech delivered in 1938 that Pétain uncharacteristically devoted to the "cult of art," wedged between "the taste for work well done" and "the sense of duty."[18] Artists did not lag behind in the critical assault, as representatives whose works were at least somewhat modern began to publicly lament the gaps in their training. Gaston Diehl, a defender of modern artists, in 1942 embarked on a survey of the "most lucid" ones who readily acknowledged their weaknesses. Francis Gruber had long thought that what artists lacked was "the desire to pursue an education,"[19] while Bazaine deplored the late age at which mastery was achieved. Whereas in the past it had been acquired before the age of twenty, now an artist had to "find it in solitude before the age of forty, by dint of battles and renunciations."[20] A single lifetime was thus too short to fill in the gaps. Of course, Diehl was content to find in certain artists a "concern for producing more accomplished works, with a more finished, stronger execution,"[21] as was the case for Roger Chapelain-Midy, André Marchand, Pierre Ino, Alfred Courmes, and even Gruber. But the art scene needed other models if the spirit of the studio, which had disappeared in the early nineteenth century, was to come alive again. The elders set the tone: "Before anything else," said Georges Rouault, "let them draw from classical antiquity, like the greatest among their peers...it was a grave mistake for young people to find being simply honest workers repugnant."[22]

Did the new circumstances affect only the artists who were the most moderate? The most modern and the most radical treated the problem "concretely," by giving up traditional materials in favor of more primitive, often unexplored ones. Could their discoveries pass for a justification

of fine craftsmanship? Their mistrust of machines, and of mass production in particular, echoed the dominant discourse, but their unsubdued spirit produced instead something like a silent grimace. Each in his own way sought, in the Western past or in primitive styles, a response to the disappearance of both man and the "precious object."[23] In addition, the work of abstract artists such as Alberto Magnelli, César Domela, and Fautrier, who privileged the "substance of the materials," not only prompted reflection on the commonplaces of the painter's and sculptor's craft but in many cases also responded to the realities of destitution and forced return to rural life. Indeed, "matterism [*matiérisme*]" also came into being through artists' prolonged contact with a natural world that they had had a tendency to abandon.[24] When Magnelli, sequestered in Grasse in 1941, ran short of canvas to paint on, he discovered engraved wood, crumpled paper and collage, gouache on slate, and little works on note paper or in school notebooks. When Domela and his family were starving in Paris, he gleaned scrap material of every kind from around craft boutiques and introduced them into his sculpture-paintings. He
Pl. 40 used brass, red copper, glass, sealskin, and sharkskin as well as precious woods of all kinds: thuja, Macassar ebony, and mangrove (the latter from Nicolas de Staël's library, smashed to pieces).

This was a long way from oil painting, denigrated for its elitism but admired for its pedigree. That grand tradition "disgusted" Fautrier,[25] who replaced it during the war with new media. To render the violence that the state of things inspired in him, he preferred to work with layers of ink, glue, colored powders, and whiting glaze. Similarly, the surrealist Victor Brauner, having settled in the *département* Basses-Alpes, created wax and candle paintings that had nothing to recommend them to the pantheon of the return to order. For that matter, such works did not appear at the Salons: they had to be unearthed in the avant-garde's tiny galleries, or await the liberation, for it to be apparent just how wide-ranging the reconsideration of the artist's craft had been. The times in fact vindicated all who preferred to identify realism with craftsmanship and labor. As Bernard Ceysson has suggested, the subject, that "fruit of invention, made each painting a masterpiece, in the sense that craftsmen give that word, where content and technique are wed." "By contrast, formalism, and especially abstraction, was defined as a kind of mechanistic mass production that privileged the technical definition at the expense of the soul."[26] The reasoning seemed sound, and it was not realized until after the liberation to what extent nonfigurative artists were thinking as much about "Man" as were the defenders of traditional fine work, whose corporatist and backward-looking interests were for the most part preponderant. At the time, the dominant voices were those who supported a return to the order of the past and to a rural France that had been led astray by nascent mechanization.

THE OLD TOOLS

In 1940, nearly half the French population was still rural, and there were some five million workers closely or remotely connected to craft enterprises. Certain for this reason of a sympathetic audience, Pétain announced that the France of tomorrow would restore "the ancient traditions that had once made its fortune and its glory" and that, as a country long known for quality, it could "restore to all its products that finish, that delicacy, that elegance in which it had no equal."[27] The theme of craftsmanship appealed to the majority of the population, even to certain modern artists nostalgic for the handmade object. "Nothing says more about the evolution of a people than the section of a molding," wrote Bazaine in the *La nouvelle revue française*, "nothing better reveals the profound character of a race, of a region, than its everyday objects."[28] Consistent with its social and economic policy, the state hastened to initiate a wide-scale movement in support of craftsmanship, setting up a vast propaganda campaign as well as the Ecole des hautes études artisanales. Praise for fine craftsmanship proliferated.[29]

Jacques Wilhelm, who was on the staff of the Musée Carnavalet, chose the journal *Atalante* to expound his definition of the role of craftsmanship in a reformed France: "to give man back the love of work well done, to place a certain beauty within everyone's reach."[30] As with all extremists, his definition of beauty vanished behind the violence and compulsion that it entailed. Order had to be imposed, "and with a firm hand," he said. It was high time, and it was just too bad if those concerned did not want to understand. It was better to rein them in, to establish strict controls over everything being built in France, than to let the country become ugly and to let that ugliness "penetrate the soul." One had to be partisan, even sectarian. One had to track down everything that contributed to perverting the tastes of the masses, those of rural inhabitants especially, with whom the chief hope of rebirth lay. And since so many things were being regulated, why not institute "true censorship, the most useful censorship of all, that of quality and taste"?[31]

The defense of craftsmanship encouraged an attack on the avant-garde movements most often reproached for having given birth to an "international style." The time had come for the return to the land, and regionalism was the order of the day, even though the regime in place had never been so violently centralizing. The rebirth of craftsmanship was thus supposed to contribute to preventing the "terrible unification"[32] of the country and to reconnecting with something that "truly comes from our homeland, by virtue of its roots and its offshoots,"[33] as the critic Louis Chéronnet said in relation to a team of decorative artists headed by Jacques Adnet[34] in winter 1941. Under the auspices of a "forward-looking tradition,"[35] conventional artists and members of the Institut de France worked in a style that brought back the good old days. There, as elsewhere, it was a matter of seizing on a moment consecrated by the reactionary forces to permanently exclude undesirables from the program. Meanwhile, the reform of the national factories, with the unification of the major artisanal centers of Gobelins, Beauvais, Sèvres, Aubusson, and Mobilier national,[36] would contribute to the artistic revolution hailed by Pétain during his visit to Aubusson in 1941.

Guillaume Janneau, who served as general administrator of the national factories and Mobilier national, had become, since the period of the Front populaire, the voice of a living tradition—in part by regularly presenting in the governmental *Revue des beaux-arts de France* the state's latest acquisitions, which gave art lovers a glimpse of its new tendencies. Rural labors, plant and animal motifs, and landscapes occupied a privileged place, as they always had in the past. The novelty came instead from the Pétainist works, whose titles, especially, no longer made use of the official republican repertoire: Alfred Auguste Janniot sold the French state *The Rebirth of France under the Auspices of the Chief of State* (Gobelins); Lucien Jonas, *Eternal France* (Gobelins);[37]
Pl. 23 and Paul Charlemagne, *Homage to Pétain* (Aubusson).

In their own way, these artists in the chief of state's service contributed to the success of the artisanal revival—even though Pétainist art consisted for the most part of mass-produced objects that the public liked to imagine were a purely artisanal product, because they so convincingly conveyed the impression by their craftsmanship that they belonged to that long French tradition of popular art and the Epinal image. These official tapestry designers, almost always painters, abandoned oils and easel painting, disparaged for their servile imitation and use of synthetic dyes, in favor of practices suited to the tastes of the day. Besides, were those countless nuances of color currently available to tapestry designers really necessary, given that over time the weavings would suffer the effects of air and light? The traditionalists decided they were not, just as the adversaries of impressionism had rejected that movement's techniques so as to undercut the form. And, this time, the innovations were accused—wrongly—of raising the cost of producing tapestry works,[38] which, it was claimed, were increasingly priced out of the reach of both private customers and public commissions.

As for the modern tradition, though an artist such as Jean Lurçat had done battle with the opposing ranks of official artists—he was at the time secretly having *Liberté* woven—he had nevertheless been in sync with them since before the war: he had revived the mural tapestry in a modernized and rationalized form[39] in response to the latitudinarianism of oil painting, whose "dictatorship over taste" imposed a "real alienation from one of the most enduring sectors of lyrical life in our country."[40] In fact, even the fresco form, returned to a place of honor between the two World Wars for its edifying qualities, tended to give way to techniques that were more explicitly "human." Tapestry combined all the advantages: it required "fine craftsmanship," that is, solid technique; it lent itself, by virtue of its monumentality, to public commissions; and, finally, it could be easily transported from one place to another—making it, as Le Corbusier's term "Muralnomad" suggested, a modern, portable form of the mural. Indeed, probably even more than the aesthetic quarrels of the day, the debate around artisanal techniques betrayed a fear of mechanization and anonymous perfection. Man, it was announced, would in the end fall wretchedly victim to these forces. Complaints about a crisis in the artisanal sector, which had been voiced since the mid-nineteenth century,[41] were now borne out by the situation of craftsmen and tapestry workers: out of twenty-five hundred in 1925, twenty-three hundred had been forced to abandon their work by 1935. The last remaining institution of learning for the traditional arts closed down in 1933. Even though the state set in place a voluntarist revival policy in 1937, tapestry remained a stricken sector.[42] The success of the major tapestry exhibition held, just after the liberation, at the Musée national d'art moderne vouched for a sensibility that went beyond the nostalgia of the dark years.[43] Under the occupation, however, excess flourished. Pl. 24

This backward march occasioned the exhibition and sale of many everyday objects that were simple enough to be manufactured industrially. Did anyone really grasp the absurdity of having to find a spiritual identity in even the most insignificant "authentic" object? To the contrary, the display of pottery, jars, wickerwork, and artisanal furniture fired the enthusiasm of the public and the critics, who were delighted that even artists were now doing "what the provincial craftsmen were doing."

ARTISTS AND ARTISANS

The world was upside down: regional craftsmen all of a sudden found themselves propelled to the forefront of a Parisian art scene that had been closed to them for some time, while urban artists were leaving the cities to return to their provincial roots and to discover the joys of handicraft. When André Lhote, a leading advocate of cubism and founder of the Académie Montparnasse, planned to settle in the little village of

Gordes in southern France with his students, he was immediately held up as an example, as were the intellectuals who had gone off to clear land in Oppède and to restore its old buildings, fallen into ruin. They had all set to work there, though no one actually knew whether theirs was the occupation of idle young bourgeois or a mass-produced ecological vocation. With the government's support, Oppède-le-Vieux was turned into a Fourierist laboratory where, gathered around Bernard Zehrfuss, winner of the Prix de Rome in 1939, some forty apprentice rebuilders dreamed up their new "garden of Provence." With their works displayed in Vichy, Marseilles, and Avignon, their project attracted the admiration of Le Corbusier as well as Georges Lamirand, of the surrealists as well as Jeune France and Groupe témoignage.[44] Alongside François Stahly, Étienne-Martin, and Zelman, everyone tried his luck at sculpture, weaving, joinery, or pottery, under the benevolent gaze of the Parisian media disgusted by the foul air of the capital. They were of course aware that this was merely an example provided by "the elite," but they were at the same time counting on it being a prelude to the attempt by "the masses themselves."[45] The earth really did not tell lies for anyone, as Pétain was wont to say, and Lhote drove the point home in 1943 by publishing with Editions Denoël his *Petits itinéraires à l'usage des artistes*, with illustrations by his own hand. There he recounted the pleasures and pains of traveling in France. He invited the French to take the scarcity of automobiles with good humor, in the hope of gaining from unprecedented contact with the land an increase in "new forces."[46]

In fact, even well before the war, artists had returned to the sources of folklore and craftsmanship, without necessarily being hostile toward all modernity. In 1939, at his Parisian gallery Matières et formes, René Breteau presented an exhibition of works by Groupe témoignage, where artisanal pieces and traditional works, modern forms and elementary materials, stood side by side with no respect for hierarchies of genre, as if Breteau wanted to demonstrate that traditional studio productions did not stand in opposition to either modernity or the avant-garde.[47] Groupe témoignage displayed the banner of its defiance before the defeat and Pétain's Révolution nationale, and its whiff of desperate spirituality did not herald the marshal's program but rather reflected a state of mind already prevalent before the war: it was time to dispose of "materialism," to pierce "the veil that hides the meaning of things." Art was no longer considered a craft higher than the others but "a simple language, a writing that [had] its utility for spiritual ends."[48] Artists were therefore prepared to place themselves on the same level as artisans. With the beginning of the occupation, official demagoguery flattered artisans—a group anxious about its fate—while trying not to offend creative artists, who did not so easily renounce their elitist traditions.

Pierre Loyer, director of the craft industry department, found the words to please the artisan, who was turned into "a master who puts his shoulder to the wheel." At the same time, the artisan's professional skill and the individualized nature of his production, so unlike industrial manufacturing, was praised. Social definitions not being in fashion, emphasis was placed on the craft, the profession, where masters and apprentices were no longer in conflict but sought a common good, in accordance with the new corporatist laws. The discourse served up to artists was not of the same vintage, as if they deserved respect due their rank. The state had affronted them by too brusquely proposing a rigid corporation plan in 1940 but made up for it in 1944 by flattering their pride. In particular, Hilaire, installed in April, presented the "corporative groups" as a tool intended to thwart the manufacture and distribution of certain furnishings or decorative objects in an "offensive" style. Craftsmanship was important because it truly "conditioned" "the popular taste." Hilaire thus called on artists to come to the rescue of artisans who were unable to find "beautiful models."[49]

Jacques Mayet, section head of the craft industry department at the industrial production ministry, had prepared the way by distinguishing, in the context of the Salon d'Automne of 1941, the artist, a "creator making only works that were proper to him and in conformity with his personal genius,"[50] from the artisan-artist, whose creative effort was not sustained, and the artisan, who executed an "inspired" body of work. Artisans were further divided into good reproducers—traditional craftsmen, good technicians—and poor reproducers destined for "reeducation." That obsessive taxonomy wittingly showed that Vichy could bend over backward to revolutionize a gravely compromised sector, too elitist without being exemplary, too intellectual but primitive, too rational but alienated.

KNOWING HOW TO FINISH

In 1929, Hautecoeur set the tone by dismissing Cézanne as pathological. Of course, he was a "kind of genius, but too often an aphasic genius." Dabbling in matters he knew nothing about, Hautecoeur isolated a set of crippling symptoms—mutism and the loss of language comprehension—that condemned the patient to no longer succeed at "expressing himself." The case of Cézanne was valuable for its exemplarity, since the malady had ultimately affected legions of painters incapable of finishing their canvases. As a precursor of modern art, Cézanne embodied the madness of the painter, which was much too quickly embraced by representatives of the various modern currents, surrealism first and foremost.

In 1942, when Hautecoeur became head of fine arts, the painter Maurice de Vlaminck held forth in response to the appointment of the former curator of the Musée national d'art moderne with a violence that he never abandoned during the occupation. Vlaminck portrayed the modern artist as one possessed, who moved from surrealism to the academism of William Bouguereau's followers and from the waxworks of the Musée Grévin to the morgue. His "sexual visions plunged him into a morbid state, where intellectual masturbation and pederasty turned him into one of those monsters that specialists in mental illnesses and invert art lovers collect." In reality, in his description, which was not at all original, the whiff of debauchery acted as a metaphor for the intellectual experiments of the avant-garde, which had been traumatizing in many respects. Indeed, since the early years of the twentieth century, traditionalists must have watched in dread as the art scene opened itself up to the primitive arts, the art of children, and, even worse, that of the insane. In 1925, drawings by mediums and the mentally ill were reproduced in *La révolution surréaliste*, and a few years later these works were exhibited by Dr. Auguste Armand Marie. Although today they are in the holdings of the Collection de l'art brut in Lausanne, at the time the sight of these works, which owed nothing to classical rules, unleashed the wrath of the proponents of order.

In 1933, the poet Camille Mauclair identified in these works signs comparable to the "techniques" and "feelings" of the avant-garde, lamenting that certain theorists of the time were no longer able to distinguish beauty from ugliness, or good taste from bad. Yet their "logic" remained sound, he said, since they declared that in art there was neither reason nor madness and that, since mental boundaries were indiscernible, everything was allowed. "We are living in the midst of a craze for 'Freudianism,'" Mauclair complained, knowing full well that the craze was confined to a well-educated elite. The traditional public remained indifferent or, more often than not, hostile to the art of the insane as well as to avant-garde art. Hence Robert Rey, former assistant curator at the Musée du Luxembourg (precursor of the Musée national d'art moderne), was not exaggerating when, in 1941, he rejoiced that the general public regarded surrealist works as "the manifestations of dementia," which the surrealists, he snickered, pretended to take as a compliment.

In reality, an enormous gap existed between the early works of the fledgling human sciences of psychoanalysis and ethnology—which modern art ventures echoed—and the general public attached to values it considered immutable. At the time, and even more than before the war, the crisis sent the public back to the most reassuring mental representations, in contrast to modern "experiments." Indeed, whatever the differences in interpretation among these new ventures, they appeared to the uninitiated if not devoid of all interest, then at least still incomplete. In 1943, the critic Jean de Beer called on artists to return to the true function of art, "a dictatorship that rules by force."[51] Denis Diderot's "clouds," which left the imagination floating and dreamy, were chased away. The creative artist had to "compel the public," which, like a bull in the bullring, would not give in before it was brought to its knees.[52] This regime of relevancy made reference to Europe's new ways, under the pretense of a return to man all the more ridiculous in that barbarism raged unchecked.

SEEK OUT THE HUMAN

On the subject of the ongoing horror, the art scene was no more knowledgeable than any other sector. It continued to call for a return to the human figure, without drawing any connection between that call and current events. It put on trial the moderns, who had privileged form at the expense of the subject and had neglected the major genres, particularly the portrait and the self-portrait, the genres believed to assure man his dignity—at least when they did not display those "features of vulgarity and obscenity" that revealed, instead, the dual shortcomings of model and artist. Just before the war, the arts journalist Bernard Champigneulle said he did not hold a grudge against Cézanne for having preferred to paint apples rather than humans, but he was worried about all Cézanne's followers. They were giving up on man, lacking the courage to deal with his "expression, the meaning of a smile, the confession of a gaze." In fact, he reproached them for painting men as they would have painted apples.

In the same manner, in 1934, Waldemar-George had served brilliantly as a pioneer in nostalgia by militating for a "new humanism" that would exalt "the magic of the human body and face." Typically, Waldemar-George, who had shaken Mussolini's hand, aspired to be neither on the right nor on the left, neither old-fashioned nor a modernist, but rather a defender of the "rights of the human person" by combining "the European blueprint" and "Latin pathos." And yet, the paintings he defended bore witness to an existential anguish that his soothing language stifled. The first portraits exhibited by one of his favorite painters, Christian Bérard, suggested motionless and dumbstruck masks. In any case, George's grandiloquent voluntarism gave rise to emulators, including Jean-Marc Campagne, author of the preface to the Breker exhibition catalog in 1942, who defended "a general conversation on the human plane" against "the flight from reality." It was necessary, he argued, "to restore to painting the dignity of thought, the cult of the poetics of the object, and the vital feeling of the greatness of man, all things that, from Jean Fouquet to Derain and the younger artists, continue to have the force of law in France, despite the adverse trends." Derain, as a renegade from fauve modernity and a theorist of the counterrevolution, constantly served to reassure the defenders of the tradition. Campagne recalled his warnings: without an alphabet, "there would be no way to read, to write, or even to think. Art is a stairway of perpetual revelations, but if you choose to misuse it, you risk falling to the ground."[53]

Human representation then occupied a prominent place within a visual vocabulary that was judged increasingly limited. The painter Philippe Besnard upped the ante in 1943 in the review *Beaux-arts*. The impressionists, like the proponents of "pure art" who followed them, practiced an art of color "without composition," in which conception and execution had been replaced by "accidents of eye and instinct." They had done without the human presence. For Besnard, the presence of man was "necessary as the very expression of intelligence, the king of creation, supreme harmony."[54]

But what was the sense of that perfect "harmony" in painting when the world was collapsing? Whatever the level of awareness of these thinkers in need of obvious truths, all hoped to ward off the crisis in values by invoking the depiction of the human that had disappeared long ago. That entailed not only attributing to the image more weight than it ever had but also compelling artists to provide an optimistic vision of humanity, when they were content to translate the rumblings of horror.

As far as the moderns were concerned, Robert Leforestier, writing in *Chantiers* in 1941, did not pass up the opportunity to mock the style of Miró's enormous panel in the "paltry Spanish pavilion" at the Exposition internationale of 1937. Miró had wanted to support the Spanish Republican cause but had found no other means to represent "the suffering of a people about to be chewed to bits" than "by a red spot, a yellow dot, and a few lines." Such "childishness" disgusted and insulted the common people. As for the traditionalists, though they could still reassure themselves by looking at the sculptures of Maillol and his emulators, painting, more tolerant of doubt, was on the whole less likely to represent the human in its best light. Even Derain, who was so often taken as exemplary, firmed up his line and muted his colors, to the point that his last canvases—even the most agreeable—were much more sinister than his early works. Those paintings, fauvist and indifferent to classical rules, quite simply hailed from a more cheerful and promising century.

One of the few artists to stay the course of the modernist adventure was undoubtedly Picasso, in disgrace for embodying everything nobody wanted any longer, if in fact they had ever accepted it.

VLAMINCK VERSUS PICASSO

In June 1942, one month after the opening of the Breker exhibition at the Orangerie, Vlaminck's attack on Picasso in the weekly *Comoedia* gave the battle against modern art its mundane and nominal dimension. It replaced the pure ideas of criticism with bitterness, a thirst for revenge, and the denunciation of a renegade artist. For Vlaminck, Picasso was finally accessible, through hatred. He was an all-too-living symbol of a youthfulness that Vlaminck execrated, the chief head to make roll while there was still time, a Catalan with "a monk's face and the eyes of an inquisitor," "a rather cheeky arrogance," with the look "of a sort of monster," "impotence in human form." Picasso was guilty of having "dragged French painting into the most deadly impasse, into an indescribable confusion," of having led it, "between 1900 and 1930, toward negation, impotence, and death."[55]

At a time when France was desperately trying to recover its lost unity, brushing away the traces of chaos as so many obstacles to its reconstruction, Picasso made a serious mistake. Instead of the artisanal and monolithic ethic that forged classical artists, he preferred the baroque heroism of a subject without a stable consciousness, always elusive, always leaping about, *singular*. Because he never projected one face in particular, he was par excellence the scapegoat who would embody a thousand and one facets of evil: displacement, disorder, blasphemy, everything that France no longer wanted and which it associated with his foreign roots. Sure of being heeded by the many who thought of Picasso as a proponent of decadence, Vlaminck aimed low, in an article that pursued a dual logic: denounce the modern venture (there was nothing original in that) and, at the same time, an artist still in Paris, just barely tolerated and only too well known for his political sympathies.

An attack that, under ordinary circumstances, would have quickly collapsed under a mountain of disgusted responses was turned deadly by the occupation.[56] The identity card permitting the Spanish immigrant to reside in France was no longer valid, and Picasso had abandoned exhibiting in public venues due to the climate of censorship. Only the imperatives of the market that, on occasion, benefited the occupier spared those of his works still sold by auction houses.[57] Works by Picasso were almost never seen except at the Hôtel Drouot or in the back rooms of a few offbeat galleries, even though his name sometimes appeared among others in the listings in arts calendars.[58] A zealous Gestapo could have had the painter arrested at any moment. After being visited by occupation authorities, Picasso continued to live on rue des Grands-Augustins until the liberation, with an almost absolute guarantee of not being harassed. He was protected on the German side by Breker, at Cocteau's request, and on the French side by André-Louis Dubois, an official dismissed by Vichy who had friends at the police prefecture in Paris.[59]

If Vlaminck's intent had been to put an end to the demiurge forever, he missed his mark, but he was able to savor the unwholesome joys of denunciation—and guilt. Indeed, he was settling old scores with the head of a family of moderns in which he himself had been a prodigal son, only to then repudiate it. Here as elsewhere, everyone, directly or indirectly, had belonged to the unclean body that was being purified. Of course, Vlaminck confessed, Picasso had been the "obstetrician" of cubism ("perversity of mind, insufficiency, amoralism"), but to continue over the long term, he needed a birthing team: Guillaume Apollinaire acted as "the midwife," Maurice Princet served as "the godfather," and "the assistants" were "Derain, Max Jacob, Braque, Juan Gris, Salmon,"[60] and finally Vlaminck himself, who now turned to easy success in the fashionable districts. In terms of numbers, his exhibited works largely dominated a more low-key art scene—one he wanted to make forget his experiments from early in the century, when uncertainty still ruled his dialogue with his friend Derain and they both loved Cézanne, van Gogh, and the Senufo statuettes from Africa they unearthed at the market in Argenteuil.[61] Primitive art was not the only passion Vlaminck shared with Picasso; there was also a joyfulness and a willpower bursting forth unreservedly, at least until 1908, when Kahnweiler brought him into his gallery and Vlaminck, like most of his friends, turned toward a "stricter" art.[62]

To assess Vlaminck's demoralization under the occupation, we have only to place side by side his dark and muddy landscapes so much in harmony with the grayness of the dark years and those from his fauve period, which really began in 1904, where each painting was an explosion of colors and abstraction. So he could well declare, in 1942, that the modern world had been drawing to an end for ages, that "the patient lacked strength, fresh and healthy blood, enthusiasm, belief in life,"[63] that he did not dream of the "living forms of landscapes, of women," but "was the victim of 'cubist' nightmares, ciphers, germs, theorems, problems."[64] In fact, his output at the start of the century expressed a vitality lacking in his mature works.

NIGHT OF THE MAGICIAN

Neither Picasso nor his friends could openly respond to Vlaminck's attack of 1942. His defenders had to be satisfied with an allusion here or there—with Bazaine's virulent reaction in a footnote of the *La nouvelle revue française*[65] or Lhote's much more cryptic response in the following week's *Comoedia*. To keep the specter of the defeat at bay, the time had come for a return to Frenchness, even for Picasso's defenders, who now found he had a very "Spanish" temperament. That was how Lhote, the industrious disciple of cubism, indicated to Vlaminck his disagreement in principle. But he defended Picasso grudgingly, announcing in his "Opinions libres... sur la peinture française" that the future of cubism went far beyond Picasso's personality, which was distinct from the French soul. Indeed, the temperament of the French, he said, was not made for "these prestidigitations." It was "slower, more attentive, more cautious than the Spanish, and, to employ a fraught vocabulary, more respectful both of the real and of the beholder." It was not fond of being compromised by disorderly outbursts: it prized "the coherence of ideas."[66]

It was a feeble defense of the accused. It put him on the side of a Francoist Spain that wanted nothing to do with him, and it once again dispatched him elsewhere—abroad—at a time when his extremist detractors were readily blacklisting him as an international Judeo-Mason. It also, once French national identity was made into a very sedate notion, gallicized the moderate part of Picasso's work and bargained away the rebellious side and everything that did not fall into the narrow categories of his cubist model. Indeed, for Lhote and his school, cubism served as a rigid model for the return to order of the interwar period, to work well done and to discipline. In Picasso's life, by contrast, it was nothing more than a passing distraction, earning him yet another reputation that he would hasten to belie. He balked on principle at the boredom of militant, aesthetic, or political agendas, participating in such battles on a whim and quickly withdrawing once the tension had eased and tedious repetition had set in.

For Picasso, exemplarity never had any value save for a brief moment, and it was always succeeded by a break that thwarted all group instinct—and all veneration of anything but the artist himself. He pushed to the limit the revolutionary function of art, which presupposed perpetual change, pilfering from every tradition, sometimes modern but more often archaic, giving a swaggering and vigorous aspect to even the most well worn. Hence, when Picasso tackled large portraits in the 1920s, producing works that recalled those of Jean-Auguste-Dominique Ingres by their "conventional attitude" and sobriety, Wilhelm Uhde wondered whether the Spanish artist was not seeking to "fall in with the characteristically French side." But, between 1919 and 1923, he once again broke with the norm of the Olympian and reasonable: his enormous bathers were much too huge and pink to be classical. In the midst of the return to order, Picasso took the most popular subjects from the zeitgeist around him and subjected them to his first experimentations with close-ups.[67]

The war and then the occupation were not going to diminish either his rebelliousness or the annoyance of his detractors, now in power, and it is not at all astonishing that Picasso should constantly return to the center of debates. Ever since *Guernica*, which had finally combined creative genius and militant protest, he was the only one in France—or abroad—to embody so perfectly the myth of the revolutionary artist, in painting and in politics. A royalist prior to Franco's reign, Picasso had quickly embraced the Republican cause before accepting the commission of the young Spanish Republic to create a piece for its national pavilion for the Exposition internationale of May 1937. He had decided "to aid" Spain, which saw him as a new Goya ready to fight the atrocities of El Caudillo, whom he immortalized as an obscene monster confronting the common people (in the guise of a raging bull) in the series of etchings *Dream and Lie of Franco*.[68] As for the famous militant commission, Picasso was short on inspiration until he saw the report of his slain compatriots in the newspaper *Ce soir* of 1 May, which published photographs of the small city of Guernica ablaze: it had been attacked four days earlier by German aircraft in the service of Francoism. He then made use of a stark black-and-white palette and violent universal "symbolism" to forever fix the cruelty of the attack, whose name and date everyone soon knew, and which thus remained on the side of Picasso's patron, the Republican and anti-Fascist left. Yet that epic canvas, which can be linked to the classic theme of the massacre of the innocents and to the apocalyptic revelation of medieval Spanish manuscripts, was far from univocal. The various protagonists—bull, horse, and so on—may embody either the common people or Fascism, the victim or the executioner. Not all the representatives of the government in Madrid accepted the work of art, which they judged hermetic and likely to be interpreted "wrongly." The reaction of Claude Roy, a young right-wing student, bore this out. For Roy, *Guernica* had nothing to say about the war in Spain, but its violence moved him, leaving him "steeped in anxiety." Time thus had to do its work for most people to accept the "masterpiece," which seemed like "a letter of bereavement" containing the terrible news: *Guernica* was the foretaste of a disaster that, as Michel Leiris said in May 1937, "was going to kill off everything we loved."[69] Besides, the lesson did not apply just in Spain, as demonstrated by the deference of engagé artists in the United States. At the American Artists' Congress of December 1937, attendees listened religiously to a message from (the ailing) Picasso read by a nurse. Picasso mentioned the measures taken to save the art treasures of the Museo del Prado during the cruel and unjust war, while recalling that he had always believed that "artists who live and work under the banner of spiritual values cannot and should not remain indifferent to a conflict in which the highest values of humanity and civilization are at stake."[70] *Guernica* soon toured the world. Just before the Munich agreement, it was exhibited in London at the New Burlington Galleries (where at the same time there was an exhibition of paintings by Ignacio Zuloaga sponsored by the Francoist government). Then, at the initiative of the Labour Party leader Clement Attlee, it was displayed in the working-class London neighborhood of Whitechapel, in Leeds, and in Liverpool, before finally arriving at the Museum of Modern Art in New York, as part of the first true retrospective of Picasso's work: *Forty Years of His Art*, which brought together 344 pieces.

Up to the war, Picasso worked at his art, which vacillated between torment (portraits of Dora Maar) and calm (those of Marie-Thérèse Walter or their daughter Maya). He was haunted by the risk he was running and regularly left Paris to seek safety.[71] He decided to leave for Royan on 29 August 1939, just after the German-Soviet Nonaggression Pact. Thanks to authorization by his friend Dubois, he was able to stay there—until the Germans arrived in Royan, on 15 August 1940, obliging him to return to Paris. The memoirs of his faithful assistant, Jaime Sabartés, recount Picasso's intense anguish upon the arrival of the Nazi troops, his return to Paris in his Hispano-Suiza crammed with recent works, his move from rue La Boétie, too close to the headquarters of the collaboration, to the studio on rue des Grands-Augustins, which brought him closer to his remaining friends in Paris, and his certainty that his works would be made to pay in his place. Those at his studio in the château de Boisgeloup were damaged when it was sacked by French soldiers, even before the Germans arrived. Others were confiscated by the Nazis during the great looting of Jewish collections, including, at a minimum, all those that had been purchased by Paul Rosenberg and Alphonse Kahn.

The reasons that impelled the artist to remain in France, in the occupied zone, in the very center of a capital patrolled by Germans and dominated by the de facto collaboration, stemmed no doubt from a strange defiance to which Picasso was not constrained, since he had ample means to leave for the United States or Latin America. The tremendous success of his recent retrospective in New York conferred a privileged status on him that he could not hope to have in Paris. Nonetheless, exile frightened him even more than remaining in France, though staying was "not really a form of courage" for him but "quite simply a form of inertia."[72] He thus arranged a tolerable mode of existence. Though he refused the supplementary rations of coal that the German embassy thought it wise to offer him—probably on the advice of Ernst Jünger—his fortune and his French supporters allowed him to live well, above the fray. He went back and forth between his studio on rue des Grands-Augustins and the restaurant Le Catalan, where the owner served him excellent chateaubriands, until the day "without meat," when the police had the establishment closed and imposed a large fine on the proprietor.[73] Discovered by Picasso, who introduced it to all his friends, Le Catalan became the headquarters of the Parisian intelli-gentsia. The surrealists—Georges Hugnet, André Thirion, Paul and Nusch Éluard, Pierre Reverdy, Robert Desnos, Jacques Prévert, and Cocteau—gathered there, as did members of the Resistance and those cultured occupiers who were on occasion lovers of "modern" painting.

THE BASHFUL LOVERS

Picasso's notorious (and uncertain) reply to the German officer who asked him if he was actually the maker of *Guernica*—"No, you are"—long remained engraved in people's memories as a brilliant affront to the enemy, though no one really wondered under what circumstances the artist might have been led to inflict it. After the liberation, Picasso boasted to Simone Téry in *Les lettres françaises* that he had distributed postcards reproducing *Guernica* to the Germans who had come to visit him, calling out "Take one! Souvenir! Souvenir!"[74] In reality, it is the memoirs of the "Francophile" occupiers, published in France in the early 1980s, that have contributed to a better understanding of the landscape of the "aesthetic collaboration." They suddenly bestow on the former enemy an immense humanity and openness of mind,[75] especially if the most untenable passages are glossed over. Thus Heller revealed, in a book of memoirs guileless enough to be reliable, that he was at the same time responsible for literary censorship and fascinated by degenerate art and letters, both the representative of official culture and a devotee of Olivier Messiaen's and Erik Satie's concerts,[76] a central figure in the Nazi intellectual machine and also a friend to Jean Paulhan, Marcel Arland, and Louis Carré. These friends led him to discover certain aspects of "modern art," to which he admitted having been converted, but not without some resistance. His account did not necessarily discredit the individuals he named, but it did suggest that, especially in matters of art, German leaders in France were allowed complete freedom to bend official policy to see works and artists that were banned in Germany.

It was at Arland's home in Brinville that Heller first saw many modern works by Picasso, Braque, and Rouault. He did not disavow Arland when the writer paid tribute to Soutine, a Lithuanian Jew, in *Comoedia*, just after the painter's death in August 1943. It was at the Galerie Louis Carré on avenue de Messine that Heller continued his heterodox apprenticeship, before pieces by Picasso (again), Klee, and Masson, all three consigned to the Nazi pyres. In 1937 alone, Klee, a former professor at the Staatliches Bauhaus who died on 29 June 1940, had 17 works shown in the *Entartete Kunst* exhibition in Munich, while 102 of his works housed in German public collections were confiscated to be auctioned off. It was by listening attentively to the gallery's owner, Louis Carré, as he praised the harshness of Delaunay's colors and Bazaine's "refined gathering together of evocations"[77] that Heller learned to understand France. Above all, he admitted, it was under Paulhan's tutelage, while standing before pieces by Braque, Fautrier, Dubuffet, Wols, Rouault, and Picasso, that Heller very happily made use of Hegelian rhetoric, a learned mix of logic and humor, to forge "the new man" within. In June 1942, the "paternal figure" Paulhan (thirty-two at the time) brought Heller to Picasso's studio, where he could contemplate, alongside the silent but "very kind, very unaffected" painter, works that, in their cruel decomposition, reminded him of "the horror of war (though never expressed)," which was "present in a way that was difficult to bear."[78]

In hindsight, Heller said he understood what Jean Cayrol[79] had meant to insinuate when he characterized Picasso as "the painter par excellence, who could have set up his easel in the roll-call area [*Appell-Platz*] at Mauthausen or Buchenwald,"[80] also confessing, with embarrassment, that he had not spoken of "those things." All in all, he was more at ease with Braque, who in his work made you forget "the heartbreaks" of the era. Forty years later, he found it painful to admit to these hours of contemplation and aesthetic happiness spent with his French "friends," speaking (exclusively or nearly so) of painting, literature, and above all music, while nearby "famine was rife, hostages were being shot, and Jewish children were being taken away by the trainload to concentration camps." "I knew," he said, but had "neither the means nor sufficient conviction nor the courage to directly resist such atrocities." He had preferred to protect what he believed to be "the true values of France,"[81] with the complicity of a few Germans in Paris, particularly the writer Ernst Jünger, to whom, in February 1943, he introduced Hans Kuhn, then a corporal assigned to the Kommandantur Gross-Paris at the Hôtel Meurice, where, in a small studio set up in a garret, the artist painted "degenerate" works informed by abstract and surrealist motifs.

The three aesthetes held forth at La Tour d'Argent on the "magical influence"[82] of Picasso, whom they all had met. Jünger had visited him for a short while on 22 July 1942, a month after Heller. Jünger, who described Picasso as "a magician," had in fact shied away from the "monstrosity" of Picasso's asymmetrical heads, preferring two more sober portraits of women and especially a piece of shoreline "that seemed, as one contemplated it, to burst forth with increasing vigor in red and yellow tones."[83] Jünger saw in Picasso's work "an objective value" that escaped comprehension and came close to being alchemical experiments, to an image of man that had not yet been born and for which the painter would have a terrible responsibility.

Picasso responded to Jünger's metaphysical temptations with curiosity of a different order. He wanted to know what color actually was and what "real landscape" should be sought behind Jünger's novel *Auf den Marmorklippen*.[84] That was just another way to return to the war and to finish off the afternoon with a display of ingenuity that has become famous: proof of Picasso's courage for some, of his impotent vanity for others. "Just the two of us," the painter supposedly declared to the writer, "sitting here as we are, could negotiate peace this very afternoon. This evening, men could rejoice."[85]

In reality, Picasso's involvement in current events took circuitous paths, allowing scope in particular for Paul Éluard's patient work to get him into the Communist Party.[86] As for the rest, he preferred to laugh about things. He had Prévert read aloud passages from *Le grand homme seul* by René Benjamin, the marshal's friend. They were, Picasso said, "incredibly comical! As fine as [Alfred] Jarry!"[87] He bragged about knowing the book by heart, particularly the moment when the members of Pétain's cabinet were discussing what the marshal ought to wear when he visited bombed cities, and Pétain's discussion with the health minister upon the latter's return from the bombed city of Lorient:

> "I've just come from Lorient."
> "What's left of it?" the marshal asks, in a muffled voice.
> "Nothing," replies the minister, in the same tone.
> "And what does the population say?"
> "Nothing, Monsieur le Maréchal," says the minister a second time.
> But he adds, "They think . . . it's the war."
> The marshal mutters, "That's fine."
> "In any case," the minister continues, "I told them you loved them."[88]

Picasso's favors to the Resistance were in fact limited to accommodating friends involved in it, such as Robert Desnos, whose *Contrée* Picasso illustrated with etchings. A few weeks after Picasso finished, on 28 February 1944, Desnos was arrested and imprisoned at Fresnes, deported to Germany and finally transferred to Czechoslovakia, where he died of typhus shortly after the liberation of Theresianstadt. Indeed, Picasso devoted himself almost exclusively to his art, never taking a break. During the occupation, he began a phase of intense productivity that lasted until the end of his life, and accordingly denied himself any activity that might take him away from that new "convict's" pace.

He made works at the time whose diversity of themes and styles responded to the state of affairs, to his status as an undesirable, and to his reclusion. He told Pierre Daix after the war, "I started a painting as it came to me. I told myself: even if it leads nowhere, this evening, you'll have made a little something.... It seems to me that I gathered up my paintings the way you had to stockpile copper and paper for engravings back then, a bit here, a bit there."[89] He transformed his bathroom, the only room that could be heated, into a sculpture studio. At a time when the occupying forces were requisitioning metals, he took to putting together all sorts of assemblages made with the means to hand, then sent his pieces to be cast in bronze.[90] He did women, nudes, portraits of children, still lifes, horses, bullfights, landscapes, *vanitas* paintings, illustrations of poems and of the comte de Buffon's *Histoire naturelle*, and sculptures of animals or friends. Current events for the most part seemed absent from his work, but they did seep in, in the form of deferred violence against subjects and models, tragically deformed and isolated from the world.

Dora Maar thus incarnates a terrifying and gnomic woman—bright or dark, but almost always shattered, in contrast to Picasso's peaceful figures of the 1920s. The painter's friends even thought they recognized a "phony war" in his *Woman Dressing Her Hair*, an image done in Royan, whose arms form a swastika, enormous and horrific. In fact, Picasso confided to Kahnweiler that after making a portrait of Maar, he discovered, when the occupation troops arrived in Royan, a striking resemblance between her head and the Nazi helmet.[91] The various realities became confused and ended up vested in an ordinary object or a familiar face. So it was not cruelty that was registered in the painted subjects, but the result of that cruelty, like a dreadful echo of the violence of war added to the violence to which the painter subjected his models—and the painting.

Indeed, Picasso's heroic theater did not fall much short of the violence of history and his logic of metaphorical play, the *greguería*,[92] could be applied to any object likely to produce something magical or bizarre. His relentless tracking of Maar's face was the result of a passionate love affair with her, but the fact that observers often recognized, well beyond his domestic conflicts, the stigmata of the war on the body of his partner shows the extent to which different emotional levels were entangled in Picasso's work. He was decidedly not "the kind of a painter" who might have "painted the war" "like a photographer."[93] And even though he always referred to a real object, he had acquired from his cubist period on the means to transform any subject in his own way, to grant it a new status that evoked less the initial object than what it had had to undergo at the painter's hands. As Malraux said in *La tête d'obsidienne*, Picasso saw Dora as a woman in tears and all women as "suffering machines,"[94] thus showing himself faithful to a conquering misogyny. There again, intrepid observers have sought Picasso's driving force in the evidence of a sexual war. They note that Picasso subjected his female figures to untenable bodily postures and constructed a carceral architecture for them that allowed him to exorcise fears that had not left him since the prewar period and that took obsessional forms during a time of curfews and German harassment.

The myth of Picasso's resistance is further put to the test by the diversity of his art and his way—more picaresque than tragic—of approaching daily life. Thus, when he alluded to the situation around
Pl. 43 him, as in *Boy with a Lobster*, executed in June 1941, Picasso did not so much denounce the privations as make fun of them, painting a naked toddler, seated, his feet too big and his manner stunned, playing with a lobster. It is the same in his *Woman with an Artichoke*, of 1941, in which the subject clings gallantly to her food as if it were a weapon. The following year, in *Seated Woman with a Fish-Hat*, a fish all ready for eating, garnished with a cut lemon, is placed on the woman's head, the fork and knife serving as hatpins. The famous *Buffet at Le Catalan* of 1943 is once again filled with food; and in his sculpture *Woman with Orange* of 1943, the narrow shaft of the body ends in a curved, scroll-like neck and a small, square lid for the head.

On the theme of privations, there was also his first theater piece, *Le désir attrapé par la queue*, begun on 14 January 1941 as an exercise in automatic writing, based on free association, in line with the surrealist game from the 1920s and the caustic spirit of Alfred Jarry and the comte de Lautréamont. The plot was inspired by the daily frustrations of hunger, cold, and love, and featured burlesque characters such as Big Foot, a poet who lived in an artist's studio and squabbled with Onion over the affections of Tart (whose role was to be performed nude), closely followed by her two friends, Skinny Anguish and Fat Anguish. The piece was read aloud at the home of Michel and Louise Leiris on quai des Grands-Augustins on 19 March 1944. It was staged by Albert Camus, who described the sets and announced the acts and the actors: Simone de Beauvoir played The Cousin; Jean-Paul Sartre, Round End; Zanie

Aubier (the actress Zanie Campan), Tart; Dora Maar, Skinny Anguish; Germaine Hugnet, Fat Anguish; Louise Leiris, The Two Bow-Wows; Michel Leiris, Big Foot; Raymond Queneau, Onion; the publisher Jean Aubier, The Curtains; and Jacques-Laurent Bost, Silence. The audience was greatly enlivened by Jacques Lacan, Brassaï, Braque and his wife, Reverdy, Valentine Hugo, and Paul Éluard's daughter Cécile. The joyous evening ended at Picasso's place, with the artist reading to his friends good passages from Jarry's *Ubu cocu*, which had inspired him. Picasso also evoked the incongruities of these years by painting, in 1943, an interior view of his studio on rue des Grands-Augustins with a (useless) radiator from a bygone age, enormous and strange. In 1943 and 1944, he evoked ever-present dangers, responding to rumors that Paris would be destroyed, with a series of realistic drawings of the Pont Neuf and places familiar from his daily walk (see, for example, the paintings titled *The Vert Galant* from 1942 and those titled *Notre-Dame* from 1943).

In contrast to his works of rampant derision undoubtedly stood *Aubade*, painted in May 1942, and his sculpture *Death's-Head (Flayed Head)*, of 1943, which evoke the tragedy most clearly. *Aubade* became his occupation masterpiece. He bequeathed it to the Musée national d'art moderne in 1947, knowing that it incarnated the dark years through its restrained despair, while opening on a future full of women prisoners and indefensible secret proceedings. In that dark and austere painting, a tragic nude lies on a striped sofa that makes her teeter in the void. At her side is seated a female companion, both musician and warden, with a mandolin. The couple might seem to parody the voluptuous concerts of Venetian painters, if one considers only the subject; in reality, however, it portended tragedy. Pl. 44

Also in the dark register were the paintings of bull skulls, dedicated to the memory of Picasso's friend Julio González, who died in March 1942. The skulls are set against flat areas of green, blue, and violet (perhaps inspired by the way the light filtered into the little church where Picasso attended the funeral in the company of the Spanish artists Louis Fernandez and Apelles Fenosa),[95] while the blue-and-mauve window in the room—in the best known canvas of the series—was perhaps inspired by the colors of the civil defense.

Finally, Picasso distanced himself from the tragedy in playful works such as his famous assemblage *Bull's Head* of 1942, made of a bicycle's seat and handlebars welded together, or in more classic themes that he developed in his own way: a large, peaceful head of Maar in 1941; in November 1942, a series on pigeons, which would later give rise to the famous *Dove of Peace* used during every pacifist campaign by the Communist Party beginning in 1949;[96] or the *Man with a Sheep* series, which culminated in a monumental sculpture realized in February 1943. In many respects, because that offering of the lamb harked back to the mind-set of a Mediterranean Picasso, calm and temperate, the work was considered after the war as a response to all his detractors, Vlaminck in the lead, who had accused him of profaning the human body—all the more so as the preliminary drawings date from July 1942, just after Vlaminck's infamous attack in *Comoedia*. For once, Picasso's work pleased popular (neo-Greek) tastes, which considered the faithful and Apollonian representation of the world the guarantee of a still-standing humanism—or of a humanism to come, for those who believed it had vanished.

Still, one would have had to see the work exhibited at a Salon to assess the degree to which Picasso was able to curb his vengeful instincts and see man as something other than a cogwheel in the midst of chaos. As Pierre Daix has rightly remarked, Picasso, like Communist poets such as Éluard and Louis Aragon, sometimes obscured the issues by embracing "the national legacy" and adopting a form that was "classic and clear,"[97] effective and popular. Temporarily at least, the observation applied only to Picasso, who was banned from exhibiting but devised other pieces better suited to his revolt, his energy, his tragic sense of a return to the human that would continue to serve as a foil to the art scene. Indeed, for a long time to come, he would be seen not as the champion of a vanishing world—which he was—but rather as the most dangerous defender of "modern art" and a society that was advancing too fast.

ON TRADITION

Every era has had its share of reactionaries who resist innovations, but the dark years seemed to assure them a lasting victory. The defeat had only accentuated the need for security in a French society long shaken by internal upheavals. In art as elsewhere, the return to "tradition" played the part of a safe investment, even if the term itself was meaningless. "Traditionalists" diverged on many points, but what united them seemed to prevail, namely, their distress in the face of the incessant onslaught of contradictory initiatives, projects, and words that presided over the democratic rule in modern times. They were exhausted by the speed at which things were changing, leaving man far behind, swathed in old values that made him nostalgic for the past. Forced to assimilate too quickly industrialization, mechanization, urbanization, and finally rationalism, which in aggregate split apart the national consciousness, France remained a rural country in which every blow to ancestral nature placed men's equilibrium in peril. Artists were not the only ones who wanted to rediscover "roots" that would hold them to the soil.

Whatever their political or aesthetic positions, most dreamed of being reborn through a healthy return to the past, keeping both adventurism and academicism at a distance. Revolution might be the order of the day, but it was to be seen primarily as a return to the past and, indeed, to the most remote time possible. One thus had to return to classical antiquity, to the Middle Ages, or even to the Renaissance, at least in words, which, for some, camouflaged the crucial thing—namely, holding the line at last, by violently purging an art scene of its troublemakers. When the extremist Lucien Rebatet rose up to defend tradition against "the graybeards of the Institut de France," he held up Derain as an example: here was a man disappointed with modernity, who claimed that to make a revolution in art was to understand its tradition, when in fact no one understood tradition any longer.[98] After Derain's trip to Germany, his aesthetic positions were suddenly marked by the seal of infamy, and his "tradition" was unable to serve all those who had adapted their artistic approach to fit the patriotic cause.

The enemies of the occupying forces felt that they too had to reappropriate the past and wrest it away from the academicians, as well as from conformism and the norm, without giving up continual movement. Léon Gischia, for example, wanted to clarify the notion of tradition and "rid it of the filth with which the evil-intentioned" had "complacently smeared" it.[99] Academicism was morbid, while tradition was "alive and in a state of perpetual becoming."[100] The exhibition *Jeunes peintres de tradition française* at the Galerie Braun in May 1941—in which Gischia participated—was meant to bear witness to this: it brought together the young guardians of tradition opposed to the oppression of the moment, by availing itself of the ambiguity of a term that designated not only the wait-and-see attitude and the reactionary forces but also their opposite.

Hence the influence of events on artistic choices must be reassessed. Let us recall World War I and the warnings of Maurice Barrès, who saw a wave of German troops thirsting for "southern" pleasures. The ancient world, especially the Romans, had abruptly taken on a nationalist meaning for the French, who became allied with the Italians in April 1915. The war of Latin classicism against Germanic barbarism supported the military battle from behind the front lines.[101] It was at this time that Cocteau celebrated the entry of the Italians into the war by drawing *Dante avec nous,* in which the poet sports a Phrygian cap as well as a laurel wreath.[102]

At the time, the majority had endeavored to demonstrate that France was the true heir to "classicism," against the mystical and medieval excesses of the German people. Even then, almost everyone hoped to oppose the enemy by laying claim to tradition and classicism. For a long time, these elastic terms responded to the imperatives of the moment and also referred to antiquity, to the Italian Renaissance and the Fontainebleau school, to Nicolas Poussin and Ingres, and finally to Despiau and Maillol. Fanette Roche-Pézard has remarked that in Europe around 1925, a polemic erupted, not for or against the return to tradition and the real, but against a certain reality and a certain tradition. It did not rule out—far from it—an escalation of conformity.[103]

The defeat and the occupation altered the consensus by revealing the well-concealed issues only to the most informed. Traditionalists were in fact divided between defenders of the Middle Ages and defenders of classical antiquity and the Renaissance. The first group returned to the wellsprings of a liveliness not based on the imitation of reality, while the second was oriented toward the classical canons of mimesis. The former gave the impression of drawing sustenance from the Frenchness of Romanesque art—in other words, from nationalism—in opposition to the latter, who returned to the European qualities of the ancient style, hence, to the aspects pledged to Fascism. The rules of the game set in 1914 seem to have been turned upside down by events and by the revival of interest in the Middle Ages prior to World War II. For the defenders of medieval traditions, the battle turned out to be particularly difficult because the classical model occupied a central place in the public's taste. The success of Maillol's *Graces* was proof of that. It was only with the "aid" of compromises by major French artists with the occupying forces that the young guard enamored of the Middle Ages arrived at its ends, and then not without difficulty. Disciples of Henri Focillon, they nonetheless fell—for the good of the cause—into the same Germanic errors identified by their master. In invoking Frenchness at every opportunity, they abandoned, at least in appearance, both Greco-Roman and "classical French" thought, which spoke "to universal reason, to man everywhere and always," in contrast to "the art of modern Germany," which was based on "the German man, German reason, German nature." The young guard thus found themselves opposed to the spirit "invented, not for the tribe, but for humanity as a whole."[104] In fact, at a fundamental level, the Jeunes peintres were moving closer to Focillon's exhortations during the German offensive of 23 May 1918: "Let us return to ourselves, to our past, to our most remote origins, to all the monuments of our exertions, to everything we have offered in the way of intelligence and virtue. History is not an arid remedy, a retreat in time. It is the people's memory. It does not distract, it exhorts, it leads to action."[105]

In this instance, the message of the enemies of the German occupation was particularly difficult because the recourse to Frenchness seemed widely shared—even by some collaborators. "The French spirit" had yet to be defined in such a way that everyone would be persuaded that it was implacably opposed to German—or even Italian—culture.

NOTES

1. Robert Leforestier, "L'art et le peuple," *Chantiers*, 14 December 1941.
2. Louis Hautecoeur, *Les beaux-arts en France, passé et avenir* (Paris: Editions A. & J. Picard, 1948), 89.
3. See the French page in the German newspaper *Pariser Zeitung*, "L'occupation des loisirs: De grands progrès à réaliser," 22 January 1941.
4. According to the figures cited in a special issue of *L'amour de l'art* in 1937: in 1936, there were some 16,000 visits by groups and 264,000 visits by individuals in France, versus, respectively, 362,000 and 757,000 to the Staatliche Museen zu Berlin.
5. The first issue of the monthly *Atalante: Revue d'art et de culture* was dated 1 December 1941, the last, June 1943; its headquarters were at 12, rue du Mont-Thabor, Paris. On the history of this review, see Anne Sogno, "La revue parisienne *Atalante* pendant l'Occupation," in Pierre Milza and Fanette Roche-Pézard, eds., *Art et fascisme: Totalitarisme et résistance au totalitarisme dans les arts en Italie, Allemagne et France des années 30 à la défaite de l'Axe* (Brussels: Editions Complexe, 1989), 213–22; and Anne Sogno's thesis on the same subject, directed by Fanette Roche-Pézard, Université Paris I–Panthéon Sorbonne, 1984.
6. Lucien Rebatet, "L'école des yeux," *Beaux-arts*, 8 August 1941, 3.
7. Abel Bonnard, "Discours prononcé...à l'inauguration de l'exposition Arno Breker à l'Orangerie des Tuileries, le 15 mai 1942," in *Exposition Arno Breker à l'Orangerie des Tuileries, Paris, mai–juillet 1942: Discours et allocutions* (Paris: E. Desfossés-Néogravure, Imprimeurs, 1943). See as well the typewritten text annotated and corrected by the author, Haute Cour trial of Bonnard, AN, series 3W 84, seal 15, docs. 61–68. See also the slightly later typewritten text hand-corrected by Bonnard presented at a luncheon in honor of Breker on 22 November 1943, Haute Cour trial of Bonnard, AN, series 3W 77, exhibit B229.
8. On the prewar period, see Pascal Ory, "La politique culturelle du Front populaire français (1935–1938)," 5 vols. (Ph.D. diss., Université Paris X–Nanterre, 1990).
9. Lucien Lautrec, "L'art pour le peuple," *Le rouge et le bleu*, 14 February 1942, 8–9.
10. Jean Bazaine, "Guerres et évasions," *La nouvelle revue française* 54 (1940–41): 622.
11. Maurice Denis, "Les besoins collectifs et la peinture—Les problèmes d'aujourd'hui"; quoted in Éric Michaud, "Art, propagande, publicité autour

de Paris, 1937," in *L'art face à la crise, 1929–1939: Actes du 4e Colloque d'histoire de l'art contemporain tenu à Saint-Étienne, les 22, 23, 24 et 25 mars 1979*... (Saint-Étienne: Centre Interdisciplinaire d'Etude & de Recherches sur l'Expression Contemporaine, 1980), 77, 91 n. 10.

12. René Borelly, "L'art au service de la Révolution nationale," *Atalante*, December 1941, 3–4.

13. René Borelly, "La plastique monumentale et la vie publique," *Atalante*, June 1943, 12–15.

14. Pierre Velut, "L'art dans la civilisation du travail," *Beaux-arts*, 24 December 1943, 1.

15. See Pierre Imbourg, "Les grandes réformes de M. Hautecoeur," *Beaux-arts*, 26 December 1940, 3.

16. Louis Hautecoeur, *Considérations sur l'art d'aujourd'hui* (Paris: Librairie de France, 1929), 66–67.

17. See AN, subseries AJ 40 1001.

18. Speech by Pétain, Metz, 20 November 1938.

19. See the survey by Gaston Diehl, "Du passé à l'avenir: Où va la peinture française?" *Comoedia*, 12 December 1942, 1, 6.

20. Diehl, "Du passé à l'avenir" (note 19).

21. Gaston Diehl, "Les étapes du Nouvel Art contemporain," *Beaux-arts*, 27 February 1942, 5.

22. Georges Rouault, quoted in René Barotte, "Georges Rouault raconte...," *Comoedia*, 11 April 1942, 1.

23. Paul Valéry, "Pensée et art français (1939)," in idem, *Regards sur le monde actuel et autres essais*, new ed. (Paris: Gallimard, 1945), 180.

24. See Jean Laude, "Problèmes de la peinture en Europe et aux Etats-Unis (1944–1951)," in *Art et idéologies: L'art en Occident, 1945–1949* (Saint-Étienne: Centre Interdisciplinaire d'Etude & de Recherches sur l'Expression Contemporaine, 1978).

25. Fautrier, quoted in André Berne-Joffroy's preface, "Franges pour un dossier Fautrier," in *Jean Fautrier, rétrospective*, exh. cat. (Paris: Musée d'Art Moderne de la Ville de Paris, 1964), n.p.

26. Bernard Ceysson, "Réalismes/figurations," in *L'art dans les années 30 en France*, exh. cat. (Saint-Étienne: Musée d'Art & d'Industrie, 1979), 39.

27. Statement by Pétain to the American press, 22 August 1940; reprinted in *Principes de la rénovation nationale: La doctrine et l'action du Maréchal* (Paris: Société d'Editions Economiques & Sociales, 1943).

28. Jean Bazaine, "Le décor et l'objet," *La nouvelle revue française* 54 (1940–41).

29. For examples, see a series of articles on "les métiers de France" (the crafts of France) by Jean Follain in the review *Chantiers;* a forum devoted to the same theme in the journal *Beaux-arts;* the campaign in support of the return to artisanal production in *Le rouge et le bleu*, beginning in 1941; and the periodicals *Métiers de France: Revue mensuelle de l'artisanat*, *La terre française: Hebdomadaire de l'agriculture et de l'artisanat rural*, *L'artisan de l'Ouest* (Saint-Brieuc), *L'artisan français: Organe officiel de la Confédération générale de l'artisanat français*, and *L'information artisanale* (n.s., Paris). In addition, see Editions du Chêne and its illustrated works on craftsmanship, a set of works edited by André Lejard that brought together, in 1942, a number of texts in the series titled "La tradition française"; Albert Coustenoble et al., *Artistes et artisans: Six conférences prononcées à l'Exposition de la sélection nationale artisanale de 1942* (Paris: Ministère de la Production Industrielle & des Communications, 1942); and Bernard Champigneulle, "Les artisans de qualité," in Bertrand de Jouvenel et al., *L'or au temps de Charles-Quint et de Philippe II* (Paris: Sequana, 1943).

30. Jacques Wilhelm, "Du rôle de l'artisanat dans l'avenir de la France," *Atalante*, January 1942, 3–4.

31. Wilhelm, "Du rôle de l'artisanat" (note 30), 3–4.

32. Wilhelm, "Du rôle de l'artisanat" (note 30), 3–4.

33. Louis Chéronnet, "Une équipe de décorateurs," *Beaux-arts*, 14 November 1941, 7.

34. Since 1928, Jacques Adnet had directed the Compagnie des arts français, founded in 1919 by Louis Süe and André Mare, under the motto, "Evolution dans la tradition." Adnet defended Brianchon, Lucien Coutaud, Legueult, Oudot, and André Planson.

35. Chéronnet, "Une équipe de décorateurs" (note 33), 7.

36. The Beauvais factory was completely destroyed in June 1940, and a few months later the *basse lisse* loom studios were transferred to the Gobelins works in Paris. The ceramics studios of the Sèvres factory (located near the Renault factories southwest of Paris) were bombed three times and were moved as well. [Mobilier national is a state institution founded by Jean-Baptiste Colbert, Louis XIV's finance minister, that conserves and commissions furnishings for a large number of public buildings in France and abroad.—Trans.]

37. See the bimonthly official organ of the general secretariat of fine arts, *Revue des beaux-arts de France*, no. 1 (1942) (chair of the editorial board, Louis Hautecoeur; secretary general, Michel Florisoone). The less bucolic works commissioned at the factories by the occupying forces received less publicity. At the Gobelins factory, in 1941, *Earthly Globe*, after a cartoon by Werner Peiner, was commissioned by Göring (26 July 1941, weaving interrupted on 5 September 1944); *Bull Cart or Ceres*, after Peiner, by Ribbentrop (fourth quarter of 1941 to 14 June 1944); *Horse Cart*, after Peiner, by Ribbentrop (fourth quarter of 1941 to 22 May 1944); *Baldachin*, after Peiner, by Göring (fourth quarter of 1941, weaving interrupted in the third quarter of 1944); see Chantal Gastinel-Coural, "Manufacture nationale des Gobelins: Etat de la fabrication de 1900 à 1990," *Bulletin du CIETA*, no. 68 (1990): 21.

38. In 1940, a square meter of tapestry from the Gobelins factory cost three thousand francs. Needlepoint tapestry from the Aubusson factory cost less, that from the Beauvais factory more: ten thousand francs per square meter. At the Aubusson factory, the work was done with shadings, using about 14,000 tones, and a square meter took four years to complete. Under the new methods used, a square meter was supposed to cost only nine thousand francs. A range of only 120 tones was to be used—a range stipulated in Jean-Baptiste Colbert's decree of 1671—along with the plant dyes reintroduced in 1938. See Guillaume Janneau, quoted in Gaston Diehl, "La renaissance d'un grand art," *Beaux-arts*, 16 May 1941, 7.

39. See his technique of coding cartoons, in which each spot was numbered so as to prevent errors in interpreting and painting the cartoon. See Michèle Heng, "Aubusson et la renaissance de la tapisserie," *Histoire de l'art*, no. 11 (1990): 61–73. The author also highlights the paradox of endeavoring to make tapestry a craft when its institutions, such as the Aubusson factory, operated as true business enterprises.

40. Jean Lurçat, "Tapisserie de haute et basse lisse," in Jean Lurçat and Marcel Gromaire, *Tapisseries contemporaines: Aubusson* (Paris: Editions Braun, 1943). See also Jean Lurçat, "Révolte contre le tableau de chevalet," *Formes et couleurs*, no. 6 (1943); and Jean Tedesco's film *Tapisseries de France* (1942).

Jean Lurçat was born in Bruyères (Vosges) on 1 July 1892 and died in Saint-Paul de Vence in 1966. His father and grandfather were postmasters. He became a student of the engraver Bernard Naudin, in 1912, at the Académie Colarossi in Montparnasse. He joined the 46th régiment d'infanterie in 1914, was wounded and then imprisoned for having written antimilitarist poems. In 1939, he moved to the Aubusson factory with Gromaire, where they worked with Derain and Dufy. Somewhat later, he was assigned to produce four wall hangings, titled *The Four Seasons*, and the Musée national d'art moderne purchased his *Garden of Roosters* and *The Poet;* the cartoon for the latter was destroyed by German forces in 1944. During the dark years, he also created *Goat (Es la verdad)* and *Liberté*, an illustration of Paul Éluard's poem of that name; later, in 1956, he designed a large tapestry (48 square meters, or nearly 58 square yards) titled *Homage to the Resistance and Deportation Dead.*

41. See Pierre Vaisse, "La querelle de la tapisserie au début de la Troisième République," *Revue de l'art*, no. 22 (1973).

42. In 1938, three artists from the Maison de la culture, Lurçat, Gromaire, and Pierre Dubreuil, were entrusted with a mission to restructure the tapestry factories. The same year, the Aubusson factory opened two studios that promoted modern artistic practices: the abandonment of perspective, simplification, economy of colors. See Ory, "La politique culturelle" (note 8), 580–82.

43. On the movement to revive tapestry, see the writings of Michèle Heng; Jean Lurçat, "Réveil d'un art mural (la tapisserie)," *Arts de France*, no. 1 (1945); Marc Saint-Saëns, "Liberté de l'art et disciplines techniques," *Arts de France*, no. 4 (1946); Jean Picart Le Doux, "Du tableau de chevalet à la tapisserie," *Arts de France*, no. 5 (1946); the special issue "Aubusson et la renaissance de la tapisserie," *Le point* 6, no. 32 (1946); Germain Bazin et al., *La tapisserie française: Muraille et laine* (Paris: Editions Pierre Tisné, 1946); and Jean Lurçat, *Tapisserie française* (Paris: Bordas, 1947).

44. Valérie-Anne Sircoulomb, "Le groupe d'Oppède pendant la Seconde Guerre mondiale: Utopie, mythe ou réalité?" (D.E.A. [*diplôme d'études approfondies*] thesis, Université Lyon II–Louis Lumière, 1990).

45. This expression is from Wilhelm, "Du rôle de l'artisanat" (note 30), 3–4.

46. André Lhote, *Petits itinéraires à l'usage des artistes* (Paris: Editions Denoël, 1943), 10.

47. At Matières et formes, Breteau presented works by members of Groupe témoignage (Jean Bertholle, Jean Le Moal, Étienne-Martin, Alfred Manessier, Lucien Beyer, René Burlet, Jean Silvant, Louis Thomas, Dimitri Varbanesco), alongside those by Charlotte Henschel, de Pettigny, Nicolas Wacker, Zelman, Kliger, François Stahly, and the "artisan artists" Beyer (stoneware), Véra Pagava (fabrics), Étienne Noël (glasswork), Bruno Simon (chess set), Talboutier-Martin (pottery), Claude Stahly-Favre (bookbinding), Marthe Verhuven (enamel), and Nelson (fabrics).

48. "Le sentiment mystique dans l'art actuel," *Connaissance des arts*, August 1960, 65; quoted in Laure de Buzon-Vallet, "Lyon, le groupe Témoignage," in *Paris 1937–Paris 1957: Créations en France*, exh. cat. (Paris: Centre Georges Pompidou, 1981), 90.

49. Georges Hilaire, report on the policy of the fine arts administration, interview in *Comoedia*, 5 August 1944.

50. Jacques Mayet, quoted in Louis Chéronnet, "À propos d'une conférence au Salon d'Automne: Conditions de l'artisanat d'art," *Beaux-arts*, 7 November 1941, 5.

51. Jean de Beer, "Notes sur l'art vivant," *Chantiers*, 25 February 1943, 7.

52. Beer, "Notes sur l'art vivant" (note 51), 7.

53. Jean-Marc Campagne, "L'objectivisme," *Beaux-arts*, 30 October 1943; and Jean-Marc Campagne, "À propos d'un titre," *Beaux-arts*, 16 January 1944, 1.

54. Philippe Besnard, "Réflexions sur les possibilités de la peinture," *Beaux-arts*, 10 September 1943.

55. Maurice de Vlaminck, "Opinions libres…sur la peinture," *Comoedia*, 6 June 1942, 1, 6.

56. Vlaminck's article against Picasso, most unusually, elicited an explicit reaction of disapproval. See Jean Bazaine's postscript to his article "Jeune peinture," *La nouvelle revue française* 56 (1942): 634.
57. For example, on 5 November 1942, at the Hôtel Drouot one Maître Blond obtained 32,500 francs for a still life by Picasso; see "Ventes de tableaux à l'étranger," *Pro arte*, February 1943, 9.
58. Announced in *Beaux-arts* in 1942: Galerie Rive Gauche and Galerie Charpentier, "Les fleurs et les fruits depuis le romantisme," works by Picasso as well as by Braque, Alix, Friesz, and others; Maison Ducrot, "Gravures de Dürer à Picasso"; at the Printemps department store art gallery, works by Picasso as well as Derain, Vlaminck, and others.
59. See André-Louis Dubois, *À travers trois républiques: Sous le signe de l'amitié* (Paris: Plon, 1972). Among the first civil servants to be dismissed, André-Louis Dubois had been part of Albert Sarraut's cabinet. He saw Picasso regularly during the occupation, almost daily by his own account.
60. Vlaminck, "Opinions libres" (note 55).
61. Vlaminck had given Derain a mask from the Ogooué region in west central Africa. The two artists would become major collectors of primitive art, most of which they acquired between 1906 and 1910. See Jean Laude, *La peinture française (1905–1914) et "l'Art nègre,"* 2 vols. (Paris: Editions Klincksieck, 1968).
62. See *Le Fauvisme français et les débuts de l'Expressionnisme allemand = Der französische Fauvismus und der deutsche Frühexpressionismus*, exh. cat. (Munich: Haus der Kunst, 1966).
63. Maurice de Vlaminck, "Sur la peinture—l'invention et le don," *Comoedia*, 5 September 1942, 1, 8.
64. Vlaminck, "Sur la peinture" (note 63).
65. See the postscript to Bazaine, "Jeune peinture" (note 56), 634.
66. André Lhote, "Opinions libres... sur la peinture française," *Comoedia*, 13 June 1942, 1, 6.
67. See the analysis in Jean Clair, "Données d'un problème," in *Les réalismes, 1919–1939*, exh. cat. (Paris: Centre Georges Pompidou, 1980).
68. That series of engravings, produced in 1937, was reprinted on postcards that were sold to benefit the Spanish Republic.
69. Michel Leiris, "Faire-part," *Cahiers d'art* 12, no. 4–5 (1937): 128.
70. Message from Pablo Picasso to the Second American Artists' Congress, New York, 23 December 1937; English version quoted in its entirety in Serge Guilbaut, *How New York Stole the Idea of Modern Art: Abstract Expressionism, Freedom, and the Cold War*, trans. Arthur Goldhammer (Chicago: Univ. of Chicago Press, 1983), 26; and also transcribed in the *New York Times*, 19 December 1937. See also the writings of Rosi Huhn.
71. Many publications have made it possible to reconstruct in detail Picasso's

existence under the occupation, particularly Jaime Sabartés's memoirs, begun in 1939 and published as *Picasso, portraits et souvenirs*, trans. Paule-Marie Grand and André Chastel (Paris: Louis Carré & Maximilien Vox Editeurs, 1946); Brassaï, *Conversations avec Picasso* (Paris: Gallimard, 1964); Pierre Cabanne, *Le siècle de Picasso*, vol. 2, *La guerre, le parti, la gloire, l'homme seul (1937–1973)* (Paris: Denoël, 1975); Pierre Daix, *Picasso créateur: La vie intime et l'oeuvre* (Paris: Editions du Seuil, 1987). On the evolution of Picasso's work and the problems of dating it, see *Picasso: Aus dem Museum of Modern Art, New York, und Schweizer Sammlungen* (Basel: Kunstmuseum Basel, 1976), which contains entries by Franz Meyer; Pierre Daix, *La vie de peintre de Pablo Picasso* (Paris: Editions du Seuil, 1977); *Picasso im Zweiten Weltkrieg, 1939 bis 1945*, exh. cat. (Cologne: Museum Ludwig, 1988), with texts by Brigitte Baer, Laurence Bertrand Dorléac, Pierre Daix, Siegfried Gohr, Remo Guidieri, Harriet Janis and Sidney Janis, Franz Meyer, Leo Steinberg, Wilfried Wiegand, and Christian Zervos.

72. Picasso, quoted in Jean Leymarie, *Picasso: Métamorphoses et unité* (Geneva: Skira, 1971), 253.

73. See Cabanne, *Le siècle de Picasso* (note 71), 83.

74. Simone Téry, "Picasso n'est pas officier dans l'armée française" (interview), *Les lettres françaises*, 24 March 1945, 6.

75. See Gerhard Heller, with Jean Grand, *Un Allemand à Paris, 1940–1944* (Paris: Editions du Seuil, 1981); Ernst Jünger, *Premier journal parisien: Journal II, 1941–1943*, trans. Henri Plard (Paris: Christian Bourgois, 1980); Ernst Jünger, *Second journal parisien: Journal III, 1943–1945*, trans. Frédéric de Towarnicki and Henri Plard (Paris: Christian Bourgois, 1980).

76. With Jünger and his French friends, Gerhard Heller was an invited guest at the Concerts de la Pléiade organized by the firm Gallimard. These concerts took place from five to seven o'clock in the evening at the Conservatoire national de musique et d'art dramatique or at the Galerie Charpentier, which exhibited paintings by Morisot, Renoir, and Braque. He heard Messiaen's *Visions de l'Amen* played by the composer and Yvonne Loriod, and Satie's *Trois morceaux en forme de poire*. See Heller, *Un Allemand à Paris* (note 75), 125.

77. Heller, *Un Allemand à Paris* (note 75), 115.

78. Heller, *Un Allemand à Paris* (note 75), 118.

79. Jean Cayrol was imprisoned in 1942 and, according to Heller's account, Pierre Drieu La Rochelle intervened in January 1943 to have Heller "do something for him."

80. See Jean Cayrol, "Pour un romanesque lazaréen," in idem, *Les corps étrangers, Pour un romanesque Lazaréen*, with "La rature" by Roland Barthes (Paris: Le Monde en 10/18, 1964), 204; quoted in Heller, *Un Allemand à Paris* (note 75), 118.

81. Heller, *Un Allemand à Paris* (note 75), 128.
82. Heller's words—"influence magique"—in his *Un Allemand à Paris* (note 75), 123.
83. Jünger, *Premier journal parisien* (note 75), 153 (22 July 1942).
84. Jünger wrote *Auf den Marmorklippen* between the end of February 1939 in Überlingen, south of Stuttgart, and 28 July of the same year in Kirchhorst, near Hanover. He proofread it in September while in the armed forces, and it was published in Germany just before the war. A romantic and mythological novel on the struggle between good and evil, it has often been interpreted as a protest against Nazism. The first French translation was published in 1942 by Editions Gallimard.
85. Jünger, *Premier journal parisien* (note 75), 154 (22 July 1942).
86. In early 1942, Éluard asked to be readmitted to the Communist Party, of which he had briefly been a member in 1926 and 1927. He joined the Communist underground in summer 1942 and kept Picasso abreast of his new political activities.
87. Quoted in Brassaï, *Conversations avec Picasso* (note 71), 77.
88. Quoted in Brassaï, *Conversations avec Picasso* (note 71), 79.
89. Quoted in Daix, *La vie de peintre* (note 71), 302.
90. He repaired the plaster casts that had been damaged when French soldiers sacked his studio at the château de Boisgeloup and had them cast in bronze at the foundry, with a few friends transporting his pieces—in plaster and then in bronze—back and forth at night in wheelbarrows, under the nose of patrols.
91. See Daniel-Henry Kahnweiler, *Mes galeries et mes peintres: Entretiens avec Francis Crémieux* (Paris: Gallimard, 1961), 190.
92. The *greguería*—very brief poetic statements characterized by a free association of words, ideas, and objects—was placed at the center of poetic life by the Spanish writer Ramón Gómez de la Serna, and Jean Cassou pointed to its importance in Spanish culture.
93. As Picasso explained to an American war correspondent in August 1944; see Peter D. Whitney, "Picasso Is Safe: The Artist Was neither a Traitor to His Painting nor His Country," *San Francisco Chronicle*, 3 September 1944.
94. André Malraux, *La tête d'obsidienne* (Paris: Gallimard, 1974), 128.
95. See Daix, *La vie de peintre* (note 71), 303; and the remarks by Fernandez recorded in Cabanne, *Le siècle de Picasso* (note 71), 77–78.
96. See, among others, works on the theme "the face of peace" in 1950; the poster for the 3rd Congrès des peuples pour la paix in Vienna, 12–18 December 1952; the front page of *L'humanité dimanche* (published by the Parti communiste français) in 1953; a scarf for the 6th World Youth Festival in Moscow, July 1957; a poster advocating peace in 1960; and the poster

for the World Congress for General Disarmament and Peace in Moscow, 9–14 July 1962.

97. See Daix, *La vie de peintre* (note 71), 308.

98. Pierre Lagarde, "André Derain révolutionnaire," *Comoedia*, 17 August 1941.

99. Léon Gischia, "Recherche d'une tradition," in Gaston Diehl, ed., *Les problèmes de la peinture* (Lyon: Confluences, 1945), 137.

100. Gischia, "Recherche d'une tradition" (note 99), 137.

101. On the opposing of Latin and Germanic, see Kenneth E. Silver, *Esprit de Corps: The Art of the Parisian Avant-Garde and the First World War, 1914–1925* (Princeton: Princeton Univ. Press, 1989).

102. Cover image for *Le mot*, 15 June 1915; reproduced in Silver, *Esprit de Corps* (note 101), 94.

103. See Fanette Roche-Pézard, "'Valori Plastici' et 'Novecento,'" in *Les réalismes, 1919–1939*, exh. cat. (Paris: Centre Georges Pompidou, 1980), 54.

104. Henri Focillon, *Technique et sentiment: Etudes sur l'art moderne* (Paris: H. Laurens, 1919), 167–76.

105. Henri Focillon, *Les évocations françaises: Les pierres de France* (Paris: H. Laurens, 1919), introduction, ii.

CHAPTER SIX

France

THE FRENCH SPIRIT

In June 1942, André Lhote, responding to Vlaminck's recent attack on Picasso, chose to take refuge behind the protective blind of the Révolution nationale to snipe at Caravaggio and Guido Reni. In his eyes, the revolution was breathing new life into "an outdated tradition" and might very well be amenable to replacement of an "imported" school responsible for the "official chiaroscuro."[1] The art historian Bernard Dorival—curator of the Musée national d'art moderne and above all suspicion of collusion with the official political program—undoubtedly provided the clearest formulation of the positions of those hostile to the occupying forces while at the same time firmly defending the return to Frenchness. Dismissing François Boucher, Voltaire, *Cyrano de Bergerac*, *La reine morte*, Jean-Baptiste Greuze, Sacha Guitry, and Ernest Meissonier as representative of "the mediocrity that a civilization drags behind it," he placed on the side of French genius,

> The most reserved, the most haughty, the most discreet sensibility of Racine and Seurat; the intelligence, both fiery and disciplined, of Claudel and Balzac, Pascal and Delacroix; reason combined with intuition to provide a serene account of the world; willpower strained to the breaking point, as in Saint Bernard [de Clairvaux] and the Messieurs du Port-Royal; along with a perpetual need for the new, a curiosity that constantly forges ahead; the taste for a certain secret heroism.[2]

Dorival was not slow to contrast this modest posture with the excesses of northern Europe. He had only to compare the expressionism of Gromaire, whose broad strokes exemplified French reason as a whole, to that of his Belgian counterparts Gustave de Smet and Constant Permeke: "In pleasure as well as in anguish, the Frenchman wants to make his own the famous words of Augustus in *Cinna:* 'I am master of myself as well as of the universe.'"[3] Such certainties may have had difficulty withstanding the tragedies imposed on France, yet Dorival was only articulating an idea deeply rooted in decades of French cultural success and quiet revolutions, intelligently tempered and co-opted by admirers of a "living" classicism or a "modern tradition."

Did not Matisse, the best representative of that revolutionary spirit turned temperate and democratic, define in his own way what ultimately constituted "the spirit" of art in France? "Expression does not lie in the passion that explodes across a face or that asserts itself by a violent movement," he confided. It lies "in the whole layout of the painting."[4] From this, his admirers concluded that the most vibrant part of French art, represented by the Jeunes peintres de tradition française (who embraced Romanesque art and modern innovation), was an "art of extreme equilibrium and in that way fully alive—a highly elaborate art, without being too learned or too refined, in which the truly human division between intelligence, emotion, and will can be traced back to the most authentic French tradition."[5] Such a definition of the French tradition dovetailed with Camus's: his was synonymous not with "the justification of instinct" but with "internal discipline," "self-control," and a "commitment to a 'rational' intelligence that has returned to the concrete and is scrupulously honest."[6]

Lhote also isolated these qualities, but in a very ambiguous manner, in *La nouvelle revue française* of November 1942, in order to restate his reservations about untidy, unmethodical Spain. "The excellent work on Picasso" recently published by Editions Hypérion was obligatory reading, but it was advisable to remember that though "the artist's constant virtues must be courage and imagination, the no less beautiful album devoted to Fouquet teaches us with an even greater timeliness that the specific qualities of the French painter are fervent application, cheerful patience, and love of the real."[7] Was it still necessary to repudiate the modern experiment undertaken by Picasso? Lhote, as we have seen, Pl. 37
preferred to salvage what he could: a tempered cubism, leading toward art for art's sake and to that "pure" (and abstract) art that Dorival soon made a very French specialty.[8]

Things became complicated in the case of sculpture, since cubism and abstraction were still largely unknown in a sector more resistant to change than painting. The few sculptors who had sought to integrate "the systematic sensibility of cubism"[9] were almost all foreigners, so that French statuary had remained "classical," as Champigneulle remarked just before the war. Moreover, that classicism did not keep such statuary from being defended, sometimes by the very critics favorable to nonfiguration in painting. What wouldn't they do to extol France? Gaston

Diehl may have been thinking of his country when he drew a laudatory portrait of Despiau in the columns of the official Italian journal *Il tempo*—undoubtedly a bastion of anti-Nazism. The subject of his praise was compromised, however: Despiau had just signed his name to a catalog of Breker's works.[10]

ON ARTISTIC NATIONALISM

The ambiguities of nationalism had their counterparts in the art world: it was possible to sell off France and invoke it at the same time. In 1941, the critic Jean-Marc Campagne declared that Paris would have no cause to envy Berlin, "if someone [wanted] to really make the effort here that [was being] made everywhere else."[11] Yet this display of patriotism did not prevent him from writing, a year later, the text for the brochure for the exhibition of Breker's works at the Orangerie. The situation seemed to have turned to the advantage of the occupying forces in the meantime. But Campagne was not the only one to run with the hare and hunt with the hounds, to support both France and Germany, national pride and Nazi pretensions.[12] Until the end, some of those who spoke out publicly paired the shame of being occupied with a whiff of chauvinism, of which the occupying forces barely took notice, since their real power made any repression on the subject pointless. The occupier responded to the toadyism of the vanquished with contempt or action: French masterpieces departed by the trainload to swell collections across the Rhine; the Orangerie hosted Breker's athletes; well-known French artists went to Germany to serve the ends of the Third Reich's propaganda machine. Anything else was a reflexive shudder quite natural on the part of a defeated country whose administration was demonstrating its de facto collaboration on a daily basis.

The vanquished sometimes went to great lengths to define the limits of a strictly French tradition. Regularly repeated, the exercise undoubtedly came to look like a revolt against the occupying forces. Still it had to be understood that only Germany was targeted (and thus Italy and Spain, owing to their misalliance with Germany), not the Jews or the foreigners or the primitive societies that, for various reasons, served as foils most of the time. In reality, the obsession with purity led everyone, modern and antimodern, to hunt down the "imported" or "semiforeign" tradition. This entailed feigning ignorance of how France had been constituted and forgetting that its fragile identity resulted from a clever mix of nationalities. Even in the underground and Resistance press, realpolitik held sway in definitions of the national tradition which usually retained a definitive and civilized version that supported the valorizing image of an invigorated France, stripped of all external influence.

In terms of living art, the French tradition was perfectly embodied in the works of Pierre Bonnard, Matisse, and Braque, and its crowning success was Braque's retrospective in 1943 at the Salon d'Automne. In 1937, Lhote recognized him as "one of the most perfect French craftsmen," stating that, as Braque was "the painter of edifying relaxation," it was in front of his works that "eventually, in museums finally modernized and open to all, the common people [would] want to rest from their troubles and anticipate their vacations, just as Americans... sated with rationalization [would] greedily lap up the disturbing phantasmagorias of surrealism."[13] It was a curious vision of a France whose avant-garde quickly settle down and dedicate itself to comforting a populace of exhausted laborers. Matisse had even announced that he wanted to paint to relax and refresh those returning home after work. For many, he magnificently embodied France. This was true even for the Communists, who considered him a friend: despite his advanced age and the apparently peaceful content of his works, he quietly rebuffed barbarism from the hilltops of Cimiez. Aragon was a devotee of Matisse's *Dessins: Thèmes et variations*, which was loosely inspired by the tales of Charles Perrault and made up of line drawings of still lifes and women (done in 1941 and 1942). Anne was no longer watching the road for her brothers to arrive and save her sister from Bluebeard. Rather, she was anticipating a squad of horsemen who would be filled with wonder at France upon discovering the painter, of whom, according to Aragon, it would later be said that "in the darkest night," at least the inspiring and comforting sound of the phrase Matisse-en-France "rang out like Le Puy-en-Velay, Marcq-en-Baroeul, and Crécy-en-Valois."[14] Pls. 25–27

The distinction between the pursuit of a national tradition and the assertion of its universal dominance became so fine that it vanished under the shock of the defeat. The humiliation of the occupation released an ad hoc egocentrism, and the situation consigned to oblivion the warnings of the prewar period. In 1938, the review *Beaux-arts* launched a campaign in support of "the renaissance of a French art, of an art of moderation, clarity, and balance, which can be achieved only through a continual struggle against easy solutions and probably also against monetary gain." Lhote agreed but with one sizable reservation: the rise of dark forces promoted "the exaltation of an art that is conformist" and "supposedly racial, at a time when 'wogs' [were] the object of unspeakable persecutions."[15] Even though the artist had proclaimed over the years that the salvation of painters from every nation depended on that of French painters and that the latter, given the crisis, had to decide "with a willful intolerance" that only "the lesson of the French masters" mattered,[16] Lhote caught wind of the tragedy and the vicious consequences of an exclusive nationalism. In this, he resembled Lurçat, fellow traveler of the left, who was persuaded that a culture, "however national it may appear, is after all only the fleeting, changeable aspect of the whole that is human culture."[17]

After the defeat, some artists, universalist on principle, did not become involved in the "national battle," out of caution or individualism. Others, in greater numbers, temporarily renounced their internationalism, finding in the various forms of withdrawal into all things French the most effective means for their resistance to the state of things. They had not the slightest sympathy for the regulations excluding foreigners and Jews, but, like many others, they regarded the German presence as their main concern.

The French art scene would shift away significantly from concern for relations with the occupiers. It began to pull back at the time of the trip by French artists to Germany, kept its distance and took stock of its position during the Breker exhibition, and recovered a modicum of hope when the Musée national d'art moderne opened its doors to the public.

THE MUSÉE NATIONAL D'ART MODERNE

The opening of the museum at the height of the occupation served as a barometer of nationalism that, in mid-summer 1942, indicated everyone's level of impatience. The exhibition of Breker's works at the Orangerie had just triumphantly imposed the German aesthetic model, sealing at the same time a new cultural pact with the occupying forces illustrated by the official reception of Hitler's favorite, the selling off of collections, and Laval's and Abel Bonnard's arrangements with Göring. The French tried to reassure themselves at the Orangerie by compiling a list of differences between the art of the two countries and by snickering at the vanquisher's grandiloquence. But to no avail: for many, the humiliation was complete. Thus, when the fine arts administration managed to prevent the Nazis from occupying the Palais de Tokyo, everyone felt a kind of relief, which was widely echoed in newspaper columns. The sparseness and mediocrity of the museum's collections, associated in great part with the deficiencies of official policy, were very quickly passed over—if they were noticed at all—in favor of pride in an achievement whose true cost most refused to assess: the ousting of Jewish artists and undesirables and the dismissal of Jean Cassou, on whom, in theory, the office of chief curator of the museum was to devolve, thus remained in the shadows during the celebration.[18] The extremist press had anticipated the regime in hunting down Cassou, that devil twice over—an old friend of the left and of modernity. When the secretary general of fine arts had come to Cassou in tears with the news that Cassou was being forced to retire, it was Cassou, a member of the Resistance from the first, who consoled Hautecoeur, predicting there would be other such disappointments under Vichy.[19]

The day of the opening, Hautecoeur once again forced the Nazi authorities in attendance to listen to him praise French art as "the flower of our nation." He made an appeal "to all the forces of our race" that this art might survive under "the sad circumstances," that these works might express "the faith of a people in an ideal that, for so many centuries, [had] never abandoned them." But as always, Abel Bonnard came right behind him, smoothing things over and reassuring the vanquishers with a battery of winks, with which they were by now familiar. Just after the opening, the press as a whole—even some extremist newspapers—joined in singing a hymn to honor restored. Tabarant wrote enthusiastically in *L'oeuvre* about the "significant artistic event";[20] and in *La gerbe*, G.-J. Gros saw it as "a milestone in the official annals of our national museums."[21] For a sense of the "paradoxes" surrounding journalism under the occupation, it is especially useful to consider the article on the new museum by the author of the Breker exhibition brochure, Jean-Marc Campagne. He confided to his readers that his visit to the only place offering an overview of contemporary art had procured him "one of the rare moments of pride" he had felt since the armistice.[22]

Because the opening of the museum, which was supposed to follow on the heels of the Exposition internationale of 1937, had been postponed—primarily due to technical errors by the architects of the Palais de Tokyo—official sites devoted to contemporary art had been scarce: the Musée du Luxembourg (the cramped precursor of the Musée national d'art moderne), the dynamic Musée des écoles étrangères contemporaines (at the Jeu de Paume), and, finally, a section of the Musée des beaux-arts de la Ville de Paris (at the Petit Palais), where Raymond Escholier promoted contemporary works.

For reasons that far transcended allegiance to the modern tradition, consensus would never be greater during the dark years than at the museum's opening. The chorus of praise with patriotic undertones was never interrupted, but was simply modified by the ill-tempered barbs of a few isolated nigglers. At *La nouvelle revue française*, Jean Bazaine in particular was too knowledgeable about painting not to make fun of the museum's assortment of the best and the worst. He was quite willing to acknowledge his masters Matisse, Braque, and Pierre Bonnard and his friends Villon and Charles Lapicque but by no means "that lovely harvest of daubs," those "bad paintings" that were not only passé but "rather genteel, rather discreet... a fashionable assortment... that Millerand still watches over, his hair falling in his eyes and his hand in his waistcoat."[23] Bazaine preferred the adventurers and the enemies of the day, such as Fernand Léger, to "so many awkward little mongrels,"[24] and he regretted that Léger was represented by only one beautiful canvas. Among the sculptors, he found Lipchitz, along with Laurens, the most "inspired" of their time. By comparison, the overrepresented Maillol, whose neo-antique *Île-de-France* had been chosen to appear on the catalog's cover, was "charming, excellent when reproduced at small sizes" but "a prisoner to the wealth of accents required by his taste for the surfaces of female flesh in full flower."[25] What in fact irritated Bazaine was the eclecticism of a presentation that condemned the best works to be "hemmed in" and finally "suffocated."[26]

That was an attack on the narrow range of the state's purchasing commissions, which had preferred a timorous policy to "adventure." To assess the mind-set of the decision makers, it suffices to cite one striking example: the refusal, in autumn 1937, by the Conseil des musées nationaux to allow the Musée des écoles étrangères contemporaines to acquire Picasso's *Still Life with Jug*, with nine of fourteen members voting no.

The absence of important artists was not merely the result of errors in judgment; it was also the logical consequence of ongoing exclusions. Thus, the fact that foreign artists (often Parisians) were not invited to exhibit considerably reduced an already limited panorama. The Musée des écoles étrangères contemporaines was the first to face the puzzle of "French art" as well as the double-edged concept of an "Ecole de Paris," a notion destined for a stormy future. In 1924, André Warnod had portrayed the latter as a school of living "French" artists, as opposed to the French academic painters, and made it the exotic refuge of émigré artists from central or southern Europe by including in its ranks Picasso, Gris, Zadkine, Modigliani, Chagall, Jules Pascin, and Soutine, among others.

Should their actual nationality be the deciding factor or rather their work, which was for the most part completed in France and generally in Paris?[27] Those most aware of the absurdity of the segregated system had suggested, back in the early 1930s, that the French collections and the holdings of the Musée des écoles étrangères contemporaines[28] should at least be assembled in the same place—but to no avail. France had everything to hope for from the already prestigious contributions of foreign artists, despite the lack of appreciation from the general public. André Dézarrois, the ambitious curator of the Musée des écoles étrangères contemporaines,[29] had amply demonstrated the existence of a major international art often linked to the history of Paris. He especially distinguished himself in presenting the major established modern artists, French and foreign—Picasso, Matisse, Braque—but also key figures kept well away from official events in 1937—abstract artists (Kandinsky, Miró, Klee) and surrealists (Tanguy, Dalí, René Magritte, Ernst)—as well as anonymous and "primitive" works, such as Oceanian or African sculptures, masks, and fetishes.

In 1937, the group exhibition *Origines et développement de l'art international indépendant*[30] was thrown together by Yvonne Zervos in a few weeks, opening at the Jeu de Paume only a fortnight after the inauguration of *Entartete Kunst* in Munich. For the first time in France, it offered a coherent landscape—a negative print as it were—of rejected modern art. The same artists who were presented in Paris under the most modern exhibition conditions were to be found deliberately displayed any which way in Germany. Even though the Parisian exhibition put on view only 177 works and had only about five thousand visitors, it made history: on the heels of *Cubism and Abstract Art*, organized by Alfred Barr and held at the Museum of Modern Art in New York in 1936,[31] it was the first coherent attempt to present modernity.

Five years later, the galleries of the new Musée national d'art moderne paled in comparison, yet they faithfully reflected the situation of the art scene as a whole, including private galleries. Over time, a multitude of those shown there have been forgotten, fallen victim to the whims of taste and conventions. Of some 327 artists represented, the works of well over half would not be recognized today, even by the most educated viewers, though at the time, they were very highly valued. Hence, it is necessary to assess the "richness" of the holdings of the Musée national d'art moderne, which has clearly changed its approach in the meantime. Its ambitious and, if need be, hermetic image must be contrasted to the aspirations of the general public during the occupation era, with its well-worn themes and treatments.[32]

Under the occupation, the human figure, particularly the female figure in its endless variety, was the preferred subject by far. Of the some 650 works shown at the Palais de Tokyo,[33] a very large number provided the visitor with a tremendously seductive (female) embodiment of an artistic France that as yet counted only a few women artists who had been elevated, with great difficulty, to the rank of "minor masters."

Graphs 5, 6

Especially in sculpture, which was more traditionalist than painting, figures of women predominated, to the point that certain spaces were set aside almost exclusively for them. Hence, in gallery 204–5, where Maillol's *Desire* set the tone, the accompanying retinue included one *Eve* each by Despiau, Louis Dejean, and François Émile Popineau, *Dancing Girl* by Émile Bernard, *Bather with Drapery* by Pierre-Marie Poisson, *Female Water Bearer* and *Woman and Child Dancing* also by Bernard, and four or five other female figures by Maillol. Beside them, Jean

Dunand's lacquered panel *The Harvest* and Félix Joffre's *The Athlete* were not nearly enough to offset the voluptuousness in the room.

By contrast, painting appeared less of a prisoner to the canons of ideal beauty, offering an eclectic mix in which landscapes, still lifes, seascapes, and human representations predominated. Here, though the elder of the major innovators drew from the same registers as the majority, their works stood out among the rest: Pierre Bonnard, with five canvases, including *Table Corner;* Matisse, with ten canvases, including *The Odalisque;* Braque, underrepresented, with only *Duo;* and Robert Delaunay, also underrepresented, with only *Portuguese Still Life.* Even *Springtime* by the rebel Picabia (in absentia in the south of France), the mysterious *Day of Slowness* by the surrealist Tanguy (exiled to the United States), and *Three Women* by Léger (also in exile), now a persona non grata, were present to brighten a rather dreary landscape. Conversely, the absence of the "foreigners" Dézarrois had wanted to include—Picasso, Miró, Klee, Ernst—and of Frenchmen such as Marcel Duchamp, Hélion, and Fautrier, marked a backing away from the push for new acquisitions during the Front populaire. Tanguy and Lapicque were exhibited, yet Kandinsky, Zadkine, and Auguste Herbin were excluded from this venue, which, all things considered, held few surprises and displayed little recklessness. The opening of the museum tended to increase national consensus around a certain notion of modern art in France: temperate and innately French. It was an economical way of responding to the occupier's titans, by displaying a national temperament that relished fleshy women and, ultimately, nature.

Among the younger generations of French artists, signs of a renewal were barely detectible. Did "the young guard" of the day, those who embraced a modern tradition, make an appearance at the Palais de Tokyo? The presence of works by Charles Lapicque, age forty-four, whose *Seascape* was displayed, and Édouard Pignon, seven years his
Pl. 34 junior, with *Red Tablecloth,* suggested that the state was beginning to take an interest in a little-appreciated group of painters who, to a degree, were headed toward new adventures.[34] The activism of a brilliant young curator, Bernard Dorival—whose very cautious superior, Pierre Ladoué, was close to retirement—was not immaterial to the arrival of the new artists recently exhibited in Paris under a polysemous sobriquet about which a great deal of ink would be spilled.

THE YOUNG GUARD

The preview of the group exhibition *Jeunes peintres de tradition française*[35] took place at 3 o'clock on Saturday, 10 May 1941, at the Galerie Braun in Paris, to sparse attendance. Organized eleven months after the start of the occupation, it was an important opening salvo in an offensive by a few artists bent on breaking the silence of the art scene. Bazaine, Beaudin, Paul Berçot, Jean Bertholle, Francisco Borès, Lucien Coutaud, Desnoyer, Gischia, Lapicque, Jean Lasne, Lautrec, Legueult, Jean Le Moal, Alfred Manessier, Marchand, Pignon, Suzanne Roger, Gustave Singier, Tal-Coat, and Walch did not form a homogeneous group. Rather, they had been hastily summoned from all over France by Bazaine and the publisher André Lejard. Their works, still figurative, were not of a nature to shock but generally subscribed to a "modern" mode, along the lines of Picasso, Matisse, and surrealism. Was that sufficient to prompt censorship by the Propaganda-Staffel Paris? Were the rules of the game not yet so clearly established that the exhibition's organizers had the impression they were breaking them and joining in "resistance"? In their own eyes at least, to defend a modern French tradition was to defend France and its "degenerate" lineage. The exhibition was thus supposed to be an initial blow struck against the occupier. Pls. 30–32, 38

Was that plan so clear-cut that, after the liberation, only it would be remembered and everything that did not enter into its positive logic forgotten?[36] The attitude of the Propaganda-Staffel Paris may have proved "disappointing," since it did not deem it necessary to intervene, preferring to focus its activities on the exclusion of Jews and Freemasons,[37] but the project to "resist" through painting itself mattered more than anything. Bazaine, the architect of the project, heralded it:

> Every war drags behind it its contingent of amnesiacs, but that is not enough to explain why all those in France who still have a little courage and freedom of thought seem to have suddenly forgotten that for the last thirty years French painting was our only effective presence in the world and one of the rare living ferments of our time....
>
> All the same, our military defeat should not admit by extension a general rout of all the best things our civilization has produced.[38]

He also evoked "a certain taste for risk and a desire to commit oneself to an art that would not be an art of escape... of all those dirty little escapes, of those lazy old cheats, of those 'returns to...' that betray the critical eras."[39] Three months after the exhibition at the Galerie Braun, despite an anonymous letter he had just received, Bazaine drove the point home in one of his reviews by affirming the need to embody tradition in a dangerous manner.[40] For him, it was time for committed words but an apolitical consensus. It was necessary to "defend openly, and apart from all politics, strong and true French values."[41]

By signing a few manifestos, Bazaine became in a way the militant leader of a generation that was succeeding a generation whose members were, in part, exiled, silent, or biding their time. The gathering in May 1941 was a prelude of sorts to the emergence of a group of artists who would say, later, that at the time they felt that the deadlock had at last been broken for them and that, despite the hard times, they were headed for alluring and unknown parts. To the initial group trained on the job were added Estève, André Fougeron, Roger Bissière, Villon, Gabriel Robin, and the sculptors Étienne-Martin and Jean Chauvin. By contrast, certain artists, such as Coutaud, Roger, Marchand, Walch, and Legueult, were for the most part no longer included in this young guard of the "French Tradition" as it presented more coherent proposals, beginning with the exhibition at the young Galerie de France in February 1943, titled *Douze peintres d'aujourd'hui*. There Bazaine, Borès, Estève, Fougeron, Gischia, Lapicque, Le Moal, Manessier, Pignon, Singier, Villon, and Chauvin exhibited works more innovative than in 1941, in some cases moving toward abstraction, at a time when all anyone was talking about was the return to the figure. In the preface to the exhibition catalog, Diehl situated these artists beyond surrealism, anecdotal art, and verbalism, on the side of discipline and a "pure" art, evocative but abstract, in which concepts of surface, color, form, and composition predominated, in the tradition of Bonnard, Braque, Matisse, and Picasso. Between their first appearance in 1941 and this exhibition, Diehl had become their impassioned advocate, while at the same time refining his choices and his tactics. In 1942, he invited them to participate in his *Les étapes du nouvel art contemporain* at the Galerie Berri-Raspail, under the patronage of a committee that included key figures from the art world.[42]

Pls. 33, 35

Behind a falsely draconian taxonomy could be detected the desire to instill a coherent order into an expanding population compromised by the lack of obvious "trends." The call for rigor, however, took up the lyrical, spiritual, and ambiguous themes of its confused age. The war had dealt a final blow to "the spirit of speculation" that drove modern art by

> again giving a primal immediacy to feeling and to life.... The games [were] over, the lyric [developed] more fully. But in many, there [sprang] up the desire to balance plastic and affective elements...the mind [had] had its say, but the heart too [had] the right to speak. Only their perfect alliance [assured] art a real and complete existence.[43]

Diehl's favorite artists would thus become "the presenters of a plastic consciousness." Among these artists, who were scattered before 1941, Bazaine, Estève, Pignon, and Fougeron had been championed by their elders Desnoyer, Goerg, and Gromaire. As for Manessier and Alfred Pellan, they were particularly close to Bissière, a master fresco painter and the influential author of many articles advocating a return to the sources of the French tradition. In fact, the Jeunes peintres de tradition française came from at least two different groups: Groupe témoignage, whose solid connection to the Révolution nationale Diehl could extol in a pinch; and Les indélicats, about which he was to remain silent given its political beliefs.

Groupe témoignage formed in Lyon in 1936 around Marcel Michaud[44] and drew young unknown artists, including Bertholle, Lucien Beyer, Réne-Maria Burlet, Le Moal, Étienne-Martin, Manessier, Jean (or Joseph) Silvant, Louis Thomas, and Dimitri Varbanesco, who exhibited that year at the Salon d'Automne in Lyon. All adhered to the pessimistic manifesto of the review *Le poids du monde*, which a year later adopted a still more dramatic name that, in translation, read "The weight of the world rests on the tenderhearted...optional subtitle:...despite the weight of the world, my heart beats and listens." They thought that, "compared to the Western civilizations of the Middle Ages and to civilizations of all times, contemporary Western civilization [was] lamentably mediocre." They wanted, "in humility, to pick up where the grand spiritual currents had left off and...begin again,"[45] via a return to the material, to folklore, and to provincial mysticisms, via a new vision, in part spiritualist and Christian, multidisciplinary, and totalizing—a vision that led them to exhibit in Lyon works of art alongside artisanal works. Did all this plant the seeds of what was going to flower after the defeat, and later, after 1940, in the activities of those of the Jeunes peintres de tradition française who had participated in events in Lyon—namely, Le Moal, Bertholle, Étienne-Martin, and Manessier? The situation changed abruptly, and their battle had an odd resonance under the new circumstances.

The other group from which the Jeunes peintres de tradition française—Estève, Fougeron, Pignon, and Robin—originated did not enjoy the same continuity. Les indélicats, formed in about 1932,[46] exhibited at the Galerie Billiet-Pierre Vorms in June 1936. They displayed albums of linoleum engravings directly inspired by political events: unemployment, the war, colonization, criticism of the elites. Indeed, these artists, like others at the time, said they were resolved to "prevail over the beast," armed with "satirical art and propaganda, revolutionary art and social demands."[47] With the defeat, these fellow travelers and loyalists to the reforming impulses of 1936 mingled with Catholic artists, revolutionary or not, who were as wary of the Soviet experiment as of the Nazi one.

At least initially, it seemed to be a time for "the eternal richness of the French sensibility"[48] which was to be opposed whenever possible to the "difficulties" of the moment. The bonds between the members of a more or less homogeneous generation, most of them born between 1903 and 1911, overcame political conflicts. These were set aside given the turn of events, in the hope of closing ranks and finally making a mark on the art scene. For consensus to exist, the agenda had to be minimal: it thus exalted above all a modern French tradition that was no longer in good repute.

Although the German authorities did not deem it necessary to censor Picasso's and Matisse's progeny, the French extremist press did, carrying out the mission that fell to it whenever an agent of "decadence" happened to compromise the purification work duly under way. Any attempt to depart from the monotony of the established program of artistic events met with an ill-tempered and revanchist reception that deployed not the usual criteria but insults and racist suspicion.

In the pages of *Je suis partout, La gerbe, La chronique de Paris,* and *Au pilori,* François Le Verrier, Kermarec, and Mosdyc attacked the Jeunes peintres de tradition française, denouncing "hipster art," the "little frauds," "practical jokers," "clowns," and "tricksters."[49] True to his usual tactics, Rebatet lamented the absence of a "true" revolution: "The most remarkable collection of errors, of laborious imitations of Cézanne, Picasso, Rouault, Lhote, of abortive offshoots, mental contortions, arbitrariness, and impotence."[50] That echoed the reflections of Alfred Cortot, now aligned with the collaborationist side, who would gibe during the preview that he was not at a "futurist" exhibition but a "pastist" one.[51]

Others, following a practice very common at the time, attacked the exhibitors' origins. Gischia? "Such a French name," a "reader" of Mosdyc's column on "hipster art" exclaimed.[52] Or Rebatet again, on the "conspiracy" of Resistance painters: "The Jewish lair from which that element [had] emerged was quickly sniffed out." Campagne held to a more traditional form of criticism, simply denouncing the "subjective" and "neotraditionalist" painters, by contrasting them to the "realists" and "objectivists" of whom Derain, he believed, constituted the best model.

By contrast, the Jeunes peintres de tradition française were of neither an age nor a disposition to compromise with the enemy[53] or to renounce the excesses of modern art. But were they necessarily presenting revolutionary works? At least until 1942, art lovers quickly recognized an energetic, youthful, and fresh interpretation of Romanesque art, cubism, fauvism, and at times surrealism. After 1942, everything that seemed to invigorate a living France, to lift the leaden pall of the return to order that had lasted since the end of the 1920s,[54] to break through the lagging spirit of the moment, was all the more striking, given that their works clashed with the ambient conformism.

Passing through Paris in 1943, the art historian Pierre Francastel, a representative of the *Annales* school of historiography, was disappointed by the monotony on view at the traditional venues. But his visit to the young Galerie de France left him in a state of jubilation that says a great deal about the climate of the time. "I have rarely had more pleasure in discovering painting," he said. "Painting—true, great, new, and all the more moving because it bears witness to the survival of Paris in wartime, the true Paris of the young, the one the philistines do not yet know, will never know even if they spend months or years on the banks of the Seine."[55]

In these paintings then, he saw the vitality of an avant-garde engaged in a quest proceeding from the major upheavals of the nineteenth century, when a new notion of space replaced the norms imposed by the Italian Renaissance.[56] Whereas Francastel refrained from announcing his discovery to the media, others less knowledgeable than he, in a steady stream of slight but no doubt effective reviews, pronounced themselves in favor of young artists, in publications broadly representative of the "spirit of the times."[57] Their contradictory remarks did not always reflect the ideas of the "activists"—far from it. Hence, for example, René Barotte, acceding to the "revolutionary" tone of the moment, stamped a work by the openly Communist Pignon with the seal of rigor. Did not our art, he asked, run the risk of dying of freedom? That canvas (*The Soccer Match*) marked "a return to a new classical order. It is, as it were, the symbol of a France that wants to live by relying on an indispensable discipline."[58]

In their day, the Jeunes peintres de tradition française were deemed answerable for supporters they did not always want or for the Nazis' tolerance toward them; at the same time, they were targeted by rightist extremists and at least some of them had joined the Resistance. In our time, they are considered either opponents or henchmen of the French state, or even of the collaboration. Their affiliation with the official organization Jeune France, which sponsored the exhibition at the Galerie Braun in 1941, ultimately marked them politically without clearing up any of the big questions.

What exactly were the political commitments of these painters, apparently torn between tradition and modernity, communitarianism and individualism, primitivism and high culture, instrumentalism and political inaction, officialdom and the Resistance? Under what circumstances did some of them join the ranks of Jeune France? And what exactly was that experiment, which is too often cursorily discussed? To date, only a single serious study on theater, rarely cited, provides the first keys to understanding it.[59]

JEUNE FRANCE

Jeune France came into being on 22 November 1940 and was banned by the government in March 1942.[60] In accordance with the Vichy policy of surrounding itself with as many satellites as possible in the service of the Révolution nationale, the organization first fell under the authority of the general secretariat of youth,[61] which encouraged idle young people to join movements, centers, or works projects. Since there was still time to kill between clearing the land and working the fields, Vichy accepted Pierre Schaeffer's proposal that he supply the cadres required for the cultural activities of the many groups dedicated to national rebirth throughout France.

Georges Lamirand was all the easier to convince because, like Schaeffer, he was a veteran of the Rover scouts, and the Vichy radio program Radio-Jeunesse, which Schaeffer had created, demonstrated the originality of the "boy scout."[62] In setting up an imaginary daily dialogue between the young and Pétain, Schaeffer allied himself with the old leader's vision and the various mythic phrases from the marshal's speeches drafted by Emmanuel Berl.[63] A few months later, Schaeffer's plan for Jeune France—drawn up with Emmanuel Mounier,[64] who had closely followed the venture—expressed a desire to legitimate the experiment but also not to serve as a tool for propaganda.

Jeune France officially adopted as its "principles, directions, spirit" the utopian core of the previous years, a curious mix of authoritarian communitarianism, decentralization, antimodernism, popular fervor, and allegiance to Pétain. "By restoring the unity of [their] generation in a new battle, in a new fervor, following the marshal," its militants would "reestablish the unity of the country" and bring about a "cultural revolution," without "making arts and culture into propaganda services," without "envisioning artists, intellectuals, and educators coming to seek their inspirational themes at some central bureau." As for the public, it said,

> we will seek it far from the cliques and the coteries of the Salon, far from the cafés, wherever the popular virtues are the least seriously compromised. Let peasants recover the desire to celebrate festivals of the earth, let workers demand and build healthy and beautiful factories, let faith shake off the blandness of a decadent piety, and we will regain true, lively, creative audiences.
>
> In working resolutely to promote the arts and to remake man and the environment, we are leading a convergent advance against modern barbarism.

> That advance makes our work a battle, which is not the most insignificant point of our enterprise.[65]

The program was sufficiently vague to attract more than one of those, whether from the left or the right, looking for a third way to change the world, to put an end to decadence, and, for some at least, to accomplish what the Front populaire had not had time to complete, by attacking two strategic sectors: culture and youth. Europe was in search of its *Gesamtkunstwerk*, the total work of art that integrated all the arts and life itself. In its own way, France had to bring about its "spiritual revolution," had to put an end to elitism, to the divorce of art from the public, and to the stultification of a soulless culture reserved for the "bourgeois." The ranks of Jeune France included, in addition to the Ecole nationale des cadres d'Uriage, the future leaders of France, those who, after the liberation, would foment its second cultural revolution. For the time being, however, they constituted a galaxy of young people resolved to take action, after years of revolutionary projects of every stripe, and assured in the bargain a decent living, which, for some at least, could be as much a determining factor as strong theoretical arguments.[66]

At the helm of Jeune France were, in the southern zone (in Lyon), Pierre Schaeffer—a graduate of the Ecole polytechnique, a Catholic, a Rover scout, the future inventor of musique concrète, a pioneer of the airwaves, and a dramatist—and, in the northern zone, Paul Flamand, who was a Catholic, eclectically educated, and the founder of Editions du Seuil. At Schaeffer's side in the southern zone were Emmanuel Mounier; the dramatist Pierre Barbier; Maurice Jacquemont, the director of the Théâtre des Quatre Saisons provinciales; and the writers Claude Roy, of the newspaper *Combat*, still associated with Action française, and René Barjavel. Alongside Flamand in the northern zone were Maurice Blanchot, likewise associated with Action française, a literary theorist and one of the major figures in modern literature after the war;[67] Xavier de Lignac, future head of Charles de Gaulle's press office;[68] Jean Vilar, future creator of the Théâtre national populaire; and Maurice Delarue, future founder of Travail et culture. Finally, in North Africa, there was the resister Max-Pol Fouchet.

The artists involved had very distinct personalities, came from various backgrounds, and had different plans. Bazaine was a personalist, while Manessier and Le Moal were faithful to the leftist struggle, and all three were about to introduce abstract art into churches. Pignon, a Communist, was closer to Picasso than to the destruction of forms undertaken by his comrades. Courmes, an anarcho-Communist, was a forerunner of the French school of pop art in the acerbic mode. Lautrec was an artisan and a pedagogue; more than the others, he was driven by the desire to set up a program for the common people.[69]

Bazaine announced at the outset that "their unity within Jeune France" would be based "neither on an aesthetic grammar nor on an orthodoxy but on a certain number of human positions and attitudes: more than ever, the problem of the artist [was] indistinguishable from the human problem, from which it should never have been separated." He demanded of painters what had to be "asked at present of every man: to commit himself." In art, Jeune France was to be open to all who were not practicing a so-called "academic art that was content to exploit dead formulas with greater or lesser skill." There was still a place for "all young people, whatever their propensities," who showed "promise, even clumsy promise, of strong work." They would find in Jeune France "material and moral support (modes of work, friendship), but also their audience, or rather the living, fertile community," which it was their task to "develop" and which ought to become involved as well. Only through that dual commitment could the isolated artist recover "his place within the polis," and only then would "the harmony between his personal language and the community to which it must give expression" come into being.[70]

THE INVIGORATING LIFE

Focusing solely on the visual arts, we find that after six months of activity, the first assessment of the arts cadres of Jeune France, which was sent to the secretary of national education and youth in July 1941,[71] expressed concern about the "profound breakdown of French popular genius" while delighting in the promise in view. The opportunity presented itself to sharpen the definition of a truly popular art. Despite its authoritarian aspect (particularly in some of Lautrec's texts),[72] the leadership of Jeune France in the occupied zone did not envision art either as "an archaism" or as "propaganda" but as a revival adapted to the contemporary world. It was not a question of replacing existing institutions but of giving rise to a "movement," of "placing life in an invigorating climate" through simple and popular means of expression, of stirring both heart and mind through technique and action.[73]

Jeune France had an ambitious pedagogical program[74] whose aim was to reach all young people, from those involved in movements and training schools for cadres, works projects, the navy, the army, and the traditional education sector to isolated individuals, whether young artists or students. To educate the public directly, the organization planned conferences; visits to museums, exhibitions, artists' or artisans' workshops, monuments, and "urban complexes"; permanent and touring exhibitions; public debates; and "traveling billboards" retracing "through photos and a few texts, and in a very direct form, the main lines of the history of the art of different peoples or of folkloric images or of the development of a minor art." In addition, it intended to set up research centers and libraries.

In its effort to educate future creative artists, Jeune France's program would aid "very young artists" and artisans in the same way, by offering them open workshops at no cost at the local youth center, or Maison de jeunesse. Such workshops were to be places not only to work but also to meet older artists and artisans. There was also talk of competitions, participation in the organization of the Maisons de jeunesse, and a folklore museum in each center.

For the most experienced artists, a nearly identical program was set aside, with the addition of group and individual exhibitions and close collaboration with architects on mural decorations of every sort—frescoes, stained glass, tapestries, and, finally, the decor in youth centers and at local festivals. In exchange, the artists committed themselves to providing ongoing educational programs and to contributing to an in-house review.

The project had both carnivalesque and edifying aspects: permanent exhibitions would take place in the foyer of the Parisian quarters of Jeune France, on rue Jean-Mermoz; traveling shows were to tour in trucks and be installed in cities and villages, in centers for youth and the unemployed or in schools. Exhibitions would have "a general theme (nature, the nation, works and days, an era in French history)," a "qualified guide" well equipped with books and records, and edifying things to see, "not only canvases but also sculptures, artisanal art objects, and beautiful reproductions or photographs—in short, all objects suitable for embellishing the home and forming the public's taste."

In fact, the task of the *maîtrises* (training programs) seemed considerable, even in its smallest details. There was even talk of publishing and selling at a modest price popular prints done by young artists and meant to replace the "countless bourgeois images..., from Millet's *The Angelus* to the post office calendar," found in working-class homes.[75] For popular taste was not innate; it had to be educated, as the plans for a national center of popular art in the so-called free zone attest. The center, to be located in Lyon, was to provide an education in music (singing, dance music, and traditional instruments), "dramatic performance" (with readings, tales, evening gatherings, mime shows, and traveling theater), and the visual arts. Apprenticeship in the visual arts was to include an education in taste, in "simple" manual and artisanal techniques, and in the design of interiors, costumes, and objects.

GLOBE-TROTTERS

When it came to training, the directives make clear the edifying and (at least seemingly) authoritarian mission of Jeune France. It was to contribute to "the new collective society" by making the artist the organizer and regulator of the artisanal sector and by uniting the "young popular forces" through the youth centers.[76]

Instructors would play the role of globe-trotters, crisscrossing France and staying at each center for eight to twelve months. Informed by their education at the *maîtrises*, they would awaken young people "to an elementary sense of the beautiful," abjuring the traditional task of copying the bust of Nero, to give them a renewed taste for a spontaneous, even clumsy, practice based on drawing. Drawing was no longer to be considered an end in itself—the accepted view in traditional sectors at the time—but simply an educational, practical, and concrete means that would appeal to the "manual workers" with whom instructors would generally be dealing. Indeed, though the task was to prove difficult and often discouraging, Lautrec, head of the *maîtrise* in visual arts in the northern zone, was moved by some of the works by his "boys" in whom the "popular vein" was very real and needed to be encouraged. In the end, the Jeune France team would turn out an "accomplished man,"[77] "cleaning up" the bad taste developed through contact with industrial products, especially in the large urban areas, where the sight of such things was all the more pernicious in that their display was repeated ad infinitum in department stores, the movies, and the press.

Jeune France was able to recruit enthusiastic young cadres and attract the support of important figures such as Jacques Copeau[78] and Paul Claudel. Hence, when Bazaine and Lautrec proposed an atelier-school to the leadership of the organization, they were assured of the support of the architect Auguste Perret, who made a commitment to work with young craftsmen on stained glass, just as Paul Beyer would teach them the art of pottery. The ideal thing, Lignac told Flamand in regard to the teachers, would be a residency that obliged them to live among their students. At the very least, a monitor had to be found, someone who would be "a mature man, of refined and obvious culture, able to make a manly and healthy impression on young minds and to ensure harmony among the master craftsmen, students, and himself."[79]

In autumn 1941, prior to undertaking any significant action, Lautrec chose to conduct a survey of the art sector to confirm his opinion that Jeune France could provide a viable alternative to official education, to the "worn-out and obsolete formulas" learned in official technical schools—even in the prestigious Ecole nationale supérieure des arts décoratifs.[80] He dreamed, in fact, of a spectacular return to the golden age of art education, when masters had not yet fled their disciples. He envisaged that, both for their personal work and for the education they would continually be instilling, masters would have a studio "next to their students' studio."[81] He wanted to point students toward the crafts that, in his view, were likely to enjoy an industrial revival. One had to be cynical and provide industry with a sound reason for hiring based on the economic demands of the moment. Those crafts with a promising future embodied "the French spirit" more than any other: the fiery arts (ceramics, metalworking, glassblowing) especially, along with stained glass, woodworking, ironworking, and letterpress printing.

Lautrec's survey of the art sector ultimately confirmed his plan to establish a school for artisans that was parallel to the traditional institutions, one that would train apprentices who were both skilled and enthusiastic about "beautiful" forms. In regard to pottery and ceramics, his on-site study uncovered a real need, though it acknowledged that one studio per region would be quite enough to satisfy demand from private households. Sounding a note of realism, he pointed out the danger of "misleading young people by launching them en masse into a career that might have no future, under cover of a snobbery just as groundless as that of the 'return to the earth.'" Indeed, he was certain that "industrial production [was] destined to completely replace artisanal production in almost all instances of objects in everyday use." One had to face the facts. The role of Jeune France could not be limited to assembly-line production; it was simply necessary to endeavor "to make the best possible use" of it. After all, "a pot stamped out by a machine [could] be just as beautiful as a pot thrown by hand (setting aside the unsteadiness of the hand)." A housewife would not hesitate between her economic interests and a little extra soul. It was better to follow the advice of André Leleu, secretary general of the Comité d'organisation de la céramique for Jeune France: invent beautiful models and try to impose them on the organizing committees for production, despite their reluctance to take an interest in aesthetic progress. In many respects, Jeune France came not as a conqueror but as a killjoy.

A few rural potters (only about a hundred in France) continued to produce strictly artisanal objects, but in limited numbers and in accordance with traditions passed from father to son. Here, Jeune France's mission was to step in when an apprentice's taste had "gradually become depraved." In fact, Lautrec especially believed in art for all: "common household production" in the areas previously overseen by Limoges and Rouen, porcelain and earthenware, provided the means to transform the corrupted tastes of the designers—ersatz rustic or ersatz modern—of which the most vulgar examples were regularly presented at the Salon de l'Imagerie Française.[82]

THE BEAUTY OF THE PEOPLE

It was also advisable to educate the public, a point on which the individuals whom Lautrec visited all agreed—René Buthaud, a master potter in Bordeaux, violently so. The government ought to create a commission charged with banning "ruthlessly all that is ugly," he said. But did everyone agree on the definition of the beautiful? Those in Jeune France seemed to be unanimous about the return to the simplicity of forms. They were wary of pottery purchased (with the best of intentions) from Le Gué, an artisan potter from Coudreceau in the *département* Eure-et-Loir, whose forms were "rudimentary, without beauty, with a shoddy glaze in extremely bad taste." Only his terra-cotta work might have been acceptable, had it not been "spoiled by aggressive two-tone coloring reminiscent of the shoes worn by bad boys in Toulon."[83]

The report of November 1941 on the stained-glass school founded the previous month, under Perret's patronage, anticipated the "recovery of lost traditions," and in particular this art of the Middle Ages that was "employed in the most commonplace household object as well as in the construction of cathedrals." Its simple and comprehensible forms were in harmony with the spirit of "purification" among the militants of Jeune France, as was the anonymity of medieval artisans and architects, who placed their genius in the service of the common good. "The retreat of artists for the last century and a half to the realm of the pure idea, which led them to abandon the public sector" and condemned the latter to ugliness, was thus to be regretted.[84] Medieval images had everyone's blessing and were in addition reassuring to beginners, whose blunders were immediately compared to the sacred naïveté of those earlier images. The exercises proposed to instructors were generally to be carried out in teams and utilized "popular" themes and techniques: linocuts, toys, prints, posters, honor rolls, chess sets, household objects, murals, wallpapers, furniture, model houses, puppets.[85] Everything had to meet rigorous methodical requirements, though, ultimately, only plastic considerations really mattered. Instructors were therefore asked to fight "slapdash tendencies" and mere "mechanics"; the form, in itself, stemmed from the "idea." The modernist lessons of Denis, Matisse, and Braque were recognized implicitly in the pedagogical exercises. It was advisable to transpose an idea with forms and colors distributed over a given surface, study contour and line as well as primary and secondary hues, transform a natural (three-dimensional) volume into a simple representation that would symbolize the volume in its main lines.[86] In not falling back on the academic use of the preponderant themes, on the human figure or edifying subject, the Jeune France cadres stood far from the dominant discourse of the Académie des beaux-arts or the secretary general of fine arts as well as from the traditional education dispensed in state art schools.

Yet the idea had to be sufficiently clear and "readable." It was therefore preferable to refer, at least initially, to Rodin, Pierre-Auguste Renoir, or Michelangelo,[87] rather than van Gogh. In the example provided—popular signs on the walls of shops—the materials could be poor in terms of color, line, and composition, but the expression was clear: the shop signs *At the Angler* and *At the Three Clodhoppers* turned out to be effective, as did Cassandre's poster *The Glass of Milk*, in contrast to Dubois's less readable *Milk*, or Carrez's even less plain advertisement for an automobile.

Signs of modernity were not ruled out so long as they met the criteria of authenticity, clarity, and fervor required by Jeune France. The images projected on 2 May 1941 before an audience of young team members provide an excellent glimpse of the effort to reconstitute a coherent, edifying history of art and the craft industry in harmony with the "spiritual" renewal of the time. The show began with a slide of a church in Loiret, and attention was drawn to the steeple, a "symbol of peasant pride and fidelity"; it ended with an image of a twentieth-century peasant at harvest time. The world depicted was not completely confined to France proper but was able to encompass images of Norwegian craft industry or the harvest bouquet of a village in central Europe, which was identified with a similar object in a village in the Vexin region of France.[88]

A "vast repertoire of images designed to touch people emotionally—still lifes, landscapes, compositions on various themes (these offered limitless possibilities, both domestic and outdoor scenes)"—were to be created for "the great masses." As long as the work remained "objective" and appeared "acceptable to their eyes, not yet accustomed to nonfigurative representation," all that did not rule out "care in the assembly of surfaces and in the choice of colors," which would create "a surface enlivened with a joyful dynamism."[89]

In fact, some imagined orienting art toward a bracing nonfigurativeness, but gradually, without "the masses" noticing. Exhibitions organized by the group were to complete with the general public the education begun in the youth sector.

FIRST ASSESSMENTS

Nevertheless, some Jeune France cadres regretted the lack of spectacular events. Of course, the social networks were working, gatherings proceeded at a good pace, artists produced many theater sets for Vilar and for Jacquemont and his company, Les quatre saisons provinciales.[90] In Paris, the exhibition by the Jeunes peintres de tradition française had not been well attended, however. In the provinces, the 1940/41 season gave rise only to *Trois réalisations de Jeune France* in Vichy, which brought together works from the architecture center in Oppède and the artisanal center in Mâcon and a tapestry cartoon by Lucien Coutaud destined for the Aubusson factory; and *Un an de théâtre*, which focused more on the stage world than the art world. Despite the privileged conditions in the "free zone," the situation was hardly better there than in the occupied zone, and people complained of difficulties, particularly in finding exhibition sites.[91] In January 1942, the leadership chose to excuse its weaknesses by citing its priorities, the first of which was to evaluate its recruits by taking a census of the most gifted young people whom the exodus had dispersed. It was completed, it seems, after the meetings in Lourmarin,[92] and the schedule of activities for January 1942 looked quite dynamic.

On 1 January, there was the exhibition of photographic art *Naissance de la forme* at the Pavillon du Parc in Vichy. On 14 January, there was the revival of *Un an de théâtre* at the Musée du Grenoble, inaugurated by the secretary general of fine arts Louis Hautecoeur and the Spanish ambassador, who had come for an exhibition of Spanish art treasures. For this revival, Jeune France assembled the costume designs and models for the sets of the "best" shows produced in the two zones of France in 1940 and 1941. There were more than three hundred models and designs by Cassandre, Jean Souverbie, Maurice Brianchon, Louis Touchagues, Cocteau, André Dignimont, Le Moal, Jean Effel, the newspaper illustrator Jacques Grange, the decorative artist Edme Lex, the as-yet unknown Christian Dior, Jean-Albert Carlotti, Yves Bonnat, and the surrealist painter Félix Labisse. On 17 January, *Le dessin français contemporain* was held at the municipal library in Lyon as a benefit for Entraide des artistes, with three hundred pieces by Rodin, Degas, Dufy, and Dunoyer de Segonzac. On 29 January, there was a display of works by artists associated with Jeune France at the Galerie des Carmélites in Lyon. Finally, on 31 January, a new exhibition of photographic art was held at the same location.

In the rivalry quickly established between the northern and southern branches of Jeune France, the group in the occupied zone could boast that it had made available to its artists a library well stocked with documentary plates and photographs. As for the southern branch, it had managed to publish a review for the *maîtrises*.[93] Still, Schaeffer's team said it was better prepared to implement the plan for a national center of popular art. In both the north and the south, the famous atelier-schools and, more generally, the education envisioned by Jeune France still had not assumed the breadth that its cadres would have liked.

In December 1941, Lautrec complained that the creator of the Musée des arts et traditions populaires, Georges-Henri Rivière, was not supporting, as Rivière had said he would, Lautrec's plan to open technical atelier-schools.[94] Did Rivière want to limit himself, as Lautrec later said, to the preservation of French patrimony, without the hope of seeing a true rebirth of the craft industry? In the end, Rivière would support Flamand's plan for a *maîtrise* in popular art, since, after all, Jeune France said it wanted not "to favor the artificial resurrection of things fallen into disuse...but to keep alive certain practices threatened by standardization...in the hope of eliciting an interest conducive to the creation of a new popular art."[95]

In these quarrels pitting the two zones against each other, it very quickly appeared to Jeune France that there was a gulf between Paris and the provinces, between the popular project of some and the more elitist project of others, between the practitioners and the theorists, between those who were urged by Vichy to envision things on a mass scale and the Parisians who valued the independence and the complexity of their work. In Paris itself, there were quarrels between the "purists," the "intransigent defenders of the artist's integrity"[96]—Bazaine, Gischia, and Pignon—and the directors of the *maîtrises* and of education, who did not necessarily have any more dealings with the rank and file than the purists, but who did not hold to the same requirements when it came to personal and original work.[97] The founders of Jeune France may have sought, originally, "to put an end to the interminable and sterile debate that pits the elite against the masses, pure art against popular art, creation against imitation,"[98] but the art scene was in fact pervaded by the same contradictions as other very active sectors of the organization, namely, theater and literature. Blanchot and Lignac were likewise accused of not wanting to share out culture. Even Schaeffer, who at the time was supposed to embody the popular purity of the so-called free zone, eventually acknowledged that he had always preferred "textual" theater to the actors' theater of Copeau or the Comédiens routiers. He even portrayed the program of the most radical pedagogues as devoid of content and similar to the "occupational therapy workshops dear to psychiatric clinics," even though such treatment was meant for "traumatized and mentally ill populations."[99] Flamand situated himself in the middle, between the elitists and "the populists."[100] He thought one could not always offer Claudel or Lope de Vega to the general public, but one could draw them in with the Compagnons de la chanson or the Comédiens routiers: though not very refined, these troupes knew how to be effective and make crowds laugh.

It was Flamand who was the recipient of the complaints. When a furious Bazaine received the new booklet concocted in the "free zone" on the "spirit" of Jeune France, he was astonished and outraged by a document he deemed to be inconsistent with the policy followed by the organization in the northern zone. Particularly when it came to "the artist's condition," Bazaine found it "sickening," in view of "the heroic and disinterested life" of his elders, to see living art treated like an "extravagant art . . . for the sake of pride, money, or little cliques." He thus threatened to resign and said he would be followed by his friends Lautrec, Manessier, and others if things were not cleared up and if such a line continued to be defended behind his back "within that costly, pointless, and lifeless bureaucracy on rue Jean-Mermoz," at the official headquarters of Jeune France.[101]

Flamand also suffered criticism from Lignac, who complained about what he had seen during the evening *maîtrise*, accusing the supervisory staff of devoting itself to "an enterprise of stultifying the mind and leading the sensibility astray," under cover of distracting uncultivated young boys while providing them access to knowledge of works of art. Rather than "vile bourgeois banalities" on the "idle, bohemian poet of genius," he said, it was a hundred times better to have "ditties, juggling, Léon Chancerel–type jokes, parlor games, and all the entertaining and good-natured paraphernalia of 'variety shows,' if they [were] not pretentious." Do not mix everything together, do not try to vulgarize high culture, he said, and everything would work out better.[102]

WHAT CONSENSUS?

An attentive reading of the archives of Jeune France hardly reveals the admirable unity that has been hastily presented in reports full of preconceptions and ungrounded in the existing sources. The organization's "line" was in fact no more univocal than the careers of its participants. It was also not merely the enactment of Mounier's personalist "catechism," as has often been claimed.[103] Its members, characteristics, and ideas diverged at an early date no doubt, but even more so when put to the test by reality and action.

Hence Schaeffer, who came from a bourgeois background, had been more hesitant than Bazaine or Flamand—faithful Catholics like him—about the youth movements of 1936. Alongside the uniformed Rover

Scouts to which he belonged, the "friends of nature" likely seemed very slovenly and debauched by an unprecedented mixing of the sexes. Schaeffer's promotion of camping indeed marked a return to nature, but it took a very different form from that of Marc Sangnier's youth hostels. More generally, Schaeffer incarnated the "grandes écoles" and "apolitical" side of the organization, an aspect that Mounier distrusted, finding it too latitudinarian, while Flamand recognized both its salutary fervor and its limitations.[104] In retrospect, Schaeffer's impression that he was in charge of collecting funds in Vichy for redistribution in Paris, where he knew he faced opposition, reinforced the tensions that may have undermined the organization at the time.[105] He maintained regular contact with certain key individuals in Vichy—Lamirand, for example—and could not evade official demands for campfires and hikes, which the northern zone happily did without. According to Schaeffer, he was thirty years old at the time and living as "a fake engineer," but he felt "a vocation as a cultural organizer," first awakened in the 1930s by the cultural gurus of the youth of the time, the heirs to the legacy of World War I, and by influences as diverse as Paul Doncoeur and Charles Péguy.[106]

When the dissolution of Jeune France was announced in spring 1942, Schaeffer and Flamand both had the sense that the situation had changed, that they would compromise themselves too much were they to continue, that they needed to become more discreet. For Schaeffer at least, "the essential" had been accomplished.[107] Jeune France had to its credit the concerts by Maurice Martenot, Olivier Messiaen, and Daniel Lesur gracing the radio waves and available to all, the continuation of the endeavors of Les Copiaux and the Comédiens routiers, the premiere of the oratorio *Jeanne d'Arc au bûcher* (text by Paul Claudel, music by Arthur Honegger), and a total of 770 theatrical performances supported by Jeune France. It had reached reconciliation with the general public, which had finally become an active participant. It had saved the honor of living French painting. It had founded ten of the cultural centers known as Maisons Jeune France throughout the country and set in place an unprecedented new education system that turned its back on established, abstract, "verbal" academicism. It fostered the beginnings of a "young" France and of a youth culture and entertained a slew of plans for more peaceful times.

The dissolution of Jeune France was explained in political terms, even though its management—supposedly faulty in the southern zone—might well have scuttled the project on their own: when Pierre Pucheu's interior ministry and the ministry of the navy wanted to attack the organization, a financial audit was all that was required.[108] The impression of some members of the Vichy government that Jeune France, even under the aegis of the regime, might constitute a state within the state and that the organization's cadres were ill disposed to docilely relay Vichy propaganda directives had bearing on the decision to ban it a few days after Laval's return to power. The surprising attitude of some when the end of the venture was announced confirmed the internal dissensions but did not lead to the hoped-for alternative—its continuation. Lignac replaced Flamand, on the condition that he be part of a triumvirate, together with Blanchot and Petitot, "three luxury coaches without a locomotive,"[109] but that lasted barely four months.[110] In fact, "the elite" seemed to have triumphed, but they did so only by abandoning the first "popular" breakthroughs, and hence Jeune France's first successes. It was better then to return to the studio or a private room.

Even before the schism, few artists in Jeune France believed in a truly popular, "quasi-folkloric" art.[111] Unquestionably there was Delarue, a fervent admirer of the anthropologist Arnold van Gennep; and in his own way there was Lautrec, more craftsman than painter, virtuous pedagogue first, artist second.[112] These two continued the fight from within Travail et culture, founded after the liberation as a successor to Jeune France. Its first director was Pierre-Aimé Touchard, who had run the Maison des lettres on rue Férou, working alongside many resisters during the occupation. Flamand, from the earlier group, was vice president, and Jean-Marie Serreau, André Bazin, Jean-Louis Barrault, and Charles Dullin, all from other milieus, also belonged.

The linkages between Jeune France, Catholicism, and Communism, if only as a result of Pignon's participation during the occupation, remained pertinent and even became considerably stronger: in the end, the Confédération générale du travail (with its ties to the French Communist Party) controlled Travail et culture to such an extent that Touchard, placed in a difficult situation, would speedily resign, followed by Flamand. The episode revealed, if there were any need, the persistently "apolitical" stance of a certain number of leaders of Jeune France, who refused to tolerate any outside intervention, whether from the left or the right. The situation became clearer after the liberation. During the occupation, however, every situation fostered ambiguity, every participant risked being co-opted—even by his worst enemies.

THE SORCERER'S APPRENTICES

On 21 February 1942, at Jeune France headquarters in Paris, a lecture by the abbé Maurice Morel, a former Oratorian and sometime painter, provided a glimpse of the potential traps. This momentous event in the life of the cultivated ecclesiastic has often been recounted as an act of resistance. At the time, the press drew different conclusions from a display meant to glorify Picasso and "decadent" art. In "L'avenir de l'art plastique," the journalist at *Beaux-arts* noted only that the subject was treated, masterfully, "by a top-quality scholar," who

> after setting out the permanence of the spirit of the tradition, identifying the major currents of French art, and decrying the masses' disaffection for the art of our time . . . condemned the pictorial excesses responsible for this state of affairs, and demonstrated, along with the richness of living art, our present need to place our trust in this school, which continues to perpetuate the supremacy our national art has always had.[113]

In the same register, it really must be asked how activities ordered by Schaeffer in the southern zone, officially linked to the regime, could have been allowed: the events in honor of Joan of Arc, for example,[114] the only figure to whom Pétain had devoted a speech;[115] or the large festivals in Bordeaux, where Lamirand took to the stage after the artists, harvesting the fruits of the operation alongside them. Such contradictions were inherent to Jeune France. Hence, in September 1941, displaying a reluctance to turn the organization into a group in the service of Vichy, Lignac refused, on behalf of the artists, to serve the cause of the Secrétariat général à la coordination des mouvements familiaux, when it wanted to gather together the masterpieces of French art devoted to the family "with an eye to a propaganda campaign for moralistic policy." Indeed, it was "almost exactly the sort of abuse against whose temptations Jeune France [had] ventured to constitute itself originally." It was better to devote Jeune France to the defense of the "independence" of artists and to flee "threats" of co-optation.[116] It was a clear position, but some deviated from it. Lautrec agreed to consider the exhibition as long as it did not have artistic pretensions; he imagined a retrospective culminating in a gallery of "moderns," from Renoir to Pignon (who painted several works titled *Madonna and Child*).[117]

Up to spring 1942, there was nothing really unanimous about Jeune France, which was neither for nor against the regime. There were only differing attitudes, more or less in favor of supporting Pétain, of waiting things out, or of resisting the occupation. From this standpoint, did not the very activities of its adherents demonstrate de facto differences in the interpretation of the circumstances? Although there were no defenders of collaboration in its midst, there were resisters, who saw no contradiction in waging their battle in the shadows while at the same time carrying out their cultural mission at Jeune France. These included Daniel Apert, an active member of the underground network "Résistance," who more than once used the organization to cross the demarcation line;[118] André Clavé, who would be deported;[119] and Pignon, who belonged to the Front national des arts.

Unlike the Ecole nationale des cadres d'Uriage, however, Jeune France did not harbor many active resisters. Rather, much of the time, its membership comprised cultural nonconformists who had the impression they were remaining true to their past commitments—communitarian, rebellious, and in large part "apolitical." The organization was to some extent the symbol of the crisis of the 1930s, the fruit of the emergence of a new social group, young people, which at the time had nothing like the group identity we see today. After the defeat, the breakdown of the nation offered those who had the desire (and who were not excluded by the rules of the game) the possibility of interfering through the meshes of what was still a loosely woven social net. Jeune France reflected the return both to nature and to the land by a hobbled, anemic youth—bourgeois or not—that suddenly believed less in the "cult of Montherlant"[120] than in a "pious naturism," in the reconciliation of the body and grace, in mountaineering, in Péguy's numinous night, in tents set up directly on the restorative ground, and in revolt. That revolt, so often commented on, was against a deadlocked, pessimistic, smothering, bourgeois, narrowly secular or piously Catholic society. Caught between Communism and the far right, the young people who enlisted in Jeune France usually chose another path: the return to an unbridled spirituality, in keeping with their exalted mind-set. They did not stage "happenings," like those in the 1960s, according to Schaeffer, because they were very "respectable" young people; they formed theater or dance troupes, groups of painters or artisans.[121] Theirs was an opportunistic apoliticism, barely camouflaged by their resounding declarations of principle.

Was it this apoliticism in particular that allowed Jeune France to move so easily from the fertile culturalist ground inherited from the Front populaire to the minefield of the Révolution nationale? Some critics, including Marc Fumaroli, have seen it merely as a project with a totalitarian aim,[122] the same project that, under the Front populaire and under the guise of "culture" and republicanism, supposedly gave birth to a "monster"—to the ideological propaganda and political hype that would flourish, after the defeat, under Mounier's leadership. Mounier was the "poor man's Heidegger,"[123] the pope of a future church "peopled" with "personalist" faithful,[124] the "almost Leninist tone" of the "culture minister"[125] of which served only to portend the dismal fate of shared knowledge. He may have opened the way for his female double, Jeanne Laurent, this time the "Lenin" of the "administrative revolution,"[126] and for the famous Malraux cultural affairs ministry in 1959, and, ultimately, for the modern religion advanced by the current cultural state, its celebrations of music, racial harmony, rock and roll, and graffiti.

Daniel Lindenberg, less susceptible to old resentments, has noted that the connection that is inevitably made between "the Jeune France experiment" and the decentralizing current of the left or even the far left was "too hastily... credited solely to the democratic impulses of the liberation." He states that "in this area as in others, one must not ignore the tangle of ambiguities contained within the 'Révolution nationale,' at least in its first months, just as one must not conceal the extent to which the achievements of 1945 were linked as much to the ideas of 1940 as to those of 1936."[127]

These ideas of 1936, which a number of Jeune France militants had embraced in their time, once more occupied a place of honor after the defeat. A continuity truly did exist between the achievements of the Front populaire and the progressive associations accompanying it, and the project of Jeune France, which planned to go "still further." We need only cite the many voluntary initiatives favoring a reconciliation between art and the general public: the associations Maison de la culture and L'art mural, with their introductory courses in the visual arts; the group Savoir, in 1937, and its introductory course in painting for the middle classes; the Académie populaire de la Union des syndicats de la région parisienne; the art clubs in the Renault, Citroën, and Marcel Bloch aircraft factories; the pedagogical excursions to museums and the traveling exhibitions of the Association populaire des amis des musées; the major socialist projects of Léo Lagrange and the Mai 1936 group; the aspiration to build, in every midsized city, art education centers whose design was astonishingly similar to the Maisons Jeune France, only more political.

Indeed, any inquiry into Jeune France runs up against a host of contradictions, which must be understood in light of the "militant apoliticism" of its cadres, still embraced today by some, Schaeffer included. He was left with the bitter aftertaste of a minority of young people who never really got involved in politics and who were in close proximity to de Gaulle without really acknowledging him. The young activists were not "warriors enough, not historians enough," "too caught up" as they were in their "little youth movement dramas."[128] Without neglecting the pioneering aspect of Jeune France's hope for cultural decentralization and diffusion, his lucid assessment puts things in place concerning the group's political role during the occupation. In the initial policy declaration, under the heading "Esprit," the notion of politics had, moreover, been articulated in an ambiguous fashion as an indispensable organicist outlook. It was said that "the most elementary chance of success [lay] in purging such activity of any political spirit, without for all that refusing or neglecting political tasks." It was understood that these political tasks demanded an immediate result and immediate success, whereas "the politics of a country also requires a long-term, organic effort, which aspires to profound and lasting reform." It was self-evident that such an effort had to entail the revolution of culture, which could not fail to attract artists. Bazaine was sufficiently persuaded to steer toward Jeune France the luminaries in his network of friends. That is because, beyond the theoretical program, what appealed to him was the implementation of the personalist "spirit," which he had embraced in 1934, drawn in by Mounier's words. Far from being simply the figurehead of Jeune France, Mounier was its only "philosophe" capable of systematizing the spontaneity of groups. He undeniably served to "rouse" a few.

NOTES

1. André Lhote, "Opinions libres... sur la peinture française," *Comoedia*, 13 June 1942, 1, 6.
2. Bernard Dorival, "Le génie français et la peinture française contemporaine," in Gaston Diehl, ed., *Les problèmes de la peinture* (Lyon: Confluences, 1945), 28–29.
3. Dorival, "Le génie français" (note 2), 37–38.
4. Quoted in Gaston Diehl, "Actualité de la peinture expressive: L'activisme," in idem, ed., *Les problèmes de la peinture* (Lyon: Confluences, 1945), 223.
5. Diehl, "Actualité de la peinture expressive" (note 4), 227.
6. Albert Camus, "Sur une philosophie de l'expression"; as quoted in Diehl, "Actualité de la peinture expressive" (note 4), 227.
7. André Lhote, "De Fouquet à Picasso," *La nouvelle revue française*, November 1942, 595. The works mentioned are Jean Cassou, *Picasso* (Paris: Editions Hypérion, 1940); and Klaus G. Perls, *Jean Fouquet* (Paris: Editions Hypérion, 1940).
8. Dorival, "Le génie français" (note 2), 33.
9. Bernard Champigneulle, *L'inquiétude dans l'Art d'aujourd'hui* (Paris: Mercure de France, 1938), 170.
10. See *Il tempo*, 17 December 1942; and Charles Despiau, *Arno Breker* (Paris: Flammarion, 1942).
11. Jean-Marc Campagne, "Propagande," *Les nouveaux temps*, 15 January 1941, 2; and Jean-Marc Campagne, "Arno Breker," in *Exposition Arno Breker à l'Orangerie, 15 mai–31 juillet 1942*, exh. brochure (Berlin: Otto von Holten, 1942).
12. See, for example, Fernand Demeure in the extremist newspaper *Le matin* of 10 October 1943: "French taste? It has never been so alive, thanks to our decorative artists."

13. André Lhote, *Peinture d'abord: Essais* (Paris: Editions Denoël, 1942), 160.
14. Louis Aragon, "Matisse-en-France," in Henri Matisse, *Dessins: Thèmes et variations* (Paris: Martin Fabiani, 1943), 39–40.
15. André Lhote, "Réponse à *Beaux-arts*," *Peintres et sculpteurs de la Maison de la culture*, no. 7, July 1938.
16. Lhote, "Réponse à *Beaux-arts*" (note 15).
17. Jean Lurçat, "La liberté dans l'art," special issue, *Peintres et sculpteurs de la Maison de la culture*, no. 7, July 1938.
18. Pierre Ladoué became the new museum's chief curator instead. He had served as an assistant to Louis Hautecoeur, who from 1927 until 1939 had been in charge of the Musée des artistes vivants (also known as the Musée du Luxembourg), housed at the Orangerie of the Palais du Luxembourg on rue de Vaugirard.
19. See the account of his dismissal in Jean Cassou, *Une vie pour la liberté* (Paris: Editions Robert Laffont, 1981), 142.
20. Tabarant, *L'oeuvre*, 7 August 1942, 1.
21. G.-J. Gros, "Courrier des arts," *La gerbe*, 27 August 1942, 6.
22. Jean-Marc Campagne, *Les nouveaux temps*, 19 August 1942, 3.
23. Jean Bazaine, "Le Musée d'art moderne," *La nouvelle revue française*, December 1942, 740.
24. Bazaine, "Le Musée d'art moderne" (note 23), 741.
25. Bazaine, "Le Musée d'art moderne" (note 23), 742.
26. Bazaine, "Le Musée d'art moderne" (note 23), 741.
27. The organization committee of *Maîtres de l'art indépendant*, the major exhibition of 1937, decided to invite only French artists or foreign-born artists who were living and had lived in France for many years, such as Picasso, Pablo Gargallo, Lipchitz, Modigliani, Soutine, Jules Pascin, and Chagall. At the time, Chagall demanded a "suitable place," mentioning that he was about to become a French citizen and citing his contribution to the development of French art; see Marc Chagall to Raymond Escholier, 29 April 1937, Archives du Petit Palais; quoted in Bernadette Contensou, "Autour de l'Exposition des maîtres de l'art indépendant en 1937," in *Paris 1937: L'art indépendant*, exh. cat. (Paris: Musée d'Art Moderne de la Ville de Paris, 1987), 13.
28. Philippe de Chennevières, curator of the Musée du Luxembourg from 1863 to 1879, had dreamed of a "palace of living art" that would bring together the various schools without distinction. In spring 1922, the foreign collections of the Musée du Luxembourg were installed, by nationality, at the Jeu de Paume, corresponding for the first time to a "diplomatic" program: the museum was answerable not only to the Direction des musées de France but also to the foreign affairs ministry. In December 1932, the Musée des écoles étrangères contemporaines at the Jeu de Paume really took off when it became independent under the authority of André Dézarrois. He was

responsible for the exhibitions *L'art espagnol contemporain* (eleven works by Picasso, five by Gris, and one by Dalí), *James Ensor*, and *Kupka-Mucha* in 1936. On the history of the Musée national d'art moderne, see Catherine Lawless, *Musée national d'art moderne: Historique et mode d'emploi* (Paris: Editions du Centre Pompidou, 1986). On the Jeu de Paume museum, see Françoise Bonnefoy, ed., *Jeu de Paume, histoire* (Paris: Editions du Jeu de Paume/Réunion des Musées Nationaux, 1991).

29. Dézarrois also edited *La revue de l'art ancien et moderne*, which ceased publication in 1937.

30. See Michel Hoog, "Sur l'exposition *Origines et développement de l'art international indépendant*," in *Paris 1937: L'art indépendant*, exh. cat. (Paris: Musée d'Art Moderne de la Ville de Paris, 1987).

31. The next major exhibition to mark the history of French museography was held at the Jeu de Paume in summer 1938: *Trois siècles d'art aux Etats-Unis*, in collaboration with the Museum of Modern Art (founded in New York in 1929). It was multidisciplinary and presented the French public with the most advanced aspects of American culture: painting, sculpture, cinema, and photography.

32. In 1982, the catalog *Chefs-d'oeuvre du Musée national d'art moderne* (Paris: Centre Georges Pompidou, 1982) included among its 120 "masterpieces" only 7 paintings acquired before 1943: Albert Marquet's *Portrait of André Rouveyre* (1904; purchased by the Réunion des musées nationaux, 1939); Henri Rousseau's *The Snake Charmer* (1907; gift of Jacques Doucet to the Musée du Louvre, 1937); Fernand Léger's *Nuptials* (1911–12; Alfred Flechtheim Bequest to the state, 1937); Jules Pascin's *Portrait of Flechtheim as Bullfighter* (1927; Alfred Flechtheim Bequest, 1938), František Kupka's *Vertical Planes–I* (1912–13; purchased by the Musée du Jeu de Paume, 1936); Salvador Dalí's *Partial Hallucination, Six Images of Lenin on a Piano* (1931; purchased by the state, 1938); and Henri Matisse's *Decorative Figure against Ornamental Background* (1925–26; purchased by the state, 1938). Of these artists, Pascin, Dalí, Rousseau, and Kupka were not represented in 1942.

33. This number, which includes paintings, drawings, watercolors, engravings, sculptures, and medals, should most likely be revised slightly upward because of the presence of series of small pieces.

34. In chronological order, the French state acquired the following works by these Jeunes peintres de tradition française: Villon's *Fight*, engraving, 9 October 1940, destination unknown; Lautrec's *Still Life with Cherries*, gouache, 25 March 1941, for the Musée national d'art moderne (order of 3 December 1942); Villon's *The Three Orders: The Church, the Castle, the Country*, engraving, 27 June 1941, for the youth movements (order of 29 June 1945); Villon's *Between Toulouse and Albi*, painting, 14 November

1941, for the Musée national d'art moderne (order of 24 March 1942); Villon's *Portrait of Young Girl*, painting, 11 April 1942, for the Musée national d'art moderne (order of 24 August 1943); Pignon's *Still Life with Red Tablecloth*, painting, 12 June 1942, for the Musée national d'art moderne (blocked) (order of 3 December 1942), at the Ministère des affaires étrangères in 1972; Villon's *Young Girl*, engraving, 7 July 1942, for the Musée national d'art moderne (order of 1942); Bazaine's sketch for a pictorial decoration for the Chapelle Saint-André, 27 December 1942, destination unknown; Gischia's *Brioches*, painting, 3 February 1943, for the Musée national d'art moderne (blocked) (order of 24 August 1943); Pignon's decorative panel for a professional school for young women in Creil, 15 November 1943 (note of 13 November 1943); Villon's *Grandmother*, engraving, 8 February 1944, for the office of Vincent Poli at the fine arts administration; Fougeron's *Soup*, engraving, 8 February 1944, destination unknown; Le Moal's *Harbor*, painting, 25 March 1944, for the Musée national d'art moderne (order of 19 June 1944); Manessier's *Fighting Cocks*, painting, 26 May 1944, for the Musée national d'art moderne (order of 19 June 1944); Lautrec, sketch for a pictorial decoration, 22 June 1944, for the council chamber for the prefecture of Versailles (note of 21 June 1944).

35. Later on, the exhibition would often be called *Vingt jeunes peintres de tradition française*—wrongly so. There were in fact twenty exhibitors, but only because Maurice Estève, whose name was listed on the invitation, had stopped displaying works.

36. A "historical" exhibition took place in Paris between 9 March and April 1967, at the Galerie Georges Bongers, 122, boulevard Raspail, for which the same artists who had exhibited in 1941 put on view both a painting from the era and a recent canvas, with text by André Lejard.

37. As was the custom from that time forward, the Propaganda-Staffel Paris, after giving its endorsement, sent its representatives to visit the exhibition: two officers went through it without comment.

38. Jean Bazaine, "Guerres et évasions," *La nouvelle revue française*, April 1941, 617.

39. Bazaine, "Guerres et évasions" (note 38), 621.

40. Encouraged by other readers of *La nouvelle revue française* at the same time.

41. Jean Bazaine, "Tour d'horizon," *La nouvelle revue française*, August 1941, 223 n. 1.

42. In this exhibition, some contributors were placed in the section titled "Liquidaters de l'après-guerre" (Étienne-Martin), others in the sections "À la recherche d'un ordre humain" (Marchand, Lautrec, Lasne, Tal-Coat, and Étienne-Martin) or "Sous le signe de l'esprit" (Desnoyer, Singier, Walch, Bazaine, Estève, Fougeron, Gischia, Lapicque, Manessier, Pignon, and the sculptor Chauvin).

43. Gaston Diehl, “Sous le signe de l’esprit,” in idem, *Galerie Berri-Raspail: Les étapes du nouvel art contemporain, I et II, 24 octobre au 13 novembre 1941,* exh. cat. (Paris: Imprimerie L. Beresniak, 1941).

44. In reality, the group adopted that name only in May 1938, for the exhibition held by René Breteau in his small Paris gallery Matières.

45. See the first issue of *Le poids du monde,* April 1937.

46. Robert Falk exhibited with the group at the time.

47. According to Jean Cassou’s preface to the catalog for the exhibition *L’art cruel,* held at the Galerie Billiet from 17 December 1937 to 6 January 1938, in which Fougeron participated alongside Dalí, Picasso, and André Masson. Fougeron exhibited again with the Association des peintres et sculpteurs de la Maison de la culture at the fledgling Maison de la culture on rue d’Anjou, alongside Pignon, Jean Amblard, and Gruber.

48. Gaston Diehl, preface to the catalog for the exhibition *Douze peintres d’aujourd’hui, sculptures de Chauvin,* held at the Galerie de France from 6 February to 4 March 1943.

49. See, for example, Mosdyc, “L’art zazou: Douze fumistes d’aujourd’hui,” *Au pilori,* 4 March 1943, 4. Mosdyc was quoting a letter from a reader of the newspaper (regarding the exhibition *Douze peintres d’aujourd’hui*).

50. Lucien Rebatet, “Révolutionnaires d’arrière-garde,” *Je suis partout,* 29 October 1943, 6.

51. Cortot belonged to the world of Groupe collaboration, which had made its presence known during the events in honor of Arno Breker.

52. Mosdyc began his career as a newspaper illustrator in the late 1930s. Under the occupation, he contributed articles and drawings to *Au pilori.* They were enough to get him to be banned from publishing for two years by the Comité national d’épuration des artistes peintres, dessinateurs, sculpteurs et graveurs in 1946.

53. Legueult, whose works were exhibited at the Galerie Braun in May 1941, was the only one of the Jeunes peintres de tradition française to take part in the offical tour of Germany later that year. He was never again found alongside the Jeunes peintres de tradition française, to whom he was not close either in spirit or in his works.

54. On the question of the *call to order* and the *return to order,* see Kenneth E. Silver, *Vers le retour à l’ordre: L’avant-garde parisienne et la Première Guerre mondiale,* trans. Dennis Collins (Paris: Flammarion, 1991); and Annick Lantenois, “Essai d’analyse critique de la formule ‘retour à l’ordre’ France, 1919–1929” (Ph.D. thesis, Université Paris I–Panthéon Sorbonne, 1992).

55. Pierre Francastel, *Nouveau dessin, nouvelle peinture: L’Ecole de Paris* (Paris: Librairie de Médicis, 1946), 15.

56. Francastel studied that shift in his *Peinture et société: Naissance et*

destruction d'un espace plastique: De la Renaissance au cubisme (Paris: Denoël, 1977).

57. In the forefront were Gaston Diehl, who praised them in the newspaper *Aujourd'hui*, the review *Beaux-arts*, *Confluences*, and the weekly *Comoedia;* Pierre d'Espezel, in *Le cri du peuple;* Pierre Imbourg, in *Beaux-arts;* Roger Lesbats, in *Le rouge et le bleu;* and Georges Theys, in *Le petit parisien.* Charles Fegdal, Brignaud, and a few others also hailed their work.

58. René Barotte, "Nos peintres au travail—Édouard Pignon," *Comoedia*, 7 August 1943, 6.

59. See Véronique Chabrol's thesis, which focuses on theater, "Jeune France—une expérience de recherche et de décentralisation culturelle, novembre 1940–mars 1942" (thèse de troisième cycle, Université Sorbonne Nouvelle–Paris III, 1974).

I am indebted to the author for allowing me to consult the Jeune France archives dealing with the artistic side of the organization, which was not part of her theater studies corpus. They are cited here as "private archive."

I benefited as well from oral statements collected from the participants Bazaine, Gischia, Le Moal, Manessier, and Pignon, and from their invaluable personal archives.

See also two studies by Véronique Chabrol: "Jeune France un 'maillon manquant' pour l'histoire de la décentralisation culturelle," *Les cahiers de l'animation*, no. 53 (1985): 85–94; and "L'ambition de 'Jeune France,'" in Jean-Pierre Rioux, ed., *La vie culturelle sous Vichy* (Brussels: Editions Complexe, 1990), 161–78.

In addition, see the precursory article by Daniel Lindenberg, "Révolution culturelle dans la Révolution nationale de Jacques Copeau à 'Jeune France': Une archéologie de la 'décentralisation' théâtrale," *Les révoltes logiques*, no. 12 (1980): 2–18; and also Archives nationales (AN), series AG II 542.

Witnesses to the Jeune France experiment have left very few written traces. For recollections, see Marc Pierret, *Entretiens avec Pierre Schaeffer* (Paris: Editions Pierre Belfond, 1969); and Pierre Schaeffer, *Les enfants de coeur: Roman* (Paris: Editions du Seuil, 1949; reprinted, 1958). See also Pierre Schaeffer, with Claude Glayman, *Les antennes de Jéricho* (Paris: Stock, 1978); and Pierre Schaeffer, *Prélude, chorale et fugue: Roman* (Paris: Flammarion, 1983).

60. The name *Jeune France* was borrowed from a group of musicians—Olivier Messiaen, André Jolivet, Daniel Lesur, and Yves Baudrier—though it is also reminiscent of the bohemian group associated with romanticism in about 1830, Les Jeunes-France, who aped the Middle Ages and boasted of drinking punch from the skulls of their mistresses. See Jerrold Seigel, *Paris bohème:*

Culture et politique aux marges de la vie bourgeoise, 1830–1930, trans. Odette Guitard (Paris: Gallimard, 1991).

61. Jeune France was an association governed by the law of 1901 and financed by the state, the Secrétariat général à la jeunesse, the Commissariat à la lutte contre le chômage, Marshal Pétain's office, and members' dues.

62. According to Claude Roy's formulation; as cited in Chabrol, "Jeune France un 'maillon manquant'" (note 59), 86.

63. After trying to get Pétain himself to read his speeches, Schaeffer entrusted the exercise to Alfred Cortot, who acquitted himself in a "quavering and earnest voice," before the speeches were commented on by others. The program lasted fifteen minutes. See Schaeffer, *Les antennes de Jéricho* (note 59), 283–85.

64. On Emmanuel Mounier and the review *Esprit*, see Michel Winock, *Histoire politique de la revue "Esprit," 1930–1950* (Paris: Editions du Seuil, 1975). It is noteworthy that the review was banned in October 1941, Jeune France in March 1942, sometime after the request by the higher echelons that Jeune France get rid of Mounier, whose ouster ultimately did not prevent the organization from being banned.

65. Quoted from *Jeune France: Principes, direction, esprit* (Paris: Imp. de M. Audin, 1941).

66. Of the artists, Bazaine, for example, did not conceal the fact that he had had financial difficulties: since 1938, he had lived on a grant from the Fondation Blumenthal, supporting his wife and two children. Manessier was living at the time in the most abject poverty, and the others were hardly in a better position. Bazaine remembers receiving about three thousand francs a month from Jeune France, a sum that seemed sufficient to live on at the time.

    Manessier received fifteen hundred francs a month as an instructor, then two thousand francs per month as an inspector (twenty-four thousand francs a year, plus six hundred francs for dependents); see Manessier to Blanche Tellier Manessier (his mother), June 1941. That allowed him to live modestly.

67. Maurice Blanchot was the foreign policy editor at the *Journal des débats* and a contributor to *La revue française*. After the latter suspended publication for financial reasons, Blanchot worked for *Le rempart*, founded by Paul Lévy, then for *Combat*, which preferred a polemical style to intellectual essays, embracing antiparliamentary and anticapitalist positions.

68. Under the name Jean Chauveau.

69. Jeune France also attracted Christiane Mathiolly, a Communist turned Carmelite; Mlle Le Floch, of the Ecole du Louvre; Pierre Hussenot, a painter; and Barr, who oversaw the exhibitions. Manessier, Le Moal, Lautrec, and Pignon were invited into Jeune France by Bazaine, who had himself been recruited by Maurice Jacquemont. Others, such as Hussenot and Courmes, joined at Lautrec's prompting.

Initially, Jeune France's board of directors, named in the late 1940s, gathered together, under very official titles, Pierre Schaeffer, general director, head of Jeune France in the southern zone, assistant section head for theater and radio in propaganda; Paul Flamand, head of Jeune France in the northern zone, assistant section head for theater and radio in propaganda; Albert Ollivier, writer for Radio-Jeunesse; Pierre Barbier, head of the first "Maison Jeune France" in Lyon; Maurice Jacquemont, director of the theater troupe Les quatre saisons provinciales; Daniel Lesur, music section; Henri Malvaux, director of the Ecole des arts professionels de Mâcon; and Claude Roy, of Editions Jeune France. Patrice de La Tour du Pin, a prisoner in Germany, was named honorary president of Jeune France at the suggestion of Claude Roy.

The research centers likewise governed "seven artistic sections" and were supposed to select works and leaders, while supervising teaching in the *maîtrises*, schools where future cadres were trained. In Paris, the research centers were staffed by Xavier de Lignac and Maurice Blanchot (literature), Jean Vilar (theater), and Jean Bazaine, assisted by Léon Gischia and André Lejard (plastic arts). Also present were Maurice Delarue and Daniel Apert (plastic arts), along with Annette Dieudonné and Jacques Chaillet (music).

In Lyon, Mounier remained close to Schaeffer. The research center was run by Pierre Barbier, Maurice Jacquemont, Olivier Hussenot, and Jean-Pierre Grenier (theater); Albert Ollivier, Claude Roy, and René Barjavel (literature); and Daniel Lesur (music). Maurice Martenot, the inventor of a new method of art education, was in charge of popular arts and crafts, while Raymond Cogniat headed plastic arts. The filmmaker Roger Leenhardt established a "Maison Jeune France" in North Africa.

In Paris, Jean Vilar, André Clavé, and Jean-Louis Barrault headed the theater *maîtrise*. In Lyon, Jean-Marie Serreau and Léon Chancerel directed the theater *maîtrise*, César Geoffray, that in music and song.

70. Jean Bazaine, typewritten document; Maurice Morel papers, private archive.

71. Leadership of Jeune France (I.D. 1607), Paris, to the minister of national education and youth, Vichy, 16 July 1941; private archive.

72. In June 1941, Manessier's wife sent her mother-in-law a letter that attested to the climate reigning at the training course for instructors that Manessier attended over the course of a month and a half. The center, she said, "is stylish in its ambiance, no dictatorship.... He has seventy boys between fifteen and seventeen years old for two hours in the afternoon. Seventy new ones every day, a rotation of five hundred. They are fairly tiring days but not boring"; Manessier archives.

73. Leadership of Jeune France (I.D. 1607), Paris, to the minister of national education and youth, Vichy, 16 July 1941; private archive.

74. This was the plan signed by Bazaine concerning the northern zone.

75. Unsigned and undated document, Pierre Schaeffer papers; private archive.

Financial questions were likewise carefully regulated: the proceeds from entry fees for the traveling exhibitions were to serve to defray the costs of the assistants (two individuals: a mechanic-driver-technician and a commentator). These assistants were supposed to find room and board among the friends of Jeune France or at youth centers, for example. A portion of the union dues (33 percent) and 15 percent of the gross from works sold were to be handed over at the end of the exhibition. More broadly, the leadership of Jeune France entrusted part of its financial and administrative management to the general secretariat of youth, while retaining "cultural oversight" of all its own activities.

76. Text by Lucien Lautrec, 21 August 1941; private archive.

77. On the plastic arts *maîtrise* and its role within Jeune France, see the text by Lucien Lautrec, 21 August 1941; private archive. It should be noted, moreover, that in Jeune France women occupied middle management, not leadership positions. Hence, for visits to museums and exhibitions, in the provinces and in Paris, provisions were made to recruit a number of former students (male and female) from the Ecole du Louvre or art schools who were "in difficult circumstances" at the time.

78. On Copeau's role in theatrical decentralization, see Lindenberg, "Révolution culturelle" (note 59).

79. Xavier de Lignac to Paul Flamand, 29 August 1941; private archive.

In November 1941, a curriculum was finally established for the stained-glass school founded on 1 October 1941, under the patronage of Auguste Perret, which would open in October 1942 at 23, rue Oudinot in Paris. The school was overseen by professors Auguste Perret (architecture), Maurice Morel, chaplain for the group (art history, humanities, and philosophy), Dulas (symbolism), Lefèvre (logic and reasoning), Father Hilaire de Barenton (world history), and Mlle Huré (technical education in stained glass).

80. Among the individuals surveyed were Jean Besnard (pottery); Meynial (ceramics); Le Gué (pottery), Eure-et-Loir; Jean Sala (glass), Paris; Lefébure, director of the ceramics and glassworks union (*chambre syndicale*), Paris; Decoeur (ceramics and pottery), Fontenay-aux-Roses; René Buthaud (pottery), Bordeaux; Francis Poulenc (pottery and ceramics), codirector of Rhône-Poulenc, Paris; André Leleu (ceramics), secretary general of the Comité d'organisation de la céramique; Edouard Goerg, painter, Paris; and Pierre du Colombier, critic, Paris. See the results of this survey by Lucien Lautrec; private archive.

81. Twenty students, fifteen to seventeen years old, selected from youth organizations or centers, met in the morning for a common program; in the afternoon, the apprentice potters and glassmakers separated into "technical" workshops. This training went on for three years.

82. The presence of Gustave Singier, one of the Jeunes peintres de tradition française, assistant head of popular imagery in the schools, had almost no impact on the reactionary line of the Société du Salon de l'Imagerie Française dominated by Paul Lavalley and Paul Charlemagne.

83. Lautrec was from Marseilles.

84. See "Suite du rapport présenté en mai 1941 à Jeune France" (concerning the founding of a stained-glass school); private archive.

85. See the plan for the curriculum in the plastic arts (7, rue Jean-Mermoz, Paris) for the use of the instructors in Jeune France, school year 1941–42; private archive.

86. Plan for the curriculum in the plastic arts (7, rue Jean-Mermoz, Paris) for the use of the instructors in Jeune France, school year 1941–42; private archive.

87. Interviews with Rodin, a series of letters from Michelangelo, and excerpts from Albert André's book on Renoir were proposed.

88. See the list of slides, 2 May 1941; private archive. According to this list, the other slides shown included

2. Basque house in Labourd. Everything under one roof.
3. Basque house in Soule. Dwelling and outbuildings separate.
4. Map of the distribution of these two types of houses, to illustrate the variety of house types within a single region.
5. Decorated lintel of a Basque house. Magico-religious emblems.
6. Alcove bed (*lis clos*) in Basse-Bretagne, second half of the seventeenth century.
7. Norwegian bed, seventeenth century. Wheel-shaped decoration already in use in the Bronze Age.
8. Hope chest, Queyras.
9. Armoire from Mâconnais, nineteenth century.
10. Glazed clay plate. Savoie, nineteenth century. Cock decoration passed down from the Celtic age.
11. Glazed stoneware crock. La Borne, Berry, simplicity of forms.
12. Ceremonial spoon, Basse-Bretagne... Celtic motif.
13. Young shepherd from Saint-Sorlin (Savoie) who sculpted the collar, dated 1937, that the ram is wearing.
14. Festival clothing for a day of grace in Perros-Guirec.
15. Work cap, winemaker from Bourgogne. Importance of work clothing for fostering a revival of traditional costumes.
16. Chief head coverings in Auvergne and Velay. Shows the diversity of head coverings within a single province.
17. Breton bagpipe players.
18. Provençal farandole. Perhaps a survival of a fertility dance.

19. Agricultural worker from Valois, engaged in archery...which brings together in a single company of men all professions and all classes.
20. Ceremonial entrance of the armoire into the bride's house, in Basse-Bretagne (celebrations marking the ages of life).
21. Cross, decorated with flowers by Loire Valley peasants for the Rogation Days procession.
22. Popular image from Chartres. Saint Crispin and Saint Crispinian, patron saints of cobblers (guild celebrations).
23. Carpenter's bouquet, in Touraine, hung by laborers on the Feast of Saint Joseph.

....

26. Earthenware plate from Rouen, eighteenth century. Locksmith in his workshop: craftsmen of the past.
27. Map compiled by Albert Dauzat, of the names given in France at the celebration of the village community.
28. Cobbler of wooden shoes displaying his stock of shoe decorations.
29. Miniature depicting French peasants at harvest time, late fifteenth century.

89. See the unsigned and undated "Suite au projet d'éditions d'estampes," Pierre Schaeffer papers; private archive.

90. In about 1941, Jean Bazaine planned to design the sets for a play written by Lope de Vega, which Vilar was to stage, *Amar sin saber a quién* (Love without knowing whom). It was not produced. He did, however, do the set for Vilar's production of Molière's *Georges Dandin*. Passionate about the theater, Le Moal worked for Jacquemont at the Compagnie des quatre saisons provinciales while running the Ateliers Jeune France.

91. In the provinces, Jeune France entered into agreements with the owners of private galleries and opened in Lyon the Galerie des Carmélites at the Carmelite convent (for major events) and the Galerie Jeune France on rue du Sergent-Blandan (for smaller exhibitions).

92. In Lourmarin, at the château in Oppède, a congress met at the initiative of Mounier and Roger Leenhardt, bringing together for ten days the vibrant and resistant elements of France, from Max-Pol Fouchet to Lanza del Vasto, Loys Masson to Pierre Seghers. See Winock, *Histoire politique* (note 64).

93. The review for the *maîtrises* in the free zone was edited by Jean de Fabrègues. Between 1925 and 1927, he had participated in the activities of the Chevaliers de Saint-Michel, a group that fought "for the return to God by both nations and the social order," seeking to revive the views of Action française. He had edited the review *Réaction* (1930–32) and *La revue du siècle* (1933–34), incarnating what Jean-Louis Loubet del Bayle has called "the second branch of the New Right."

94. At the time, Rivière was still involved in setting up the Musée national des arts et traditions populaires, which opened in 1937. During the occupation, the government, with Edmond Humeau as an intermediary and within the framework of the Commissariat à la lutte contre le chômage, assigned a research program on traditional settlements to Rivière. That allowed him to put multidisciplinary teams to work in the service of the new discipline of French ethnography. On this subject, see Georges-Henri Rivière, "Le chantier 1425: Un tour d'horizon, une gerbe de souvenirs," *Ethnologie française* 3, no. 1–2 (1973): 9–14; see also Georges-Henri Rivière, interview by Laurence Bertrand Dorléac, Paris, 2 October 1982, in Laurence Bertrand Dorléac, "Art, culture et société: L'exemple des arts plastiques à Paris entre 1940 et 1944" (habilitation thesis, Institut d'études politiques de Paris, 1990), 2:640–52.

95. See the "Project d'une maîtrise des arts populaires" (initiated by Paul Flamand; the head of the *maîtrise* was Delarue, its committee members were Rivière, Mlle Le Floch, Poulaille, and Chasse), undated; private archive.

96. According to Pierre Schaeffer's formulation; see Schaeffer, *Les antennes de Jéricho* (note 59), 278.

97. Bazaine in particular did not like teaching, systematically avoiding it during his career to have time to devote himself to his art.

98. See *Jeune France: Principes, direction, esprit* (note 65).

99. See Schaeffer, *Les antennes de Jéricho* (note 59), 276.

100. Flamand held firmly to this line after the war, in his work as a publisher.

101. Jean Bazaine to Paul Flamand, 10 October [1941], private archive.

102. X[avier de] L[ignac], "Note du Secrétariat des études à Paul Flamand," undated; private archive.

103. See especially "the line" of Mounier's personalist manifesto of 1934.

104. Pierre Schaeffer was born into a family of musicians in Nancy in August 1910. He entered the Ecole polytechnique in 1929. He was appointed to the post of PTT engineer in Strasbourg in 1934 and transferred to Service de la radiodiffusion in Paris in 1936. Passionate about philosophy and literature since his youth, he wrote many books in his spare time over the course of his long career at the Office de radiodiffusion télévision française. During the occupation, he wrote "Esthétique et technique des arts-relais" (first published in 1977); and he later published *Traité des objets musicaux: Essai interdisciplines* (Paris: Editions du Seuil, 1966). He was also the author of stories, novels, plays, and many musical works for radio.

Of all the participants in Jeune France, he undoubtedly had the most eclectic career. That career also followed most closely the multidisciplinary project of the organization, with his innovative musical experiments, and conformed the least to the accessible and "popular art" he had promoted.

105. Well after the war, Schaeffer would say that, at least initially, he managed to get subsidies more easily then than during the Fifth Republic.

106. Pierre Schaeffer papers; private archive.

107. He continued his activities with the training program in Beaune in 1942, alongside Jacques Copeau. At that time, he introduced young actors, technicians, and musicians to radio broadcasting techniques. This program gave rise to the Studio d'Essai, which in 1944 launched the first appeals on Radio libre.

The vagaries of Schaeffer's memory are to be noted: he was certain that Jeune France had lasted less than a year, when in fact it lasted sixteen months. See Pierret, *Entretiens avec Pierre Schaeffer* (note 59), 132.

108. The man who liquidated Jeune France was Jacques Hillairet, a well-educated navy officer and an old friend of Bazaine's who believed he could remedy the situation. Hautecoeur, who saw Jeune France as a state within the state that was impeding his plans for decentralization and for the creation of multidisciplinary "art centers," was careful not to intervene.

On Hautecoeur's indecisive plans, see Serge Added, "Le théâtre en France dans les années-Vichy 1940–1944," 2 vols. (Ph.D. thesis, Université de Reims, 1990); and, on the same subject, Serge Added, *Le théâtre dans les années-Vichy, 1940–1944* (Paris: Editions Ramsay, 1992).

109. At least some members of Jeune France went along with the change: Lautrec, for example, continued to be remunerated until June 1942. On 4 May 1942, Manessier wrote to his mother, "Jeune France is still just as obscure. I have been renewed for another month, which is good, but no fresh news for the long term"; Manessier archives.

110. The dissolution order appeared in the *Journal officiel* of 11 July 1942.

111. In the words of Daniel Apert, head of the plastic arts.

112. In 1948, Lautrec founded the Académie populaire d'arts plastiques in Paris, where he put his pedagogical methods into practice. These methods are also set out in his *Le dessin gestuel: Exercices pratiques et notes* (Paris: n.p., 1974), published with the help of the secrétariat d'Etat à la Jeunesse et aux Sports, which also subsidized the other activities of Lautrec's academy—classes, training programs, and "pedagogical exhibitions."

113. "L'avenir de l'art plastique," *Beaux-arts*, 27 February 1942, 3.

When Morel gave a similar lecture after the liberation, at the Université de la Sorbonne under the aegis of Travail et culture, Picasso could only view the "homage" of a man in a cassock with reservations, even joking that Morel had wanted Picasso dead. During that event, tracts were supposedly distributed in which Picasso was depicted wearing a cassock and Morel was decked out with a hammer and sickle. During the lecture, the abbé displayed Picasso's series of increasingly spare drawings of bulls.

114. For the celebration of Joan of Arc in May 1941, Pierre Schaeffer and Pierre Barbier wrote *Portique pour une fille de France: Dix tableaux*, with music

by Yves Baudrier, Léo Preger, and Olivier Messiaen. The project assembled 175 actors and 15,000 extras recruited from Jeune France's youth centers and *maîtrises*. They performed before more than 130,000 spectators.

115. See his message to the population of Savoie at the inauguration of the statue of Joan of Arc in Chambéry on 10 May 1942; Haute Cour de Justice trial of Philippe Pétain, AN, series 3W 290, seal 16, exhibit 49.

116. X[avier de] L[ignac], note to the leadership of Jeune France, 8 September 1941; private archive.

117. Response to a note from Paul Flamand, 2 September 1941, regarding Lucien Lautrec, "Avant-projet à l'exposition ayant pour thème: 'La famille dans l'art français,' à proposer à M. Hourdin, secrétaire général à la coordination des Mouvements familiaux"; private archive.

118. One of Apert's leaders was supposedly Ronet, a medical doctor who later became a senator. Also reportedly participating were Mme Claude Edmond, Jean-Louis Cavaillès, and Jean Gosset. Cavaillès was shot in 1944; Gosset was deported and died in Neuengamme. See Daniel Apert, interview by Véronique Chabrol, 26 March 1974.

119. Lautrec was once entrusted with a letter from Clavé. He was arrested, then released about two weeks later, not knowing what it contained.

120. Still very much in vogue.

121. Schaeffer's comments about the events of May 1968 were pessimistic. He saw the same signs of revolt and boredom among the young people, made more violent in a more violent world; and the failure of the solutions they had envisioned, since both communitarianism (southern zone) and art for art's sake (northern zone) had led to the contemporary "decadence."

122. See Marc Fumaroli, *L'Etat culturel: Une religion moderne* (Paris: Editions de Fallois, 1991).

123. Fumaroli, *L'Etat culturel* (note 122), 103.

124. Fumaroli, *L'Etat culturel* (note 122), 102.

125. Fumaroli, *L'Etat culturel* (note 122), 100.

126. Fumaroli, *L'Etat culturel* (note 122), 81.

127. Lindenberg, "Révolution culturelle" (note 59), 9.

128. On Schaeffer's apoliticism, see both Pierret, *Entretiens avec Pierre Schaeffer* (note 59); and Schaeffer, *Les antennes de Jéricho* (note 59), in which he relates the events of the period after the liberation: his difficulty finding his place for himself there, the consequences of his refusal to participate in a purging committee and to join what seemed to him to be "cliques" unworthy of past battles, his declared incapacity to "negotiate," his feeling that he was neither Gaullist nor Communist and thus was marginalized or even attacked (especially by the Communists).

CHAPTER SEVEN

The Red and the Blue

THE ARTISTIC *ESPRIT*

Emmanuel Mounier's personalist program was a skillful blend of revolutionary and utopian impulses with serious and sacred undertones. Though only a few artists officially approved of it, it had attracted, beginning in the 1930s, a certain number more or less eager to take a stand off the beaten paths of the Communist Party. Among its first adherents, Gromaire, Goerg[1] (also affiliated with the Communist-led Maison de la culture in Paris), and Jean Labasque were not part of the young guard of the Jeunes peintres de tradition française exhibited at the Galerie Braun in 1941,[2] but Bazaine, another of Mounier's followers, was the show's coordinator. It was he who had assembled the young painters and who had invited some of them to work with Jeune France. The circumstances would turn to advantage his talents as an organizer, yet he never abandoned his two priorities, painting and literature. A remarkable individual who had known Marcel Proust and Léon Blum, this child of the enlightened bourgeoisie preferred, from the very start of his literary studies, to choose his intellectual guides from the progressive pantheon. In 1940, however, Bazaine was working as a critic for *La nouvelle revue française*—after extracting a promise from Pierre Drieu La Rochelle, who had just recruited him, and despite not concealing his fundamental differences with Drieu, that he could express himself freely in its pages.[3] Drieu records this clearly in his *Journal.* At least until Drieu turned thirty, whenever he found himself casting "a doleful eye" on his books, he had only "to see a beautiful painting to be cheered up." Painting had always saved him, because it was "the warmest act of accepting life—even when the painter was Picasso, that beautiful triumphant victim of Parisian desolation."[4]

For Drieu, who was familiar with Bazaine's prewar writings, was not the important thing, at least at first, to share the hope of a "total revolution"? We need to go back in time to grasp the extent to which the situation, before it became a minefield, presented the painter with an opportunity to establish the failure of a materialist society that was rotten to the core. From the early 1930s on, Mounier had invited artists and intellectuals to foment against that society a "personalist and communitarian revolution" that would necessarily entail a "temporary and limited" dictatorship.[5] He scored a hit with artists by attacking the modern capitalist model, which "casts aside the unemployed as a waste product of the mechanization of their bodies . . . [and] the artist as a waste product of the mechanization of his soul." There was even a chance that they would assent when he denounced the artist's role "in the service of money and its castes" or art's divorce from the "popular masses."[6] All that was much in the air at the time. By contrast, Mounier winnowed down his audience when he held himself aloof from Communism and Fascism alike. He paid tribute to surrealism for deliberately fostering a purifying revolt by renouncing mediocrity and conformism, "the worst enemies of art as well as the inner life,"[7] only to accuse the movement soon after of stagnating at "anarchy" or even, in certain cases, of delivering itself up to Moscow and thus rushing headlong into a "new servitude."[8] For Mounier, the (Marxist) Association des écrivains et artistes révolutionnaires was mired in error, which could be avoided only by inventing a third way free of external influences. As for Hitler's Fascism, it likewise served Mounier as a foil: at the cultural level, it had exiled everything that mattered in Germany. Bolshevists and Fascists had made culture march in lockstep, and Mounier warned people to be wary of decrees from any state, even if, as in the best-case scenario, it was decentralized and "softened up."[9]

BAZAINE AGAINST THE STATE

In terms of cultural achievements, Bazaine likewise largely deplored the poverty of Soviet and German works shown to the public in 1937, during the Exposition internationale des arts et techniques dans la vie moderne.[10] The Soviets presented " 'popular' canvases of a nauseating vulgarity," reminiscent of "the most vile products of a decadent bourgeois art," while the Nazis camouflaged a comparable, "purely materialist" ideal under a classical facade. In both cases, there was a kind of total objectivity and an identical "dupery . . . the pretense of a living tradition perpetuated." The Russians were still cultivating "muddy" chiaroscuro; the Germans, in memory of Dürer's splendid lyricism, pursued "an artificial dryness."[11]

Beginning in 1941, Bazaine thus appealed for a characteristically French art that would not have such flaws, while refusing to support official France when he judged that refusal necessary. His "political" positions followed from that stance. He had seen totalitarian regimes hamper creativity, and he would act against such efforts on the part of the French state under Pétain's regime. In 1941, as we have seen, he ironically denounced the plan for a graphic and plastic arts corporation—a scheme strongly encouraged by the occupier and implemented by the Vichy government—reminding people of the state's incompetence in the arena of the fine arts. In contesting the state's desire to make artists comply with aesthetic and racial criteria, he repudiated in his own way Jeune France's initial allegiance to Pétain—just as he was joining its ranks—while using *La nouvelle revue française* to parade his refusal to swallow all the regime's lies. Drieu may simply have been lax in his "rereading" of the proofs, or he may well have decided, from that time on, to allow through some attacks on the regime, which was too timorous for his taste. This was odd at the very least, given that it was precisely on the matter of the artists' corporation that the government seemed to be displaying zeal. In fact, Bazaine and Drieu had very few tastes in common—a distrust of academicism, no doubt, and a taste for "political engagement" and for "grandeur" that was completely at odds with the corporation project. On that point as well, Bazaine remained in agreement with Mounier, who denounced the artist's isolation but envisioned the remedy in "a strength, a harshness, and a grandeur, or even, in counterreaction, a high degree of serenity that a servile art or an art of the ivory tower would never give him."[12] It was necessary, wrote Mounier, "to struggle against academicism, not to remove artists from certain natural contexts existing apart from the Parisian landscape eroded by capitalist trusts, art dealers, and the rich."[13]

On this, a good part of the art scene during the occupation could still agree. But not all artists had the same desire to push the French people far beyond the limits of the person "constrained by the narrowness of his instincts and the poverty of his introversion." The "vast educational" effort was undertaken by only a small number, who were more or less resolved to instill a new taste worthy of the general renaissance. Within Jeune France, the Jeunes peintres de tradition française thus began to put Mounier's "solutions" into practice, just as most of these artists found a personal response to universal and spiritual aims in a revitalized Catholicism.

Given the general character of his revolt, Mounier could hope for the support of at least part of the art scene, when it refused to be confined "to either the right or the left." Indeed, art was supposed to come to terms with the common people at church as well as at the factory, across traditional political lines. Mounier chose to scoff at the categories that were foundering in the prevailing confusion. "Charity was on the right," he said, "along with the Académie [française], religion, the war minister, the soul, [Paul] Bourget, Latin, the liberal economy, notaries, and families. Justice was on the left, along with Picasso, civil servants, Monsieur Homais, public health, feminism, freedom, and experimental psychology."[14]

His list was not only "paradoxical;"[15] it was dripping with contempt for both camps. His logic, though it did not compromise on the need for radical change, seemed to undermine his political lucidity. Even if the personalists had slipped into "the magnetic field of Fascism,"[16] they still held humanist convictions that kept them away from extremism. Although the utopian aspect of their revolt made them give up on democratic liberalism, they still maintained that the individual could not be relegated to the bottom rung of "the bamboozled community" but was to take its place in a universal being and also in a restored human society. The defeat and its ramifications transformed their arguments, articulated in a theoretical manner before the war, into slogans of national reform or resistance to the status quo. Their criticism of reality was so radical, however, that they saw no other solution than to help the modern world die, once more reducing it to the metaphor of a moldering old tree: "a collapse of all its worm-eaten mass" was necessary for the "coming of new growth."[17] By virtue of a very religious attachment to the individual, they preferred to be redeemed by the Middle Ages rather than the Renaissance, which, according to them, had neglected the communitarian element.

THE RENAISSANCE ROMANESQUE

In June 1942, Bazaine was hoping for a naïve young painting that had escaped an "increasingly unsettled, complex, and compromised" world.[18] It would resemble "that nakedness before a virgin world, that purity and that simplicity of intentions and of means, that frankness and that freedom of approach which some call clumsiness."[19] This assigned quite a precise meaning to the famous tradition to which he laid claim. It was not conservative but rather open to permanent adventure, to chance, and to the mystery of a state of nature as opposed to the old rigid world of men and cities.

For the most part self-taught, the Jeunes peintres de tradition française thus enjoyed an advantage over those of their fellows who had received an academic education.[20] Their apologia for primitivism arose from a great visual erudition, however. They were steeped in the sources of the era. Romanesque art was among the specialties sampled by intellectuals in the 1930s, succeeding the vogues for the Ballets Russes and African art (*art nègre*).[21] The educated public had become infatuated with it as well. Bazaine, Gischia, and Beaudin took courses in medieval art at the Institut d'art et d'archéologie on rue Michelet and read the works of Focillon;[22] Manessier, Le Moal, and Bertholle put their interests into practice, studying fresco under Roger Bissière at the Académie Ranson. Literature on the subject became more available, including books illustrated with the Romanesque frescoes at Saint-Savin-sur-Gartempe or Tavant, the Beatus manuscript of Saint-Sever, and articles in the reviews *Verve* and *Minotaure*.[23] Knowledge of medieval culture was enriched as well by a few excellent exhibitions: in 1937, the Bibliothèque nationale de France presented *Les enlumineurs français du VIIIe au XVIe siècle;* the same year, Catalan works of art from the tenth to the fifteenth century were assembled first at the Musée des écoles étrangères contemporaines at the Jeu de Paume and then outside Paris at the château de Maisons-Laffitte; and many major pieces were displayed at the exhibition *Chefs-d'oeuvre de l'art français*, which welcomed several million visitors to the Palais de Tokyo.

But it was probably the opening of the galleries of the Musée national des monuments français at the new Palais de Chaillot that allowed the faithful easiest access to the art they loved. Inaugurated during the Exposition internationale of 1937, these new galleries were the result of a tremendous labor of reproduction undertaken by Prosper Mérimée in the nineteenth century, and they replaced the first outcome of his efforts, the Musée des moulages at the (since demolished) Palais du Trocadéro in 1882. For a century, the Direction générale des beaux-arts had commissioned small-scale watercolors of the frescoes decorating the walls of several hundred French medieval churches. The works had been reproduced life-size at the museum, on canvases covered with a special coating that made them look like stone. Without leaving Paris, visitors could come to admire the images of Christ of Montoire-sur-le-Loir, the *Christ in Majesty* of Berzé-la-Ville, the *Virgin and Child* of Montmorillon, the equestrian *Constantine* of the Saint-Jean de Poitiers baptistery, the scenes in the crypt at Tavant, and the *Christ* of the church at Saint-Savin-sur-Gartempe.[24]

Like many artists since the late 1920s, the painters in Jeune France saw in these frescoes an artistic rebirth that superseded the decadence of the art of antiquity.[25] They called for a renunciation of the banalities of a falsely rationalist Renaissance. The world had to once more "crackle with angels and demons," and, as in the Middle Ages, a commission had to provide the pretext for expressing such fervor. The artist's modern condition discouraged his anonymity; consequently, he would sign his masterpieces while aspiring to the modesty of the craftsman. He did not always have the opportunity to work on a team, but his vision would expand beyond his easel when he studied the exacting rules of fresco and mural art. The passion for the Romanesque was in step with the demands of the time: if you wanted to attract crowds, works had to grow larger in size and they had to leave the museum.

A NEW SACRED ART

During the Front populaire, Bazaine, Lautrec, Le Moal, and Pierre Vérité had accepted a commission from the undersecretary for sports, Léo Lagrange: they decorated one of the first French youth hostels with images of the four natural elements. And most of the Jeunes peintres de tradition française had participated, alongside their famous elders Léger, Picasso, and Matisse, in the successive exhibitions of mural art held before the war. In 1937, they honed their skills decorating the avant-garde pavilions of the Exposition internationale, under the watchful eyes of the masters. Bissière, Bertholle, Estève, Beaudin, Manessier, and Le Moal (who had all taken architecture classes) worked with the Delaunays and Aublet;[26] Gischia, Estève, and Chauvin were with Le Corbusier and Léger; and Lapicque labored, by himself, at the Palais de la découverte. As for Bazaine, he created his first stained-glass window for a private chapel. When it came to murals, some artists came out ahead, particularly Bissière, an instructor at the Académie Ranson, who in 1937 had begun work on the frescoes for the oratory of the little chapel neighboring his home in Boissierette in the *département* Lot;[27] and Le Moal, his student, who in 1939 had had the opportunity to work with a team on a monumental ceiling decoration for the New York World's Fair. Although they sometimes painted on a grand scale, if only for the theater, Le Moal, Gischia, and Bazaine[28] had to await the end of the war, when sacred art would begin its true revolution, for the Jeunes peintres to really give free rein to their taste for mural art and stained glass.

This revival of interest in Romanesque art in fact entailed a certain conception of the sacred[29] that sharply recoiled from the banalities of pious conformism as represented, ultimately, by text-heavy and obviously emotive images such as those published in the Saint-Sulpice district of Paris. To that "decadence" of faith, many writers had already attested, including Péguy, Gide, Paul Claudel, and Bergson.

In July 1934, Bazaine complained in *Esprit* that "sacred art" had made a name for itself by renouncing the task of being "the complete expression of life and of human concerns."[30] Denis and Desvallières had actually anticipated his warning in the 1910s, but their conception of a renaissance predicated on the mysticism of the Nabis or Rosicrucians brought about only a timid renewal. Nonetheless, their Ateliers d'art sacré, inaugurated in Paris in 1919, created a precedent. Beginning in 1920, new workshops by master glassworkers opened in which the defense of tradition and the primacy of technique still prevailed. The Exposition internationale des arts décoratifs et industriels modernes, held in Paris in 1925, which restored the prestige of craftsmen; the first major exhibition of "present-day" religious art, held at the Palais Rohan in Strasbourg in 1934; and the building projects of the Chantiers du Cardinal—all these prefigured, barely, the real upheavals desired by Bazaine. In laying the theoretical foundations for a true renewal, he was probably the only one to announce clearly that religious art could no longer limit itself to being a pale reproduction of a lackluster reality but instead had to move in the direction of "suggestion" and transposition. It should no longer countenance the dichotomy between life and religion—an idea that led Bazaine to advocate authentic "human emotion" by an artist who was a nonbeliever over the candied exercises of religious but subdued painters.

THE OUTSTRETCHED HAND

History would vindicate Bazaine, as fervent but rarely religiously observant artists were called on to produce sacred art. In the 1940s, for example, Matisse, Léger, Braque, Lurçat, Lipchitz, and Chagall all contributed to the decoration of Notre-Dame de Toute Grâce at Plateau d'Assy. Before the war, Pignon had painted the first version of *The Dead Worker:* as Bernard Ceysson remarked, even as this piece referenced the history of the workers' movement, within the tradition of a tempered cubism and the *return to order*, it could also be regarded "in terms of a reference to Christian pietà." The Communist painter Fougeron shared the Jeunes peintres de tradition française's enthusiasm for Romanesque art, and he set out on a tour of France to discover it in situ. This was a nod not only to the consequences of the party's policy of *the outstretched hand* toward Catholics but also to the art sector's propensity to renounce religious sectarianism.

The Dominican priests Marie-Alain Couturier and Pie-Raymond Régamey (who together edited *L'art sacré* beginning in 1937),[31] the canon Lucien Ledeur, and the abbé Maurice Morel joined Bazaine in a fight that ran counter to the interests of the conservative clergy but met with an increasingly positive public response. Exhibitions in which profane and sacred works appeared side by side,[32] the enthusiasm of certain critics, and the atmosphere of the time, which favored the reform of catechisms and forms, all prepared the way for the new order. The battle against the old institutions proved difficult, but they ultimately yielded in the face of the reformers' vitality. The church in Les Bréseux decorated by Manessier in 1947 disconcerted the conservative authorities. Then the church of Plateau d'Assy, inaugurated in 1950, to which Bazaine contributed,[33] along with almost all the major artists from the first half of the twentieth century, believers or not, gave rise to attacks from fundamentalist circles. They appealed to Rome—to no avail. In point of fact, nonfigurative art ran counter to the legibility required by Catholic doctrine and brought to mind the iconoclasm of the Reformation.[34] Nonetheless, Ledeur responded by stepping up the implementation of his renovation program for the small churches of Franche-Comté, an effort Le Moal joined. And Matisse pressed on with the creation of the Dominican chapel in Vence, opened in 1951, shortly before the consecration of Sacré-Coeur d'Audincourt. This church, built by the architect Maurice Novarina, features a large mosaic on the facade made by Bazaine, seventy meters of stained glass designed by Léger, a stained-glass window in the baptistery by Miró, and—a later addition—stained-glass windows in the crypt by Le Moal. In claiming that all art is religious, Bazaine likely wanted above all to highlight the spiritual nature of the artist's work, not only in its themes but also in its daily practice.

During the occupation, the French state would continue to commission church works from pious but conventional artists. It preferred, like its friends, to disregard the compromises of the time. It immersed itself in saints' lives,[35] persuaded that a fruitful dialogue could be established across time between the sacred Middle Ages and the twentieth century, between two groups of artists bound together by "emotional affinities."[36] The Jeunes peintres, according to their leaders at least, believed in a reformative and fervent art, an art vested with universal values and reconciled to existence, as in the past. What the Jeunes peintres liked about medieval art, in addition to its monumentality and its strong colors, was its "craft," which contrasted with the logic of technology, whose morbid aspects World War I had revealed. They liked its focus, its tenor, but also its license, which reminded them of modernity's freedoms. The distance that separated the naïveté of medieval artisans from the learned reflections of a contemporary artist hardly mattered. The tenets of abstract art showed that Gromaire had been right to see, in 1935, the Middle Ages as the first great age of visual realism, which the common people ought to embrace as its own and which had to be studied with respect.[37]

THE SHATTERED MIRROR

The young primitives retired the old categories that obscured the relativity of the systems for interpreting the world. Perspective was replaced with a skillful organization that referenced a mobile world, where shapes flow over the beholder or vanish into matter and color.

Lapicque, the eldest of the group of Jeunes peintres, began creating his *Figures* in 1939,[38] while thinking of champlevé enamelwork from the twelfth century as well as stained-glass windows. He liked champlevé enameling for its "barely suggested spaces, at the same time flattened and infinite, defying all corporeal evaluation and yet present."[39] That remark applied to his future works such as, from 1940, *Joan of Arc*
Pl. 28 *Crossing the Loire*,[40] *Sainte-Catherine-de-Fierbois*,[41] and *The Maritime Vocation*,[42] which, despite their dense armature of crisscrossing bars, compel beholders to lose themselves in a space without perspective and without bounds. That sensation recurs in Bazaine's works from 1941 on. A small watercolor on cardboard dating to 1941[43] rendered any traditional reading impossible; a year later, his oil painting *Swimmers in the Wave*[44] broke even more resolutely with what was being produced at the time.

Mobilized during the phony war as part of a reconnaissance unit destined for the front, Bazaine had discovered a disturbing and haunting natural world. Rather than simply being faced with the spectacle of the world, he was deeply "inside" it, and from that experience derived his interest in a new, mobile, and incomprehensible landscape.[45] Later, without painting "from nature," he would dissolve his human figures in a preexisting natural world,[46] especially water,[47] the generic and boundless element. Similarly, his oil painting *Still Life in Front of a Window* of 1942[48] granted neither the subject matter its central place (only a chair in the foreground is recognizable) nor the window its function of differentiating spaces. Instead, he dispersed objects across a network, a parceled-out space, where inside and outside mingle together. That still life, the first of his nonfigurative paintings, exhibited at the Galerie de France in 1943, seemed to be part of a cycle of artistic reappraisals shared by other young painters such as Manessier and Le Moal and also
Pl. 36 to echo the experiments of Villon[49] and Lapicque.

The intention here is not to establish primacy but to note a convergence of singular works. A reconsideration is now under way regarding the original reception of these artists. They were seen by their detractors, and by parochial advocates of a supposedly more "radical" American school, as mere followers of Pierre Bonnard, the fauves, or the cubists. Their present-day exponents say that such a view confines them within a tradition that these artists undoubtedly embraced, but only as part of their search for a new path.

Their predecessors had demonstrated that they could do without linear perspective by privileging the line, the arabesque, expressive distortion, and repetition of decorative motifs. In works by the Jeunes peintres, drawing was still employed, but its function was to divide up a surface, to organize, to domesticate color, to establish a cadence—without necessarily "depicting." The results they produced urged the viewer toward fantasy, imagination, and freedom. Standing before their works, the attentive art lover could recognize the imprint of the "moderns" who had embraced "primitivism": Cézanne, Bonnard, the fauves, the cubists, Matisse, Braque, and Picasso—but also Robert Delaunay and, finally, Jacques Villon. From Delaunay, they learned the Orphism that had allowed him to be done with the dark period of cubism; and they were influenced by Villon and his personal vision of cubism, the golden section, and exotic art.

The Jeunes peintres were not, for that matter, the only ones to endorse these discoveries: Lhote, Walch, Desnoyer, and Gromaire, whose works were to be seen in galleries or Salons at the time, had already learned certain lessons from them. With the younger artists, however, the license became greater, the tone less didactic, the desire to break away more obvious, and the old romantic opposition between color and drawing increasingly outdated.

We probably should distinguish artists such as Bazaine, Lapicque, and Manessier, who beginning in 1942 made their figures unrecognizable, from the others, who confronted the strangeness of the world in a different way. Pierre Francastel has aptly spoken of their monstrous universe, as in works by Estève, where "trees grow out of housetops" and the figures "have nothing in common with humanity."[50] Estève's figures are monsters with "bean heads" and "moon faces,"[51] while Gischia's have barbaric or Carolingian visages, and Fougeron's are topped with a "piece of pumpkin."[52] It was something of a joke to pronounce such works "Snow White for grownups" when the public clamored for "topicality,"[53] but the works also pointed out the distance that separated the will of the majority from the rebellious spirit of the Jeunes peintres. The official taste for a faithful and reassuring representation of the world was a long way from their refusal to bow to the diktat of lies and to the "humanist" figuration of man that had lost all its meaning now that chaos had set in.

To grasp the spirit of the Jeunes peintres de tradition française, we must consider their disenchantment with a deadlocked world whose faithful representation seemed to acknowledge an impasse. We thus will have to place their paintings side by side with conventional works conforming to the taste of the majority and clinging to the old rules of imitative continuity: only then will we be able to evaluate the power attributed to a group of works that would not have the same significance after the liberation. In fact, the Jeunes peintres seemed to hew to the heroic line, while seeking that unstable equilibrium point between order and chaos, reason and utopia, continuity (which was opposed to the "pure present" of barbarism) and change.

THE MEANING OF COLORS

The Jeunes peintres, heirs to a "classical" tradition that culminated in Matisse and Braque, retained above all their sense of order and rigor. Their grids, armatures, spirals, and arabesques may have reflected preoccupations different from those of their predecessors, but their apparent structuring of space still reminded some of the asceticism of the most austere advocates of the call to order during the previous period: Henri Jannot, Robert Humblot, Claude Venard, Georges Rohner, and Gruber. Yet the Jeunes peintres radically distanced themselves from these predecessors, if only in their violent treatment of reality and their use of color. For them, color was the "keystone of the art of painting," "loud, intense, frenetic."[54] It generated movement, created volume, made light dance. Cubism had overused muted nuances, and the prewar *return to order* had exhausted the dark range of colors.

Léger, citing World War I, had expressed the need to respond to the grayness and muck of "four years without color"[55] by setting free the most violent and pure tones he had ever used.[56] Once again, and this time out of the trenches, life was "groping" along; man was "hidden, concealed, on all fours, the color of earth." To this earth lauded by official voices, the young guard, resolved to fight against the darkness of the time and the prevailing artistic currents, responded with a debauchery of garish colors. For Estève, color was "emotionally moving"; it had "a life, a mystery, a possibility of direct contact with vision"[57] and was in that respect superior to drawing. Only color could "interpret the human emotion" that rose up in Manessier, responding to a "more abstract, more profound feeling." The colors that expressed emotion "managed to spread out more and more, to almost devour the objects themselves."[58] For those who were moving toward abstraction, color imposed unity and the free and nonfigurative transposition of reality. For everyone, it acted like a primitive weapon, capable of triggering strong sensations without using sophisticated arguments that, especially after the defeat, seemed rendered null and void. For Bazaine, it was, more specifically, what would put their paintings in the thick of the current battle.[59]

His statements on the use of color went beyond what the Jeunes peintres de tradition française were generally doing. But they became a sort of manifesto at a time when the lack of freedom compelled painters to deviate from the traditional codes. In January 1943, Bazaine published an article in *Comoedia* titled "Peinture bleu, blanc, rouge." In it, he declared that a nation does not choose its flag at random and that "there would be a great deal to say about this type of colored crystallization of a people's deep-seated instincts."[60] What followed was an openly nationalist text that could easily be understood as a declaration of war against the foreign presence. In reality, it echoed a text by Matisse, an excerpt of which Bazaine had published in 1942, and which he turned to his own account. After too much refinement, it was necessary to return to the essential principles that had formed human language. "Paintings that are refinements, subtle gradations, blendings without energy, call for beautiful blues, beautiful reds, beautiful yellows, materials that stir the sensual depths of men."[61]

A year later, for the needs of the cause, Bazaine replaced yellow with white, moving color into symbolic and militant categories. His "political" position opportunely coincided with formal reflections that had preceded the occupation and that did not have the same charge before the defeat. In 1936, Bazaine had spoken of a "dynamic balance of warm tones, the reds and yellows, and cool tones, the blues," capable of transposing "space and depth."[62] As of 1938, shades of red and blue dominated in his work. Yet, even as it accommodated "French" colors, that use of red and blue in permanent tension was in line with Bazaine's interest (shared by the Jeunes peintres de tradition française) in Romanesque and popular art. Without being a faithful application of Lapicque's dogmatic conclusions, it was reminiscent as well of that artist's scientific remarks on color.

In the 1930s, Lapicque—a painter, a graduate of the Ecole centrale des arts et manufactures, and a laboratory assistant at the Faculté des sciences in Paris between 1931 and 1943—developed a theory of fragmentation of color that challenged Isaac Newton's conclusions about the chromaticism of the eye, disputed Hermann von Helmholtz's conclusions about the dispersion of light in the retinal image, and even disagreed with the research of his own teacher, Professor A. Polack, on color sight.[63] The practical effects of his theory called into doubt the application of a notion of color perception adapted by artists during the Renaissance.

According to Lapicque, the primary colors did not refract in the same manner in the eye and they faded differently over time. Thus, because of its darkening qualities, blue was the appropriate color to use to transpose a nearby reality, fixed and dense. Red, yellow, and their variations, which brightened while remaining luminous, ought to be used for everything that was distant and changeable. Lapicque cited as examples certain Romanesque works as well as decorative arts from the eighteenth century, which, according to him, presupposed a knowledge of the optical effects he had observed.[64] For him, as for the other Jeunes peintres de tradition française, this use of color was undoubtedly limited to finding efficient "equivalencies" for what was still going to be represented. This importance granted to "technical" requirements, however, moved away from naturalistic aims and contributed to a modern evolution that made those requirements more interesting than the painting itself. Lapicque, moreover, had no illusions about the "realism" of his paintings, particularly as he had pinpointed not only the chromatic function of colors but their emotional and ethical function as well. As a devotee of philosophy, a faithful reader of Plato, George Berkeley, and Bergson (a passion he shared with Bazaine), and a participant in the debates raging about realism at the Maison de la culture in the 1930s,[65] Lapicque understood perfectly why using red and yellow (or gold) to suggest a "luminous" and "transcendent" sky could both lead to "admirable creative works" and get away from "intellectual neutrality." It could attest to "a certain implicit belief, namely, that light comes to us from infinite spaces." In the same way, using blue "because of the dark principle in which it participates"[66] (according to Leonardo da Vinci) expressed a hierarchy of values that went beyond mere prettiness and technique.

JOAN OF ARC AND *THE ARMED MAN*

Joan of Arc Crossing the Loire, Lapicque's most significant work, produced at the start of the occupation, would need to be interpreted in light of these remarks. It was a painting of its historical moment, the first in a series of works constructed more or less on the same model by the Jeunes peintres de tradition française (Bazaine and Manessier in particular). It expressed the anguish of the time, despite the almost definitive disappearance of any legible figure. The predominant use of a dark blue, which crisscrosses a space weakly illuminated by a few splashes of red and yellow, sufficed to express the pessimism of the painter a few days after the defeat. Just as economically, Bazaine would likewise broadcast a more optimistic message, just before the liberation
Pl. 29 of Paris, in his *Mass for the Armed Man*. In that painting, the prevailing use of red and its variants (vermilion, crimson, pink, and so on) pushed back a few steel-blue verticals, while a tangle of short horizontals passed over and under them, to temper their action. The center was constituted by the point of intersection of what some saw as a Saint Andrew's cross (others would see it as a cross of Lorraine, associated with de Gaulle and

the Free French Forces, or as a Chi-Rho), around which was organized a fairly complex network of straight lines disrupted at six or seven points by fragments of curves.

Despite their sufficiently explicit layout, in Lapicque's painting as well as Bazaine's, the meaning was not spoon-fed to viewers, as it was in figurative or narrative works. Even their titles, which by tradition should point to an interpretation, gave rise to discomfort and a polysemy of clandestine messages. *Joan of Arc Crossing the Loire* referred to a well-known figure, both emblematic and ambiguous, claimed throughout history by the right and the left, including the Freemasons and the pacifist Alain. For the far right, Joan of Arc remained a myth—according to Michel Winock, the mythic converse of the Jew for anti-Semites. For all, she was the principal figurehead of nationalism, even of patriotism. At the time, depending on who was using her, she served both the anti-German cause and the anti-English war.[67] *Mass for the Armed Man*, a title Bazaine chose for his transparent and evanescent figure while listening to Josquin des Prez's *Missa L'homme armé*, referred to the registers of religion as well as war—to religious war, something that, in the mid-twentieth century, could disconcert the viewer.

The works they exhibited after the liberation would appear to have opposed the occupation through a series of more or less readable signs running counter to the leanings of the majority: recourse to a medieval and French tradition, distortion of the subject, deconstruction, and the use of symbolic colors, forms, and titles. All in all, the Jeunes peintres de tradition française demonstrated the extent to which their formal commitments tended to take the place of traditional militant action. Bazaine accompanied his revolution of forms with a certain number of declarations of principle that stemmed from his status as a scholar. On the whole, however, he asserted throughout his life a libertarian vocation and a commitment to the artist's work in itself,[68] a desire to change the world from the place where he accomplished his daily tasks. It was a widely shared position among modern artists, whose refusal to embrace the official cultural project and the status quo often involved intensive, vigorous, intransigent labor.

NOTES

1. After the suicide of Roger Salengro, Blum's interior minister, who had been wrongly accused of having deserted in 1916, Goerg signed the petition "Pour l'honneur," published in *L'aube*, 21 November 1936, 1.
2. Goerg, Gromaire, and Labasque all wrote for *Esprit* before the war. In the arts, other contributors to *Esprit* included Jean Lurçat, Pierre Courthion, Pierre Vérité, and Marcel Moré.

3. Drieu La Rochelle, who had read the pieces that Bazaine published in the review *Esprit* before the war, had convinced Bazaine to write for *La nouvelle revue française* by reassuring him that art would remain "free"...
4. Pierre Drieu La Rochelle, *Journal 1939–1945*, ed. Julien Hervier (Paris: Gallimard, 1992), 208 (entry dated 20 May 1940).
5. Emmanuel Mounier, *Révolution personnaliste et communautaire* (Paris: Fernand Aubier, 1935), 133.
6. Mounier, *Révolution personnaliste* (note 5), 172, 173, 175.
7. Mounier, *Révolution personnaliste* (note 5), 174.
8. Mounier, *Révolution personnaliste* (note 5), 174.
9. Mounier, *Révolution personnaliste* (note 5), 186.
10. See Jean Bazaine, "La peinture à l'exposition," *Esprit: Revue internationale*, 1 December 1937, 450–55.
11. Bazaine, "La peinture" (note 10), 453–54.
12. Mounier, *Révolution personnaliste* (note 5), 176.
13. Mounier, *Révolution personnaliste* (note 5), 187–88.
14. Mounier, *Révolution personnaliste* (note 5), 17. [Monsieur Homais is the pompous, irreligious, and morally and intellectually vacuous apothecary in Gustave Flaubert's *Madame Bovary*.—Trans.]
15. Mounier, *Révolution personnaliste* (note 5), 17.
16. To use Philippe Burrin's expression, in his "La France dans le champ magnétique des fascismes," *Le débat* (Paris), no. 52 (1984): 52–72.
17. Mounier, *Révolution personnaliste* (note 5), 30.
18. Jean Bazaine, "Jeune peinture," *La nouvelle revue française*, June 1942, 634.
19. Bazaine, "Jeune peinture" (note 18), 633.
20. See, in particular, the monographs developed at the time of the major retrospective exhibitions devoted to these artists at the Grand Palais.
21. See Pierre Francastel, *Nouveau dessin, nouvelle peinture: L'Ecole de Paris* (Paris: Librairie de Médicis, 1946), 168.
22. Henri Focillon's *L'art des sculpteurs romans: Recherches sur l'histoire des formes* was published in 1931; and both his *Art d'Occident: Le Moyen Âge roman et gothique* and his *Peintures romanes des églises de France* appeared in 1938.
23. There was a vast body of literature on Romanesque art published at the time. See in particular Louis Bréhier, *Le style roman* (Paris: Librairie Larousse, 1941); Marius Balmelle, *L'art pré-roman et roman au musée de Mende* (Mende: Imprimerie de Chaptal, 1942); Victor Allègre, *L'art roman dans la région albigeoise* (Albi: Imprimerie Coopérative du Sud-Ouest, 1943); Pierre Lavedan, *Histoire de l'art*, vol. 2, *Moyen Âge et temps modernes* (Paris: Presses Universitaires de France, 1944); Léon Gischia and Lucien Mazenod, eds., *Les arts primitifs français: Art mérovingien, art carolingien, art roman* (Paris: Arts & Métiers Graphiques, 1939); Pierre

Francastel, *L'humanisme roman: Critique des théories sur l'art du XIe siècle en France* (Rodez, France: Imprimerie P. Carrère, 1942); and the essay by Georges Bataille on the *Apocalypse de Saint-Sever*, initially published in the 2 May 1929 issue of *Documents* and reprinted by Editions de Cluny in 1943.

24. The project continued during the occupation under the direction of Jean Verrier, assisted by students from the Ecole des beaux-arts.

25. See Léon Gischia, "Recherche d'une tradition," in Gaston Diehl, ed., *Les problèmes de la peinture* (Lyon: Confluences, 1945).

26. In 1935, Robert Delaunay and Aublet had created the association Art et lumière, which many artists joined.

27. Bissière stopped working during the occupation. For his work, I referred to Jean Laude's (unpublished) lecture introducing the exhibition *Paris 1937–Paris 1957: Créations en France*, which opened at the Centre Georges Pompidou on 28 May 1981.

28. Le Moal began in 1939, Bazaine in 1941. They worked for the theater directors Maurice Jacquemont and Jean Dasté, among others.

29. On the Jeunes peintres de tradition française and the sacred, see especially Gérard Monnier, "Actualité de l'art sacré," in Jacques Beauffet et al., *L'art en Europe: Les années décisives, 1945–1953* (Geneva: Skira/Musée d'Art Moderne de Saint-Étienne, 1987), 48–53; *Groupe Témoignage: 1936–1943*, exh. cat. (Lyon: Musée des Beaux-Arts, 1976); and Jean-Pierre Greff, *Asse, Bazaine, J. Bony, Collot, Gutherz, Elvire Jean, Lautrec, Le Moal, Manessier, C. de Rougemont: Maquettes des vitraux de la cathédrale et oeuvres récentes*, exh. cat. (Saint-Dié: Musée de Saint-Dié, 1988).

30. Jean Bazaine, "Note sur l'art religieux 'moderne,'" *Esprit: Revue internationale*, 1 July 1934, 658–59.

31. The review was founded in 1935 with the support of Paul Claudel, Copeau, François Mauriac, Robert Mallet-Stevens, Perret, Georges-Henri Pingusson, and the priests Couturier, Paul Doncoeur, and Régamey.

32. In particular, the *Exposition des vitraux et tapisseries modernes* held at the Petit Palais, 4–30 June 1939.

33. Bazaine contributed three stained-glass windows for the facade: *King David*, *Saint Cecilia*, and *Saint Gregory the Great*. He began working on the latter two in 1943, and the first versions he produced are installed in a chapel at the Couvent Saint-Jacques in Paris.

34. See *L'art sacré*, no. 9–10 (1952).

35. See René Barotte, "Nos peintres au travail: Jean Bazaine," *Comoedia*, 23 October 1943, 6.

36. Francastel, *Nouveau dessin* (note 21), 168.

37. See "Premier débat: Marcel Gromaire," in Jean Lurçat et al., *La querelle du réalisme: Deux débats organisés par l'Association des peintres et sculpteurs* *de la Maison de la culture* (Paris: Editions Sociales Internationales, 1936), 23–36; quoted in Bernard Ceysson, "Realismes/figurations," in *L'art dans les années 30 en France*, exh. cat. (Saint-Étienne: Musée d'Art & d'Industrie, 1979), 41.

38. See, for example, *Portrait* (1939), 50 × 45 cm; illustrated in Jean Lescure, *Lapicque* (Paris: Editions Galanis, 1956), 52.

39. Lescure, *Lapicque* (note 38), 51.

40. *Joan of Arc Crossing the Loire* (1940), 100 × 81 cm; illustrated in Lescure, *Lapicque* (note 38), 45.

41. *Sainte-Catherine-de-Fierbois* (1940), 92 × 73 cm; illustrated in Lescure, *Lapicque* (note 38), 86.

42. *The Maritime Vocation* (1940), 65 × 81 cm; illustrated in Lescure, *Lapicque* (note 38), 55.

43. *Untitled* (1941), 35 × 48 cm; illustrated in *Bazaine*, exh. cat. (Geneva: Skira/Centre National des Arts Plastiques, 1990), 30.

44. *Swimmers in the Wave* (1942), 160 × 160 cm; illustrated in *Bazaine* (note 43), 31.

45. Jean Bazaine, interview by Laurence Bertrand Dorléac, 20 March 1992, Clamart.

46. He stopped working while he was mobilized in Lorraine in 1939.

47. See *The Bath* (1939); *The Children in the Wave* (1939–41); *The Swimmer* (1943), 65 × 100 cm; and *Swimmer in the Reeds* (1943), 44 × 116 cm.

48. *Still Life in Front of a Window* (1942), 116 × 89 cm; illustrated in *Bazaine* (note 43), 32.

49. See, for example, Villon's treatment at about this time of the human figure, which disappears into the ground and walls, in oil paintings such as *Portrait in Green* (1942), 92 × 73 cm; and *Portrait of Camille Renault* (1944), 130 × 97 cm.

50. See Francastel, *Nouveau dessin* (note 21), 25.

51. Francastel, *Nouveau dessin* (note 21), 27.

52. Francastel, *Nouveau dessin* (note 21), 21.

53. Francastel, *Nouveau dessin* (note 21), 28. [Francastel is claiming that paintings by Estève and his fellow artists are of a piece with Walt Disney's *Snow White and the Seven Dwarfs* (1937) and Mickey Mouse cartoons—that is, such art is just Disney for the adults of the time, who prize old tales, primitivism, imagination, and spontaneity.—Ed.]

54. See Bernard Dorival, *Les étapes de la peinture française contemporaine*, vol. 3, *Depuis le cubisme, 1911–1944* (Paris: Gallimard, 1946), 307.

55. See Fernand Léger, lecture: "Peintre-1937—Couleur dans le monde," *Peintres et sculpteurs de la Maison de la culture.*

56. See "Fernand Léger retrouve la France," *Arts de France*, no. 6 (1946): 33–42.

57. Estève, as quoted in Gaston Diehl, "Primauté de la couleur," in idem, ed., *Les problèmes de la peinture* (Lyon: Confluences, 1945), 234.

58. Manessier, as quoted in Diehl, "Primauté" (note 57), 234.

59. On Jean Bazaine and color, see Laurence Bertrand Dorléac, "Jean Bazaine 1940–1944: Imaginaire politique et modernité picturale: Remarques sur le rouge et le bleu," in *Image et histoire: Actes du colloque Paris-Censier, mai 1986* (Paris: Publisud, 1987), 220–35.

60. Jean Bazaine, "Peinture bleu, blanc, rouge," *Comoedia*, 30 January 1943, 1.

61. Quoted in Bazaine, "Jeune peinture" (note 18), 634 n. 1.

62. Unpublished lecture by Bazaine on Cézanne, 1936; quoted in Jean-Pierre Greff, "Bazaine 1941–1947: Les années décisives," in *Bazaine*, exh. cat. (Geneva: Skira/Centre National des Arts Plastiques, 1990), 146.

63. See his theoretical studies: Charles Lapicque, "Les contrastes adoptés par les peintres," *Réunions de l'Institut d'optique* 6, no. 3 (1935): 33–35; "Le rouge et le bleu dans les arts," *Réunions de l'Institut d'optique* 6, no. 4 (1935): 11–26; "Les images rétiniennes régulières, leurs déformations par irrégularités optiques de l'oeil," *Réunions de l'Institut d'optique* 7, no. 2 (1938): 12–38; "La couleur picturale du ciel et de la terre," in *Deuxième Congrès international d'esthétique et de science de l'art, Paris, 1937* (Paris: Librairie Féliz Alcan, 1937), 2:274–76; and "L'optique de l'oeil et la vision des contours" (Ph.D. diss., Université de Paris, 1938).

In late 1939, he was mobilized by the Centre national de la recherche scientifique. As a member of the Commission supérieure technique de camouflage, he performed experiments on night vision in airplanes, with Professor Holweg and Antoine de Saint-Exupéry.

64. See Denis Dorio to the contrôleur général des finances Nicolas Desmarets, 26 April 1708; quoted in André Pottier, *Histoire de la faïence de Rouen* (Rouen: Auguste Le Brument, 1870), 17, 116.

65. On 24 June 1938, during a fiery debate on the subject of freedom in art, he took a position alongside Louis Lapicque (his father), Maximilien Luce, Jean Perrin, and Henri Le Sidaner.

66. Charles Lapicque, *Peintres et sculpteurs de la Maison de la culture*, no. 7, July 1938.

67. See Michel Winock, *Nationalisme, antisémitisme et fascisme en France* (Paris: Editions du Seuil, 1990); and Michel Winock, "Jeanne d'Arc," in Pierre Nora, ed., *Les lieux de mémoire*, vol. 3, *Les France*, pt. 3, *De l'archive à l'emblème* (Paris: Gallimard, 1992), 675–733.

68. When he was invited to the Soviet Union in the 1960s, Bazaine delivered a lecture in which he declared that the purpose of painting is "to prove that man is free."

CHAPTER EIGHT

In the Shadows

THE "RESISTANCE"

Whether in the case of the artists of the Jeunes peintres de tradition française specifically or modern artists more generally, their spontaneous, empirical, at times ambiguous revolt obliges us to reconsider the notion of resistance to the occupation, its signs, and its internal logic. One could rightly speak of intellectual resistance in connection with certain poets and writers, credited, by turns, with an admirable courage or a culpable ineffectiveness. Everyone concurs, however, that at least their intention was to revolt against the loss of freedom.[1] What actually came of their action, what hope and inefficacy ensued, might well be compared to the fate that awaited the art world. Far removed from the weapons used by the actual Resistance—propaganda, counterpropaganda, remarkable feats, sabotage, intelligence operations—the artists' responses seem quite absurd.

Though it is impossible to estimate accurately the percentage of resisters by socioprofessional category, artists do not seem to have distinguished themselves by a unified attitude, in one direction or the other, toward the regime. Even if we knew where artists ranked among executed Resistance fighters,[2] we would hardly be the wiser about the actions of the group as a whole. Their art will not bear witness either. Naturally, some artists could have joined the Resistance but continued to paint still lifes and nudes, while others could incarnate the battle against oppression in their works without ever being part of a Resistance network.[3]

To put things back in their context, however, we will have to assess each particular action on its own terms. The range of responses was broad, from the (very rare) refusal to express oneself publicly to (occasional) transgressions of the accepted codes. It was so broad that, for the majority, it ultimately extended to the act of simply continuing to live, work, and exhibit under the occupier's nose. Once the occupying forces positioned themselves in opposition to culture and freedom of expression, it became easy to interpret any free manifestation of thought as a form of courage. The continuing work and activism of artists—to which the public responded—could well be taken as a palliative, an exorcism, a way like any other of resisting the reigning barbarism. The problem for the historian, however, stems from the concordance between their acts and the demands of the German powers, which called for art to be seen as a remedy for the crisis, as a slightly decadent but effective bauble that could distract the population without necessarily making it think. Let us recall that one of the first demands made by the occupying forces was to have Paris return to its life "as usual" as a brilliant capital of the arts, letters, and spectacles. Within that logic, the artists were only responding to the Germans' demands, while serving as regulators, accepting de facto the rules of the game, the villainous laws, humiliation, and self-censorship. But there were also works that disregarded the rules then in force.

German censorship targeted artists for racial or political reasons. It did not target their works, whose content and form were left "free." Yet in reality, from the start of the occupation, the German presence on the art scene fostered a system of widespread self-censorship, and works that were openly subversive in their subject or form were mostly relegated, voluntarily, to the intimate galleries of the avant-garde. The traditional Salons maintained an innocuous ambience that suggested nothing of the extraordinary circumstances, so much so that they seemed to visitors a little like havens of peace that the external world had not managed to disturb. To that apparent absence of reaction, a certain number of artists quickly responded with codes of rebellion that very often only the initiated were able to understand.

Nothing in these codes could trouble the occupier's calm, at least until the constant threat posed by the Resistance turned the quest for rebels into an obsession. In the art world as elsewhere, isolated initiatives occasionally contributed to the worries of the upholders of public order. In 1944, just before the Salon des Tuileries, the word spread that artists ought to submit their most "advanced" and "bold" pieces against "the Nazi barbarism."[4] Yet the response to that instruction could range from a nonfigurative work of art to the inclusion of a simple tricolor cloth as a sign of patriotism. The initiative was enough to make Rebatet seethe when he happened upon the unsigned and clandestine proclamation. Still, he could take comfort in the thought that the Jew behind the conspiracy was quickly sniffed out.[5]

Obvious representations of the battle being waged in the shadows were actually very rare. There again, resistance via the image took circuitous routes. To get a fix on the problem of artists' attitude during the occupation, we must revisit a model of political engagement constructed in the 1920s against the backdrop of political crisis and revolt targeting the individualist status of "genius." It was during that era that the fate of "engagé" work that assumed a speculative and critical "modern" attitude, rather than adhering to a rigidly "Zhdanovist" content, was negotiated.

Although the moderation of their militancy during the occupation might suggest artists were depoliticized, the previous phase had indicated, on the contrary, a widespread sensitivity to contemporary movements of thought, a responsiveness that would persist into the dark years.

GENESIS OF A POLITICAL COMMITMENT

There was no dearth of militant experience among artists. Pascal Ory's study of the Front populaire's cultural policy recounts in detail the situation in the 1930s and before.[6] Beginning in the 1920s, the Section française de l'Internationale ouvrière, the Confédération générale du travail, and the cooperative movement placed their hopes in the *atelier social* (theory discussion group), which confined itself to minor commemorative creations, before the Communist Party intensified militant action, first within the Association des écrivains et artistes révolutionnaires (AEAR), then within the Maison de la culture. Even before the May 1936 movement, it was the Communist Party that responded, in an ecumenical mode, to the expectations of all those wanting to become involved in social and antifascist struggle. That move would mark the modalities of political commitment in the art sector during the occupation.

The "associations" advanced by the Communist Party in the 1930s increased the number of initiatives. Among these were the creation of the group Les indélicats in 1932 and the exhibition in 1936 of albums (in a militant style that found few imitators) by its members Robert Falk, Fougeron, and Pignon; the Salon featuring the revolutionary painters of the AEAR in 1934; and in 1935, a major exhibition under the aegis of the Maison de la culture. It was at that time as well that the Maison de la culture formed an alliance with the particularly dynamic association L'art mural, run by Saint-Maur, which organized four major Salons between June 1935 and June 1938.[7] The Maison de la culture[8] especially showed a considerable amount of work by increasing the number of exhibitions and publications. The relative eclecticism of its program and its leaders reflected more or less faithfully the atmosphere of the time. Léger, Lhote,[9] Lipchitz, Frans Masereel, and Lurçat (the one closest to the

Communist Party) participated,[10] but so did honorary presidents who would follow very different paths: Friesz would join the official trip to Germany in 1941, Gromaire became a member of the Resistance, Marquet entered the Communist Party immediately after the liberation, and Matisse explored new artistic forms from Cimiez. The most active participants were often younger and less famous. They included the newspaper illustrator Jean Effel, Albert Laforêt, Pignon, Gruber, Goerg, Edmond Kuss, Boris Taslitzky, and Marc Saint-Saëns. Their noticeable aesthetic differences did not particularly bother an association ready to compromise so long as it could score points in the arena of cultural hegemony. The program proved to be acceptable to many progressives open to solutions offering "art for all." The Maison de la culture welcomed volunteers, even those that the Communist Party had rejected—Le Corbusier, for example. At the time, its power lay less in its propensity to solve the "immediate," "socioeconomic" problems of artists than in the privilege it granted the fundamental debates of the day, under the leadership of not only Aragon (who was already defending socialist realism) but also Malraux, Georges Sadoul, and Francis Jourdain. Malraux evoked the intensity of the debates, which could unleash such a passion "nowhere but in Paris and in another time."[11]

Even as the proper remedies remained a matter of debate, everyone agreed on the need to bring art and "the people" together. Hence we need to understand the prevailing watchwords of the 1940s as a curious sequel to the Front populaire: the aspiration for teamwork and for collective masterpieces, the call for discipline, the return to reality,[12] the revival of mural art and realism, and the promotion of museums and art education for all. The differences lay primarily in terminology. When Cassou spoke of "popularization," he was clearly evoking the communication that ought to be established between "the masses, the great mass of laborers, and museums,"[13] whereas the Révolution nationale prohibited addressing the "people" as a class. Even the struggle against academicism and traditional education, and more generally against the modalities for legitimating artists, began prior to the defeat and continued after it. This struggle against academicism, as we have seen, gave new power to the Institut de France, even though the institution itself, "undermined" from within, left room for independent art, through isolated key individuals such as the young curator Bernard Dorival at the Musée national d'art moderne.

Pressed by Aragon to take a position in support of realism, as early as the Front populaire years, the art sector could not resolve to opt for a concerted course of action. Even the Communist Party and its fellow travelers preferred to create some slack by finding an imbricate definition that nevertheless privileged two popular forces. In 1936, Gromaire called to the rescue "pictorial folklore" and its presiding genius, Henri Rousseau; at his side was Madeleine Rousseau, attached to the Musée du Luxembourg, who privileged the phrase "maîtres populaires de la réalité" (popular masters of reality) under which rubric she brought together a number of naïve works in 1937. Photography, which Aragon saw as a weapon in the service of a new realism, also figured prominently among the "popular" arts.[14] Any of its different aesthetic variants could be deemed acceptable, including surrealist photomontage in the style of John Heartfield, directly inspired by contemporary political events. It was thus no longer the physical world that was sacrosanct, but the artist's intention and his "project"—what Aragon called "human forces" as opposed to the "forces of nature." And it was again in the name of a certain aesthetic ecumenism that the Maison de la culture entrusted to the surrealist painter André Masson the decorative arts studio Jeunes 37, which was supposed to compete with the traditional instruction of the Ecole des beaux-arts and the Ecole nationale supérieure des arts décoratifs.[15]

All in all, on the eve of war, a good portion of the left in France, and especially the French Communist Party, rejected both abstract and propaganda art for the most part, though not without a few contradictions. Abstract art was defended by Blum, who had rallied behind the Delaunays when they were in difficulty. Even Aragon clung to a very French definition of the cultural "party line" in calling for work on subjects with collective overtones and a mysteriously "dialectical" content. Even when Lurçat and Gromaire recommended "serious" approaches, not everyone followed them. Far from it: many thought that Matisse and even Bonnard embodied the salutary relaxation of workers.

Following Ory, we should notice to what extent the visual and architectural works by leftist militants and sympathizers stood out neither for their perfect unity nor for their distinctive features nor for their "political" coherence before or after the artists' political engagement—even though certain themes clearly reference their choices of the moment.[16]

All the same, could the events of the 1930s have left the artists indifferent? Goerg, torn between personalism and the Maison de la culture, declared that no artist should still paint the same way after 6 February 1934.[17] Likewise, the Front populaire episode, in bringing out a certain mordancy in artists, had not left them untouched. From that standpoint, Picasso's *Guernica* remained the most successful example of the direct influence current events could have on a sensitive observer. The growing triumph of Nazism on French soil itself led some at least to believe that an adequate response on the part of artists was called for.

CONQUER, BUT HOW?

If we set aside attitudes that seem to have been unaffected by the new situation, three groups of protagonists in particular responded to the state of affairs with works characterized by sarcasm, dissolving figures, dream states, or militant "realism": artists exiled either within or beyond the borders of France, "modern" artists and surrealists. The first group was heterogeneous, made up of exiles within or outside of France who refused to collaborate with official artistic life as they awaited the outcome of the war as well as, more generally, those who refused to let democracy founder. Masson, for example, resumed the maturation process he had begun, building on his experiences of World War I, the Spanish civil war, and the political battles of the surrealists. He left France, calling future generations to witness that the surrealists had been clairvoyant in opposing the dictators by absenting themselves.

In the United States, the Voice of America, exhibitions of modern art, the review *VVV*, and lectures all demonstrated a staunch refusal to submit on the part of French artists who could take advantage of being at a favorable distance for free speech. On the other side of the Atlantic, the (minority) attitude of those who remained in France and kept silent—Matisse, for example—seemed all the more stoic given that the occupation authorities were inviting artists to "participate." A large portion of the most radical modern artists,[18] while grasping how unfavorable their situation was, continued to step forward. Still it should be made clear how intimate, secretive even, were these appearances—already largely restricted before the war—which gave them a rebellious side. Whereas the Jeunes peintres de tradition française, thanks to their group stratagem, were able to impose their presence more or less by force, the intermittent presence of isolated individuals, sometimes known and watched by the occupying forces, remained much more discreet. The program of activities, meager compared to the usual schedule of artistic events, appeared all the more radical because it ran counter to the climate of pervasive self-censorship. As of 1941, some dealers took the risk of disregarding the occupier's (supposed) orders by exhibiting works whose spirit resolutely clashed with the traditional output and antidecadent norms of Nazi Germany. Save for the Jeunes peintres de tradition française, Galerie Jeanne-Bucher regularly presented disconcerting works in the backyard and on the fourth floor of a bourgeois home. The visitors book attests to the loyalty of the modernist inner circle: it bears the names of Lurçat, Maar, Georges Braque, Nicolas de Staël, André Lanskoy, Henri Laurens, Pignon, Véra Pagava, Domela, Georges Vantongerloo, and Kandinsky.[19] Kandinsky, whose works Bucher had exhibited in 1936, figured among the key individuals targeted by

German censorship, even though he had rejected any clear political engagement. For a certain time at least, he accommodated himself to Nazism,[20] wanting to keep the "drama" from finding expression in his painted work. Instead, he wished to provide joy and serenity, and "through his paintings to touch spirits in order to make them find hope, the intangible, poetry, and the sublimity of colors."[21] The delicate tensions in his pieces of the time amply attest to that sentiment: *Sky Blue* (1940), *Green and Red* (1940), *Joyous Theme* (1942), *Circle and Square* (1943), and *Simplicity* (1943).[22] Even so, Kandinsky's works were censored at Galerie Jeanne-Bucher in July 1942: they remained the too glaring symbol of a decadence banned in Germany and of the modernity taught at the Bauhaus.

That did not prevent Bucher from again exhibiting Kandinsky's paintings and gouaches in January and February 1944, alongside works by Domela and de Staël, though she took care not to send out invitations this time. Hers was an exceptionally courageous attitude, and it came with the desire to hold the "line," whatever the circumstances, by showing "difficult" artists: Laurens, Léger, Ernst, Louis Marcoussis, Hans Reichel, Klee, Maar, Pagava, Miró, Domela, and de Staël. A certain number of insiders could admire the same stubborn desire to go against the spirit of the time among those running the little gallery L'esquisse, which conducted Resistance activities while exhibiting the anti-Nazi artists Domela, Magnelli, de Staël, and Kandinsky, once again censored.[23] The same held for Galerie de Berri, which displayed the works of Vantongerloo and Olivier Debré; Galerie Jeanne Castel, which exhibited Fautrier; Galerie de l'Abbaye, where Léon Zack showed Henri Michaux; Galerie Louis Carré, which featured Dominguez; and Galerie René Drouin, which offered Fautrier and Dubuffet. Thus were presented, in the shadows, artists whose importance would be fully recognized only later, when their singular works could again be seen, discussed, and measured by the standard of a modernity hungry for change. These works were far from constituting a homogeneous current: each contradicted in its own way the art that had prevailed for a
Pls. 39, 40 greater or lesser period of time. They deployed cold or lyrical abstraction, subverted fine craftsmanship and traditional tools, pulverized matter, and engaged in fanciful distortions. Each viewer, depending on his level of awareness, would see more or less freedom and insolence there, though it was the rare work that portrayed events in an explicit manner.

THE VALLÉE-AUX-LOUPS

From this standpoint, Fautrier's famous *Hostages* series remains exemplary, responding to reality with formlessness and to suffering with ideograms. Fautrier painted these works while listening to the sinister sounds of hostages being executed in the forest near the suburban house (close to Vallée-aux-Loups) where he had taken refuge in 1940, after being harassed for his Resistance activities.[24] The very title he gave his works is enough to indicate the artist's interest in ongoing events without ruling out a certain freedom of interpretation, in the places where the narration leaves room for equivalents full of poignancy in the very matter and form of the painting. Malraux saw in the series a timeless incarnation of torture; Francis Ponge, a "stubborn resistance" through the affirmation of beauty and "the heroic lie";[25] Paulhan, the ambiguity and the tenuous balance between "horror and recognition."[26] Daniel Wallard took away the idea that Fautrier had not looked at his hostages "before or during the event, but after, and, it seems, long after, at the moment when these bloody, profaned, torn-apart martyrs"[27] were losing their human form and decomposing. Their reactions point toward the preeminence of matter and formlessness in these works, the disappearance of the historical subject behind the painter's transfigured reality. At the sight of Fautrier's thick pink and greenish paints, Ponge spoke of a martyrdom where "horror and beauty [were] mingled together in detached observation."[28] His blunt remark takes us back to the fascination almost always exerted by horror combined with the effects of art, from Goya to *Guernica* and the works of Zoran Music, who lived through the extreme experience of the Dachau camp, among deportees who often sought to bear witness to their wretched condition in a comprehensible way. Pl. 41

Their reactions also underscore the ability of modern artists to remove themselves from the most fraught and painful reality by radically transposing it. Who, then, could be sure of the content of their works? Among the French, traditionalists hostile to any mischief relentlessly continued, in the name of humanism, to attack abstraction, intellectualism, phantasmagoria, and distortion. The occupying forces, apart from choosing a few prime targets (Kandinsky and Picasso), seemed to have internalized Hitler's advice to let artistic France degenerate. They were in attendance at least during officially advertised events, and their reactions occasionally proved to be excellent indicators of the interpretation that could be given to "freedom." From that standpoint, the exquisitely insolent acts of certain surrealists cruelly demonstrated the limits of a formal political engagement that was as radical as it was ambiguous.

LE GRAND JEU

The eruption of hostilities and the defeat had brought about the departure for the New World of those surrealist artists and writers who preferred to fire off their chants of solidarity from afar. In many respects, everything occurring outside France had a greater impact than the cultural events in occupied France itself. All the same, surrealists who remained behind risked some poorly known actions, whose provocative power and impasses have been pointed out by Michel Fauré[29] and by witnesses. Internal disagreements within the decimated ranks of the movement did not prevent any number of fine and more or less "considered" activities. In 1938, the group Les réverbères had taken a position violently opposed to the Nazi cultural oppression policy,[30] while remaining divided on the role to be granted to political engagement.

By spring 1939, dissensions had surfaced: Jean-François Chabrun and Diamant-Berger left the surrealist movement, arguing that "the poet has the right to live only if he aids in the international Marxist revolution of the proletariat," given that "political games" in themselves "are only the intellectual aspect of the egotistical cowardice of the bourgeoisie."[31] The majority of the group, while remaining sensitive to the Communist cause, retorted by championing the original principles: political abstention, total independence, and the revival of play, which were incompatible with any preconceived doctrine. In summer 1940, Les réverbères, untroubled by the political qualms of their former friends, published a few deluxe albums of color engravings[32] that retained the pre-1940 spirit—jazz, abstraction, automatism, Dada provocation. Gatherings quickly resumed at the home of Jean Marembert and Geneviève La Haye, where many faithful from the prewar period came and went: Noël Arnaud, Henri Bernard, Simone Bry, Jacques Bureau, Maurice Frédéric, Aline Gagnaire, André Guilliot, Jean Hoyaux, Jean Janin, Jean Jausion, Marcel Laloë, Olga Luchaire, Marc Patin, Simone Prégnon, Ulrich Senn, Michel Tapié, and Pierre Vérité. Those who could not return to the capital were replaced by new recruits: Freist, Goebel, Jean Lucas, Michel Lasserre, Marthe Verhuven, François Voirin, and Gérard Vulliamy.

As in the period before 1940, there was a great deal of discussion preliminary to a big event. The political analysis was succinct and optimistic: the Germans did not intend to censor artistic and literary life. Marembert had gotten wind of the "liberal" projects of Abetz, who would conduct an investigation of the avant-garde, of course, but with peaceful intentions. Les réverbères could strike just as they had in the good old days. And so much the better if the artistic life was not yet moving forward, with the exception of the exhibition invoking "French

Tradition" by the Jeunes peintres, which had been on display at the Galerie Braun since May. Breteau, who lent his large gallery in Saint-Germain-des-Prés to Les réverbères, was the friend of both groups. For the optimists, the summer was thus taking shape as the occasion for an artistic and literary offensive.

The first public gathering was set for 20 July 1941 at three o'clock in the afternoon, in the far end of the courtyard of 70, rue Bonaparte. The old hands might be fighting it out behind the scenes, but the younger members preferred action to the founders' quarrels: Tapié criticized Marembert for centralizing all the documents at his place and for delaying preparation of the catalog, the poster, the recordings, and the masks for the event. In any case, only a simple tract-manifesto signed by Arnaud was distributed at the event, and everything was nearly in place the day of the opening. The full schedule provided plenty of distractions for the many initiates, who witnessed one of those spectacles that had amused them before the occupation. The exhibition brought together paintings, drawings, poems, and sculptures, along with recordings, plaques, and enamels by the twenty-six members of Les réverbères. Shortly before five o'clock in the evening, Voirin, dressed as a Swiss guard and armed with a halberd, channeled the crowd in to see the show. Since there was a great shortage of chairs, someone went to borrow some from the nearby public school. As it was the afternoon, the wild evenings of the prewar period took on the air of a slightly daring church youth group. The bogeyman was in the room, discreet, represented by three members of the Propaganda-Staffel Paris. Olga Luchaire sang pieces by Satie and Claude Dubosq, accompanied on the piano by Henri Sauguet. La Haye, Lucas, and Frédéric interpreted a poem mimed by Arnaud,[33] and Tapié praised the genius of Clément Pansaers,[34] a Belgian Dada poet and author of *Bar Nicanor* and *Le pan-pan au cul du nu nègre*. Finally, Arnaud, Hoyaux, and Patin presented with great seriousness three painting by Pansaers—who had never painted in his life—lifting the cloth that protected them as if they were unveiling an official statue. Witnesses remember that on one of these paintings was spread out a blotch topped by an old cigarette butt and that this last part of the show, meant to be very comical, made the audience uncomfortable. Its members remained rather inert, except for the Germans, who saw these jokes as a sincere attack on the fraud of the avant-garde. The troublemakers reacted to the flop by throwing the artificial fruit serving as decorations at the spectators, and, this time, the farce did not meet with resistance. The party ended with a general letting off of steam, everyone launching harmless projectiles at one another under the amused gaze of the Propaganda-Staffel Paris.

That first and last event put on by Les réverbères met with a reception that educated its authors for good about the impact of their strategy. Ten days after the opening, Campagne, in the collaborationist newspaper *Les nouveaux temps,* heaped terms of endearment on the conspirators, like a good father moved by the first burps of his offspring. Even their manifesto seemed too literary to be taken seriously. And, besides, was it quite clear that one did not want to approve it? In it, Les réverbères railed against the "fishers in troubled waters" and against the "unused civil servants" who had assumed "they could, in the uncertainty surrounding the aftermath of tragedy, beat their tight drums, exude their venom, traffic, falsify, pervert." It also attacked "the firemen in their freshly shined helmets," the spineless critics of course, and the unscrupulous dealers. To all this corruption, the rebels opposed an ethics that remained equally aloof from academic honors and the triviality of the market. In short, there was something to satisfy a good majority, and Campagne prided himself on being part of it.[35] His show of understanding was all the more humiliating in that it appeared side by side with the most vile news items in Jean Luchaire's daily. The same issue covered, for example, "the incident" of 28 July 1941 at the Institut d'études des questions juives, which was "invaded by 150 foreign Jewesses, carrying or dragging children, all the wives of detainees." Driven out by the special section, "though the police forces avoided brutality," these women took the opportunity "to stir up a part of the population in Yid," before the special section could "clear" the crowd.[36] In fact, even before the publication of Campagne's laudatory review in *Les nouveaux temps,* the atmosphere of Les réverbères's meeting at the Café de Flore just after the show was freighted with failure. Arnaud was particularly aware of the ineffectiveness of a neodadaist action whose burlesque destroyed all its political charge. He was quite ready to join the team of more politically committed surrealists who had resumed their activities after the "major players" had left the country and were publishing a review with a Rimbaudian title, *La main à plume.*[37]

LA MAIN À PLUME

The two former members of Les réverbères who rallied to André Breton's cause, Jean-François Chabrun[38] and Gérard de Sède, had attended their friends' performance; they had no trouble convincing the others to join them. A short time later, only the group La main à plume was fighting against the state of affairs and keeping the surrealist spirit alive in occupied France. Prepared for official reprisals, it observed security measures so far as possible, masking in anonymity most of the names of the artists and writers.[39] In late August 1941, the new *La main à plume* reprinted "Etat de présence," Chabrun's editorial-manifesto, in which the author announced that it was necessary at all costs to stay and do battle in the field... of poetry. A few days later, four hundred copies of *Géographie nocturne* appeared, printed on a black ground and in dark blue type. The invitation to a nocturnal journey opened with a line from Herakleitos: "Those who are asleep are workers and collaborators in what goes on in the universe" (Frag. 75 Diels-Franz). The text that followed invoked German romanticism and everything the surrealists had drawn from it, yet distinguished its "worst intellectual ambiguities"—even though the praise of the night as "conquest toward action" sounded odd, a touch too literary or metaphorical. The only real novelty for aficionados was no doubt *L'usine à poèmes*, cooked up from collective texts on the initiative of Chabrun and Patin. Did not the times favor making the authors behind a work disappear? Surrealists dared to push that logic to its extreme while the communitarian traditionalists saw anonymity as the best guarantee of both discretion and the general public's sympathy. The third issue of *La main à plume* was to be remembered as the group's most original publication. *Transfusion du verbe*[40] was in every respect more substantial than the previous issues. In particular, it adopted the arrogance that had always brought the surrealists success. Picasso, Dominguez, Raoul Ubac, Tita, Gagnaire, and Vulliamy signed the illustrations, which appeared only in the margins of the texts but had a singular impact. Chabrun and Bureau were enthusiastic about black jazz, suppressed in France at the time: Chabrun saw it as a model of collective improvisation applicable to the written word and to painting. And Paul Éluard, who had just joined the team, offered his poem "Les raisons de rêver," accompanied by a drawing by Picasso dedicated to the poet and dating back to May 1936.

Éluard's collaboration, in the midst of the occupation, was a response of sorts to the exclusion Breton had pronounced against him before the war, after Éluard had contributed, in May 1938, to Aragon's literary review *Commune;* his character, too civilized for Breton's taste, and his concessions to traditional literature made Éluard a poor apostle of surrealist dogma. Despite the reluctance of some, La main à plume welcomed Éluard in October 1941, in the interest of expanding its membership and closing ranks in the occupied zone. The poet proved to be in top activist form, attending many meetings of the work group at the Café des Quatre Sergents, on the corner of rue Campagne-Première and boulevard Raspail. It was Éluard who, along with the Spanish Republican Manuel, maintained relations between Picasso and his friends. Nevertheless, he did not manage to entirely convince some persnickety members: Adolphe Acker, Chabrun, and Robert Rius criticized him in particular for his unconditional friendship with Hugnet, whom Éluard wanted to bring into the group. On Tuesday, 17 March 1942, a stormy session ended with an agreement in principle, although serious grievances had been put forward by the opposition. Acker, supported by Chabrun—who also opposed Éluard—went so far as to deny him the right to lecture them on ethics, since "he [made] a living by selling paintings to the Germans."[41] Though no one knew the details of the two poets' financial operations, it was clear that, at least in the case of Hugnet, who ran a shop at 9 *ter*, boulevard du Montparnasse, business was thought to motivate him at least as much as poetry. A storekeeper and an art dealer, he accumulated surrealist objects of every kind as well as other, more traditional pieces that, in the midst of the occupation, could indisputably garner him a certain commercial success. Arnaud, Bureau, and Patin had, in any case, managed to demonstrate to the group that its own best interests lay in bringing Hugnet in, if only to distribute its publications or to ensure Éluard's and Picasso's loyalty to its cause. The group's obsession with maintaining a semblance of concord would prevail over everything else, at least until 1943. On 2 May 1943, Éluard was ousted from the group, and on 6 October, it was Hugnet's turn. In the bargain, the latter received a good thrashing in the brawling surrealist tradition. The two poets, just as in 1938, were no longer aligned with the majority and were thus deemed undesirable.

In the meantime, *La main à plume* had had to respond to a few important events. In spring 1942, the inquiry into poetry it launched augured a lively work of analysis whose results were to be published in *La conquête du monde par l'image*. The last German order regarding censorship intervened to disrupt the diversions of the happy band. Up to that time, small publishing houses could still escape the drastic regulation of the "free" zone, but the order of 27 April 1942, with the rational utilization of printing paper as an excuse, subjected the issues of *La main à plume* to prior approval by the representative of the German military command (*Militärbefehlshaber*). In addition to the intolerable requirement of having to ask for an official certificate for publication, censorship could now affect the group, in whose works references to banned Marxist authors were fairly easily identified even if their names were not given. Moreover, the occupation authorities would have had no difficulty effecting some fine hauls of rebels in a sector directly or indirectly linked to political groups on the far left.

Arnaud had the idea of responding to this adversity by consolidating the "friendly" small reviews into a single publication. Talks began but ran up against the implacable vanity of each of the participants. Citing ideological disagreements, the publication directors, as close-knit as they were, insisted on preserving their autonomy. On several occasions, La main à plume was appalled by the compromises some were making. The first issue of the review *Messages*, which came out on 16 March 1942 and was prepared by the poet Jean Lescure with the support of Pierre Emmanuel, Jean Follain, Eugène Guillevic, Jean-Pierre Grenier, Pierre Bodin, and Ubac, had some appeal for the surrealists. By contrast, the second issue triggered the ire of La main à plume, who found the participation of Paul Claudel and Loÿs Masson an unacceptable betrayal. Not only were the two poets Christians but Claudel was the author of an already-famous ode to Pétain. The third installment rankled because of the assistance that Ubac, an artist and poet for *La main à plume*, gave to *Messages*, which would be spurned from then on.

In early summer 1942, what did defectors and traitors matter? *La conquête du monde par l'image* demonstrated the vitality of La main à plume, which brought together the many surrealists then at liberty, not only the faithful but also the poets Maurice Blanchard; Léo Malet, repatriated from a German prison camp for reasons of health; and Marcel Mariën, who was writing the first monograph on Magritte.[42] Magritte himself joined in, alongside the artists Paul Delvaux, Magritte's compatriot; Valentine Hugo; and Hans Arp, on whose resources Hugnet happily drew without always waiting for the artist's consent. Finally, Maurice Henry, a loyal surrealist since the 1920s who would remain loyal until 1951,[43] contributed his absurd humor to the illustrated part of *La conquête du monde par l'image*. To the great displeasure of the group, which clung to its purity with regard to collaboration with the enemy, it was discovered—too late, after the issue was published—that the illustrator had offered his best pages to the Fascist daily *L'oeuvre*, run by Marcel Déat. With the exception of that false note, the review cut a fine figure with, on the cover, the photograph of a sculpture by Picasso destined for posterity: the famous *Bull's Head* made from the handlebars and seat of a bicycle and baptized *Object* for the occasion. Picasso had presented the group something tenderly and comically poetic, a piece that held enough surprises to delight his advocates and scandalize his many adversaries when it was exhibited at the Salon d'Automne after the liberation. (The artist proved generous, moreover, as he could be from time to time, in donating two works to *La main à plume*.) In that same issue, which invoked Johann Wolfgang von Goethe and the liberation of images—"these idols left in the organism, in the memory, in the imagination"[44]—the privileged place that Chabrun's writing accorded to representation recalled its telluric force in producing immediate and brutal sensations. The fate of poetry also depended on advances made by artists in visual representation, and henceforth the group could

boast of talented experimenters in its ranks: Dominguez and his four-
Pl. 42 dimensional paintings; Ernst and his frottages, invented in the concentration camps; Ubac and his photographs; and Malet and his *décollage*, discovered in the streets of Paris. Malet had taken to tearing pieces off posters, in order to discover, under the first layer, strange visions other than the banal sense of the original message. Before the future Nouveaux réalistes Jacques Villeglé and Raymond Hains who paid homage to him in the late 1940s, Malet realized that, by suppressing a letter here and adding one there, the entire "physiognomy of the streets" could be turned upside down, allowing the passerby to become a poet and dreamer in spite of himself.[45] A mere acronym could grab his attention—for example, there was the Société anonyme de distribution d'eau, which he preferred to call SADE.

His *décollage* put to good use city walls emptied of industrial advertising and reserved for propaganda first and foremost. It also proposed a form of defacement of imposed messages, an approach that already had its tradition and its theorists. Although Malet confined himself to the poetic form of revolt, others, persuaded that effectiveness lay in comprehensibility, used defacement for distinctly propagandist ends. Of them, the (nonsurrealist) Communists were undoubtedly the best prepared to organize a militant action. They set up a resistant or underground force, in the strict sense of those terms, but without entirely resolving the question of what defined the "subversive" content of a work of art or the problem of the participation of the artist in a life managed by the occupier.

THE FRONT NATIONAL DES ARTS

When compared to modern works protesting the oppression of the time, images produced by the Resistance were rare and also conformed to a different logic. They acted like fun-house mirrors, turning the enemy's own weapons and content—its messages and its major motifs—back against it. Before the war, Sergeĭ Chakhotin, once an assistant to Ivan Petrovich Pavlov at the Academy of Sciences of the USSR, had established a doctrine that made it possible to fight "the violation of the masses." At a time when city walls in Germany were covered with swastikas drawn in chalk, Chakhotin came across one crossed out with a diagonal stroke. Inspired, he transformed the stroke into a downward-slanting arrow across the swastika, a combination that soon became a sign of opposition among anti-Nazi youth. Chakhotin's innovative and militant book, published in France as *Le viol des foules par la propagande politique* in 1939, was censored two months into the war because of its passages against Hitler and Mussolini.[46] Nonetheless, his message seems to have produced emulators, less among the occupying forces—quick learners—who co-opted the first *V*'s for "Victory" that appeared on Parisian walls in 1941,[47] than among members of the Resistance. They used the letters in "Laval" to form a swastika or the slogan "Vive la Relève" (Long live the Relève) to draw the Führer's face.[48] Or they used the opposite tack, for example, with the poster published by the Commissariat génèral à la famille for Mother's Day, 31 May 1942: the plump offspring carried in triumph by a Frenchwoman dressed up like a German *Mädchen* in the official poster was replaced by a dark and frowning mother displaying a long, half-starved baby.[49] It was likewise the counterpropaganda branch of the Resistance that supervised the production of a small poster praising sabotage, which depicted a prisoner behind barbed wire.[50] It was perhaps only the children who departed from the usual vocabulary, with their drawings of Mickey Mouse cheering for de Gaulle or an airplane nose down in a field of flowers under the valorous slogan "DEGAULE [*sic*] VICTOIRE."[51]

The imagery produced as part of the Resistance was confined to these sorts of scattered actions, which also included illustrations for political poems, particularly by Lurçat, who executed cartoons for the tapestries *Es la verdad* and *Liberté*, which featured a poem by Éluard; and, ultimately, the creation, in 1944, of the underground album *Vaincre*, by militants and sympathizers of the Communist Party resolved to act not only on the traditional art scene but also underground. There as elsewhere, the Communist Party, which made propaganda a key element in its struggle, showed itself to be better organized than the rest of the French Resistance and was determined to carry out concrete, even spectacular, action. Its artistic troops, however, had to reckon with the reservations of a specific sector resistant to any overzealous recruitment, whose apparent neutrality embarrassed the militants. The party had entrusted the artistic battle to the Front national des arts,[52] a branch of the vast Front national, which in 1941 was composed of many currents and covered the entire country.[53] Run by Goerg, Pignon, and especially the young painter André Fougeron, who had come from anarcho-syndicalist circles and had joined the Communist Party when it was banned in 1939,[54] the Front national des arts went to great lengths to constitute centers of resistance, with forces that were few in number but active. Fougeron turned his studio on rue Marcel-Sembat in Montmartre into an underground print shop, where he illustrated the headlines for the Resistance publications that his friends were manufacturing alongside him: *L'art français*, *L'université libre*, *Les lettres françaises*, and *Le palais libre*. He rallied artists he had known at the Maisons de la culture on rue de Navarin and rue d'Anjou between the time of the Front populaire and the outbreak of war: Pignon, Goerg, Desnoyer, Montagnac, and Walch. In 1942, the agent who was the Montmartre workshop's liaison with the Resistance was arrested, after which the equipment was moved to a new, less conspicuous studio, in a neighborhood where official painters had chosen to live in the past. This time, it was the scene painter Paul Goyard who rented in his own name an office in the 17th arrondissement, until he was discovered and sent to Buchenwald. A longtime fellow traveler of the Communist Party, he thus resumed an activism put to the test in 1936, when his studio in Saint-Denis was used for the manufacture of signs and banners for street demonstrations and of scenery designed by Fernand Léger for Jean-Richard Bloch's dramatic spectacle *Naissance d'une cité*.[55]

From Goyard's office, the small periodical *L'art français*, clandestinely created by Fougeron in 1941, could thus continue to express a viewpoint sharply critical of the policy of the Nazi and Vichy powers.[56] The particulars of artists' political involvement were treated less harshly in its pages, and the conclusions drawn rapidly led to a realism that chose not to disregard the rank and file. In November 1942, however, "an art lover" who had been through the Salon d'Automne flatly accused the art scene of lacking nerve. He preferred a perfect nobody who had not necessarily produced a beautiful painting but had "spoken" to the art lover with a depiction of a prisoner behind barbed wire. As for the rest, he had wondered while looking at all those works with their tame subjects whether it was really true that "outside, on this misty morning, long lines of shivering women [were] waiting in front of empty shops, that a million prisoners, sentenced to forced labor, starving, [were] languishing in the camps."[57] A year later, this appeal for more political paintbrushes found a response in the directives of the Front national des peintres et des sculpteurs: creative artists were to join the Resistance group Francs-tireurs et partisans, form committees in every housing or studio complex, fight against the deportations, provide papers, hiding places, ration coupons, money, and work. In terms of art, it was understood that the resisters' assignment was to extol, "with their own means, pencil and brush, . . . the heroism of fighting France." But, given that the program had to be placed within reach of everyone, each artist's daily conduct would likewise be regarded as constituting an assault on the occupier. Even if it consisted only of "that aspect of fidelity to the spirit of honest and audacious exploration that has earned our country its renown as a nation of arts and artists, we would have to celebrate it as a demonstration of resistance to the barbarian invader."[58] Resistance to the status quo thus took on an unprecedented scope, and, in theory at least, countless works now served the cause. Aragon made Matisse the symbol of the true France against Nazi Germany, and even artists close to the Communist Party usually privileged form in their works, at the expense of a readable and militant message. The few rare exceptions would prove the rule: in 1943, André Fougeron's *Rue de Paris*, exhibited at the Salon des Tuileries;[59] and, in April 1944, *Vaincre*, an underground album of lithographs by various artists sold to benefit the Francs-tireurs et partisans. Fougeron's painting divided in two the wretched of France: on the right, against a bright ground, are a mother and her naked and emaciated children, one of them thrown against a trash can; on the left, against a dark sky, a group of somber spectators. Since the piece is clearly dated "Paris 43," the scene left the symbolic field and entered into history, in stark contrast to the still lifes and landscapes of a peaceful France on show. The painting borrowed its forms from the history of modernity and the Middle Ages, of which the artist was particularly fond. It was shocking less for its style than for its explicit subject, which went against the grain of official Franco-German discourse: the idyllic family was reduced to degeneracy, and the famous young people coddled by the regime were shown growing up amid the rubbish heaps of the capital. With that painting, Fougeron demonstrated that it was possible to hoodwink the Nazis out in the open. Yet he seems not to have inspired imitators, though evidence is lacking. Fougeron himself later made similar paintings, but in a different, much more militant context. Pl. 46

The twelve plates of the album *Vaincre* responded to the desire of a number of artists to clearly express their violent denunciation of the state of affairs with means other than writing. In 1944, Fougeron brought together therein works by eight artists,[60] including Boris Taslitzky, who had been deported to Buchenwald. The usual style of each of these artists did not belong to the propagandist register, far from it. But for the circumstances, it voluntarily verged on caricature. Assured that the album would be sold clandestinely, the artists could not have made their works more explicit: scenes of German torture, Laval depicted as *Bougnaparte*,[61] Pétain as a Nazi officer, camps, prisons, distended bodies, distorted expressions, texts and symbols granted key importance. Pl. 47

Éluard was supposed to write the preface for the collection. He came to see the plates with Pierre Villon, head of the Front national as of 1943, but the liaison officer to whom he entrusted his text, Annie Hervé, was arrested and had to swallow the paper on which it was written. The bulk of the work was done, however, and distribution began nearly four months before the liberation. As always for publications sold clandestinely, the clientele was handpicked and already won over to the cause. The twelve plates had been printed on a handpress by Marcel Mannequin, in an edition of only three hundred numbered copies. The most important thing was not the number, it was said, but the manifestation of a revolt by the painters who, "after the poets," united with "the sublime effort by the country of France."[62]

That episode remained an exception in every respect and stood in stark contrast, by its uniqueness, to the positions on resistance adopted by most in the arts sector. The awful void was soon filled by the myth of Picasso as Communist resister, who, since he had painted *Guernica*, had masterfully succeeded, even before his militant avowal, in incarnating the rejection of barbarism, though he had never protested by any means other than painting—and words. He explained to Malraux one day: to the question of why artists never went to prison, Picasso responded that, because they could not paint there, they preferred never to venture inside.

PICASSO'S STAND

Picasso's membership in the Communist Party established the party's reputation in France as the natural family of intellectuals and artists, while bluntly reinstating an orthodox logic of political commitment, in an art scene that was having difficulty establishing its corporate image as "resisters" and its "sense of history."[63] Picasso's stand returned the refugee to the bosom of France, by making the painter a true Frenchman practicing a very French art, at least for those finally willing to admit that, in exchange, the national tradition would be advantageously turned on its head.

In 1932, Picasso had announced that the work one creates is a way of keeping a journal. But it was in 1937, with his anti-Francoist paintings, that he made his militant positions clear, though he as yet belonged to no party. "I have always believed, and still believe," he said in May of that year, "that artists who live and work in accordance with spiritual values cannot and should not remain indifferent to a conflict in which the highest values of humanity and civilization are at stake."[64] It was only after joining the Communist Party (in 1944) that he refined his position by providing justifications for his not having "painted the war," though he left to future historians the difficult task of finding in his body of work the transformations related to those circumstances. Kahnweiler, one of his most discerning critics, saw the presence of the war everywhere in Picasso's output from the dark years, even in "imperceptible things," adding that it could not be otherwise for "a great painter."[65] Other critics sought telltale signs and found them clearly inscribed in a fairly large number of particularly painful, dark, or even ironic works. We have seen how Picasso's work responded, above all, to the vagaries of his passions and of a life that did not always leave room for political events. Above all, we have noted the extent to which any given event rapidly mutated as he worked, mingling with a store of rebellion and cruelty that he could then apply to the most anodyne or familiar subjects, by dropping the initial object to concentrate on metaphorical play. Thus, the liberation of Paris that was brewing in April 1944 inspired calmer works: a profile of a young man, a female nude, a woman washing her feet, a tender portrait of his former lover Marie-Thérèse Walter. Even as battles were raging in Paris, he focused on repainting in his own manner Poussin's *The Triumph of Pan,* as a prelude to his dialogue with Velázquez, Delacroix, and Manet. Picasso seems not to have wanted to make a clear-cut choice between his baroque inspiration, violent and hardly comprehensible to the general public of the time, and the famous "current" of French culture "drawn to classic and clear form," in Pierre Daix's words.[66] But he did allow himself to drift toward something more calm and temperate, thus making it possible for his works to become part of the new national pantheon. In reality, the price Picasso paid for joining the Communist Party[67] in autumn 1944 was an allegiance of another sort, to the values of French culture that had been called into question for four years by the very fact of the occupier's presence.

To the Communist Party, conformist by nature, fell the difficult task of curbing the rebellious side of Picasso's temperament so that he could represent the revolution in a manner orthodox enough to suit the outlook of his audience. His dove series fully satisfied the apparat, as did his harmless human figures that served its struggle for peace. Only his portrait of Joseph Stalin of 1953 would cause embarrassment: it was too vigorous, too dark, too perfectly rendered, without the gloss of official pieces. The incident would have to be buried, by a return to the obligatory doves and to popular figures reminiscent of those done at the start of his career, but more vapid.[68] It was as if he had held, from the start, to an exemplary standard, which made him give the Communist Party his most innocuous works, while jealously holding on to the others, always divided between classical and baroque, peaceful and turbulent, dark and bright. In reality, the gap between his militant "intentions" and his desire to paint freely, without making direct reference to current events, widened with the news he had joined the Communist Party, which was announced to great fanfare on the front page of *L'humanité* on 5 October 1944. The news broke just before the opening of the Salon de la Libération—as that year's Salon d'Automne was officially known—which paid tribute to the artist, and well before the end of the month, when Picasso publicly explained the reasons for his act. The party could be proud of its new recruit: a symbol of the Resistance to the occupying forces (though no one ever wondered what his action had consisted of), the painter, already world famous, was joining the camp of the executed.

The news presaged the impact and significance of the Salon de la Libération, which opened the next day, on 6 October.[69] The shock registered by the public, which had come out in droves, was all the more violent. In the end, friends of the left who had not understood the freedom of *Guernica* were bewildered by his art, which they would have preferred more didactic and militant. For the conservatives on the right, Picasso's works continued to be an offense to the French tradition, incarnating more than ever the point of view of the foreigner. For the best informed, the artist's career and stature in France was appreciably changing course. By joining the Communist Party in France and by participating in an established Salon for the first time, Picasso became the first foreigner to whom such a tribute had been paid, and he was integrated with great fanfare into the French scene.

THE SALON DE LA LIBÉRATION

After four years of restrictions on thought, the influential members of the Salon d'Automne wanted to break taboos by presenting works that were more radical than usual, as witnesses to recovered freedom. Picasso had always steered clear of the event, which was too conventional for his tastes, but his young admirers had persuaded him to allow them to prepare a room in his honor.[70] Seventy-four paintings[71] and five sculptures were exhibited, most completed after 1939. Large paintings occupied pride of place, particularly *Aubade*, *Woman with Artichoke*, and *Chair with Gladiolus*. Once again, his pieces were shocking for their style and not for their subject matter, astonishing a public that had never had any real contact with his work.

Just after the exhibition opened, a few people attacked the Picasso hall. Shouting "Refund!" and "Take them down!" they removed a number of canvases, "which they would have trampled if the artists present had not snatched them from their hands."[72] They threatened to destroy the exhibited pieces without further explaining their actions. Was it a revolt against Picasso the militant, Picasso the modern painter, or Picasso the foreigner? The motives were as always mixed, each person privileging his own version of an incident that, as it happened, strengthened the victim's party. Lhote, whom we last saw in 1942 claiming, in opposition to Vlaminck, that French cubism extended far beyond the figure of Picasso, now took the side of the painter's unconditional defenders. He intervened after witnessing the event, claiming that it was an attack by "young scatterbrains with the look of Doriotists, who had better things to do than to enlist in the FFI [Forces françaises de l'intérieur], and of self-righteous middle-aged gentlemen."[73] In reality, the various versions of this event invite caution and do not rule out other interpretations. The reaction of students from the still very conservative Ecole des beaux-arts cannot be dismissed, nor can that of particular political groups. Picasso's adversaries were legion and still had their hearts set on denouncing a body of work about to be integrated into the nation's imaginary museum. After the disturbance, the gallery was well guarded by a contingent of young artists camped in front of the works. It was safeguarded as well by a published protest, bearing the distinguished names of the intelligentsia of the time: Communists such as Éluard and Aragon and non-Communists such as Sartre, François Mauriac, and even Valéry, who came forward more on principle than out of aesthetic sympathy.

At the end of the month, Picasso decided to break his silence and explain the reasons that had impelled him to join the Communist Party, seizing an opportunity given him not by the party but by the Marxist American magazine *New Masses*.[74] In the most complete justification he ever provided, he made his decision seem self-evident, something that followed naturally from his entire life and work. He deliberately confused the artistic and the political realms and shattered the image of braggart with which he had often been saddled. In the end, he imitated the surrealists, who had never stopped reiterating that the aesthetic revolution was inevitably the counterpart of a political revolution. He was, he announced, proud to say that he had "never considered painting an art of mere enjoyment, of distraction." And he added, "Through design and through color, since those were my weapons, I have tried to penetrate deeper and deeper into a knowledge of the world and of men, so that such knowledge would free us more each day.... Yes, I am aware that I have always fought, through my painting, as a true revolutionary."[75]

Picasso was thus paving the way for the future, giving himself complete freedom to conduct a battle "for internal use," whose protagonists would be only himself and painting. He accordingly dismissed in advance the possibility of letting others take over the fight in his place and, as a precaution, suggested that his art and his person were truly two distinct things: "These years of terrible oppression showed me that I had to fight not only with my art but with my person.... And so I went to the Communist Party without the slightest hesitation because, deep down, I had always been with it.... If I had not yet officially joined, it was out of 'innocence' in a way, because I believed that my work, the allegiance I felt in my heart, was sufficient; but it was already my party."[76]

Finally, Picasso laid bare the true nature of his enlistment, on behalf of a political family, a flesh-and-blood community, and, in the end, a nation, if only a temporary one. The notions of party, apparat, and political line were alien to him, auguring the future limits of his militancy. But Picasso would provide tremendous and lasting support to a milieu that included his own friends above all and to which he thus remained attached. By contrast, he abandoned the elementary militant imperatives, which were not at all part of the contract he had signed at the start. He was in such a rush, he said, to find his homeland again: "I have always been an exile. Now I am no longer; as I wait for Spain to finally be able to welcome me, the French Communist Party has opened its arms to me, and there I have found everyone I respect."[77]

Soon after the first emotional and intentionally naïve declarations came more cynical reflections from Picasso about the Communist Party. He confided to Claude Roy that he had gone there as "one goes to the source" but that over time he had come to grasp the disadvantages of that filial charge, comparing himself to a son who dreamed of being a poet when his parents saw him as a lawyer.[78]

No doubt he was likewise rather ill at ease after the liberation, when—a few days before the announcement that he had joined the Communist Party—he was asked, as one who incarnated the spirit of resistance, to preside over a commission to purge his profession.

THE PURGE

The history of the purge, in the grip of the debates still raging about individual responsibility under the occupation, deserves particular attention. Its historiography—leaving aside the cultural scene—has evolved considerably,[79] bringing the major problems to the fore once again: the purpose of the purge and the stakes involved at the time of the liberation and after; the disproportion between the acts committed and the offenses prosecuted; the difference in treatment across the various professions; the difficulty of defining what collaboration was. In fact, in addition to the human factor, the complexity of the purge subsisted in the diversity of the behaviors judged.

The justice meted out on the art scene was less spectacular than on the literary scene, which staged the major show trials, Brasillach's in particular.[80] Although writers had, for the most part, resisted in a manner just as enigmatic as that of artists, the positions writers took were often more explicit, hence easier to judge. A work of art was not governed by the same codes of legibility. Very few works clearly revealed a villainous "collaborationist" content, and even the mass producers of marshal art were unlikely to be brought to trial, given their haste, oftentimes, to promote the new political messages of the liberation. Once content was set aside as the criterion for selecting who would be purged, what remained was the individual's attitude. On the art scene as elsewhere, participants were judged less as a function of what they had actually done than by their nominal function. Hence, while art dealers who got rich at the expense of the Jews might have been considered effective agents of the collaboration, they were not brought to trial, because they were protected by their cynicism and their lack of real ideological motivations.

The civil servants in charge of fine arts were no more likely to be brought to justice, especially when they had continued to "manage" administrative affairs without taking any spectacular initiatives. By contrast, Abel Bonnard, well known for his extremism, was sentenced to death (in absentia), and Georges Hilaire, to five years in prison (in absentia), primarily for his police activities. Hilaire's support of the fine arts administration was not at issue; if anything, it counted in his favor, particularly when his action on Jean Cassou's behalf was recalled.[81] The penalties incurred by the administrative staff at museums and the fine arts administration were laughable in comparison. Georges Grappe, curator of the Musée Rodin, who had run the plastic arts section of Groupe collaboration, was relieved of his duties as curator. So too was the curator of the Musée national du château de Pau, who had distinguished himself in the affair of the Ghent altarpiece; likewise, certain minor functionaries known for the favors they had done for the occupying forces were dismissed.[82] Jacques Beltrand, an engraver, a professor at the Ecole des beaux-arts, the president of the Société des peintres-graveurs français, and a member of the professional committee of the nascent arts corporation, had served the occupier munificently by agreeing to play the part of the official appraiser charged with giving an assessment (as low as possible) of the value of the stolen collections. Although he was a true French supporter within the ranks of the looters, the tribunal of the court of justice in Paris, after launching an inquiry against him for "breaching the external security of the state" (in October 1944), closed the case without reaching a verdict: Beltrand had "unconsciously" played "the representative role that the enemy [sought] to have him play." Moreover, he had no competence in the field of appraisal—had he not valued a painting by Jan Vermeer (from the Rothschild collection) at 100,000 francs when it was worth 2 million? His judges deduced from this that his (very low) estimates had been forced out of him and that, in the end, more accurate appraisals "would not have impeded the spoliations."

Among the writers on art, Rebatet, the most loquacious, seemingly paid the price for his pamphlets and his columns in *Je suis partout*. He was found guilty, belatedly, after public condemnation had subsided, of complicity with the enemy. His death sentence was commuted to life with hard labor, and he was granted amnesty after a few years spent at Clairvaux prison.[83] By comparison, the fortunes of Jean-Marc Campagne, who might have come up on charges for serving Germany by welcoming Breker, went largely unnoticed. The case against him was weak and barely mentioned his tribute to the Third Reich's sculptor. His deposition (on 28 February 1945) begins with this little phrase, which summed up fairly well the art world's defense at the time: "I was never involved in politics." As for his notorious essay on Breker's work, he had endeavored to show in it what Breker owed to his French masters. Campagne also denied having belonged to Groupe collaboration. He was found innocent by the court of justice of the Seine. A few years later, he could be found writing a monograph on the painter Alfred Courmes, who was a part of one of the committees purging the art scene.[84] As for Séverin Faust, who was better known by the name Camille Mauclair and who had fled in August 1944, his death in April 1945 put an end to all proceedings. The case file on him, found in the archives, was hardly thick, composed of a few of his articles published in the press and largely devoid of his invectives as a longtime pamphleteer.

Did these judgments form a consensus? The purge had the peculiarity of revealing the internal tensions within the Resistance and within the new administration. The brief tenure at the Direction des beaux-arts of the Communist Joseph Billiet (where he was assisted by André Fougeron)—Billiet was very quickly replaced by Jacques Jaujard—said a great deal about the fratricidal relationship between the Communist Party and the non-Communists, between, that is, the French Communist Party, the Gaullist forces, and the different Resistance movements. In addition to these general political forces, there were rivalries between local and central agencies, and between "legal" and ad hoc purge committees.[85] Hence, the artists who were targeted complained that they had to answer to a variety of different judges who did not necessarily agree on how their "trial" would unfold.[86]

As one might expect, on the art scene, it was the Communist Party that proved the most active and radical, serving as the real driving force behind a purge movement very much focused on Paris. It followed a regular pattern, and its aftermath is still perceptible today. In general, passions flared upon the liberation, fueling the purge, then again when the surviving deportees returned to France in spring 1945. That event served as the backdrop for the Laval and Pétain trials, before things calmed down in 1946, a year before the first amnesty decrees.[87] The purge of artists, which was essentially sanctioned by the professional committees and the Comité national d'épuration des artistes peintres, dessinateurs, sculpteurs et graveurs, established on 30 May 1945,[88] reached its height with the liberation, before giving way to clemency, then to one last thrust in early 1946, and finally to the last convictions in spring of that year.

The most vehement attack came from Communist youth, the young painters of the Front national des étudiants. They issued a tract denouncing the artists who had "committed treason,... accomplices of the agents of Nazi propaganda." Despiau, Derain, Dunoyer de Segonzac, Friesz, Vlaminck, van Dongen, Legueult, Oudot, Belmondo, "and those gentlemen of official art," Landowski, Bouchard, and Lejeune, having been solicited by the Reichsministerium für Volksaufklärung und Propaganda, had all "dishonored [themselves] by agreeing to participate in a trip to Germany." Once there, "the herd was trotted out across the Reich, and on its return was eager to publish in the rotten press statements of friendship and admiring gratitude." Because they had pledged "the prestige of French art" along with their own reputations, it was "intolerable that the Comité du Salon d'Automne, which met on 7 September [1944] for a purge session, did not judge it proper to exclude a single one of these artists." Calling for "the total purge," "here and everywhere," the young Communists set forth criteria for judgment sufficiently precise to make a minority of artists feel that they were being targeted: those who had gone on the trip to Germany, those who had participated in Groupe collaboration, and, finally, those who had "worked for the enemy," a fuzzier notion.

The young Communists' wish to see a national committee of painters and sculptors formed by "all patriotic artists" was soon granted—by the Communist Party, which oversaw the events that followed. On 3 October 1944, the steering committee of the Front national des arts, with Picasso as its chair, asked the public prosecutor for the arrest and trial

> of artists who by their attitude of collaboration with the enemy gravely compromised the good name of French art.... Henri Bouchard, sculptor, 25, rue de l'Yvette, Paris (16th), member of the Institut [de France], former president of Artistes français, who participated in the propaganda trip to Germany, served on the Arno Brecker [*sic*] honor committee, and was president of the plastic arts section of Groupe collaboration. Othon Friesz, painter, rue Notre-Dame-des-Champs, Paris (6th), vice president of the Salon des Tuileries, who participated in the propaganda trip to Germany, served on the Arno Brecker honor committee, and was vice president of the plastic arts section of Groupe collaboration. Paul Belmondo, sculptor, 77, rue Denfert-Rochereau, Paris, member of the Salon des Tuileries committee, who participated in the propaganda trip to Germany, served

> on the Arno Brecker honor committee, and was vice president of the plastic arts section of Groupe collaboration. Paul Landowski, sculptor, 12, rue Max-Blondat, Boulogne-s[ur]-Seine, member of the Institut [de France], who participated in the propaganda trip to Germany and served on the Arno Brecker honor committee. Jacques Beltrand, engraver, 3, rue Max-Blondat, Boulogne-sur-Seine, president of the Société des [peintres-]graveurs français, member of the [Salon des] Tuileries committee, appraiser on behalf of the German authorities for the acquisition of works of art for the Reich. Jean-Marc Campagne, art critic, 25, place de la Madeleine, Paris, vice president of his section of Groupe collaboration, author of Nazi propaganda brochures against French art. Camille Mauclair, art writer, 98, rue du Cherche-Midi, Paris, president of his section of Groupe collaboration, author of Nazi propaganda brochures against French art.[89]

Among the impromptu judges assembled were Communists such as Fougeron, Pignon, and Picasso, but above all there were fellow travelers who may or may not have participated in Resistance activities: Montagnac, Goerg, and Pierre Ladureau, who had contributed to the album *Vaincre*, sold to benefit the Francs-tireurs et partisans; Brianchon, Emmanuel Auricoste, Desnoyer, Walch, Georges Emile Capon, Gruber, Camille Berg, and Roger Eskenazi, who had not particularly distinguished themselves as resisters; and, finally, Lhote, who had defended "orthodox" cubist and nationalist positions, and Courmes, a former member of Jeune France, who had maintained his anarchistic views.

The committee's head, André Fougeron, legitimated by his actions for the Resistance and his stint on the staff of the fine arts directorate under Billiet, took his duties seriously enough to open an independent investigation of those accused. The association of those individuals with the Salon d'Automne, whose committee had opted for clemency in early September, was an invitation to take a close look at the career of each. The initial accusatory tenor rapidly softened in a written text. The committee changed its mind about calling for arrests before an investigation, and now envisioned "clearing up a murky atmosphere and distinguishing errors from offenses as soon as possible."[90]

The initial conclusions already presaged the outcome and the preponderance of "errors" over "offenses." Belmondo had been registered as a member of Groupe collaboration unbeknownst to him, and he vehemently protested against that liberty taken with his name. Friesz also claimed on his honor that he had been enrolled in error in the group by Grappe. Jacques Beltrand and Campagne had recently cleared themselves of the activities for which they were criticized. Ultimately, the possibility of redemption was held out. In the case of Landowski, for example, one could point to his "admirable activity on behalf of students threatened with deportation," which served to counterbalance his trip to Germany and his support of the Breker committee.[91]

When we last saw Landowski, he was director of the Ecole des beaux-arts and had agreed to go to Germany, believing he would have prisoners released but knowing himself condemned in advance for his decision. Thanks to his journal, we find him again in 1944, confiding his anger—and his remorse. He tells of his reunions with his previously outcast Jewish friends; the judgment of his comrades; the nauseating sight of those who had sincerely made their peace with the occupying forces; the impossibility, now, of speaking or writing freely to denounce what he did not like; his examinations as witness and accused during the purge inquiries; his enthusiasm for de Gaulle; his "shame...at not foreseeing it," at having shaken the hand of a German and gone to Germany; his impression that all his "troubles" of the moment were, after all, well justified.[92]

He bowed with good grace to the successive summonses from the purge commissions. During the fourth examination, in November 1945, he saw evaporate all the reasons that had led him to agree to go to Germany. He felt he had ill-served the memory of the historical figures who had formed the nation, and whom he was then depicting in the embroidery on the gown of his latest statue, *France*. On 22 November, he noted that the session had gone well and that, when it was over, all the members of the commission had stood to shake his hand before leaving. On 25 November, he had a talk with Dunoyer de Segonzac, who suggested to him that the "campaign against the trip to Germany originated in the cubist contingent of the Salon d'Automne" and that the press found it impossible to print a single line criticizing the Front national. In February 1946, apparently at Fougeron's initiative, Landowski was again obliged to answer not for the trip but for his participation in the events surrounding the Breker exhibition, particularly those at the Musée Rodin, under the auspices of Groupe collaboration. Finally, the verdicts were reached.

Landowski's final impression was that "the commission was composed of good people who, in some cases, [had] been very indulgent.... In others, too harsh perhaps." Finally, on 6 April 1946, the artist received confirmation that he was exonerated and indicated he was "excessively satisfied," thinking that, this time, it was all "really over." The previous day, his wife had attended a lecture on the matter by Minister of Justice Pierre-Henri Teitgen, during which he had declared that "all purge cases would be closed in July."

In substance, Teitgen had suggested on that day that the "collaborators" had gone astray less by being supporters of Fascism or Nazism than by behaving like traitors to the nation and to "its soul," composed of that long heritage of Christian humanism, of that belief we all have in a natural right that governs men, families, governments, nations, and states, and that, for everyone, discerns... good and evil, honor.... It is composed of that fundamental belief in the primacy of man.... It is composed—that French tradition, that French vocation—of that faith that drives us all, of the basic qualities of men of all colors, all races, all nations, and all beliefs, of all territories and all horizons. It is composed of that vocation, of that sense of the universal.... And yet, the acceptance of the policy of collaboration resulted in all those values being forgotten.... It was the betrayal of the very core of France's strength. What [the collaborators] did was not a political error, it was not a false policy, it was a disavowal of our country's very reasons for existence.[93]

In the art world, the purge, despite its deficiencies, restored the sector's capacity to openly judge uncivic and "anti-French" actions. By putting to one side the broader responsibility of all those who continued to work despite the villainous laws and the climate of oppression, the sanctions imposed were meant to be exemplary. Just like the overall purge, they dealt a deathblow to the true extremists (Mauclair and Rebatet) and unleashed the need for revenge—and for violence—against those who, even without ideological purpose, had gone off with the occupiers. In other words, most often, they served less as actual reparation for the real victims of that era than as an exorcism for all who, most of the time, had been content to lament while biding their time.

The time for reconstruction had begun, and the artistic schedule was full. The upshot was the normalization of the social status of artists, which would slowly come into line with that of the rest of the population; the emphasis on the patrimony of the modern tradition, by Jean Cassou, who had returned to the Musée national d'art moderne and who proclaimed the need to reconcile "art and the nation";[94] the diffusion and decentralization of art initiated by the Front populaire and, above all, Jeune France; and, finally, the restored sense of pride in the French art world and the certainty that it would win back its worldwide supremacy, even as the economic and cultural war that threatened was giving the advantage to New York City.[95] Strengthened by European emigration, that city would henceforth benefit from an unprecedented displacement, definitively settling its score with an Ecole de Paris exhausted by the war. Defeat and dictatorship had forced Europe into exile and submission, and it would take some forty years for it to recover from the bloodletting.

NOTES

1. See Louis Parrot, *L'intelligence en guerre: Panorama de la pensée française dans la clandestinité* (Paris: La Jeune Parque, 1945); Jacques Debû-Bridel,

La résistance intellectuelle (Paris: Julliard, 1970); Vercors, "La résistance intellectuelle," in Jacques Meyer, ed., *Vie et mort des Français, 1939–1945* (Paris: Hachette, 1971); Claude Greis, "L'idée de 'résistance intellectuelle' à travers les revues *Fontaine, Poètes casqués, Poésie 40* et *Les lettres françaises,* de leur création à la Libération" (M.A. thesis, Université Paris IV–Paris Sorbonne, 1972); Pierre Seghers, *La Résistance et ses poètes, France 1940–1945* (Paris: Seghers, 1974); Jacques Gaucheron, *La poésie, la Résistance, du Front populaire à la Libération* (Paris: Les Editeurs Français Réunis, 1979); *La littérature française sous l'Occupation: Actes du Colloque de Reims (30 septembre–1er et 2 octobre 1981),* 2 vols. (Rheims: Presses Universitaires de Reims, 1989); James Steel, *Littératures de l'ombre: Récits et nouvelles de la Résistance, 1940–1944* (Paris: Presses de la Fondation Nationale des Sciences Politiques, 1991).

2. No statistical study on the Resistance by professional sector is as yet usable. The existing data must be considered with caution: for example, the list by professional category (in percentages) of those in an R.S. military network who were shot (266 authorized networks, including 254 fighting units), in which artists occupy the penultimate position, wedged between teachers and women with no profession. See Marie-Madeleine Fourcade, "Les réseaux," in Jacques Meyer, ed., *Vie et mort des Français, 1939–1945* (Paris: Hachette, 1971), appendix 1, 355.

3. Somewhat paradoxically, Jean Moulin, the head of the French Resistance charged by de Gaulle with uniting the covert fighters, camouflaged his clandestine activities by opening Galerie Romain—at 22, rue de France in Nice—which he entrusted to the intrepid Colette Dreyfus (Colette Jacques at the time), with whom he traveled, ostensibly in search of works of art, but actually on Resistance missions. The inauguration of his gallery, which he wanted to be legitimate, took place in February 1943 (see the Nice newspaper *La page*). The gallery displayed modern works from Moulin's personal collection and from those of dealers (sometimes exiled Jews): Gustave Courbet, Degas, Forain, Giorgio de Chirico, Maurice Utrillo, Tal-Coat, Dufy, Rouault, and so on, but also Friesz (who had gone on the trip to Germany in 1941).

   On 16 July 1943, Jacques received a telegram: "Sell as agreed." She was to flee and evacuate the collection: Moulin had been arrested. The occupying forces were there the next day; see Michelle Michel, *Exposition Résistance-déportation: Création dans le bruit des armes,* exh. cat. (Paris: Chancellerie de l'Ordre de la Libération, 1980), cat. no. 722.

   On that gallery, see the Colette Dreyfus archives; and Michel, *Exposition Résistance-déportation* (this note), cat. nos. 719–22, which reference Moulin's handwritten letter of 16 October 1942 to the prefect of the Alpes-Maritimes soliciting his authorization to open a gallery, as well as

Friesz's *Bec-de-l'Aigle at La Ciotat*, oil on canvas, 38.5 × 46.8 cm (private collection of Jean Moulin; bequest by Laure Moulin to the Musée des beaux-arts de Béziers), which was on display at *Exposition Résistance-déportation.*

On Moulin's artistic life, see Daniel Cordier, *Jean Moulin: L'inconnu du Panthéon*, vol. 1, *Une ambition pour la République, juin 1899–juin 1936* (Paris: J.-C. Lattès, 1989), esp. 465–72. On Moulin's brief life as a "dealer," we await the remainder of Cordier's biography, to be published. [The third volume, covering the period of November 1940 through December 1941, appeared in 1993.—Trans.]

After giving the press a few drawings, Moulin, who was employed by the prefectural administration, exhibited his works for the first time, under the name "Romarin," at the Salon de Chambéry of 1922. He had moved toward a quick or lively art and the appropriate techniques: pen, pencil, charcoal, pastel, watercolor.

4. Lucien Rebatet, "Le Salon des Tuileries," *Je suis partout*, 23 June 1944, 4.
5. Rebatet, "Le Salon des Tuileries" (note 4), 4.
6. See Pascal Ory, "La politique culturelle du Front populaire français (1935–1938)," 5 vols. (Ph.D. diss., Université Paris X–Nanterre, 1990).
7. Created by the painter Saint-Maur in 1934 and defended by Jean Cassou and the critics Louis Chéronnet and Jean-Marc Campagne (future author of the introduction to the Breker exhibition at the Orangerie), L'art mural was led by Saint-Maur, Colette Rodde, and R. Schoedelin; Jean Cassou (vice president); and Amédée Ozenfant, who was also the director of his own academy. L'art mural was supported by an eclectic and prestigious honorary committee, composed of Pierre Bonnard, Jean Carlu, Chagall, Paul Colin, Derain, Dufy, Gromaire, Max Jacob, Kandinsky, Lhote, Lipchitz, Malraux, Marquet, Anatole de Monzie, Perret, Henri de Régnier, Henri Sellier, and Zadkine.
8. A year later it was called the Association des peintres, sculpteurs, dessinateurs, graveurs de la Maison de la culture; then Association des peintres et sculpteurs de la Maison de la culture.
9. Lhote also ran his own academy and at the time was beginning his *Traité du paysage*, which was published in 1939.
10. Lurçat was editor in chief of *Russie d'aujourd'hui* and contributed to *Cahiers du bolchévisme* in 1938, before editing a Communist provincial daily after the liberation.
11. André Malraux; quoted in Ory, "La politique culturelle" (note 6), 496, 497.
12. See Jean Cassou, "La liberté dans l'art," *Peintres et sculpteurs de la Maison de la culture*, February 1938; quoted in Ory, "La politique culturelle" (note 6), 498.
13. See Louis Chéronnet, "Popularisation," *Le musée vivant par l'APAM*, no. 4 (May 1937); and Ory, "La politique culturelle" (note 6), 500.
14. See Louis Aragon, review of Gisèle Freund's *La photographie en France au*

dix-neuvième siècle (Paris: La Maison des Amis des Livre, A. Monnier, 1936), *Commune*, June 1936, 1267; quoted in Ory, "La politique culturelle" (note 6), 511.

15. In 1937, fourteen hundred students and two schools were located there. See Ory, "La politique culturelle" (note 6), 554.
16. See Ory, "La politique culturelle" (note 6), 597ff.
17. See Ory, "La politique culturelle" (note 6), 507.
18. A category with uncertain boundaries, whose representatives we define, by convention, as having emerged after the liberation; they remained obscure during the occupation.
19. See the visitors book for the Galerie Jeanne-Bucher, 53, rue de Seine, Paris.
20. See Elodie Vitale, "Le Bauhaus et la République de Weimar: Trois fermetures," in Pierre Milza and Fanette Roche-Pézard, eds., *Art et fascisme: Totalitarisme et résistance au totalitarisme dans les arts en Italie, Allemagne et France des années 30 à la défaite de l'Axe* (Brussels: Editions Complexe, 1989).
21. According to Magnelli's remarks on Kandinsky; quoted in Michel, *Exposition Résistance-déportation* (note 3), cat. no. 499.
22. See Christian Derouet and Jessica Boissel, eds., *Kandinsky: Oeuvres de Vassily Kandinsky (1866–1944)*, exh. cat. (Paris: Centre Georges Pompidou, 1984).
23. After the visit of the Propaganda-Staffel Paris, whose representatives threatened to return, Domela was given the task of taking home his own canvases as well as those of Kandinsky.
24. See Gerhard Heller's account, in his *Un Allemand à Paris, 1940–1944* (Paris: Editions du Seuil, 1981), 121.
25. Francis Ponge, *Note sur les otages, peintures de Fautrier* (Paris: Pierre Seghers, 1946).
26. Jean Paulhan, *Fautrier l'enragé* (Paris: Gallimard, 1962), 34.
27. Daniel Wallard, "Les arts:... Les otages de Fautrier," *Poésie*, no. 29 (1946): 89.
28. Ponge, *Note sur les otages* (note 25).
29. See Michel Fauré, *Histoire du surréalisme sous l'Occupation: Les réverbères–La main à plume* (Paris: La Table Ronde, 1982); the documentation of which Fauré availed himself, particularly the dossier compiled by Nadine Lefébure for France-Culture, winter 1965–66; José Pierre, "La Seconde Guerre mondiale et le deuxième souffle du surréalisme," in *Paris 1937–Paris 1957: Créations en France*, exh. cat. (Paris: Centre Georges Pompidou, 1981), 136–40.
30. See the text by Jean-François Chabrun, "*Entartete Kunst*," *Les réverbères*, no. 3 (1938): 1–2.
31. See their open letter to Les réverbères of March 1939, and the group's

response, signed by most of its members, published in *Les réverbères*, no. 4 (1939): 1.

32. In 1940: *Cheval à quatre*, 12 pp., edition of 32, texts and illustrations by Henri Bernard, Simone Bry, Aline Gagnaire, Maurice Frédéric, Jean Jausion, and Michel Tapié; *Dédale*, 12 pp., edition of 31, texts and illustrations by Noël Arnaud, Henri Bernard, Simone Bry, Maurice Frédéric, Aline Gagnaire, Jean Jausion, Jean Marembert, Loys Masson, André Poujet, and Michel Tapié. In 1941: *Huit poèmes pour Cécile*, 32 pp., edition of about 150, text by Noël Arnaud, illustrations by Aline Gagnaire and Michel Tapié.

33. *L'enfant au visage* became *L'enfant au visage de vent.*

34. Actually Clément Pansaert.

35. See Jean-Marc Campagne, "La république des arts," *Les nouveaux temps*, 30 July 1941, 3.

36. "Un incident à l'Institut d'études des questions juives," *Les nouveaux temps*, 30 July 1941, 2.

37. For the title, Gérard de Sède was inspired by a line from "Mauvais sang" in Arthur Rimbaud's *Une saison en enfer* (1873): "La main à plume vaut la main à charrue" (The hand with a pen is as good as the hand on a plow).

38. Jean-François Chabrun had been incarcerated by the French authorities in spring 1940, after circulating a book containing a political tract against the occupation and the Vichy regime. After additional searches, Benjamin Péret, Léo Malet, and Bruno Stenberg were imprisoned as well. They were released after the bombing of Rennes, just before the arrival of German troops. Malet was intercepted by the occupying forces as he was returning to Paris and sent to Germany, where he remained a prisoner for a year and a half.

39. Only the names of the printer and agent (*dépositaire*) actually appeared: respectively, Cario and Marc Patin (who had served as an intermediary between the two surrealist groups before they merged); then Noël Arnaud, who replaced Patin.

40. Issue dated December 1941–March 1942, 32 pp., 400 copies printed, including 20 deluxe copies.

41. See Fauré, *Histoire du surréalisme* (note 29), 116. On this point, see the account given by André Thirion, interview by Laurence Bertrand Dorléac, 12 January 1983, Paris, in Laurence Bertrand Dorléac, "Art, culture et société: L'exemple des arts plastiques à Paris entre 1940 et 1944" (habilitation thesis, Institut d'études politiques de Paris, 1990), 2:665.

42. See *Magritte*, preface by Marcel Mariën (Brussels: Editions "La Boétie"/Les Auteurs Associés, 1943).

43. Maurice Henry, born in Cambrai in 1907, had participated in the surrealist group Le grand jeu (which published an eponymous journal) between 1928 and 1931.

44. Fauré, *Histoire du surréalisme* (note 29), 139.

45. See Jacques Villeglé, *Urbi et Orbi* (Mâcon, France: Editions W, 1986).

46. See Sergeĭ Chakhotin, *Le viol des foules par la propagande politique*, rev. ed. (Paris: Gallimard, 1952). First published in French in 1939.

47. In Morse code, the resisters' *V* is composed of three dots and a dash, which echoes, as mentioned by Jean Guéhenno in his *Journal*, the distinctive opening motif of Ludwig van Beethoven's Symphony no. 5 in C Minor, op. 67. The occupying forces hoisted large white flags adorned with a monumental *V* and put up red posters with a black *V* above the swastika, but to no avail: the French continued to cut out *V*'s, *H*'s (for "honneur"), and crosses of Lorraine from their metro tickets, with which the sidewalks of Paris were strewn. See Jean Guéhenno, *Journal des années noires (1940–1944)* (Paris: Gallimard, 1947), 125 (entry for 30 June 1941), 140 (entry for 17 August 1941).

48. Handbills reproduced in Philippe Buton, "La contre-propagande de la Résistance intérieure et extérieure," in Laurent Gervereau and Denis Peschanski, eds., *La propagande sous Vichy, 1940–1944*, exh. cat. (Nanterre: Bibliothèque de Documentation Internationale Contemporaine, 1990), 243. [The Relève was a program that recruited French workers to go to Germany in exchange for French POWs and as replacements for German workers serving in the military.—Trans.]

49. In answer to the official poster, by the artist Phili, was an anonymous hand-drawn poster calling on mothers to demonstrate "Pour le pain et la liberté" (For bread and freedom) on 31 May 1942. For both posters, see Buton, "La contre-propagande" (note 48), 243.

50. This Roneographed work is reproduced in Buton, "La contre-propagande" (note 48), 241.

51. Reproduced in Buton, "La contre-propagande" (note 48), 244, 246.

52. The Front national des arts was dissolved in 1946 and replaced by the Union des arts plastiques, which was associated with the Union nationale des intellectuels.

53. The Front national came into being at the home of the exiled Jacques Lipchitz, where Pignon was living. Armed by General Henri Giraud, the organization fomented the insurrection of Corsica in September 1943. Its leadership was composed of Pierre Villon, Georges Maranne, Irène Joliot-Curie, Justin Godart, and Monsignor Chevrot. For Pignon's account of the first meetings, see Debû-Bridel, *La résistance intellectuelle* (note 1), 217–29.

54. Fougeron was among those mobilized on the Belgian border and was imprisoned in Stenay, from which he escaped to the free zone before being demobilized and returning to Paris. The underground leader of the Front national des arts (under the name "Marcel"), he was officially the assistant of Jacques Villon, who produced, for the Galerie Louis Carré between

1942 and 1946, a series of lithographs after watercolors by Pierre Bonnard. Fougeron would become secretary general of the Union des arts plastiques from its creation in 1945 until 1950 and incarnated the French version of socialist realism.

On Fougeron, and on realism and political engagement more generally, see Simone Flandin, "André Fougeron: Le parti pris du réalisme 1948–1953" (M.A. thesis, Université Blaise Pascal–Clermont-Ferrand II, 1982); *André Fougeron: Pièces détachées, 1937–1987*, exh. cat. (Paris: Galerie Jean-Jacques Dutko, 1987); Boris Taslitzky, introduction to *Fougeron: De 1936 à aujourd'hui*, exh. cat. ([Gentilly]: Editions Musée de la Résistance Nationale, 1992). On his socialist-realist choices, and on artists and the Communist Party more generally, see Anatole Jacovsky, "Quelques mots sur quelques tableaux d'André Fougeron," *Le point*, no. 36 (1947); Louis Aragon, preface to *Dessins de Fougeron* (Paris: Editions Les 13 Epis, 1947); Pierre Daix, *Nouvelle critique et art moderne: Essai* (Paris: Editions du Seuil, 1968); Roger Garaudy, *Pour un réalisme du XXe siècle: Dialogue posthume avec Fernand Léger* (Paris: Editions Bernard Grasset, 1968); Andreĭ Aleksandrovich Zhdanov, *Sur la littérature, la philosophie et la musique* (Paris: Editions Norman Bethune, 1970); Vladimir Il'ich Lenin, *Sur l'art et la littérature*, ed. Jean-Michel Palmier, 3 vols. (Paris: Union Générale d'Editions, 1975–76); Avner Ziss, *Eléments d'esthétique marxiste*, trans. Antoine Garcia (Moscow: Editions du Progrès, 1977); Marc Lazar, "Le réalisme socialiste aux couleurs de la France," *L'histoire*, no. 43 (1982); Jeannine Verdès-Leroux, *Au service du parti: Le parti communiste, les intellectuels et la culture (1944–1956)* (Paris: Fayard/Editions de Minuit, 1983); Dominique Berthet, *Le P.C.F., la culture et l'art (1947–1954)* (Paris: La Table Ronde, 1990); Ory, "La politique culturelle" (note 6); Sarah G. Wilson, "Art and the Politics of the Left in France, c. 1935–1955" (Ph.D. diss., Courtauld Institute of Art, University of London, 1991).

55. Created and presented at the Vélodrome d'Hiver in October 1937.

56. *L'art français* was subtitled "Organe des comités de peintres, sculpteurs, graveurs du Front national de lutte pour l'indépendance de la France," and there were five issues: no. 1 (1941), no. 2 (October 1942), no. 3 (November 1942), no. 4 (November 1943), no. 5 (March 1944). The press run was between 1,500 and 2,000 copies for each issue. Founder: Joseph Billiet; editors: Desnoyer, Goerg, Fougeron, Montagnac, Walch. The review was initially printed at Fougeron's home, 3, rue Marcel-Sembat; in 1942, after the arrest of a Resistance liaison agent, it was printed at the home of Paul Goyard, a painter and decorative artist associated with the Communist Party since 1936. After the liberation, *L'art français* became the "revue mensuelle des arts plastiques," *Arts de France*. On that new review, see Jean-Philippe Chimot, "Avatars de la théorie de l'art dans *Arts de France* (1945–1949)," in *Art et idéologies: L'art en Occident, 1945–1949* (Saint-Étienne: Centre Interdisciplinaire d'Etudes & de Recherches sur l'Expression Contemporaine, 1978), 145–58.

57. "Propos d'un amateur," *L'art français*, no. 3 (1942).

58. "Propos d'un amateur" (note 57).

59. André Fougeron, *Rue de Paris*, 1943, oil on canvas, 130 × 95 cm.

60. Works by other artists were to have been included in the project: Maurice Denis had died in the meantime; Jean Amblard was detained by the regional branch of Arts et traditions populaires in Auvergne; and Desnoyer (at Montauban), Marquet (in Algiers), Gromaire (at Aubusson), and Lurçat (at Saint-Céré) could not submit their works because of circumstances.

61. [*Bougnaparte* is a portmanteau word combining "Bonaparte" and *bougnat*, "coal merchant," used to refer to natives of Auvergne.—Trans.]

62. See the "preface," issued after the album's publication, by Joseph Billiet ("Raoul" in the underground), director general of the fine arts administration after the liberation, in *La Marseillaise*, 28 September 1944, 1.

63. See Louis Parrot, "Picasso au Salon," *Les lettres françaises*, 7 October 1944, 7.

64. Jean Leymarie, *Picasso: Métamorphoses et unité* (Geneva: Skira, 1971), 100.

65. See Daniel-Henry Kahnweiler, *Mes galeries et mes peintres: Entretiens avec François Crémieux* (Paris: Gallimard, 1961), 191.

66. Pierre Daix, *La vie de peintre de Pablo Picasso* (Paris: Editions du Seuil, 1977), 313. [The current location of Picasso's *The Triumph of Pan, after Poussin* (1944)—which is sometimes called *Bacchanale*—is unknown; Poussin's *The Triumph of Pan* (1635–36) is at the National Gallery, London.—Trans.]

67. Éluard supposedly announced to his friends a month after the liberation that the news about Picasso joining the Communist Party would be made public shortly.

68. See in particular Picasso's *The Clown*, published in 1957 on the front page of *L'humanité dimanche*.

69. The Salon d'Automne of 1944 ran until 5 November, at the Petit Palais, described on the catalog as the "Palais des beaux-arts de la Ville de Paris, avenu[e] de Tokyo et avenue du Président Wilson."

70. These were artists exhibiting at the Salon d'Automne: Fougeron, Montagnac,...

71. Or seventy-five, depending on the source.

72. See André Lhote's articles for the arts page (p. 7) of the issues of *Les lettres françaises* for 16, 23, 30 September and 14, 29 October 1944.

73. See André Lhote, "Quand les 'collaborateurs' se font critiques d'art," *Les lettres françaises*, 14 October 1944, 7; and Parrot, "Picasso au Salon" (note 63).

74. His declarations, contained in a cable he "sent specially to *New Masses*," were first published as Pablo Picasso, "Why I Became a Communist," *New Masses*, 24 October 1944, 11; and then in fuller form in Pol Gaillard, "Pourquoi j'ai adhéré au parti communiste: Une interview de Picasso à la revue américaine *New Masses*," *L'humanité*, 29–30 October 1944, 1–2. *New Masses* took orthodox Communist positions and had been used to support the Communist Party in a violent campaign against Leon Trotsky in the 1930s. See Serge Guilbaut, *Comment New York vola l'idée d'art moderne: Expressionnisme abstrait, liberté et guerre froide* (Nîmes: Editions Jacqueline Chambon, 1983), 26.

75. Gaillard, "Pourquoi j'ai adhéré" (note 74), 1, 2.

76. Gaillard, "Pourquoi j'ai adhéré" (note 74), 2.

77. Gaillard, "Pourquoi j'ai adhéré" (note 74), 2.

78. See Claude Roy, *Nous* (Paris: Gallimard, 1972), 369.

79. On the question of individual responsibility, the archives relating to the purge are incomplete. See, in the Archives nationales, series Z (subject to restrictions), which contains the archives of the court of justice of the Seine; and the few archives from the purge commissions included in series F 21, on the fine arts. See also the journals and private archives of artists, those of André Fougeron in particular; the overview by Henry Rousso, "L'épuration en France: Une histoire inachevée," *Vingtième siècle*, no. 33 (1992); and Claude Lévy and Dominique Veillon, "L'épuration en France: Approche bibliographique," *Bulletin de l'Institut d'histoire du temps présent*, no. 4 (1981).

On the purge of the cultural scene, see Pierre Assouline, *L'épuration des intellectuels: 1944–1945* (Brussels: Editions Complexe, 1985). See in particular, in his appendix 5, the list of 148 undesirable writers compiled (primarily for internal use) by the Comité national des écrivains, which included—among those who concern us here—the names of Abel Bonnard, Jacques Benoist-Méchin, Pierre Drieu La Rochelle, Pierre d'Espezel, Camille Mauclair, George Montandon, Anatole de Monzie, Lucien Rebatet, André Salmon, and Maurice de Vlaminck. See also Pascal Mercier, "Le Comité national des écrivains, 1941–1944" (thesis, Université Sorbonne Nouvelle–Paris III, 1980).

On newspaper illustrators, see Christian Delporte, "Dessinateurs de presse et dessin politique en France des années 1920 à la Libération," 4 vols. (Ph.D. diss., Institut d'études politiques de Paris, 1991). On theater, see Serge Added, *Le théâtre dans les années-Vichy, 1940–1944* (Paris: Editions Ramsay, 1992), 311–17.

80. A number of artists signed a petition addressed to General de Gaulle supporting Brasillach's petition for reprieve. Desvallières signed, as did Vlaminck and Derain, who were themselves targeted by the purge committees.

81. Abel Bonnard and Georges Hilaire were convicted on 4 July 1945 and 7 March 1947, respectively, by the Haute Cour de Justice, which was established by the order of 18 November 1944 and composed of three magistrates and twenty-four jurors chosen by the members of the Assemblée consultative provisoire of Algiers. This court tried 108 state ministers and senior civil servants, the head of state, and the head of the government. On the Haute Cour de Justice, see Raymond Lindon and Daniel Amson, *La Haute Cour, 1789–1987* (Paris: Presses Universitaires de France, 1987).

82. Both the deputy chief clerk and the auditor of the fine arts administration were relieved of their duties.

83. Rebatet's novel *Les deux étendards* was published by Gallimard in 1951. Rebatet regularly wrote for the right-wing and far right-wing press under his own name as well as under the pseudonym François Vinneuil.

84. Jean-Marc Campagne, *Alfred Courmes: Prospecteur de mirages entre ciel et chair* (Paris: Éric Losfeld, 1973).

85. On political forces in France after the liberation, see Philippe Buton and Jean-Marie Guillon, *Les pouvoirs en France à la Libération* (Paris: Belin, 1994); Comité d'histoire de la 2e Guerre mondiale, *La Libération de la France: Actes du colloque international tenu à Paris du 28 au 31 octobre 1974* (Paris: Editions du Centre National de la Recherche Scientifique, 1976); Jean-Pierre Rioux, *La France de la IVe République*, vol. 1, *L'ardeur et la nécessité, 1944–1952* (Paris: Editions du Seuil, 1980). On the party, see Philippe Buton, "Le Parti communiste français à la Libération: Stratégie et implantation," 2 vols. (Ph.D. diss., Université Paris I–Sorbonne, 1988).

86. On this matter, see Paul Landowski's unpublished journal. The major figures on the art scene were judged by the Haute Cour de Justice (Abel Bonnard and Georges Hilaire), by the court of justice of the Seine (Jacques Beltrand, Othon Friesz, Jean-Marc Campagne, and Camille Mauclair), or, in most cases, solely by the professional committees.

87. Amnesties continued to be granted from 1947 to 1953.

88. The courts of justice were set up in accordance with the order of June 1944 at de Gaulle's request, in order to keep the purge from being sanctioned only by military tribunals. Two other bodies were also convened to judge the guilty parties: the civic chambers (order of 28 August 1944) and the Haute Cour de Justice (order of 18 November 1944).

These courts of justice consisted of a magistrate and four jurors chosen by the local Comité départemental de Libération from the citizens who had distinguished themselves by "demonstrating their national feeling." The courts were often criticized for lapses in their procedural rules, particularly where the defense was concerned. It is still difficult to establish with accuracy a numerical assessment of this purge sanctioned by the courts of justice. Generally, the figure of about 350,000 individuals who faced legal charges is advanced, based not on the number of cases in which a judgment was handed down but on the number of cases handed over to the legal authorities. In addition, 124,613 people were to be judged by the courts of justice, with a conviction rate of slightly more than 76 percent.

See Rousso, "L'épuration en France" (note 79). On the legal foundations for the purge, see Émile Garçon, *Code pénal annoté*, vol. 1, *Art. 1 à 294*, ed. Marcel Rousselet, Maurice Patin, and Marc Ancel (Paris: Recueil Sirey, 1952).

89. Document, private archives; reproduced in the third volume of Bertrand Dorléac, "Art, culture et société" (note 41).

90. Undated document signed by Auricoste, Berg, Jean Eugène Bersier, Brianchon, Capon, Courmes, Desnoyer, Fougeron, Goerg, Gruber, Lhote, Montagnac, Pignon, Marc Saint-Saëns, and Walch. Note the disappearance of the names Picasso, Ladureau, and Eskenazi, and the appearance of those of Bersier and Saint-Saëns. Document, private archives; reproduced in the third volume of Bertrand Dorléac, "Art, culture et société" (note 41).

91. Exhibits relating to the defense of artists accused of collaboration, André Fougeron's private archives.

92. For these reflections, see the unpublished journal of Paul Landowski for the years 1944 to 1946.

93. Pierre-Henri Teitgen, *Les cours de justice, conférence prononcée le vendredi 5 avril 1946 au théâtre Marigny sous les auspices des Conférences des ambassadeurs* (Paris: Editions du Mail, 1946), 16.

94. See the first issue, published in December 1945, of the review *Arts de France*, which was linked to the Communist Party.

95. See Guilbaut, *Comment New York vola l'idée* (note 74); and Serge Guilbaut, *Reconstructing Modernism: Art in New York, Paris, and Montreal, 1945–1964* (Cambridge, Mass.: MIT Press, 1990).

CONCLUSION

In looking back, let us keep in mind the exceptional character of these four years of gestation, despite their substantial continuities with what came before and after. History put an end, finally, to the Nazi plan to impose military discipline on a French society that was undoubtedly more recalcitrant than we have indicated but was held at bay by an increasingly violent regime. In the realm of art, the significant episodes of the time portended the worst abuses of the era.

France was treated by the occupiers like a fief to be pillaged at will but gifted in the area of the arts. It was still "decadent" but was about to undergo its cultural revolution, after decades of democracy and artistic modernity that had placed it in the forefront of European consciousness. History will not soon forget Vlaminck's public criticism of himself and his time. His dark and thickly painted landscapes acknowledged the death of the moment, the end of color, the desolate terrain. He turned against his youthful fauvism the way his compatriots buried the hopes raised by the early part of the century. After the first cataclysm, of 1914 to 1918, artists had begun to believe in disaster, repeatedly issuing warnings and statements of principle. Until 1939, political debate often took the place of works of art, which were already marked by the stamp of restrictions and the moral order. There was a tremendous need to settle the social question of the function of art via an authoritarian summoning of artists to account. Vichy, and all who continued to express themselves after the defeat, would try to resolve that question by every available means. Indeed, it was during the dark years and the dictatorial Vichy regime that the major reform of art and artists came about—corporatism, a reappraisal of the educational system, an increase in the powers of the Institut de France, the exclusion of symbols of "decadence" and of continuous movement, the irrational quest for a strong identity and a strong social bond, the return to unadulterated Frenchness, and tired depictions of the leader.

In political terms, this would be seen as the revenge of the "outcasts" of 1936, as involving not only the triumph of the rightists over the Front populaire that, it was said, had encouraged chaos but also the return of those disappointed with socialism and of all who regarded Pétain's words as inexorably following from "the renaissance" of the Révolution nationale that had been undertaken but left incomplete. One of the strengths of Pétain's regime was to have pulled off, at least initially, the feat of drawing to itself the vital and "revolutionary" forces of the past. That produced a contradiction inherent in the period, which witnessed the rise, in the midst of the occupation, of a generation that was of two minds, Christian and Communist. Stemming in great part from the movement of 1936, that new generation of artists was intoxicated by change, colors, and pedagogy, opportunistic enough to take handouts from the French state while calling for intransigence in the creative process. For the Christians at least, creation was a higher form of commitment against which the regime could do nothing.

A product of the 1930s, this generation was consecrated with the liberation as the guardian, during the worst moments, of the modern tradition in France. It had not braved the occupier's wrath with weapons in hand, but it had produced ambiguous, violently colored, and unstructured works at odds with the general *doxa* of the time. Parallel to that surprising *public opinion* whose forms of resistance have been uncovered by Pierre Laborie,[1] the Jeunes peintres de tradition française staunchly refused to submit to the state of things, oscillating between order and chaos, tolerance and revolt, traditions and modernities, individualism and communitarianism.

The revolution in sacred art, the introduction of abstract art into churches, and socialist realism awaited their champions. These trajectories, with their opposing forms and logics, each appealed to a social conception of art and of artists inherited from the prewar period. Yet France, which up to that point was firmly planted in the nineteenth century, now entered, once and for all, an era where critical consciousness would begin to shift. In that respect, the failure of socialist realism, the ebb of realism generally, and the success of nonfigurative art attested less to the crisis of humanism—announced by the long-standing detractors of modern art—than to the universal desire to reconnect with individualism, which had been in ill repute for years. Representations of the world in which no preestablished discourse came to arrest the solitary progress of eyes and minds prospered as a result.

This artistic abstraction was new: it appealed primarily to existentialist freedom and archaic lyricism, much less to the geometric forms that had emerged at the Bauhaus to glorify rationality. With the instrumentalization of "progress" in 1914 to 1918 and its tragic implementation in the death camps, barbarism had become technological. At

Hiroshima and Nagasaki, "justice" itself had been meted out with the help of a great many scientific advances. The faithful representation of a world haunted by the ghosts of recent massacres became impossible, but so were allegories stamped with the mark of the machine. The body and matter would be at the center of the artistic deliverance of the postwar period in Europe and the United States—not the hygienic, high-performance body of Leni Riefenstahl or Montherlant, but an unruly, belching body; not matter tamed and subdued, devoted to the benefits of "fine craftsmanship" that the Révolution nationale harped on a hundred times, but matter in its raw state, a sign of chaos and of the refusal to believe in the omnipotence of reason, harmony, and history.

The black works of Pierre Soulages, Hans Hartung, and Olivier Debré; the formless and always on edge figures of Jean Fautrier; the poetic drifting of Gaston Chaissac; the poster *décollage* of Raymond Hains and Jacques Villeglé; the emaciated sculptures of Alberto Giacometti; the riot of matter and color in the art of the Nordic group Cobra; the dark battles of Lucio Fontana; the scars of Antoni Tàpies's Spain—in some sense, all these came to purge the body and the disorder of an unending series of legislative acts whose barbarism had overtaxed Europe. The real succès de scandale of the immediate postwar period (and hence its first major triumph) came from Jean Dubuffet, who during the occupation had begun to avenge the teeming masses crushed by the weight of oppression. His exhibition of 1946, *Mirobolus, Macadam et Cie, Hautes Pâtes*, constituted one of the high points in the revolt against learned culture and the *logos*, against the renowned French tradition that was forever limited to levelheadedness and fine craftsmanship. His vociferations against reason as well as his sardonic and distorted subjects still referred to the carnage more than to the reconstruction under way.

Democracy was once again the order of the day: artists could revolt, vituperate, remember, prophesy disaster. Outrageous art was, so to speak, the barometer of recovered health. Under the guise of the Révolution nationale and of rebirth, the crisis had kept revolt in check; democracy liberated the insurrectionary forces of artists determined to exorcise five somber and earth-toned years.

NOTE

1. See Pierre Laborie, *L'opinion française sous Vichy* (Paris: Editions du Seuil, 1990).

PLATES

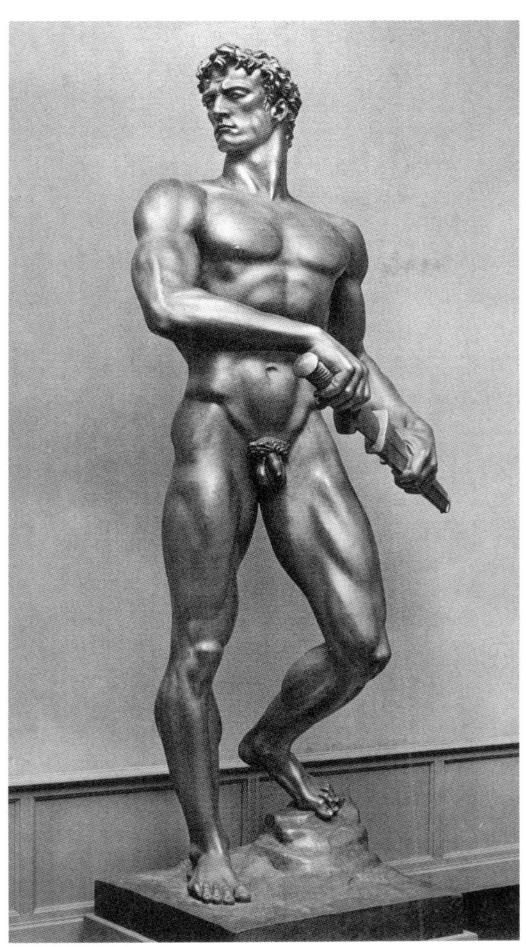

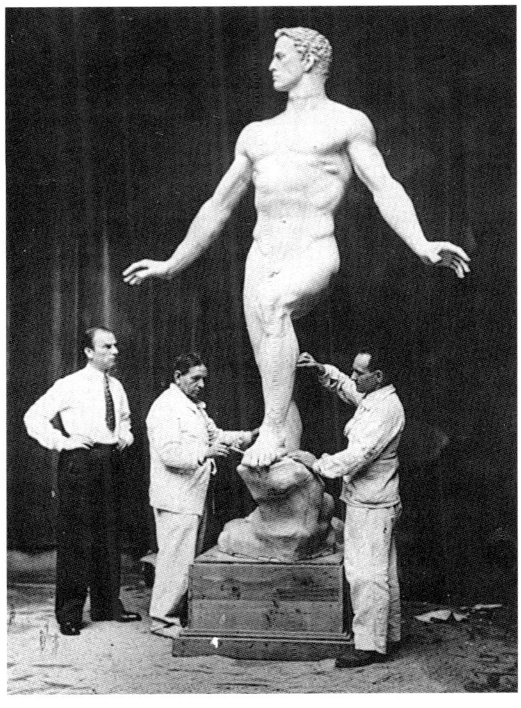

Pl. 1. Arno Breker (German, 1900–1991)
Readiness, 1939

Pl. 2. Arno Breker supervising the installation of one of his sculptures for the exhibition of his works at the Orangerie des Tuileries, Paris, May 1942

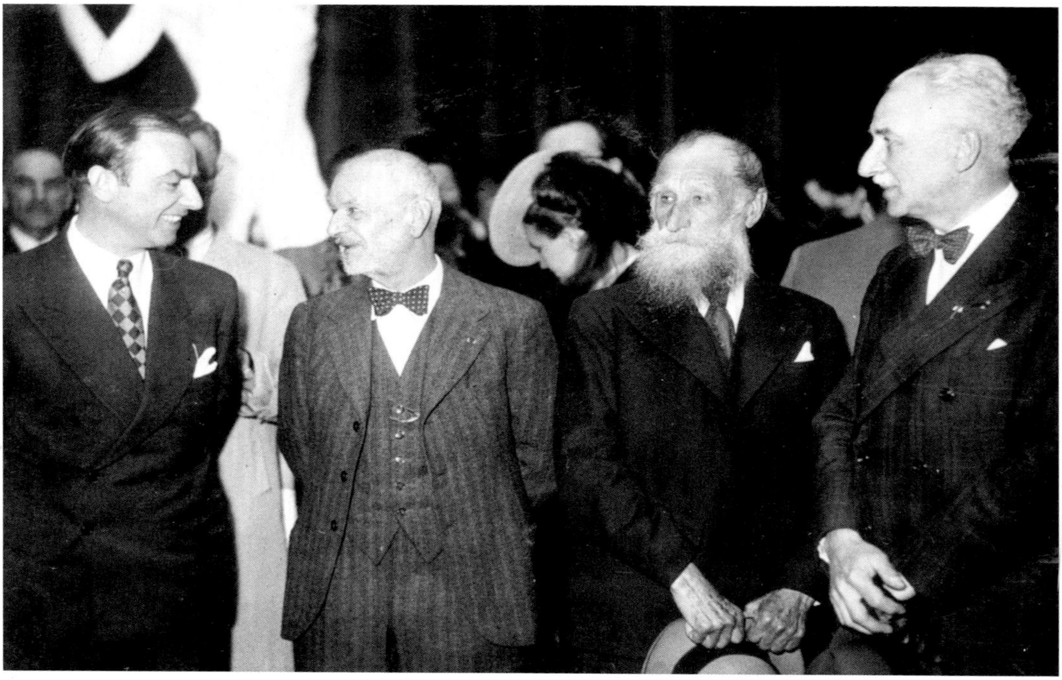

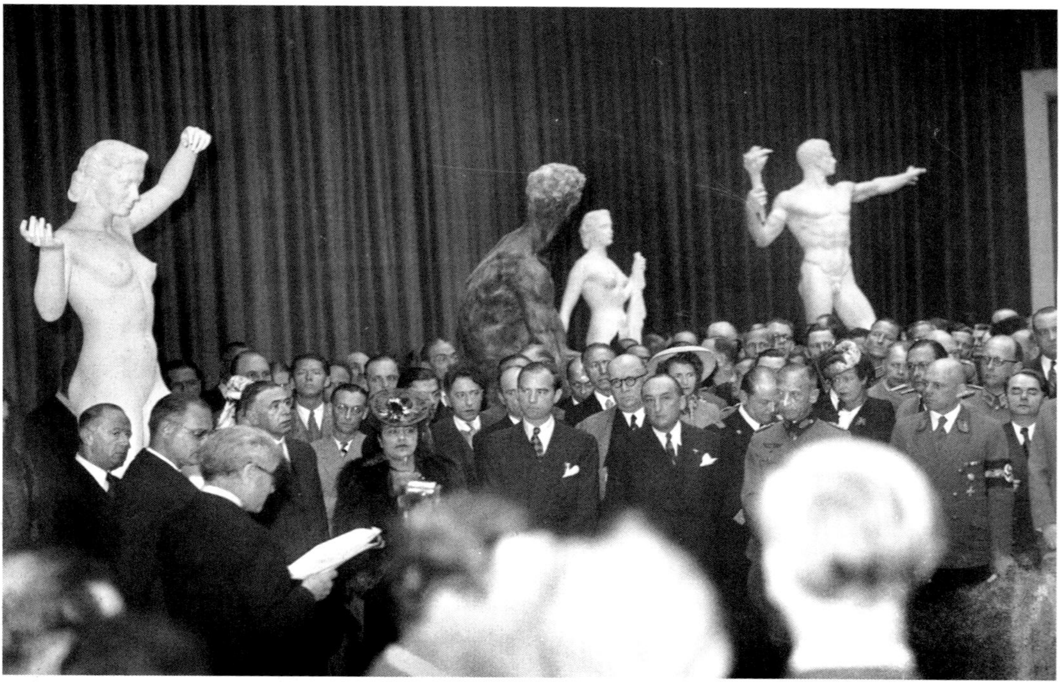

Pl. 3. The sculptors Arno Breker, Charles Despiau, and Aristide Maillol and the fine arts minister Louis Hautecoeur at the Arno Breker exhibition, Orangerie des Tuileries, Paris, May 1942

Pl. 4. Speech by the minister of national education and youth, Abel Bonnard, at the inauguration of the Arno Breker exhibition, Orangerie des Tuileries, Paris, May 1942. Among those in attendance are Otto Abetz, Jacques Benoist-Méchin, Arno Breker, Fernand de Brinon, Jean Cocteau, and Serge Lifar

Les Lettres françaises accueillies en Allemagne

Sur invitation du Dr Goebbels, ministre du Reich, des écrivains et poètes français se sont rendus en Allemagne. Les voici dans le studio d'Arno Breker, le célèbre sculpteur allemand

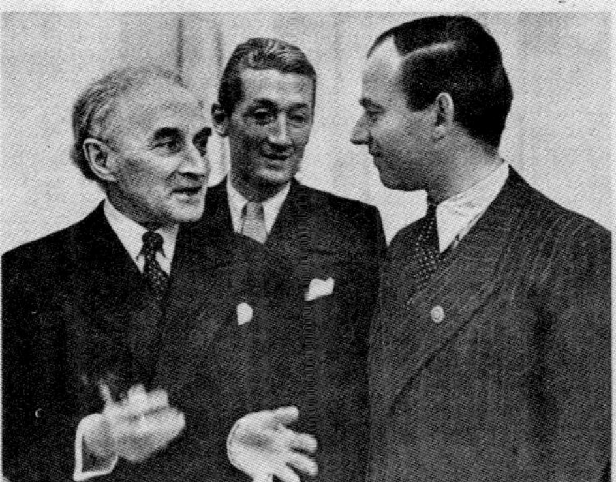

M. ABEL BONNARD, de l'Académie Française, est, parmi les auteurs philosophiques, un des plus connus pour l'élégance de son style. Il est ici en conversation animée avec le professeur Breker et un autre écrivain français, M. André Fraigneau (au centre)

CONDUITS PAR LE PROFESSEUR BREKER, les invités ont eu l'occasion de se faire une idée du travail de l'artiste et de s'entretenir des problèmes de l'art allemand et français. Ici, le professeur Breker (à droite) présente à ses hôtes une de ses dernières créations

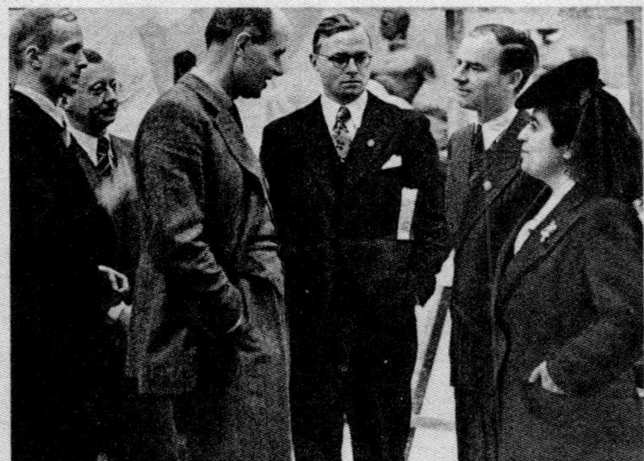

AVEC VIF INTERET, le professeur et Mme Breker écoutent les explications de M. Pierre Drieu La Rochelle. Cet écrivain appartient à la «Nouvelle Revue Française», revue qui s'intéresse aux problèmes nationaux-socialistes et fascistes

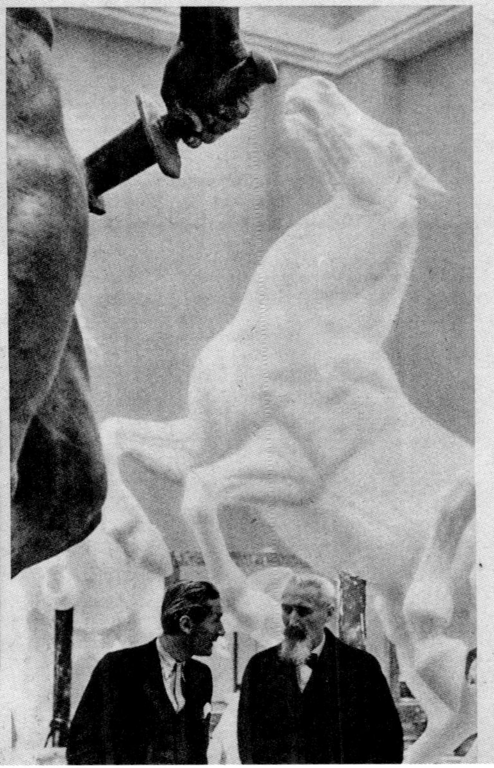

AU PIED DE PLASTIQUES MONUMENTALES, deux invités français s'entretiennent de leur voyage en Allemagne qui leur a fait tant d'impressions. Clichés Rohrlack

Pl. 5. French writers and poets visiting the studio of Arno Breker during the official trip to Germany, November 1941
From *Signal*, no. 1, January 1942

LE DON A LA PATRIE JUIN 1940

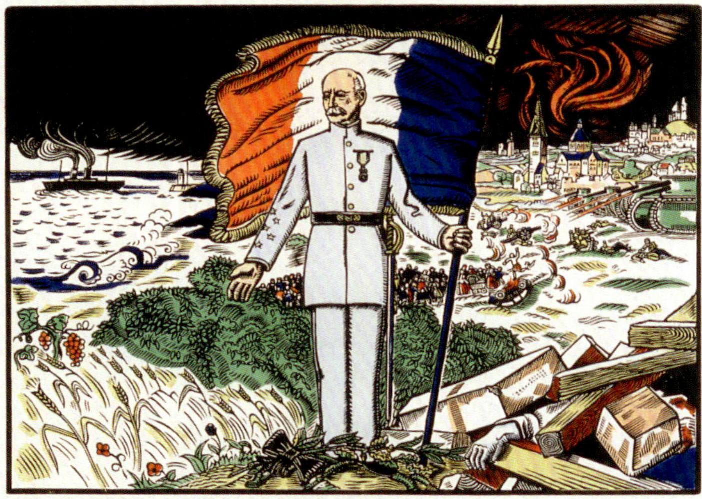

Depuis la Victoire, L'ESPRIT DE JOUISSANCE L'A EMPORTÉ SUR L'ESPRIT DE SACRIFICE. On a revendiqué plus qu'on n'a servi. On a voulu épargner l'effort, on rencontre aujourd'hui le malheur. – JE FAIS À LA FRANCE LE DON DE MA PERSONNE, pour atténuer son malheur. – Je ne serais pas digne de rester à votre tête, si j'avais accepté de répandre le sang français pour prolonger le rêve de quelques Français mal instruits des conditions de la lutte. Je n'ai voulu placer hors du SOL DE FRANCE ni ma personne, ni mon espoir. (Paroles du Maréchal – 1940).

IMAGERIE DU MARÉCHAL – Imprimé à LIMOGES 1941

LA RELÈVE DES ÉTOILES

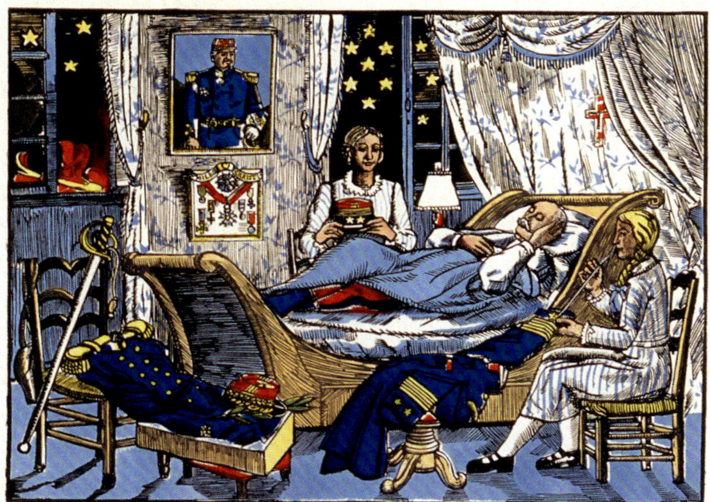

SOUS un régime indifférent au seul mérite, il n'avait eu qu'un avancement très lent. Aux prises avec l'action, sa supériorité s'avéra éclatante. Après quinze jours de campagne, il est nommé GÉNÉRAL. Ce soir-là, il cantonne dans la demeure des petites-filles du Général de SONIS. Elles gardaient avec piété les reliques de celui qui naguère avait chargé à la tête des ZOUAVES PONTIFICAUX, à LOIGNY : Tandis que leur hôte repose, elles entrent sur la pointe des pieds. Elles ont dégarni de ses insignes l'uniforme vénéré du HÉROS DE LA LOIRE, leur aïeul. Et, telles de bonnes fées attentives à filer le destin de la Patrie, elles recousent les étoiles sur la tunique du futur HÉROS DE VERDUN.

IMAGERIE DU MARÉCHAL – Imprimé à LIMOGES 1941

Pl. 6. Gérard Ambroselli (French, 1906–2000)
Le don à la patrie juin 1940 (Gift to the nation, June 1940), 1941
From the series of prints *Imagerie du maréchal,* Limoges

Pl. 7. Gérard Ambroselli (French, 1906–2000)
La relève des étoiles (The changing of the stars), 1941
From the series of prints *Imagerie du maréchal,* Limoges

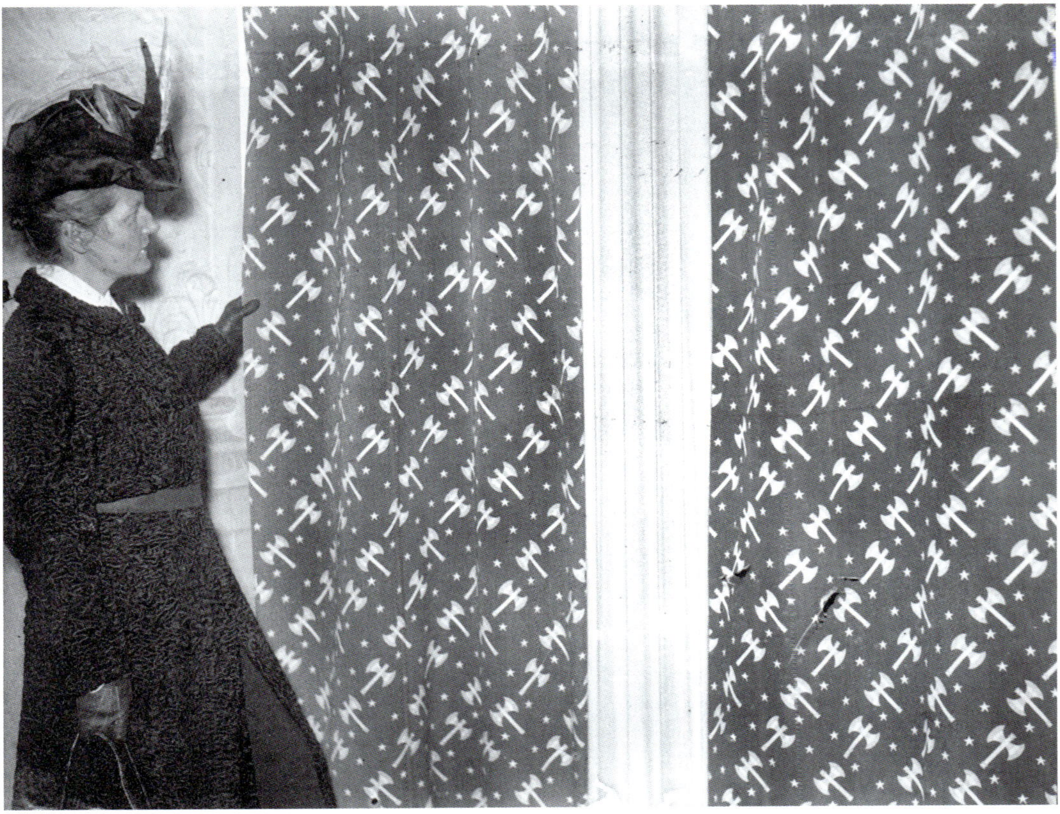

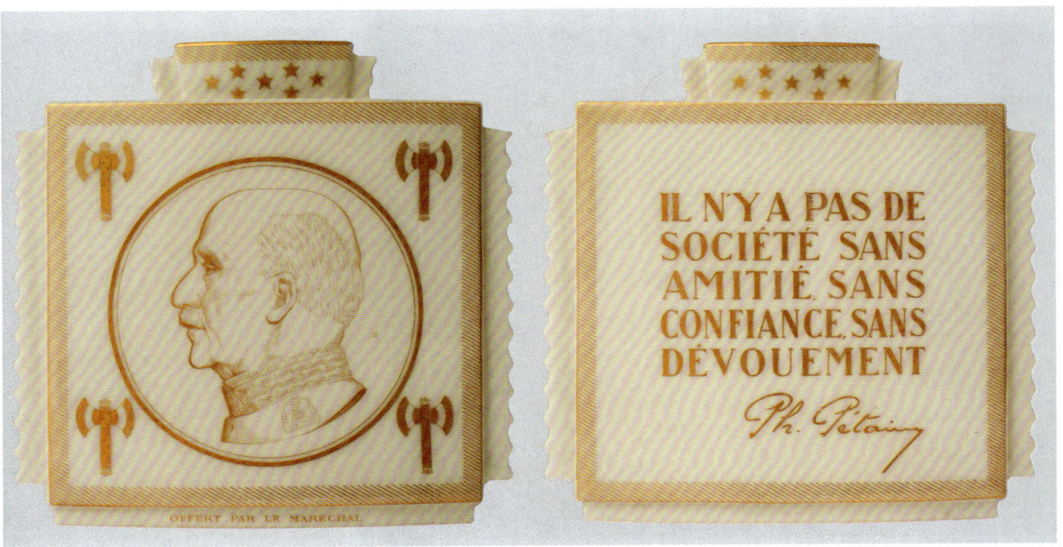

Pl. 8. Lyonnaise silk decorated with the *francisque*, on display at an exhibition at the Pavillon de Marsan, Musée des arts decoratifs, Paris, March 1943

Pl. 9. Sèvres Porcelain Manufactory, after a design by Robert Lallemant (French, 1902–54)
Vase with a portrait of Philippe Pétain on the obverse and an inscription signed "Ph. Pétain" on the reverse, 1944

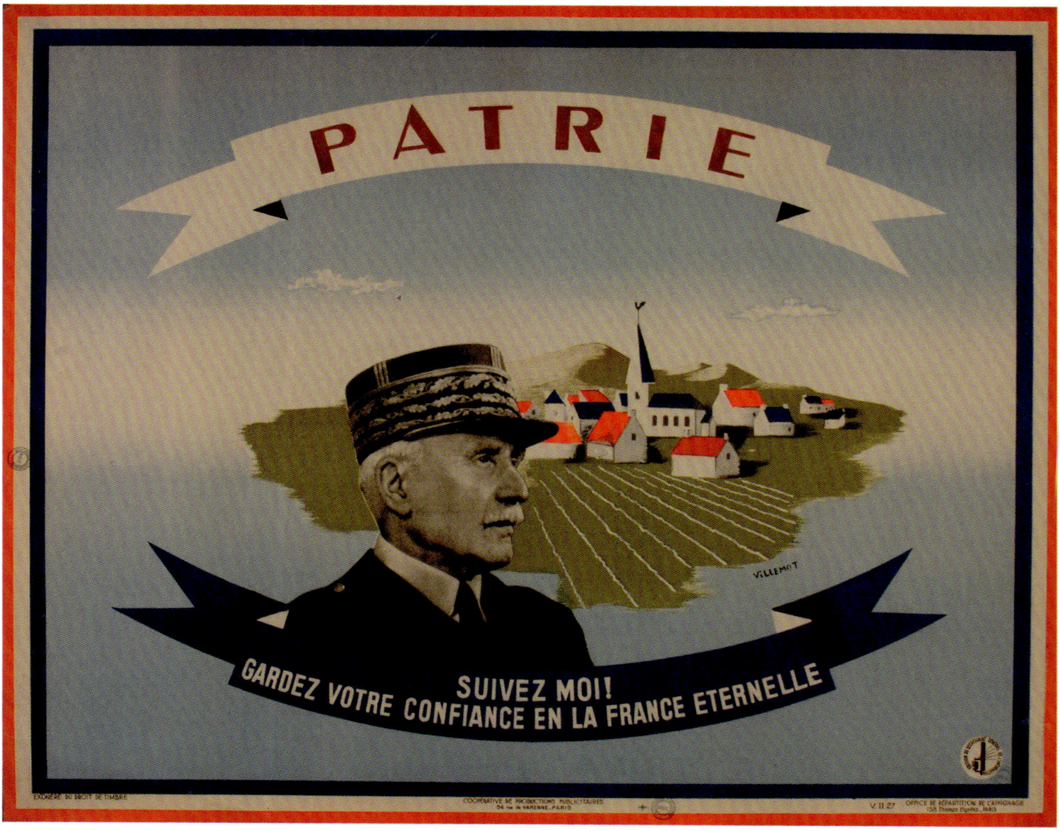

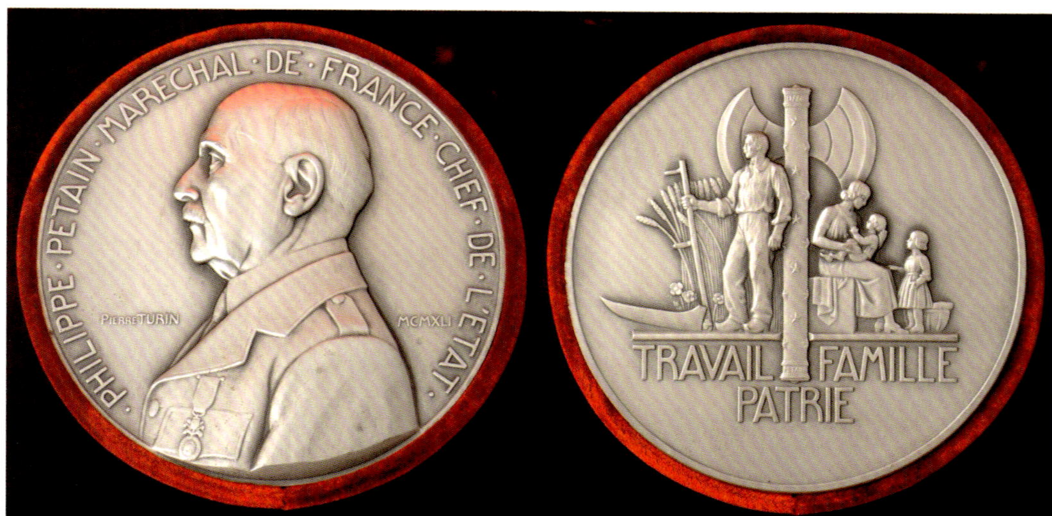

Pl. 10. Bernard Villemot (French, 1911–89)
Patrie, suivez moi! Gardez votre confiance en la France éternelle (Countrymen, follow me! Keep your faith in eternal France), 1941
Poster issued by the Edition du Secrétariat général de l'information

Pl. 11. Pierre Turin (French, 1891–1968)
Medal with a portrait of Philippe Pétain on the obverse and the Vichy motto "Travail, famille, patrie" (Work, family, nation) inscribed and illustrated on the reverse, 1941

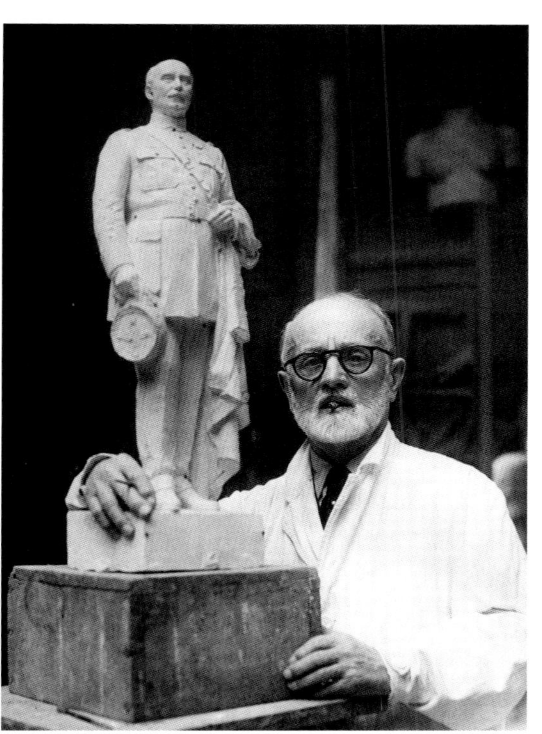

Pl. 12. François Cogné with his maquette of Philippe Pétain, which was exhibited at the Salon des Artistes Français, Paris, April 1942

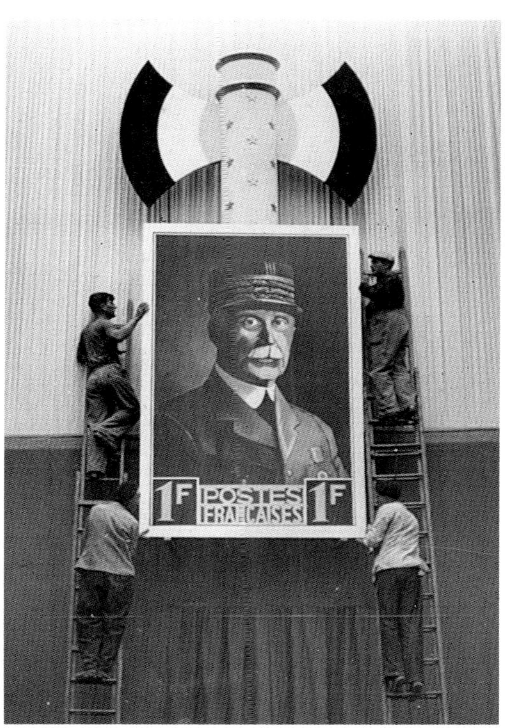

Pl. 13. Workers attaching a poste
stamp depicting Philippe Pétain t
artisans français, Palais de la pc

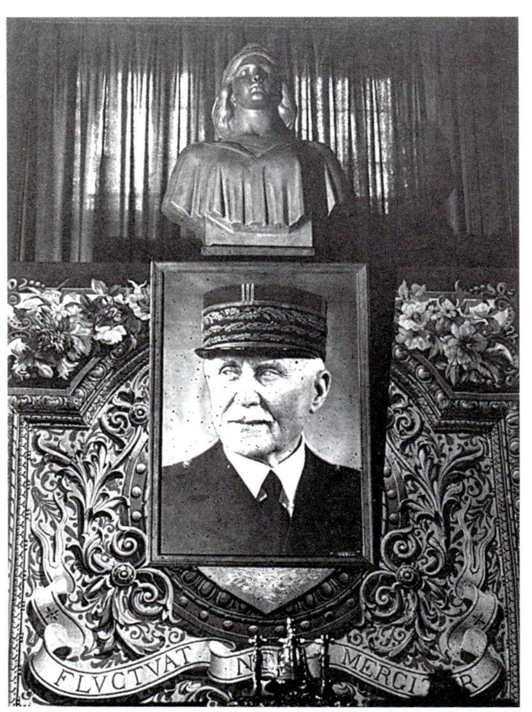

` Portrait of Philippe Pétain, installed under a bust
ne, Salle des séances, Hôtel de Ville de Paris,
`42

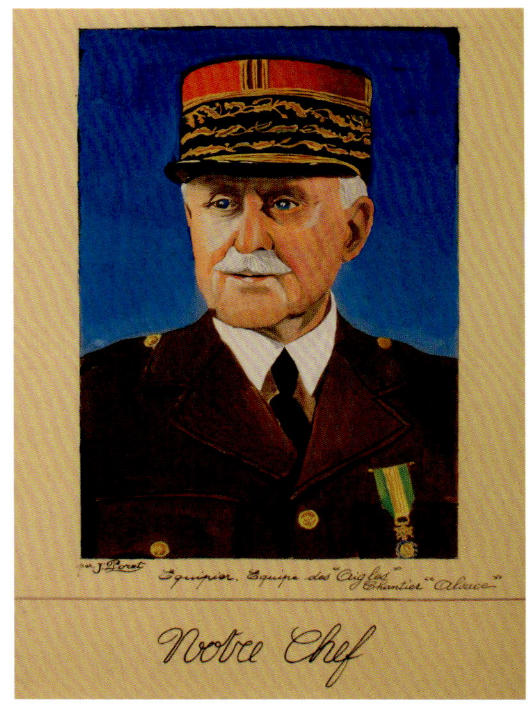

Pl. 15. J. Porat
Notre chef (Our leader), [ca. 1942]
Gouache portrait in an album offered to Philippe Pétain by the Chantier de Normanville, Haute-Normandie, France

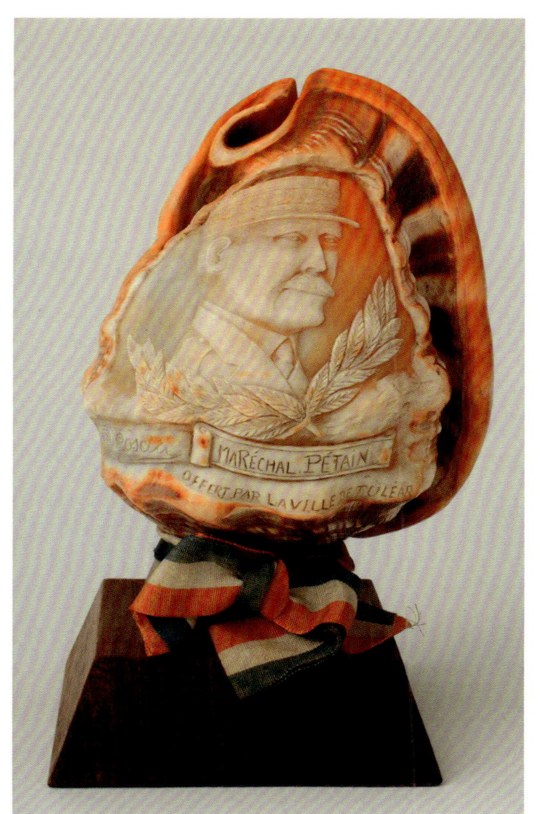

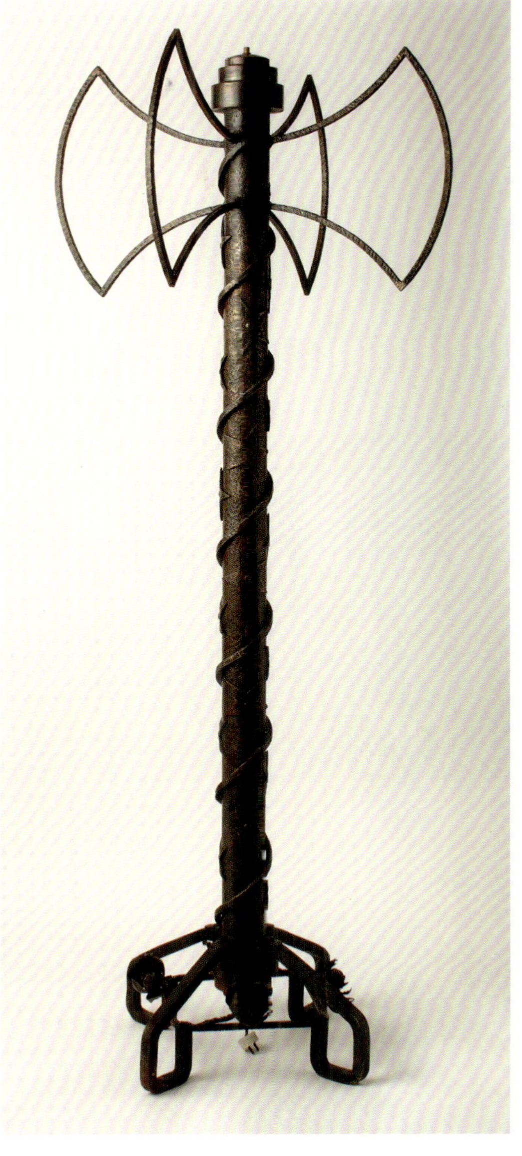

Pl. 16. Coscia
Maréchal Pétain, [ca. 1942]
Sculpted shell offered to Philippe Pétain by the city of Tuléar [Toliara], Madagascar

Pl. 17. *Francisque*-shaped lamp stand offered to Philippe Pétain by the youth of a professional development center in the 13th arrondissement of Paris, [ca. 1942]

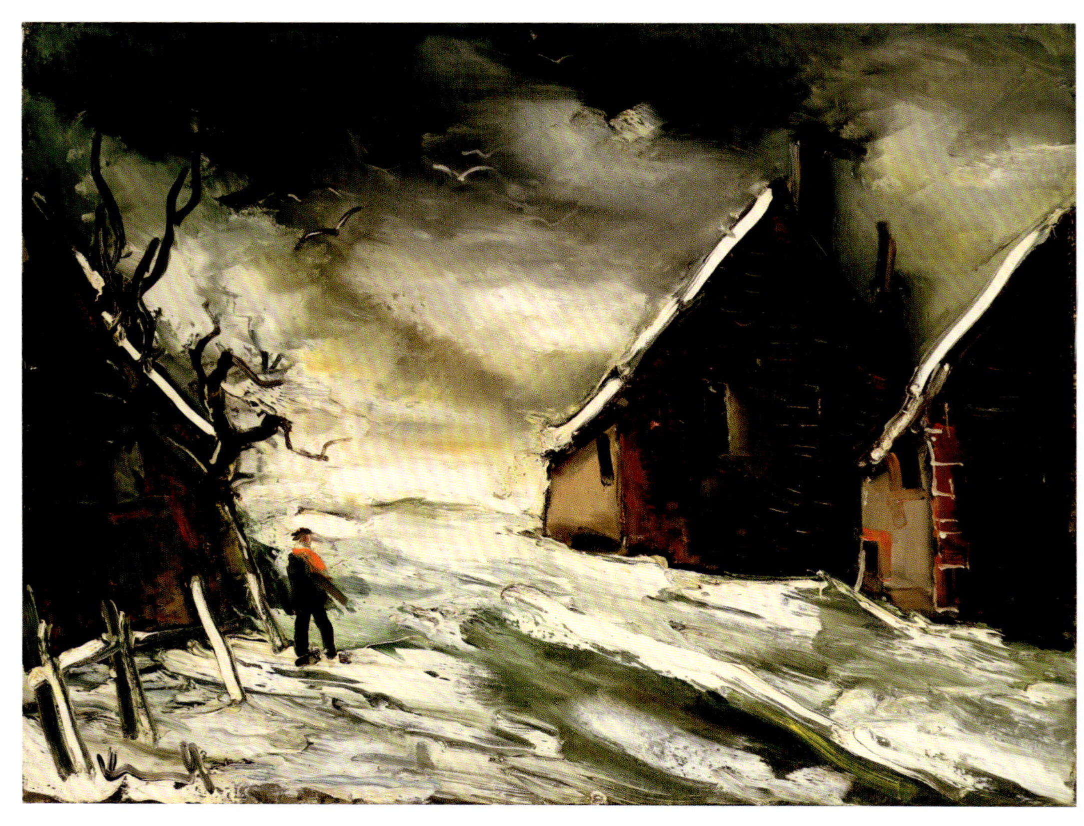

Pl. 18. Maurice de Vlaminck (French, 1876–1958)
The Village in Winter, n.d. [probably 1940s]

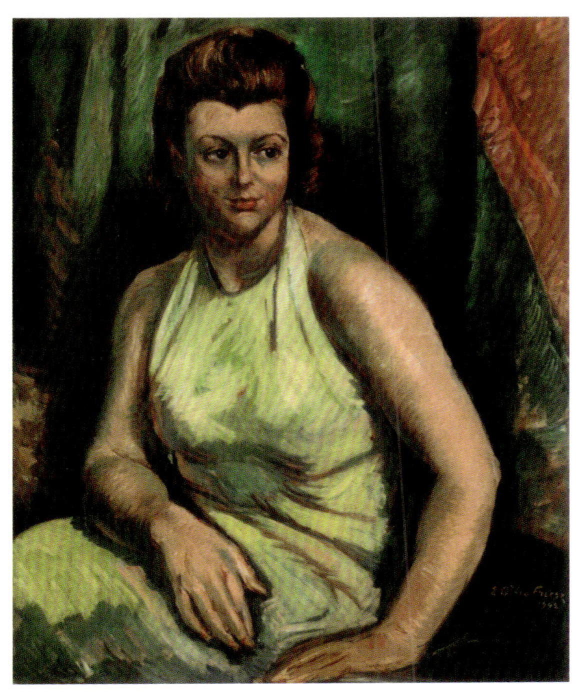

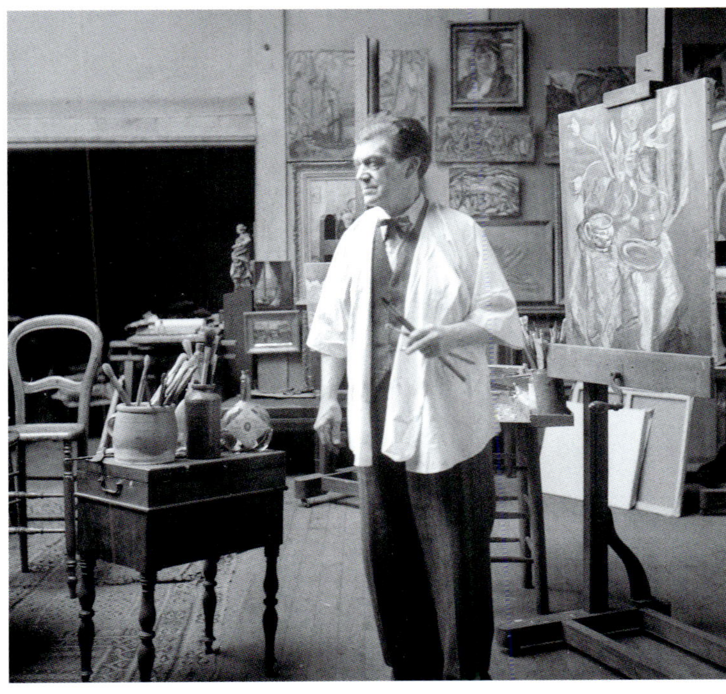

Pl. 19. Othon Friesz (French, 1879–1949)
Portrait of Winnie, 1942

Pl. 20. Othon Friesz in his studio, 1943

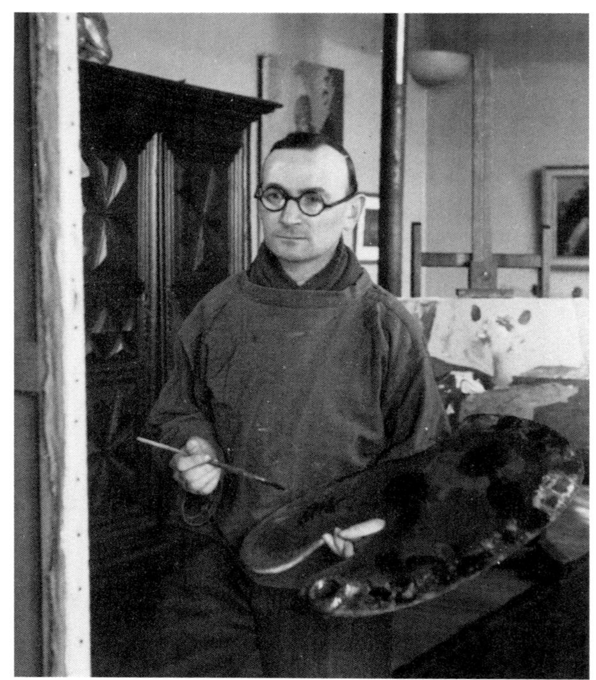

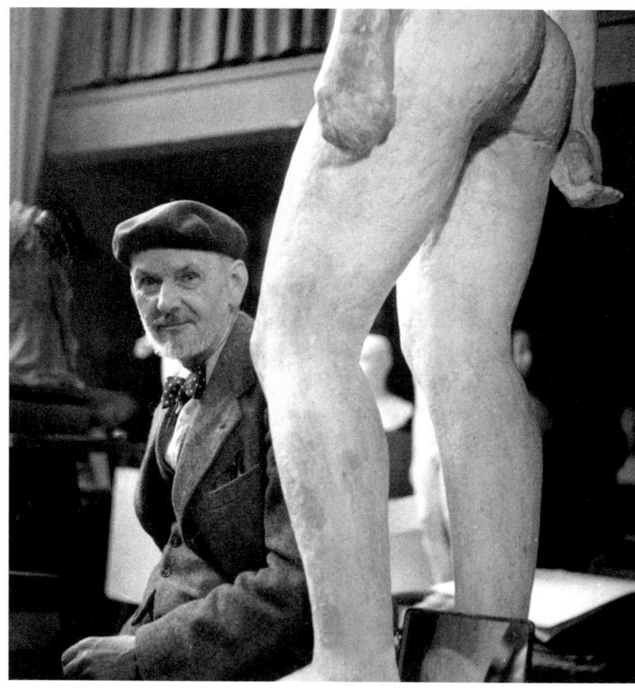

Pl. 21. Roland Oudot in his studio, n.d.

Pl. 22. Charles Despiau in his studio, 1943

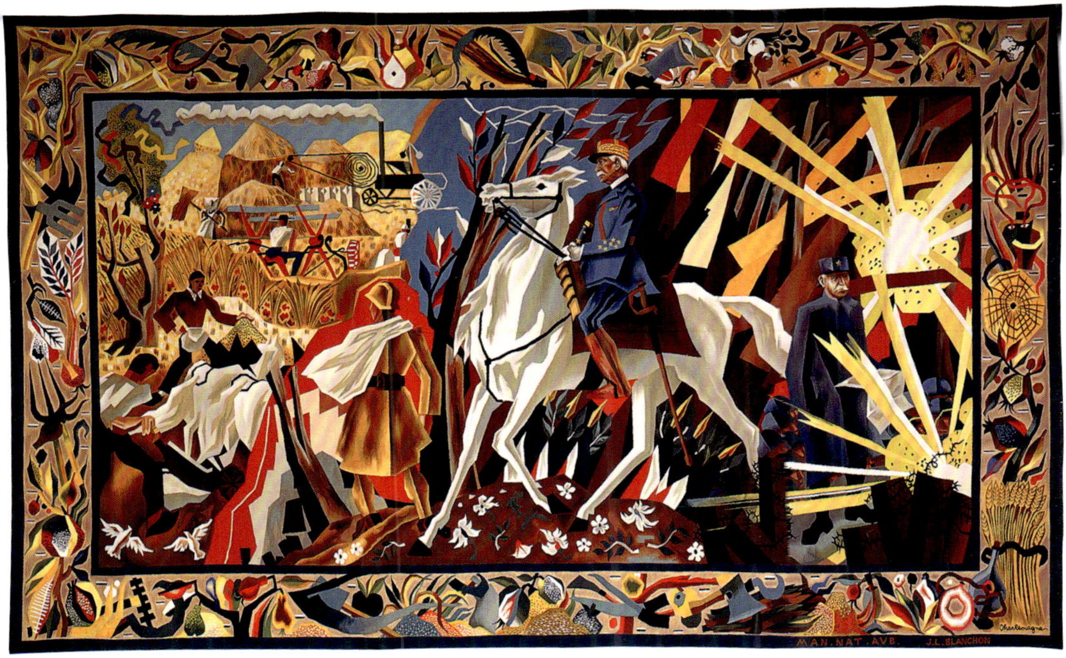

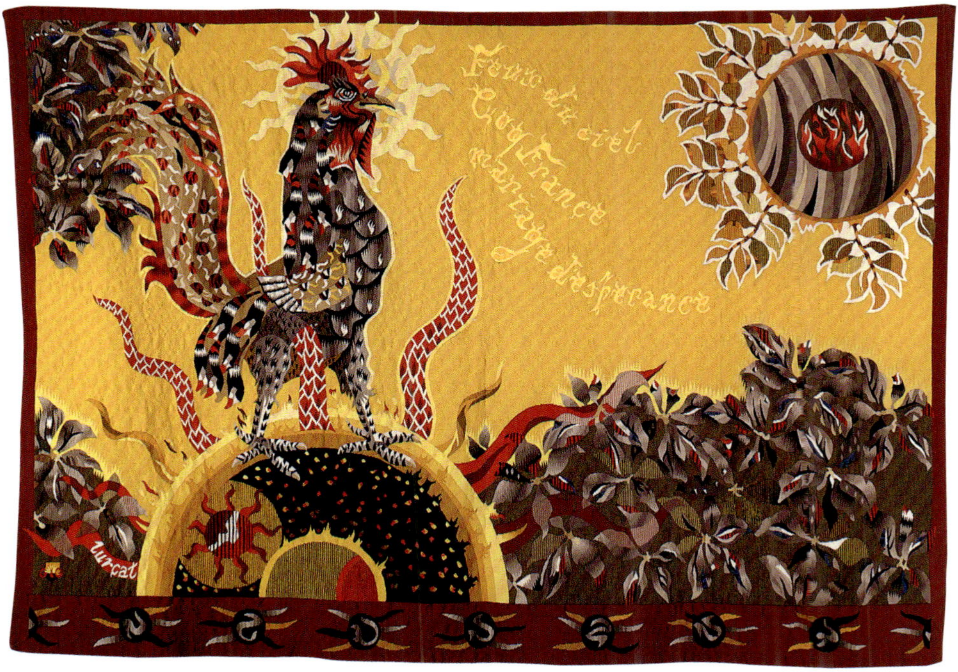

Pl. 23. Aubusson Tapestry Manufactory, woven after a cartoon by Paul Charlemagne (French, 1892–1972)
Homage to Pétain, 1942

Pl. 24. Aubusson Tapestry Manufactory, woven after a cartoon by Jean Lurçat (French, 1892–1966)
Spirit of France, 1943

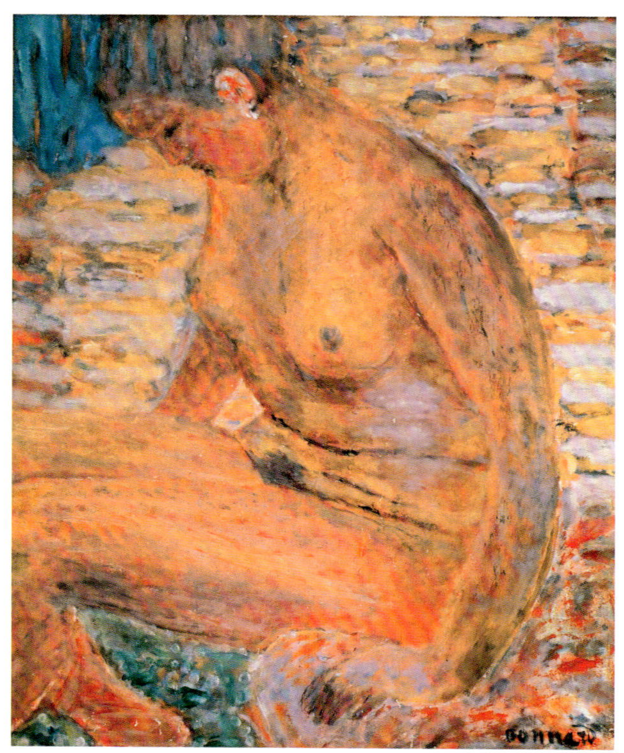

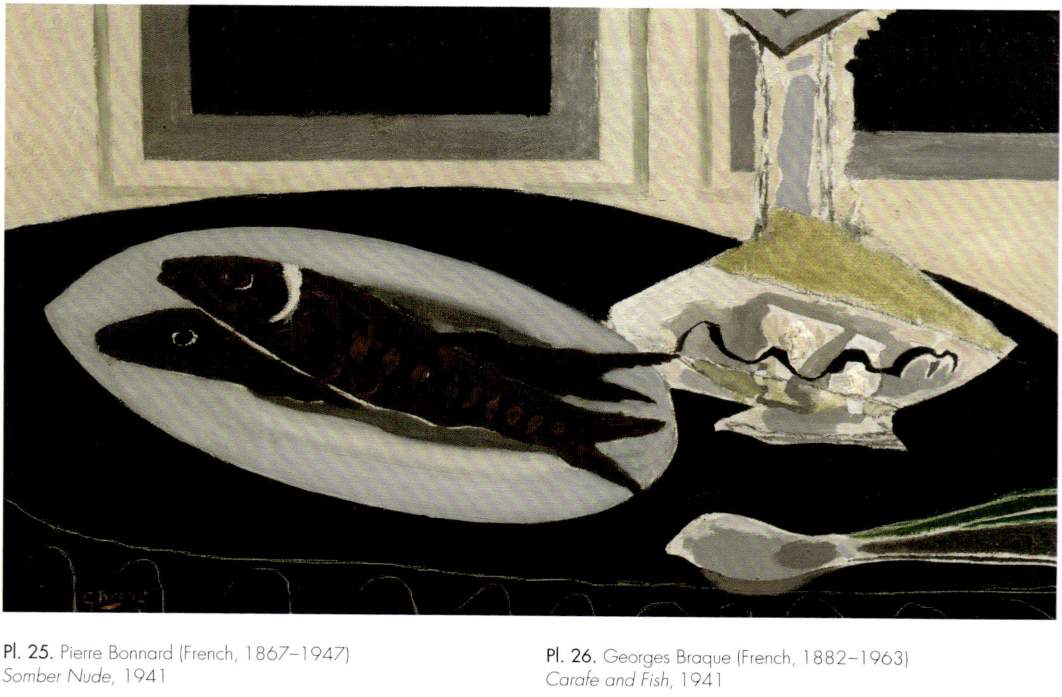

Pl. 25. Pierre Bonnard (French, 1867–1947)
Somber Nude, 1941

Pl. 26. Georges Braque (French, 1882–1963)
Carafe and Fish, 1941

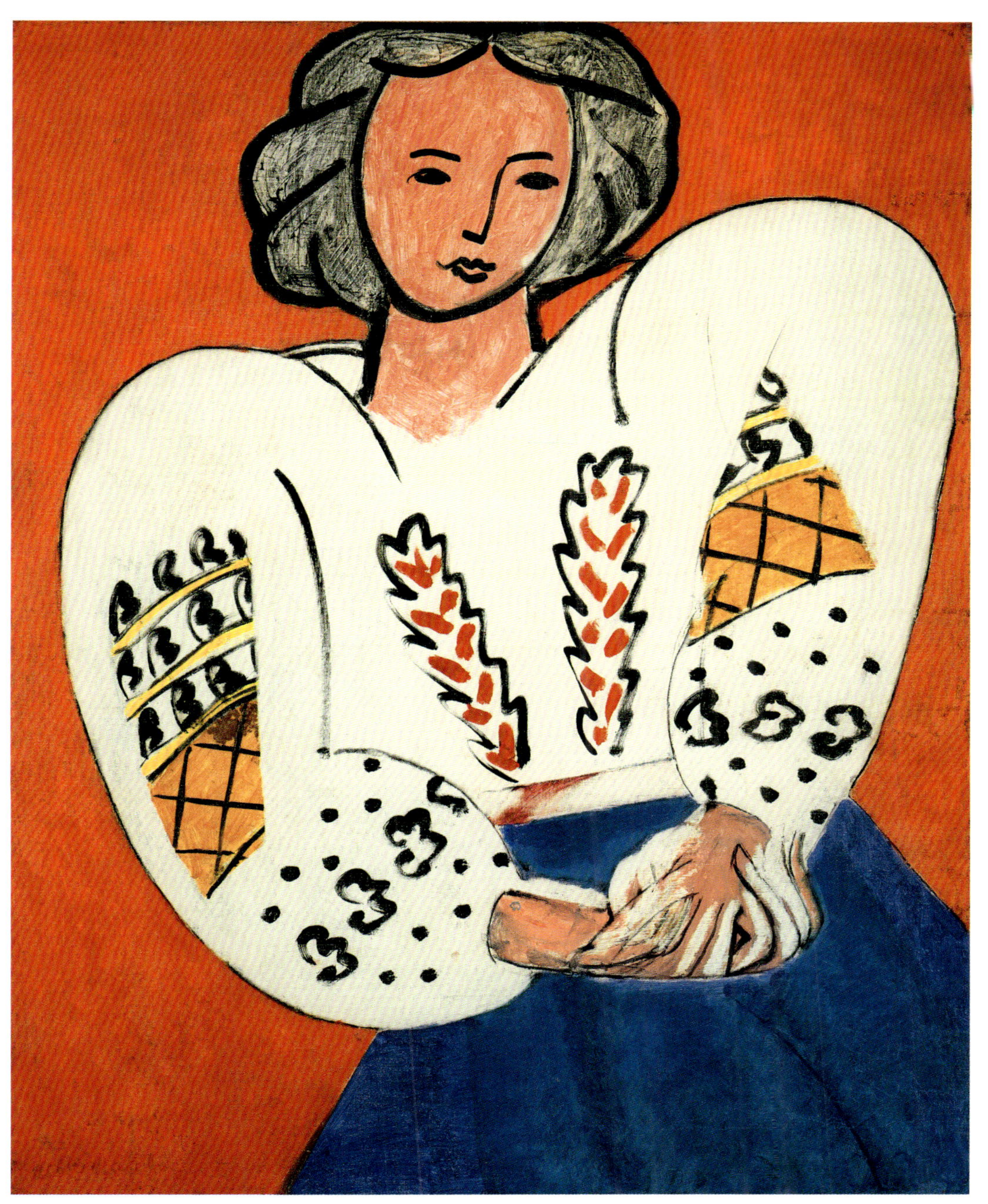

Pl. 27. Henri Matisse (French, 1869–1954)
The Romanian Blouse, 1940

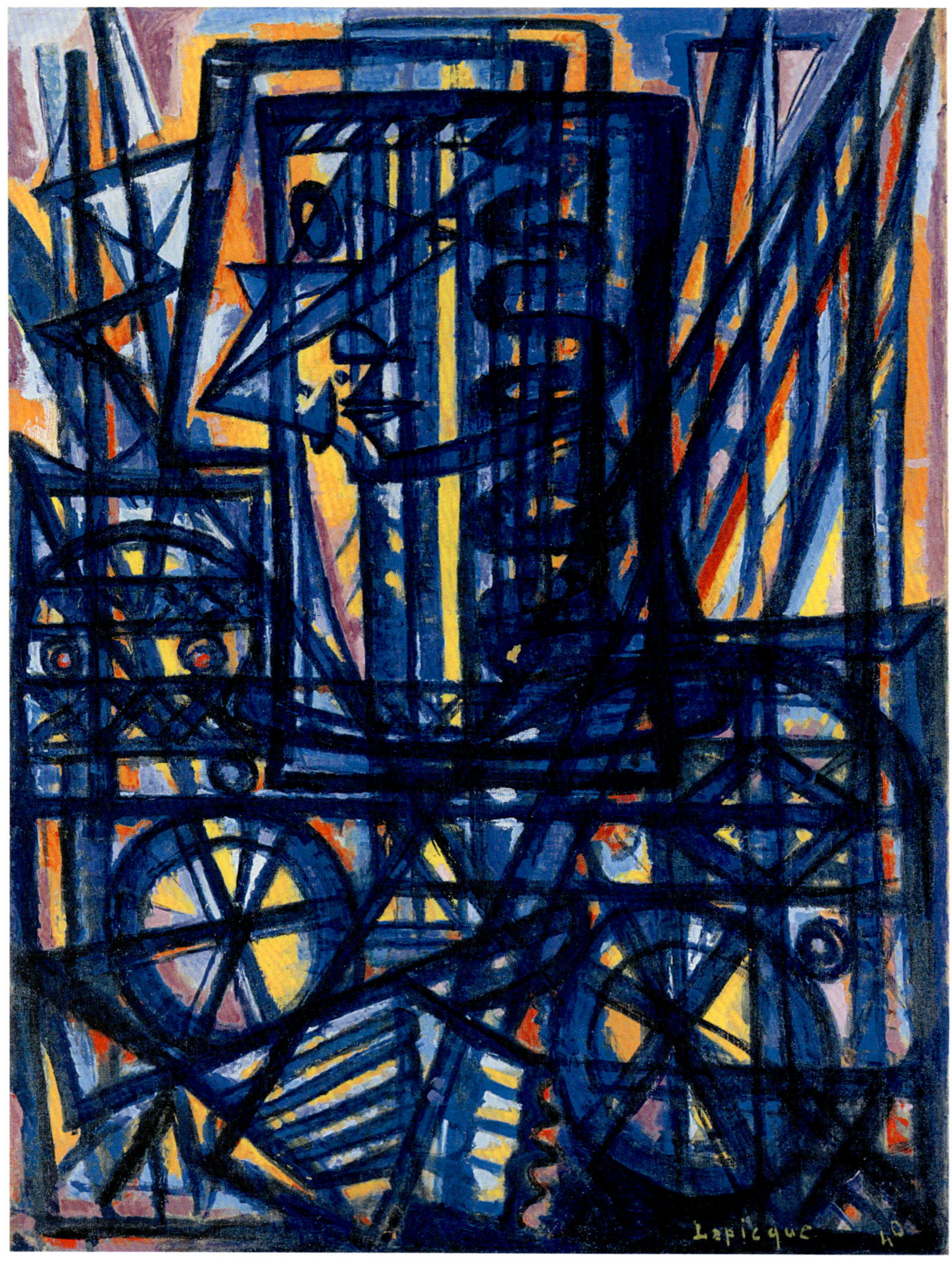

Pl. 28. Charles Lapicque (French, 1898–1988)
Joan of Arc Crossing the Loire, 1940

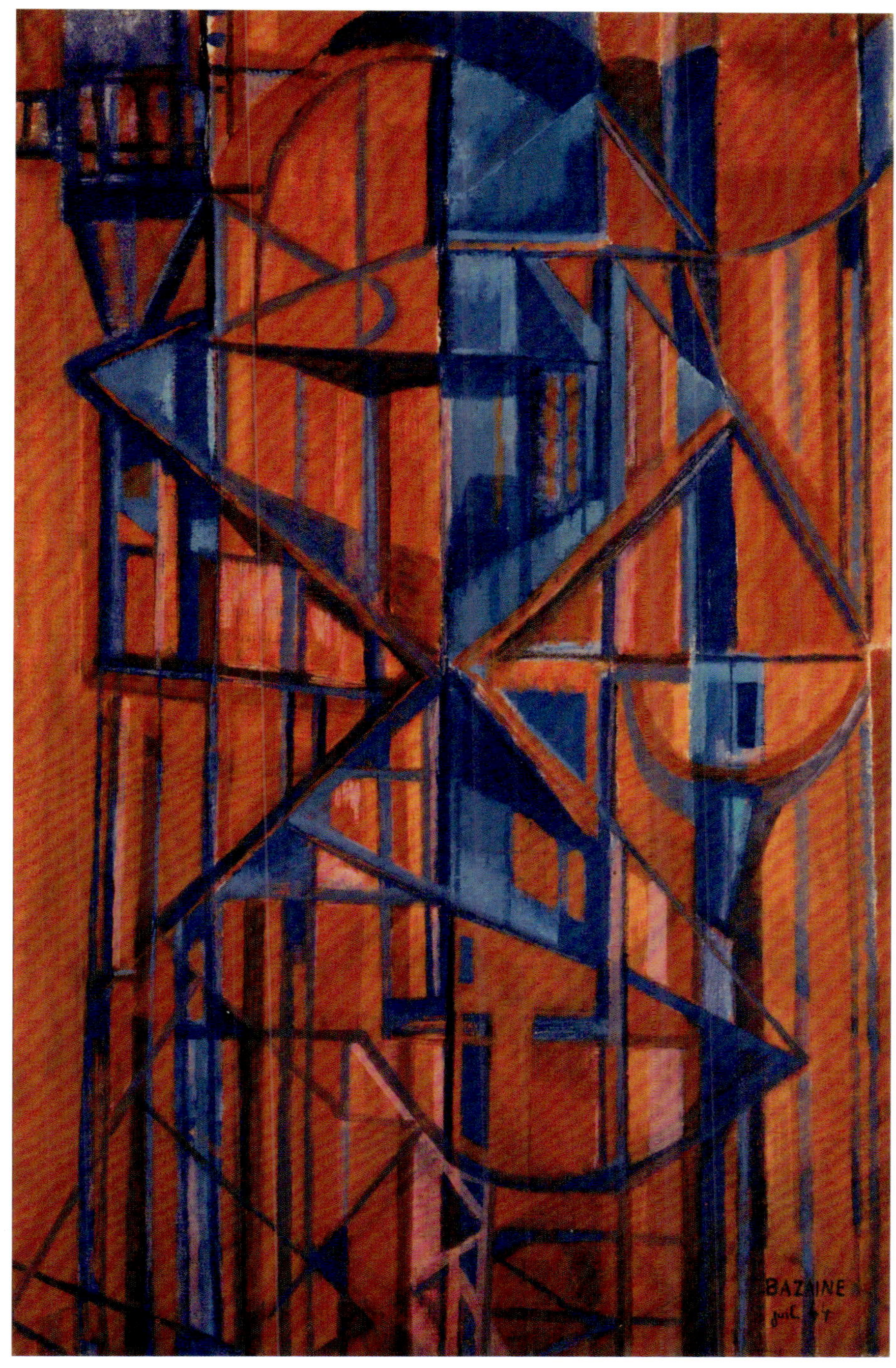

Pl. 29. Jean Bazaine (French, 1904–2001)
Mass for the Armed Man, 1944

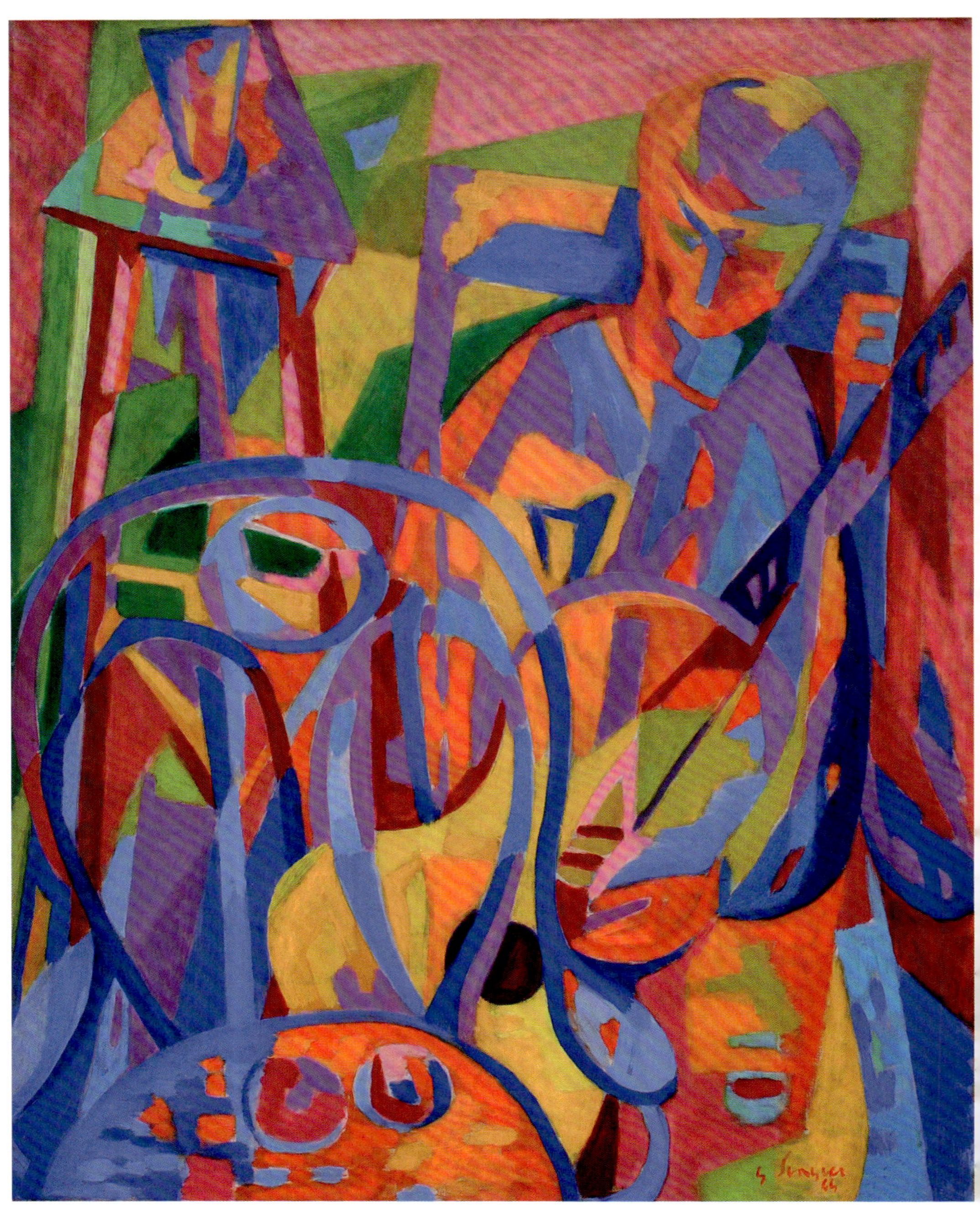

Pl. 30. Gustave Singier (French, 1909–84)
The Guitar, 1944

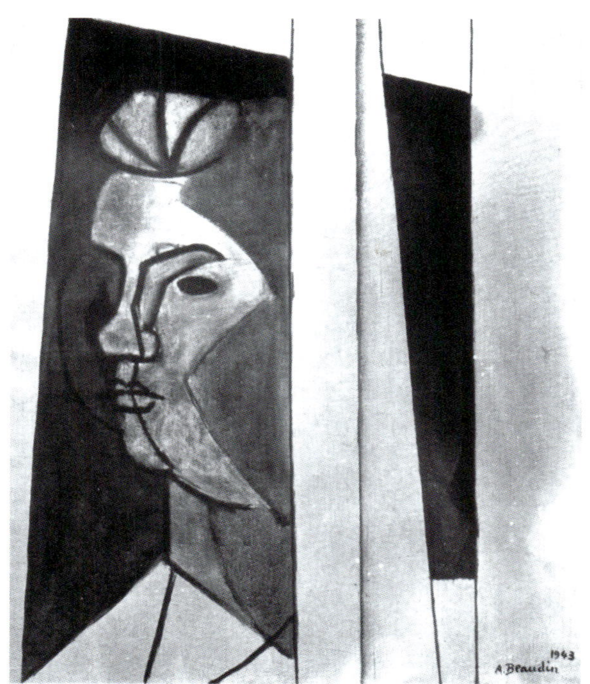

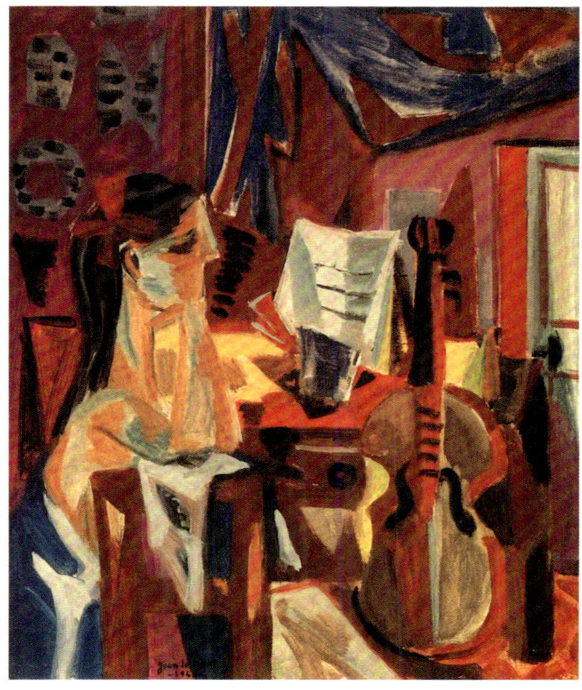

Pl. 31. André Gustave Beaudin (French, 1895–1979)
The Head at the Window, 1943

Pl. 32. Jean Le Moal (French, 1909–2007)
Figure and Musical Instruments, 1943

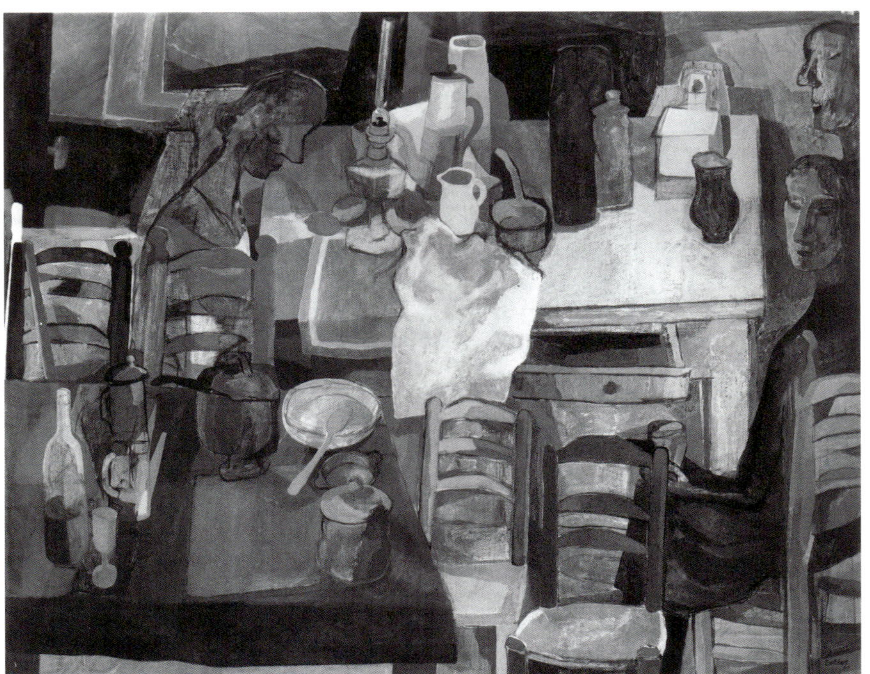

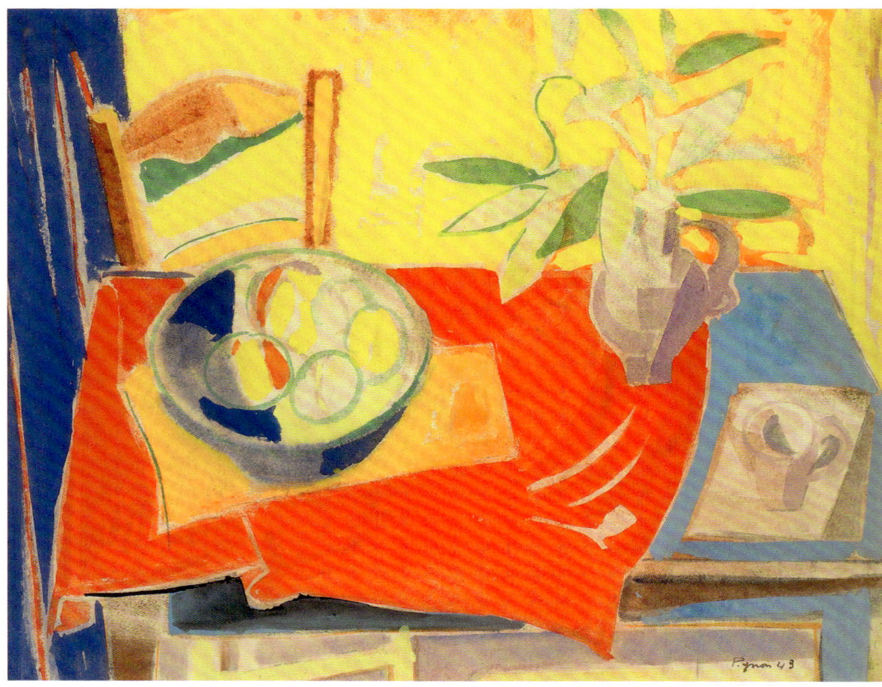

Pl. 33. Maurice Estève (French, 1904–2001)
Interior with Mauve Woman, 1941

Pl. 34. Édouard Pignon (French, 1905–93)
Still Life with Red Tablecloth, 1943

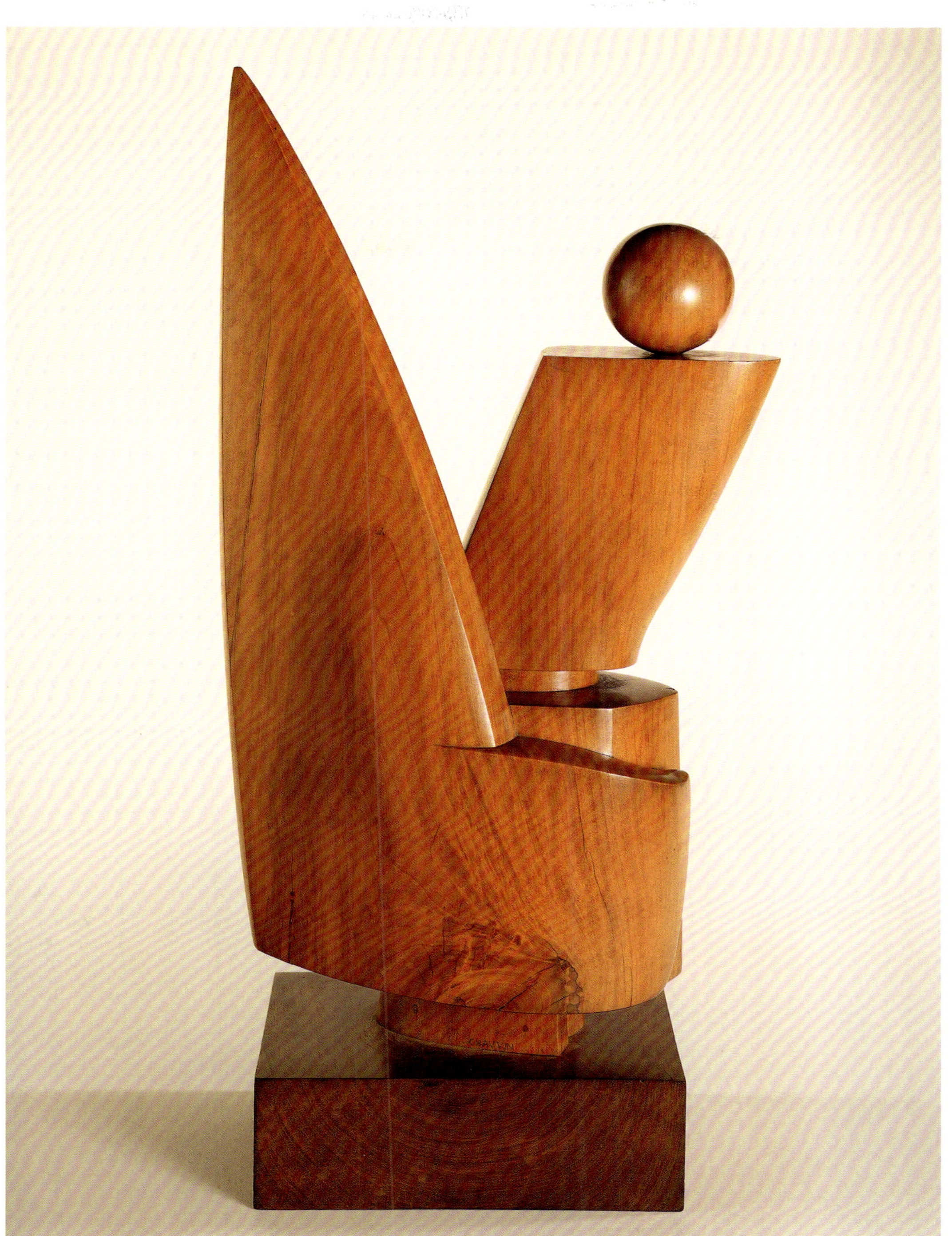

Pl. 35. Jean Chauvin (French, 1889–1976)
The Sacred Flame, 1940

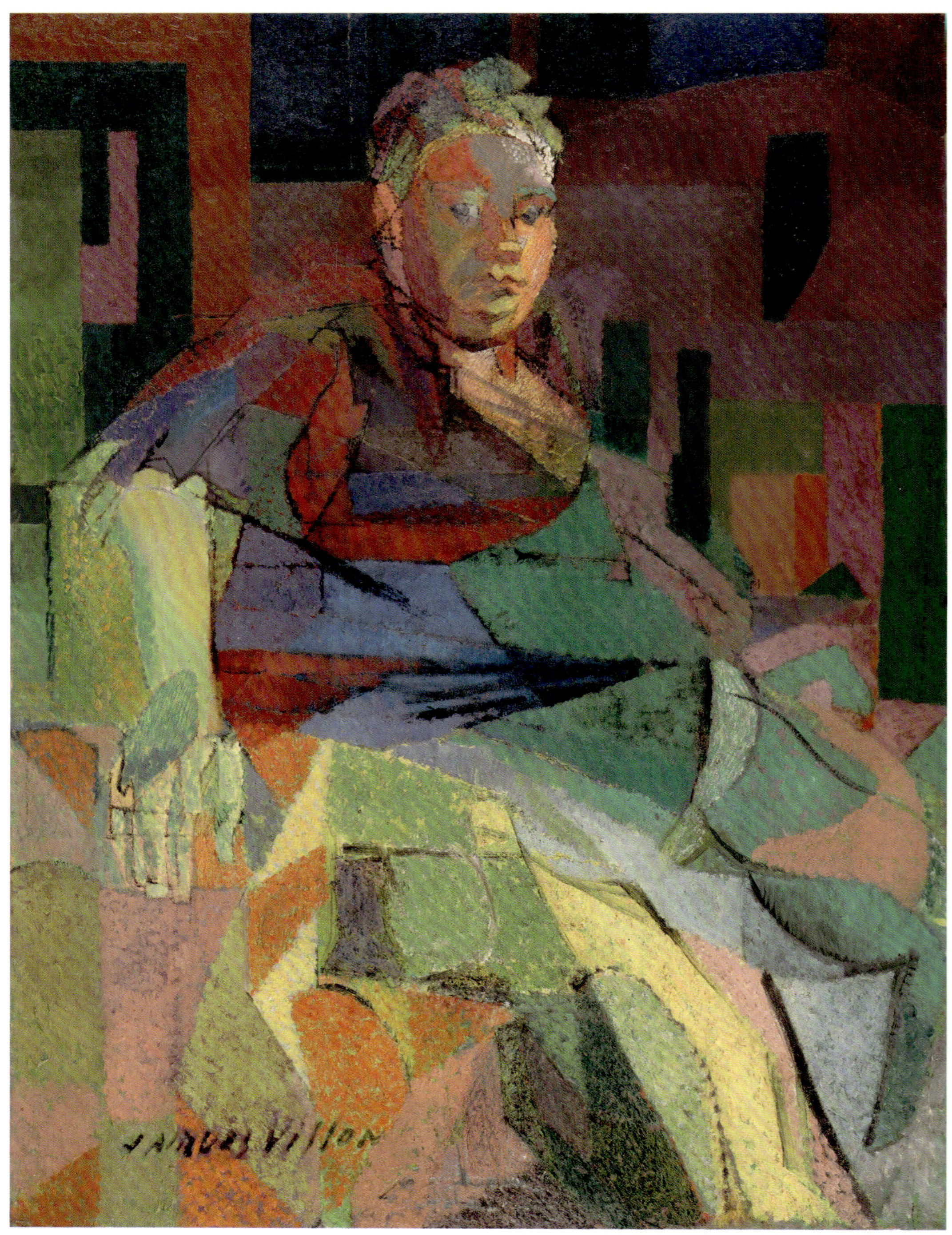

Pl. 36. Jacques Villon (French, 1875–1963)
Portrait of Camille Renault, 1944

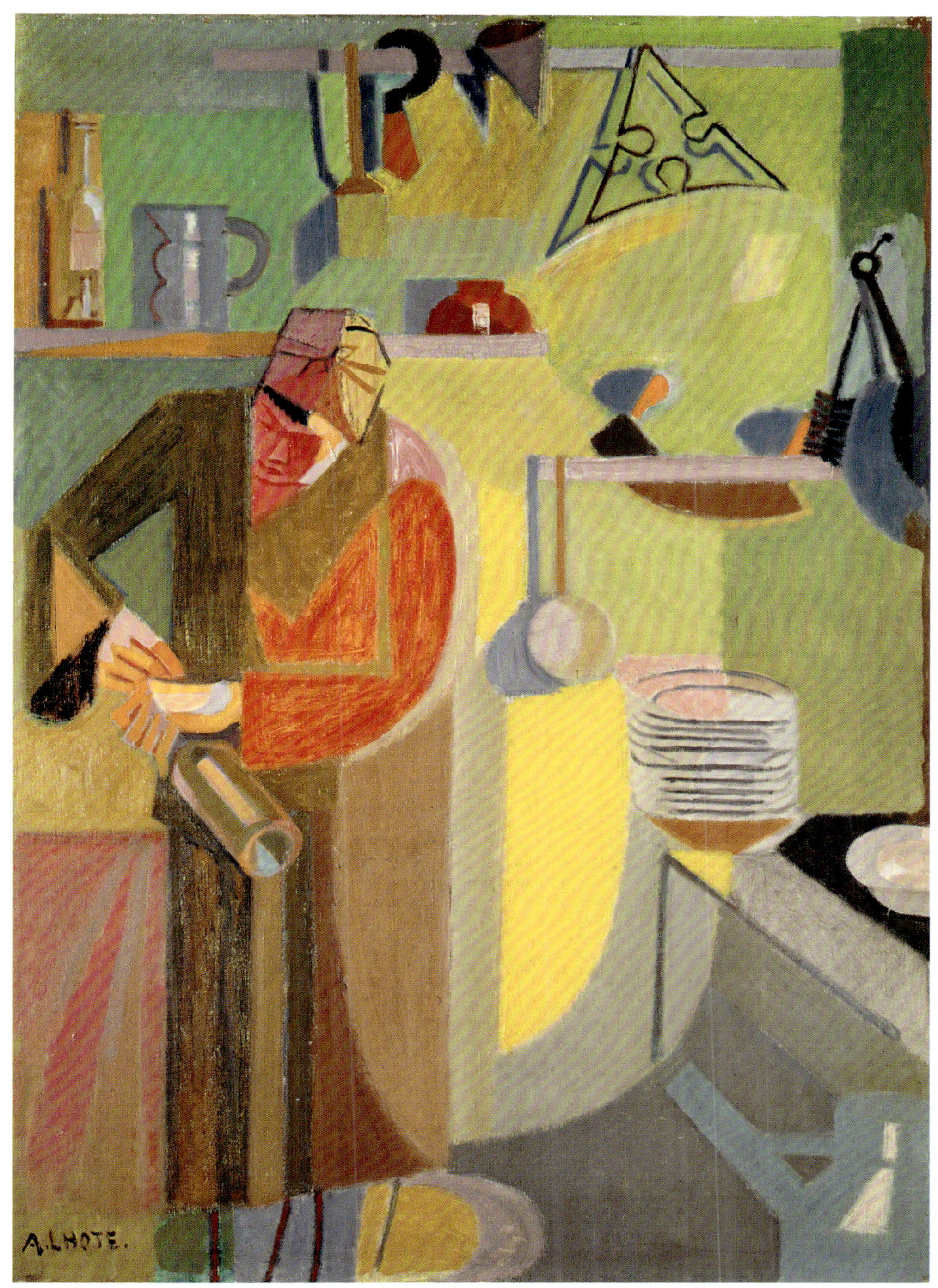

Pl. 37. André Lhote (French, 1885–1962)
Kitchen at Gordes, n.d.

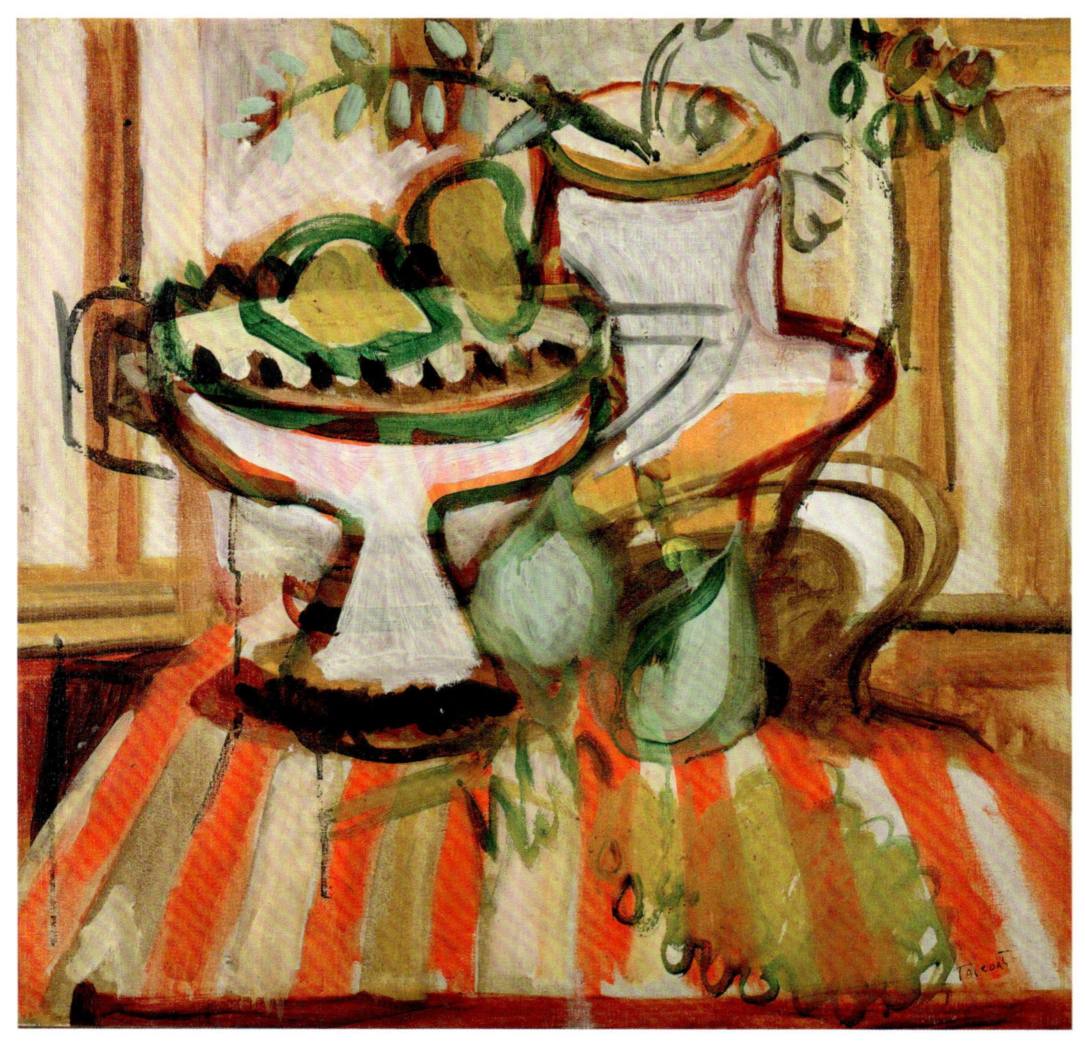

Pl. 38. Tal-Coat (French, 1905–85)
Still Life with a Fruit Bowl, 1942–43

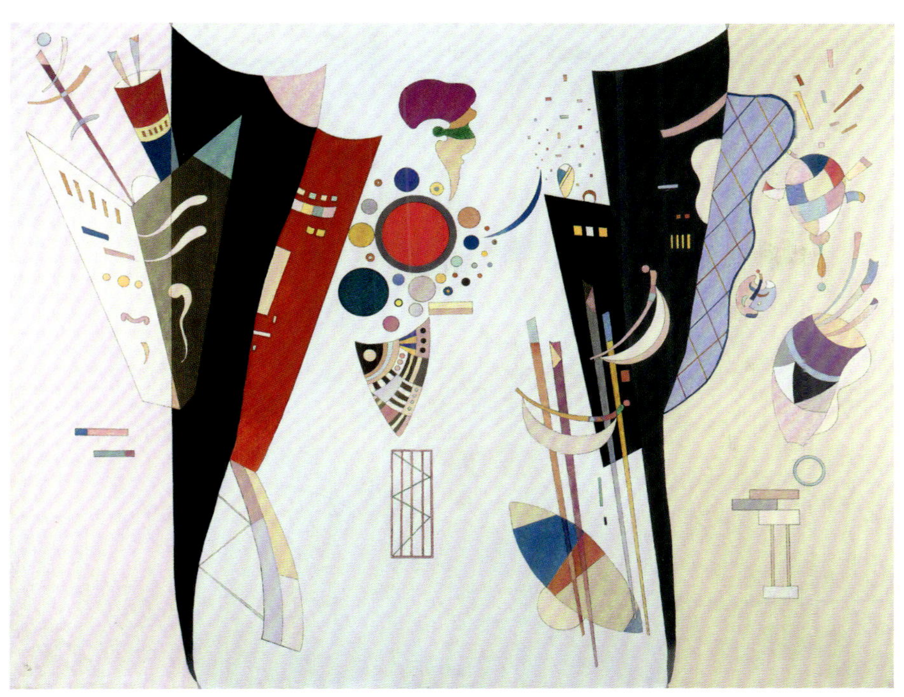

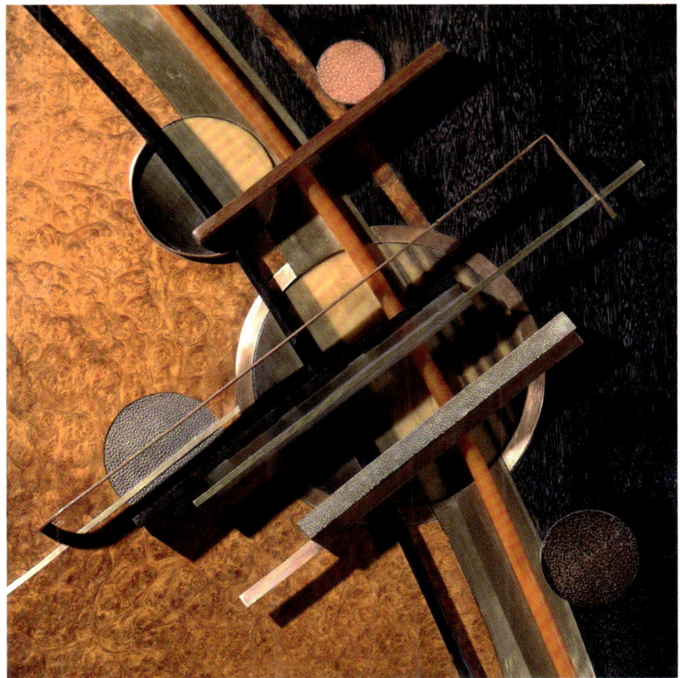

Pl. 39. Vasily Kandinsky (Russian, 1866–1944)
Reciprocal Accord, 1942

Pl. 40. César Domela (Dutch, 1900–1992)
Relief No. 15E, 1941

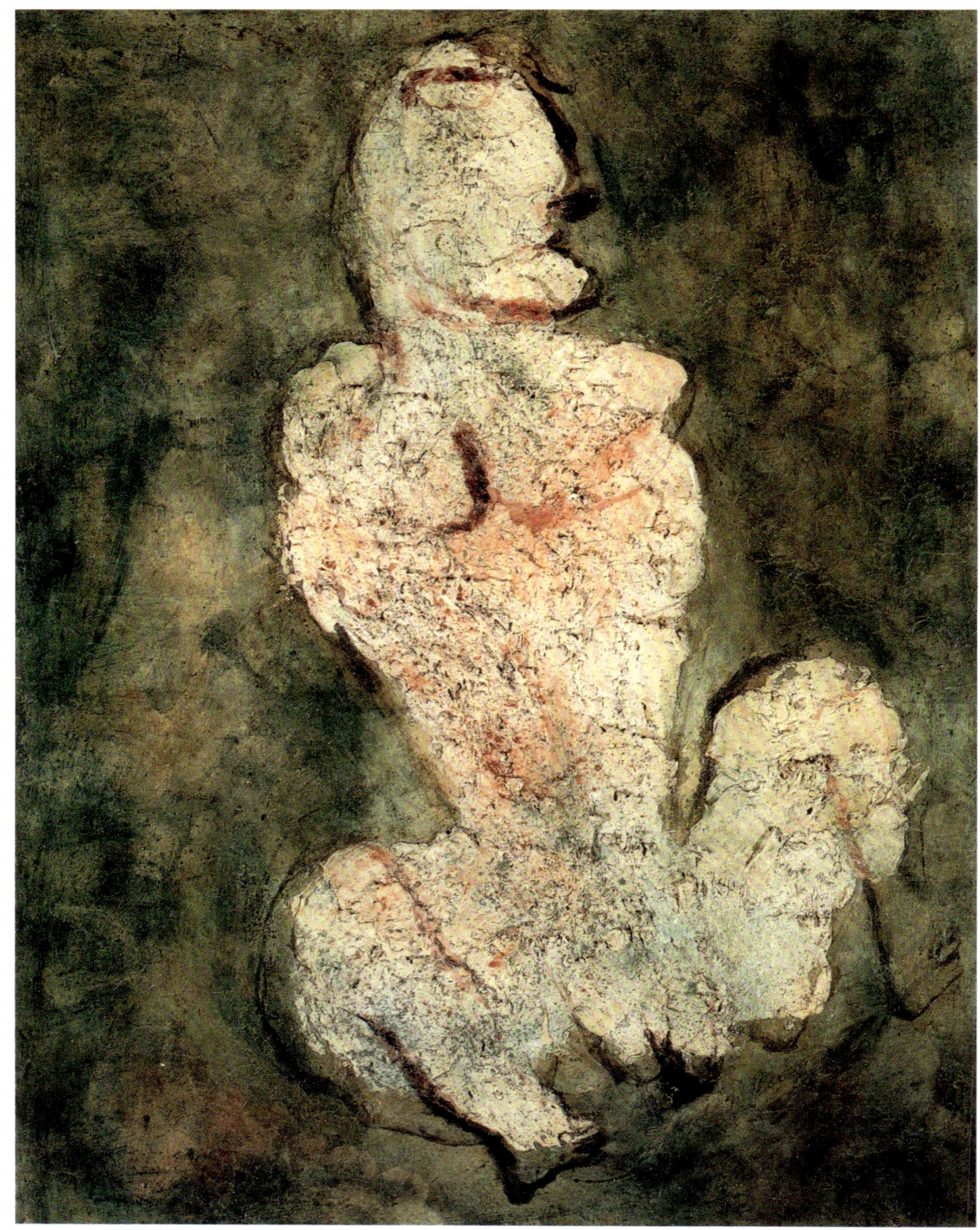

Pl. 41. Jean Fautrier (French, 1898–1964)
Hostage's Body, 1943

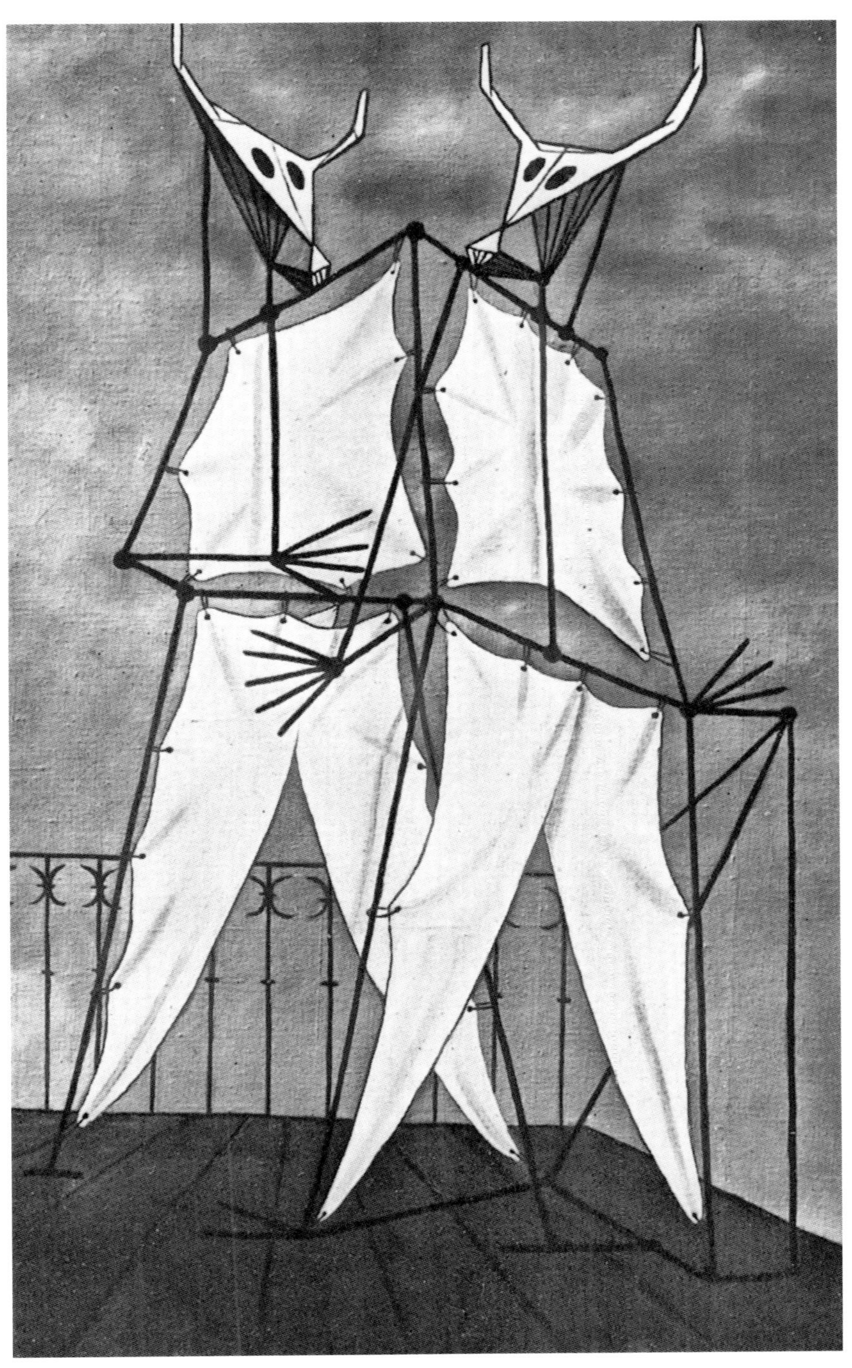

Pl. 42. Oscar Dominguez (Spanish, 1906–57)
The End of the War, 1943

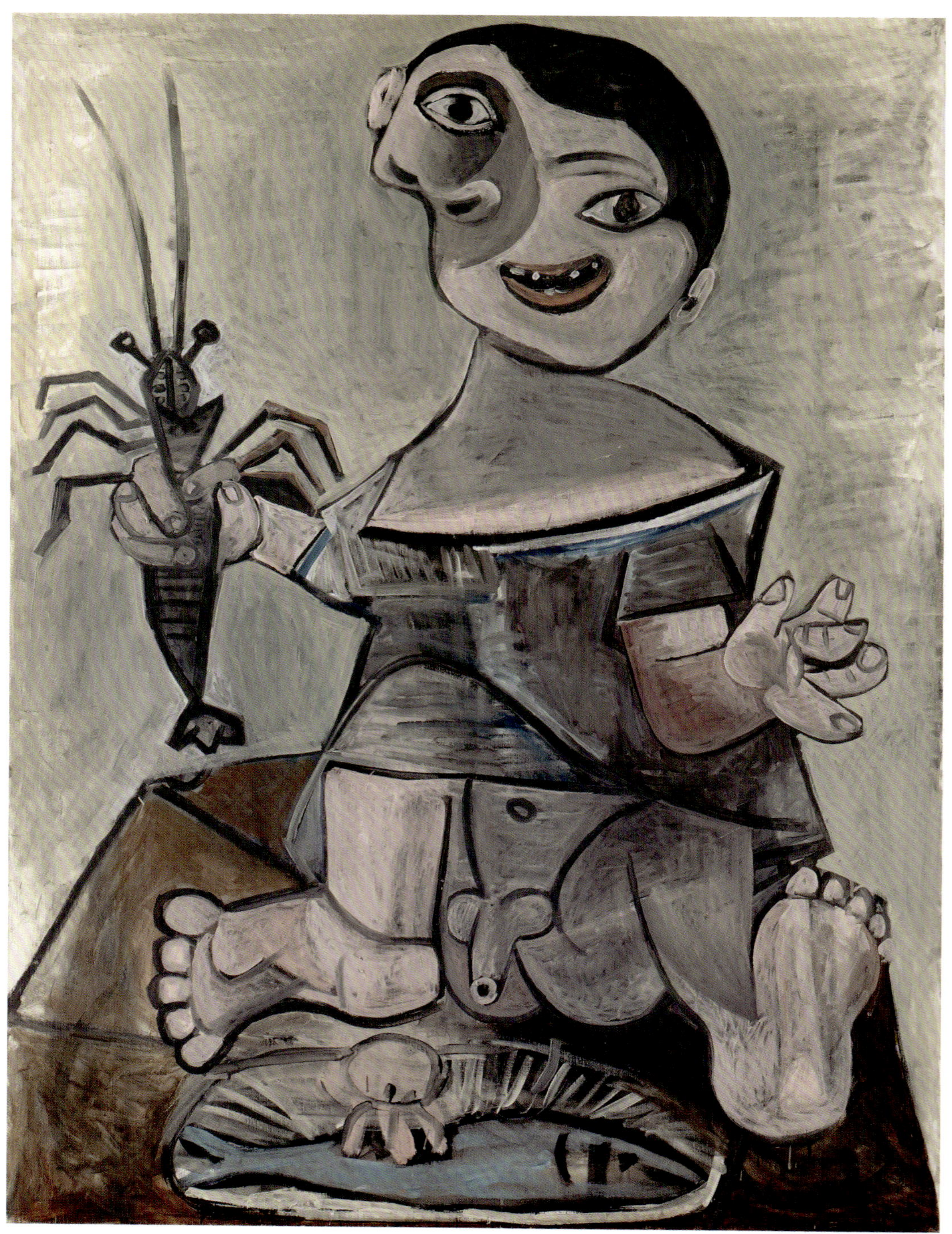

Pl. 43. Pablo Picasso (Spanish, 1881–1973)
Boy with a Lobster, 1941

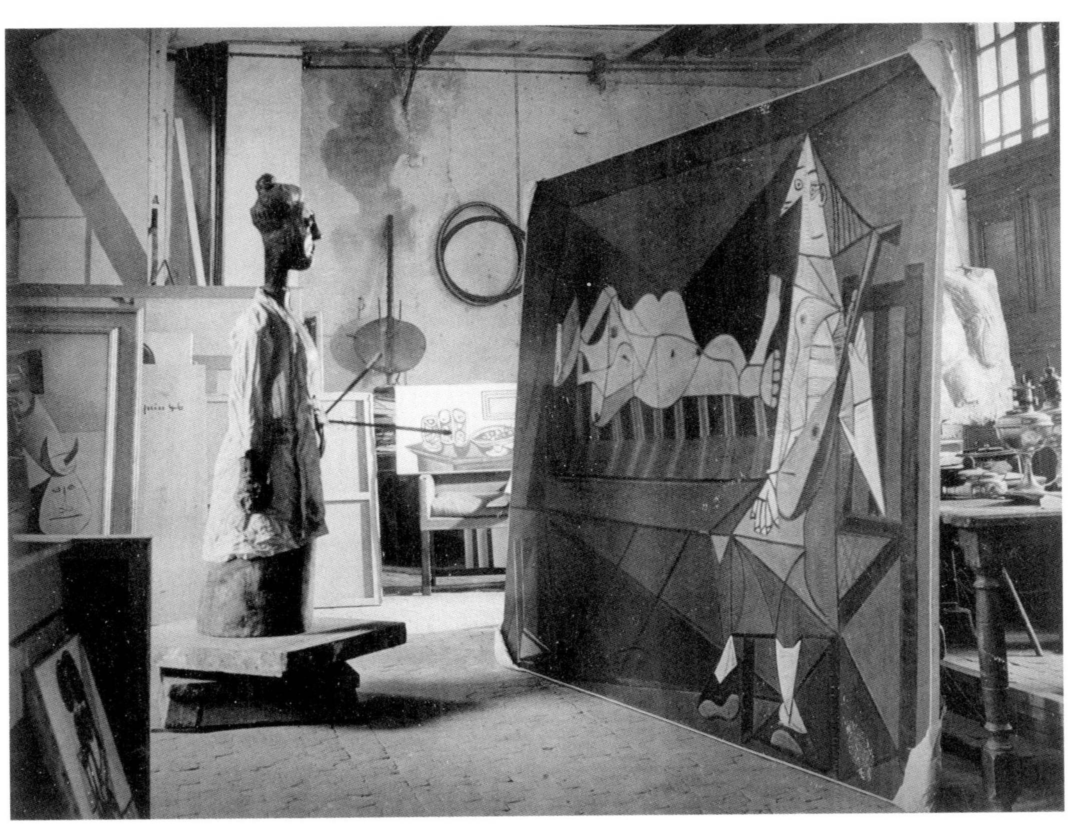

Pl. 44. Brassaï (French, 1899–1984)
Pablo Picasso's *Aubade* in the artist's studio on rue des Grands-Augustins, Paris, 1946

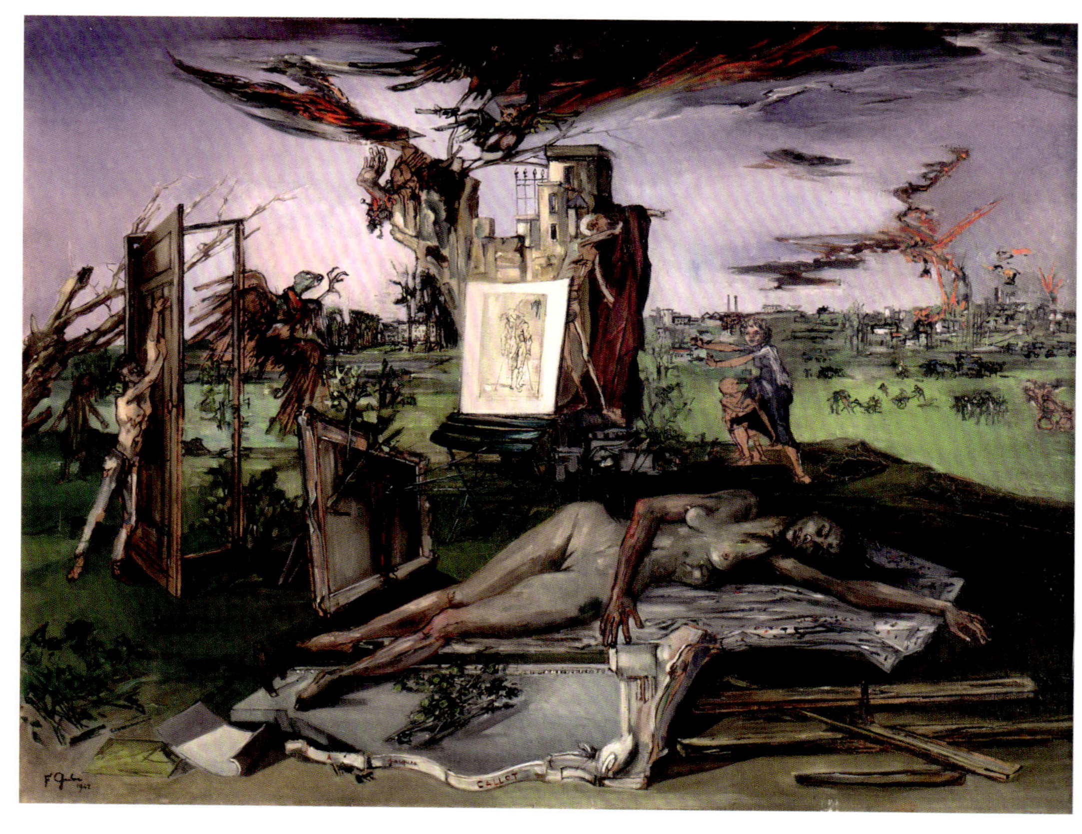

Pl. 45. Francis Gruber (French, 1912–48)
Homage to Jacques Callot, 1942

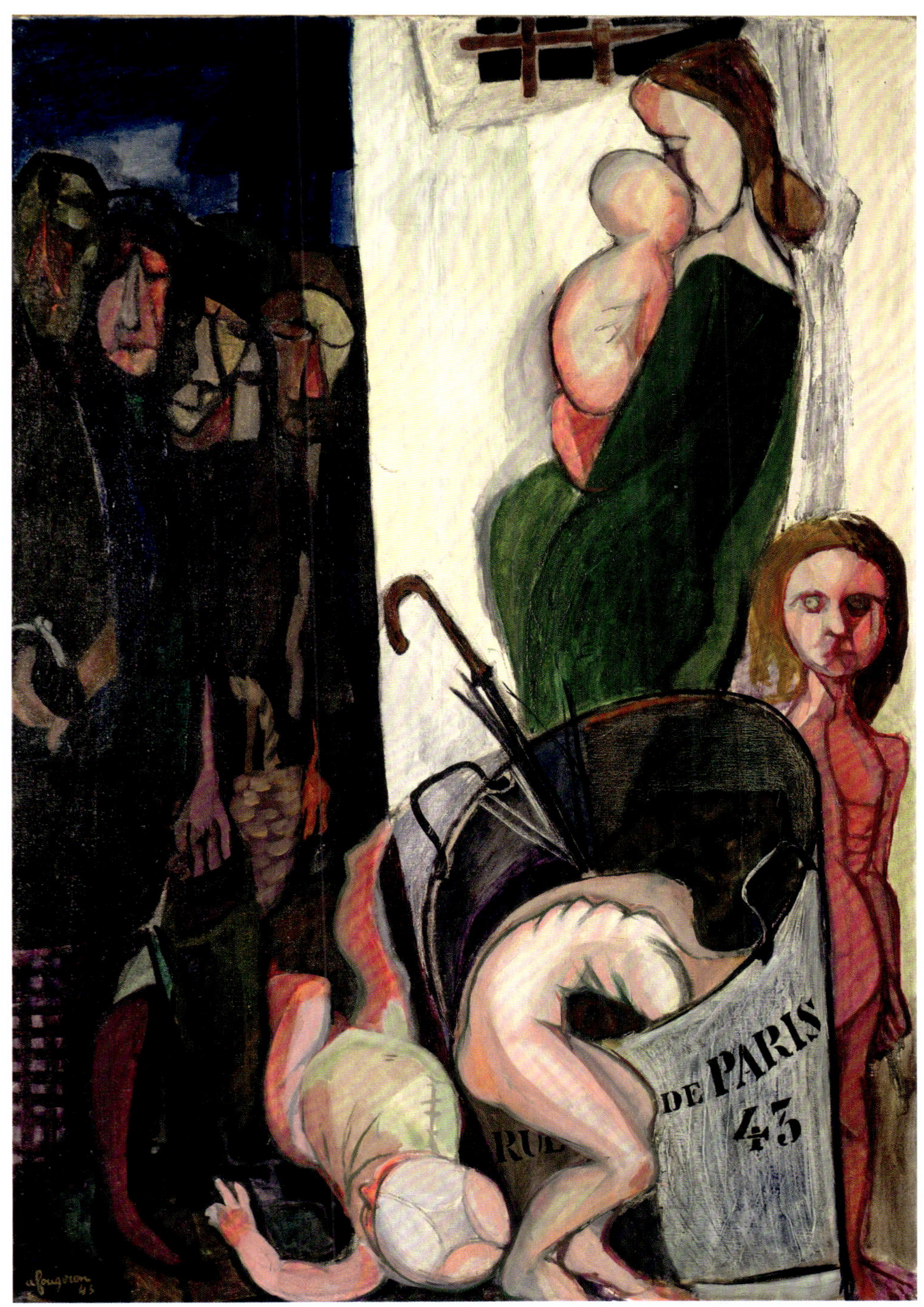

Pl. 46. André Fougeron (French, 1912–98)
Rue de Paris, 1943

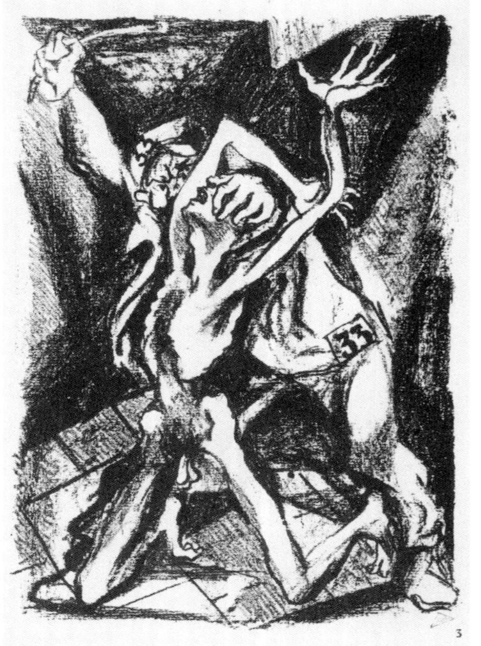

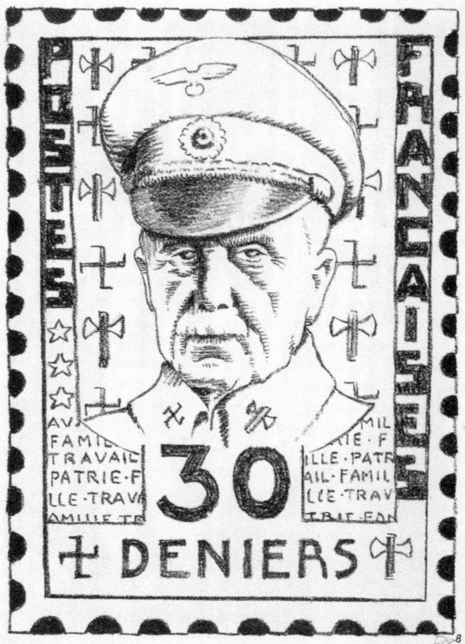

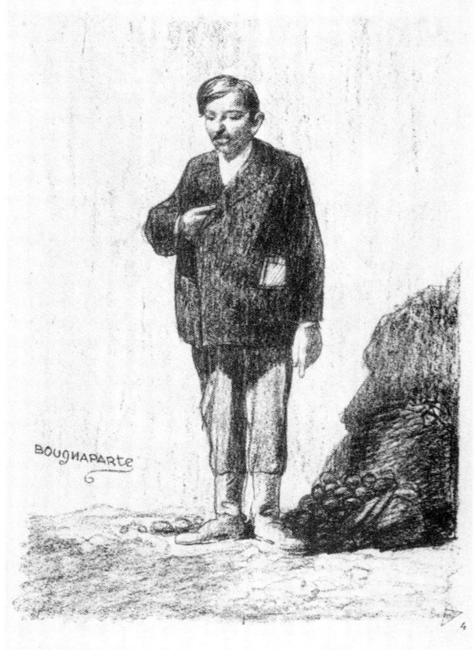

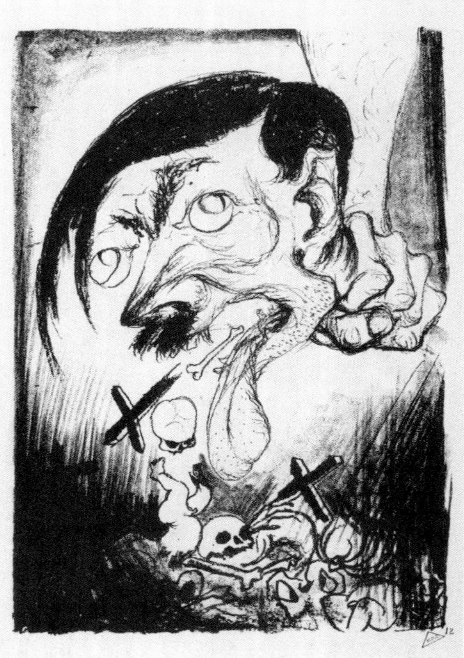

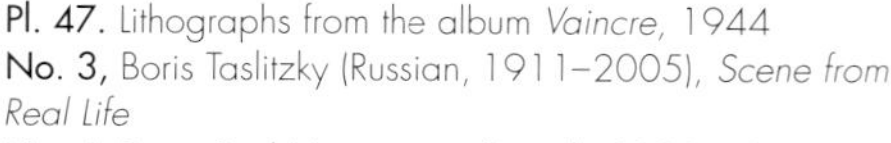

Pl. 47. Lithographs from the album *Vaincre,* 1944
No. 3, Boris Taslitzky (Russian, 1911–2005), *Scene from Real Life*
No. 4, Pierre-Paul Montagnac (French, 1883–1961), *Bougnaparte*

No. 8, Pierre Ladureau (French, 1882–1974), *Judas*
No. 12, André Fougeron (French, 1912–98), *Death to the Beast*

APPENDIX

Table 1. Involvement of selected artists in various significant events, 1940–1944

Profession	Name	Trip to Germany (1941)	Corporation of artists (1940–1944)			Breker exhibition honorary committee (1942)	Letter from Hilaire (1944)			Accused of collaboration during the postwar purge
			Study committee	Professional organization committee	Specialized bureau		Received	Reply		
								Yes	No	
PAINTER	Aujame						•	•		
	Berthommé-Saint-André						•	•		
	Bonnard						•	•		
	Brianchon						•	•		
	Denis*		•							
	Derain	•				•	•			•
	Desvallières*		•	•	•					
	Dunoyer de Segonzac	•		•	•		•			•
	Dupas*			•						
	Estève						•		•	
	Friesz	•				•	•			•
	Goulinat						•	•		
	Gromaire						•		•	
	Guy-Loë						•			
	Legueult	•				•	•	•		•
	Lhote				•			•		
	Manguin						•	•		
	Pougheon*			•						
	Puy						•	•		
	Waroquier, de						•	•		

	Wild, R.						•	•		
ENGRAVER	Beltrand			•						•
	Dautel			•						
	Jacquemin						•	•		
SCULPTOR	Belmondo	•			•	•				•
	Bouchard*	•	•	•	•	•				•
	Couturie						•		•	
	Despiau	•			•	•	•	•		•
	Drivier*						•	•		
	Gimond						•		•	
	Landowski*	•	•	•		•				•
	Lejeune*	•			•					•
	Maillol					•	•	•		
	Niclausse*						•	•		
	Osouf						•	•		
	Yencesse						•	•		
ART CRITIC OR WRITER	Campagne						•	•		•
	Champigneulle						•	•		
	Chéronnet						•	•		
	Colombier, du						•	•		
	Diehl						•	•		
SET DESIGNER	Dignimont						•	•		
	Oudot					•	•	•		•
	Touchagues						•	•		
DECORATIVE ARTIST	Dutrène		•	•						
	Montagnac			•						

* Member of the Académie des beaux-arts of the Institut de France prior to 1944.

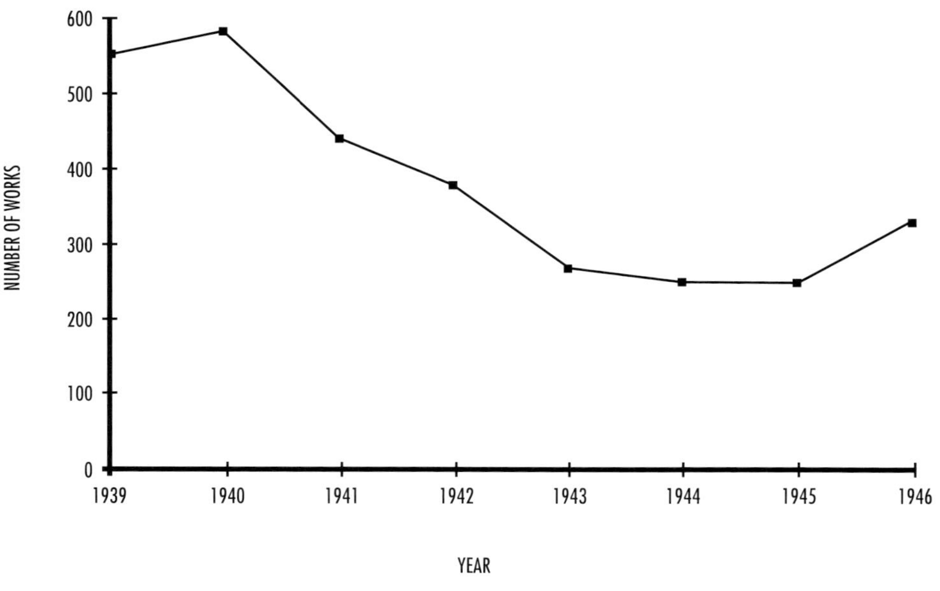

Graph 1. Annual purchases of works of art by the French state, 1939–June 1946. Source: Inventory book, Archives nationales

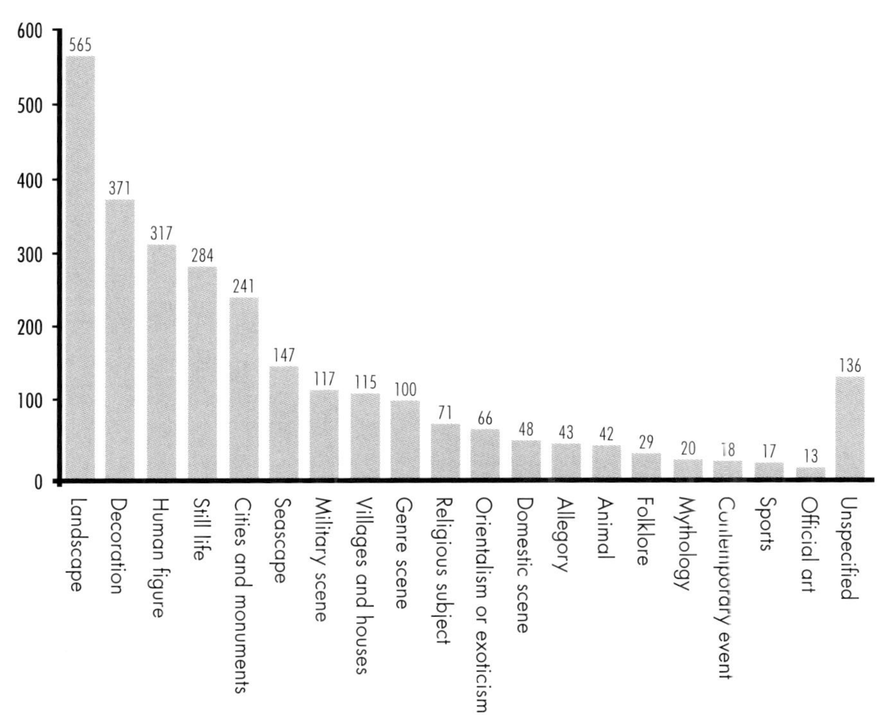

Graph 2. Distribution by subject of the paintings, drawings, and decorations acquired by the French state, 1939–1945 (*N* = 2,760 works). Source: Inventory book, Archives nationales

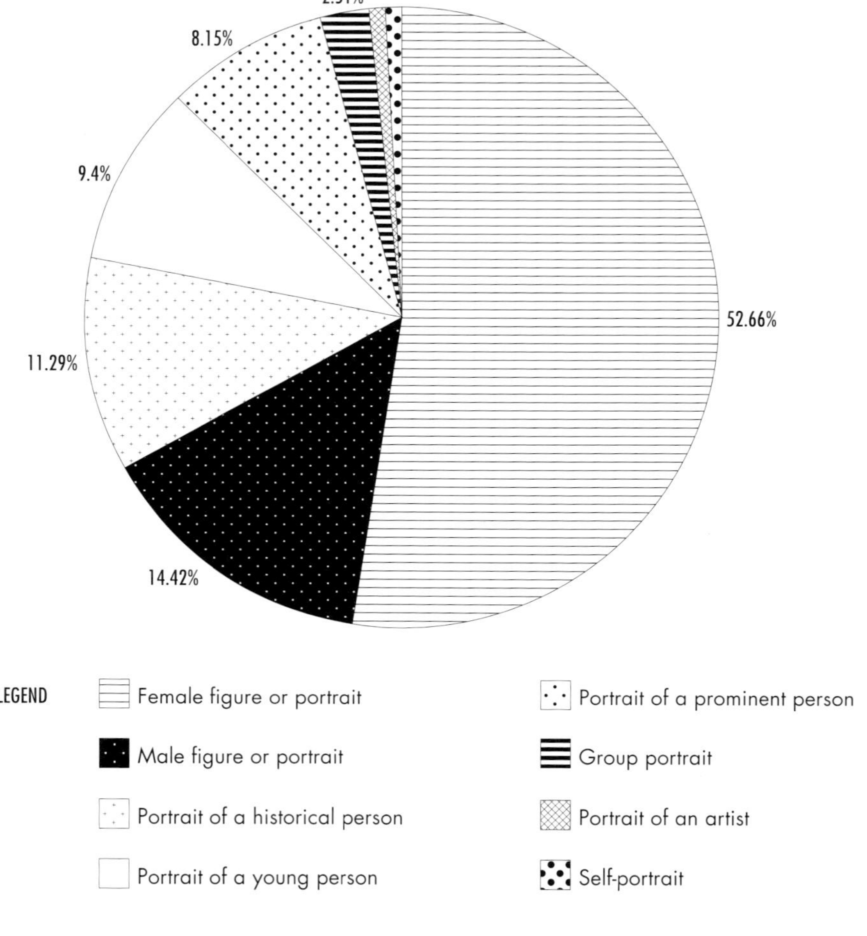

Graph 3. Distribution of representations of human figures acquired by the French state, 1939–June 1946. Source: Inventory book, Archives nationales

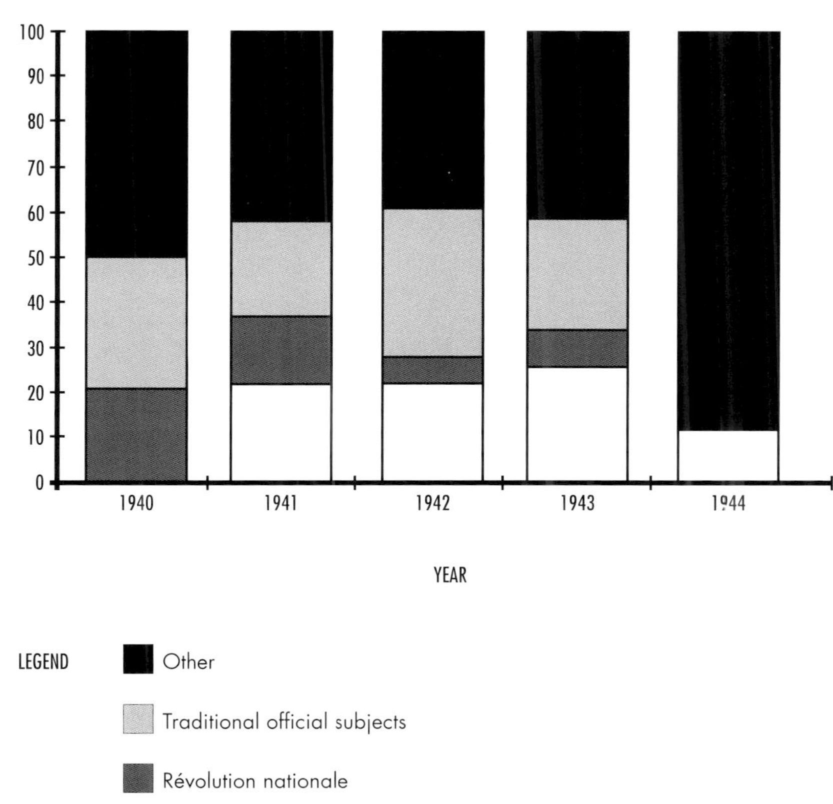

Graph 4. Distribution of subjects on stamps, by series issued, July 1940–August 1944 (*N* = 63 series). Source: Jean Storch, Jean-François Brun, and Robert Françon, *Timbres de France: Marianne, 1983–1984: Catalogue fédéral* (Paris: Fédération des Sociétés Philatéliques Françaises, 1983)

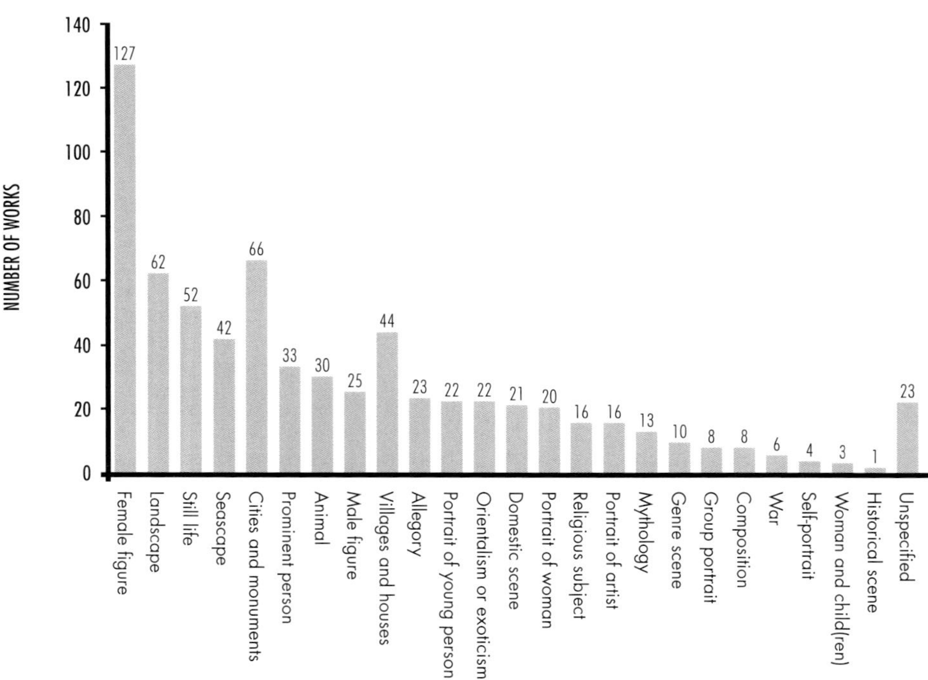

Graph 5. Distribution by subject of the works of art exhibited at the Musée national d'art moderne, August 1942 (N = 697 works). Source: *Musée national d'art moderne: Exposition permanente: Catalogue* (Paris: Musée National d'Art Moderne, 1942)

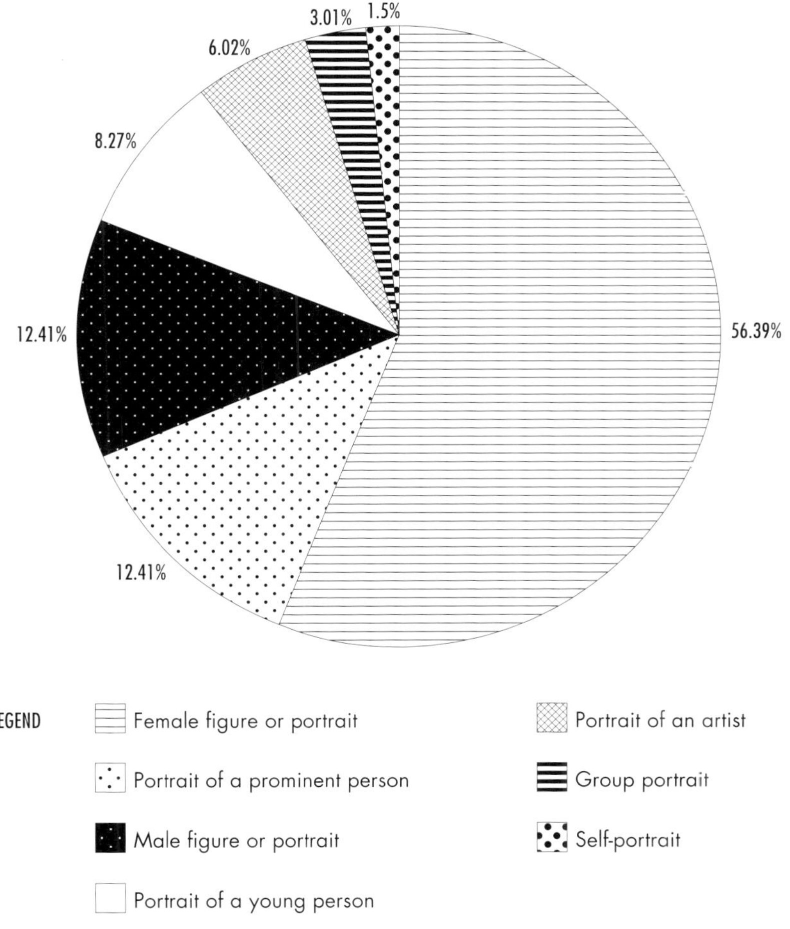

Graph 6. Distribution of representations of human figures exhibited at the Musée national d'art moderne, August 1942. Source: *Musée national d'art moderne: Exposition permanente: Catalogue* (Paris: Musée National d'Art Moderne, 1942)

JUNE 1940–OCTOBER 1944

Chronology

Artistic or cultural events are set in the serif font, and items relating primarily to politics, government, or the war are set in the sans serif font. Some items are listed generally, under a year or under a month within a year, rather than being associated with a particular day.

1940

First plan for a corporation of the graphic and plastic arts.

Sculpture and mural painting public works projects organized in the Paris region.

Les réverbères resumes its activities.

Jean Cassou, *Picasso* (Ed. Hypérion), a book that will remain in circulation during the occupation.

Fourth issue of the revue *Le poids du monde repose sur les sensibles*, published in Lyon by members of Groupe témoignage.

Lapicque, *Joan of Arc Crossing the Loire, Sainte-Catherine-de-Fierbois, The Maritime Vocation.*

Creation of the Salon de l'Imagerie Française.

JUNE

Propaganda-Abteilung Frankreich moves into 52, avenue des Champs-Elysées.

10 French government leaves Paris for Bordeaux.

14 Paris occupied by the Germans.

16 Reynaud resigns as premier of France. Pétain replaces him as head of state.

17 Formation of the Pétain cabinet.

17 Rivaud named minister of national education.

18 From London, de Gaulle appeals to the French to resist.

21 The ship *Massilia* leaves France for North Africa.

21 Hitler arrives at Rethondes.

22 Signing of the armistice.

22 Death of Edouard Vuillard.

23 Hitler visits Paris accompanied by Speer, Breker, Brandt, Bormann, and Bodenschatz.

25 The armistice goes into effect.

25 Pétain calls for "intellectual and moral" recovery in France.

29 Death of Paul Klee.

30 Beginning of the German inventory of French and Jewish collections.

JULY

Dunoyer de Segonzac founds the Ecole nationale des cadres d'Uriage with Bertrand d'Astorg, Hubert Beuve-Méry, Paul-Henry Chombart de Lauwe, Joffre Dumazedier, Olivier Hussenot, Simon Nora, and others.

The two legislative chambers of the French Parliament decide to revise France's constitutional laws.

First issue of the French-language edition of the German review *Signal*.

Maurice Denis notes in his journal: "Saturday three of us were at the Institut de France, Cognacq, Tournaire, and I. And Bouteron. The conversation suggested that people are turning toward the hope of a new dictatorial regime, in short, toward Germany. It makes you want to cry."

8 The railway car of the 1918 armistice "returned" to Germany.

9 The Third Reich's propaganda ministry declares that France will play the role of an expanded Switzerland in Europe and will become a country of tourism, possibly involved in the manufacture of goods in the field of fashion.

10 The National Assembly grants full powers to Pétain.

12 Mireaux replaces Rivaud to become education and fine arts minister.

15 Hilaire named *préfet* of the *département* Aube.

15 Vollard-Bockelberg's decree on the "safeguarding" of works of art in occupied France.

21 Hautecoeur named director general of fine arts (appointment confirmed on 9 August).

30 Decree regarding youth groups, the future Chantiers de la jeunesse, which are placed under the authority of général de division, and former scoutmaster, Joseph de La Porte du Theil.

30 Establishment of the supreme court of Riom to judge the leaders of the French Third Republic.

AUGUST

The first agents of Free France arrive in France.

Abetz named the Third Reich's ambassador to Paris.

The general secretariat of youth creates a department for arts initiatives.

Picasso returns to 7, rue des Grands-Augustins in Paris.

16 Establishment of the provisional organization committees.

18 The Propaganda-Abteilung Frankreich placed in charge of all cultural activity.

22 Pétain tells the U.S. press that the France of tomorrow "will restore the ancient traditions that had once made its fortune and its glory. The traditional country of quality, it will be able to give to all its products that finish, that delicacy, that elegance in which it had no equal."

29 Creation of the Légion française des combattants.

SEPTEMBER

Art français contemporain at the Musée de l'Orangerie.

6 Cabinet reshuffled: most parliamentarians are eliminated.

7 Ripert replaces Mireaux and becomes education and youth minister.

17 Rationing of basic foodstuffs.

17 Expansion of Rosenberg's powers regarding the pillage of works of art belonging to Jews and to Freemasons.

27 German promulgation of a decree concerning the Jews.

27 Signing of the Tripartite Pact by Germany, Italy, and Japan.

28 Convention signed with the occupying forces by the Syndicat des éditeurs.

OCTOBER

Organization of the Resistance in France.

Reopening of some galleries at the Musée du Louvre.

Pierre Imbourg argues for the arts corporation plan in the review *Beaux-arts*.

Beginning of the systematic seizure of Jewish collections.

Reform of fine arts education.

3 The Conseil des ministres passes the first Statut des Juifs.

5 Law entrusting the inventorying, management, and liquidation of property in sequestration to the Vichy administration.

11 Creation of the Commissariat à la lutte contre le chômage.

19 First issue of the weekly *Compagnon*.

22 Pétain authorizes Cogné to mass-produce his official bust.

23 Meeting in Montoire-sur-le-Loir: Hitler promises Pétain to make a place for France in the new Europe, in exchange for French collaboration.

30 Message from Pétain: the French must agree to collaborate.

NOVEMBER

Mounier points out the need for a "total revolution."

Monet-Rodin retrospective at the Orangerie des Tuileries organized by Entraide des artistes.

3 Göring visits the haul of looted works at the Jeu de Paume.

9 Decree dissolving the trade unions.

11 Student demonstration in Paris.

22 Birth of the association Jeune France, under the aegis of the general secretariat of youth and the patronage of the education ministry.

30 At his Galerie folklore in Lyon, Michaud presents the works of Groupe témoignage—Bertholle, Beyer, Burlet, Pernin, Silvant, Thomas, Chardon, Gleizes, Le Moal, Niogret, Étienne-Martin, Salendre, Stahly—accompanied by poetry sessions, a conversation on "painting and spirituality," concerts, and a display of French and foreign arts and crafts.

DECEMBER

Creation of the Commissariat au chômage des jeunes.

Survey by Arts et traditions populaires on traditional housing.

1 Decree stipulating the reorganization of the Direction générale des beaux-arts.

13 Ripert resigns his posts and is replaced by Chevalier as minister of education and youth.

13 Laval dismissed by Pétain and arrested by the Vichy regime but soon released at the behest of the Germans. Flandin is named foreign affairs minister in his stead.

14 Circular from the secretary general of fine arts to academy superintendents, relating to the suspension of Jews dictated by the law of 3 October 1940.

15 First issue of the first underground newspaper, *Résistance,* run by the Resistance network based at the Musée de l'homme in Paris.

15 Two million children's drawings glorifying Pétain are sent to Vichy.

19 First major jazz festival, held at the Salle Gaveau in Paris.

31 Creation of the Ordre des architectes.

1941

Georges Lamirand, *Messages à la jeunesse* (Ed. F. Sorlot).

Abel Bonnard, *Des jeunes gens ou une jeunesse?* (L'Artisan du Livre).

Max Ernst goes into exile in the United States.

Exhibition of thirty-three paintings (1892–1941) by Denis at Galerie Louis Carré.

Exhibition of a few works by Pierre Bonnard at Galerie Pétridès.

Salon de l'Imagerie Française.

Competition on the theme of Pétain's image.

Pétain visits Aubusson.

First Salon du Dessin et de la Peinture à l'Eau (summer).

Un an de théâtre, an exhibition organized in Vichy by Jeune France, with more than three hundred maquettes for plays produced during the 1940/1941 season. Illustrations by Touchagues, Cocteau, Le Moal, Effel, Dior, and others.

Exhibition of the Paul Jamot bequest.

Morisot exhibition at the Orangerie des Tuileries. Catalog preface by Paul Valéry.

Decoration of the town hall of Brou (Eure-et-Loir) by Lautrec.

Magnelli in Grasse, turns to wood engravings, crumpled paper, collages, gouaches on slate, works on notepaper, staff paper, and school notebooks.

Pierre Bonnard begins *Nude in the Bath* (completed 1946).

Gruber, *Portrait of the Artist in His Studio.*

Belmondo, *Bust of Louis Hautecoeur.*

Start of *La main à plume*, an underground surrealist publication by Chabrun and Arnaud, who publish *Transfusion du verbe*, illustrated by Tita, Gagnaire, Picasso, Dominguez, and Ubac; Duchamp's *Box in a Valise;* and Picasso's *Le désir attrapé par la queue;* and the presentation of Hans Arp's first papers.

Creation of the Front national des arts, with Aujame, Denis, Fougeron, Goerg, Lurçat, and Pignon.

First issue of the clandestine periodical *L'art français*, founded by Billiet and edited by Desnoyer, Goerg, Fougeron, Montagnac, and Walch.

Campaign promoting the craft industry in the socialist review *Le rouge et le bleu.*

The painter Guy-Loë replaces the recently deceased poet Garnier as head of Entraide des artistes.

Trip to Germany by Belmondo, Bouchard, Derain, Despiau, van Dongen, Dunoyer de Segonzac, Friesz, Landowski, Legueult, Lejeune, Oudot, and Vlaminck.

Jeune France publication: *Principe, direction, esprit* (Imp. Audin).

Lucien Rebatet, *Les tribus du cinéma et du théâtre* (Nouvelles Editions Françaises).

Robert Rey, *La peinture moderne, ou l'Art sans métier* (PUF), a violent criticism of modern art.

Alfred Rosenberg, *Tradition und Gegenwart* (Franz Eher Nachf.).

Secrétariat d'Etat aux Communications, Commissariat Technique à la Reconstruction Immobilière, *Charte de l'architecte reconstructeur* (Imp. Nationale).

Élie Faure, *Histoire de l'art*, vol. 4, *L'art moderne* (Plon).

Charles [Sterling], *Les peintres du Moyen Âge* (Ed. P. Tisné/Bibliothèque Française des Arts).

Étienne Saint-Léon, *Histoire des corporations de métiers* (PUF).

Louis Bréhier, *Le style roman* (Larousse).

Jeanne Bucher, *L'artisanat hier et aujourd'hui* (Les Livres Nouveaux).

Louis-Ferdinand Céline, *Les beaux draps* (Nouvelles Editions Françaises).

Paul Éluard, *Le livre ouvert* (Ed. Cahiers de l'Art).

Jean Paulhan, *Les fleurs de Tarbes, ou La terreur dans les lettres* (Gallimard).

Louis Aragon, *Le crève-coeur* (Gallimard).

Pierre de Lescure and Vercors found Les Editions de Minuit.

Maurice Blanchot, *Thomas l'obscur* (Gallimard).

Jean Cocteau, *La machine à écrire* (Gallimard).

Death of Henri Bergson.

Olivier Messiaen, *Quartet for the End of Time.*

Two million art objects pass through the Hôtel Drouot.

JANUARY

Exhibition on the peasantry at Galerie La Boétie.

Establishment of a chair of ethnography at the Ecole du Louvre.

8 Jean-Marc Campagne, "L'art facile et la décadence du goût," *Les nouveaux temps.*

10 Renewal of the German-Soviet Nonagression Pact.

10 New series of the newspaper *Beaux-arts* coincides with "certain undeniable indications of revival," announces Louis Réau, professor at the Sorbonne and member of the editorial board.

15 Campagne declares in *Les nouveaux temps*, "We wish to indicate that Paris already has no cause to be envious of Berlin."

FEBRUARY

The leaders of the Musée de l'homme network are the first Resistance fighters to be executed.

Darlan becomes Pétain's heir apparent.

Le Juif süss (dir. Harlan) in Paris movie theaters.

1 Founding of the collaborationist Rassemblement national populaire (RNP) by Déat and its amalgamation with Deloncle's Mouvement social révolutionnaire.

7 *Je suis partout* resumes publication.

14 Rebatet criticizes the Institut de France in *Je suis partout.*

17 Decree on the reorganization of architectural education.

17 Establishment of a study committee for the graphic and plastic arts.

MARCH

The Main-d'oeuvre immigrée gains strength.

15 The occupying forces call for an arts corporation.

19 *Le sport dans l'art* exhibition opens at the Musée Galliera.

23 Carcopino named minister of education and youth.

23 Hautecoeur named secretary general of fine arts (he had been its director).

26 Creation of the artisanal bureaus for distributing materials.

29 Creation of a Commissariat général aux questions juives.

APRIL

Daily ration of bread: 275 g (10 oz.).

Jean Bazaine, "Guerre et évasions," *La nouvelle revue française.*

21 The Librairie Rive-Gauche at 47, boulevard Saint-Michel, becomes the "Franco-German" bookstore.

MAY

Chagall goes into exile in the United States.

Arrest of the artist Berline.

Jean Bazaine, "Le décor et l'objet," *La nouvelle revue française.*

2 Decree issued by the interior minister Pierre Pucheu regulating the use of the *francisque.*

8 New Nazi order concerning the Jews in the occupied zone

8 Pierre du Colombier, "Belles images d'autrefois," *Beaux-arts,* calls on artists to do what provincial artisans once did.

8 Jean-Marc Campagne, "Quelle place va-t-on faire à l'art dans la réforme de l'enseignement?" *Beaux-arts.*

10 Preview of the exhibition *Jeunes peintres de tradition française* at Galerie Braun: Bazaine, Beaudin, Berçot, Bertholle, Bores, Coutaud, Desnoyer, Gischia, Lapicque, Lasne, Lautrec, Legueult, Le Moal, Manessier, Marchand, Pignon, Roger, Singier, Tal-Coat, Walch.

14 Arrest in Paris of foreign Jews.

22 Pierre d'Espezel, "Les peintres de la Jeune France," *Le cri du peuple.*

24 Drafting of a corporation organization plan.

31 *La France européenne* exhibition at the Grand Palais.

JUNE

Picasso, *Boy with a Lobster.*

2 Carcopino reminds academy superintendents of students' obligation to display political reserve.

7 New Statut des Juifs set in place by the Vichy government.

15 First issue of the new *Pariser Zeitung*. Contributors covering the arts: Paul Strecker, Albert Buesche, Hans Haveman, Martin Raschke, Wolf Schramm.

21 Quota on Jews enrolled at universities.

22 Germans invade the USSR.

23 Law banning the display of artworks executed prior to 1900.

JULY

5 Jean Giraudoux, "L'art et le sport au stade Roland-Garros," *Comoedia,* argues that the nations "that have the highest percentage of art reviews are also those that have the highest percentage of gymnasts: Germany and Finland."

5 Creation of professional crafts groups.

6 Constitution of the Légion des volontaires français contre le bolchevisme.

7 Decree relating to the provisional organization of industrial production, in accordance with the law of 16 August 1940. It calls for the creation of an organization committee for the graphic and plastic arts.

18 Léandre Vaillat, "La sculpture devant l'urbanisme," *Beaux-arts.*

20 Exhibition by Les réverbères.

AUGUST

Government reorganization that results in the education ministry no longer reporting to the army but to the interior minister, Pierre Pucheu.

Bernard Faÿ, "Caractères de l'esprit français," *La nouvelle revue française.*

Jean Bazaine, "Tour d'horizon," *La nouvelle revue française.*

5 Denis refuses to chair the Ordre des artistes.

8 Lucien Rebatet, "L'école des yeux," *Beaux-arts.*

10 Decree stipulating that some provincial museums be attached to the Direction des musées nationaux and others be subject to state control.

14 High-level officials, magistrates, and soldiers required to take an oath of allegiance to Pétain.

17 Pierre Lagarde, "André Derain révolutionnaire," *Comoedia*.

21 Pierre Georges, better known as Colonel Fabien, kills a German officer in the Barbès-Rochechouart metro station.

22 Hostage decree.

31 Provincial festivals in Vichy.

SEPTEMBER

Beginning of the activities of the Front national.

Georges Hilaire becomes acting *préfet* of the interior ministry in the occupied zone.

Festival Swing held at the Salle Pleyel in Paris.

Reconstitution of the Comité national du folklore.

5 The exhibition *Le Juif et la France* opens in Paris.

26 In London, de Gaulle constitutes the Conseil national de la France Libre.

OCTOBER

Exhibition of artworks by mobilized German soldiers at the requisitioned Galerie Bernheim-Jeune.

Start of the series of exhibitions organized by Gaston Diehl, *Les étapes du nouvel art contemporain*, at Galerie Berri-Raspail.

First Salon des Moins de Trente Ans at Galerie royale.

1 Edmond Humeau, "Le chômage intellectuel," *Chantiers*.

4 Promulgation of the Charte du travail.

15 Carcopino announces that the sale of portraits and objects glorifying Pétain has brought in 16,846,000 francs.

16 Pétain orders the internment of Daladier, Blum, and Gamelin.

16 Law regarding the wearing of the *francisque*.

22 Execution of ninety-eight hostages.

22 Death of Louis Marcoussis.

23 Twenty-seven executed by firing squad in Châteaubriant.

25 Decree announcing the resignation of Denis and his replacement by Dupas, also a member of the Institut de France.

25 Death of Robert Delaunay.

NOVEMBER

First issue of *Cahiers du Témoignage chrétien*.

Exclusion measures against the Jews, regarding awards and travel grants.

First volume in the series Cahiers de l'Institut allemand, published under the direction of Epting.

Creation of the Ecole des hautes études artisanales.

Exhibition of recent india ink and charcoal drawings by Matisse at Galerie Louis Carré.

1 First issue of *Le rouge et le bleu*, titled "Le sport vaincra la décadence physique des Français."

8 Guillaume Durance, "Peinture romane," *Le rouge et le bleu*.

15 First bulletin issued by Secours national.

16 *Kunst der Front*, an exhibition of works by German soldiers, opens at the Jeu de Paume.

19 One hundred thousand French workers depart for Germany.

22 Bernard Poissonnier, "Peintres et sculpteurs français en Allemagne," *Comoedia*.

29 Maximilien Gauthier, "Impressions d'Allemagne," *Comoedia*.

DECEMBER

Germany and Italy declare war on the United States.

Jean Bazaine, "Masques corporatifs," *La nouvelle revue française*, opposes the Vichy plan for an arts corporation.

First issue of *Atalante: Revue d'art et de culture*, directed by René Borelly, which includes his "L'art au service de la Révolution nationale."

German exhibition of various freestanding pieces and busts of Hitler in imitation bronze and other materials at the Petit Palais in Paris.

Exhibition of thirty charcoal, chalk, and pencil drawings of nudes by Maillol, with texts by Denis and du Colombier, at Galerie Louis Carré.

La femme, les peintres et les sculpteurs contemporains, at the just reopened Galerie Charpentier.

8 German reprisals in Paris after attacks on members of the Wehrmacht.

12 Arrest in Paris of 750 key Jewish individuals.

14 Robert Leforestier, "L'art et le peuple," *Chantiers*.

19 Salon de la Paysannerie Française in Paris.

1942

New exclusion measures against secret societies.

Pétain calls the French to a "community of souls."

Le bolchevisme contre l'Europe exhibition.

Claude-Joseph Gignoux, Marcel Felgines, and Maurice Bouvier-Ajam, *Le corporatisme français* (Ed. CEP), which includes a declaration by the Office central d'organisation corporative.

Anatole de Monzie, *Pétition pour l'histoire* (Flammarion).

Joseph de La Porte du Theil, *Les chantiers de la jeunesse ont deux ans* (Sequana).

Conference of leaders of the Resistance: de Gaulle, Moulin, d'Astier, Pineau, Frenay, and others.

Arrest of the artist Gotko.

Pierre Ladoué, chief curator of the Département d'art moderne, in charge of the Inspection générale des beaux-arts, declares that "in the year of war 1942," he wants to privilege works that will serve the intellectual development of "the mob."

State commission for a decorative group intended to embellish the Autoroute de l'Ouest awarded to Belmondo, Joffre, Lagriffoul, Grattesat, Cadenat, and others.

Acquisition by the state of seven ancient Gobelins tapestries from the *Esther* series, woven after François de Troy's cartoons.

Poster competition organized by the Commissariat général à l'éducation générale et aux sports.

The state's policy on acquiring works of art affects 241 artists in Paris and the provinces.

Acquisition by the state of a *Still Life* by Pignon and Gischia, a *Portrait of a Young Girl* by Villon, and a sculpture by Chauvin.

Campaign promoting the architectural design for the Porte Maillot, by Perret and Maillol.

Poster competition on the theme of anti-Communist propaganda.

Tribute to Pétain by the children of France at the Musée Galliera.

Tournon replaces Landowski as head of the Ecole des beaux-arts and Ecole nationale supérieur des arts décoratifs.

Arrest of the Resistance contact for the clandestine and resistant review *L'art français.*

Artists in Exile at the Pierre Matisse Gallery in New York.

Domela, *Composition.*

Estève, *Figure with Blue Tablecloth.*

Manessier, *Man with a Branch.*

Chauvin, *Figure* (bronze).

Lurçat, *Cock of France 1942* (tapestry).

Picasso, series of seven paintings dedicated to Julio González; studies for *Man with a Sheep* and on the theme of pigeons; *Buffet at Le Catalan; Woman with Orange.*

Lapicque, *Recruit Joining His Regiment.*

De Staël, *Portrait of Jeannine.*

Bazaine, *Swimmers in the Wave.*

Villon, *Portrait of the Artist.*

First abstract paintings by Debré.

Charles Despiau, *Arno Breker* (Flammarion).

Second edition of Fritz René Vanderpyl's pamphlet *L'art sans patrie, un mensonge: Le pinceau d'Israël* (Mercure de France).

John Hemming Fry, *Art décadent sous le règne de la démocratie et du communisme* (Ed. H. Colas).

Set of works edited by André Lejard brings together a number of texts in a series entitled "La tradition française."

André Lhote, *Peinture d'abord* (Denoël).

Clémence-Paul Duprat, *Enquête sur la peinture murale en France à l'époque romane* (Ed. Bulletin Monumental).

André Lejard, *Les tapisseries de l'Apocalypse de la cathédrale d'Angers, accompagnées du texte de l'Apocalypse de saint Jean dans la traduction de Le Maistre de Sacy* (Ed. A. Michel).

Pierre Francastel, *L'humanisme roman* (Imp. P. Carrère).

Louis Hautecoeur, *Littérature et peinture en France du XVIIe au XXe siècle* (A. Colin).

La main à plume publishes Christian Dotremont's "La conquête du monde par l'image," Raoul Ubac's "Note sur le mouvement et l'oeil," Oscar Dominguez's "La pétrification du temps," and illustrations by Arp, Delvaux, Henry, Magritte, Picasso, Hugo, Tita, Dominguez, and Vulliamy; then twelve booklets devoted to texts by Arnaud,

Blanchard, de Sède, Chabrun, Breton, Malet, Manuel, Péret, Iché, Ruis, Dotremont, and Picasso, with illustrations by Tanguy, Dalí, Miró, Picasso, and Magritte.

Dinner party at the Buttes-Chaumont brings together artists, art lovers, and critics, in memory of the "fauve" adventure (spring).

Le Corbusier works on his "Modulor," a scale of mathematical proportions.

Jean Genet, *Le condamné à mort* (n.p.).

Paul Éluard, *Poésie et vérité 1942* (Ed. de la Main à Plume).

Francis Ponge, *Le parti pris des choses* (Gallimard).

Saint-John Perse, *Exil* (Ed. des Lettres Françaises).

Albert Camus, *Le mythe de Sisyphe* (Gallimard).

Louis Aragon, *Les voyageurs de l'impériale* (Gallimard).

Louis Aragon, *Les yeux d'Elsa* (Ed. de la Baconnière).

Honegger, Symphony no. 2 for String Orchestra and Trumpet.

Jolivet, *Dolores, ou Le miracle de la femme laide* (opera).

Schoenberg, Concerto for Piano and Orchestra, op. 42.

Prokofiev, Piano Sonata no. 7 in B Flat Major, op. 83.

L'assassin habite . . . au 21 (dir. Clouzot).

Les inconnus dans la maison (dir. Decoin).

La nuit fantastique (dir. L'Herbier).

JANUARY

Franco-German negotiations (Darlan, Benoist-Méchin, Abetz).

In *Atalante*, Jacques Wilhelm, attaché at the Musée Carnavalet, calls for a renaissance in the craft industry and champions the "true censorship, the most useful of all, that of quality and taste."

Resignation from Secours national by Robert Guillou, founder of the Commission des lettres et des arts, and Jacques Devaux, member of the high council of the Ordre des architectes, both of whom had denounced Secours national's duplicity.

Exhibition of children's drawings glorifying Pétain at the Musée Galliera.

Exhibition of charcoals by Redon at Galerie de France.

Jeune France holds the exhibition *Dessins français contemporains* in Lyon, with works by Gromaire, Lhote, Derain, Kisling, Dufy, Matisse, Dunoyer de Segonzac, Picasso, and others.

1 Exhibition of photographs organized by Jeune France at the Pavillon du Parc in Vichy.

14 *Un an de théâtre,* organized by Jeune France in Grenoble.

18 Inauguration of Galerie Friedland: Alix, Brianchon, Coutaud, Despierre, Estève, Goerg, Gruber, Marchand, Legueult, Jannot, Oudot, Pignon, Planson, Tal-Coat, Walch.

FEBRUARY

Borelly argues for the arts corporation plan in *Atalante.*

At the Paris headquarters of Jeune France, Morel gives a lecture on the subject of "l'avenir de l'art plastique."

Jean Bazaine, "Dessins de Matisse et de Dufy," *La nouvelle revue française.*

Vercors, *Le silence de la mer* (Ed. de Minuit).

Borotra and Carcopino inaugurate the exhibition *L'art et le sport* at Vichy's town hall.

3 Mass arrest and deportation of Jews and Communists in Paris.

7 Henri Bouchard, "La vie de l'artiste dans l'Allemagne actuelle," *L'illustration.*

8 Inauguration of Galerie de France, run by P. Martin and J. Lambert, with a show of works by Dufresne.

14 Lucien Lautrec, "L'art pour le peuple," *Le rouge et le bleu.*

15 Order regarding the new organization of the general secretariat of youth.

19 Beginning of the trial of Gamelin, Daladier, Blum, Jacomet, and La Chambre at the supreme court of Riom.

24 The title of architect can no longer be given to anyone who is not a registered member of the Ordre des architectes.

27 Gaston Diehl, "Les étapes du Nouvel Art contemporain," *Beaux-arts.*

MARCH

The curator Georges-Henri Rivière provides the broad outline for the organization of the Musée national des arts et traditions populaires.

Exhibition of works by Laurens, Léger, and Kandinsky at Galerie Jeanne-Bucher.

Specialized bureaus and key players named for the Ordre des artistes.

1 Inauguration of the exhibition *Le bolchevisme contre l'Europe*.

1 Attack on a German military post in Paris: a sentry is killed.

3 Heavy bombing of the Paris suburbs by the British air force.

16 Publication of the review *Messages*, put together by Jean Lescure.

20 The association Jeune France dissolved by the Vichy regime (dissolution order issued on 11 July 1942).

27 First convoy of Jewish deportees to the East.

27 Death of Julio González.

APRIL

Exhibition-competition sponsored by the state on the theme "Youth festivals in the France of tomorrow" at the Musée Galliera.

2 On orders from the Germans, Pétain reinstates Laval as head of government.

11 René Barotte, "Georges Rouault raconte . . . ," *Comoedia*.

18 Constitution of the new government by Laval, who holds the offices of head of government and minister of the interior and of foreign affairs.

18 Abel Bonnard becomes education minister.

18 Laval names Hilaire secretary general for the administration of the interior ministry.

18 First issue of the Institut allemand's review *Deutschland-Frankreich*, with texts by Abetz, Sieburg, Dujardin, Jünger, Brasillach, and others.

MAY

Picasso, *Aubade*.

Exhibition of works by Vuillard, Pierre Bonnard, and Utrillo at Galerie de l'art moderne.

Exhibition of works by Beauchant, Lurçat, Klee, Laurens, Braque, and Léger at Galerie Jeanne-Bucher.

Exhibition of works by Dufy, Goerg, Picasso, and Levavasseur at Galerie Drouant.

Exhibition of watercolors and tapestries by Gromaire at Galerie Renou et Colle.

Rouault exhibition, text by Dorival, at Galerie Louis Carré.

Exhibition of works and manuscripts by Audiberti, Cocteau, Éluard, Fargue, Follain, Hugnet, Tardieu, Valéry, and others.

Grand Prix du Trophée sportif at the Pavillon de Marsan at the Louvre.

1 In his May Day speech, Pétain praises the merits of "work well done."

4 Cortot named official representative in the cabinet of the education minister.

6 Darquier de Pellepoix named general commissioner of Jewish questions.

6 Creation of Ecole des hautes études architecturales.

6 Reception at the Hôtel Ritz in honor of Breker.

15 Inauguration of the Breker exhibition at the Orangerie des Tuileries, with speeches by the education minister Abel Bonnard and Benoist-Méchin.

16 Statement by Despiau regarding his trip to Germany appears in *Comoedia*.

18 Germany demands that qualified workers be sent across the Rhine.

20 Tribute to Breker by Brasillach at the Théâtre des Arts-Hébertot.

23 Cocteau's "Salut à Breker" appears on the front page of *Comoedia*.

29 By order of the Germans, Jews in the occupied zone older than age six must wear the yellow star.

30 Execution of hostages at Mont Valérien.

30 Signing at a German bookstore on place de la Sorbonne of Despiau's book on Breker, with Breker in attendance.

31 Mother's Day.

JUNE

Dismissal of Metternich, head of the German Kunstschutz, following the Ghent altarpiece affair.

Heller, in charge of literary censorship, meets with Picasso.

Epting recalled to Berlin, where he will remain until January 1943.

Major crafts exhibition at the Orangerie at the Château de Versailles, in which painters, ceramists, workers in wrought iron, embroiderers, cabinet makers, stringed instrument makers, and others participate.

Le paysage français de Corot à nos jours exhibition at Galerie Charpentier. Catalog preface by Jean-Marc Campagne.

Exhibition of Vuillard's works (1868–1940) at Galerie Louis Carré.

Exhibition-homage at Galerie Friedland, with Gruber's *Homage to Jacques Callot*.

Exhibition of works by Picasso, Dufy, Léger, Coutaud, and Souverbie.

Exhibition of fauve paintings by Braque, Derain, Friesz, Linaret, Manguin, Marquet, Matisse, Puy, Rouault, Valtal, van Dongen, and Vlaminck.

Exhibition of works by Dufy, Léger, Picasso, Coutaud, Souverbie, Terechkovitch, and others at Galerie Rive Gauche.

Exhibition of recent works by Fautrier at Galerie Alfred Poyet.

Exhibition of watercolors by Michaux at Galerie de l'Abbaye.

Exhibition of sculptures and drawings by Laurens at Galerie Jeanne-Bucher.

Kandinsky, *Delicate Tensions, An Intimate Feast, Three Variegated Figures, Joyous Theme.*

Jean Bazaine, "Jeune peinture," *La nouvelle revue française:* we need to find, the painter writes, "the primitive purity of an increasingly unsettled, complex, and compromised world."

3 Farewell reception for Breker organized by de Brinon.

6 Maurice de Vlaminck, "Opinions libres . . . sur la peinture," *Comoedia*, offers a violent denunciation of Picasso.

13 André Lhote, "Opinions libres . . . sur la peinture française," *Comoedia*, an ambiguous response to Vlaminck.

22 The French government decides to send French workers to Germany.

22 In a speech, Laval says: "I desire the victory of Germany because without it bolshevism would tomorrow establish itself everywhere."

22 Accord between de Gaulle and the underground networks of the Resistance. Publication of the Charte française.

JULY

Primitifs du XXe siècle at Galerie René Drouin.

Exhibition of gouaches and paintings by Kandinsky at Galerie Jeanne-Bucher is canceled by the German authorities.

Buffon's *Histoire naturelle* published by Editions Fabiani, with illustrations by Picasso, who is beginning *Man with a Sheep.*

Albert Camus, *L'étranger* (Gallimard).

8 Georges Limbour, "Révélation d'un peintre: Jean Dubuffet," *Comoedia*, illustrated with Dubuffet's *The Metro.*

10 In Vichy, exhibition of tributes to Pétain by students from the Paris schools.

15 Gaston Diehl, "Naissance du fauvisme," *Comoedia.*

16–17 Roundup of the Vélodrome d'Hiver (Rafle du Vel d'Hiv).

24 The Vichy government abolishes the committees of the Senate and the Chamber of Deputies at the National Assembly.

25 Marcel Raval, "Paris ne doit pas être un musée," *Le rouge et le bleu.*

29 Oberg-Bousquet police pact.

AUGUST

Mass arrest of Jews in the occupied zone.

Letter from Monsignor Saliège protesting the persecutions of the Jews.

Félix-Olivier Martin named inspector general of youth.

3 Van Eyck's *Adoration of the Mystic Lamb* handed over to the occupying powers.

6 Inauguration of the Musée national d'art moderne at the Palais de Tokyo.

15 Interview with Le Corbusier regarding "La cité de demain" published in *Le rouge et le bleu:* "More than anything else, the housing problem is the source of the great malaise of our time," he states.

29 Marguerite Bouvier, "Georges Braque sculpteur," *Comoedia.*

SEPTEMBER

Jeanneret resigns from Abel Bonnard's cabinet, which he judges too latitudinarian, and is replaced by Giraudet.

Jean Bazaine, "Autour d'une dispute," *La nouvelle revue française,* the painter's reply to Pierre Drieu La Rochelle on the question of the French tradition.

4 Beginning of the battle of Stalingrad.

4 French citizens between twenty-one and thirty-five years old are from now on subject to the Service du travail obligatoire.

5 Maurice de Vlaminck, "Sur la peinture—L'invention et le don," *Comoedia,* denounces modernity.

20 First issue of *Les lettres françaises.*

20 Gait becomes assistant director in Abel Bonnard's cabinet.

OCTOBER

Lucien Rebatet, *Les décombres* (Denoël).

16 In Lyon, creation of the Académie du Minotaure in Burlet's studio, with Burlet, Idoux, Le Norman, and Étienne-Martin participating.

31 Jean Paulhan, "Braque," *Comoedia.*

NOVEMBER

Establishment of the first Resistance maquis in the southern zone

Picasso working on a *Pigeon* series.

Van Dongen exhibition at Galerie Charpentier.

In Lyon, Jean-Pierre Chevalier, Camille Bryen, Stanislas Fumet, André Warnod, and Raymond Cogniat discuss the "relationship between signs, rite, and sounds."

5 The lawyer Blond sells a "still life" by Picasso for 32,500 francs at the Hôtel Drouot.

8 Allied landing in French North Africa.

9 Laval meets with Hitler at Berchtesgaden, Germany.

11 Germans invade the southern zone.

17 Constitutional act giving Laval the power to issue decrees and laws at his sole discretion.

27 French fleet scuttled at Toulon. Demobilization of the French Armistice Army.

DECEMBER

Exhibition of drawings by Matisse, Picasso, Derain, and others.

Jean Bazaine, "Le Musée d'art moderne," *La nouvelle revue française.*

Les visiteurs du soir (dir. Carné) in Paris movie theaters.

2 Premiere of Montherlant's *La reine morte* at the Comédie-Française.

8 National crafts exhibition at the Pavillon de Marsan at the Louvre.

12 Gaston Diehl, "Du passé à l'avenir: Où va la peinture française?" *Comoedia.*

17 Gaston Diehl, "Une journée avec Charles Despiau," *Tempo.*

24 In Algiers, Admiral Darlan shot by Bonnier de La Chapelle (who would be executed two days later).

28 De Gaulle appeals to Giraud to create a provisional government.

1943

Gait becomes general commissioner of youth.

First series of "Doctrines," a set of publications issued by the Office central d'organisation corporative.

Freundlich deported to Lublin-Majdanek.

Braque retrospective at the Salon d'Automne.

Exhibition of recent pastels and drawings by Maillol at Galerie Louis Carré.

Kandinsky, *Circle and Square, Seven, Simplicity, Two Rays, Three Rays.*

Dominguez, *Dreaming Woman, The End of the War.*

Brauner working on *Number* and *Object of Counterenchantment* series.

Picasso, *Bull's Head, Death's Head.*

Le Moal, *Boat at Noon.*

Bazaine, *Saint Cecilia* and *Saint Gregory the Great* (stained-glass windows).

Singier, *The Siesta.*

De Staël, *Composition.*

Pignon completes a monumental decoration for the Ecole professionelle de jeunes filles in Creil, exhibited at the Salon d'Automne.

Lapicque, *African Figure, Oceanian Figure.*

Manessier, *Crucifixion.*

Fougeron, *Rue de Paris* (two versions, only one extant).

Bazaine, *Still Life in Front of the Window, The Swimmer, The Swimmer in the Reeds.*

Jean Lurçat and Marcel Gromaire, *Tapisseries contemporaines (Aubusson, Lurçat, Gromaire)* (Ed. Braun), which promotes the renaissance of tapestry.

Jean Lurçat, "Révolte contre le tableau de chevalet," *Formes et couleurs.*

André Lhote, *Petits itinéraires à l'usage des artistes* (Ed. Denoël), which encourages artists to rediscover the joys of hiking and of the land.

Gaston Diehl, ed., *Peintres d'aujourd'hui: Les maîtres* (Ed. Charpentier).

Maurice Denis, *L'inquiétude spirituelle de l'art contemporain* (Ed. J. Peyronnet); excerpted from *L'art.*

Louis Hourticq, *Génie de la France* (PUF).

Arnold Van Gennep, *Manuel de folklore français contemporain*, vol. 1.1, *Introduction générale: Du berceau à la tombe*... (Ed. A. Picard).

Émile-Aurèle Van Moé, *L'Apocalypse de Saint-Sever, manuscrit latin 8878 de la Bibliothèque nationale (XIe siècle): Notice descriptive* (Ed. de Cluny).

Marcel Gromaire, "À propos des Vierges romanes," in Émile Mâle, Louis Bréhier, and Marcel Gromaire, *Vierges romanes d'Auvergne* (Ed. Le Point).

Paul Valéry, preface to *Les Fouquet de la Bibliothèque nationale* (Ed. de la revue Verve).

Robert Desnos, *Picasso, seize peintures, 1939–1943* (Ed. du Chêne).

Louis Aragon, "Matisse-en-France," in Henri Matisse, *Dessins: Thèmes et variations* (Ed. M. Fabiani).

George Besson, *Charles Walch* (Ed. Braun & Cie, Coll. "Initier").

Gaston Diehl, *Les fauves* (Ed. du Chêne); translated into German as *Der Fauvismus* (Bücher der Eiche).

Vlaminck, *Portraits avant décès* (Flammarion).

Special issue of *Cahiers de poésie*, published by Jean Simonpoli, with illustrations by Lam, Tita, Brauner, Tanguy, Masson, and a drawing collectively done by Brauner, Breton, Lam, and Hérold.

Clandestine publication of André Thirion's erotic text, *Le grand ordinaire*, illustrated with works by Dominguez.

René Borelly, "La plastique monumentale et la vie publique," *Atalante*.

Nos tailleurs d'images (dir. Lucot) shown at the Champs-Elysées cinema.

Gaston Bachelard, *L'air et les songes* (J. Corti).

Gustave Thibon, *Retour au réel* (H. Lardanchet).

Georges Bataille, *L'expérience intérieure* (Gallimard).

Simone de Beauvoir, *L'invitée* (Gallimard).

Jean Giono, *L'eau vive* (Gallimard).

André Malraux, *La lutte avec l'ange*, pt. 1, *Les noyers de l'Altenburg* (Ed. du Haut-Pays).

Jean-Paul Sartre, *L'être et le néant* (Gallimard), *Les mouches* (Gallimard).

Elsa Triolet, *Le cheval blanc* (Denoël).

Antoine de Saint-Exupéry, *Le petit prince* (Reynal & Hitchcock).

Michel Leiris, *Haut mal* (Gallimard).

François Mauriac, *Le cahier noir* (Ed. de Minuit).

Marcel Aymé, *Le passe-muraille* (Gallimard).

Colette, *Gigi* (J. Ferenczi & Fils).

Jean Giraudoux, *Sodome et Gomorrhe* (B. Grasset).

Bartók, *Concerto for Orchestra.*

Poulenc, *Figure humaine.*

Stravinsky, *Ode.*

Messiaen, *Visions de l'Amen.*

Le corbeau (dir. Clouzot).

L'éternel retour (dir. Delannoy)—from a script by Cocteau.

Les anges du péché (dir. Bresson).

Douce (dir. Autant-Lara).

Lumière d'été (dir. Grémillon).

JANUARY

Galerie Jeanne-Bucher discreetly exhibits works by Kandinsky, Domela, and de Staël.

1 Closing of the Ecole nationale des cadres d'Uriage.

13 Death of Sophie Taeuber-Arp.

14 Casablanca Conference brings together Roosevelt, Churchill, de Gaulle, and Giraud.

30 Creation of the paramilitary force Milice.

30 Jean Bazaine, "Peinture bleu, blanc, rouge," *Comoedia:* "A nation does not choose its flag at random."

FEBRUARY

Picasso, *Man with a Sheep.*

Solo exhibition of works by Vantongerloo, *Trente années de recherches*, at Galerie de Berri.

Jacques Wilhelm, "Le futur Musée des arts et traditions populaires," *Atalante.*

2 German field marshal Paulus surrenders in Stalingrad.

6 Preview of *Douze peintres d'aujourd'hui* at Galerie de France, an exhibition of thirty-six works by Bazaine, Bores, Estève, Fougeron, Gischia, Lapicque, Le Moal, Manessier, Pignon, Singier, Villon, and Chauvin. Catalog preface by Gaston Diehl.

10 Marcel Raval, "Sport et tradition," *Beaux-arts.*

25 Robert Da, "Crise de la peinture," *Chantiers.*

25 Jean de Beer, "Notes sur l'art vivant," *Chantiers.*

26 *Retour de captivité* exhibition opens at the Musée Galliera.

MARCH

Cabinet shake-up in Vichy.

Le sport dans l'art at the Musée Galliera.

Exhibition of engravings by Callot at Galerie René Drouin.

4 Mosdyc comes out against the Jeunes peintres de tradition française in *Au pilori.*

5 The Commissariat général aux Chantiers de la jeunesse placed under the control of Laval rather than, as previously, the ministry of national education and youth.

24 Law abolishing the Secrétariat adjoint à la jeunesse.

24 Félix-Olivier Martin replaces Lamirand as head of the general secretariat of youth.

APRIL

Weekly ration of meat: 120 g (4 oz.).

19 Warsaw Ghetto Uprising begins.

MAY

Maillol visited by Pascot, general commissioner of sports.

Twelve paintings by Braque at Galerie de France.

Hilaire asks Bousquet to release Cassou.

27 First meeting of the clandestine Conseil national de la Résistance under the presidency of Moulin.

29 Claude Roy, "Maillol devant la caméra," *Comoedia.*

JUNE

3 In Algiers, formation of the Comité français de libération nationale, chaired jointly by de Gaulle and Giraud.

5 Jean Bazaine, "Braque au Salon d'Automne," *Comoedia.*

21 Moulin arrested in Caluire-et-Cuire.

27 Assembly of Rassemblement national populaire (RNP) militia members at Stade Pierre de Coubertin.

JULY

Death of Gotko in a German camp.

Exhibition on the old convents of Paris organized by Entraide des artistes.

14 Editions de Minuit publishes *L'honneur des poètes*, with a preface by Paul Éluard.

17 Groupe collaboration conference.

24 Fall of the Fascist regime in Italy.

27 Rose Valland witnesses the destruction of "degenerate" works of art in Paris.

AUGUST

Brasillach and his adherents leave *Je suis partout*.

Death of Chaïm Soutine.

7 René Barotte, "Nos peintres au travail: Édouard Pignon," *Comoedia*.

14–15 Former Vichy interior minister Pucheu arrested in Morocco.

17 Extremists publish a "plan for French national recovery."

SEPTEMBER

Publication of "Le chant des partisans" in the first issue of *Les cahiers de Libération*.

Jean Georges becomes head of Abel Bonnard's private secretariat.

Exhibitions of works by Denis, Dufy, Vlaminck, Picasso, and others at the gallery in the Printemps department store.

Manessier goes on a three-day retreat to the Cistercian La Trappe abbey in Soligny-La-Trappe, in the company of Camille Bourniquel.

15 Many Resistance fighters arrested in the northern zone.

OCTOBER

Cinq peintres d'aujourd'hui exhibition at Galerie de France: Bores, Beaudin, Gischia, Estève, and Pignon.

3 In *Je suis partout*, Pierre Jeannet notes the Parisian "vogue" for Vlaminck.

23 René Barotte, "Nos peintres au travail: Jean Bazaine," *Comoedia*.

29 Lucien Rebatet, "Révolutionnaires d'arrière-garde," *Je suis partout*, denounces the pictorial activities of the Jeunes peintres de tradition française.

30 Jean-Marc Campagne defends "objectivism" in *Beaux-arts*.

NOVEMBER

Exhibition of works by Fautrier—forty-six paintings (twenty-six of them recent), plus five sculptures, engravings, and drawings—at Galerie René Drouin.

Exhibition of tapestries at the Compagnie des arts français.

Exhibition of ceramics and pottery at Magasins réunis de l'Etoile.

Salon de l'Orfèvrerie in Paris.

First issue of *La chronique de Paris*, directed by Henri Jamet, for which Rebatet edits the section on art.

3 In France, first meeting of the Comité central des mouvements de Résistance.

12 A. Paille, "Joan Miró," *Beaux-arts*.

13 On the order of the Germans, Pétain is forbidden from making radio broadcasts.

26 Gaston Diehl, "Les exigences de demain," *Beaux-arts*.

27 Premiere of Claudel's *Le soulier de satin* at the Comédie-Française.

DECEMBER

La Porte du Theil, former head of Chantiers de la jeunesse, is deported.

Adolphe Feder deported to Auschwitz.

Exhibition of modern cartoons and tapestries from the Manufactures nationales at the Musée de l'Orangerie.

Exhibition of recent paintings by Dominguez, with text by Éluard, at Galerie Louis Carré.

Tribute to Groupe témoignage in the form of a dialogue between artists and the public at the Académie du Minotaure in Lyon.

Paul Landowski, *Peut-on enseigner les beaux-arts?* (Ed. Baudinière).

4 Breker declares in *Comoedia* that he chooses his models from among "the splendid men belonging to a revived and very pure race."

10 Edmond Humeau, "Un problème d'Etat—l'avenir des intellectuels," *Chantiers*.

18 Pétain accepts the conditions imposed by the Germans.

24 Pierre Velut (assistant secretary to the Confédération de l'éducation), "L'art dans la civilisation du travail," *Beaux-arts*.

31 General secretariat of youth replaced by a Commissariat général à la jeunesse headed by Maurice Gait, who replaces Félix-Olivier Martin.

1944

Salon des Provinces Françaises organized by the review *Beaux-arts* at the Musée Galliera.

Kandinsky, *Isolation, Black Stripes.*

Laurens, *The Farewell.*

Magnelli, *Composition.*

Lapicque, *The Liberation of Paris.*

Bazaine, *Swimmer, Mass for the Armed Man.*

Manessier, *Grande Trappe, Pilgrims at Emmaus.*

Estève, *Meditation.*

Gischia, *Madonna and Child, Still Life with Bowl of Fruit.*

Pignon, *Madonna and Child on Blue and Red Ground, Sleeping Woman on Blue Carpet.*

Vaincre, a clandestine album of twelve lithographs by nine artists denouncing the German occupation and the Vichy regime.

Georges Bataille, *Histoire de l'oeil* (n.p.), new edition illustrated by Bellmer.

Pierre Bonnard, *Correspondances* (Ed. Verve).

Paul Éluard, *À Pablo Picasso* (Ed. des Trois Collines).

André Lhote, *Bonnard: Seize peintures, 1939–1943* (Ed. du Chêne).

Pierre Lavedan, *Histoire de l'art,* vol. 2, *Moyen Âge et temps modernes* (PUF).

Camille Mauclair, *La crise de l'art moderne* (Ed. C.E.A.).

Paul Valéry, *Propos me concernant* (Plon).

Louis Aragon, *Aurélien* (Gallimard).

Death of Jean Giraudoux.

Death of Antoine de Saint-Exupéry.

Death of Vasily Kandinsky.

Bartók, Sonata for Solo Violin.

Messiaen, *Trois petites liturgies de la présence divine* and *Vingt regards sur l'Enfant Jésus.*

Olivier Messiaen, *Technique de mon langage musical* (A. Leduc).

Stravinsky, *Babel.*

Premier de cordée (dir. Daquin).

Le ciel est à vous (dir. Grémillon).

JANUARY

Discreet exhibition of works by Kandinsky, Domela, and de Staël at Galerie Jeanne-Bucher.

Exhibition of five painters *de la réalité* at Galerie Chardin: Henri Cadiou, Philippe Rouart, Augustin Rouart, René Cottet, and Robert Jeannisson.

1 Death of Piet Mondrian in New York.

1 Darnand named "secrétaire général au Maintien de l'ordre."

4 Official abolition of Chantiers de la jeunesse.

6 Henriot named information and propaganda minister.

15 Political meeting organized by the staff of *Je suis partout* at Salle Wagram.

16 Jean-Marc Campagne, "À propos d'un titre," *Beaux-arts*.

20 Establishment of expedited courts martial.

27 The Milice extends its activities to the northern zone.

FEBRUARY

Arrest of Max Jacob.

1 Creation of the Forces françaises de l'intérieur (FFI).

4 Premiere of Anouilh's *Antigone* at the Théatre de l'Atelier.

11 Preview of the exhibition of twenty-nine works by Bertholle, Bissière, Le Moal, Manessier, Singier, and Étienne-Martin at Galerie de France.

21 Execution of the militants of the Main-d'oeuvre immigrée (trial of the Affiche Rouge).

MARCH

German attack on the maquis of Glières.

Hautecoeur replaced by Hilaire as secretary general of fine arts.

Exhibition of recent wall tapestries by Lurçat at Galerie Louis Carré.

Exhibition of engravings by Dürer, Picasso, and others at the Maison Ducrot.

Martial d'Auvergne, *Prière pour les déshérités*, illustrated by Fougeron (Ed. R. Mostier).

5 Death of Max Jacob.

15 The Conseil national de la Résistance publishes its program.

16 Marcel Déat named secretary of state.

19 Picasso's *Le désir attrapé par la queue* performed at the Leiris home, with Raymond Queneau, Simone de Beauvoir, Jean-Paul Sartre, Albert Camus, Georges Hugnet, and others in attendance.

22 Brossolette tortured by the Gestapo: he throws himself out a window.

APRIL

Peintures abstraites—Compositions de matières at the gallery L'esquisse.

Circular from the Service artistique du Maréchal, directed by Robert Lallemant, in which the vision of a Maréchal art project is defended.

Publication *Je vous hais!* (Impr. spéciale du Bureau central de presse et d'informations), an anti-Semitic pamphlet signed by Maurice-Ivan Sicard, Émile Bougère, Jehan Teisseire, Henry Coston, and Father Montandon.

4 Cabinet shake-up.

4 Heavy bombardment of Paris and the northern suburbs by Allied forces.

26 Pétain in Paris.

28 In an address, Pétain condemns "le terrorisme."

MAY

Designation of the Commissaires de la République, which are to establish civic order in France in the name of de Gaulle's provisional government.

First exhibition sponsored by the Service artistique du Maréchal.

5 Interview with Camille Mauclair published in *Revivre*.

27 Premiere of Sartre's *Huis clos* at the Théâtre du Vieux-Colombier.

JUNE

Decree concerning the courts of justice.

6 De Gaulle calls on the French to revolt.

6 D-day for the Normandy Invasion.

6 *Dix peintres subjectifs* exhibition at Galerie de France: Desnoyer, Despierre, Fougeron, Gischia, Gruber, Marchand, Pignon, Robin, Tailleux, Tal-Coat. Catalog preface by Bernard Dorival.

7 Bayeux becomes the first city in France to be liberated.

8 Mobilization of the Milice.

10 German troops massacre the inhabitants of Oradour-sur-Glane.

20 Jean Zay assassinated by the Milice.

23 In *Je suis partout*, Rebatet denounces "the conspiracy" of Resistance painters.

JULY

Scholz, who heads the painting office of the ERR, reports that 203 collections comprising 21,903 art objects of every kind have been confiscated by the Nazi authorities.

Hilaire, in his capacity as secretary general of fine arts, sends a personal letter to some one hundred artists, inviting them to join a new "active and useful council" to reform the arts.

Vingt et un paysages exhibition, which includes a painting by Dubuffet, at Galerie René Drouin.

Contemporary decorative ceramics at the Compagnie des arts français.

3 The "Republic of Vercors" is proclaimed by the French Resistance.

5 Manifesto by collaboration extremists.

12 Last council of ministers in Vichy.

AUGUST

1 The Second Armored Division (France) commanded by General Leclerc lands in Normandy.

5 Pétain disavows the Milice.

5 Interview with Hilaire regarding his report on the state of the fine arts published in *Comoedia*.

16 Germans execute thirty-five young people (most of them resisters) in the Bois de Boulogne.

17 The official press stops publishing in Paris.

19 Truce in Paris.

20 German authorities arrest Pétain.

22 De Gaulle's Comité d'action militaire du Conseil national de la Résistance breaks the truce in Paris.

22–25 Battles in Paris between the Forces françaises de l'intérieur and the German forces. Barricades erected.

22–25 The Resistance press becomes the liberation press and takes possession of the offices of the collaborationist press.

25 Second Armored Division enters Paris. General von Choltitz surrenders to General Leclerc and Henri Rol-Tanguy at the Gare Montparnasse.

26 De Gaulle enters Paris.

26 Bombing of the capital by the Germans.

26 In all, the Forces françaises de l'intérieur hold back ten enemy divisions, liberate fourteen *départements* and forty-four cities, and take fifty thousand prisoners.

28 Decree establishing civic chambers to judge the collaborators.

SEPTEMBER

Between the liberation and November 1944, Joseph Billiet, the curator at the Musée national du château de Malmaison charged with protecting provincial collections, oversees the Direction des arts et des lettres. He will be replaced by Jacques Jaujard, director of the Musées nationaux.

5 Publication of an initial list of members of the provisional government.

9 Constitution in Paris of the provisional government under the presidency of de Gaulle.

16 Death of Aristide Maillol.

OCTOBER

Women granted the right to vote.

Abstract art shown at Galerie Berri-Raspail.

3 The steering committee of the Front national des arts (painting, sculpture, and engraving branch) meets in Paris under Picasso's leadership and calls for the arrest of a number of artists and art critics. That call will be modified a few days later after a defense of the accused.

5 *L'humanité* announces that Picasso has joined the Communist Party.

6 "Salon de la Libération" (Salon d'Automne): Picasso exhibits 74 canvases; Hommage aux Anciens et aux Jeunes peintres de tradition française. Shortly after the Salon opens, a few outraged attendees remove some of Picasso's works from the walls and threaten to destroy them.

23 The Second Armored Division enters Strasbourg.

23 Meeting between Hitler and Doriot at German GHQ.

28 Dissolution of the Milices patriotiques is a setback for plans to build a popular democracy in France.

SOURCES AND BIBLIOGRAPHIC OVERVIEW

SOURCES

Few of the sources for this book are still inaccessible. Although many documents have unfortunately vanished, due to the upheavals associated with World War II, hasty liquidations, or natural catastrophes, the available records, whether freely accessible or subject to restrictions, are plentiful. They are conserved in various locations, public and private. The following sources are recommended in particular.

A. PUBLIC ARCHIVES

At the Archives nationales, the series and subseries

- 3W (subject to restrictions), Haute Cour de Justice trials
- F21, Fine arts
- 2AG (subject to restrictions), Archives of the French state
- AJ 40, German archives from World War II
- AJ 52, Ecole nationale supérieure des beaux-arts
- AJ 53, Ecole nationale supérieure des arts décoratifs
- AJ 39, Chantiers de la jeunesse
- Z (subject to restrictions), Civic chambers of the court of justice of the Seine
- Arts corporation (currently being cataloged)
- Louis Carré papers

At the Archives du ministère des affaires étrangères, the so-called Rose Valland archives, actually Fonds OBIP, or Office des biens et intérêts privés (currently being cataloged)

At the Archives du ministère de la culture, the series

- 880306, art. 12, Export and exchange of works of art
- 880465, arts. 1–19, Bureau des travaux d'art
- 880465, arts. 75–76, The art business
- 900423, arts. 1–2, Allocation of works of art owned by the state
- 900621, arts. 13–15, Salons and Biennials

At the Archives de Paris, the series and subseries

VR, Beaux-arts de la Ville de Paris

VM, Municipal buildings

DZ, Scholarly collections and papers

At the Archives du ministère de l'économie et des finances, the series

B 8806 (subject to restrictions), Plundering of works of art

Archives de l'Institut de France

B. PRIVATE ARCHIVES

Centre de documentation juive contemporaine
Entraide des artistes
Galerie de France
Galerie Jeanne-Bucher
Louis Carré
Paul Flamand
André Fougeron
Robert Lallemant
Paul Landowski

C. ORAL ACCOUNTS

The retrospective oral accounts I have collected from witnesses have only a very limited place in my text. (Transcripts of some of these accounts have been deposited at the Archives nationales.) I have never felt that the many interviews I have conducted since I began my studies in 1979 should be put to use in the same way as traditional historical sources, that is, documents or images dating to the period in question. Exercises in hindsight, the testimony I gathered in so-called open-ended interviews—I always preferred to let the witnesses speak spontaneously rather than ask them a set series of precise questions—was often, though not always, at odds with my conclusions. In any event, such statements made "in retrospect," and by nature reflecting the vagaries of memory, were able to serve as one avenue of research. They also serve a purely theoretical function for me: they are a judicious reminder that history finds its sustenance primarily in flesh and blood. My thanks to all those I interviewed for their valuable contributions to an undertaking whose conclusions are not necessarily those they expected.

In particular, I wish to thank Gérard Ambroselli, painter, engraver, and sculptor; Jean Bazaine, painter; Paul Belmondo, sculptor; Benn, painter; Arno Breker, sculptor; Pierre Cabanne, art writer; Henri Cadiou, painter; Gildo Caputo, art writer and dealer; Jean Cassou, curator of the Musée national d'art moderne and writer; Roger Chapelain-Midy, painter; Georges Cheyssial, curator; Robert Couturier, sculptor; Jean-Baptiste Denis, psychoanalyst; Gaston Diehl, art writer; César Domela, artist; Bernard Dorival, curator and art historian; Jean Effel, newspaper illustrator; André Fougeron, painter; Sylvie Galanis, art dealer; Marcel Gili, sculptor; Maurice Guy-Loë, painter and head of Entraide des artistes; André Hambourg, painter; Hans Hartung, painter; Jean Hélion, painter; Gerhard Heller, publisher; Monsieur Herbet, art dealer; Mme Robert Lallemant; Hubert Landais, honorary director of the Réunion des musées nationaux; Colette Lasne, painter; Lucien Lautrec, painter; Jacques Villeglé, artist; Father Lecoeur; Jean Le Moal, painter; Jean Lescure, poet and writer; Roger Limouse, painter; Edouard Georges Mac-Avoy, painter; Alfred Manessier, painter; Jean Marzelle, painter; Maurice Mazo, painter; Father Morel, painter and art writer; Jean Osouf, sculptor; Roland Oudot, painter; Georges Pacouil, painter; Édouard Pignon, painter; Valentine Prax, painter; Georges-Henri Rivière, founder and curator of the Musée national des arts et traditions populaires; Émile Sabouraud, painter; Sennep, newspaper illustrator; Pierre Soulages, painter; Jean Tardieu, poet and writer; André Thirion, writer; Dina Vierny, art dealer; Yankel, painter; Hubert Yencesse, sculptor; and Marcel Zahar, art writer.

BIBLIOGRAPHIC OVERVIEW

In the French edition of this book, published in 1993, I provided an overview of the publications I consulted, which is translated here, but slightly expanded to give some indication of the historiographical progress made over the past fifteen years. For additional and topically specific bibliography, the reader should consult the notes, which for the most part remain faithful to the original edition.

Prior to 1993, numerous exhibitions and exhibition catalogs contributed to enriching our knowledge of the artistic scene during the dark years, starting with *Exposition Résistance-déportation: Création dans le bruit des armes*, organized by Michelle Michel and held at the Musée de l'Ordre de la Libération in 1980. Also important were shows at the Musée national d'art moderne, the Musée d'art moderne Saint-Étienne Métropole, and the Musée municipal de Boulogne-Billancourt. Not focused solely on the occupation years, these were especially instructive regarding the periods before and after the war. They further opened my eyes to the larger context for my research on the artistic question, which I began in 1979 and the results of which I have been publishing since 1986, starting with *Histoire de l'art, Paris 1940–1944: Ordre national, traditions et modernités* (Paris: Publications de la Sorbonne, 1986).

The first surveys related to culture during the dark years must be consulted—specifically, Hervé Le Boterf, *La vie parisienne sous l'Occupation, 1940–1944*, 2 vols. (Paris: Editions France-Empire, 1974–75), André Halimi, *Chantons sous l'Occupation* (Paris: O. Orban, 1976), and Gilles Ragache and Jean-Robert Ragache, *La vie quotidienne des écrivains et des artistes sous l'Occupation, 1940–1944* (Paris: Hachette, 1988). The theoretical framework for thinking about the occupation began to develop only later, however, in the context of pioneering exhibitions and scholarly forums. Here I will note three foundational initiatives in this area. In 1987, a roundtable led by Jean-Pierre Rioux brought together researchers for the first time to discuss cultural life in the Vichy era—the plastic arts, but also theater, cinema, radio, fashion, history, literature, and sports. The proceedings have been published in Jean-Pierre Rioux, ed., *La vie culturelle sous Vichy* (Paris: Editions Complexe, 1990). In 1988, a colloquium led by Pierre Milza and Fanette Roche-Pézard on concepts of totalitarianism and resistance to totalitarianism in the arts in Italy, Germany, and France provided the occasion to look beyond France proper. For the proceedings, see Pierre Milza and Fanette Roche-Pézard, eds., *Art et fascisme: Totalitarisme et résistance au totalitarisme dans les arts en Italie, Allemagne et France des années 30 à la défaite de l'Axe* (Brussels: Editions Complexe, 1989). I refer the reader as well to the work published elsewhere by the numerous authors invited to participate in these two gatherings. Finally, the exhibition *La propagande sous Vichy, 1940–1944*, held in 1990 at the Musée d'histoire contemporaine de la Bibliothèque de documentation internationale contemporaine, and its invaluable accompanying catalog, edited by Laurent Gervereau and Denis Peschanski, offered the first historical and systematic presentation of that issue.

At the opposite end of the spectrum, works grounded in memory or caprice have continued to play a part in multiplying the gray areas. Here we find writings ranging from the autobiographical narrative of the curator Germain Bazin, *Souvenirs de l'exode du Louvre, 1940–1945* (Paris: Somogy, 1992), published without notes and subject to the approximations of memory, to the short study by Michèle C. Cone, *Artists under Vichy: A Case of Prejudice and Persecution* (Princeton: Princeton Univ. Press, 1992), larded with misinterpretations and inaccuracies.

The increasing number of scholarly publications on the cultural aspects of France during the dark years have been most useful, and I have cited many such works in the notes to this book. Here, I will distinguish Christian Faure, *Le projet culturel de Vichy: Folklore et révolution nationale, 1940–1944* (Lyon: Presses Universitaires de Lyon/CNRS, 1989); Rémy Handourtzel, *Vichy et l'école, 1940–1944* (Paris: Editions Noêsis, 1997); Pierre Giolitto, *Histoire de la jeunesse sous Vichy* (Paris: Perrin, 1991); Myriam Chimènes, ed., *La vie musicale sous Vichy* (Brussels: Editions Complexe, 2001); on fashion, Dominique Veillon, *La mode sous l'Occupation: Débrouillardise et coquetterie dans la France en guerre, 1939–1945* (Paris: Payot, 1990); on theater, Serge Added, *Le théâtre dans les années-Vichy, 1940–1944* (Paris: Editions Ramsay, 1992); and on artists and the war, Lionel Richard, *L'art et la guerre: Les artistes confrontés à la Seconde Guerre mondiale* (Paris: Flammarion, 1995). Herman Lebovics's book on historical anthropology is essential reading: *True France: The Wars over Cultural Identity, 1900–1945* (Ithaca: Cornell Univ. Press, 1992), translated into French by Geoffroy de Laforcade as *La vraie France: Les enjeux de l'identité culturelle, 1900–1945* (Paris: Belin, 1995). On intellectuals, several important studies have been published: Gérard Loiseaux, *La littérature de la défaite et de la collaboration: D'après "Phönix oder Asche?" (Phénix ou cendres?) de Bernhard Payr*, new ed. (Paris: Fayard, 1995); Claude Singer, *Vichy, l'université et les Juifs: Les silences et la mémoire* (Paris: Les Belles Lettres, 1992); Pierre-André Taguieff, ed., *L'antisémitisme de plume, 1940–1944: Etudes et documents* (Paris: Berg International, 1999); and Gisèle Sapiro, *La guerre des écrivains, 1940–1953* (Paris: Fayard, 1999). On women, see Francine Muel-Dreyfus, *Vichy et l'éternel féminin: Contribution à une sociologie politique de l'ordre des corps* (Paris: Editions du Seuil, 1996).

In 1992, the international colloquium "Le régime de Vichy et les Français," organized by the Institut d'histoire du temps présent, evaluated the state of historiography regarding the dark years. In the wake of pioneering works by Yves Durand, Robert O. Paxton, Jean-Pierre Azéma, Stanley Hoffman, Pascal Ory, and Claire Andrieu, increasingly focused and insightful research is appearing, including the publications by Pierre Laborie on the imagination of France and the French, Philippe Burrin on the collaboration, Jean-François Muracciole and Olivier Wieviorka on the Resistance, Marc-Olivier Baruch on the French administration, and Denis Peschanski on control.

Since 1993, there has been ongoing research into the history of the economic pillage of Jewish possessions and of their restitution, based on research conducted by the so-called Mission d'étude sur la spoliation des Juifs de France de 1940 à 1944, or Mission Mattéoli. See, in particular, Claire Andrieu, ed., *La persécution des Juifs de France, 1940–1944, et le rétablissement de la légalité républicaine: Recueil des textes officiels, 1940–1999* (Paris: La Documentation Française, 2000).

In terms of the fate of artworks, the foundational work was published in 1947 by the Centre de documentation juive contemporaine: Jean Cassou, ed., *Le pillage par les Allemands des oeuvres d'art et des bibliothèques appartenant à des Juifs en France: Recueil de documents* (Paris: Editions du Centre de Documentation Juive Contemporaine, 1947). See also the series of articles by Janet Flanner published in the *New Yorker* in 1947; Michel Florisoone, Carle Dreyfus, and Jeanine Lemoine, *Les chefs-d'oeuvre des collections françaises retrouvés en Allemagne par la Commission de récupération artistique et les services alliés*, exh. cat. (Paris: Ministère de l'Education Nationale, 1946); and Rose Valland, *Le front de l'art: Défense des collections françaises, 1939–1945* (Paris: Librairie Plon, 1961). On Rose Valland as curator and witness, see Corinne Bouchoux, *Rose Valland: Résistance au musée* (La Crèche: Geste, 2006).

Recent research has contributed considerably to filling in the history of Nazi plundering and reparations. Here the essential publication is Isabelle Le Masne de Chermont and Didier Schulmann, eds., *Le pillage de l'art en France pendant l'Occupation et la situation des 2000 oeuvres confiées aux musées nationaux* (Paris: La Documentation Française, 2000). This study responded to the urgent questions posed in my earlier works, as well as to Hector Feliciano's *Le musée disparu: Enquête sur le pillage des oeuvres d'art en France par les nazis* (Paris: Austral, 1995). On this same subject, it is also necessary to cite Lynn H. Nicholas, *The Rape of Europa: The Fate of Europe's Treasures in the Third Reich and the Second World War* (New York: Knopf, 1994), translated into French by Paul Chemla as *Le pillage de l'Europe: Les oeuvres d'art volées par les nazis* (Paris: Editions du Seuil, 1995). See also Jonathan Petropoulos, *Art as Politics in the Third Reich* (Chapel Hill: Univ. of North Carolina Press, 1996); the proceedings of a colloquium organized by the Direction des musées de France, *Pillages et restitutions: Le destin des oeuvres d'art sorties de France pendant la Seconde Guerre mondiale* (Paris: Adam Biro, 1997); Peter Harclerode and Brendan Pittaway, *The Lost Masters: The Looting of Europe's Treasurehouses* (London: Gollancz, 1999); and, at least for the iconography, Robert M. Edsel, *Rescuing Da Vinci: Hitler and the Nazis Stole Europe's Great Art, America and Her Allies Recovered It* (Dallas: Laurel, 2006).

Of late, several important works have emerged from the region of Provence. Regarding art and culture, see *Varian Fry et les candidats à l'exil, Marseille, 1940–1941: Arp, Bellmer, Brauner,..., Wols*, exh. cat. (Arles: Actes Sud, 1999); *Varian Fry: Du refuge à l'exil: Actes du colloque des 19 [et] 20 mars 1999*, 2 vols. (Arles: Actes Sud, 2000); and Danièle

Giraudy et al., *Le "Jeu de Marseille": Autour d'André Breton et des surréalistes à Marseille en 1940–1941*, exh. cat. (Marseilles: Alors Hors du Temps, 2003).

New studies on French detainment camps have appeared as well. See, in particular, Denis Peschanski, *La France des camps: L'internement, 1938–1946* (Paris: Gallimard, 2002); and Jean-Marc Dreyfus and Sarah Gensburger, *Des camps dans Paris: Austerlitz, Lévitan, Bassano, juillet 1943–août 1944* (Paris: Fayard, 2003).

ILLUSTRATION CREDITS

The reader will have to excuse the more noticeable gaps in the illustration program, some of which are due to the refusal of a copyright holder, an artist, or an artist's estate to allow a work to be reproduced here.

Every effort has been made to locate and contact copyright holders for their permission to reprint images. The publisher would be grateful to hear from any copyright holder who is not acknowledged below. The following sources have granted permission to reproduce illustrations in this book.

P. xiv, pl. 8
Photo: © LAPI/Roger-Viollet

Pl. 1
© Breker-Archiv/Marco-VG. Photo: Charlotte Rohrbach © Breker-Archiv/Marco-VG

Pl. 2
© Photograph History Paris/Marco-VG. Photo: Bibliothèque de documentation internationale contemporaine (BDIC) et Musée d'histoire contemporaine, Paris

Pls. 3, 4
Photo: © LAPI/Roger-Viollet. Reproduced with the permission of History Paris-Archive/Marco-VG

Pl. 5
From *Signal*, no. 1, January 1942. Photo: Rohrlack [Charlotte Rohrbach?]. Photo: Bibliothèque Kandinsky, Centre Pompidou, Paris. Reproduced with the permission of History Paris-Archive/Marco-VG

Pls. 6, 7, 10, 47 (nos. 3, 12)
© 2008 Artists Rights Society (ARS), New York/ADAGP, Paris. Photo: Bibliothèque de documentation internationale contemporaine (BDIC) et Musée d'histoire contemporaine, Paris

Pls. 9, 11, 13–17, 47 (nos. 4, 8)
Photo: Bibliothèque de documentation internationale contemporaine (BDIC) et Musée d'histoire contemporaine, Paris

Pl. 12
Photo: courtesy Keystone/Eyedea Press, Paris/Établissement de Communication et de Production Audiovisuelle de la Défense, Ivry-sur-Seine

Pl. 18
© 2008 Artists Rights Society (ARS), New York/ADAGP, Paris. Photo: Private collection/The Bridgeman Art Library

Pl. 19
© 2008 Artists Rights Society (ARS), New York/ADAGP, Paris. Photo: © Christie's Images Ltd. 2003

Pls. 20, 22
© 2008 Artists Rights Society (ARS), New York/ADAGP, Paris. Photo: © Laure Albin-Guillot/Roger-Viollet

Pl. 21
© 2008 Artists Rights Society (ARS), New York/ADAGP, Paris. Photo: Fonds Marc Vaux, Bibliothèque Kandinsky, Centre Pompidou, Paris

Pl. 23
© 2008 Artists Rights Society (ARS), New York/ADAGP, Paris. Photo: Mobilier National, Manufactures Nationales, Gobelins-Beauvais-Savonnerie

Pl. 24
© 2008 Artists Rights Society (ARS), New York/ADAGP, Paris. Fine Arts Museums of San Francisco, Gift of

Mrs. Marie Stauffer Sigall in memory of her father, John Stauffer, 1950.3. Photo: Fine Arts Museums of San Francisco

Pl. 25
© 2008 Artists Rights Society (ARS), New York/ADAGP, Paris. Photo: © Fondation Dina Vierny–Musée Maillol, Paris, France/The Bridgeman Art Library

Pls. 26, 36, 39, 40
© 2008 Artists Rights Society (ARS), New York/ADAGP, Paris. Photo: CNAC/MNAM/Dist. Réunion des Musées Nationaux/Art Resource, New York

Pl. 27
© 2008 Succession H. Matisse, Paris/Artists Rights Society (ARS), New York. Photo: Erich Lessing/Art Resource, New York

Pl. 28
© 2008 Artists Rights Society (ARS), New York/ADAGP, Paris. Photo: Private collection, Switzerland

Pl. 29
© 2008 Artists Rights Society (ARS), New York/ADAGP, Paris. Collection Mr. and Mrs. Adrien Maeght, Paris. Photo: From Michèle C. Cone, *Artists under Vichy: A Case of Prejudice and Persecution* (Princeton: Princeton Univ. Press, 1992), pl. 3

Pl. 30
© 2008 Artists Rights Society (ARS), New York/ADAGP, Paris. Photo: courtesy Hanina Fine Arts Ltd., London

Pl. 31
© 2008 Artists Rights Society (ARS), New York/ADAGP, Paris. Photo: courtesy Galerie Louise Leiris S.A.S., Paris

Pl. 32
© 2008 Artists Rights Society (ARS), New York/ADAGP, Paris. Photo: From Michel-Georges Bernard, *Jean Le Moal* (Neuchâtel: Editions Ides & Calendes, 2001), 73

Pl. 33
© 2008 Artists Rights Society (ARS), New York/ADAGP, Paris. Photo: courtesy Musée Estève, Bourges

Pl. 34
© 2008 Artists Rights Society (ARS), New York/ADAGP, Paris. Photo: Artcurial, Briest-Le Fur-Poulain-F. Tajan, Paris

Pl. 35
© 2008 Artists Rights Society (ARS), New York/ADAGP, Paris. The Metropolitan Museum of Art, Purchase, Anonymous Gifts, 1991 (1991.78). Photograph © 1991 The Metropolitan Museum of Art

Pl. 37
© 2008 Artists Rights Society (ARS), New York/ADAGP, Paris. Photo: Giraudon/Art Resource, New York

Pl. 38
© 2008 Artists Rights Society (ARS), New York/ADAGP, Paris. Photo: © Musée d'Art Moderne de la Ville de Paris, Paris, France/Lauros/Giraudon/The Bridgeman Art Library

Pl. 41
© 2008 Artists Rights Society (ARS), New York/ADAGP, Paris. Photo: From Yves Peyré, *Fautrier, ou, Les outrages de l'impossible* (Paris: Editions du Regard, 1990), 10

Pl. 42
© 2008 Artists Rights Society (ARS), New York/ADAGP, Paris. Photo: From *Dominguez, du 1er au 14 décembre 1943* (Paris: Galerie Louis Carré, 1943), n.p.

Pl. 43
© 2008 Estate of Pablo Picasso/Artists Rights Society (ARS), New York. Photo: Réunion des Musées Nationaux/Art Resource, New York

Pl. 44
© 2008 Artists Rights Society (ARS), New York/HUNGART, Budapest. Photo: © Estate Brassaï–RMN

Pls. 45, 46
© 2008 Artists Rights Society (ARS), New York/ADAGP, Paris. Photo: © Private collection/Lauros/Giraudon/The Bridgeman Art Library

INDEX

ART OF THE DEFEAT, FRANCE 1940–1944

Laurence Bertrand Dorléac
Translated by Jane Marie Todd

Laurence Bertrand Dorléac is Professeur des universités and a senior member of the Institut Universitaire de France. She has written widely on the relations between art and history in the twentieth century. Her publications include *Histoire de l'art, Paris 1940–1944: Ordre national, traditions et modernités* (1986), *L'ordre sauvage: Violence, dépense et sacré dans l'art des années 1950–1960* (2004), and the proceedings volume *Picasso, l'objet du mythe* (edited with Androula Michaël, 2005). Currently, her research is focused on the definition and various functions of art in Western society since World War II. She teaches a seminar at the Centre d'Histoire de Sciences Po.

Jane Marie Todd is a full-time translator and copy editor who has translated some forty books in the fields of art criticism, philosophy, history, biography, literary criticism, and women's studies. She holds a doctorate in comparative literature and has taught at Reed College and the University of Oregon. Her translation of Benjamin Stora's *Algeria, 1830–2000: A Short History* (2001) was a finalist for the French-American Foundation Translation Prize. Other recent translations include Michel Winock, *Nationalism, Antisemitism, and Fascism in France* (1998); Brassaï, *Conversations with Picasso* (1999); and Julia Kristeva, *Colette* (2004).

OTHER TRANSLATIONS PUBLISHED BY THE GETTY RESEARCH INSTITUTE

IN PRINT

Jacqueline Lichtenstein, *The Blind Spot: An Essay on the Relations between Painting and Sculpture in the Modern Age* (2003)
Translation by Chris Miller
ISBN 978-0-89236-892-1 (paper)

Le Corbusier, *Toward an Architecture* (1924)
Introduction by Jean-Louis Cohen
Translation by John Goodman
ISBN 978-0-89236-899-0 (hardcover), ISBN 978-0-89236-822-8 (paper)

Johann Joachim Winckelmann, *History of the Art of Antiquity* (1764)
Introduction by Alex Potts
Translation by Harry Francis Mallgrave
ISBN 978-0-89236-668-2 (paper)

Jacob Burckhardt, *Italian Renaissance Painting according to Genres* (1885–93)
Introduction by Maurizio Ghelardi
Translation by David Britt and Caroline Beamish
ISBN 978-0-89236-736-8 (paper)

Gottfried Semper, *Style in the Technical and Tectonic Arts; or, Practical Aesthetics* (1860–63)
Introduction by Harry Francis Mallgrave
Translation by Michael Robinson and Harry Francis Mallgrave
ISBN 978-0-89236-597-5 (hardcover)

Julien-David Le Roy, *The Ruins of the Most Beautiful Monuments of Greece* (1770)
Introduction by Robin Middleton
Translation by David Britt
ISBN 978-0-89236-669-9 (paper)

Giovanni Battista Piranesi, *Observations on the Letter of Monsieur Mariette; with Opinions on Architecture, and a Preface to a New Treatise on the Introduction and Progress of the Fine Arts in Europe in Ancient Times* (1765)
Introduction by John Wilton-Ely
Translation by David Britt and Caroline Beamish
ISBN 978-0-89236-636-1 (paper)

Carl Gustav Carus, *Nine Letters on Landscape Painting, Written in the Years 1815–1824; with a Letter from Goethe by Way of Introduction* (1831)
Introduction by Oskar Bätschmann
Translation by David Britt
ISBN 978-0-89236-673-4 (paper)

Karel Teige, *Modern Architecture in Czechoslovakia and Other Writings* (1923–30)
Introduction by Jean-Louis Cohen
Translation by Irena Žantouská Murray and David Britt
ISBN 978-0-89236-596-8 (paper)

Jean-Nicolas-Louis Durand, *Précis of the Lectures on Architecture* (1802–5) with *Graphic Portion of the Lectures on Architecture* (1821)
Introduction by Antoine Picon
Translation by David Britt
ISBN 978-0-89236-580-7 (paper)

Walter Curt Behrendt, *The Victory of the New Building Style* (1927)
Introduction by Detlef Mertins
Translation by Harry Francis Mallgrave
ISBN 978-0-89236-563-0 (paper)

Aby Warburg, *The Renewal of Pagan Antiquity: Contributions to the Cultural History of the European Renaissance* (1932)
Introduction by Kurt W. Forster
Translation by David Britt
ISBN 978-0-89236-537-1 (hardcover)

Sigfried Giedion, *Building in France, Building in Iron, Building in Ferroconcrete* (1928)
Introduction by Sokratis Georgiadis
Translation by J. Duncan Berry
ISBN 978-0-89236-319-3 (hardcover)

Hermann Muthesius, *Style-Architecture and Building-Art: Transformations of Architecture in the Nineteenth Century and Its Present Condition* (1902)
Introduction and translation by Stanford Anderson
ISBN 978-0-89236-282-0 (hardcover), ISBN 978-0-89236-283-7 (paper)

Friedrich Gilly: Essays on Architecture, 1796–1799
Introduction by Fritz Neumeyer
Translation by David Britt
ISBN 978-0-89236-281-3 (paper)

Nicolas Le Camus de Mézières, *The Genius of Architecture; or, The Analogy of That Art with Our Sensations* (1780)
Introduction by Robin Middleton
Translation by David Britt
ISBN 978-0-89236-235-6 (paper)

Claude Perrault, *Ordonnance for the Five Kinds of Columns after the Method of the Ancients* (1683)
Introduction by Alberto Pérez-Gómez
Translation by Indra Kagis McEwen
ISBN 978-0-89236-232-5 (hardcover), ISBN 978-0-89236-233-2 (paper)

Heinrich Hübsch, Rudolf Wiegmann, Carl Albert Rosenthal, Johann Heinrich Wolff, and Carl Gottlieb Wilhelm Bötticher, *In What Style Should We Build? The German Debate on Architectural Style (1828–47)*
Introduction and translation by Wolfgang Herrmann
ISBN 978-0-89236-199-1 (hardcover), ISBN 978-0-89236-198-4 (paper)

Otto Wagner, *Modern Architecture: A Guidebook for His Students to This Field of Art* (1902)
Introduction and translation by Harry Francis Mallgrave
ISBN 978-0-226-86938-4 (hardcover), ISBN 978-0-226-86939-1 (paper)

IN PREPARATION

Régis Michel, *Ideal Beauty: A Western Phantasy* (1989)
Translation by Simon Pleasance and Fronza Woods
ISBN 978-0-89236-768-9

Designed by Stuart Smith
Production coordinated by Anita Keys
Type composed by Diane Franco in Century Expanded and Futura
Printed in China through Asia Pacific Offset, Inc., on Gold East Matte